'This textbook is like no other. It provides a gro
hensive approach to organizational behavior from a p..... ...
readers to engage in approaches to being an employee, manager or leader that take seriously
the challenges of creating and building positive organizations or positive organizing that fosters employee flourishing, engagement, psychological safety, well-being and purpose beyond
simply profit maximization. The textbook covers traditional topics such as teams, emotions,
job design and leadership but covers them in a way that focuses on deepening understanding
of how these topics constrain or enable processes of positive organizing. The textbook also
addresses pivotal new subjects such as individual strengths, generative interactions, great
workplaces, powering positivity and the positive organization of progress. The authors
address these core ideas from an empowering, easy-to-understand, actionable perspective,
while also addressing the complexities, paradoxes and trade-offs involved in a focus on
a positive perspective. The textbook fosters understanding, constructive action and an
expansion of our imagination around management as a force for good.'

*Jane Dutton, Robert L. Kahn Distinguished University Professor
Emerita of Business Administration and Psychology, Ross School
of Business, University of Michigan, USA*

'This is an especially insightful and engaging book on Positive Organizational Behavior. It
is an ideal introduction for those scholars and students unfamiliar with POB and a splendid
guide for managers who see their role not narrowly technically, nor merely as the "agents"
of "principals", but as a force of positive change. Miguel Pina e Cunha, Arménio Rego,
Ace Simpson and Stewart Clegg do not preach but invite the reader to think about ways
of creating organizational contexts that bring out the best in people. Importantly, their
good advice comes with a health warning: what is positive is not absolute, can be manipulated, and is dialectically related to the negative. If you care for a subtle, rigorous and
utterly relevant argument, you will find it here.'

*Haridimos Tsoukas, The Columbia Ship Management Professor of Strategic
Management, University of Cyprus and Distinguished Research
Environment Professor of Organization Behavior,
Warwick Business School, UK*

'Organizations dominate modern society, be it multinational corporations, government agencies or large non-profit organizations. They are capable of the best or the worst outcomes for
clients, employees and other stakeholders. How can leaders ensure that their organizations are
managed positively and deliver the best? This book is a tour de force on positive organizing,
written by some of the best organizational scholars in the world. It will be an indispensable
reference for organizational researchers and for thoughtful business leaders.'

*Filipe Santos, Chaired Professor of Social Entrepreneurship, Dean of
CATÓLICA-LISBON School of Business & Economics, Lisbon, Portugal*

'Positivity rooted in reality, recommendations anchored by science, this book marshals surprising stories and rigorous research to bring a fresh and hopeful view of what organizations can become.'

*Bradley Owens, Marriott School of Management at
Brigham Young University, Salt Lake City, USA*

'Enlightening, fulfilling, bringing new positivity concepts every organization should know of to overcome in an innovative way challenges, be more competitive while impacting positively human wellbeing.'

Leila Triki, Dean, Mediterranean School of Business, Tunisa

'This is one of those rare books that provides both scientific insight and practical relevance. It is an important contribution to our understanding of what makes good management in both its ethical and performance dimensions. In fact the book shows that one can support the other. A must for executives and scholars alike willing to make a real difference in the field of management.'

Milton Sousa, Associate Professor, Universidade Nova de Lisboa, Lisbon, Portugal

'This book is a gift to both the scientific community and a wider audience. As far as I know, the research on the topic of positive management has not yet been translated into the format of a book aiming at a wider and structured dissemination of that knowledge. Scholars, students, practitioners, citizens from all over the world should definitely fast-read this magnificent work.'

Miguel Pereira Lopes, Associate Professor, ISCSP,
Universidade de Lisboa, Lisbon, Portugal

'This book effectively and comprehensively presents research on the "positive lens" – a lens focused on thriving and flourishing in organizations. I particularly value the discussion of positive leadership and the description of character strengths and virtues such as humility and authenticity. Without humility, without authenticity, and without the development of other strengths such as courage, humanity, and temperance, organizations cannot achieve sustainable excellence. This book will inspire many great conversations with leaders.'

Dusya Vera, Professor of Strategy, C.T. Bauer College of Business,
University of Houston, USA

'This book outlines and extends the field of positive organization studies in a way that is accessible and hugely readable, yet rigorously detailed and nuanced. Full of pleasant surprises and riveting illustrations it brings the field alive to show the power of organizing in a way that promotes both human excellence and excellent performance, affirms strengths and emphasizes the good in the human condition. The duality of positivity and negativity weaves its way throughout this work and defines the authors' approach and the book is hopeful and yet full of realism. A powerful and hugely enjoyable book that sets out an important research and teaching agenda.'

Rebecca Bednarek, Senior Lecturer, Victoria Business School,
Victoria University, Wellington, New Zealand

'This is simply a superb textbook on positive organizational research. It covers a lot of ground without being superficial. It combines knowledge of historical roots with current practical advice and cases. It is accessible and written with an appealing light tone that brims with engagement. And the book takes steps towards something that is rare and much needed – the blending of positive and critical perspectives in our understanding of organizations as engaged in the quest for human betterment.'

Arne Carlsen, Professor, BI Business School, Oslo, Norway

'The authors have done a great job describing the essence of positive organizational behavior and its potential for building work places that are both admired and beneficial for the people working in it. I recommend this book for readers who like to get a contemporary overview of this field and its practical implications.'

Dirk van Dierendonck, PhD, Professor of HRM, Vice Dean of Faculty,
Rotterdam School of Management, Erasmus University, Netherlands

'An alternative, engaging and provoking book about positive organizational scholarship research. It provides a reflective perspective on POS at individual, organizational and social level. Beautifully written, engaging, transformative.'

Antonino Vaccaro, Academic Director CBS-IESE Business School, Navarra, Spain

'Positivity is precious for people who seek to perceive and manage contemporary organizations, often caught in the risks of linear, unidimensional and dichotomous thinking. This textbook aids, engages and fuels all of us in understanding how good, beautiful, complex and socially relevant the positive knowledge can be in practice. It's pedagogically and conceptually brilliant!'

Eduardo Davel, School of Management, Federal University of Bahia, Brazil

'The book departs from the mere opposition of the "banality of evil" and the (supposed) indispensable forces for "good management". Later it soon moves away from such a simplistic approach and it presents a grand finale where positive and negative management are dialectically intertwined. To achieve that the authors acutely elaborate on the fundamental opposition lying at the very core of organization between humanistic and managerial approaches to management and organization. An opposition that eventually mirrors the diversity of consideration about humans: are they people or resources? Or both? The book provides multiple answers at different levels of aggregation. As the authors brilliantly synthetize: "good management is much rarer than usually assumed!" Hence, works like that are to be spread in the managerial world! A must-read for Organization Studies scholars too!'

Luca Giustiniano, Director of CLIO (Center for research in Leadership,
Innovation and Organisation), Luiss University, Italy

'An excellent and thoughtful research-oriented review of the positive organizational behavior literature. Key concepts, ideas, and studies are presented in an concise, creative, and organized way.'

Joana Story, Associate Professor, Fundação Getúlio Vargas, São Paulo, Brazil

'This book places values and ethics where they should be in organizations – right in the center. Rather than assume that positive values and ethical beliefs are a nice addition to a profit seeking, efficiency oriented organization, Cunha, Rego, Simpson and Clegg offer us pragmatic, specific, and thoughtful advice about how to create organizations, institutions and civilizations founded on positive values and ethics. This should be the central textbook for all students of organizations, management and leadership.'

Wendy Smith, University of Delaware, USA

'How pleasant it is to read a book that being ideological doesn't disguise itself behind "irrefutable" theories describing "reality". Instead, it openly used ideology as a tool to sculpture an equally possible, albeit better, form of managing and organising. Its theoretical acumen and powerful illustrations lend it both legitimacy and currency to become mandatory reading in the organisational behaviour field for students and managers alike. This is the kind of book that should, at least, complement more traditional perspectives, if not replace them, thus bending back double hermeneutics forces towards a better world.'

Nuno Guimaraes da Costa, Associate Dean, Faculty and Research,
ICN Business School, France

'This insightful and inspiring book examines the myriad ways in which organizations and their members can help make the world a better place. In an era where almost everything is viewed as "disruption", the authors successfully restore a more balanced and timely appreciation of how the good and bad intertwine in organizations as they do in life itself.'

Moshe Farjoun, Professor, York University, Canada

'I am impressed with all dimensions of your book (writing, reference base, comprehensive coverage and application examples). I know it will be successful.'

Fred Luthans, University of Nebraska, USA

'GEM Anscombe, in her landmark article "Modern Moral Philosophy" (1958) decried the lack of an appropriate psychology for the study of virtue to move forward. This present volume is a decisive contribution to this effort, particularly in the fields of business and organizations.'

Alejo José G. Sison, Universidad de Navarra, Spain

'*Positive Organizational Behaviour* is a gift for anyone interested in positive organizational behaviour. This book is a compendium of theoretical and practical knowledge of workplace emotion, positive leadership styles, and many other exciting and new developments within the scholarship of positive organizational behaviour. Essential reading for any leader who wants to understand the impacts of positive organizational behaviour in the 21st century.'

Kai Chi Yam, NUS Business School, Singapore

'The authors of *Positive Organizational Behavior* have produced a unique and endlessly fascinating approach to this subject, using vivid examples and an impressive array of sources to show how people can make a positive difference in organizations. The book will be an invaluable resource for students of management and organizations, and an inspiration to researchers who're seeking new and original insights.'

Peter Fleming, Professor of Management, University of
Technology Business School Sydney, Australia

'A marvelous, unique book! The first textbook in the flourishing field of Positive Organizational Scholarship, *Positive Organizational Behaviour* makes an invaluable contribution to our understanding of positive organizing. Sharing research across a vast range of core OB topics in a concise, accessible, and engaging way, it offers a wonderful resource both for students new to positive ways of organizing and for seasoned scholars alike. But what makes this book especially distinctive and refreshing is the lens through which this accomplished team of authors looks. Warning us against a naïve exaltation of the positive, *Positive Organizational Behaviour* offers a reflective perspective that encourages us to appreciate the emancipatory potential of positive organizing while remaining alert to the shadow side of positivity. A must-have for all who research and teach about organizational behavior!'

Sally Maitlis, Professor of Organisational Behaviour and Leadership,
Saïd Business School, University of Oxford, UK

Positive Organizational Behaviour

Positive Organizational Behaviour: A Reflective Approach introduces the most recent theoretical and empirical insights on positive organizational practices, addressing emerging topics such as resilience, job crafting, responsible leadership and mindfulness. Other books on positive approaches tend to gloss over the limitations of the positive agenda, but this textbook is unique in taking a reflective approach, focussing on the positive while also accommodating critical perspectives relating to power and control.

Positive Organizational Behaviour provides an integrated conceptual framework, evidence-based findings and practical tools to gain an understanding of the potential of positive organizational practices.

This innovative new textbook will provide advanced management and psychology students with a grounding in the area, and help them develop strategies for building effective and responsible organizations.

Miguel Pina e Cunha is the Amélia de Mello Foundation Professor of Leadership at the Nova School of Business and Economics, Universidade Nova de Lisboa, Lisbon, Portugal.

Arménio Rego is Professor at Católica Porto Business School, Portugal.

Ace Volkmann Simpson is Reader in Human Resource Management and Organizational Behaviour at Brunel University, London, UK.

Stewart Clegg is Professor in Management at the University of Technology Sydney, Australia.

Positive Organizational Behaviour

A Reflective Approach

Miguel Pina e Cunha, Arménio Rego, Ace Volkmann Simpson and Stewart Clegg

Routledge
Taylor & Francis Group

LONDON AND NEW YORK

First published 2020
by Routledge
2 Park Square, Milton Park, Abingdon, Oxon OX14 4RN

and by Routledge
52 Vanderbilt Avenue, New York, NY 10017

Routledge is an imprint of the Taylor & Francis Group, an informa business

British Library Cataloguing-in-Publication Data
A catalogue record for this book is available from the British Library

Library of Congress Cataloging-in-Publication Data
A catalog record has been requested for this book

ISBN: 978-1-138-29308-3 (hbk)
ISBN: 978-1-138-29309-0 (pbk)
ISBN: 978-1-315-23224-9 (ebk)

Typeset in Bembo
by Swales & Willis, Exeter, Devon, UK

Contents

PART IV
Building contexts   **307**

Author biographies

Miguel Pina e Cunha is the Fundação Amélia de Mello Professor of Leadership at Nova School of Business and Economics, Universidade Nova de Lisboa, Lisbon, Portugal. Miguel feels an attraction to what Gail Whiteman called 'management studies that break your heart'[1] and his research deals, mostly, with the surprising (paradox, improvisation, serendipity, zemblanity, vicious circles) and the extreme (positive organizing, genocide). Miguel has published more than 150 papers on these and related topics. He recently co-authored the *Elgar Introduction to Theories of Organizational Resilience* (Elgar, 2018), and co-edited *Management, Organizations and Contemporary Social Theory* (Routledge, 2019).

Arménio Rego is Professor at Católica-Porto Business School, Universidade Católica Portuguesa, Portugal. He has published in journals such as *Human Relations, Journal of Business Ethics, Journal of Business Research, Journal of Management* and *The Leadership Quarterly*, among others. His research examines positive organizational behaviour. He is the lead author of *The Virtues of Leadership: Contemporary Challenge for Global Managers* (with Cunha and Clegg, Oxford University Press, 2012), and co-author of the *Elgar Introduction to Theories of Organizational Resilience* (Elgar, 2018). His main research focus is on virtuous leadership, organizational virtuousness, team processes, and individual performance and well-being.

Ace Volkmann Simpson is Reader in Human Resource Management and Organizational Behaviour at Brunel Business School, Brunel University London and Research Advisory Board member at the Center for Positive Organizations, Ross School of Business, University of Michigan. Ace has a strong interest in human well-being, flourishing and social justice, and his research brings a critical-social perspective to positive organizational practices such as humility, psychological safety, paradox transcendence and love. His main research focus is on the cultivation of organizational compassion, which he is currently studying as a missing factor in most programmes aiming to address the persistent problem of workplace bullying. Ace's research has been published in journals such as *Academy of Management Review*, the *Journal of Management*, the *Journal of Business Ethics* and the *Journal of Management Inquiry*.

Stewart Clegg is Distinguished Professor in Management at UTS Business School, University of Technology Sydney, Australia. Before moving to UTS he was Reader at Griffith University (1976–1984), Professor at the University of New England (1985–1989), Professor at the University of St Andrews (1990–1993) and Foundation Professor at the University of Western Sydney, Macarthur (1993–1996). He currently holds a small number of Visiting Professorships at prestigious European universities and research centres. He is one of the most published and cited authors in the top-tier journals in the Organization Studies field and the only Australian to be recognized by a multi-method ranking as one of the world's top 200

'Management Gurus' in *What's the Big Idea? Creating and Capitalizing on the Best New Management Thinking* by Davenport, Prusak and Wilson (Harvard Business Review Press, 2003). The central focus of his theoretical work has always been on power relations, enabling him to write on many diverse and ubiquitous topics – as power relations are everywhere! He is the author of two widely used textbooks: *Management & Organizations: An Introduction to Theory and Practice* (with Kornberger and Pitsis) and *Strategy: Theory and Practice* (with Schweitzer, Whittle and Pitelis), both published by Sage. He is also the chief editor of the *Handbook of Organization Studies* (with Hardy, Nord and Lawrence), *Handbook of Power* (with Haugaard) and *Handbook of Macro-Organizational Behavior* (with Cooper), all published by Sage. He has published numerous other books, including a book with Oxford University Press on *The Virtues of Leadership: Contemporary Challenges for Global Managers* (with Rego and Cunha, co-authors of this text). He is a prolific contributor to leading journals in the fields of Organization Studies, Political Power and Management.

Note

1 Whiteman (2010).

Reference

Whiteman, G. (2010). Management studies that break your heart. *Journal of Management Inquiry*, 19, 328–337.

Acknowledgements

A book is a collective project, involving names that go well beyond its authors. This book is no exception and all of us have to acknowledge the contributions of a great number of people in several institutions.

Miguel thanks his colleagues at Nova with whom he discussed, throughout the years, the ideas that materialized in this book: Daniel Traça, Filipa Castanheira, Emanuel Gomes, Miguel Alves Martins, Pedro Neves, Sónia Oliveira, Filipa Rodrigues, Milton Sousa, Samantha Sim and Joana Story. Luca Giustiniano has offered ideas from the very beginning to the very end of the project. Miguel Pereira Lopes, a long-time fellow co-worker in the positive field, provided important feedback and insights. Herminia Martins, as always, played a crucial role in the back office. Miguel is also grateful to the Facultad de Administracion of the Universidad de Los Andes (Bogotá, Colombia) and LUISS Guido Carli University (Rome, Italy), where part of this work has been prepared. Uniandes and LUISS have been, over the years, great examples of organizational hospitality.

Arménio thanks his MBA students, at Católica Porto Business School, for helping him in testing the practicality of several approaches and ideas presented in this book. He is thankful to his colleagues from LEAD.Lab. He also gratefully acknowledges the support from CEGE at Católica Porto Business School (particular thanks go to Ricardo Gonçalves, Nuno Martins and Sofia Salgado Pinto) and the Business Research Unit at ISCTE – ISCTE-Instituto Universitário de Lisboa (particular thanks to Sílvia Silva, Maria de Fátima Salgueiro and Rui Costa Pinto).

Ace gratefully acknowledges scholarly colleagues Jane Dutton, Gretchen Spreitzer, Kim Cameron and Bob Quinn from the University of Michigan, Center for Positive Organizations. Their courageous trailblazing research into the positive and enthusiastic inclusiveness of a global scholarly and practitioner community in this positive project has established Positive Organizational Scholarship as a recognized and respected field of academic engagement. This book stands on the shoulders of these academic giants. Ace also thanks the CompassionLab micro-community, particularly Monica Worline, for the ongoing opportunities for regular mutual scholarly engagement. Finally, he thanks colleagues and students at the UTS Business School, where he previously worked as Lecturer and Senior Lecturer (2013–2019), for their enthusiastic interest and encouragement of his research and teaching on positive organizational practices.

Stewart thanks his colleagues Miguel, Arménio and Ace, for their work on this project and for involving him in the team. He would not have been involved at all had it not been for the trailblazing example of a dear friend, sadly departed. Peter Frost was that friend, a remarkable scholar who blended practical insight and theoretical acumen and who wrote from the heart. It was his experiences recovering from surgery in an oncology ward from the cancer that eventually killed him in 2004, experience that led to his path breaking book on Toxic Emotions at work and what you can do about them (Frost 2007), that introduced Stewart to the field of Positive Organization Scholarship. Peter showed Stewart that a concern with the positive was not some kind of managerial con-trick designed to deepen corporate hegemony but a significant and important response to the alienated and estranged world of work that organization designs impose on so many of us. There are better ways to live and work and Peter showed the way, academically and in his life.

The *tripalium* figure in Chapter 5 was generously offered by Vasco Cunha.

Funding

Part of this book was written in the always hospitable environment of Nova Busines School. This work was funded by Fundação para a Ciência e a Tecnologia (UID/ECO/ 00124/2013, UID/ECO/00124/2019, UID/GES/00315/2019, and Social Sciences DataLab, LISBOA-01-0145-FEDER-022209), POR Lisboa (LISBOA-01-0145-FEDER-007722, LISBOA-01-0145-FEDER-022209) and POR Norte (LISBOA-01-0145-FEDER-022209).

Two important notes before we start

1 A note on positive examples

Throughout this book you will find cases and descriptions of organizations (as well as individuals and teams) that have adopted some characteristics of positive organizing. We use these examples for illustrative purposes and make no claims about the positiveness of the organizations, teams and individuals in other respects. In other words, we are not making endorsements. We recognize that even positive organizations can become toxic (or reveal, sometimes, negative features). And toxic organizations can regenerate themselves. Reflecting on historical cases (e.g., shortly before collapsing, Enron had been named as one of the '100 Best Companies to Work for in America'), it is also important to acknowledge that some positive *narratives*, as conveyed by organizations and leaders, disguise negative and toxic *practices*. We therefore ask our readers to approach the examples as illustrations based on the best possible information for educational purposes only.

2 A note on positive research and researchers

Throughout the book we support the topics presented with hundreds of studies that have contributed to the development of a positive approach to organizations. Some of the authors cited identify themselves with the positive organizational scholarship movement. Others do not. And still others may even dislike the notion of 'positivity'. In this sense, the fact that we use a reference to support a point does not mean that the author is a supporter of the vision discussed in the book – or that he/she is a POS (Positive Organizational Scholarship) or a POB (Positive Organizational Behaviour) scholar. The fact is, she/he may even be a critic.

Part I

Prologue

Introduction

In the past, the authors of this book have written about evil organizations at length.[1] Our interests in the 'banality of evil', to quote Hannah Arendt's telling phrase,[2] is not due to a fascination with the dark side per se; instead, the fascination we have is, from our perspective, a necessary antidote to the often panglossic tendencies of management and organization studies to always look on the bright side of life. To focus on exemplars of evil organization is to throw the characteristics of negative organization into sharp relief. Many contemporary organizations might not be out-and-out evil but they are extremely bad. From four management professors such a verdict may seem surprising; management is more often associated with a Whiggish enthusiasm that one must admit that things are getting better, all the time, a belief in the perfectibility of things worthy of Pollyanna. That such enthusiasm might be overstated is warranted by Jeffrey Pfeffer, a management professor at Stanford University, who recently noted 'only four companies made both *Fortune*'s most admired and best places to work lists in 2015'.[3] The small number indicates the difficulty of being both admired and positive. More often than not, as the *Financial Times*' William Skidelsky described them:

> Offices are often spirit-sapping places, incompatible, for many, with a sense of agency and self-respect. People also dislike having bosses: the prospect of not having one, surveys have shown, is a major motivation for going freelance. Having the freedom to work where you want, in your own time, rather than among people and in a place not of your choosing, are things that people increasingly value, and not only those at the top end of the pay-scale.[4]

Pfeffer's observation is consistent with much negative portrayal of managers and organizations in popular culture and the media.[5] It is also consistent with evidence suggesting that organizations and leaders can sometimes be a source of toxicity damaging to individuals' health and life.[6] Several factors explain the lack of positivity in popular representations of management and organizations.

First, there is a fundamental opposition at the very core of organization between (a) humanistic approaches to management and organization, emphasizing intrinsic, non-instrumental approaches to motivation and efficiency and (b), managerial approaches narrowly focussed on productivity with an instrumental view of motivation. These two views can be represented as antithetical[7] and this opposition may ultimately be unresolvable. Debate hinges on opposing notions about humans: as people or as resources. Because of the importance of the 'resource' paradigm, people are often treated as just another factor of production, without giving serious consideration even to the most basic human rights such as respect, dignity and health.[8] The result can be extreme, as some waves of recent workplace-related suicides signify.[9]

Second, the importance of a positive perspective may be discounted in its own right. So-called 'soft skills' can be viewed as *nice to have* rather than *must have* competences or, more formally, as preferential rather than constitutive attributes of managing and organizing.

Third, even organizations that aim to develop 'soft' attributes may discover that such development can represent 'the *hardest* work of all'.[10] As a result, given that talk is cheap, what distinguishes truly positive organizations is the fact that they practice what they preach: 'At other places, managers say that people are their most importance resource, but nobody acts on it. At Southwest, they have never lost sight of the fact', an observer of the airline industry exclaimed.[11]

Fourth, good management is much rarer than usually assumed. As revealed in a Gallup report on the quality of workplaces, managers account for a significant percentage of variance in worker engagement, as much as 70 per cent according to some authors (see Box I.1 on what good managers do). Furthermore, only 15 per cent of the global workforce is actively engaged[12] (18 per cent is actively disengaged). The lack of quality and consistency in how people are managed complicates the creation of positive organizations.

Box I.1 What do great managers do?[13]

The Gallup organization defines five qualities of great managers. They:

- Motivate employees and engage them with a valuable organizational mission.
- Express the levels of assertiveness and grit necessary to get things done and overcome adversity.
- Create cultures of accountability.
- Build positive relationships.
- Make decisions oriented to productivity, not politics.

This book contrasts with most other organizational behaviour textbooks, which tend to be embedded in managerialist assumptions. Managerialism holds efficiency, productivity and profit maximization as the ultimate objectives of good management.[14] It further sees the manager as the main legitimate source of decision-making authority. It is these assumptions, we hold, that make work in so many organizations painful, with destructive effects on people's lives in the broader society and the environment. Unfortunately, toxic managers and toxic organizations are often admired – since ruthless exploitation makes them appear to be efficient and to become rich (Box I.2).

The research on which this book is founded has been conducted by scholars engaged in what has come to be known as Positive Organizational Scholarship (POS), a movement within academia that emerged at the turn of the millennium (discussed in Chapter 1).[15] In adopting a positive focus, this textbook follows Kim Cameron, Jane Dutton and Robert Quinn, founders of the POS movement, in inviting you to imagine alternative possibilities for how we organize:

Imagine another world in which almost all organizations are typified by appreciation, collaboration, virtuousness, vitality and meaningfulness. Creating abundance and human well-being are key indicators of success. Imagine that members of such organizations are characterized by trustworthiness, resilience, wisdom, humanity, and high levels of positive energy. Social relationships and interpretations are characterized by compassion, loyalty, honesty, respect, and forgiveness. Significant attention is given to what makes life worth living.[16]

This textbook makes such positive imagining possible, as it is based on scholarly research, supplemented with copious real-life examples from exemplary organizations. Although we classify the research that is the basis for this textbook as positive organizational scholarship, not all of the academics who published these studies self-identify as POS scholars. Indeed, there is much research into extraordinary organizational practices that has been conducted outside of the POS movement. Some of this work, in fact, preceded the POS movement by decades. We nonetheless see this work as contributing to the objectives of POS, which informs the development of positive organizational behaviour. Accordingly, we hold that it is important to include this body of research within our textbook on positive organizational behaviour.

The scholarship presented in this textbook clarifies why being positive and admired, humane and lucrative, must not be opposite goals. Our defence of the idea may appear deceptively simple but a plethora of evidence suggests otherwise: being positive takes work. As we will discuss throughout the book, the positive and the negative interact (Box I.2). For example, seemingly positive processes of market growth may produce the sort of collective euphoria that has been associated with asset bubbles.[17] Conversely, being optimistic may not be a recommendable trait for leaders responsible for running a nuclear power plant.

Box I.2 Should we deplore some admired entities?

On August 16, 2016, Amazon.com was depicted by *The New York Times* as a 'bruising workplace'.[18] Jeffrey Pfeffer commented on the article in *Fortune* magazine as follows:[19]

> The recent *New York Times* profile of Amazon.com describing its relentless, high-pressure, measurement-obsessed culture is scarcely the first to depict what it is like to work there, either in its warehouses or its offices. While CEO Jeff Bezos has denied (no surprise) the accuracy of the reporting, a quick Web search reveals numerous articles painting a picture remarkably consistent with this most recent portrayal: Amazon is a tough place to work, Bezos is famous for his temper and put-downs of employees, and many people who cannot stand the stress and pressure leave. There are numerous lessons to be gained from considering Amazon, its culture, and its success – lessons that pertain to many other workplaces. Here are three: The leaders we admire aren't always that admirable … Economic performance and costs trump employee well-being … People participate in and rationalize their own subjugation.

The roadmap for the book

The book follows a well-known, some would say conservative, logic: we move from micro to macro. Although this classification can be problematic due to thematic overlaps, we move from individual-level themes to organizational-level dimensions. In real life, things are necessarily more complicated as processes do not stop at the boundary between levels. Moreover, some topics cross over different levels and other topics could be included in different chapters. Overall, however, this logic offers a workable roadmap for the journey, which we organize as follows.

In this introduction we establish the background for the ensuing discussion. Recognizing some of the problems with the contemporary organizational landscape of theory and practice, including cynical managerial views of human nature, loss of public confidence in companies and institutions, and low levels of employee engagement with high levels of employee stress, we present positive organizational behaviour as a promising alternative. Application of a positive lens enables observation of the desired outcomes of positive organizing discussed in this book including: employee flourishing, engagement, psychological safety, wellbeing, a sense of meaning and a purpose beyond mere profit maximization, as well as the vital importance of virtues and an ethical approach to management. Adopting a positive lens is not only an *intellectual* endeavour – it also affects how individuals *act*. As Ghoshal observed:[20]

> A theory of subatomic particles or of the universe – right or wrong – does not change the behaviors of these particles or of the universe. If a theory assumes that the sun goes around the earth, it does not change what the sun actually does. So, if the theory is wrong, the truth is preserved for discovery by someone else. In contrast, a management theory – if it gains sufficient currency – changes the behaviors of managers who start acting in accordance with the theory. A theory that assumes that people can behave opportunistically and draws in conclusions for managing people based on that assumption can induce managerial actions that are likely to enhance opportunistic behaviour among people (Ghoshal & Moran, 1996). A theory that draws prescriptions on corporate governance on the assumptions that managers cannot be trusted can make managers less trustworthy (Osterloch & Frey, 2003). Whether right or wrong to begin with, the theory can become right as managers – who are both its subjects and the consumers – adapt their behaviors to conform with the doctrine.

In Chapter 1 we present the **foundations** of positive organizational behaviour (which, as discussed above, academics study as POS). This chapter defines the meaning of positive, briefly traces the inception of positive approaches in organizational studies and clarifies the mutual relationship between positive and negative. Reflecting on this relationship is an important consideration that you, the reader, will be invited to undertake as you journey throughout the book: positive does not mean the exclusion of negative. In fact, purely positive organizations would be dead organizations. Reality involves friction and discomfort, and these are part, inevitably, of an organization's existence. Hence, we introduce boxes throughout the book exemplifying the positive in the negative and the negative in the positive.

The second and third chapters discuss **personal strengths**. While Chapter 2 considers the importance of personal dispositions, Chapter 3 focusses on state-like characteristics, specifically psychological capital (i.e., hope, self-efficacy, resilience and optimism). Positive approaches emphasize the importance of what is teachable and developable and the second and third chapters illustrate that emphasis. What distinguishes positive organizations is their role in emphasizing individual strengths to develop positivity as a personal attribute. The core assumption underlying the two chapters is that while a focus on weaknesses and criticisms makes employees defensive and less prone to change, a focus on strengths leads them to flourish and, in the process, contributes to team and organizational excellence. An emphasis on strengths does not mean that organizations should ignore weaknesses. The two capability streams, though not unrelated, are also different in their effects.

Chapter 4 discusses **emotions**. Emotions are integral to organizational behaviour. This chapter considers emotions as an evolutionary tool and discusses the importance of cultivating positive emotional capabilities within an organizational context, along with the significance of what has been termed emotional intelligence in organizational life. We also consider the role of mindfulness and its implications for management. The topic of emotions extends well beyond the individual level; emotions can be cultivated collectively as organizational climate. A core assumption underlying this chapter is that organizations can facilitate organizational thriving by cultivating positive emotions and developing competences in regulating negative emotions. The chapter however refuses the 'Pollyanna mindset' that considers positive emotions as always positive in their effects and negative emotions as always engendering negative consequences. Negative emotions play a role in organizations and the interplay between positive and negative emotions may be crucial for individual and organizational flourishing.

Chapter 5 explores the importance of **work design** for human flourishing. Work occupies a substantial part of our lives and, as such, it should ideally be a source of potential human growth rather than its restriction. Often it is not. In this chapter we situate the development of job design theories historically and present recent developments stressing that organizations should design jobs for meaning, wellbeing and health. As a tripartite goal these objectives are noble but the chapter also indicates that in some cases jobs can become so central in their meaning that they fundamentally conquer the space deserved by other spheres of life, thus harming wellbeing and health.

Chapter 6 considers the importance of **relationships**. Organizations are typically portrayed in textbooks as groups of individuals working in coordinated ways, often as teams, to achieve higher order goals. As an illustration of organizations this is limited. Relationships, we consider, are the fabric of organizing that makes or breaks organizations. In this chapter we discuss organizations as relational spaces by considering the nature of positive, generative relationship as well as the difference made by conversations in establishing organizational patterns of communication. We also problematize relations by considering why negative and intoxicating relationships, expressed as uncivil behaviours, are so prevalent in organizations.

Teams constitute the theme of Chapter 7. Team dynamics are fascinating human processes. From the outside teams normally look alike while in reality they express very different realities. Some teams are rich with potential and growth, whereas others are highly dysfunctional. Diversity within teams can be highly positive or fundamentally negative. Learning may be rich or nonexistent. The question we pose in this chapter is: what factors explain differences in team success? We discuss the critical dimensions and predictors of team effectiveness and the hardware and software of teaming. We pay special attention to team psychological safety, team learning and collective intelligence, including how it can be promoted or not by leaders.

Chapter 8 is about **leadership**. Leadership is a core theme in organizations because leaders are highly influential in terms of organizational functioning. Leaders have often been approached as romantic and heroic figures. In this chapter we avoid such approaches and present leaders as potential agents of positivity. Positive leaders are those who create organizations characterized by a respect for diversity, the cultivation of virtues such as humility, while creating well-led organizations. This, of course, contrasts with what happens in many organizations, in which leaders create 'subordinates'. The chapter focusses specifically on humble leadership, ethical leadership, authentic leadership and servant leadership, considering these approaches as routes through which positive leadership may be enacted. Seeing just the positive in positive leadership approaches can be a source of negativity because it is too one-sided; hence, undesirable potential effects of these positive 'styles' are also discussed.

Positive leaders create **positive workplaces**, discussed in Chapter 9. These have been variously described as the best places in which to work, best workplaces, authentizotic organizations and cultures of abundance. What they have in common is a number of characteristics that revolve around appreciating individuals with all their differences. These ideal type organizations are certainly not perfect but they do present a number of similarities. Their merits notwithstanding, it is important to keep in mind that positive workplaces are ongoing projects, always incomplete, and always in a process of becoming something different – more positive but also always potentially more negative. Conservatism, faith in existing solutions and exploitative inclinations are all enduring threats to positive organizations, a paradox that positive leaders must learn to navigate.

The tenth chapter discusses **power**. Power is often viewed as a negative, corruptive force. It certainly can be. But power is also an indispensable force for good. Without power, nobody 'changes the world'. We start this chapter, given its huge historical lineage, with an introduction to several major theorists of power. We are especially interested in different expressions of power: as an instrument of domination but also as a shared relational force. Power can be used to liberate as much as it can be used to dominate. We consider cases of positive deviance as well as processes organizations can adopt to generate positive approaches to power: creating cultures of speaking up, moving from command and control to empowering, stimulating divergence through devil's advocacy, among others. By powering positivity, organizations are doing a service to themselves as major corporate scandals are, to some extent, a product of the misuse or the abuse of power, as documented in recent scandals such as those involving VW or Wells Fargo.

Chapter 11 considers the potential of organizations as **engines of progress**. Moving to a macroscopic level, our approach becomes more philosophical and sociological as we trace contested relationships between companies and society. The business firm can be an admirable engine of progress but can also be a force with potentially destructive attributes. Organizations oftentimes solve societal problems at the same time as they create further problems. This chapter discusses the conflicting relationship between business and society. Without discounting the dangers ahead, including new ones resulting from digitalization, whose implications may well include job destruction and unemployment with the deepening of the gap between the included and the excluded, the chapter dwells on the creation of more sustainable organizations.

Our final chapter, 12, revisits the overall themes of the book and considers the perils behind the promises, problematizing the relationship between **the positive and the negative** and raising questions of ethics and virtue. This chapter extends the discussion initiated in the introduction and explains why, in each topic, the positive can produce intended or unintended negative effects. We consider this chapter important for countering simplistic representations of what positive means and to underline the paradoxical side of organizations, including positive organizations. We also discuss why being positive is still so rare.

Intentions and a credo

Sometimes the best way to describe a thing is by explaining what it is not: we do not intend to offer the reader infallible solutions. Pop psychology books and the $12 billion self-help industry are rife with remedies for life's uncertainties and miseries.[21] We do not discuss these approaches. In line with Fred Luthans, a pioneering researcher of positive organizational behaviour, we aim to avoid the 'surface positivity' often adopted in texts that promise miraculous solutions.[22] We do not want to be Pollyannaish in naively persuading our readers about the power of the positive as a given. In fact, we believe that the paradigm of positivity can be harmful in the wrong hands, much as the proverbial road to hell that is paved with good intentions. Fostering positivity may be used as an instrumental tool, a moral technology[23] aimed at gaining more effort from more satisfied employees, much as contented cows allegedly produce more milk.[24]

People spend a significant part of their lives at work. Yet, for many, work life is far from fulfilling. As displayed in movies as old as *Modern Times* or as recently as *Horrible Bosses*, life in organizations can be punishing, as expressed in the deaths resulting from work-related suicide in places such as France, China and Japan. Work too often sucks rather than sustains, negating rather than nourishing the spirit, a dismal reality that we would not contest. Aware of these tendencies, we rather seek to make a modest contribution through a positive lens on organizational phenomena, seeking to identify that which is generative, life-affirming and contributory to wellbeing in organizational life. As will be discussed in this volume, there is abundant research suggesting ways to manage people decently, rather than dreadfully. Our credo is presented in Box I.3.

Box I.3 Our credo

1 We believe that no miraculous solutions exist to organizational problems.
2 We believe that positive solutions in one place or time can be undesirable in another time and space.
3 Prescriptions should be approached with a critical distance.
4 Positive principles can be used manipulatively.
5 An excess of something positive can become negative.
6 One positive characteristic does not neutralize other negative characteristics.
7 One person's positive can be another's negative.
8 Positivity may emerge as a consequence of negative experiences (e.g., post-traumatic growth) – but this does not legitimize 'doing the evil' to 'build the good'.
9 Life, including organizational life, has positive and negative sides, and ignoring or underestimating the negative side only brings more negativity.
10 The fact that something is stigmatized as evil is not enough to delegitimize it as such, as expressed by slavery, anti-Semitism or many other examples of applied evil.

Is studying evil a positive endeavour?

In adopting a positive lens on organizational phenomena, we necessarily adopt a positive bias.[25] We seek to understand from a scholarly perspective the organizational factors that contribute towards exceptional human behaviours and states, extraordinary interpersonal relations and generative organizational outcomes. Yet, in the same way that we defend the importance of a field of positive organizational scholarship and practice, we also defend the need for a field dedicated to evil organization studies, but not practices.[26] This field could reveal some interesting possibilities. For example:

- Evil practices are often wrapped in positive descriptors such as honour, decency, purity and tradition.
- Positive processes such as the desire to belong can be exploited and abused to perpetrate evil.
- Discourses replete with positive references are often filled with toxic potential.
- Bad is stronger than good[27] which means that in trying times people may revert to basic, instinctual behaviours.

The study of evil in organizations puts managerialist assumptions under the spotlight, questioning their veracity; it highlights power imbalances that contribute towards life-sucking and dehumanizing employee exploitation, domination and control and it provides a voice for stakeholders whose concerns have too often been silenced. Such scholarship has traditionally been the domain of the field of Critical Management Studies (CMS).[28] In fact, one of us (Stewart) is a founding contributor to the CMS movement. The objective of critical scholarship is to create awareness of structures of domination that underpin managerial agendas – providing informed citizens with the means of liberation from these overarching systems of control.

POS has a similar emancipatory objective but with a different approach.[29] In promoting positive organizational practices, POS is not value neutral but normative, prescribing practices that generate human thriving and flourishing in organizations and the communities in which they operate.[30] While adopting a positive lens is in itself a critique of managerialist business as usual practices, there is nonetheless the potential for managerial co-opting or colonizing of positive organizational practices in the service of managerialist agendas. In such a scenario, positive practices are used as mere means towards the ends of greater efficiency, productivity and profitability.[31] There are no guarantees that positive practices may not become structures of domination and control. Being inattentive towards potential toxicity may be as negative as ignoring the possibilities a positive perspective opens up. Accordingly, we include as the subtitle to this book 'a reflective approach', inviting you to reflect on the motivations and effects at play when positive organizational principles are applied within specific contexts. By 'reflective' we refer to an analysis that considers both the opportunities as well as the risks underpinning the positive perspective. Such an approach allows us to focus on the positive but with mature reflexivity regarding the inherent limitations of a naive ideological commitment to positivity.

Publications on POS have seen significant growth in the last decade but so far this has resulted only in the publication of articles and edited volumes. To the best of our knowledge no textbook is available on organizations and their practices from a positive perspective. It is this gap that the book aims to fill. Further, existing literature tends to ignore limitations and critiques. Accordingly, our more specific objectives are:

- To provide a framework for students, practitioners and academics to analyze, understand and act according to principles of POS.
- To provide a reflective perspective on the implications of POS for the understanding of organizational behaviour.
- In doing so, we complement existing textbooks on organizational behaviour. The framework presented in the book provides concepts with which to analyze and manage positively.
- The book explores the potentials of Positive Organizational Behaviour (POB) as an alternative, empirically based approach to traditional organizational behaviour.
- The book will provide readers with the conceptual language and theoretical frameworks to address some of the main problems facing organizational members by offering them a positive but not naive approach to the problems faced within and by organizations.

A reading grid

Writing a book on what makes a positive organization is a risky endeavour: organizations are processes, dynamic and unstable. As Bob Quinn, a POS researcher at the University of Michigan Center for Positive Organizations, points out, organizations are constantly in the process of becoming more positive or more negative.[32] For this reason, the book should be read with a number of precautionary notes in mind:

- The book presents numerous illustrations of organizations. But illustrations are not endorsements: positive organizations can become negative (or reveal a negative face) and negative organizations can become positive (or contain positive features).
- It is possible that the book uses examples of companies that one day will be known for their negative practices. Had the book been written five years earlier, we might have featured the cases of VW and Wells Fargo[33] as illustrative of companies with solid sustainable practices. We now know that this would have been an empirical *faux pas*. There is no solution to this other than removing examples, trusting sources or offering these types of disclaimers or warnings. Realities are not always what they are represented as being.
- We aim to achieve a combination of rigour and relevance, hence the presentation of examples and illustrations.
- Yet, leading positively is more than *knowing a lot about management*. Engaging with literature can also help with developing interpersonal and reflective skills, skills that are so important for any manager. The reader will thus find examples, illustrations, digressions and provocations coming from the arts.
- For the same reason, when justified, we precede our explorations of the positive in organizations with historical or philosophical considerations. This is important, we think, as management as a deeply institutionalized process is informed by history and ideas, even where it is not evidently the case. Indeed, to recall Keynes, we are often slaves of defunct and mad ideas, in management no less than economics.
- As explained, we do not see positive and negative as opposites. They are parts of a paradoxical interdependence (see, e.g., Chapter 12). For this reason, in each

chapter the reader will find examples of this interpenetration, with boxes on the positive in negative, and the negative in positive.

- At the end of each chapter you will find some suggestions that may facilitate subsequent exploration of each topic.

It is also worth noting that the traditional approach of separating organizational phenomena into various categories of study (such as leadership, individual differences, team and group dynamics), although helpful for analyzing and learning about organizational behaviour, is artificial. In reality these topics all blur into each other, with significant overlaps between them. Accordingly, we present Table I.1 to give some sense of how these topics overlap within this textbook.

Table I.1 How traditional organizational behaviour (OB) topics overlap with the contents of this textbook

Traditional OB topics	This textbook
Individual characteristics	Ch. 2: Leveraging on individual strengths Ch. 3: Psychological capital: the 'HERO' effect Ch. 7: Real teams: supporting learning and change
Emotions and moods	Ch. 4: Emotions and happiness at work
Values	Ch. 6: Generative interactions in organizations Ch. 8: Leveraging on individual strengths Ch. 9: Great workplaces Ch. 10: Powering positivity Ch. 11: The positive organization of progress Ch. 12: The positive–negative dialectic
Motivation concepts	Ch. 3: Leveraging on individual strengths Ch. 3: Psychological capital: the 'HERO' effect Ch. 5: Designing work for meaning, learning and health Ch. 9: Great workplaces
Teams and groups	Ch. 6: Generative interactions in organizations Ch. 7: Real teams: supporting learning and change
Power and politics	Ch. 10: Powering positivity Ch. 11: The positive organization of progress
Leadership	Ch. 8: Positive leadership: humble, ethical, authentic and servant (Almost all chapters discuss topics related to leadership)
Innovation and creativity	Ch. 7: Real teams: supporting learning and change Ch. 10: Powering positivity
Organizational culture	Ch. 6: Generative interactions in organizations Ch. 7: Real teams: supporting learning and change Ch. 9: Great workplaces Ch. 10: Powering positivity
Human resource policies	Ch. 2: Leveraging on individual strengths Ch. 3: Psychological capital: the 'HERO' effect Ch. 5: Designing work for meaning, learning and health
Organizational change	Ch. 7: Real teams: supporting learning and change Ch. 9: Great workplaces
Ethics and sustainability	Ch. 8: Positive leadership: humble, ethical, authentic and servant Ch. 10: Powering positivity Ch. 11: The positive organization of progress Ch. 12: The positive–negative dialectic

Table I.2 A positive lens: does it matter to my organization?

Think about your employer or an organization you know. Ask the following questions:

- How do we frame effectiveness? As job performance without a more encompassing consideration of elements of human flourishing and personal growth?
- Do we assume that the place makes the people? In other words that people are moulded by their environments?
- Do we represent individuals rather than relationships as the building blocks of organizations?
- Do we assume that organizations and the people inside them compete for scarce resources in a sort of war for talent and other resources?
- Do our assumptions admit that resources (e.g., intelligence) are mostly fixed and pre-determined?
- Do we assume that personal growth is hard and perhaps impossible after a limit?
- Do we represent development as transferring and accumulating knowledge?
- Is the language in use a source of dehumanization – for example treating people as disposable human resources?
- Do we mostly focus on the negative side?
- Do we assume that people are motivated first and foremost by individual self-interest?

In case you have answered yes to any of the questions, we suspect that this book is for you.

The table provides a guide to students and academics studying or teaching organizational behaviour, a guide for understanding how the usual topics and chapters included in organizational behaviour textbooks map against the chapters included in this textbook on positive organizational behaviour.

Having clarified the objectives and guidelines, it is time to assess how much this discussion matters to organizations around us (see Table I.2) and then turn the page to explore the book.

Notes

1 Cunha, Rego, Silva and Clegg (2015); Cunha, Clegg and Rego (2015); Simpson et al. (2014); Cunha, Rego and Clegg (2014); Cunha, Clegg, Rego, & Gomes (2015).
2 Arendt (1963).
3 Pfeffer (2016, p. 1).
4 Skidelsky (2017, p. 9).
5 Parker (2018).
6 Goh, Pfeffer and Zenios (2015a, 2015b, 2016); Pfeffer (2016).
7 Alvesson (1982).
8 Pfeffer (2018).
9 Clegg, Cunha and Rego (2016).
10 Waytz (2016, p. 73, italics in the original).
11 O'Reilly and Pfeffer (1995, p. 14).
12 Beck and Harter (2014); Gallup (2017).
13 Source: Beck and Harter (2014).
14 Klikauer (2013); Parker (2002).
15 Bernstein (2003).
16 Cameron, Dutton and Quinn (2003, p. 3).
17 Teeter and Sandberg (2017).
18 Kantor and Streitfeld (2015).
19 Pfeffer (2015).
20 Ghoshal (2005, p. 77).

21 Oettingen (2017).
22 Luthans (2002).
23 Foucault (1975/1979).
24 Scott (1992).
25 Cameron, Dutton and Quinn (2003).
26 Clegg (2006).
27 Baumeister, Bratslavsky, Finkenauer and Vohs (2001).
28 Alvesson and Willmott (1992); Fournier and Grey (2000).
29 Caza and Carroll (2012).
30 Cameron, Dutton and Quinn (2003).
31 Fineman (2006).
32 Quinn (2015).
33 Independent Directors of the Board of Wells Fargo and Company (2017); Tayan (2019).

References

Alvesson, M. (1982). The limits and shortcomings of humanistic organization theory. *Acta Sociologica*, 25(2), 117–131.
Alvesson, M., & Willmott, H. (1992). *Critical management studies*. London: Sage.
Arendt, H. (1963). *A report on the banality of evil*. London: Faber.
Baumeister, R. F., Bratslavsky, E., Finkenauer, C., & Vohs, K. D. (2001). Bad is stronger than good. *Review of General Psychology*, 5(4), 323–370.
Beck, R., & Harter, J. (2014). Why good managers are so rare. *Harvard Business Review*, March 13 (https://hbr.org/2014/03/why-good-managers-are-so-rare?cm_sp=Article-_-Links-_-Comment).
Bernstein, S. D. (2003). Positive organizational scholarship: Meet the movement. An interview with Kim Cameron, Jane Dutton, and Robert Quinn. *Journal of Management Inquiry*, 12(3), 266–271.
Cameron, K. S., Dutton, J., & Quinn, R. E. (2003). *Positive organizational scholarship: Foundations of a new discipline*. San Francisco, CA: Berrett-Koehler.
Caza, A., & Carroll, B. (2012). Critical theory and positive organizational scholarship. In K. S. Cameron, & J. P. Schneider (Eds.), *The Oxford handbook of positive organizational scholarship* (pp. 965–978). New York: Oxford University Press.
Clegg, S., Cunha, M. P., & Rego, A. (2016). Explaining suicide in organizations. Durkheim revisited. *Business & Society Review*, 121(3), 391–414.
Clegg, S. R. (2006). Why is organization theory so ignorant? *Journal of Management Inquiry*, 15, 426–430.
Cunha, M. P., Clegg, S. R., & Rego, A. (2015). The institutionalization of genocidal leadership: Pol Pot and a Cambodian Dystopia. *Journal of Leadership Studies*, 9(1), 6–18.
Cunha, M. P., Clegg, S., Rego, A., & Gomes, J. F. (2015). Embodying Sensemaking: Learning from the Extreme Case of Vann Nath, Prisoner at S–21. *European Management Review*, 12(1), 41–58.
Cunha, M. P., Rego, A., & Clegg, S. R. (2014). The ethical speaking of objects: Ethics and the "object-ive" world of Khmer Rouge Young Comrades. *Journal of Political Power*, 7(1), 35–61.
Cunha, M. P., Rego, A., Silva, A. F., & Clegg, S. R. (2015). An institutional palimpsest? The case of Cambodia's political order, 1970 and beyond. *Journal of Political Power*, 8(3), 431–455.
Fineman, S. (2006). On being positive: Concerns and counterpoints. *Academy of Management Review*, 31(2), 270–291.
Foucault, M. (1975/1979). *Discipline and punish: The birth of the prison*. New York: Vintage Books.
Fournier, V., & Grey, C. (2000). At the critical moment: Conditions and prospects for critical management studies. *Human Relations*, 53(1), 7–32.
Gallup. (2017). *State of the global workplace*. New York: Gallup Press.
Ghoshal, S. (2005). Bad management theories are destroying good management practices. *Academy of Management Learning and Education*, 4(1), 75–91.
Goh, J., Pfeffer, J., & Zenios, S. (2015a). Exposure to harmful workplace practices could account for inequality in life spans across different demographic groups. *Health Affairs*, 34(1), 1761–1768.

Goh, J., Pfeffer, J., & Zenios, S. A. (2015b). Workplace stressors & health outcomes: Health policy for the workplace. *Behavioral Science & Policy*, 1(1), 43–52.

Goh, J., Pfeffer, J., & Zenios, S. A. (2016). The relationship between workplace stressors and mortality and health costs in the United States. *Management Science*, 62(2), 608–628.

Independent Directors of the Board of Wells Fargo & Company. (2017). *Sales practices investigation report.* April 10 (https://08.wellsfargomedia.com/assets/pdf/about/investor-relations/presentations/2017/board-report.pdf)

Kantor, J., & Streitfeld, D. (2015). Inside Amazon: Wrestling big ideas in a bruising workplace. *The New York Times*, August 16, A1.

Klikauer, T. (2013). *Managerialism: A critique of an ideology.* London: Palgrave Macmillan.

Luthans, F. (2002). The need for and meaning of positive organizational behavior. *Journal of Organizational Behavior*, 23, 695–706.

O'Reilly, C., & Pfeffer, J. (1995). *Southwest Airlines (A), Case HR-1A.* Stanford Graduate School of Business.

Oettingen, G. (2017). Don't think too positive. *Aeon*, July 25 (https://aeon.co/essays/thinking-positive-is-a-surprisingly-risky-manoeuvre).

Parker, M. (2002). *Against management: Organization in the age of managerialism.* New York: Polity Press and Blackwell.

Parker, M. (2018). Employing James Bond. *Journal of Management Inquiry*, 27(2), 178–189.

Pfeffer, J. (2015). 3 lessons from the Amazon takedown. *Fortune*, August 18 (http://fortune.com/2015/08/18/amazon-new-york-times/).

Pfeffer, J. (2016). Why the assholes are winning: Money trumps all. *Journal of Management Studies*, 53(4), 663–669.

Pfeffer, J. (2018). *Dying for a paycheck: How modern management harms employee health and company performance – and what we can do about it.* New York: Harper.

Quinn, R. E. (2015). *The positive organization: Breaking free from conventional cultures, constraints, and beliefs.* San Francisco, CA: Berrett-Koehler.

Scott, W. R. (1992). *Organizations: Rational, natural, and open systems.* (3rd ed.). Englewood Cliffs, NJ: Prentice Hall.

Simpson, A. V., Clegg, S. R., Lopes, M. P., Pitsis, T., Rego, A., & Cunha, M. P. (2014). Doing compassion or doing discipline? Power relations and the Magdalene Laundries. *Journal of Political Power*, 7(2), 253–274.

Skidelsky, R. (2017). A job for life. *Financial Times Life & Arts*, April 22/23, 9.

Tayan, B. (2019). The Wells Fargo cross-selling scandal. Stanford Closer Look Series (https://www.gsb.stanford.edu/sites/gsb/files/publication-pdf/cgri-closer-look-62-wells-fargo-cross-selling-scandal.pdf).

Teeter, P., & Sandberg, J. (2017). Cracking the enigma of asset bubbles with narratives. *Strategic Organization*, 15(1), 91–99.

Waytz, J. (2016). The limits of empathy. *Harvard Business Review*, 94(1), 70–73.

1 Positive organizations

The foundations

Summary and objectives

In this chapter we explain the background of positive approaches to organizations and their applications. The study of organizations from a positive perspective: (1) articulates a focus on strengths; (2) aims to achieve excellent results across broad categories of stakeholders; (3) and does so in a virtuous and socially responsible manner. In this chapter we consider the duality between positive and negative, compare and contrast the assumptions underpinning classical management and positive management and discuss the practical consequences of positive assumptions.

Organizing 'for good'

Do we really need a focus on the positive side of organizing? Let us consider evidence from distinct sources:

- Gallup studies on the state of the global workplace indicate that the vast majority of employees around the world *do not* feel engaged with their work.[1]
- Corporate scandals propelled by greed seem to be here to stay, wave after wave.
- One of the darling companies of the new economy, Uber, has been found to have established a 'toxic' culture that bred sexism and sexual harassment.[2]
- Work-related suicidal waves have hit major companies such as France Telecom and Foxconn.
- Organizations around the world promote modern forms of slavery, human trafficking and other means of human exploitation.[3] For example, in Southeast Asia, fishing boats crewed by forced labourers never dock to impede the slaves from escaping. Fish catches and supplies are received at sea.[4]
- Stress has been qualified as a modern malaise, an epidemic.

The list could go on but this sample of evidence indicates organizations that are often spaces rife with negativity. Although frequently presented as tools for human progress, organizations often end up producing oppression and exploitation.[5] For too many people, work is not a personally fulfilling experience; indeed, in some cases organizations produce negative externalities for their communities as well as the governments and societies that embed them, and as well as the natural environment that sustains all species. Organization and management studies often ignore non-consumers: people at the fringes, the poor, the disenfranchised, the creatures of the land, air and sea. Positive organizational studies aim to create scientifically validated conceptual frameworks and modes of intervention destined to reverse this sad state of affairs. Instead of taking the negative as normal, positive organizational studies invests its energies into ways of promoting organizations as engines of social, economic and environmental progress. From a positive perspective, human variables, such as satisfaction and well-being, become 'dependent variables',[6] i.e., valuable outcomes in and of themselves, rather than causes of other valuable outcomes, such as productivity. Positive organization aims at developing forms of organizing 'for good'[7] that contribute towards the creation of better organizations, more fulfilled people, more balanced communities.

Positive organizational studies: the principles

The field of positive organizational studies, including the different streams of POB or POS, constitutes a new area of research and intervention in organizations and management. The different approaches, as will be discussed below, are varied but compatible in their ultimate intentions. They all aim to construct a theory of management oriented towards what is good and beneficial rather than to what is problematic. Throughout this book we refer to POB as organizational behaviour with a positive, balanced focus. The label 'positive organizational studies' as we use it here combines the two domains of POB and POS. From Fred Luthans and colleagues, we derive the importance of measurement and impact; from the POS community we derive a regard for human virtues, in the Aristotelian sense we discuss below, as ends in themselves. Performance without virtue is flawed and potentially unsustainable.[8]

A literature search in the field of psychology conducted by Luthans found 375,000 articles about negatives and only about 1,000 on positives, which corresponds to a negative/positive publication ratio of 375/1.[9]

- Negatives refer to debilitating processes such as illness, fear, anxiety.
- Positives refer to facilitative processes such as love, flourishing, courage or optimism.

The orientation towards that which is problematic, exhibiting a 'repair shop' logic (see Figure 1.1),[10] is prevalent in the field of management and organizational studies, where researchers have been interested mostly in solving problems and addressing issues defined as such by management rather than those upon whom management's decisions have considerable impact. Yet, a balanced view of management should not ignore the values that count the most. Dean Ornish, a professor of medicine at the University of California, explains that 'Science is documenting the healing values of love, intimacy, community, compassion, forgiveness, altruism and service'.[11] He added that, given this, being selfless may constitute the most self-serving approach to life.

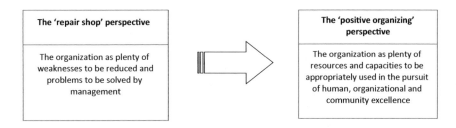

Figure 1.1 Two perspectives on organizational functioning and management.

What does positive mean?

Positive organizing involves three interrelated dimensions: excellence, 'affirmative dynamics' and eudemonia. First, as previously noted, the positive organizational perspective defends the proposition that 'positive' refers to outcomes in two dimensions: human excellence and excellent performance.[12] An organization qualifies as positive to the extent that it expresses superior effectiveness, sustainably. Research has shown that organizations with positive practices, such as those that signify great workplaces, are more effective and resilient. One explanation for this is the fact that the goodwill these organizations build in good times allows them to withstand difficulties in bad times, namely because of the degree of commitment of their employees[13] and other stakeholders.

Second, a positive organization is one that affirms strengths instead of tackling weaknesses, a characteristic known as 'affirmative dynamics':[14] the organization is approached from the perspective of the resources it has rather than by those it does not possess. A logic of resourcefulness replaces one of resource scarcity. The farmer-entrepreneur Tim Grayson, studied by Baker and Nelson, epitomizes this logic at work.[15] Instead of viewing his plot of land as useless (it was crisscrossed by abandoned coal mines, which tended to collapse, releasing large quantities of methane when they did so), he created a series of business opportunities by activating resources seemingly invisible to others. He created business opportunities 'out of nothing': he converted methane into energy, sold this energy to a local utility, using part of it to heat a greenhouse in which he cultivated hydroponic tomatoes. In the water that bathed the tomato roots he raised tilapia, a fish increasingly perceived as a delicacy in the US. Fish waste was used as fertilizer. Instead of considering lack, Grayson adopted a positive logic, seeing resources where others had only noticed resource voids.

Box 1.1 The positive in the negative: reframing autism as a form of talent[16]

Autism is a broad-spectrum syndrome that refers to challenges related to language social skills and to repetitive behaviours, among other conditions. It is normally presented as an impediment to living a fulfilling work life. But our readers who watched the movie *Rain Man*, featuring Tom Cruise and Dustin Hoffman, have possibly retained the observation that the character played by Hoffman (Raymond) presented some exceptional qualities. The syndrome he suffered from could be represented as meaning that the behaviours that are normally represented as problematic can in fact carry many positive implications. For example, Raymond's mathematical thinking was superb as was his attention to detail and unparalleled memory.

These skills are, in fact, so notable that some companies are trying to make use of them. These companies include SAP, which is hiring people with autism to work as software evaluators, programmers and data quality experts. Vodafone Germany is paying attention to the specific skills of these people, as is Microsoft. As a result, these companies, in a disposition aligned with the positive view of organization, have tapped a talent pool where others would normally see a handicap.

Third, positive refers to a eudemonic assumption, emphasizing what is virtuous and good in the human condition. Well-functioning human groups aspire to excellence and virtue; they strive to succeed through the polar opposites of vice and mediocrity. Being successful is important but so are the ways in which success is achieved: the best results should be obtained in the right way. Success in the absence of excellence is potentially problematic: it is tempting to cut corners and engage in excess in the pursuit of results but doing so lays shaky foundations for the future and presents evident risks in the here-and-now. Recall the case of Enron.[17] Results obtained at any cost can be unsustainable and jeopardize the reputation and sometimes even the very continuity of an organization. Numerous examples illustrate this possibility, including not only those of Enron but also Wells Fargo[18] in the US and Banco Espírito Santo[19] and VW[20] in Europe. In the case of VW, an orientation to win 'with all means' meant that ethical issues did not stop the organization from winning its 'wars' against competitors.[21] A practice of prioritizing profits over stakeholders (such as the environment, society, employees, customers, suppliers, distributors and shareholders) partly explains the emissions scandal that shredded Enron's reputation into tatters – and damaged customers and fostered cynicism and suspicion against (other) corporations.

By aligning its triangle of definitional elements, a positive organization is one that sustainably obtains superior performance in a virtuous way, via an emphasis on strengths. Organizations qualify as positive when they get the right results, using appropriate, ethical and sustainable means. In so doing, they do not create social pollution but rather contribute towards the strengthening of ties between businesses and communities. Positive organizations are porous to their environments and see balance as an important aspirational goal. Instead of focussing on the finalities of one stakeholder, they embrace a holistic understanding of organizational goals and responsibilities, and they see themselves as embedded in societies rather than as independent legal mechanisms of production. Their ultimate goal or reason for being is not profit at all cost but the 'overall well-being' of stakeholders.[22] Note, however, that the emphasis on positive does not entail the denial or the removal of negative, as we discuss next.

The positive–negative duality

The notion that positive and negative are two sides of the same coin is an old one. In this sense, the positive is not the exclusion of negative for that would be impossible. As the Greek philosopher Heraclitus (540–480 BC) observed, life is simultaneously tragic and comic. Those you meet on the way up will be the same folk you meet on the way down.[23] It is being denied what we want that gives value to what we prize.[24] A meaningful life is not one devoid of negative experiences but rather one in which such experiences help to enhance the meaning of life.[25]

A logic of duality then does apply to positive organizational behaviour: it acknowledges the simultaneity of positive and negative, as in the Yin-Yang, an ancient Taoist symbol that represents the duality of the world (see Figure 1.2). Duality refers to opposites as mutually constituting – there is white in black and black in white. For instance, good and evil, day and night, love and hate, imply one another. In organizations, the same applies with regard to the simultaneous need for competing values of stability and change, autonomy and control, exploration and exploitation, differentiation and integration.

Throughout this textbook a number of positive processes will be discussed. But the negative is integral to positive organizations. We thus invite you to think about

Figure 1.2 Yin-Yang: the 'bright' and the 'dark' need each other.

positive and negative as duality, two sides of the same coin. This happens because positive processes can turn negative, namely because the excess of a good thing can become bad. For example, the pursuit and experience of happiness might sometimes lead to negative outcomes.[26] Negative experiences may be a source of personal and collective development (i.e., 'poison' may be changed into 'medicine').[27] Positive and negative are inextricably linked. A positive organization is not one that has eradicated the negative but one that incorporates the negative in the process of building positivity; such attempts at developing a positive approach to organizations are a long-standing endeavour. We next consider some fundamental contributions.

POB: key historical contributions

The field of positive organizational studies emerged as a new management idea in the 1990s but it descends from a long lineage with roots in philosophy, psychology and the social sciences. We briefly trace the history of the idea by considering the contributions of Aristotle (384–322 BC), Mary Parker Follett (1868–1933), Abraham Maslow (1908–1970), Douglas McGregor (1906–1964), Martin Seligman, and the recent POS and POB streams.

Aristotle, hedonism and eudemonism

Positive organizational behaviour is sometimes perceived as a new idea. But the roots of a positive approach to society can be traced a couple of millennia back, to the Greek philosopher Aristotle (384 BC–322 BC). In the *Nicomachean Ethics*, Aristotle established a difference between two distinct forms of happiness: hedonic and eudemonic.[28] Hedonism associates wellbeing with pleasure and is based on the pursuit of sensory experiences that gratify the tongue, eyes, ears, nose and skin. It is a type of pleasure that is based upon subjective experience that dissipates quickly. Eudemonic happiness refers to the search for purpose and meaning, involving the cultivation of virtuous character that contributes to the greater good. It is associated with the long term, with enduring goals rather than with short-term experiences. Self-development and contribution are central to the achievement of eudemonic happiness.

Research contrasting eudemonic and hedonic conceptions of wellbeing (see Table 1.1) shows that the impact of the eudemonic orientation tends to be superior, suggesting that

Table 1.1 Contrasting hedonic and eudemonic conceptions of wellbeing

Hedonism	Eudemonism
Cultivation of pleasure	Cultivation of virtue and character strengths along with contribution to the greater good
Subjective sensory experience of pleasure	Searching for purpose and meaning gives satisfaction
Superficial pleasures cause happiness	Long-term enduring gains cause happiness
Pleasure dissipates	Meaning persists over time
Feeling good	Doing good
Sensation-seeking	Meaning-seeking

organizations should appreciate the difference between these two approaches.[29] Instead of framing satisfaction as a superficial process with mostly hedonic dimensions, managers may consider the eudemonic forces that confer meaning as a source of enduring satisfying experiences. When the big tech corporations pamper their employees with lunches that look to be a 'Rio Carnival of delicious food aimed at keeping the talent happy',[30] they are investing in the hedonic dimension of wellbeing. If hedonic experiences matter, they do not substitute for the role of the eudemonic dimension. In other words, good food does not substitute for a sense of purpose but neither does a sense of purpose oppose good food or pleasant facilities.

Wright argued for the importance of eudemonism for positive organizational studies in the following way:

> more than just considering employees as a means to the desired end of higher organizational productivity, to make a truly valuable contribution to the field the mission of POB must ... include the pursuit of employee happiness, health, and betterment issues as viable goals or ends in themselves. Highly consistent with Aristotle's centuries old quest of *eudaimonia*, to provide a value-added contribution to organizational research, POB must consider issues of employee betterment as intrinsic goods for which all should work and strive. Pursuit of good or worthwhile life deserves no less.[31]

The implications are clear: organizations should invest in both eudemonic and hedonic dimensions, as each of these have different consequences.

Box 1.2 Arts and music in schools – what do they have to do with happiness and positivity?[32]

Andria Zafirakou, a British teacher, launched her charity 'Artists in Residence' at Alperton community school in Brent. In 2018, she was awarded a $1 million global teaching prize. What would you do if you won a $1 million prize? Consider what Zafirakou did, according to an article published in *The Guardian*:[33]

> After winning a $1 million global teaching prize, Andria Zafirakou could have paid off her mortgage, bought a Ferrari and put her feet up for the rest of her

life. Instead, the north London teacher has announced she is using the money she won in March with the Varkey Foundation global teacher prize – a kind of Nobel prize for teaching – to set up a campaigning charity to get more artists and arts organisations into Britain's schools.

... Many will see it as an extraordinary act of altruism given there were no obligations attached to the prize money. "If this was the lottery it would have been a different situation, but it's not the lottery," Zafirakou said. "This is something I won because I'm a teacher so it's right to give it back to the profession."

... Schama, a professor of art history at Columbia University in the US, said Zafirakou was a force of nature and he was happy to be an artist-in-residence at Alperton ... He said it was a mistake to see arts and music in schools as a luxury or an add-on. "It is an indispensable centre. What will remain of us when AI takes over will be our creativity, and it is our creative spirit, our visionary sense of freshness, which has been Britain's strength for centuries."

The article also quoted Lord Bragg, who said:

The curious thing, and it has baffled me for years, is that the only people in the country who don't get it are the politicians. I go to the theatre quite a bit and I never see a politician ... I wonder if they read books.

Figure 1.3 Andria Zafirakou, winner of the Global Teacher Prize for 2018.[34]

Questions for reflection

- What kind of happiness is Zafirakou likely to experience – hedonic or eudemonic?
- Is a Ferrari a source of hedonic or of eudemonic happiness?
- Why was Schama happy to be an artist-in-residence at Alperton? What was his argument about AI and the future of work?
- Do you consider that bringing arts to schools would educate students to flourish and be better employees and better leaders? Or not? Why?
- Could managers build more positive workplaces if they read more books and appreciated arts? Or not? Why?

Mary Parker Follett, the 'prophet of management'

Mary Parker Follett (1868–1933), an American social worker, social and organizational theorist and management consultant, developed a stream of management ideas with a positive orientation. She viewed management less as a tool for efficiency and more as a form of organizing that made human flourishing possible via the articulation of solutions to human problems in an integrative way. For her, leadership ought to contribute to the creation of a common purpose that would integrate organizations with their surrounding communities. She saw economic and ethical problems as two sides of the same coin.[35] Because of the embeddedness of organizations within their communities, economic decisions are necessarily imbued with an ethical dimension.[36]

Follett also pioneered an integrative approach to power by defending the superiority of thinking in terms of *power-with* rather than *power-over*. She anticipated the notion of empowerment by arguing the need for managers and workers to cooperate in achieving common objectives that benefit each group. In summary, a number of themes to be explored in this book have a clear Follettian resonance (for more information on Follett see Chapter 10).

Maslow's eupsychia[37]

Eupsychian was a term coined by psychologist Abraham Maslow (1908–1970), well known for his hierarchy of needs. In his book *Eupsychian Management*[38] he refers to 'the wellbeing of psyche'. Maslow was mainly interested in the possibility that employment could provide people with the opportunity to satisfy their higher order needs for self-esteem and self-actualization. Self-actualizing managers would create self-actualizing organizational members across levels, in a virtuous circle of psychological growth that would benefit organizations and society as a whole.[39] In his view, this would require that organizations and human resource systems should be designed according to 36 assumptions (a sample, with adaptations, is presented in Table 1.2). Organizing, in accordance with these principles, would be good for employee wellbeing and organizational performance. In order to succeed in this purpose, Maslow held, several barriers need to be removed.[40] Managers must self-actualize themselves to produce virtuous circles in organizations, i.e., self-actualization in other people. After satisfying their lower order needs (i.e., physical, safety and social ones), people

Table 1.2 A sample of Maslowian principles of enlightened management[41]

- Everyone is to be trusted.
- Everyone can enjoy good teamwork, friendship, good group spirit.
- Hostility is reactive rather than character-based.
- Everyone prefers to feel important and respected, rather than unimportant, anonymous and wasted.
- Everyone prefers to love and respect the boss (rather than to hate or disrespect him/her).
- People prefer to work rather than to be idle.
- People prefer meaningful work to meaningless work.
- People prefer uniqueness as persons, in contrast to being anonymous or interchangeable.
- Everyone likes to be justly and fairly appreciated.
- People prefer to identify with more and more of the world, toward a fusion with the world or peak experience.

---

internalize the B values, i.e., intrinsic values of Being (e.g., wholeness, truth, beauty, goodness, justice, completion, playfulness) and develop a sense of pride in their work that can eradicate faulty products and poor services.

McGregor's theory Y

Another important precursor of the field is Douglas McGregor (1906–1964), with his notion of theory Y management. McGregor published the influential book *The Human Side of Enterprise* in which he contrasted two approaches to management. One, theory X, sees management as an authoritarian practice. The other, theory Y, is management that is empowering and participative. The application of these two theories will lead to highly distinct organizations. When managers assume the principles of theory X, they enact a number of practices that will potentially confirm their expectations; the same occurs with theory Y. The manager's implicit theories therefore play a fundamental role in the way managers manage.

Theory X represents an authoritarian approach to organization. It assumes that people are lazy and untrustworthy and will avoid work if they can and for this reason they need to be controlled. Work is perceived as an unpleasant activity conducted for external reasons and out of necessity. Workers, according to theory X, are motivated by the extrinsic reward of their paycheck. Organization, in this sense, is mostly about control through the provision of external rewards and punishments.

Theory Y portrays a different view of organizations and their members. Work is perceived as part of an individual's identity: it is important in defining who one is. When organizations are designed adequately – for example, when they provide psychological safety (see Chapter 7) – people are willing to accept responsibility and to be accountable. Workers, according to theory Y, are motivated by intrinsic rewards of personal achievement and contribution. At work, people can control themselves and be empowered. Instead of mindlessly repeating work, they prefer to approach it mindfully and to change it in order to improve the system. Even routine work can be rich in adaptation and micro-creative moves.[42]

One might think that the adoption of theory X or Y (see comparison in Table 1.3) would depend on the industry and that some sectors are more prone than others to one theory or the other. Research shows that this is not necessarily the case, and that

Table 1.3 The principles of theories X and Y[43]

Dimensions	Theory X	Theory Y
Relation to work	People tend to dislike work	Work is integral to individual identity
Relations with responsibility	People prefer to avoid responsibility	In the appropriate conditions people accept accountability
Control	People have to be controlled	People can control themselves
Supervision	Supervision must be permanent	People can supervise themselves
Motivations	People work because of external rewards	People work for intrinsic rewards

people in different sectors can be responsive to the principles of theory Y, including organizations in traditional manufacturing such as Toyota.[44] Even bureaucratic organizations are compatible with the principles of theory Y. Bureaucracy is not necessarily merely mindless repetition: it can be creative and innovative.

Martin Seligman and positive psychology

The field of POB can also be considered an 'offshoot of positive psychology'.[45] Positive psychology was officially launched and promoted by Seligman[46] and refers to the intention to 'catalyze a change in the focus of psychology from preoccupation only with repairing the worst things in life to also building positive qualities'.[47] It has been defined as

> the scientific study of optimal human functioning. At the meta-psychological level, it aims to redress the imbalance in psychological research and practice by calling attention to the positive aspects of human functioning and experience, and integrating them with our understanding of the negative aspects of human functioning and experience. At the pragmatic level, it is about "understanding the *well-springs*, *processes* and *mechanisms* that lead to desirable *outcomes*."[48]

Positive psychology departs from the prevailing quest for 'fixes' that often characterizes psychological approaches.[49] However, it does not aim to project a 'rose-coloured' view of reality nor does it ignore the suffering, selfishness and dysfunctional institutions so often surrounding many people's work and life.[50] It also does not mean that the rest of psychology is negative. Positive psychology rather aims to study the entire range of human experiences. In this sense, it aims to rebalance the attention given to human phenomena beyond the traditional mainstream focus on the negative. Such a negative focus is the result of several causes: bad is stronger than good, i.e., people tend to pay more attention to what is dangerous and threatening, something evident every day from that which the news. There are, however, additional explanations: post-World War II, US funding agencies prioritized research on mental problems, namely to help returning war veterans.[51] Clinical psychology traditionally focussed on illness rather than health, while positive psychology aims to study factors that make life good without denying the full experience of being human, including its tragic dimension.

POB and POS

In the 1990s, the positive psychology movement inspired two main streams within management and organizational studies. One group was formed in the University of Michigan and included researchers such as Kim Cameron, Jane Dutton, Robert Quinn and Gretchen Spreitzer, who founded the Centre for Positive Organizations. They labelled their approach Positive Organizational Scholarship. POS is defined by the following main principles:[52]

- *Emphasizing the positive.* POS refers to an alternative perspective to mainstream organizational theory, one that emphasizes the positive. It represents organizations as capable of emphasizing what is good and constructive. In this alternative view, challenges and obstacles are presented as inevitable to life. They are not avoided but rather embraced as sources of growth, even when painful. The positive perspective does not render them pleasant but rather as integral moments to human existence that permit growth. As is often said, no pain no gain.
- *Focus on superior performance.* POS is sometimes associated with superior outcomes, sometimes with spectacular results. Positive forms of organizing can trigger transformative accomplishments, as exemplified by the case of Nelson Mandela's leadership in South Africa. An organization that offers good feelings for members but then fails in terms of outcomes can hardly be considered positive. Positivity is not sustainable when organizations fail to create value and to achieve results ensuring sustainability.
- *An affirmative bias.* POS is deliberately biased in the direction of the positive. This bias is known as the heliotropic effect. The effect refers to the orientation to light. In the case of POS, the focus is on strengths and opportunities rather than on weaknesses and threats. The world of POS is a world of possibility rather than of constraint.
- *Eudemonic assumption.* POS assumes that excellence and virtue are important for their own sake, as ends, not as means. The positive view is thus marked by a deep ethical commitment (i.e., ethics and goodness are at the heart of the discipline).

In Nebraska, US, a team led by Fred Luthans developed the idea of Positive Organizational Behaviour, which he defined as 'the study and application of positively oriented human resource strengths and psychological capacities that can be measured, developed, and effectively managed for performance improvement in today's workplace'.[53] POB is anchored in the idea that a number of psychological strengths can be developed, and that this development will produce a positive impact. The most famous of these strengths are the components of positive psychological capital (PsyCap): hope, efficacy, resilience and optimism (see Chapter 3).

By preparing leaders and creating suitable contexts, organizations may promote the construction of these psychological strengths – seen as state-like characteristics. They are neither pure states (such as emotions) nor traits (i.e., stable dispositions). The emphasis on state-like characteristics means that positive attributes can be developed and are not necessarily related to the possession of special and stable personal attributes. The two schools of POB and POS have differences but also a common ground, they:

- Both emphasize strengths
- Aim to develop the human side of organization

- Have a propensity for change
- Have affirmative objectives
- Seek to influence real organizations in the direction of improvement

A key distinction between POS and POB is that whereas POS tends to focus more broadly on scholarship concerning the macro/organizational level of organizational processes, POB tends to focus more narrowly on the micro- and meso-levels of individual behaviours and states (see Table 1.4). Although we have titled this textbook *Positive Organizational Behaviour*, our area of concern is broader than that of Luthans and his micro definition of POB. It is also broader than POS with its focus on scholarship. We are concerned with equipping students, practitioners and researchers with a broad understanding of positive organizational practices. In doing so, we primarily draw from these two established positive schools to offer a refreshing and empirically grounded perspective on the possibilities for thinking differently about organizations. We also draw from the research of scholars from outside of these two streams who we see as contributing findings relevant to promoting positive organizational processes.

The assumptions of POB

The way managers represent organizations (and people) influences the way they manage them. The assumptions they use to design and run organizations constitute a template that will shape organizational functioning, as Keynes implied. People look at organizations from the vantage point of a number of assumptions. Assumptions frame the way we make sense of the world and influence how we behave. They refer to ideas that are accepted as true without questioning or justification. An assumption may not be real in itself but once it is used by people to frame something as real, it becomes real in its consequences. It generates self-fulfilling prophecies. If we assume that organizational members are foremost self-interested and see organizations as places operating according to the Darwinian notion of the 'survival of the fittest', we will act accordingly. Others will accordingly likely react in self-protective and competitive ways – thus corroborating our assumption. Assumptions about organizations make our understanding of them simpler but the fact that they go unquestioned creates a number of consequences that are not necessarily positive.

Table 1.4 Compatible but different: distinguishing POS and POB[54]

Positive organizational behaviour (POB)	*Positive organizational scholarship (POS)*
Mostly concerned with individual psychological qualities and their impact on performance improvement.	Mainly concerned with the positive aspects of the organizational context.
Studies having been conducted primarily at the micro- and meso-levels of analysis (using survey research).	Studies having usually been conducted at the organizational level of analysis (using diverse qualitative and quantitative research methods).
Has tended to develop from individual to group to organizational levels of analysis.	Has developed in the opposite direction.

The power of assumptions and their self-fulfilling consequences can be illustrated by the placebo effect. Placebos have been traditionally defined as inert agents used with the goal of convincing a patient that a given (non-existing) substance will produce an effect. Interestingly, these inert agents often do produce positive effects. As Jeffrey Pfeffer documented, organizational equivalents of placebos do matter and some of them are highly consequential for positive organizing. For example, people tend to have a positive view of themselves. We normally think we are above the average. This preference collides with the willingness to receive honest negative feedback. Consequently, people prefer to validate their positive self-views than to see them countered.

It was commonly thought that placebos work because subjects trusted that the placebo contained an active substance. Recent evidence shows, however, that such deception may not be necessary: even open-label placebo treatments (i.e., treatments in which the placebos were openly presented as such) may relieve pain. In short: even when people are informed about the true nature of the placebo, they still end up benefitting from its effects.[55] Researchers are now trying to explain this effect and one possible explanation being offered is that the simulation of a therapeutic process with its meanings and rituals in a given psychosocial context can produce positive effects. Placebos express the power of thoughts and assumptions for life in general. But how do assumptions work in the organizational world? In response, we discuss assumptions regarding: human nature, trust, categories, organizations, leadership and talent. Other assumptions could also have been considered but this palette illustrates the way established assumptions influence the organizations we build.

Box 1.3 A positive provocation: should organizations contemplate the use of open placebos?

Pfeffer has defended the importance of being untruthful in some organizational circumstances.[56] His defence is based on the argument that we are hardwired to lie to ourselves about our competencies. Asked anonymously, people claim that they are above average in positive traits, from intelligence to sense of humour to physical attractiveness. The phenomenon is known as the 'above average effect' and it is a result of people's desire to hold a positive image of themselves.[57]

People tend to develop a positive self-esteem. When they receive positive feedback, they will perceive it as being consistent with the knowledge they already hold. For example, people generally like those who flatter them.[58] Negative feedback can potentially create dissonance and will certainly not contribute towards subordinates appreciating a candid leader. This is not meant to say that leaders should not tell the truth. They should be honest without ignoring the importance of appreciation and praise: tell the negative things but also the positive and do not forget to put more emphasis on the positive – if possible.

The implication is clear: an emphasis on the positive is potentially better received because it is aligned with human preferences. Because people strive to be liked and admired, any attempt at change will be better received if it is aligned with people's self-concepts.

One implication for organizations is that leaders can provide 'open organizational placebos' about their employees: open, positively distorted information about their employees. Done openly they do not raise ethical issues and can activate a Pygmalion sort of effect, i.e., causing leaders to develop positive expectations about their employees by focussing on their strengths,[59] a process which will potentially activate a self-fulfilling dynamic. The effect has been documented in organizational analysis[60] and it should be noted that low expectations are also self-fulfilling, the so-called Golem effect.

Tools such as the *My Reflected Best Self*[61] exercise (see Chapter 2) can be used to leverage the initiative. It consists of asking a number of people (co-workers, supervisors, etc.) to describe an employee when he or she is at her/his best. Analysis of the collected feedback for overriding themes helps to identify a number of strengths and illustrations of these strengths, showing a person's best side. It can help individuals to identify professional paths that might suit them best and to remember that every person has a bright side.

Assumptions about human nature

Central among assumptions of a discipline of positive organizations are those referring to the nature of humans. Herbert Simon, Winner of the Nobel Memorial Prize in Economic Sciences, pointed out:

> Nothing is more fundamental in setting our research agenda and informing our research methods than our view of the nature of human beings whose behaviors we are studying ... It makes a difference to research, but it also makes a difference for proper design ... of institutions.[62]

Sumantra Ghoshal argued that the field of management and organizations is dominated by negative assumptions resulting in and reinforcing bad management theories. These theories hold pessimistic views about human nature and result in the design of organizations aimed at impeding the negative expressions that would otherwise emerge. These negative expressions can be found in the canonical model of the *Homo Economicus*. According to such a view, people are naturally inclined to fulfil their personal goals, with no consideration for the interests of others. As a result, organizations should be designed to create the right incentives for people to behave properly. Theories can become self-fulfilling.[63] In a context centred on goals and rewards, people focus their attention on what matters the most: goals and rewards. In such a model of self-focussed maximizers, behaviours guided by justice or altruism should be understood as 'aberrations', as they manifestly diverge from the expected model.[64]

Positive psychology introduced a different set of assumptions. It views human nature under a different light, departing from the premises of the *Homo Economicus*, which do not, as a matter of record, hold up to the scrutiny of research.[65] Departing from the 'disease' or 'repair' mentality, positive psychology assumes human beings are oriented towards loyalty and cooperation,[66] that they are capable of performing admirable acts. Human beings can orient themselves and others to what is excellent, abundant, virtuous, sustainable and resilient. Instead of focussing on the 'badness'[67] of human nature, positive scholars focus on its inherent goodness. A 'positive psychology' is one focussed on the nurturing of good rather than the suppression of bad.[68]

Assumptions about trust

Organizations can assume that people should be trusted or, conversely, that they should rather be controlled and monitored (consider theory X). Strickland advanced a fundamental contribution to this process that he called the dilemma of the supervisor.[69] The dilemma refers to the fact that when managers design organizations as control mechanisms they communicate that people should be distrusted. When intense control processes are in place, they start to justify their very existence. Faced with intense control mechanisms, people try to craft some level of autonomy and to evade the supervision (i.e., psychological reactance;[70] see Box 1.4), a behaviour that itself justifies not only the existing control mechanisms but also their possible intensification. The process may initiate a negative spiral: people comply only perfunctorily, they decrease their intrinsic motivation and decrease of voluntary cooperation and genuine commitment justifies further reinforcement of external control. As in any other vicious circle, at a certain point each new attempt to solve a problem ends up aggravating it.[71] In the end those exercising surveillance decrease the levels of trust and intrinsic motivation of their targets and thus intensify the very problems they intended to solve. Their intervention is now part of the problem. Therefore, assumptions about trust are critical in defining the type of organization one builds. Positive organizations are built on trust.[72]

Box 1.4 How do employees react to being technologically monitored?

Jeffrey Pfeffer argued that, although employing technology to monitor the employees' web usage may sound 'like a smart way to keep them focused on work', the consequence is actually perverse. A kind of boomerang effect unfolds:[73]

> It's no secret that plenty of workers use their company's high-speed Internet access to shop, make travel arrangements, or just surf the Web ... In light of this, it would seem to make sense for managers to keep track of their workers' Web habits. Shouldn't employees conduct personal business on their own time? Think of all the lost productivity! Not so fast. There are problems with this logic. First, while employers have increasingly been taking the Big Brother approach, thanks to software that tracks Internet usage and even lets the boss read a worker's e-mails, the proportion of absenteeism attributable to personal needs has also been on the rise – almost doubling in 2002 to 21 per cent. Notice the lesson here: If you don't want your people missing work to take care of personal business, maybe it would be better to let them take care of some of that business at work. Losing a few minutes here or there – or even a couple of hours – is cheaper than losing entire days.
>
> Other unintended consequences of electronic monitoring are more difficult to measure but potentially worse for business. Studies show, for instance, that electronic monitoring results in lower job satisfaction, in part because people begin to believe the quantity of their work is more important than the quality.

Monitoring also induces what academics call psychological reactance: the tendency of people to rebel against constraints. Tell people they can't shop, they can't use corporate networks for personal business, they can't make personal phone calls, and their desire to do all those things goes up. Another worrisome consequence stems from the self-fulfilling prophecy, which simply means that people behave as they are expected to. So, if you expect an employee to do a good job, he or she probably will. Act as though you distrust people, and you create employees who are, in fact, less trustworthy.

Assumptions about labels

Names or ideas also carry weight. Liberman, Samuels and Ross carried out experimental studies in which they manipulated the name of a Prisoner's Dilemma type of game.[74] Some subjects were told that they were going to play the Wall Street Game; others were told that the game was called the Community Game. The name of the game influenced the willingness of the subjects to cooperate (in the case of the community game) or to compete (in the Wall Street game). The study shows that individual inclinations to compete or to collaborate may result from simple cues which subtly indicate something about expected behaviour. The way organizations signal their prevailing assumptions, therefore, has an impact on the unfolding of their social dynamics.

Assumptions about organizations

Before you read Table 1.5, think about your own assumptions regarding organizations. How do you generally describe the organizations you know? Possibly as hierarchies. In such hierarchies, people have different ranks. There are bosses and subordinates. Bosses command and subordinates obey. Leadership is a positional attribute: the leaders are those in positions of authority and leaders are often portrayed as organizational heroes. Because bosses often feel special and endowed with natural privileges,[75] it is best to be careful

Table 1.5 Mainstream vs positive assumptions[77]

Mainstream organizational assumptions – or normal management	Positive organizational assumptions – or positive management
People follow primarily their self-interests.	People are also interested in the common good.
People pursue extrinsic rewards.	People have intrinsic motivations.
People exchange.	People contribute.
People minimize their costs.	People exceed expectations.
People tend to support the status quo.	People are inclined towards change.
People lose trust.	People build trust.
People engage in political communication.	People enjoy authentic communication.
People see constraints.	People see possibilities.
People assume hierarchy.	People assume equality.
People compete for resources that are scarce by definition.	People increase the resource pool.

when communicating with them. In other words, you don't say what you think, you say what protects you: you communicate politically, with tact. This organization can be described as an internal market, where people compete for resources. Resources are scarce by definition: bonuses, promotions, attention. Thus, collaborating with one's colleague can be problematic as you will be helping your potential competitor. Relationships are, consequently, characterized more by exchange than by generosity or consideration. You help someone in case you can benefit from the relationship. Of course, this limits the trust you can put in those around you. It stimulates a focus on personal goals and minimizing the rest. What is not measured is not managed. Employees conceive their roles as consisting of doing what they have to do rather than in changing to improve the system. You mind your own thing – and if everyone does the same, everything should be alright. Success, at the end, is measured by how much you gain, materially speaking.

This description, overall, corresponds to what many organizations actually do look like and it certainly fits the description of business and organization contained in many management textbooks.[76] Organizations such as these can be very successful according to a number of indicators. But there are alternative assumptions about what an organization is and how it operates. Now consider the right column of Table 1.5. Here, is proposed a different type of organization, a positive organization.

Organization represented according to the tenets of positive organizing looks different from that which prevails in the contemporary world of work, as depicted, for example, in Gallup's survey mentioned at the opening of this chapter. Positive organizations are built on what Monica Worline and Jane Dutton have called a positive default assumption.[78] A positive default assumption states that people are essentially good and capable; that employees are interested in their personal gains but also in the common good. Positive assumptions consider that people feel that they are part of something bigger than themselves and that they have a duty to contribute. They are connected to something that transcends them: a purpose, a community of peers, a team. People are motivated by intrinsic causes: their sense of self-worth, personal growth, bonds with others, sense of impact, the extraction of meaning from what they do, which leads them to see new opportunities. For example, a job can be transformed, adapted, made more interesting (please refer to the discussion about job crafting in Chapter 5). Colleagues can be made part of the process, co-designers of more interesting and rewarding organizational contexts. In this type of organization, people are willing to give to others and engage in mutual helping. This is an organization where acting generously does not mean being a sucker in a company of takers: giving and helping is normal, expected and reciprocated.[79]

In a positive organization, resources can be multiplied and everyone is assumed to be endowed with some talent, some natural charisma. Normal people can build extraordinary organizations and talent is not necessarily obtained through 'wars'.[80] These organizations are aware that positive forms of mutuality can be jeopardized by free-riding. As such, organizations weed out those employees whose behaviours can endanger this logic. They are not complacent. They expand the talent of their members and counter the complacency that creates 'niceness' but not vitality.

Organizations with a positive inclination reduce hierarchy to what is necessary. Some hierarchy is facilitative of coordination and purpose but hierarchy does not define competence or responsibility for specific tasks.[81] Speaking up and initiating change is acceptable and welcome. People stimulate one another's curiosity. Asking 'why' is perceived as beneficial rather than menacing (see Box 1.5).

> **Box 1.5 'Asking why' at OutSystems**
>
> OutSystems is a multinational software company that defined a number of cultural values and practices distilled in a document called *The Small Book of the Few Big Rules*. The booklet can be downloaded from the company's website[82] and defines the behavioural rules for employees. One of these rules is the 'Ask Why' rule. It establishes that employees should avoid doing tasks whose finality they are not aware of.
>
> The *Ask Why* rule has a number of positive effects. First, it assures that people know why they do things, which potentially facilitates the attribution of meaning to work. Second, it facilitates coordination, as managers must explain why something is supposed to be done. Third, it reduces hierarchical distance, as managers cannot rule by decree. Fourth, it stimulates discovery and creativity, as by discussing the whys, new possibilities are open for discovery.
>
> The *Ask Why* rule was inspired by Toyota, whose *Five Whys* Technique is well known: people should consecutively ask why until they get close to the root of a problem. Asking why, at Toyota, OutSystems, or any other organization, taps the potential of positive assumptions as it counters several well-established truths of normal management (i.e., management based on command and control, mindlessness and mere repetition).

Assumptions about leadership

Wiseman has contributed to debate on the importance of leadership assumptions by contrasting two types of leaders: diminishers and multipliers. Diminishers are those leaders that see themselves as the dynamos of organizations: things happen or fail to happen because of them and the things they do. Multipliers have a more expansive view of leadership and talent, admitting that good ideas can potentially originate in any part of the organization and any individual. As a result, they develop very different expressions of leadership, as portrayed in Table 1.6.

Diminishers are inclined to create *followers*, whereas multipliers aim at developing *other leaders*. For someone to act like a multiplier, he/she can adopt a number of practices, such as asking questions instead of providing answers; dispensing their ideas in small doses in order not to asphyxiate the ideas of others; expecting complete work from others instead of asking them for bits and pieces of work with no holistic meaning.

The challenge of creating more multiplicative leaders entails, first, recognizing that one acts as a diminisher by choice, not necessarily by need. Managers typically justify the behaviours on the left side of Table 1.6 not as a choice of their own but as a result of subordinates lacking qualification. By adopting these behaviours, they impede their followers from developing the competences that would have allowed them to act as multipliers. In other words, they create a negative spiral and a self-fulfilling prophecy that will progressively render their employees less prepared for the logic of multiplication, thereby confirming the goodness of their own assumptions.

Table 1.6 Multipliers and diminishers[83]

Diminishers	Multipliers
Empire builder: hoards resources and underutilizes talent.	**Talent magnet**: attracts talented people, develops them and uses them to their highest potential.
Tyrant: creates a toxic and psychologically unsafe environment that suppresses people's thinking and capabilities.	**Liberator**: creates an intense environment where people have permission (and are encouraged) to think, to speak, to act and to be themselves.
Know-it-all: is presumptuous; has all the answers; gives directives aiming at demonstrating how much he or she knows.	**Challenger**: asks questions that impel people to find the answers; creates opportunities for people to stretch their thinking and behaviours.
Decision maker: makes centralized, abrupt decisions that confuse followers, both individually and collectively; at best, gets input from just a small inner circle of advisers.	**Debate maker**: cultivates rigorous debate among team members; gives people a chance to weigh in and consider different possibilities – and therefore strengthens the team members' understanding of the issue and makes them more able to carry out actions are required.
Micromanager: pays excessive attention to details, drives results through his or her personal involvement, do it by him/herself; sees him/herself as 'the smartest person in the room'.	**Investor**: gives other people ownership of results and invests in their success; coaches and develops people; enables people to operate independently.

Box 1.6 The positive in negative, the negative in positive

Do multipliers, or givers (see Box 6.5 in Chapter 6), or other people with positive profiles, have perfect personalities? No! People can be disagreeable givers. Disagreeable givers can be disagreeable because they are over-demanding, because they speak up when it is better to shut up, because their high moral standards are not matched by others, because their perfectionism can reach extreme heights. Therefore, it is important not to establish a correspondence between being positive and being nice. Positive is not always nice and nice is not always positive. A nice boss is not necessarily a good leader, as research demonstrates: some leaders express tough forms of care.[84] Nice bosses may evade problems to keep social harmony, they can stimulate the idea that good team workers do not make waves, they can have difficulties in handling conflicts.

Assumptions about talent

Another set of assumptions that helps with understanding why some organizations are more positive than others has been advanced by psychologist Carole Dweck. Dweck conducted extensive human-talent-related research on two types of mindsets: fixed and growth (see Table 1.7). People with a growth mindset enjoy challenges, view success as the outcome of hard work, learning and preparation, view failures as learning opportunities and systematically identify possibilities for furthering the acquisition of new skills. People with a 'fixed mindset' view success as based upon the deployment of innate gifts of intelligence, see failure as threatening, and seek to avoid challenges as constituting a source of distress (see the sub-section 'Antecedents of grit' in Chapter 2).

Table 1.7 Describing fixed and growth organizational mindsets[86]

	Fixed mindset	*Growth mindset*
Assumptions	Intelligence and talent are a given: people have what they have.	Intelligence and talent can be magnified: people can grow.
	It is all about the outcome.	It is all about the process.
	People want to look smart.	People want to learn and grow.
	People avoid challenges.	People like to be challenged.
	People desist when confronted with obstacles.	People can persist to reach their goals.
	People perceive effort as potentially irrelevant.	People perceive effort as the path to mastery.
	People discount feedback.	People learn from feedback and criticism.
	People feel threatened by the success of others.	People feel inspired by the success of others.
Organizational HRM practices and policies	Emphasis on applicant's past credentials and past accomplishments.	Emphasis on applicant's potential and passion for learning.
	Control cultures.	Innovation cultures.
	Risk-avoidance.	Risk taking.
	A propensity to hire outsiders.	A preference to hire from within.
	War for talent.	Multiplication of talent.

The fixed vs growth mindset offers a third window of observation on positive assumptions. In some organizations talent is taken as fixed, in the sense that it is thought to exist in limited quantities that are pre-determined. According to this perspective, talent is more or less determined and companies have to fight for it. The result is the so-called 'war for talent' in jobs markets, with organizations competing for talent that is fixed and rare. The notion of the 'war for talent' became so prevalent that it was almost left undiscussed. However, it is underpinned by a normal assumption: that talent is fixed.

In organizations with a fixed mindset, people are seen as endowed with specific quantities of intelligence that cannot be expanded. Differently, a great organization is one that uses the talent of its extraordinary employees. A growth mindset adopts a different starting point: talent can be expanded and ordinary people can create extraordinary organizations. Collective mindsets have consequences for employees' commitment and performance:[85]

> When entire companies embrace a growth mindset, their employees report feeling far more empowered and committed; they also receive far greater organizational support for collaboration and innovation. In contrast, people at primarily fixed-mindset companies report more of only one thing: cheating and deception among employees, presumably to gain an advantage in the talent race.

Good organizations espouse a growth mindset. They expand the talent pool of the collective. Instead of seeing great organizations as the product of extraordinary individuals, they are conceived as the result of normal persons doing extraordinary things together.[87] As Hill observed, even genius can be a collective endeavour,[88] rather than an expression of some extraordinary individual capacity.

A fixed organizational mindset can lead to a performance goal orientation: it is important to give people goals within their reach and to accept the status quo. People under this mode operate in order to obtain success. The growth mindset, in turn, supports a learning goal orientation: individual qualities can be expanded and failure is not necessarily an indication of the lack of some quality but a trigger for development. The brain is perceived as a muscle: the more you exercise it, the stronger it gets. Failure is framed as meaning that new learning and new approaches are being cultivated – with their inevitable costs. A growth mindset equips individuals and teams with more adaptive responses that subsequently may facilitate higher performance in the future, given the emphasis on learning.

Box 1.7 The positive of the negative: the paradox of excellence

As explained by Dweck, the experience of failure is painful even under a growth mindset. Failing confronts us with our limitations and projects an image of incompetence. For people in a growth mindset failure does not define them. As explained by DeLong and DeLong, individuals are confronted, over a career's span, with the need to learn new skills to assume new responsibilities. Imagine a salesperson that is promoted to a sales leadership position.[89]

As they assume new responsibilities, individuals move out of their comfort zone. They will probably see a reduction in their effectiveness as they have to learn new tasks. However, they are aware of the fact that this learning curve precedes a subsequent, higher level of competence. Hence the paradox: to become better, individuals start by getting worse. And those professionals that prefer to stay in the comfort zone will remain as competent as before but their skills will potentially become obsolete. Sustained excellence thus implies that, from time to time, individuals will accept that they will be less competent than before.

At this stage one might ask: if positive assumptions are so powerful, why aren't they more abundant? In the following section we discuss this by asking: are positive assumptions realistic?

POB is positive – but is it realistic?

Can organizations function according to the positive assumptions discussed in this chapter? Evidence suggests that 'business history is replete with examples of companies run by tyrant-like CEOs and managers – people more focused on their own interests than working for the good of the company or their employees'.[90] Positive organizations seem to characterize only a minority of organizations. In order to clarify the meaning of positivity and positive assumptions, it should be noted that normal and positive assumptions correspond to two ideal types, ideal in the sense that they describe pure types rather than real cases (i.e., without any organization being fully represented as predicted by the paradigm's principles). Therefore, positive does not mean perfect.

Organizations typically combine characteristics of the two sets of assumptions, but some organizations are closer to the positive paradigm than others. Throughout the book, we will present cases and descriptions of organizations that have adopted positive organizing. Before we move to the next chapter, it is important to make some clarifications:

- As noted, some organizations are more positive than others.
- Positive organizations remain positive because they establish positivity in the organization's culture and practices *on an ongoing basis.*
- Positive organizing is more than the output of having good people on board. As pointed out by Culbert, good people can be bad managers – their good nature and good intentions notwithstanding – because the prevailing business culture corrupts positive intentions.[91]
- Positive organizations are aware of the importance of positive institutional work – the need to create and maintain 'institutional patterns that express mutually constitutive experiential and social goods'.[92]
- They are also mindful that positive values and practices are constantly 'vulnerable to erosion'.[93]

As a result, positivity is more than goodness or noble intentions. It is an unfinished effortful construction, a practice, whose anchoring is embedded in institutionalized organizational patterns. This effort must be consistent across levels and over time.

Final comments

The field of positive organization studies is a 'big tent'[93] that integrates existing research streams (e.g., positive psychology, social responsibility, organization development) and opens up new and promising opportunities for studying and designing organizations. It offers an alternative or complementary view to common management assumptions, one that emphasizes organizations as spaces rich in possibility. In this sense, a positive approach to management and organization represents a critical view of mainstream management and organization theory. Such an approach synthesizes the contributions of sub-disciplines that, in spite of their differences,[95] share a common concern for human flourishing via the construction of better organizations.

   In this chapter we have traced the history and underlying assumptions of positive organizational approaches and prepared foundations for the forthcoming chapters. Before we close, it is important to note that positivity is a process more than a condition. Consequently, organizations are not positive or negative: they are always in the process of becoming something more positive or more negative.[96] Managing positively consists in maintaining the momentum for organizational flourishing, thriving and wellbeing.

Want more?

The field of positive organizing is relatively new but already rich in bibliography. A critical source to understand the discipline is the volume edited by Cameron, Dutton and Quinn (2003), *Positive Organizational Scholarship: Foundations of a New Discipline.* This book put together a number of authors who shaped the field. Cameron and Spreitzer (2012a) later organized a monumental *Handbook of Positive Organizational Scholarship* that possibly represents the most complete overview of the positive in organizations. Cameron (2008) also wrote *Positive Leadership* and *Practicing Positive Leadership*. Also, from the Michigan group, Dutton and Spreitzer (2014) published *How to Be a Positive Leader*. Luthans, Youssef and Avolio (2007) authored *Psychological Capital*, which summarizes the work on the concept of PsyCap. Robert Quinn (2015) published *Positive Organizations*. In a different tone, Robert Sutton (2007) criticized the tolerance of organizations for uncivil behaviour in *The No Asshole Rule*, recently complemented by *The Asshole Survival Guide*.

Glossary

Assumptions   Something considered to be truth without proof or questioning.

Eudaimonia   A central concept in Aristotelian thinking, which refers to human flourishing.

Golem effect   The Pygmalion effect in reverse: subordinates realize the low expectations of their leaders.

Hedonism   A school of thought according to which the pursuit of pleasure is the primary or most important goal of mankind.

Heliotropism   The tendency of living systems towards what is positive and life-giving.

Homo economicus   The model of the 'Economic Man', a model of human nature that represents people as rational and self-interested maximizers.

Organizational circles   Organizational processes with a cyclical re-occurrence that form recurrent patterns. They can be positive (virtuous) or negative (vicious).

Placebos   Inert agents used with the purpose of pleasing a patient rather than to express a specific therapeutic effect.[97]

Positive organizational principles   Value-laden ideals that seek to elevate organizations and their contribution to society, forming the core of the positive organizational disciplines (e.g., emphasis on strengths, exceptionality of performance, and virtuous inclination).

Positive organizational behaviour   'The study and application of positively oriented human resource strengths and psychological capacities that can be measured, developed, and effectively managed for performance improvement in today's workplace'.[98]

Positive organizational scholarship   'A new movement in organizational science that focusses on the dynamics leading to exceptional individual and organizational performance such as developing human strength, producing resilience and restoration, and fostering vitality'.[99]

Positive organization studies   The study and application of positive principles to micro, meso and macro organizational levels, focussing on processes and outcomes.

Positive organizations   Organizations that sustainably obtain superior performance in a virtuous way, through an emphasis on strengths.

Positive psychology   The study of the processes that contribute to the optimal functioning of individuals, groups and organizations.

Pygmalion effect   Inspired by the Greek myth in which Pygmalion creates and falls in love with a statue of Galatea. It was subsequently popularized by the story of *My Fair Lady*. The effect states that people's behaviour and performance is influenced by the expectations of others.

Self-fulfilling prophecies   According to Merton 'the self-fulfilling prophecy is, in the beginning, a false definition of the situation evoking a new behaviour which makes the originally false conception come true'.[100]

Virtues   'Individual attributes that represent moral excellence, inherent goodness, and what represents humanity's very best qualities'.[101]

Notes

1 Gallup (2013, 2017).
2 Hook (2017, p. 9).
3 Crane (2013).
4 *The Economist* (2018).
5 Martí (2018).
6 Mitchell (2018).
7 Martí (2018).
8 Rego, Cunha and Clegg (2012); Tsoukas (2017).
9 Luthans (2002b).
10 Keyes and Haidt (2003).
11 Ornish (2005).
12 Spreitzer and Cameron (2012, p. 85).
13 Carvalho and Areal (2016).
14 Spreitzer and Cameron (2012, p. 85).
15 Baker and Nelson (2005).
16 Source: Sproud (2016).
17 McLean and Elkind (2013).
18 Independent Directors of the Board of Wells Fargo & Company (2017).
19 Schein and Hawbecker (2016).
20 Brown and Worthington (2017).
21 Ewing (2017, p. 62).
22 Meyer (2015).
23 Dylan (1991).
24 Nayak (2014).
25 Vohs, Aaker and Catapano (2019).
26 Gruber, Mauss and Tamir (2011).
27 Clair and Dufresne (2007).
28 Aristotle (2000).
29 McMahan and Estes (2011).
30 Broughton (2017, p. 18).
31 Wright (2003, p. 441).
32 We are grateful to Filipe Novais for having called our attention to the case.
33 Brown (2018).
34 Image source: Author: Fuzheado. Retrieved from https://commons.wikimedia.org/wiki/File:Andria-zafirakou-gtp-winner-2018.jpg. This file is licensed under the Creative Commons Attribution-Share Alike 4.0 International license.
35 Follett (1987).
36 Melé (2007); Tsoukas (2017).
37 This section partially draws on Rego, Cunha and Oliveira (2008).
38 Maslow (1965).
39 Payne (2000).
40 Payne (2000).
41 Source: Maslow (1965).
42 Reay, Golden-Biddle and Germann (2006).
43 Adapted from McGregor (1960).
44 Takeuchi, Osono and Shimizu (2008).
45 Meyer (2015, p. S175).
46 Seligman (1999).

47 Seligman and Csikszentmihalyi (2000, p. 5).
48 Linley, Joseph, Harrington and Wood (2006, p. 8, italics in the original).
49 Sheldon and King (2001, p. 216).
50 Gable and Haidt (2005, p. 1095).
51 Seligman (2002).
52 Cameron and Spreitzer (2012a, 2012b).
53 Luthans (2002a, p. 59).
54 Based on Donaldson and Ko (2010). The differences between POS and POB are debatable. For example, Lopes (2013) considered that, 'whereas POS is an umbrella concept, POB focuses more on specific positive constructs'.
55 Carvalho et al. (2016).
56 Pfeffer (2016).
57 Brown (1986).
58 Vonk (2002).
59 Rosenthal and Jacobson (1968).
60 Kierein and Gold (2000).
61 Roberts et al. (2005).
62 Simon (1985, p. 293).
63 Ferraro, Pfeffer and Sutton (2005).
64 Ghoshal (2005, p. 83).
65 Henrich et al. (2001).
66 Brewer and Caporael (1990).
67 Ghoshal (2005, p. 86).
68 Peterson and Seligman (2003).
69 Strickland (1958).
70 Brehm and Brehm (1981).
71 Tsoukas and Cunha (2017).
72 Fox (1974).
73 Pfeffer (2003).
74 Liberman, Samuels and Ross (2004).
75 Keltner (2016).
76 Collinson and Tourish (2015).
77 Source: Heynoski and Quinn (2012, p. 120, with minor changes).
78 Worline and Dutton (2017).
79 Dutton (2003); Grant (2013).
80 O'Reilly and Pfeffer (2000).
81 Child (2019).
82 See www.outsystems.com/the-small-book/.
83 Adapted from Wiseman and McKeown (2010).
84 Zhang, Waldman, Han and Li (2015).
85 Dweck (2016).
86 Built from Dweck (2006, 2014).
87 O'Reilly and Pfeffer (2000).
88 Hill, Brandeau, Truelove and Lineback (2014).
89 DeLong and DeLong (2011).
90 Buchko, Buscher and Buchko (2017, p. 731).
91 Culbert (2017).
92 Nilsson (2015, p. 373).
93 Nilsson (2015, p. 392).
94 Mitchell (2018).
95 Rich (2018).
96 Quinn (2015).
97 Price, Finniss and Benedetti (2008).
98 Luthans (2002b, p. 698).
99 Cameron and Caza (2004, p. 731).
100 Merton (1948, p. 195).
101 Cameron and Win (2012, p. 232).

References

Aristotle. (2000). *Nicomachean ethics*. Oxford: Oxford University Press.

Baker, T., & Nelson, R. E. (2005). Creating something from nothing: Resource construction through entrepreneurial bricolage. *Administrative Science Quarterly*, 50(3), 329–366.

Brehm, S. S., & Brehm, J. W. (1981). *Psychological reactance: A theory of freedom and control*. New York: Academic.

Brewer, M. B., & Caporael, L. R. (1990). Selfish genes vs selfish people: Sociobiology as origin myth. *Motivation and Emotion*, 14(4), 237–243.

Broughton, P. D. (2017). In praise of lunch. *Financial Times Life & Arts*, June 10, 18.

Brown, H., & Worthington, R. (2017). Corporate culture: Reflections from 2016 and lessons learnt. *Governance Directions*, 69(2), 100–102.

Brown, J. A. D. (1986). Evaluations of the self and others: Self-enhancing biases in social judgments. *Social Cognition*, 4, 353–476.

Brown, M. (2018). Teacher who won $1m will use windfall to get artists into schools. *The Guardian*, June 26 (www.theguardian.com/education/2018/jun/26/1m-teaching-prize-winner-launches-uk-school-arts-charity).

Buchko, A. A., Buscher, C., & Buchko, K. J. (2017, p. 2 do artigo). Why do good employees stay in bad organizations? *Business Horizons*, 60(5), 729–739.

Cameron, K. S. (2008). *Positive leadership: Strategies for extraordinary performance*. San Francisco, CA: Berrett-Koehler.

Cameron, K. S., & Caza, A. (2004). Introduction: Contributions to the discipline of positive organizational scholarship. *American Behavioral Scientist*, 47(6), 731–739.

Cameron, K. S., Dutton, J., & Quinn, R. E. (2003). *Positive organizational scholarship: Foundations of a new discipline*. San Francisco, CA: Berrett-Koehler Publishers.

Cameron, K. S., & Spreitzer, G. M. (2012a). *The Oxford handbook of positive organizational scholarship*. Oxford: Oxford University Press.

Cameron, K. S., & Spreitzer, G. M. (2012b). What is positive about positive organizational scholarship? In K. S. Cameron, & G. M. Spreitzer (Eds.), *The Oxford handbook of positive organizational scholarship* (pp. 1–14). Oxford: Oxford University Press.

Carvalho, A., & Areal, N. (2016). Great places to work®: Resilience in times of crisis. *Human Resource Management*, 55(3), 479–498.

Carvalho, C., Caetano, J. M., Cunha, L., Rebouta, P., Kaptchuk, T. J., & Kirsch, I. (2016). Open-label placebo treatment in chronic low back pain: A randomized controlled trial. *Pain*, 157(12), 2766–2772.

Child, J. (2019). *Hierarchy: A Key Idea for Business and Society*. London: Routledge.

Clair, J. A., & Dufresne, R. L. (2007). Changing poison into medicine: How companies can experience positive transformation from a crisis. *Organizational Dynamics*, 36(1), 63–77.

Collinson & Tourish. (2015). Teaching leadership critically: New directions for leadership pedagogy. *Academy of Management Learning and Education*, 14(4), 576–594.

Crane, A. (2013). Modern slavery as a management practice: Exploring the conditions and capabilities for human exploitation. *Academy of Management Review*, 38(1), 49–69.

Culbert, S. A. (2017). *Good people, bad managers: How work culture corrupts good intentions*. New York: Oxford University Press.

DeLong, T. J. & DeLong, S. (2011). Managing yourself: The paradox of excellence. *Harvard Business Review*. 2011, 119–123.

Donaldson, S. I., & Ko, I. (*2010*). Positive organizational psychology, behavior, and scholarship: A review of the emerging literature. *Journal of Positive Psychology*, 5(3), 177–191.

Dutton, J. E. (2003). *Energize your workplace*. San Francisco, CA: Jossey Bass.

Dutton, J. E., & Spreitzer, G. M. (2014). *How to Be a Positive Leader: Small Actions, Big Impact*. San Francisco, CA: Berrett-Koehler.

Dweck, C. (2012). *Mindset: Changing the way you think to fulfil your potential.*. London: Hachette UK.

Dweck, C. (2014). Talent. How companies can profit from a 'growth mindset'. *Harvard Business Review*, November, 28–29.

Dweck, C. (2016). What having a "growth mindset" actually means. *Harvard Business Review*, 13, 213–226.

Dylan, B. (1991). Foot of pride. In *The bootleg series volumes 1–3: Rare and unreleased*. New York: Columbia.

The Economist. (2018). Traffic jammers. May 5, 70.

Ewing, J. (2017). *Faster, higher, farther: The inside story of the Volkswagen scandal*. London: Bantam Press.

Ferraro, F., Pfeffer, J., & Sutton, R. I. (2005). Economics language and assumptions: How theories can become self-fulfilling. *Academy of Management Review*, 30, 8–24.

Follett, M. P. (1987). *Freedom and co-ordination*. New York: Garland.

Fox, A. (1974). *Beyond contract: Work, power and trust relations*. London: Faber & Faber.

Gallup. (2013). *State of the global workplace*. New York: Gallup Press.

Gallup. (2017). *State of the global workplace*. New York: Gallup Press.

Ghoshal, S. (2005). Bad management theories are destroying good management practices. *Academy of Management Learning and Education*, 4(1), 75–91.

Grant, A. (2013). In the company of givers and takers. *Harvard Business Review*, 91(4), 90–97.

Gruber, J., Mauss, I., & Tamir, M. (2011). A dark side of happiness? How, when, and why happiness is not always good. *Perspectives on Psychological Science*, 6(3), 222–233.

Henrich, J., Boyd, R., Bowles, S., Camerer, C., Fehr, E., Gintis, H., & McElreath, R. (2001). In search of homo economicus: Behavioral experiments in 15 small-scale societies. *AEA Papers and Proceedings*, May, 73–78.

Heynoski, K., & Quinn, E. R. (2012). Seeing and realizing organizational potential: Activating conversations that challenge assumptions. *Organizational Dynamics*, 41(2), 118–125.

Hill, L. A., Brandeau, G., Truelove, E., & Lineback, K. (2014). Collective genius. *Harvard Business Review*, 92(6), 94–102.

Hook, L. (2017). Crisis inside the 'cult of Travis'. *Financial Times*, 10 March, 9.

Independent Directors of the Board of Wells Fargo & Company. (2017). Sales practices investigation report. April 10 (www08.wellsfargomedia.com/assets/pdf/about/investor-relations/presentations/2017/board-report.pdf)

Keltner, D. (2016). *The power paradox*. New York: Allen Lane.

Keyes, C. L. M., & Haidt, J. (2003). Introduction: Human flourishing: The study of that which makes life worthwhile. In C. L. M. Keyes, & J. Haidt (Eds.), *Flourishing: Positive psychology and the life well-lived* (pp. 3–12). Washington, DC: American Psychological Association.

Kierein, N. M., & Gold, M. A. (2000). Pygmalion in work organizations: A meta-analysis. *Journal of Organizational Behavior*, 21, 913–928.

Liberman, V., Samuels, S. M., & Ross, L. (2004). The name of the game: Predictive power of reputations versus situational labels in determining prisoner's dilemma games. *Personality and social Psychology Bulletin*, 30(9), 1175–1185.

Linley, P. A., Joseph, S., Harrington, S., & Wood, A. M. (2006). Positive psychology: Past, present, and (possible) future. *Journal of Positive Psychology*, 1(1), 3–16.

Lopes, M. P. (2013). A dialectical approach to positive organizational studies. *American Journal of Industrial and Business Management*, 3, 185–195.

Luthans, F. (2002a). Positive organizational behavior: Developing and managing psychological strengths. *Academy of Management Executive*, 16(1), 57–72.

Luthans, F. (2002b). The need for and meaning of positive organizational behavior. *Journal of Organizational Behavior*, 23, 695–706.

Luthans, F., Youssef, C. M., & Avolio, B. J. (2007). *Psychological capital*. Oxford: Oxford University Press.

Martí, I. (2018). Transformational business models, grand challenges, and social impact. *Journal of Business Ethics*. doi:10.1007/s10551-018-3824.3.

Maslow, A. H. (1965). *Eupsychian management*. Homewood, IL: Irwin.

McGregor, Douglas, and Warren, Bennis. *The Side of Enterprise*. McGraw-Hill, 1985.

McLean, B., & Elkind, P. (2013). *The smartest guys in the room: The amazing rise and scandalous fall of Enron*. London: Penguin.

McMahan, E., & Estes, D. (2011). Hedonic versus eudaimonic conceptions of well-being: Evidence of differential association with self-reported well-being. *Social Indicators Research*, 103, 93–108.

Melé, D. (2007). Ethics in management: Exploring the contribution of Mary Parker Follett. *International Journal of Public Administration*, 30, 405–424.

Merton, R. K. (1948). The self-fulfilling prophecy. *The Antioch Review*, 8(2), 193–210.

Meyer, M. (2015). Positive business: doing good and doing well. *Business Ethics: A European Review*, 24(S2), S175–S197.

Mintzberg, H., Simons, R., & Basu, K. (2002). Beyond selfishness. *MIT Sloan Management Review*, 44(1), 67.

Mitchell, T. R. (2018). A dynamic, inclusive, and affective evolutionary view of organizational behavior. *Annual Review of Organizational Psychology and Organizational Behavior*, 5, 1–19.

Nayak, A. (2014). Heraclitus (540-480 BC). In J. Helin, T. Hernes, & R. Holt (Eds.), *The Oxford handbook of process philosophy and organization studies* (pp. 32–47). Oxford: Oxford University Press.

Nilsson, W. (2015). Positive institutional work: Exploring institutional work through the lens of positive organizational scholarship. *Academy of Management Review*, 40(3), 370–398.

O'Reilly, C. A., & Pfeffer, J. (2000). *Hidden value: How great companies achieve extraordinary results with ordinary people*. Boston, MA: Harvard Business Press.

Ornish, D. (2005). Love is real medicine. *Newsweek*, October 17, 43.

Payne, R. L. (2000). Eupsychian management and the millennium. *Journal of Managerial Psychology*, 15(3), 219–226.

Peterson, C. M., & Seligman, M. (2003). Positive organizational studies: Lessons from positive psychology. In K. S. Cameron, J. E. Dutton, & R. E. Quinn (Eds.), *Positive organizational scholarship: Foundations of a new discipline* (pp. 14–27). San Francisco, CA: Berrett-Koehler.

Pfeffer, J. (2003). Why spy? Technology that monitors employees' Web usage sounds like a smart way to keep them focused on work. Wrong. Let 'em surf. *CNN Money*, February 1 (http://money.cnn.com/magazines/business2/business2_archive/2003/02/01/335973/index.htm).

Pfeffer, J. (2016). Tell me lies, tell me sweet little lies: The many positive functions of being untruthful. *People + Strategy*, 39(4), 32–35.

Price, D. D., Finniss, D. G., & Benedetti, F. (2008). A comprehensive review of the placebo effect: Recent advances and current thought. *Annual Review of Psychology*, 59, 565–590.

Quinn, R. E. (2015). *The positive organization: Breaking free from conventional cultures, constraints, and beliefs*. San Francisco, CA: Berrett-Koehler.

Reay, T., Golden-Biddle, K., & Germann, K. (2006). Legitimizing a new role: Small wins and microprocesses of change. *Academy of Management Journal*, 49(5), 977–998.

Rego, A., Cunha, M. P., & Clegg, S. (2012). *The virtues of leadership: Contemporary challenge for global managers*. Oxford: Oxford University Press.

Rego, A., Cunha, M. P., & Oliveira, M. (2008). Eupsychia revisited: The role of spiritual leaders. *Journal of Humanistic Psychology*, 48(2), 165–195.

Rich, G. J. (2018). Positive psychology and humanistic psychology: Evil twins, sibling rivals, distant cousins, or something else? *Journal of Humanistic Psychology*, 58(3), 262–283.

Roberts, L. M., Spreitzer, G., Dutton, J., Quinn, R., Heaphy, E., & Barker, B. (2005). How to play to your strengths. *Harvard Business Review*, 83(1), 74–80.

Rosenthal, R., & Jacobson, L. (1968). Pygmalion in the classroom. *The Urban Review*, 3, 16–20.

Schein, J. B., & Hawbecker, J. P. (2016). *The fall of Banco Espírito Santo: Holy Spirit or Devil in disguise?* Northwestern Kellogg School of Management. Case # 5-116-004.

Seligman, M. (1999). The President's address. *American Psychologist*, 54, 559–562.

Seligman, M. (2002). Positive psychology, positive prevention, and positive therapy. In C. R. Snyder, & S. Lopez (Eds.), *Handbook of positive psychology* (pp. 3–9). New York: Oxford University Press.

Seligman, M., & Csikszentmihalyi, M. (2000). Positive psychology: An introduction. *American Psychologist*, 55, 5–14.

Sheldon, K. M., & King, L. (2001). Why positive psychology is necessary. *American Psychologist*, 56(3), 216–217.

Simon, H. (1985). Human nature in politics: The dialogue of psychology with political science. *American Political Science Review*, 79, 293–304.

Spreitzer, G., & Cameron, K. S. (2012). Applying a POS lens to bring out the best in organizations. *Organizational Dynamics*, 41, 85–88.

Sproud, J. (2016). Há talentos por aproveitar. *Executive Digest* (Portugal), December, 75–76.

Strickland, P. (1958). Surveillance and trust. *Journal of Personality*, 26, 200–215.

Sutton, R. (2007). *The No Asshole Rule: Building a Civilised Workplace and Surviving One That Isn't*. London: Sphere.

Takeuchi, H., Osono, E., & Shimizu, N. (2008). The contradictions that drive Toyota's success. *Harvard Business Review*, June, 96–104.

Tsoukas, H. (2017). Strategy and virtue: Developing strategy-as-practice through virtue ethics. *Strategic Organization*. doi:10.1177/1476127017733142.

Tsoukas, H., & Cunha, M. P. (2017). On organizational circularity: Vicious and virtuous circles in organizing. In M. W. Lewis, W. K. Smith, P. Jarzabkowski, & A. Langley (Eds.), *The Oxford handbook of organizational paradox: Approaches to plurality, tensions, and contradictions* (pp. 393–412). New York: Oxford University Press.

Vohs, K. D., Aaker, J. L., & Catapano, R. (2019). It's not going to be that fun: Negative experiences can add meaning to life. *Current Opinion in Psychology*, 26, 11–14.

Vonk, R. (2002). Self-serving interpretations of flattery: Why ingratiation works. *Journal of Personality and Social Psychology*, 82(4), 515–526.

Wiseman, L., & McKeown, G. (2010). *Multipliers: How the best leaders make everyone smarter*. New York: HarperCollins.

Worline, M., & Dutton, J. (2017). *Awakening compassion at work*. Oakland, CA: Berrett-Koehler.

Wright, T. A. (2003). Positive organizational behavior: An idea whose time has truly come. *Journal of Organizational Behavior*, 24(1), 437–442.

Zhang, Y., Waldman, D. A., Han, Y.-L., & Li, X.-B. (2015). Paradoxical leader behaviors in people management: Antecedents and consequences. *Academy of Management Journal*, 58(2), 535–565.

Part II

Positivity and the self

2 Leveraging on individual strengths

Summary and objectives

This chapter looks at the individual level of analysis, considering the meaning of 'positive individuals' and how they can be developed. By 'positive individuals' we mean those who can leverage their organizational context to grow not only as individual contributors but also as human beings. Specifically, we discuss the importance of trait-like strengths: virtues and character strengths, core self-evaluations and grit (the state-like strengths that represent positive psychological capital are discussed in the next chapter). Overall, the chapter focusses on how individuals may identify and use their own strengths and how those strengths may be identified, facilitated and developed via both personal and organizational actions.

Affirmative dynamics

A positive organization affirms strengths instead of tackling weaknesses, creating 'affirmative dynamics'[1] that produce positive upward spirals. While the focus on weaknesses and criticisms makes employees defensive and less prone to change, the focus on strengths can lead them to grow, flourish and contribute for the team and the organization. Therefore, the main assumption of this chapter (and the next) is that a focus on employees' strengths may help them become more self-effective, feel more valued, more willing to perform better and to fulfill their potential. Such a focus results in benefits for both individuals and organizations. Such benefits will be particularly apparent as trends such as automation and the introduction of artificial intelligence reduce the need for human work involved in routine tasks and increase the need for work related to creativity and relational competence. To obtain these competences, most organizations will need to revise the way they manage people, namely by focussing on specific strengths. As Roberts and colleagues stated:[2]

> A focus on problem areas prevents companies from reaping the best performance from its people. After all, it's a rare baseball player who is equally good at every position. Why should a natural third baseman labor to develop his skills as a right fielder? ... The alternative ... is to foster excellence in the third baseman by identifying and harnessing his unique strengths.

A question emerges from such an approach: what is a strength? According to Clifton and Harter, a strength 'is the ability to provide consistent, near-perfect performance in a given activity. An individual strength might be the person's ability to manage several activities at the same time flawlessly, or an organizational strength might be its capacity for constant innovation'.[3] This chapter focusses on individual strengths, a term we use in a broad sense: 'the characteristics of a person that allow them to perform well or at their personal best'.[4]

We acknowledge, however, that any individual characteristic is a strength to the extent that it promotes adjustment to the environment: 'whether a characteristic is a strength depends on its match to the person's context, suggesting that a strength in one situation may be a weakness in another'.[5] From this perspective, any personality characteristic can be considered as a potential strength.[6] (Box 2.1 discusses a tool to identify personal strengths; see also Box 2.2). We focus on three high-order individual strengths that are potentially relevant in the workplace: character strengths, core self-evaluations and grit (the next chapter, Chapter 3, discusses psychological capital). These three have played central roles in the POS movement.

Box 2.1 Composing your best self-portrait?

The Reflected Best Self Exercise™ as a source of self-knowledge

Individuals who are aware of their strengths and understand when they are at their best are more likely to use their strengths and thus be more productive and happier.[7] You may develop such self-knowledge through the Reflected Best Self Exercise™ (RBSE™). RBSE is a tool developed by scholars at the Center for Positive Organizations[8] (Ross School of Business, University of Michigan) to help an individual 'discover' his/her main strengths and talents (i.e., 'the best self') from the perspective of others and then to compose their self-portrait. 'Reflected' means that the self-portrait is based on individual perceptions of how others perceive them. The exercise is supported by three theoretical points.[9] First, changes in self-knowledge are critical in explaining how and why individuals change what they do and how they feel. Second, individuals are active participants in constructing their organizational experience. Third, the relational context in which individuals are embedded influences significantly how they themselves define and feel about that context. Through the RBS exercise, an individual may gather and analyze data about their best self, tapping into recognized and unexplored areas of potential, and thus improve performance and make better career decisions. The exercise involves four steps:

1 **Identifying respondents/observers and asking them for feedback**. Collect feedback about your best self (i.e., your main strengths and positive qualities) from a variety of people (e.g., your past and present supervisors, subordinates, friends, teachers and family members) who know you well. Ask the respondents to identify your main strengths and positive qualities, to provide examples of how and in which situations you have expressed them.

2 **Recognizing patterns**. After gathering feedback from respondents, search for common themes and add to the examples with observations of your own. Organize the main themes into a table composed of three columns. In the first column, include the common theme (e.g., perseverance). In the second, include

examples given by the respondents (e.g., 'when you have an important goal in mind, you are persistent in pursuing it, despite obstacles and drawbacks; for example, for five months, you worked relentlessly to persuade our CEO to ...'). In the last column, include your interpretation (e.g., 'I am very diligent in following my dreams').

3   **Composing the self-portrait**. Based on the information you gathered and your interpretation of the data compose your self-portrait: 'an insightful image that you can use as a reminder of your previous contributions and as a guide for future action'.[10] In 'drawing' your self-portrait, develop a narrative. Complete sentences such as 'When I am at my best, I ...', or 'My best qualities are revealed when ...'.

4   **Redesigning your job (and/or making career decisions)**. Reflect on your self-portrait, considering if there is fit between your self-portrait and your current job. Ask yourself questions such as: (1) 'How may I put my strengths into play in my current job?' (2) 'How may I craft my current job to get a better fit between what I do and my best self?' (3) 'What career decisions should I make to get an optimum fit?' (4) 'How I can develop my strengths to be happier and more successful?'

To be effective, the RBS exercise 'requires commitment, diligence, and follow-through'.[11] Don't use the RBS exercise to stroke your ego, or to stealthily impress your observers with a portrait of how great you are. Create conditions such that the gathered feedback is reliable and not used by your observers to flatter you. There is a specific RBSE instrument that can be used to facilitate the RBS process.[12] It is a proprietary tool, however, so you need permission to use it. No permission is required to undertake the RBS process described above on your own, however, as it is in the public domain, published in journals such as the *Harvard Business Review*[13] and the *Academy of Management Review*.[14]

Strengths are placed in the trait–state continuum represented in Figure 2.1. Character strengths are positive trait-like characteristics, with moral value being attached to most of them.[15] Core self-evaluations and grit are also positive trait-like characteristics but no moral value is placed on them. In contrast, as discussed in the next chapter, psychological capital is a state-like construct, which is amenable to cultivation and development. From a practical point of view, trait-like characteristics may be managed mainly through selection and by creating team/organizational conditions that encourage individuals to use their strengths. Conversely, state-like characteristics may be managed through leadership and organizational practices that develop the employees' strengths. Note, however, that several individual characteristics have been considered as both trait-like and state-like. For example, core self-evaluations (such as self-esteem, generalized self-efficacy, locus of control, and emotional stability, discussed below) are, as originally conceptualized, dispositional traits and thus relatively stable over time and across situations[16] although some authors suggest that they may fluctuate around a relatively stable set point.[17]

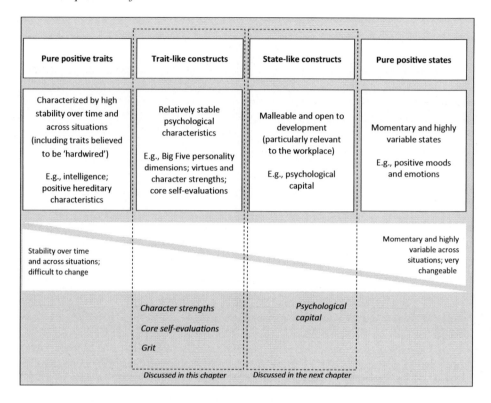

Figure 2.1 The trait–state continuum.[18]

Character strengths

Positive and virtuous habits

Virtues and character strengths are central to POS.[19] A virtue is 'a disposition to act, desire, and feel that involves the exercise of judgment and leads to a recognizable human excellence or instance of human flourishing. Virtuous activity involves choosing virtue for itself and in light of some justifiable life plan'.[20] Therefore, virtue refers to 'singular attributes that represent moral excellence'.[21] Six core virtues identified by Peterson and Seligman[22] through a broad sweeping factor analysis of the values espoused in world wisdom traditions, philosophy, psychology and even greeting cards are: wisdom, courage, humanity, justice, temperance and transcendence. They further identified 24 character strengths that they described as 'the psychological ingredients – processes or mechanisms – that define the virtues'. These strengths represent 'the distinguishable routes to displaying one or another of the virtues'.[23] For example, the virtue of wisdom is displayed through character strengths such as creativity, curiosity and love of learning.

Character strengths are *habits* emerging from the association between thoughts, feeling and actions.[24] For example, the character strength of love involves *thinking* about close relations with others, *feeling* empathy and compassion for others and *acting* accordingly. These thoughts, feelings and actions may be considered as character strengths if they are *habits* – a disposition to think, to feel, to act virtuously. Therefore, character strengths are trait-like, in that they are relatively stable across time and situations.

What distinguishes these positive traits from other traits, such as openness to experience or introversion-extraversion, is their moral content. Character strengths are 'the subset of personality traits on which moral value is placed'.[25] Openness to experience, introversion-extraversion, or even the positive core self-evaluations are traits with no obvious moral weight.[26] In contrast, the character strengths of kindness, teamwork, prudence, honesty and justice are morally valued, which qualifies them as character strengths.

The Values in Action (VIA) classification includes the 24 character strengths discussed above,[27] organized according to the six core virtues, also mentioned above (Table 2.1). Every individual has *some* character strengths (his/her 'signature strengths'); it is very unlikely that there is a 'perfect' human-being endowed with *every* strength.[28] Even the most virtuous individuals have weaknesses and flaws. A curious, creative, honest and persistent individual may be unkind and socially unintelligent. Nelson Mandela was not a saint.[29] Therefore, character '"is individualized and idiosyncratic", such that everyone has a unique profile of character strengths. Character is plural … Individuals are not simply honest or kind, brave or wise, humble or fair; rather an individual's character is best understood as a profile of strengths'.[30]

Table 2.1 Classification of character strengths – the VIA model.[31]

Virtue	Character strengths[32]
Wisdom and knowledge 'Good judgement and advice about important but uncertain matters of life.'[33]	*Cognitive strengths entailing the acquisition and use of knowledge* **Creativity** (originality; ingenuity): 'thinking of novel and productive ways to do things'. **Curiosity** (interest; novelty-seeking; openness to experience): 'taking an interest in all of ongoing experience'. **Judgement and open-mindedness** (critical thinking): 'thinking things through and examining them from all sides'. **Love of learning**: 'mastering new skills, topics, and bodies of knowledge'. **Perspective** (wisdom): 'being able to provide wise counsel to others'.
Courage 'Doing what is right, even when one has much to lose.'[34]	*Emotional strengths involving the exercise of will to attain goals in the face of opposition (external or internal)* **Honesty** (authenticity; integrity): 'speaking the truth and presenting oneself in a genuine way'. **Bravery** (valour): 'not shrinking from threat, challenge, difficulty, or pain'. **Perseverance** (persistence; industriousness): 'finishing what one starts'. **Zest** (vitality; enthusiasm; vigour; energy): 'approaching life with excitement and energy'.

(Continued)

Table 2.1 (Cont.)

Virtue	*Character strengths*[32]
Justice Justice 'refers generally to that which makes life fair'.[35] In the Western culture, the notion of justice is strongly associated with equity – the belief that 'rewards should be apportioned according to contributions or merit'.[36] Collectivistic cultures tend to prefer the notions of equality (the same for everyone) or need (one should receive according to his/her needs).	*Civic strengths underlying healthy/fair community life* **Fairness**: 'treating all people the same according to notions of fairness and justice'. **Leadership**: 'organizing group activities and seeing that they happen'. **Teamwork** (citizenship; social responsibility; loyalty): 'working well as member of a group or team'.
Humanity A disposition to 'tend and befriend'.[37] 'Whereas the virtue of justice lies in impartiality, the virtue of humanity relies on doing more than what is only fair – showing generosity even when an equitable change would suffice, kindness even if it cannot (or will not) be returned, and understanding even when punishment is due'.[38]	*Interpersonal strengths involving 'tending and befriending' others* **Kindness** (generosity; compassion; nurturance; care; altruistic love; 'niceness'): 'doing favours and good deeds for others'. **Love** (capacity to love and be loved): 'valuing close relations with others'. **Social intelligence** (emotional intelligence; personal intelligence): 'being aware of the motives and feelings of self and others'.
Temperance 'The virtue of control over excess.'[39]	*Strengths protecting against excess* **Forgiveness and mercy**: 'forgiving those who have done wrong'. **Modesty and humility**: 'letting one's accomplishments speak for themselves'. **Prudence**: 'being careful about one's choices; not saying or doing things that might later be regretted'. **Self-regulation** (self-control): 'regulating what one feels and does'.
Transcendence The 'connection to something higher – the belief that there is meaning or purpose larger than ourselves'.[40]	*Strengths forging connections to the larger universe and provide meaning* **Appreciation of beauty and excellence** (awe; wonder; elevation): 'noticing and appreciating beauty, excellence, and/or skilled performance in all domains of life'. **Gratitude** (optimism; future-mindedness; future orientation): 'being aware of and thankful for the good things that happen'. **Hope (optimism)**: 'expecting the best and working to achieve it'.[41] **Humour** (playfulness): 'liking to laugh and joke; bringing smiles to other people'. **Spirituality** (faith; purpose): 'having coherent beliefs about the higher purpose and meaning of life'.

Virtue is in the middle

Virtues and character strengths have a paradoxical nature in that the highest, or optimal, point is in the middle. For example, courage is the middle ground between foolhardiness and cowardice. This perspective corresponds to Aristotle's 'doctrine of the mean':[42] virtues and character strengths work best in the range of the 'golden mean' between the extremes of excess and deficiency (Table 2.2). An extreme level of a virtue may be dysfunctional. Excessive demonstrations of virtues are, in essence, not virtue but vices. For example:[43]

- An excessive appreciation of beauty may lead one to lose contact with rude or trivial realities. And an excessive appreciation of excellence may lead to perfectionism.
- Excessive hope/optimism may lead individuals to unrealistic optimism that, in turn, leads to neglecting risks and problems, and to a commitment to solutions, decisions or strategies that are not feasible.
- An excess of humour may give rise to inconvenient and disrespectful behaviours, thus hurting personal relationships, trust and credibility.
- Excessive creativity may give rise to fanciful or unrealistic ideas – or behaviours that, although creative, are foolish in the context where the individual is operating.
- Excessive curiosity may lead people to ask inconvenient questions or to incur unnecessary risks when confronting unfamiliar situations.
- Even an excess of honesty – in case you can imagine that – may lead one to tell the truth regardless of the nature of the situation and of perverse consequences for others. This may lead to the diminishing of others and to perceptions of moral arrogance.[44]

Adam Grant illustrated the relevance of the golden rule in his commencement speech to Utah State University's graduating class of 2017:[45]

> In graduation speeches, three of the most popular virtues are generosity, authenticity, and grit. If you want to live by these virtues you need resilience. You need resilience to stay generous on the days when you lose faith in humanity. You need resilience to stay true to yourself on the days when others lose faith in you. And you need resilience to persevere on the days when you lose faith in yourself. But if you're too obsessed with any of these virtues, you might undermine your own resilience. Virtues can be a little bit like vitamins. Vitamins are essential for health. But what if you get more than your body needs? If you take too much Vitamin C, it won't hurt you. If you overdose on Vitamin D, though, it can do serious harm: you could wind up with kidney problems. A great philosopher named Aristotle thought virtues were like Vitamin D. Too little of a virtue is bad, but so is too much. He believed that every virtue lies between vices of deficiency and excess. Too little humour is dry; too much is silly. Too little pride makes us meek; too much breeds narcissism. Too much self-restraint leaves you doing homework while your friends are tailgating. Too little self-restraint means you'll really regret eating that fourth Scotsman Dog.

Therefore, an individual gives proof of virtuousness when, in the presence of a specific situation, that person uses reason and experience to interpret the idiosyncrasies of the situation, charting a course of action located between the extremes of deficiency and excess. Behaving virtuously thus requires adopting the right combination of strengths, expressing them to the right degree and in the right situation. For example, when one team member discovers that another is adopting an ethically questionable behaviour, it is important to be *wise*: having the discernment to assess the situation realistically, being prudent to avoid unfair accusations, being as kind as possible, adopting an open-minded approach to assess the complexity of the situation and being courageous to do the right action in face of risks, pressures and obstacles. In addition, a close look at virtues such as hope offers a mixed combination of positive and negative. As Carlsen et al. have pointed out, hope has 'a shadow of despair and risk'. And, they added, it 'is not an undifferentiated positive experience but rather a positively charged quality of experiencing that may be heightened by the totality of what is a stake'.[46]

The fruits of character strengths

Peterson and Park pointed out that 'character matters in part because it leads people to do the right thing, and the right thing can be productive and profitable'.[48] Research has suggested that character strengths are positively associated with individuals' resilience, health and wellbeing, and are a cause of healthy long-life development.[49] Experiencing life as fulfilling is more likely when individuals identify their own signature strengths of character and use them as much as possible on a regular basis.[50] Individuals endowed with character strengths garner higher levels of interpersonal trust, engage in more effective workplace relationships, show higher job satisfaction and obtain better performance.[51]

Executives who demonstrate character strengths such as integrity, bravery, perspective and social intelligence are also more effective.[52] This happens because virtuous leaders are more likely to take the lead on unpopular but necessary decisions, to develop more fruitful relationships and to make more ethical and wiser decisions.[53] They evoke more loyalty and trust (from both internal and external stakeholders), thus acting as positive role models. Organizations whose members are more virtuous outperform those who are less virtuous.[54] A possible explanation is that virtuous members develop more trustful relationships, tend to cooperate more, be conscientious and more committed to their jobs.

Virtuous organizations also deal more appropriately with crises. After the tragedy of 11 September 2001, many airlines adopted downsizing and layoff strategies. However, other companies followed a different approach in facing the crisis. Southwest Airlines refused to lay off its employees. Former CEO Jim Parker explained the decision as follows:[55]

> Clearly, we can't continue to do this indefinitely, but we are willing to suffer some damage, even to our stock price, to protect the jobs of our people ... You want to show your people that you value them, and you're not going to hurt them just to get a little more money in the short term. Not furloughing people breeds loyalty. It breeds a sense of security. It breeds a sense of trust.

Southwest Airlines also profited from being prudent. The company could resist Wall Street pressure to take on more debt to respond to the crisis because it had built up healthy financial reserves for such a contingency.[56] As Cameron pointed out, it is unrealistic to assume that companies can always avoid downsizing.[57] However, based on empirical research,[58] he stated:[59]

Table 2.2 Negative in the positive: virtue is in the middle.[47]

Insufficient ←	The virtuous strength	→ Excess
	Wisdom and knowledge	
Dullness; unimaginativeness; insipidity	**Creativity**	Excessive fantasy; lack of realism
Disinterest; boredom; ennui; world-weariness	**Curiosity**	Inconvenience; bedazzlement with novelty; adventurism
Inflexibility; rigidity; ethnocentrism; dogmatism; stereotyping	**Judgement and open-mindedness**	Naivety; chameleonic behaviour, switching views without regard to the quality of the evidence as different interpretations emerge
Intellectual resistance; ignorance	**Love of learning**	Obsessive passion; not knowing when to stop learning and start practicing
Thoughtlessness; foolishness; idiocy	**Perspective/wisdom**	Self-righteousness; fundamentalism; idealism; arrogance
	Courage	
Deceitfulness; insincerity; falseness; pho-niness; dishonesty	**Honesty**	Honesty is 'excessive' when, for example, the truth is told even if it is uncalled for or is harmful. Some kinds of purity for preserving an important value may be unrealistic and/or jeopardize more important values.
Cowardice; spinelessness	**Bravery**	Recklessness; foolishness; self-righteousness
Laziness; vacillation; cutting corners	**Perseverance**	Obstinacy; stubbornness
Sluggishness; dullness; lethargy; listless-ness; sloth	**Zest**	Restlessness
	Justice	
Favouritism; one-sidedness; prejudice; caprice; unfairness	**Fairness**	Insisting on equality when equity is due; exceeding in equity (i.e., creating excessive wage dispersion)
Clumsiness to influence/inspire others toward collective action	**Leadership**	The dark side of charisma; cultism
Selfishness; self-centredness; egotism	**Teamwork**	Forgetting oneself; megalomaniac 'altruism'
	Humanity	
Stinginess; mean-spiritedness; wrath; coldness; indifference	**Kindness**	Intrusiveness; unctuousness; mawkishness
Alienation; estrangement; loneliness; aloofness; envy; selfishness	**Love**	Over-zealousness; sentimentality; paternalism
Inaccurate self-understanding and social and emotional inability in social relation-ships; cluelessness; self-deceit	**Social intelligence**	Intrusiveness; manipulation; chameleon-like behaviour
	Temperance	
Unforgivingness; mercilessness; ven-geance; spitefulness	**Forgiveness and mercy**	Sanctimoniousness
Immodesty; grandiosity; pomposity; pride; arrogance; vanity; bragging	**Modesty and humility**	Self-mortification; unctuousness
Imprudence; recklessness; irresponsibility; carelessness	**Prudence**	Timidity; risk aversion

(Continued)

Table 2.2 (Cont.)

Insufficent ←	The virtuous strength	→ Excess
Intemperance; impulsiveness; explosiveness; wildness; libertinage; lust	**Self-regulation**	Rigidity
	Transcendence	
Mindlessness; insensibility; philistinism; shallowness; triviality	**Appreciation of beauty and excellence**	Bewitchment; 'the optimum is enemy of the good'
Ingratitude; ungratefulness	**Gratitude**	Excessively 'indebted' to everything and anything
Helplessness; pessimism; gloom	**Hope**	Over-optimism; unrealism; risk neglect
Humourless; sourness; tediousness; dourness	**Humour**	Inconvenience; no sense of seriousness; buffoonery
Spiritual emptiness; godlessness; purposelessness	**Spirituality**	Out-of-this-worldliness; undue proselytism

My research on downsizing over the last 20 years has found that the way downsizing occurs is more important than the fact that it occurs. In a study of a large number of downsizing firms in 16 different industries, strong and statistically significant relationships were found between virtuous practices – characterized by high levels of compassion, forgiveness, gratitude, integrity, optimism, trust, and so on – and both objective outcomes such as profitability, productivity, and quality and subjective outcomes such as morale, customer loyalty, and employee engagement. Organizations that implemented virtuous practices performed significantly better than those that did not.

Different profiles of character strengths have different consequences for individuals, teams and organizations. To be effective as a team member, an individual must be not only humble but also perseverant and courageous. Humility without perseverance and courage may become a weakness in that the person is unable to act vigorously when necessary. A team full of creative, curious, humorous and learning-oriented people is different from a team whose character signature includes judgement, perspective and persistence. Different roles, situations and contexts require different strengths. Curiosity and creativity are more relevant for jobs that require new solutions to problems. Prudence, judgement and perspective are more crucial for making complex decisions. Honesty and bravery are particularly important in situations that are critical from an ethical point of view. Modesty is more highly prized in leaders who act in Singapore than in the US, for example: context is important.[60]

A fruitful approach towards virtues and character strengths in the workplace is the perspective of person–work fit.[61] According to the perspective of *supplementary* fit, individuals are more likely to flourish and achieve higher performance[62] if there is convergence between the person and the context:

For example, someone who is kind presumably is more satisfied with and more successful at work that entails individual service to others. Someone who is creative presumably flourishes at a job that requires new solutions to problems. Someone who is curious presumably does well with work that is complex and varied.[63]

Distinctly, the perspective of *complementary* fit considers that the strengths of the employee fulfill the needs of the work environment through compensating for what is missing in other employees, therefore leading to greater satisfaction:

> For example, bravery is a character strength to the degree that the setting presents challenges and threats. In occupations where bravery is rare, an individual who exercises this strength as needed achieves greater fulfilment and satisfaction. In other words, complementary fit leads to the prediction that character strengths less common among those in a given occupation should contribute more to satisfaction with that work.[64]

The complementary view may be considered for other virtues as well. For example, a prudent individual may be especially valuable in a team of risk takers. Therefore, both the supplementary and complementary perspectives are valid for different virtues and character strengths, in different situations.

Box 2.2 Measuring your character strengths

You may identify your main character strengths (i.e., your signature strengths) by answering the 'VIA Survey of Character Strengths' available in the 'Authentic Happiness' website.[65] By answering the 240 questions, you get information about your 'top strengths'. A shorter self-assessment (120 questions) may be found on the website of the VIA Institute on Character.[66] After completing the survey, you get your character strengths profile. By being aware of your strengths, you are better able to explore how and in which situations you may best use them. You may also consider developing and applying an action plan.[67] You may also assess your strengths via the StrengthsFinder 2.0, now CliftonStrengths 34 (www.gallupstrengthscenter.com/home/en-us/strengthsfinder).

How do character strengths form and unfold?

Character strengths may be considered as 'malleable positive traits'[68] in that they are both stable and developable. They are moderately heritable but they are also influenced by family and other socializing environments (e.g., teachers and peers).[69] They may also change as a consequence of important life events, including dramatic ones (see Box 2.3). A study indicated that recovery from illness and disorder may benefit character.[70] A different study showed that seven character strengths of Americans increased after September 11: gratitude, hope, kindness, leadership, love, spirituality and teamwork.[71] Other studies have discovered that growth following traumatic events may entail a strengthening of character.[72]

Box 2.3 The positive in the negative: is a prison experience a source of strengths' development?[73]

Thomas Middelhoff, the former CEO of the German media group Bertelsmann (as well as of Arcandor and the Thomas Cook Group), was 'the embodiment of a new generation of self-confident German business leaders – among them Jürgen Schrempp at Daimler and Rolf-Ernst Breuer at Deutsche Bank – doing mega-deals in the US'.[74] He was known for his lavish spending, arrogance and big ego. Having been convicted of fraud, he lost health, wealth, reputation and personal freedom. His 'picture-perfect family life' disintegrated. And he nearly died in jail after developing an incurable, life-threatening autoimmune disease. After being released from prison (where he spent almost three years), he told the *Financial Times*: 'It's so strange, but internally I'm stronger than I was beforehand. I have the feeling that I'm in a really thrilling stage of my life'. The key mistake that led him to prison, he said, 'was a disrespect for procedure, in particular his failure to get formal board approvals for the birthday present and the flights'. He acknowledged: 'I was out of touch with reality and thought that certain rules did not apply to me'.

He also came to realise ('that was a colossal mistake') that a key flaw in his character was vanity, a constant thirst for public attention and affirmation, a strong wish to be in the limelight. He said that, over the years, he became a narcissist attracted by hedonism and a lavish lifestyle. When the interviewer commented that it is very difficult to change one's character, he replied: 'I'm monitoring myself very closely today … Am I again trying to dominate a conversation? … Am I again trying to show that I know something better?'

The turning point occurred when he started to develop self-awareness about his inauthenticity, with the key moment being when he found himself standing naked in front of a prison officer. He acknowledged that such experience 'was appalling' but, at the same time, led him to learn a lesson: 'You cannot survive in such an environment if you constantly reject your situation and feel sorry for yourself'. He further expressed that, helped by his rediscovered faith, he 'learned a lot about humility and emotions'.

Questions for reflection

- What personal strengths do you identify in Middelhoff?
- Why (and how) might a personal strength turn into a weakness?
- Why was narcissism problematic for Middelhoff?
- Why did Middelhoff lose touch with reality (see Chapter 8)?
- In what conditions or cases is an 'appalling' experience a source of personal development?
- Take into account what the interviewer wrote about Middelhoff: 'I think not for the first time, [he] is a man of contradictions. Take his claim that he doesn't care about his reputation any more. When I mention in passing that his bestselling book about his time in jail received some mixed reviews, he embarks on a lengthy analysis of media reviews and readers' feedback on

Amazon. "Within eight weeks, I had 40 reviews, and only one was truly negative", he says, adding that the book's average rating was 4.7 out of 5. A few days after our meeting, his publisher calls me to make the same point. Middelhoff is defeated by his schnitzel. We are both so full that we do not even mention the possibility of having dessert. He asks me if I want an espresso, orders two and then – well aware that the *FT* will pay for the lunch – asks the waitress for the bill. This is the Thomas Middelhoff who is used to running the show.'

What does this tell you about the difficulties in changing one's character?

We do not cite these findings to suggest that people *need* to experience adversity to develop their character strengths. Although recovering from adversity may lead some individuals to become stronger, it is also possible that character strengths work as buffers and help individuals to maintain or even increase their wellbeing after dramatic events.[75] It is also likely that some character strengths contribute towards developing other character strengths after recovering from dramatic events. For example, an individual inclined to appreciate beauty and excellence may be more motivated to develop prudence after recovering from an illness caused by bad habits: being prudent is perceived as a route to living better and enhancing appreciation of beauty and excellence. An employee endowed with gratitude may develop kindness after having been supported and helped by others during a traumatic organizational restructuring: kindness is a way to reciprocate the kindness of others.

As habits, character strengths are established by practice. Therefore, they may unfold via deliberate or conscious actions.[76] An employee may develop prudence if he/she wishes and *thinks* about being prudent, *believes* in the value of prudence and *makes recurrent efforts* to be prudent. Being self-aware is necessary for starting a process of personal development. A self-unaware employee who does not acknowledge the imprudence of his/her habits does not embark on such a development process.

Character strengths are habits established by prevailing rewards and punishments, as well as social modelling.[77] (See Box 2.4 for possible gender differences.) If an organization rewards (even if only socially and symbolically) bravery and modesty, it is more likely that the employees develop bravery and modesty. Cowardice and immodesty will be socially punished with people feeling more inclined to leave the organization. If the team environment where the employee works is characterized by honesty, it is more likely that they will develop honesty, otherwise their dishonesty will be punished. Working for a leader who is a paragon of virtues may also contribute to developing character strengths. Organizations may encourage employees to apply their strengths at work in several ways:[78]

- Helping employees to identify strengths.
- Enabling people to engage in tasks and jobs that are in line with personal strengths.
- Creating conditions for job crafting (see Chapter 5), thus aligning jobs with individual character strengths and the things that provide meaning to people.
- Allowing employees with complementary strengths to join forces.

Through these actions, employees may develop higher engagement, performance, wellbeing and psychological capital, potentially becoming more successful in achieving their goals.

Box 2.4 Do males and females express different character strengths?

A meta-analysis[79] has found that males and females are mostly similar in their character strengths, although females score higher in four strengths: appreciation of beauty and excellence, kindness, love and gratitude.

Questions for reflection

*   How do you explain these gender differences?
*   What consequences may emerge from these differences in interactions between males and females within the workplace?

Core self-evaluations

Core self-evaluations (CSE) constitute a high-order trait composed of four lower-order traits: self-esteem, generalized self-efficacy, neuroticism/emotional stability and locus of control[80] (Table 2.3). These four traits are characterized by three criteria: evaluation focus, fundamentality and scope.[81] First, they represent an evaluation (rather than a description) of the self. Second, they are fundamental in that they are central to the self-concept. Third, they are broad in that they represent generalized self-evaluation (in contrast, e.g., with *organization-based* self-esteem,[82] which is an evaluation focussed on a specific domain). These four dispositional traits have usually been studied separately. However, because of commonalities between them, CSE may be considered as a broad, general, positive self-regard or self-concept.

CSE may be defined as a 'fundamental appraisal of one's worthiness, effectiveness, and capability as a person'.[83] Individuals with positive CSE appraise themselves in a consistent positive way across situations. They see themselves as capable, valuable, worthy and in control of their lives. In contrast, individuals with negative CSE appraise themselves as less capable and less worthy and valuable than others, and they respond negatively to failure, error and deficiency, seeing themselves as less competent at being in control of their lives.

Studies have suggested that individuals with a positive CSE denote higher levels of job satisfaction, life satisfaction, organizational commitment, job engagement, motivation and job performance.[97] They are also more able to develop social ties and get more social support while living abroad, thus adapting better as expatriates. One possible explanation for the relationship between CSE and satisfaction is that individuals with more positive CSE choose and pursue goals that are in line with their ideals, interests and values, making them happier.[98] In contrast, individuals with a negative CSE are more likely to pursue avoidance or prevention goals (i.e., 'goals that entail moving away from a negative outcome or state or averting a negative result'),[99] leading to dissatisfaction.

Individuals with a more positive CSE (see Box 2.5, which presents a self-report measure) perform better because they are more motivated and engaged at work.[100]

Table 2.3 The four components of CSE.

Definition	Sample items to measure the component	Comments
Self-esteem The overall value that the individual places on him/herself as a person.	'I feel that I am a person of worth, at least on an equal basis with others.'[84] 'At times I think I am no good at all' (reverse scored).[85]	Self-esteem and self-efficacy may be interrelated, but they represent different constructs. While self-esteem represents feelings of self-acceptance, goodness and self-respect,[86] self-efficacy represents the sense that one can be effective and successful. An individual may have high self-esteem and, at the same time, lack confidence in effectively carrying out their job.
Generalized self-efficacy The evaluation of how well the individual believes he/she can perform across a variety of situations.	'I am strong enough to overcome life's struggles.'[87] 'I often feel that there is nothing that I can do well' (reverse scored)[88]	Generalized self-efficacy differs from specific self-efficacy in that the later represents the evaluation within a specific domain. An individual with a high generalized self-efficacy tends to be self-effective (self-confident) across multiple domains. But an individual with a high level of self-efficacy in a specific domain (e.g., in leadership roles) is not necessarily self-effective in other domains (e.g., as a golf-player or as a writer) (see Box 2.6).
Emotional stability (low neuroticism) Emotional stability (neuroticism): the tendency to have a positive (negative) cognitive/explanatory style and to focus on positive (negative) aspects of the self.[89] Represents the propensity to be calm and secure.	'I rarely feel fearful or anxious' (emotional stability)[90] 'When I'm under a great deal of stress, sometimes I feel like I'm going to pieces' (neuroticism)[91]	Like the other three CSE traits, emotional stability may have a dark side, including in leaders (e.g., 'unemotional leaders may hamper employees who value frequent interaction with their supervisors, and derive a sense of their own job satisfaction based in large part on feedback they get from supervisors').[92]
(Generalized) locus of control Beliefs about the causes of events in one's life.[93] Internal locus of control: the individual sees events as contingent on his/her own behaviour. External locus of control: the individual sees events as dependent on factors outside his/her control (e.g., luck or bad look).	'I am the master of my fate' (internal).[94] 'A great deal that happens to me is probably a matter of chance' (external).[95]	Locus of control is often studied as a generalized belief, but it may also be considered at a specific domain level (e.g., work locus of control).[96]

They feel more capable of dealing with job demands and are more 'psychologically available'.[101] Thus, they are more prepared to put their physical, cognitive and emotional energies into job performance. Individuals with a more positive CSE also are more likely to thrive at work[102] (i.e., they experience both a sense of vitality and a sense of learning).[103] By feeling worthy, competent and capable, they focus on their everyday work, develop a sense of control over their work environment, seek out stimulating roles that provide intrinsic motivation, feel less threatened by new or challenging situations, help others and provide social support and thus feel positive energy and engage more in learning. They denote higher affective organizational commitment and motivation at work, better health, superior individual performance and contribute more for collective performance.[104]

Because individuals with high CSE view situations more positively, it is possible that they see themselves as worthy of the advantages and benefits offered by those situations and are more likely to work harder to extract those benefits.[105] For example, it is likely that they benefit more from the socialization process, which may have positive consequences for newcomer adjustment, performance and career success.[106] It is also possible that individuals with a positive CSE have a propensity towards the manifestation of servant leadership (see Chapter 8).[107] And employees with positive CSE react positively to servant leadership behaviours, such as empowerment.[108]

Box 2.5 Measuring your CSE[109]

To what extent do you agree with the 12 sentences below? Use the following five-point scale to answer.

1	2	3	4	5
Strongly disagree	Disagree	Neutral	Agree	Strongly agree

1. I am confident I get the success I deserve in life. ☐
2. Sometimes I feel depressed. ☐
3. When I try, I generally succeed. ☐
4. Sometimes when I fail I feel worthless. ☐
5. I complete tasks successfully. ☐
6. Sometimes, I do not feel in control of my work. ☐
7. Overall, I am satisfied with myself. ☐
8. I am filled with doubts about my competence. ☐
9. I determine what will happen in my life. ☐
10. I do not feel in control of my success in my career. ☐
11. I am capable of coping with most of my problems. ☐
12. There are times when things look pretty bleak and hopeless to me. ☐

For the questions 2, 4, 6, 8, 10 and 12, reverse the scores (see the next equivalence table). If you have answered 1, replace that score by 5, and vice-versa. If you have answered 2, replace that score by 4, and vice-versa. If you have answered 3, maintain the score. For the questions 1, 3, 5, 7, 9 and 11, keep your original answer.[110]

If your original answer is:	1	2	3	4	5
Replace it by:	5	4	3	2	1

Then, sum the 12 scores and divide by 12. This is your CSE score. Judge, Bono, Erez and Thoresen[111] found scores ranging from 3.8 to 4.0. Is your score lower or higher that those scores?

One implication of the research is that CSE should be used in selection processes. However, caution is necessary to avoid developing a hyper-CSE, which may lead to hubris[112] (see also Chapter 8). Hubris is the 'overestimation of one's own abilities resulting in overconfident, overambitious judgment and decision making, associated with the acquisition of significant power, invulnerable to and contemptuous of the advice and criticism of others'.[113] This overestimation is especially problematic in executives,[114] leading to 'more value-destroying merger-and-acquisition activities', greater acquisition premiums, higher chances of venture failure, investment distortions, excessive risk taking and poorer performance.[115] The syndrome of hubris affects individuals operating in different domains, including sports (see Box 2.7).

Box 2.6 The absolute self-confidence of an under-confident French actress

I ask her [Isabelle Huppert, a famous French actress] whether she has absolute confidence in herself. 'Yes,' she replies. 'I have absolute confidence in my acting abilities, since the beginning. It may sound arrogant. I never doubt. I have absolutely no fear. I have unlimited self-confidence. There are so many other areas where I am not that, I am not ashamed to say it.' What makes her doubt? 'Crossing the street, meeting people ... Everything that's vital. But acting, nothing can intimidate me. Acting is never an obstacle. I do it without thinking. It's like eating or drinking. It's a non-event ... Of course it's an enormous pleasure, but there's no stress.'[116]

Figure 2.2 Isabelle Huppert, 4 November 2010, at Cinemania.[117]

Hyper-CSE may also lead to a costly investment in self-esteem, with negative consequences for individual wellbeing: individuals invest in their work and success because 'they have to rather than want to',[118] thus losing autonomy; they become focussed on themselves at the expense of others, losing their relationships and social and emotional wellbeing.

Some character strengths, such as modesty/humility, perspective/wisdom, prudence and self-regulation, may be especially effective to prevent the possible negative consequences of CSE. Therefore, the positive effect of CSE depends significantly on an individual's virtuousness. If an individual with a very high CSE is imprudent and intemperate, it is more likely that he/she becomes a megalomaniac pursuing unfeasible goals and projects and persisting at them for too long. Or, it may be that he/she underestimates the risks of dangerous and intemperate behaviours (see Box 2.7). This determining role played by character strengths helps to explain their moral nature – a feature that is not necessarily present in CSE.

Box 2.7 Hubris in sports: how heroes fall from the pedestal

In May 2012, an article published in *The Atlantic* explained the fall of Tiger Woods as follows:[119]

> After more than a decade as the greatest golfer in history and the most famous athlete on the planet, Tiger Woods crashed on Thanksgiving weekend 2009, ramming his SUV into a fire hydrant and then having his myriad infidelities, along with humiliating text messages, exposed in the tabloids. Since then, he has been treated for sex addiction, been divorced, changed coaches, and lost not only his way but his golf game.

More than two years before, John Feinstein, an American sportswriter, described Woods as follows:

> **All of which leads to the most oft-asked question** in this entire tangled web: how could one of the great control freaks of history allow himself to completely lose control of his life this way? Anyone who claims it was an unhappy marriage or an over-developed sex drive entirely misses the point. Tiger Woods went on these binges for one simple reason: hubris. He did it because he believed he could do it and no one would catch him and, if someone did somehow catch him, they wouldn't dare out him.[120]

Buzz Bissinger explained how 'Tiger Woods finally fell from his pedestal':[121]

> Woods, to the bitter end and with a kind of hubris that revealed his fundamental arrogance, still felt he could beat the tidal wave back. When he was taken to the hospital for injuries, a fake name was used. When the highway patrol came knocking, he refused to speak to them for three straight days. It was only when his paramours started pouring out of every cupboard like tenement cockroaches that Tiger expressed some sort of awareness that he was in deep shit, though he

did not do so in person but on his Web site ... Once again it was sheer arrogance from a 33-year-old man ... who continued to think he could fool the world.

Woods is not alone in the hall of fallen heroes. Roger Abrams, Professor of Law at Northeastern University, in an article called 'Incivility, taunting and hubris in sports', wrote that 'Long before Donald Trump perfected the public art of the obnoxious swagger, sports at all levels had been consumed by arrogance and pomposity'.[122] Harvey Araton wrote in *The New York Times* that 'Phil Jackson's beloved triangle' was 'a symbol of hubris'.[123] Christopher Bergland explained that 'pride comes before fall', and that Lance Armstrong (seven times winner of the Tour de France, who was banned for life, in 2012, from Olympic sports as a result of longstanding use of doping) was one of those 'hubris-filled heroes' who have fallen 'from their pedestals in mythic proportions'.[124]

Questions for reflection

- Why are sports a domain in which hubris so often develops? Is hubris the downside of a 'thirst to win'?
- How do you interpret the idea, quoted below, that 'There is a sweet spot between hubris and humility that is the key to greatness'?[125]

Grit

Perseverance toward long-term goals

Imagine that you are passionate about a long-term goal – in your personal life, in your job, or in a hobby. Will you be successful in achieving such a goal? It depends on how perseverant you are. Imagine now that you are perseverant in your goal pursuits. Will you be successful in reaching them? It depends on how consistent your interests are. If you change your interests and goals frequently, you don't have enough time to gain the necessary competence to excel in those activities. Therefore, both perseverance and consistency of interests are important to achievement. This is what grit means: perseverance and passion for long-term goals.[126] Angela Duckworth, the scholar who has done the most to popularize the notion of grit, shared her own experience:[127]

I was a good fourth-year math teacher relative to other fourth-year math teachers. But I was not nearly as good as the master teachers who had been doing it for 25 years. And I would never be that good, unless I decided to spend 20 more years working really hard at it. I realized that just shifting, shifting, shifting every two or three years was not going to add up to what I wanted. I thought, 'I'm very ambitious. I want to be world class at something. And this is not a recipe for it'.

Grit has been extoled as crucial for success in multiple life domains (e.g., academic achievement, teaching effectiveness, success in the military context, workplace sales, marriage and sports).[128] As Duckworth pointed out, 'Grit predicts success over and beyond talent. When you consider individuals of equal talent, the grittier ones do better'[129] (see Box 2.8).

Box 2.8 The chicken and the egg: how do talent and grit interrelate?

1 Talented *and* gritty

Angela Duckworth replied in the following way to the question about what research finding had most surprised her:[130]

'Probably the finding that most surprised me was that in the West Point data set, as well as other data sets, grit and talent either aren't related at all or are actually inversely related. That was surprising because rationally speaking, if you're good at things, one would think that you would invest more time in them. You're basically getting more return on your investment per hour than someone who's struggling. If every time you practice piano you improve a lot, wouldn't you be more likely to practice a lot? We've found that that's not necessarily true. [For example], in terms of academics, if you're just trying to get an *A* or an *A*–, just trying to make it to some threshold, and you're a really talented kid, you may do your homework in a few minutes, whereas other kids might take much longer. You get to a certain level of proficiency, and then you stop. So you actually work less hard. If, on the other hand, you are not just trying to reach a certain cut point but are trying to maximize your outcomes – you want to do as well as you possibly can – then there's no limit, ceiling, or threshold ….

When I look at people whom I really respect and admire, like psychology professor Walter Mischel or economist Jim Heckman, these people are extremely talented … Still, they work 17 hours a day. Jim Heckman won the Nobel Prize in Economic Sciences in 2000, and if he were working to get to a cut point, he should now be coasting. But he's not. I think he wants to win another Nobel! The people who are, for lack of a better word, 'ambitious' – the kids who are not satisfied with an *A* or even an *A+*, who have no limit to how much they want to understand, learn, or succeed – those are the people who are both talented *and* gritty. So, the inverse relationship between talent and grit that we've found in some of our studies doesn't mean that all talented people are un-gritty. That's certainly not true. The most successful people in life are both talented and gritty in whatever they've chosen to do.'

2 Which came first: the chicken or the egg? Both!

The notion that grit and deliberate practice is more important than talent, or that talent may develop as the consequence of deliberate practice, must be approached with caution. Deliberate practice may also result from talent: 'deliberate practice may be correlated with success because it is a proxy for ability: We stop doing what we do not do well and feel unrewarded for'.[131] In summary: grit builds talent, talent makes individuals grittier and success and performance are affected by talent, grit and many other factors.

The idea of grit was adopted and then diffused by the media. Baer wrote in *Fast Company* that 'to be successful, grit is a most valuable asset'.[132] Martins, Dias and Khanna considered that grit helps to explain 'what makes some Silicon Valley companies so successful'.[133] Foote, Eisenstat and Fredberg also argued that, to navigate the difficult and often unforeseen challenges of today's organizations, leaders need 'grit, persistence, and focus'.[134] Policy makers in the UK and US have implemented training programmes that cultivate grit in children, teenagers and adults.[135] A report by The US Department of Education, Office of Educational Technology advocated the promotion of grit, tenacity and perseverance because these characteristics are 'critical factors for success in the 21st century'.[136]

One possible reason why grit leads to success is because gritty individuals spend more time and effort in 'deliberate practice':[137] that is, practising activities aimed at improving specific aspects of performance (e.g., spending day after day, month after month, year after year, in playing piano, running, playing chess, writing, etc., with a focus on mastering and excelling in those activities). Even the success of The Beatles may be explained, in part, by the band's 'deliberate practice'[138] (Box 2.9). The notions of grit and deliberate practise are represented in Gladwell's 'ten thousand hours' rule[139] (see Box 2.9). Gladwell, citing the neurologist Daniel Levitin, wrote:[140]

> In study after study, of composers, basketball players, fiction writers, ice skaters, concert pianists, chess players, master criminals, and what have you, this number comes up again and again. Of course, this doesn't address why some people get more out of their practice sessions than others do. But no one has yet found a case in which true world-class expertise was accomplished in less time. It seems that it takes the brain this long to assimilate all that it needs to know to achieve true mastery. This is true even of people we think of as prodigies. Mozart, for example, famously started writing music at six. But, writes the psychologist Michael Howe in his book *Genius Explained*, by the standards of mature composers, Mozart's early works are not outstanding … The music critic Harold Schonberg goes further: 'Mozart', he argues, actually 'developed late', since he didn't produce his greatest work until he had been composing for more than twenty years.

Box 2.9 The Beatles: confidence and grit were more important than effortless inspiration

The Beatles were one of the most successful rock bands of all time. Was their success a fruit of talent and inspiration, luck, or grit? Peter Aspden, a former arts editor and writer at the *Financial Times*, wrote that 'Luck, genius and sheer grit all played a part in launching The Beatles'.[141] On the relevance of grit (and confidence), Aspden wrote:

John Lennon's profanity ends the volume [The Beatles: *All These Years*, Volume One: *Tune In*]:[142] 'We were the best fucking group in the goddamn world ... It was just a matter of time before everybody else caught on.' It wouldn't take them very long. The Beatles never lacked for confidence ... The Beatles came back from Hamburg having played music together for 415 hours in the space of just 14 weeks. Their trials would become a key illustration of Malcolm Gladwell's '10,000 hours' thesis ... on the importance of serious and substantial practice. Part one of The Beatles' story is as much about grit and drive as about effortless inspiration. As they moved through the beginning of the 1960s, their homework began to yield results. They always remained ahead of the game.

Is grit enough to be successful?

The impact of employee grit on performance is understudied, and Ion, Mindu and Gorbanescu even argued that the relevance of grit in the workplace should be treated with caution. These authors suggested that 'Grit is dispensable in explaining the personality-job performance and job satisfaction relationships'.[144] Observations of this type, however, are debatable in that they do not consider that the effects of grit on performance depend on other factors. As Gladwell explained:[145]

> Practice isn't a SUFFICIENT condition for success. I could play chess for 100 years and I'll never be a grandmaster. The point is simply that natural ability requires a huge investment of time in order to be made manifest.

Therefore, grit is a necessary but not a sufficient condition for success. Grit leads to long-term success only if the individual also has other capacities and personal characteristics. Virtues and character strengths may be especially valuable – in that they work as facilitators of the positive effects of grit, and as buffers of its potential negative effects (see the next sub-section on humility). It is difficult to imagine how a gritty

Figure 2.3 The Beatles, after arriving at Kennedy Airport, 7 February 1964.[143]

employee who is dishonest, cognitively limited and socially inept can be successful.[146] It is also difficult to imagine how a gritty *and* arrogant leader may be successful in fostering team flourishing and effectiveness.

Contextual conditions (both at the task and social climate levels) are also necessary for grit to be productive and a source of personal flourishing. Employee grit translates into better performance if the gritty employee has autonomy to carry out the job.[147] In contrast, if the rules, structures and factors that lead to success in the activity change often, the impact of grit and deliberate practice on performance is weakened:[148]

> In tennis, chess, and classical music, the rules never change, so you can study up to become the best. But in less stable fields, like entrepreneurship and rock and roll, rules can go out the window. Richard Branson started in the record business but quickly branched out into fields well beyond music: Virgin Group has 400 companies and is launching people into space. Then there's a band like the Sex Pistols, who took the world by storm even though Sid Vicious could barely play his bass. So mastery is more than a matter of practice.

Moreover, in the contemporary workplace, many tasks are now performed in teams. For grit to turn into higher performance, it is necessary that the employee experience a supportive context and a supportive leader (see Chapter 8).[149] Being gritty implies taking risks, innovating, overcoming obstacles through creativity, being perseverant when others give up. If a gritty employee feels like working in an unsupportive context, it is likely that he/she refrains from embracing risky and innovative projects.

The downside of grit as counterweighted by humility

Gritty individuals are more susceptible to the sunk-cost fallacy,[150] i.e., the tendency 'to honor prior costs by holding on to failing projects'.[151] They are also more likely to persist too long in unfeasible goals and projects,[152] less open to information that contradicts their beliefs, and more likely to be 'handicapped by judgment and decision-making biases'.[153] By staying the course, gritty individuals may also miss new and relevant opportunities because they are so focussed on their passionate goal.[154] Therefore, 'putting all eggs in one basket' may be risky, even dangerous.[155] The challenge is thus paradoxical: the focus on passionate long-term goals must coexist with an active and open-minded judgement and decision-making.[156] Such a challenge requires a humble perspective (Box 2.10).

Research[157] suggests that humble individuals are better able to develop positive social relationships through helpfulness, generosity, social bonding, forgiveness and social justice commitment. They also experience more psychological and emotional wellbeing and obtain better learning and performance outcomes. Studies also indicate that humble leaders foster several positive outcomes (including performance and effectiveness) in employees, teams and organizations. Humility may unlock the positive potential of employee grit and help individuals to avoid incurring the risks associated with grit. Without humility, gritty individuals are less open to information that contradicts their beliefs, less willing to abandon unfeasible projects, more obstinate in pursuing original goals and more likely to miss new opportunities. Humility may be the ingredient that reconciles a focus on valued long-term goals with active, open-minded judgement and decision-making.[158] It seems plausible that successful individuals are both gritty *and* humble:[159]

When Robert Noyce, the founder of Intel, was asked how he felt about being known as the 'Father of Silicon Valley' he responded, 'You know it makes me a little bit proud, and a little bit humble'. There is a sweet spot between hubris and humility that is the key to greatness. Bob Noyce was like a rare alloy that blended ambition and confidence with conscientiousness and compassion.[160]

Box 2.10 Humility: the sense that one is not the 'centre of the universe'

The word 'humility' comes from the Latin *humus*, meaning 'earth' or 'ground', and from the Latin word *humilis*, 'on the ground'.[161] Being humble thus means having a grounded view of oneself and others,[162] and reflects 'a self-view that something greater than the self exists' (see also Chapter 8).[163] Humble individuals 'acknowledge their personal strengths and weaknesses (as well as those of others), without leading themselves to develop feelings of superiority or inferiority'.[164] Humility is a foundational principle of all major world religions; it is at the core of several philosophical discussions about morality,[165] being described by some philosophers as a meta-virtue foundational to other virtues.[166]

This apparent simplicity hides the lack of consensus among researchers about the definition of humility. Some literature even equates humility with modesty, honesty, empathy, low self-esteem, low narcissism, integrity.[167] The conceptual debate can also be found in the consideration of humility as a virtue, a personality trait, a psychological strength, a value or an orientation.[168] Moreover, different authors have indicated different sets of key components of humility. Owens and colleagues[169] proposed the 'first comprehensive, empirically-based conceptualization of leader humility',[170] focussed on 'expressed humility' (i.e., on observable behaviours interpreted by observers/followers as reflecting humility). The expressed humility construct reflects the *interpersonal* nature of humility and comprises three dimensions: (1) capacity or willingness to evaluate oneself without positive or negative exaggeration; (2) viewing others in an appreciative non-threatened way; and (3) teachability (i.e., openness to new ideas, feedback and advice). Nielsen and Marrone considered these three components as the 'conceptual core of humility'.[171] Their literature review also suggested the following additional seven components: (4) transcendence/perspective; (5) low self-focus; (6) self-transcendent pursuit; (7) no desire for control; (8) recognition of luck and good fortune; (9) relational/collective orientation; (10) lack of concern for superiority.

Antecedents of grit

There are reasons to believe that grit is associated with several individual characteristics. For example, it is possible that optimistic individuals,[172] as well as those who have the capacity to delay gratification,[173] are grittier. It is also possible that overconfident and hyper-optimistic individuals are less gritty. These individuals may be so self-confident and so optimistic that they feel no need to persevere in efforts to achieve their goals (i.e., why be perseverant if success is guaranteed?). Another important predictor of grit is a growth mindset (Box 2.11 and Chapter 1, including Table 1.7): individuals with a growth mindset are grittier than those with a fixed mindset.[174]

Individuals with a fixed mindset believe that their capacities, strengths, talent, intelligence and gifts are immutable. For them, performing poorly on a task or assignment demonstrates that they lack capacities rather than that they have more to learn. They give up and invest in easier tasks or assignments. In contrast, individuals with a growth mindset see their abilities as flexible and developable through dedication, input from others, good strategies and hard work. Individuals with a growth mindset are less likely to get frustrated when they experience failure or make a mistake. They put more energy into learning. They are more perseverant toward their goals, in spite of failures and mistakes. They are grittier.[175] Therefore, they tend to outperform those with a fixed mindset.[176]

'Mindsets' may be mental constructions but they profoundly affect our actions. Is the growth mindset affected by our brain? Grit may have a neuroanatomical basis. Does this mean that the growth mindset is 'fixed' – one has it or has not? The answer is negative. Research suggests that training interventions may change mindsets.[177] The type of feedback provided also reinforces mindsets. If a supervisor, teacher or parent attributes achievement to intelligence, it reinforces a fixed mindset. Conversely, attributing a report's success to preparation and effort reinforces the growth mindset. Moreover, according to research on brain plasticity,[178] people's brains change with experience; thinking about growth and behaving accordingly affects the brain.

Box 2.11 Do you have a growth or a fixed mindset?

To what extent do you agree with the following sentences?[179]

1 'You have a certain amount of intelligence and you really can't do much to change it.'
2 'Your intelligence is something about you that you can't change very much.'
3 'You can learn new things, but you can't really change your basic intelligence.'
4 'You either are creative or you are not – even by trying very hard you cannot change much.'
5 'You have to be born a creator – without innate talent you can only be a scribbler.'
6 'Some people are creative, others aren't – and no practice can change it.'
7 'A truly creative talent is innate and constant throughout one's entire life.'
8 'Everyone can create something great at some point if he or she is given appropriate conditions.'
9 'Practice makes perfect – perseverance and trying hard are the best ways to develop and expand one's capabilities.'
10 'Rome wasn't built in a day – each creativity requires effort and work, and these two are more important than talent.'

If you agree strongly with the first seven sentences, and disagree strongly with the last three, it is likely that you have a fixed mindset. If you disagree with the first seven sentences, and agree with the last three, it is more likely that you have a growth mindset.

Questions for reflection

- What kind of mindset do you have? If you have a fixed one, do not blame yourself!
- What kind of mindset do your peers or employees have? If they have a fixed one, don't blame them – by doing so you would inadvertently reinforce their mindset. Instead, challenge and support them, and build a psychologically safe environment (see Chapter 7).
- Do you reward others just because of great efforts, regardless of the performance and learning outcomes? In that case, be careful: reward both efforts *and* learning.
- Take into account that the *growth mindset* is a journey, not a proclamation, a fashion or a destination.[180]

Having a meaningful purpose and performing meaningful work also nourishes grit[181] (see Chapter 5). If employees are motivated by a meaningful purpose or if they have the opportunity to perform meaningful work, it is more likely that they persevere toward such meaningful purposes. As David Brooks explained in *The New York Times* article about University of Pennsylvania Professor Angela Duckworth, a leading grit researcher and former public-school teacher:[182]

I don't know about you, but I'm really bad at being self-disciplined about things I don't care about. For me, and I suspect for many, hard work and resilience can only happen when there is a strong desire. Grit is thus downstream from longing. People need a powerful why if they are going to be able to endure anyhow. Duckworth herself has a very clear telos. As she defines it, 'Use psychological science to help kids thrive.' Throughout her book, you can feel her passion for her field and see how gritty she has been in pursuing her end.

Developing grit

The idea of grit as malleable and developable has found empirical support in the work of several researchers.[183] While, for example, conscientiousness is a (more) stable trait, grit may be motivation-based and developable.[184] Organizations may foster their employees' grit in several ways, including allowing the employees to carry out meaningful work and pursuing a meaningful purpose. Employees feel more engaged at work when they consider that the mission or purpose of their company makes an important contribution to society, enabling the employee to view their job as important.[185]

Considering that one 'person's grit enhances the grit of others',[186] and that more important than the 'message' a leader aims to deliver is the 'message' the employee receives/perceives,[187] it is likely that grit in leaders is transferred to employees. Two main processes may explain this influence: social learning[188] and social contagion.[189] Social learning theory suggests that employees' behaviours, beliefs and attitudes are learned from the environment via the process of observational, or vicarious, learning. The social contagion literature suggests that employees display behaviours, attitudes, emotions and beliefs that are similar to those observed in their leaders.

A high level of grit in leaders is not enough to foster grit in employees. Considering the challenges and risks associated with grit, it is important that leaders are not only gritty but also supportive. Duckworth has suggested that individuals' grit develops as a consequence of both demanding/challenging and supportive relationships (i.e., 'tough love') with authority figures[190] (see Box 2.12). She notes, 'supportive and demanding parenting is psychologically wise and encourages children to emulate their parents. It stands to reason that supportive and demanding leadership would do the same'.[191] Assuming that a gritty leader is perceived as challenging and demanding, it makes sense to expect that leaders perceived as *both* gritty and supportive, versus those who are *only* gritty, are more likely to foster employee grit. Since the time-scale for a gritty employee's goal pursuit is long, the employee needs a sense of support from his/her leader and to feel that there are (material, emotional, informational, relational) resources available for the pursuit of that goal.[192] Support from a highly regarded leader may signal that such resources are available to assist the pursuit of long-term goals.

Box 2.12 Challenging and supporting: a necessary duet to developing grit?

A report of The US Department of Education, Office of Educational Technology, made several recommendations to help schools in fostering the students' grit. One consisted of combining challenge with support. The rationale is as follows:

> Our research pointed to two potentially important factors. *First, students need opportunities to take on 'optimally challenging' goals that, to the student, are worthy of pursuit.* Optimally challenging goals are those that are within the student's range of proximal development – not too difficult and not too easy. Students will find goals worthy of pursuit when the goals resonate with their personal values and interests. *Second, students need a rigorous and supportive environment to accomplish these goals and/or develop critical psychological resources.* As students engage in pursuing their goals, there is a wide range of challenges they may encounter, such as conceptual complexity, distractions and boredom, lack of resources, and adverse circumstances. Students will be more likely to persevere when the learning environment has a fair and respectful climate, conveys high expectations, emphasizes effort over ability, and provides necessary tangible resources – materials, human, and time.[193]

Questions for reflection

- May the same approach (challenging and supporting) be adopted by leaders in order to develop employees' grit?
- Why would just challenging *or* just supporting be problematic? What happens when a leader challenges and is very demanding but unsupportive? And what happens when the leader is supportive but is not challenging?

Final comments

Several important assumptions underpinned this chapter. First, employees grow and contribute to team and organizational flourishing when they have opportunities to use their strengths. Second, some strengths are more plastic than others. However, to a certain extent, all strengths are developable. Third, employees are more likely to flourish if they identify their own strengths, make deliberate efforts to develop them, and work in contexts where they may use and develop their best-selves. Fourth, organizations may reap the benefits of employees' strengths in several ways: (1) selecting individuals with positive traits; (2) creating conditions so that employees may use their strengths; (3) helping employees to discover their own strengths and allowing them to work on jobs that fit those strengths; (4) develop employees' strengths.

The chapter also discussed how strengths may become weaknesses when they are excessive or unaccompanied by other strengths. Self-confidence may turn into overconfidence and hubris if individuals are not endowed with strengths such as wisdom, prudence, humility and self-regulation. Gritty individuals are more likely to flourish if they are endowed with those virtues. The moral nature of character strengths operates as a 'virtuous frame' that reinforces the positive effects of other strengths and acts as a buffer against the risks associated with those other strengths. In summary, every strength has a downside and it is the interplay between virtues and strengths that makes individuals, teams and organizations more likely to flourish. As Park, Barton and Pillay explain:

> Good character is important in the daily lives of individuals and families, in the workplace, in school, and in the larger community. Good character is what citizens look for in their leaders, what we seek in a spouse, what friends and colleagues look for in each other, and what parents wish for and try to encourage in their children. Strengths of character are foundation of optimal life-long human development and thriving.[194]

These authors also stated that 'positive institutions like families, schools, and communities make it easier or harder for individuals to have and display good character but these institutions are only positive in the first place when comprised of people with good character'.[195] We consider that positive organizations are comprised of employees with positive psychological strengths and good character, with these positive qualities being encouraged and developed through positive leadership (Chapter 8) and positive organizational practices. The final message is that organizations can develop normal heroes by emphasizing and cultivating the positive core of individuals.

Want more?

A good review of virtues and character strengths may be found in Park, Barton and Pillay.[196] Peterson and Seligman's[197] classic VIA handbook is crucial for understanding the rationale behind the classification and receiving a granular analysis of each virtue and character strength. Harzer and Ruch[198] discuss signature strengths at work, while Peterson, Stephens, Park, Lee and Seligman[199] discuss the relevance of character strengths at work. A literature review of positive CSE may be found in Chang, Ferris, Johnson, Rosen and Tan,[200] while Judge and Hurst[201] discuss both benefits and costs of positive CSE. Duckworth's[202] book may help with understanding the relevance of grit in different life domains and how grit may be nourished and developed. Furthermore, Disabato, Goodman and Kashdan[203] have examined, in a sample of 7,617 participants from six of the seven continents, how each grit facet relates to wellbeing and personality strengths. Readers with research goals may benefit from the meta-analysis of grit by Credé, Tynan and Harms.[204]

Glossary

Character strengths   'The distinguishable routes to displaying one or another of the virtues.'[205]

Core self-evaluations   A 'fundamental appraisal of one's worthiness, effectiveness, and capability as a person'.[206] Covers self-esteem, generalized self-efficacy, emotional stability (neuroticism) and locus of control.

Courage   'Doing what is right, even when one has much to lose.'[207]

Emotional stability   The propensity to be calm and secure.

Fixed mindset   The belief that abilities and intelligence are immutable.

Generalized self-efficacy   The evaluation of how well the individual believes he/she can perform across a variety of situations.

Golden mean   Virtue defined as the middle (between the extremes of excess and deficiency).

Grit   Passion and perseverance for long-term goals.

Growth mindset   The belief that abilities and intelligence may be developed.

Hubris   Extreme pride or self-confidence.

Humanity   Disposition to 'tend and befriend'.[208]

Locus of control   Beliefs about the causes of events in one's life.[209]

Pollyanna effect   *Pollyanna*, by Eleanor H. Porter (1913), is a classic of children's literature. The character, Pollyanna, is an overoptimistic young orphan who sees a bright side in every situation and circumstance, regardless of how bad the circumstance may be. The Pollyanna effect thus represents the tendency to be overoptimistic, to underestimate the negative circumstances, and to look for the bright side of everything, including misfortune.

Reflected Best Self Exercise[TM]   An exercise developed by scholars at the Center for Positive Organizations[210] (Ross School of Business, University of Michigan) to help individuals to 'discover' their main strengths and talents (i.e., 'the best self') from the point of view of others.

Self-esteem   The overall value that the individual places on him/herself as a person.

Temperance   'The virtue of control over excess.'[211]

Transcendence   The 'belief that there is meaning or purpose larger than ourselves'.[212]

Virtue   'A disposition to act, desire, and feel that involves the exercise of judgment and leads to a recognizable human excellence or instance of human flourishing.'[213]

Wisdom   'Good judgment and advice about important but uncertain matters of life.'[214]

Notes

1 Spreitzer and Cameron (2012, p. 85).
2 L. M. Roberts et al. (2005a, p. 75).
3 Clifton and Harter (2003, p. 114).
4 Wood, Linley, Maltby, Kashdan and Hurling (2011, p. 15).
5 King and Trent (2013, p. 199).
6 Sheldon, Jose, Kashdan and Jarden (2015).
7 Bakker and van Woerkom (2018).
8 L. M. Roberts et al. (2005a, 2005b).
9 L. M. Roberts et al. (2005a).
10 L. M. Roberts et al. (2005b, p. 78).
11 L. M. Roberts et al. (2005b, p. 76).
12 http://positiveorgs.bus.umich.edu/cpo-tools/rbse/.
13 L. M. Roberts et al. (2005b).
14 L. M. Roberts et al. (2005a).
15 Park, Barton and Pillay (2017).
16 Chang, Ferris, Johnson, Rosen and Tan (2012).
17 Nübold, Muck and Maier (2013).
18 Built from: Avey, Luthans and Youssef (2010); Luthans and Youssef (2007); Luthans, Avolio, Avey and Norman (2007).
19 Cameron and McNaughtan (2014); Cameron and Spreitzer (2012).
20 Peterson and Seligman (2004); Peterson, Stephens, Park, Lee and Seligman (2010).
21 Cameron (2011, p. 27).
22 Peterson and Seligman (2004).
23 Peterson and Seligman (2004, p. 13).
24 Park, Peterson and Seligman (2004); Peterson and Seligman (2004).
25 Peterson, Stephens, Park, Lee and Seligman (2010, p. 222).
26 Peterson, Stephens, Park, Lee and Seligman (2010).
27 The classification of some strengths is debatable (e.g., the humour strength under the transcendence virtue; leadership under virtue of justice). Consider, for example, Ruch and Proyer (2015) who tested the factorial structure of the 24 strengths model. Park, Barton and Pillay (2017) stated that several character strengths are not 'moral traits' per se. They pointed out individuals who, although endowed with the 'leadership' strength, cannot be considered virtuous. They also discussed the potential negative side of emotional intelligence. These authors also argued that the VIA classification is a 'work in progress'.
28 Park, Barton and Pillay (2017).
29 A. Roberts (2008).
30 Niemiec (2013, p. 15).
31 Built mainly from: Park, Peterson and Seligman (2006); Peterson and Seligman (2004); Peterson, Stephens, Park, Lee and Seligman (2010).
32 Quotes from Park, Peterson and Seligman (2006).
33 Baltes and Smith (1990, p. 87).
34 Peterson and Seligman (2004, p. 36).
35 Peterson and Seligman (2004, p. 36).
36 Peterson and Seligman (2004, p. 37).
37 Peterson and Seligman (2004, p. 293).
38 Peterson and Seligman (2004, p. 37).
39 Peterson and Seligman (2004, p. 38).
40 Peterson and Seligman (2004, p. 38).
41 This conceptualization of 'hope' differs from the one adopted by the psychological capital scholars, and is more aligned with the concept of optimism. See the next chapter.
42 Aristotle (2009).
43 See Rego, Cunha and Clegg (2012).
44 Stouten, van Dijke, Mayer, De Cremer and Euwema (2013).
45 See 'USU 2017 Commencement Speech – Dr. Adam Grant' in www.youtube.com/watch?v=YJeLTHsbSug. The text was published by Grant (2017).

46 Carlsen, Hagen and Mortensen (2012, p. 296).
47 Built from Rego, Cunha and Clegg (2012).
48 Peterson and Park (2006, p. 1149).
49 Hausler et al. (2017); Martínez-Martí and Ruch (2017); Niemiec (2013); Park, Peterson and Seligman (2004); Peterson and Park (2011).
50 Peterson, Stephens, Park, Lee and Seligman (2010).
51 Harzer and Ruch (2014); Niemiec (2013); Peterson and Seligman (2004); Sosik, Centry and Jae (2012).
52 Peterson and Seligman (2004); Sosik, Centry and Jae (2012).
53 Crossan, Mazutis and Seijts (2013).
54 Cameron, Bright and Caza (2004).
55 In Cameron (2010, p. 47).
56 Cameron (2010).
57 Cameron (2010).
58 See Bright, Cameron and Caza (2006).
59 Cameron (2010, p. 48).
60 Oc, Basshur, Daniels, Greguras and Diefendorff (2015).
61 Harzer and Ruch (2014); Peterson, Stephens, Park, Lee and Seligman (2010).
62 Harzer and Ruch (2014).
63 Peterson, Stephens, Park, Lee and Seligman (2010, p. 221).
64 Peterson, Stephens, Park, Lee and Seligman (2010, p. 224).
65 www.authentichappiness.sas.upenn.edu/questionnaires/survey-character-strengths.
66 www.viacharacter.org/survey/Account/Register.
67 Niemiec (2013).
68 Sosik, Centry and Jae (2012, p. 367).
69 Peterson and Park (2011).
70 Peterson, Park and Seligman (2006).
71 Peterson and Seligman (2003).
72 Peterson, Park, Pole, D'Andrea and Seligman (2008).
73 All quotes are from Storbeck (2018, p. 3).
74 Storbeck (2018, p. 3).
75 Peterson and Park (2011).
76 Niemiec (2013).
77 Park, Barton and Pillay (2017); Peterson and Park (2011).
78 Bakker and van Woerkom (2018); Harzer and Ruch (2012).
79 Heintz, Kramm and Ruch (2019).
80 Judge, Locke and Durham (1997); Judge, Bono, Erez and Thoresen (2003).
81 Chang, Ferris, Johnson, Rosen and Tan (2012).
82 Organization-based self-esteem is 'the degree to which an individual believes him/herself to be capable, significant, and worthy' as an organizational member (Pierce & Gardner, 2004, p. 593).
83 Judge, Bono, Erez and Thoresen (2003, p. 304).
84 Rosenberg (1965).
85 Rosenberg (1965).
86 Lyubomirsky, Tkach and DiMatteo (2006).
87 Judge, Locke, Durham and Kluger (1998).
88 Judge, Locke, Durham and Kluger (1998).
89 Judge, Bono, Erez and Thoresen (2003).
90 Costa and McCrae (1992).
91 Costa and McCrae (1992).
92 Judge, Piccolo and Kosalka (2009, p. 868).
93 Rotter (1971).
94 Rotter (1971).
95 Rotter (1971).
96 Spector (1988).
97 Hsieh and Huang (2017); Judge and Bono (2001); Judge, Bono, Erez and Locke (2005); Judge, Bono, Erez and Thoresen (2003); Judge and Hurst (2012); For a meta-analysis, see Chang, Ferris, Johnson, Rosen and Tan (2012).

 98 Judge, Bono, Erez and Locke (2005); Sheldon, Jose, Kashdan and Jarden (2015).
 99 Judge, Bono, Erez and Locke (2005, p. 257).
100 Rich, Lepine and Crawford (2010).
101 Rich, Lepine and Crawford (2010).
102 Porath, Spreitzer, Gibson and Garnett (2012); Walumbwa, Muchiri, Misati, Wu and Meiliani (2017).
103 Spreitzer, Sutcliffe, Dutton, Sonenshein and Grant (2005).
104 Walumbwa, Muchiri, Misati, Wu and Meiliani (2017).
105 Judge and Hurst (2007).
106 Fang, Duffy and Shaw (2011).
107 Liden, Panaccio, Meuser, Hu and Wayne (2014).
108 Liden, Panaccio, Meuser, Hu and Wayne (2014).
109 'This measure is non-proprietary (free) and may be used without permission' (Judge, Bono, Erez & Thoresen, 2003, p. 315).
110 Some research (Arias & Arias, 2017; Beléndez, Gómez, López & Topa, 2018) suggests that the items worded positively (1, 3, 5, 7, 9 and 11) and those worded negatively (2, 4, 6, 8, 10 and 12) represent different constructs: positive core self-evaluation and negative core self-evaluation, respectively.
111 Judge, Bono, Erez and Thoresen (2003).
112 Hiller and Hambrick (2005); Sadler-Smith, Akstinaite, Robinson and Wray (2017).
113 Sadler-Smith, Akstinaite, Robinson and Wray (2017, p. 531).
114 Tang and Yang (2015).
115 Synthesis in Tang, Li and Yang (2015).
116 Chassany (2017, p. 3).
117 Author: Cinemania film festival. Retrieved from https://commons.wikimedia.org/wiki/File:Isa belle_Huppert_Cinemania.jpg. File licensed under the Creative Commons Attribution-Share Alike 4.0 International license.
118 Judge and Hurst (2012, p. 166).
119 Heineman Jr. (2012).
120 Feinstein (2010, bold in the original).
121 Bissinger (2010).
122 Abrams (2016).
123 Araton (2017).
124 Bergland (2013).
125 Bergland (2013).
126 Duckworth, Peterson, Matthews and Kelly (2007, p. 1087).
127 In Perkins-Gough (2013, p. 18).
128 Credé, Tynan and Harms (2017); Duckworth (2016); Macnamara, Hambrick and Oswald (2014).
129 In Perkins-Gough (2013, p. 16).
130 In Perkins-Gough (2013, pp. 15–16; italics in the original).
131 Sternberg (1996, p. 350); see also Macnamara, Hambrick and Oswald (2014).
132 Baer (2013).
133 Martins, Dias and Khanna (2016).
134 Foote, Eisenstat and Fredberg (2011, p. 100).
135 Credé, Tynan and Harms (2017); Ion, Mindu and Gorbanescu (2017).
136 Shechtman, DeBarger, Dornsife, Rosier and Yarnall (2013).
137 Duckworth, Kirby, Tsukayama, Berstein and Ericsson (2011); Ericsson, Krampe and Tesch-Römer (1993); Hambrick et al. (2014).
138 Gladwell (2009).
139 Gladwell (2009).
140 Gladwell (2009, p. 238).
141 Aspden (2013, p. 12).
142 Lewisohn (2013).
143 Retrieved from https://commons.wikimedia.org/wiki/File:The_Beatles_in_America.JPG. This work is in the public domain in the United States because it was published in the US between 1923 and 1977 without a copyright notice.

144 Ion, Mindu and Gorbanescu (2017, p. 167).
145 In Baer (2014a).
146 Hambrick et al. (2014); Meinz and Hambrick (2010).
147 Gilson, Diz and Lochbaum (2017).
148 Baer (2014b). See Macnamara, Hambrick and Oswald's (2014) meta-analysis about the relationship between deliberate practice and performance in different fields.
149 Duckworth (2016).
150 Arkes and Blumer (1985).
151 Van Putten, Zeelenberg and van Dijk (2010, p. 33).
152 Macnamara, Hambrick and Oswald (2014).
153 Duckworth and Eskreis-Winkler (2013).
154 Duckworth and Eskreis-Winkler (2013).
155 In Useem (2016).
156 Duckworth and Eskreis-Winkler (2013).
157 See Nielsen and Marrone (2018).
158 Duckworth and Eskreis-Winkler (2013).
159 Collins (2001).
160 Bergland (2013).
161 Argandoña (2015); Owens, Rowatt and Wilkins (2012).
162 Owens, Rowatt and Wilkins (2012).
163 Ou et al. (2014, p. 37).
164 Rego et al. (2019).
165 Argandoña (2015); Owens, Rowatt and Wilkins (2012); Owens, Johnson and Mitchell (2013).
166 Owens and Hekman (2012).
167 De Vries, Lee and Ashton (2008); Ogunfowora and Bourdage (2014); Tangney (2009). See Nielsen and Marrone (2018) for a review.
168 Owens, Johnson and Mitchell (2013).
169 Owens and Hekman (2012); Owens, Rowatt and Wilkins (2012); Owens, Johnson and Mitchell (2013).
170 Oc, Basshur, Daniels, Greguras and Diefendorff (2015, p. 69).
171 Nielsen and Marrone (2018).
172 Duckworth and Eskreis-Winkler (2013).
173 Wang et al. (2018).
174 Dweck (2016, 2017).
175 Wang et al. (2018).
176 It is important to note that there are not 'pure' mindsets: 'Everyone is actually a mixture of fixed and growth mindsets, and that mixture continually evolves with experience' (Dweck, 2016).
177 Blackwell, Trzesniewski and Dweck (2007).
178 Ng (2018).
179 Dweck, Chiu and Hong (1995); Karwowski (2014).
180 Dweck (2015).
181 Vainio and Daukantaite (2016); Von Culin, Tsukayama and Duckworth (2014).
182 Brooks (2016, p. A23).
183 Duckworth and Gross (2014); Hill, Burrow and Bronk (2016); Mueller, Wolfe and Syed (2017); Wang et al. (2018).
184 Vainio and Daukantaite (2016).
185 Gallup (2017).
186 Duckworth (2016, p. 263).
187 Duckworth (2016).
188 Bandura (1977).
189 Aarts, Gollwitzer and Hassin (2004); Chartrand and Lakin (2013).
190 Duckworth (2016).
191 Duckworth (2016, p. 266).
192 Vainio and Daukantaite (2016).
193 Shechtman, DeBarger, Dornsife, Rosier and Yarnall (2013, p. vii; italics in the original).
194 Park, Barton and Pillay (2017, p. 73).

195 Park, Barton and Pillay (2017, p. 75).
196 Park, Barton and Pillay (2017).
197 Peterson and Seligman (2004).
198 Harzer and Ruch (2012).
199 Peterson, Stephens, Park, Lee and Seligman (2010).
200 Chang, Ferris, Johnson, Rosen and Tan (2012).
201 Judge and Hurst (2012).
202 Duckworth (2016).
203 Disabato, Goodman and Kashdan (2019).
204 Credé, Tynan and Harms (2017).
205 Peterson and Seligman (2004, p. 13).
206 Judge, Bono, Erez and Thoresen (2003, p. 304).
207 Peterson and Seligman (2004, p. 36).
208 Peterson and Seligman (2004, p. 293).
209 Rotter (1971).
210 L. M. Roberts et al. (2005a, 2005b).
211 Peterson and Seligman (2004, p. 38).
212 Peterson and Seligman (2004, p. 38).
213 Peterson and Seligman (2004); Peterson, Stephens, Park, Lee and Seligman (2010).
214 Baltes and Smith (1990, p. 87).

References

Aarts, H., Gollwitzer, P. M., & Hassin, R. R. (2004). Goal contagion: Perceiving is for pursuing. *Journal of Personality and Social Psychology*, 87, 23–37.

Abrams, R. I. (2016). Incivility, taunting and hubris in sports. *Huffington Post*, January 15 (www.huffingtonpost.com/roger-i-abrams/incivility-taunting-and-h_b_8993698.html).

Araton, H. (2017). Phil Jackson's beloved triangle: A symbol of hubris. *The New York Times*, June 30, B13.

Argandoña, A. (2015). Humility in management. *Journal of Business Ethics*, 132, 63–71.

Arias, V. B., & Arias, B. (2017). The negative wording factor of Core Self-Evaluations Scale (CSES): Methodological artifact, or substantive specific variance? *Personality and Individual Differences*, 109, 28–34.

Aristotle. (2009). *The Nicomachean ethics* (translated by David Ross; revised by Lesley Brown). Oxford: Oxford University Press.

Arkes, H. R., & Blumer, C. (1985). The psychology of sunk cost. *Organizational Behavior and Human Decision Processes*, 35 (1), 124–140.

Aspden, P. (2013). The fab before. *Financial Times*, September 28–29, 12.

Avey, J. B., Luthans, F., & Youssef, C. M. (2010). The additive value of positive psychological capital in predicting work attitudes and behaviors. *Journal of Management*, 36 (2), 430–452.

Baer, D. (2013). To be successful, grit is a most valuable asset. *Fast Company*, October 1, www.fastcompany.com/3018841/leadership-now/to-be-successful-is-grit-more-important-than-intelligence.

Baer, D. (2014a). Malcolm Gladwell explains what everyone gets wrong about his famous '10,000 hour rule'. *Business Insider*, June 2 (www.businessinsider.com/malcolm-gladwell-explains-the-10000-hour-rule-2014-6).

Baer, D. (2014b). New study destroys Malcolm Gladwell's 10,000 hour rule. *Business Insider*, July 3 (www.businessinsider.com/new-study-destroys-malcolm-gladwells-10000-rule-2014-7).

Bakker, A. B., & van Woerkom, M. (2018). Strengths use in organizations: A positive approach of occupational health. *Canadian Psychology/Psychologie Canadienne*, 59 (1), 38–46.

Baltes, P. B., & Smith, J. (1990). Toward a psychology of wisdom and its ontogenesis. In R. J. Sternberg (Ed.), *Wisdom: Its nature, origins, and development* (pp. 87–120). Cambridge: Cambridge University Press.

Bandura, A. (1977). *Social learning theory*. Oxford: Prentice-Hall.

Beléndez, M., Gómez, A., López, S., & Topa, G. (2018). Psychometric properties of the Spanish version of the Core Self-Evaluations Scale (CSES-SP). *Personality and Individual Differences*, 122, 195–197.

Bergland, C. (2013). The sweet spot between hubris and humility. *Psychology Today*, March 3 (www.psychologytoday.com/intl/blog/the-athletes-way/201303/the-sweet-spot-between-hubris-and-humility).

Bissinger, B. (2010). Tiger in the rough. *Vanity Fair*, January 4 (www.vanityfair.com/culture/2010/02/tiger-woods-201002).

Blackwell, L. S., Trzesniewski, K. H., & Dweck, C. S. (2007). Implicit theories of intelligence predict achievement across an adolescent transition: A longitudinal study and an intervention. *Child Development*, *78* (1), 246–263.

Bright, D., Cameron, K., & Caza, A. (2006). The amplifying and buffering effects of virtuousness in downsized organizations. *Journal of Business Ethics*, 64, 249–269.

Brooks, D. (2016). Putting grit in its place. *The New York Times*, May 10, A23.

Cameron, K. (2010). Five keys to flourishing in trying times. *Leader to Leader*, 55, 45–51.

Cameron, K., & McNaughtan, J. (2014). Positive organizational change. *The Journal of Applied Behavioral Science*, *50* (4), 445–462.

Cameron, K. S. (2011). Responsible leadership as virtuous leadership. *Journal of Business Ethics*, *98*, 25–35.

Cameron, K. S., Bright, D., & Caza, A. (2004). Exploring the relationships between organizational virtuousness and performance. *The American Behavioral Scientist*, 47 (6), 766–790.

Cameron, K. S., & Spreitzer, G. M. (Eds.) (2012). *The Oxford handbook of positive organizational scholarship*. Oxford: Oxford University Press.

Carlsen, A., Hagen, A. L., & Mortensen, T. F. (2012). Imaging hope in organizations. In K. S. Cameron, & G. Spreitzer (Eds.), *The Oxford handbook of positive organizational scholarship* (pp. 288–303). Oxford: Oxford University Press.

Chang, C., Ferris, D. L., Johnson, R. E., Rosen, C. C., & Tan, J. A. (2012). Core self-evaluations: A review and evaluation of the literature. *Journal of Management*, 38, 81–128.

Chartrand, T. L., & Lakin, J. L. (2013). The antecedents and consequences of human behavioral mimicry. *Annual Review of Psychology*, 64, 285–308.

Chassany, A.-S. (2017). Lunch with FT: Isabelle Huppert, 'I have unlimited self-confidence'. *Financial Times, Life & Arts*, July 29/30, 3.

Clifton, D. O. & Harter, J. K. (2003). Investing in strengths. In A. S. Cameron, B. J. E., Dutton, & C. R. E., Quinn (Eds), *Positive Organizational Scholarship: Foundations of a new discipline*, (pp. 111–121). San Francisco: Berrett-Koehler.

Collins, J. (2001). Level 5 leadership: The triumph of humility and fierce resolve. *Harvard Business Review*, January, 67–76.

Costa, P. T., & McCrae, R. R. (1992). *The revised NEO personality inventory (NEO-PI-R) and NEO five factor inventory (NEO-FFI) professional manual*. Odessa, FL: Psychological Assessment Resources.

Credé, M., Tynan, M. C., & Harms, P. D. (2017). Much ado about grit: A meta-analytic synthesis of the grit literature. *Journal of Personality and Social Psychology*, *113* (3), 492–511.

Crossan, M., Mazutis, D., & Seijts, G. (2013). In search of virtue: The role of virtues, values and character strengths in ethical decision making. *Journal of Business Ethics*, 113, 567–581.

De Vries, R. E., Lee, K., & Ashton, M. C. (2008). The Dutch HEXACO Personality Inventory: Psychometric properties, self-other agreement, and relations with psychopathy among low and high acquaintanceship dyads. *Journal of Personality Assessment*, 90, 142–151.

Disabato, D. J., Goodman, F. R., & Kashdan, T. B. (2019). Is grit relevant to well-being and strengths? Evidence across the globe for separating perseverance of effort and consistency of interests. *Journal of Personality*, 87, 194–211.

Duckworth, A. L. (2016). *Grit: The power of passion and perseverance*. New York: Scribner.

Duckworth, A. L., & Eskreis-Winkler, L. (2013). True grit. *Observer* (Association for Psychological Science) 26 (4) (www.psychologicalscience.org/index.php/publications/observer/2013/april-13/true-grit.html).

Duckworth, A. L., & Gross, J. (2014). Self-control and grit: Related but separable determinants of success. *Current Directions in Psychological Science*, 23 (5), 319–325.

Duckworth, A. L., Kirby, T., Tsukayama, E., Berstein, H., & Ericsson, K. (2011). Deliberate practice spells success: Why grittier competitors triumph at the National Spelling Bee. *Social Psychological and Personality Science*, 2, 174–181.

Duckworth, A. L., Peterson, C., Matthews, M. D., & Kelly, D. R. (2007). Grit: Perseverance and passion for long-term goals. *Journal of Personality and Social Psychology*, 92 (6), 1087–1101.

Dweck, C. S. (2015). Carol Dweck revisits the growth mindset. *Education Week*, 35 (5), 20–24.

Dweck, C. S. (2016). What having a 'growth mindset' actually means. *Harvard Business Review*, January 23 (https://hbr.org/2016/01/what-having-a-growth-mindset-actually-means)

Dweck, C. S. (2017). *Mindset: Changing the way you think to fulfil your potential.* New York: Ballantine.

Dweck, C. S., Chiu, C., & Hong, Y. (1995). Implicit theories and their role in judgments and reactions: A world from two perspectives. *Psychological Inquiry*, 6, 267–285.

Ericsson, K. A., Krampe, R. T., & Tesch-Römer, C. (1993). The role of deliberate practice in the acquisition of expert performance. *Psychological Review*, 100, 363–406.

Fang, R., Duffy, M. K., & Shaw, J. D. (2011). The organizational socialization process: Review and development of a social capital model. *Journal of Management*, 37 (1), 127–152.

Feinstein, J. (2010). The disappearance of Tiger Woods. *The Guardian*, February 7 (www.theguardian.com/sport/2010/feb/07/tiger-woods-john-feinstein).

Foote, N., Eisenstat, R., & Fredberg, T. (2011). The higher ambition leader. *Harvard Business Review*, September, 95–102.

Gallup. (2017). *State of the global workplace.* New York: Gallup Press.

Gilson, T. A., Diz, M. A., & Lochbaum, M. (2017). 'Drive on': The relationship between psychological variables and effective squad leadership. *Military Psychology*, 29 (1), 58–67.

Gladwell, M. (2009). *Outliers: The story of success.* New York: Penguin.

Grant, A. (2017). To be resilient, don't be too virtuous. *Linkedin*, May 13 (www.linkedin.com/pulse/resilient-dont-too-virtuous-adam-grant).

Hambrick, D. Z., Oswald, F. L., Altmann, E. M., Meinz, E. J., Gobet, F., & Campitelli, G. (2014). Deliberate practice: Is that all it takes to become an expert? *Intelligence*, 45, 34–45.

Harzer, C., & Ruch, W. (2014). The role of character strengths for task performance, job dedication, interpersonal facilitation, and organizational support. *Human Performance*, 27 (3), 183–205.

Hausler, M., Strecker, C., Huber, A., Brenner, M., Höge, T., & Höfer, S. (2017). Distinguishing relational aspects of character strengths with subjective and psychological well-being. *Frontiers in Psychology*, 8, 1159.

Heineman, B. W., Jr. (2012). The self-destruction of Tiger Woods. *The Atlantic*, May 9 (www.theatlantic.com/entertainment/archive/2012/05/the-self-destruction-of-tiger-woods/256939/)

Heintz, S., Kramm, C., & Ruch, W. (2019). A meta-analysis of gender differences in character strengths and age, nation, and measure as moderators. *The Journal of Positive Psychology*, 14(1), 103–112.

Hill, P. L., Burrow, A. L., & Bronk, K. C. (2016). Persevering with positivity and purpose: An examination of purpose commitment and positive affect as predictors of grit. *Journal of Happiness Studies*, 17 (1), 257–269.

Hiller, N. J., & Hambrick, D. C. (2005). Conceptualizing executive hubris: The role of (hyper) core selfevaluations in strategic decision-making. *Strategic Management Journal*, 26 (4), 297–319.

Hsieh, H. H., & Huang, J. T. (2017). Core self-evaluations and job and life satisfaction: The mediating and moderated mediating role of job insecurity. *The Journal of Psychology*, 151 (3), 282–298.

Ion, A., Mindu, A., & Gorbanescu, A. (2017). Grit in the workplace: Hype or ripe? *Personality and Individual Differences*, 111, 163–168.

Judge, T. A., & Bono, J. E. (2001). Relationship of core self-evaluation traits - self-esteem, generalized self-efficacy, locus of control, and emotional stability - with job satisfaction and job performance: A meta-analysis. *Journal of Applied Psychology*, 86 (1), 80–92.

Judge, T. A., Bono, J. E., Erez, A., & Locke, E. A. (2005). Core self-evaluations and job and life satisfaction: The role of self-concordance and goal attainment. *Journal of Applied Psychology*, 90, 257–268.

Judge, T. A., Bono, J. E., Erez, A., & Thoresen, C. J. (2003). The Core Self-Evaluations Scale (CSES): Development of a measure. *Personnel Psychology*, 56 (2), 303–331.

Judge, T. A., & Hurst, C. (2007). Capitalizing on one's advantages: Role of core self-evaluation. *Journal of Applied Psychology*, 92, 1212–1227.

Judge, T. A., & Hurst, C. (2012). The benefits and possible costs of positive core self-evaluations: A review and agenda for future research. In D. Nelson, & C. L. Cooper (Eds.), *Positive organizational behavior: Accentuating the positive at work* (pp. 159–174). London: Sage.

Judge, T. A., Locke, E. A., & Durham, C. C. (1997). The dispositional causes of job satisfaction: A core evaluations approach. *Research in Organizational Behavior*, *19*, 151–188.

Judge, T. A., Locke, E. A., Durham, C. C., & Kluger, A. N. (1998). Dispositional effects on job and life satisfaction: The role of core evaluations. *Journal of Applied Psychology*, *83*, 17–34.

Judge, T. A., Piccolo, R. F., & Kosalka, T. (2009). The bright and dark sides of leader traits: A review and theoretical extension of the leader trait paradigm. *The Leadership Quarterly*, 20, 855–875.

Karwowski, M. (2014). Creative mindsets: Measurement, correlates, consequences. *Psychology of Aesthetics, Creativity, and the Arts*, *8* (1), 62–70.

King, L. A., & Trent, J. (2013). Personality strengths. In H. A. Tennen, J. I. Suls, & I. B. Weiner (Eds.), *Handbook of psychology Vol. 5. Personality and social psychology* (2nd ed., pp. 197–222). New York: Wiley.

Lewisohn, M. (2013). *The beatles – Volume 1: Tune in*. London: Little, Brown.

Liden, R. C., Panaccio, A., Meuser, J. D., Hu, J., & Wayne, S. (2014). Servant leadership: Antecedents, processes, and outcomes. In D. V. Vay (Ed.), *The Oxford handbook of leadership and organizations* (pp. 357–379). New York: Oxford University Press.

Luthans, F., Avolio, B. J., Avey, J. B., & Norman, S. M. (2007). Positive psychological capital: Measurement and relationship with performance and satisfaction. *Personnel Psychology*, 60 (3), 541–572.

Luthans, F., & Youssef, C. M. (2007). Emerging positive organizational behavior. *Journal of Management*, 33, 321–349.

Lyubomirsky, S., Tkach, C., & DiMatteo, M. R. (2006). What are the differences between happiness and self-esteem. *Social Indicators Research*, 78 (3), 363–404.

Macnamara, B. N., Hambrick, D. Z., & Oswald, F. L. (2014). Deliberate practice and performance in music, games, sports, education, and professions: A meta-analysis. *Psychological Science*, 25, 1608–1618.

Martínez-Martí, M. L., & Ruch, W. (2017). Character strengths predict resilience over and above positive affect, self-efficacy, optimism, social support, self-esteem, and life satisfaction. *The Journal of Positive Psychology*, 12 (2), 110–119.

Martins, H., Dias, Y. B., & Khanna, S. (2016). What makes some Silicon Valley companies so successful. *Harvard Business Review*, April 26. Available at (https://hbr.org/2016/04/what-makes-some-silicon-valley-companies-so-successful)

Meinz, E. J., & Hambrick, D. Z. (2010). Deliberate practice is necessary but not sufficient to explain individual differences in piano sight-reading skill: The role of working memory capacity. *Psychological Science*, 21(7), 914–919.

Mueller, B. A., Wolfe, M. T., & Syed, I. (2017). Passion and grit: An exploration of the pathways leading to venture success. *Journal of Business Venturing*, 32 (3), 260–279.

Ng, B. (2018). The neuroscience of growth mindset and intrinsic motivation. *Brain Sciences*, 8 (2), 20. doi: 10.3390/brainsci8020020.

Nielsen, R., & Marrone, J. A. (2018). Humility: Our current understanding of the construct and its role in organizations. *The International Journal of Management Reviews*, 20, 805–824.

Niemiec, R. M. (2013). VIA character strengths: Research and practice (The first 10 years). In H. H. Knoop, & A. Delle Fave (Eds.), *Well-being and cultures: Perspectives on positive psychology* (pp. 11–30). New York: Springer.

Nübold, A., Muck, P. M., & Maier, G. W. (2013). A new substitute for leadership? Followers' state core self-evaluations. *The Leadership Quarterly*, 24 (1), 29–44.

Oc, B., Basshur, M. R., Daniels, M. A., Greguras, G. J., & Diefendorff, J. M. (2015). Leader humility in Singapore. *The Leadership Quarterly*, 26, 68–80.

Ogunfowora, B., & Bourdage, J. S. (2014). Does Honesty–Humility influence evaluations of leadership emergence? The mediating role of moral disengagement. *Personality and Individual Differences*, 56, 95–99.

Ou, A. Y., Tsui, A. S., Kinicki, A. J., Waldman, D. A., Xiao, Z., & Song, L. J. (2014). Humble chief executive officers' connections to top management team integration and middle managers' responses. *Administrative Science Quarterly*, 59, 34–72.

Owens, B. P., & Hekman, D. (2012). Modeling how to grow: An inductive examination of humble leader behaviors, contingencies, and outcomes. *Academy of Management Journal*, 55 (4), 787–818.

Owens, B. P., Johnson, M. D., & Mitchell, T. R. (2013). Expressed humility in organizations: Implications for performance, teams, and leadership. *Organization Science*, 24 (5), 1517–1538.

Owens, B. P., Rowatt, W. C., & Wilkins, A. L. (2012). Exploring the relevance and implications of humility in organizations. In K. S. Cameron, & G. Spreitzer (Eds.), *The Oxford handbook of positive organizational scholarship* (pp. 260–272). Oxford: Oxford University Press.

Park, N., Barton, M., & Pillay, J. (2017). Strengths of character and virtues: What we know and what we still want to learn. In M. Warren, & D. Stewart (Eds.), *Scientific advances in positive psychology* (pp. 73–101). Santa Barbara, CA: Praeger.

Park, N., Peterson, C., & Seligman, M. E. (2006). Character strengths in fifty-four nations and the fifty US states. *The Journal of Positive Psychology*, 1 (3), 118–129.

Park, N., Peterson, C., & Seligman, M. E. P. (2004). Strengths of character and well-being. *Journal of Social & Clinical Psychology*, 23 (5), 603–619.

Perkins-Gough, D. (2013). A conversation with Angela Lee Duckworth. *Educational Leadership*, September, 14–20.

Peterson, C., & Park, N. (2006). Character strengths in organizations. *Journal of Organizational Psychology*, 27, 1149–1154.

Peterson, C., & Park, N. (2011). Character strengths and virtues: Their role in well-being. In S. I. Donaldson, M. Csikszentmihalyi, & J. Nakamura (Eds.), *Applied positive psychology: Improving everyday life, health, schools, work, and society* (pp. 49–62). New York: Psychology Press.

Peterson, C., Park, N., Pole, N., D'Andrea, N. P. W., & Seligman, M. E. P. (2008). Strengths of character and posttraumatic growth. *Journal of Traumatic Stress*, 21 (2), 214–217.

Peterson, C., Park, N., & Seligman, M. (2006). Greater strengths of character and recovery from illness. *The Journal of Positive Psychology*, 1 (1), 17–26.

Peterson, C., & Seligman, M. E. P. (2003). Character strengths before and after September 11. *Psychological Science*, 14 (4), 381–384.

Peterson, C., & Seligman, M. E. P. (2004). *Character strengths and virtues: A handbook and classification.* New York: Oxford University Press.

Peterson, C., Stephens, J. P., Park, N., Lee, F., & Seligman, M. E. (2010). Strengths of character and work. In P. A. Linley, S. Harrington, & N. Page (Eds.), *Oxford handbook of positive psychology and work* (pp. 221–231). New York: Oxford University Press.

Pierce, J. L., & Gardner, D. G. (2004). Self-esteem within the work and organizational context: A review of the organization-based self-esteem literature. *Journal of Management*, 30 (5), 591–622.

Porath, C. L., Spreitzer, G., Gibson, C., & Garnett, F. G. (2012). Thriving at work: Toward its measurement, construct validation, and theoretical refinement. *Journal of Organizational Behavior*, 33 (2), 250–275.

Rego, A., Cunha, M. P., & Clegg, S. (2012). *The virtues of leadership: Contemporary challenge for global managers.* Oxford: Oxford University Press.

Rego, A., Owens, B., Yam, K. C., Bluhm, D., Cunha, M. P., Silard, T., Gonçalves, L., Martins, M., Simpson, A. V., & Liu, W. (2019). Leader humility and team performance: Exploring the mechanisms of team psychological capital and task allocation effectiveness. *Journal of Management*, 45(3), 1099–1033.

Rich, B. L., Lepine, J. A., & Crawford, E. R. (2010). Job engagement: Antecedents and effects on job performance. *Academy of Management Journal*, 53 (3), 617–635.

Roberts, A. (2008). Nelson Mandela is a hero, but not a saint. *The Guardian*, June 26 (www.theguardian.com/commentisfree/2008/jun/26/nelsonmandela.zimbabwe).

Roberts, L. M., Dutton, J. E., Spreitzer, G., Heaphy, E., & Quinn, R. (2005a). Composing the reflected best-self portrait: Building pathways to becoming extraordinary in work organizations. *Academy of Management Review*, 30, 712–736.

Roberts, L. M., Spreitzer, G., Dutton, J., Quinn, R., Heaphy, E., & Barker, B. (2005b). How to play to your strengths. *Harvard Business Review*, 83 (1), 75–80.

Rosenberg, M. (1965). *Society and the adolescent self-image*. Princeton, NJ: Princeton University Press.

Rotter, J. B. (1971). External control and internal control. *Psychology Today*, June, 37, 38, 40, 42, 58–59.

Ruch, W., & Proyer, R. T. (2015). Mapping strengths into virtues: The relation of the 24 VIA-strengths to six ubiquitous virtues. *Frontiers in Psychology*, 6, 460. doi: 10.3389/fpsyg.2015.00460.

Sadler-Smith, E., Akstinaite, V., Robinson, G., & Wray, T. (2017). Hubristic leadership: A review. *Leadership*, 13 (5), 525–548.

Shechtman, N., DeBarger, A. H., Dornsife, C., Rosier, S., & Yarnall, L. (2013). *Promoting grit, tenacity, and perseverance: Critical factors for success in the 21st century*. Washington, DC: U.S. Department of Education.

Sheldon, K. M., Jose, P. E., Kashdan, T. B., & Jarden, A. (2015). Personality, effective goal-striving, and enhanced well-being: Comparing 10 candidate personality strengths. *Personality and Social Psychology Bulletin*, 41, 575–585.

Sosik, J. J., Centry, W. A., & Jae, U. (2012). The value of virtue in the upper echelons: A multisource examination of executive character strengths and performance. *The Leadership Quarterly*, 23 (3), 367–382.

Spector, P. E. (1988). Development of the work locus of control scale. *Journal of Occupational Psychology*, 61 (4), 335–340.

Spreitzer, G. M., & Cameron, K. S. (2012). Applying a POS lens to bring out the best in organizations. *Organizational Dynamics*, 41, 85–88.

Spreitzer, G. M., Sutcliffe, K., Dutton, J., Sonenshein, S., & Grant, A. M. (2005). A socially embedded model of thriving at work. *Organization Science*, 16, 537–549.

Sternberg, R. J. (1996). The costs of expertise. In K. A. Ericsson (Ed.), *The road to excellence: The acquisition of expert performance in the arts and sciences, sports, and games* (pp. 347–354). Mahwah, NJ: Lawrence Erlbaum.

Storbeck, O. (2018). Lunch with the FT – Thomas Middelhoff: 'I thought certain rules didn't apply to me'. *Financial Times Europe, Life & Arts*, May 12/13, 3.

Stouten, J., van Dijke, M., Mayer, D. M., De Cremer, D., & Euwema, M. C. (2013). Can a leader be seen as too ethical? The curvilinear effects of ethical leadership. *The Leadership Quarterly*, 24 (5), 680–695.

Tang, Y., Li, J., & Yang, H. (2015). What I see, what I do: How executive hubris affects firm innovation. *Journal of Management*, 41 (6), 1698–1723.

Tangney, J. P. (2009). Humility. In S. Lopez, & C. Snyder (Eds.), *Oxford handbook of positive psychology* (pp. 483–490). New York: Oxford University Press.

Useem, J. (2016). Is grit overrated? *The Atlantic*, May (www.theatlantic.com/magazine/archive/2016/05/is-grit-overrated/476397/).

Vainio, M. M., & Daukantaite, D. (2016). Grit and different aspects of well-being: Direct and indirect relationships via sense of coherence and authenticity. *Journal of Happiness Studies*, 17 (5), 2119–2147.

Van Putten, M., Zeelenberg, M., & van Dijk, E. (2010). Who throws good money after bad? Action vs. state orientation moderates the sunk cost fallacy. *Judgment and Decision Making*, 5 (1), 33–36.

Von Culin, K. R., Tsukayama, E., & Duckworth, A. L. (2014). Unpacking grit: Motivational correlates of perseverance and passion for long-term goals. *The Journal of Positive Psychology*, 9 (4), 306–312.

Walumbwa, F. O., Muchiri, M. K., Misati, E., Wu, C., & Meiliani, M. (2017). Inspired to perform: A multilevel investigation of antecedents and consequences of thriving at work. *Journal of Organizational Behavior*. doi: 10.1002/job.2216.

Wang, S., Dai, J., Li, J., Wang, X., Chen, T., Yang, X., Chen, T., Yang, X., He, M., & Gong, Q. (2018). Neuroanatomical correlates of grit: Growth mindset mediates the association between gray matter structure and trait grit in late adolescence. *Human Brain Mapping*. doi: 10.1002/hbm.23944.

Wood, A. M., Linley, P. A., Maltby, J., Kashdan, T. B., & Hurling, R. (2011). Using personal and psychological strengths leads to increases in well-being over time: A longitudinal study and the development of the strengths use questionnaire. *Personality and Individual Differences*, 50 (1), 15–19.

3 Psychological capital
The 'HERO' effect

Summary and objectives

This chapter considers four state-like strengths that compose psychological capital (PsyCap): self-efficacy, hope, optimism and resilience. The core assumption is that these four psychological resources can be developed and deployed to a greater extent and more effectively than the strengths discussed in Chapter 2. The chapter explains why the four psychological resources are considered as a core-confidence strength, their consequences for individuals' attitudes and behaviours (including performance) and how PsyCap may be developed. Reinforcers and neutralizers of PsyCap are also discussed.

A 'core confidence' strength

University of Nebraska-Lincoln Professor Fred Luthans introduced the concept of Positive Organizational Behaviour (POB),[1] proposing several psychological capacities for inclusion in the POB framework.[2] The five POB inclusion criteria he used to determine which capacities to include are:[3]

- The construct/strength 'must be theory- and evidence-based, in order to lend itself to scientific study'.
- It must be positively-oriented.
- It should be validly and reliably measurable, thus allowing for rigorous research.
- It needs to be open to development and management.
- It must be related to desired work attitudes, behaviours and performance criteria.

To date, the psychological capacities deemed to best fit the POB inclusion criteria are **h**ope, (self)**e**fficacy, **r**esilience and **o**ptimism (i.e., HERO; Table 3.1).[4] These four make up the constitutive dimensions of psychological capital (PsyCap). In contrast with character strengths, CSE and grit, which are trait-like, PsyCap is a 'state-like' construct, meaning that the construct is more stable over time than a pure state but less stable than a trait. PsyCap has been defined as an individual's positive psychological state of development characterized by

> (1) having confidence (efficacy) to take on and put in the necessary effort to succeed at challenging tasks; (2) making a positive attribution (optimism) about succeeding now and in the future; (3) persevering toward goals and, when necessary, redirecting paths to goals (hope) in order to succeed; (4) when beset by problems and adversity, sustaining and bouncing back and even beyond (resilience) to attain success.[5]

Table 3.1 HERO resources: the four components of PsyCap

	Definition	Characterization
Hope	'A positive motivational state based on an interactively derived sense of successful (a) agency (goal-directed energy) and (b) pathways (planning to meet goals).'[6]	Hopeful employees denote willpower and 'waypower'. They look for alternative pathways (i.e., 'waypower') when the old ones are blocked.[7] They enjoy goal pursuit, being more intrinsically motivated and looking for creative ways to implement their 'agency energy'.[8] When they do not attain goals, they use the feedback to improve goal pursuit and strategies, thus being more energetic in looking for alternative and creative ways to overcome obstacles.
(Self)-efficacy	'The individual's conviction or confidence about his or her abilities to mobilize the motivation, cognitive resources or courses of action needed to successfully execute a specific task within a given context.'[9]	Self-efficacious employees choose challenging tasks and endeavours, apply their efforts and motivational resources to accomplish their goals, and persevere in the face of obstacles and difficulties.[10]
Resilience	'The capacity to rebound or bounce back from adversity, conflict, failure or even positive events, progress and increased responsibility.'[11]	Resilient employees are able 'to overcome, steer through, bounce back and reach out to pursue new knowledge and experiences, deeper relationships with others and [find] meaning in life'.[12] They have zestful and energetic approaches to life, are curious and open to new experiences,[13] and improvise in situations predominantly characterized by change and uncertainty.[14]
Optimism	'A positive explanatory style that attributes positive events to personal, permanent, and pervasive causes and interprets negative events in terms of external, temporary and situation-specific factors.'[15]	Optimistic employees take credit for favourable events, strengthening their self-esteem and morale, which in turn may lead to greater creativity.[16] They distance themselves from unfavourable life events, thus diminishing the likelihood of experiencing depression, guilt, self-blame and despair. They are less likely to give up and more likely to have a more positive outlook on stressful situations, to experience positive emotions, to persevere when facing difficulties and to look for creative ways to solve problems and take advantage of opportunities.[17]

PsyCap is a kind of 'core confidence'[18] that represents 'one's positive appraisal of circumstances and probability for success based on motivated effort and perseverance'[19] (see Box 3.1 for how to measure PsyCap). These four capacities reinforce and nourish each other. They can be taken as 'resource caravans'[20] constituted by 'psychological resources that may travel together and interact synergistically to produce differentiated manifestations over time and across contexts'.[21] As suggested by Stajkovic, 'it is hard to imagine one without the other(s)'.[22] For example, a resilient individual is more likely to restore self-efficacy and hope after experiencing a failure. An optimistic individual is more likely to persevere toward his/her goals (i.e., to be hopeful) if he/she is self-confident. While hope leads individuals to set goals and to be more determined in pursuing them, self-efficacy ensures that these goals are challenging such that optimism fuels positive expectations of success. Optimistic, hopeful and self-efficacious people are potentially more resilient to adversity.[23] If a self-efficacious employee is more creative because he/she accepts significant challenges and carries out cognitive and creative efforts to achieve goals, such a propensity is stronger if s/he also has high hope:[24] s/he does not only accept challenges and make an effort to achieve goals but also identifies sub-goals and creative pathways to achieve those goals, overcoming such obstacles by pursuing multiple and creative pathways.

Box 3.1 Measuring PsyCap

PsyCap may be measured with five main tools. First, PCQ-24 (Psychological Capital Questionnaire, 24 items, 6 items for each PsyCap component) is a self-report measure used in most PsyCap studies.[25] Sample items include the following:[26]

- 'I feel confident helping to set targets/goals in my work area' (self-efficacy).
- 'If I should find myself in a jam at work, I could think of many ways to get out of it' (hope).
- 'When things are uncertain for me at work, I usually expect the best' (optimism).
- 'When I have a setback at work, I have trouble recovering from it and moving on' (resilience; reverse coded).

Second, the PCQ-12[27] (12 items) is the short version of PCQ-24. Because self-report measures are amenable to faking and social-desirability biases, Harms and Luthans (2012) developed and validated an implicit measure of PsyCap (I-PCQ).[28] Third, the I-PCQ is a semi-projective technique that uses written situational prompts (individuals are invited to generate stories about someone, not themselves) that are followed by 'normal' questions/items. A fourth procedure consists in analyzing the content of computer-aided text.[29] Fifth, some authors have suggested measuring PsyCap through other-reports,[30] where acquaintances are invited to report the PsyCap of the focal individual. It is debatable if self-reports and other-reports measure the same construct. Some authors[31] have suggested that while self-reports measure self-attributed (innerly experienced) PsyCap, other-reports measure conveyed PsyCap (i.e., PsyCap as perceived by others). Several reasons support such a conceptual differentiation. First, individuals manage impression tactics[32] to convey a strength that they do not actually possess as measured via self-attributed PsyCap. Second, some situations in which the individuals operate are so strong[33] that the individuals are led to *convey* behaviours that reflect more the situational requirements than their *inner* PsyCap. Third, individuals behave differently toward different observers.[34] Therefore, different observers will describe the same focal individual in different ways. Fourth, conveyed PsyCap is in the eye of beholder, the consequence being that different observers see the same observed individual differently.[35] If we ask different team members to report the

PsyCap of a target, it is likely that they rate him/her differently. Self-attributed PsyCap and conveyed PsyCap are therefore conceptually different, as measured by self-reports and other-reports, respectively.

Consequences of PsyCap

Individuals with higher PsyCap develop higher job satisfaction, commitment, engagement, well-being, creativity, thriving and performance[36] (but see Box 3.2). PsyCap is related to increased efforts and better performance by *enabling* the motivational potential emerging from the individuals' skills and 'desires' (i.e., goals).[37] Without PsyCap, such potential remains untapped. Moreover, PsyCap nourishes the setting of ambitious goals, and makes individuals more focussed on developing skills to reach them.[38] PsyCap also neutralizes undesirable attitudes and behaviours.

Scholars have identified several reasons for the positive effects PsyCap produces, including the effects on individual performance.[39] Individuals with higher PsyCap are more proactive and energized toward goal-pursuit and more motivated to find resources (emotional, cognitive, behavioural and material) that allow them to overcome obstacles and face challenges. They assess problematic situations in a more positive light, making them more motivated to develop efforts to overcome obstacles and persevere in pursuit of goals. They experience more positive emotions, which broadens thought–action repertoires,[40] leading to superior creativity. Positive emotions also facilitate the building and restoration of physical, social and psychological resources depleted in problematic situations (e.g., failures and errors).

Box 3.2 Are both self-confidence and under-confidence associated with success?

1 Self-confidence of the 'Special One'

José Mourinho, who successfully coached football teams such as FC Porto, Chelsea, Internazionale, Real Madrid and Manchester United, has been considered one of the best in the *métier*. Several players have stated that one of the best strengths of Mourinho is his own self-confidence and his capacity to foster self-confidence in the players. Footballer Frank Lampard, who worked with Mourinho at Chelsea FC (July 2004–September 2007), said in an interview:

> We were changing the face of English football via the personality of Mourinho himself. The biggest thing José brought me, more than anything tactical, was self-confidence. His own self-confidence rubbed off on me. The way we played, we had determination and flair and I loved it. It was a period of my life when I didn't even have to think about playing.[41]

In another interview, when asked about what makes Mourinho so successful, Lampard told *talkSPORT*:[42] 'It's a presence and an aura and a way with people. He galvanizes people. His own self-confidence reflects back on his teams. He did that to me personally'. Lampard further stated:[43]

> I've had really good managers and different managers at times. It's the ones that get the best out of you, individually. We're all human beings and if a manager doesn't talk to you and tell you what they want or whether they're happy with you … we've all got confidence that is up and down. Mourinho was the best. For me he was. He brought my confidence to a level it had never been.

Mourinho himself has a 'theory' about the importance of his self-confidence. *The New York Times* asked him:[44] 'Your self-confidence is well documented. But what do you say to the people who say you are arrogant?' Mourinho replied:

> I say, I am not. I say, I am not. I say that at this level of pressure – if you can use the word pressure because I don't like to use it very, very much because I have so many pleasures in what I am doing – that you can cope well with that pressure. But that is well: If you are not self-confident, if you don't believe in your work, you are a step down. If you are a leader and you can influence people's attitudes and you want people to follow you up and be as strong as you are, you must be strong. I used to say that normally the team is the face of its coach. So if the coach is not brave enough, self-confident enough, arrogant enough, the team will lose qualities. And I believe that is why my teams are always very, very difficult teams to beat.

The *New Statesman* magazine elected Mourinho as the 2015 Man of the Year. Jason Cowley described the 'Special One' as follows:[45]

> Mourinho's confidence is that of a man at the head of the wealthiest football club in the world, a club whose very mission … is to become the best, a 'global brand' or 'franchise' surpassing even Manchester United or Real Madrid. It is the confidence of a man who has the resources to buy whoever he wishes to enhance his formidable squad of champions and who is paid as much as £100,000 per week, but still takes time out to endorse anything from mobile phones to credit cards. It is the confidence of a man who as a coach is used to winning, who is defined by winning, and for whom defeat is intolerable. But it is also the confidence of a man who is his own creation – one who dared to dream what he might become and became all that he wanted to be. He is, in every sense, a man of our times, and for our times.

Figure 3.1 José Mourinho, 28 September 2017.[46]

2 A fearful and underconfident star?

Pepe Guardiola, a former successful football player and another successful coach, said, in April 2018:[47] 'I'm happy we will receive the Premier League trophy and [have] the chance to be the best team in history in England, with the most points'. Does this represent self-confidence? Hans-Wilhelm Muller-Wohlfahrt, an orthopaedic surgeon who had worked at Bayern for more than 35 years by the time Guardiola was appointed as head coach of the team in 2013 (he left in 2017 for Manchester City), wrote in his controversial autobiography:[48]

> I think Pep Guardiola is a person with a weak self-confidence who does everything to hide that from other people ... Because of that, he seems to live in a constant fear. Not so much of defeats, but of the loss of power and authority.

Questions for reflection

- Is it possible to be successful with both low and high self-confidence? If so, how?
- Reflect on the idea of the insecure overachiever in Box 3.4. What does it mean to be an insecure overachiever? Can Guardiola be considered an insecure overachiever?

PsyCap 'goes beyond'[49] other forms of capital (i.e., economic, human and social; see Table 3.2) and thus constitutes a source of sustainable competitive advantage in today's highly competitive environments.[50] Think about an organization rich in financial, structural/physical and technological capital, whose employees have been educated in the best schools but do not trust or cooperate with each other. In the long run, this organization may be less competitive than an organization that, as well as being strong financially is composed of employees that do trust and cooperate with each other and who are psychologically stronger in consequence.

High levels of social and psychological capital may compensate for a modest level of human capital. Imagine two soccer teams, say HumanCap FC and PsyCap United, that are playing a match against each other. HumanCap, composed of highly skilled and cooperative players, is winning 1–0. The players of PsyCap United are slightly less skilled but more hopeful, resilient and optimistic. Being a cohesive team and never giving up, United manages to score a goal five minutes before the end of the match. The highly skilled players of the team HumanCap feel frustrated and the team collapses psychologically in the face of adversity. They blame each other. Meanwhile, players of team PsyCap do not give up, they persevere and, four minutes later, they manage to score again. A higher level of social and psychological capital of PsyCap wins over the higher level of human capital of team HumanCap. In short, to be competitive and successful, teams and organizations must invest not only in economic and human capital but also in social and psychological capital.

At the individual level, the possession of high PsyCap produces similar advantages. Imagine an employee who is highly skilled, both in the technical and social realms, educated in a very prestigious university, extremely competent technically, trustworthy and able to build rich social relationships. However, after experiencing a setback, self-confidence is lost, willpower decreases and they become pessimistic. It is likely that success and career advancement are affected by a modest PsyCap. The person may even be

Table 3.2 Economic, human, social and psychological capital – assess yourself

Forms of capital	What kind of capital do you have? Ask yourself
Economic capital	• Am I economically rich?
	• Do I have money and several sources of income?
	• Do I finance myself to gain excellent training?
Human capital	• Have I been educated in a good university?
	• Do I have extensive training in my area?
	• Am I technically skilled?
	• Am I an expert in the area?
Social capital	• Am I trustworthy?
	• Is it easy for me to develop social relationships?
	• Am I a cooperative coworker?
	• Am I able to get support from others when I need technical advice?
Psychological capital	• Do I believe in my capacities?
	• Do I set challenging goals for myself?
	• Do I have willpower to overcome obstacles?
	• Am I able to find several pathways to overcome obstacles and pursue my goals?
	• Am I perseverant?
	• Do I envisage the future optimistically?
	• When things are uncertain for me at work, do I usually expect the best?
	• Do I see opportunities in problems?
	• Am I always able to get up after 'falling'?

Table 3.3 Guidelines for developing employee PsyCap

Self-efficacy	• Give the employee opportunities to experience success (i.e., mastery experiences). • Help the employee to set challenging, achievable, concrete and specific goals. • Provide the employee with a mentor. • Help the employee to learn with relevant role-models (i.e., successful exemplary people). • Tell success stories about how goals were attained. • Help the employee to develop 'imaginal experiences' (the employee imagines him/herself succeeding in effectively dealing with difficult situations and challenges). • Provide positive feedback. • Create conditions such that the employee may experience psychological and physiological health.
Hope	• Help the employee to set challenging, achievable, concrete and specific goals. • Break down complex, difficult or long-term goals into manageable sub-goals (i.e., 'stepping'), thus allowing the employee to experience gradual progress and 'small wins'. • Provide opportunities for the employee to participate in decision-making (via, e.g., delegation and empowerment). • Show confidence in employees and treat them 'as if they are going to succeed'. • Carry out scenario analysis experiences in which the employee explores alternative courses of action and prepares for multiple possibilities. • Encourage/help employees to carry out 'mental rehearsals', in which the employee 'visualizes important upcoming events, anticipates possible obstacles, and mentally pictures alternative pathways to overcome those obstacles, enhancing preparedness to handle blockages'.[51] • Help the employee to 're-goal' when he/she faces absolute goal blockages, thus helping him/her to avoid the trap of 'false hope'.
Optimism	• Help the employee to develop 'leniency for the past', i.e., to reframe and accept his/her past failures and setbacks, to give him/herself the benefit of the doubt, to forgive him/herself for mistakes that he/she can no longer reverse. • Help the employee to develop 'appreciation for the present', i.e., thankfulness and contentment about the positive sides of his/her current life, including both the things that he/she can control and those he/she cannot. • Help people to see the future and its uncertainties as opportunities for growth and advancement and help them build a positive and confident attitude. • Provide positive feedback. • Promote 'realistic optimism' (e.g., help people understand that a past failure does not mean that a similar failure will happen again in the future, without leading people to consider that failure is a consequence of others' actions or bad luck).
Resilience	• Provide healthcare benefits, wellness and employee assistance programmes to the employee in order to reduce the probability of physical and psychological risks (e.g., stress, burnout, health problems). • Provide training and development opportunities to help the employee face obstacles and problems more effectively.

(*Continued*)

Table 3.3 (Cont.)

- Foster a positive and compassionate social climate in which the employee may benefit from high-quality relationships[52] (see Chapter 6) and gain from social support during critical times and situations.
- Help people shift from cause-oriented thinking (what happened?) to response-oriented thinking (how to address the problem).[53]
- Help the employee to develop the virtue of forgiveness and turn 'poison into medicine'.[54]
- Provide 'human moments' to the employee.
- Create conditions for people to rest and 'recharge'.[55]

---

overtaken by a less skilled colleague who is psychologically stronger. It is important to note, however, that team and organizational PsyCap is not the mere sum of the individual PsyCap of team and organizational members (see the last section of this chapter).

Developing PsyCap

One of the most important POB criteria is the plasticity or malleability of psychological resources, which make them open to development. Research indicates that the four components of PsyCap change over time; thus, they can be developed. They are not pure momentary states (i.e., 'plastic', such as moods) nor are they trait-like characteristics (e.g., relatively fixed, much as 'plaster'; e.g., character strengths, CSE and grit) – they are state-like resources. In other words, PsyCap is amenable to development.[56] Luthans and colleagues[57] have suggested guidelines for developing each component (see Table 3.3), and several studies[58] have revealed that interventions based on those guidelines are effective in fostering PsyCap.[59]

Appreciative Inquiry (AI) is also an effective way to foster PsyCap. AI is a strengths-based approach (see Box 3.3)[60] aimed at producing positive change in individuals, teams and organizations. Individuals who participate in AI activities may develop PsyCap because those activities allow for the satisfaction of fundamental psychological needs:[61] the need for competence (i.e., to do something well, to learn new skills, to feel the pleasure of being effective); the need for autonomy (i.e., the innate propensity of self-choice and self-control) and the need for relatedness (i.e., the desire to connect with others, to love and to be loved). For example, by identifying the situations when they are at their best, individuals become more self-effective. By asking people to idealize a better future, individuals become more optimistic. Through collective appreciative activities, the quality of relational space improves, an important factor in nurturing resilience.

Organizations may foster PsyCap through designing jobs with appropriate characteristics (e.g., jobs that allow relatedness, competence and autonomy needs: see Box 3.3) and creating a supportive team/organizational climate[62] or culture. By performing jobs that are challenging and facilitate learning new skills, employees develop self-confidence. By working within a positive social climate and satisfying relatedness needs, employees are more likely to see the future in a more optimistic way, and are more inclined to get social support and help in critical moments (thus developing resilience). In contrast, a stressful working environment and high levels of work–family conflict may lead to a lower level of PsyCap.[63] Such conditions are more likely to harm resilience.

Leaders (see Chapter 8) are particularly well-positioned to improve followers' PsyCap. Studies have suggested that transformational leadership,[64] authentic leadership,[65] ethical leadership[66] and social support[67] assist in developing people's PsyCap. For example, by intellectually stimulating their followers, a transformational leader may foster a sense of efficacy and lead them to discover novel pathways, thus developing their hope. By respecting and welcoming critical opinions and contributions from his/her followers and listening to alternative perspectives before reaching a conclusion, an authentic leader makes his followers develop self-confidence and willpower. By behaving with fairness and sharing power with his/her followers, an ethical leader may lead them to develop greater self-efficacy and to be more optimistic about the future.

Studies also suggest that, via role modelling and social contagion, leaders with higher PsyCap[68] are better able to develop PsyCap in their followers. Leader humour may also build follower PsyCap. A possible explanation is that humorous leaders foster positive emotions (and decrease negative ones) in followers, and this positive affect builds PsyCap.[69]

Box 3.3 Appreciative Inquiry

1 A strength-based approach

The method of AI involves the 4-D cycle intervention that concretizes these five principles:

1   **Discovery** involves engaging employees in a rigorous exploration of their best past experiences to identify existing positive core organizational assets related to an affirmative question such as 'how can we enhance the quality of our workplace relationships', or 'how can we enhance the quality of our customer experience'.
2   **Dream** involves inviting members to reflect on the insights that emerged from the discovery phase and use it to envisage new possibilities about the most preferred future.
3   **Design** is where members are invited to build on the outcomes of the dream process to co-design concrete actions and activities.
4   **Destiny** involves helping members, in groups, to self-organize to implement activities and projects in order to achieve their common wished-for future.

2 Resources about AI

The readers may find resources about AI (e.g., articles, videos, interviews) in David Cooperrider's blog at www.davidcooperrider.com/.

Reinforcers and neutralizers of PsyCap

The effects of employee PsyCap for their performance may depend on several conditions. Some conditions may operate as reinforcers, or facilitators, while others may be neutralizers. Reinforcers and neutralizers co-exist in context. For example, an employee with high PsyCap is more likely to translate PsyCap into more effort and better performance if he/she feels that the team context is psychologically safe and the leader is supportive and respectful (see Chapters 7 and 8). A service provider is more likely to translate PsyCap into better customer service if he/she works in a team characterized by a positive service climate.[70] In contrast, some factors may neutralize the positive effect of high PsyCap on employee performance.[71] For example, the absence of continuous feedback may neutralize the positive performance impact of self-efficacy:

> [The absence of continuous feedback leaves subordinates] to play a guessing game concerning whether to continue on the current path of work-related behavior or to chart another course. The communication received through performance appraisal feedback is essential for encouraging employees to continue on a positive trajectory or to guide employees in improving problem areas.[72]

Considering that hopeful employees tend to be independent thinkers, and to possess an internal locus of control, they need a high degree of autonomy to express and utilize their agency. If they work in contexts where their proactivity and search for autonomy are restrained, it is possible that they 'may feel that their willpower and waypower are irrelevant, even detrimental, to performance evaluation'. It is also possible 'that "they withdraw into their shell" and refrain from investing their hope resources in performing tasks'.[73] In summary: some contexts are conducive to developing and nurturing PsyCap, while others make it difficult for the employees' strengths to flourish.

Reinforcers and neutralizers may also reside in the individual him/herself, i.e., in other individual characteristics. For example, humility may reinforce, while arrogance may neutralize, the potential positive effect of self-confidence. In some conditions, and for some activities, a grain of pessimism may help optimistic individuals to be more creative.[74] This reasoning is based on the assumption that optimism and pessimism represent different constructs,[75] not opposite poles of the same construct. The interplay between optimism and pessimism may predict employee creativity:[76]

> Although optimism may lead individuals to respond to opportunities with novel ideas, and to continue to strive and cope actively with the problems encountered in seeking desirable outcomes, some degree of pessimism may lead them to develop dissatisfaction or frustration with the status quo ... and help them to be more realistic when they face problems that block the path to their goals ... If a high level of optimism is not accompanied by a certain level of pessimism, employees may be caught up in a kind of Pollyanna effect ... facing organizational problems and opportunities without realism, underestimating obstacles, and becoming unable to propose new *and* useful ideas for dealing realistically with problems and opportunities.

It is also important to note that the effects of the four components of PsyCap are not linear: after a certain threshold, the positive effects decrease or even become negative. A strength may turn into a weakness when it is excessive. The excess of a good thing becomes a bad thing. Overoptimistic individuals may be caught up in a kind of 'Pollyanna' effect: they face organizational problems and opportunities with a lack of realism, overestimate benefits and underestimate costs, do not recognize the severity of problems, neglect risks and underestimate the likelihood of negative events, perceive no harm in problematic and dangerous situations and expect the best regardless of a situation.[77]

Overconfidence may also produce negative consequences, unless individuals are humble enough to mitigate those negative effects (see Box 3.4). Excessively confident individuals overestimate their skills and their ability to affect future outcomes. They also take credit for past positive outcomes without acknowledging the role of chance.[78] They may pursue unrealistic goals and make irrational decisions. They are 'incurious when it comes to learning because they feel they know most of what there is to know'.[79] Their propensity is toward excessive optimism.[80] As Gladwell pointed out, 'one of the things that happen to us when we become overconfident is that we start to blur the line between the kinds of things that we can control and the kinds of things that we can't'.[81] Excessive optimism and overconfidence are among the causes of overpriced acquisitions,[82] such as that which led to the collapse of Bear Stearns, for example, as a trigger of the 2008 financial crisis.

Box 3.4 Negative in positive and positive in negative

1 Is there 'nothing good about being confident'?

Lucy Kellaway wrote about confidence. She quoted celebrities such as Michelle Obama, who told students that 'Your success will be determined by your own confidence and fortitude'. Cicero also considered that 'With confidence you have won before you have even started'. Samuel Jackson believed that 'self-confidence is the first requisite to great undertakings'. Kellaway pointed out:

> There is nothing good about being confident ... It's better to be unconfident.[83] For a start, the unconfident try harder as they are driven on by anxiety. They also listen to criticism and try to adjust accordingly. And they are far less likely to become arrogant, hubristic monsters ... Barack Obama, Sir Richard Branson and Madonna might all be confident. But their confidence didn't cause their success: it was the success that caused their confidence ... We should stop our obsession with self-belief – which risks turning us all into lazy narcissists – and focus on competence. We should not aim to believe we are good at what we do, we should instead aim simply be good at it.[84]

David Brooks[85] also wrote about 'The problem with confidence', noting that:

> I almost never see problems caused by underconfidence, but I see (and create) problems related to overconfidence every day ... So my first reaction when reading of female underconfidence is not simply that this is a problem. It's to ask, how can we inject more of this self-doubt and self-policing into the wider culture. How can each of us get a better mixture of 'female' self-doubt and 'male' self-assertion? ... In the very act of trying to think about self-confidence, your vanity is creating this ego that is unstable and ethereal, and is thus painfully fragile, defensive, boasting and sensitive to slights.

As Kellaway considers that 'Competence beats confidence every time at the office', so Brooks argued that 'It's probably a better idea to think about competence, which is task-oriented. If you ask, "Am I competent?", at least you are measuring yourself according to the standards of a specific domain'.

2 The negative and the positive in the negative

Manfred Kets de Vries argued that 'Many stars can, in reality, be insecure overachievers'.[86] Insecure overachievers are successful individuals who are insecure about their own capacities.[87] They are so insecure that they work relentlessly to excel in what they do. Andrew Hill discussed the 'virtues' of these individuals:[88]

> When I speculated a few years ago about self-doubt in the Davos set, several chief executives confessed the description resonated with their own occasional lapses of self-confidence. You will find more than a few insecure overachievers in the media, from the BBC to the *Financial Times*. And most organisations would rather employ anxious, praise-hungry perfectionists than happy but smug under performers.[89]

The dark side of insecure overachievers is that they overwork at the expense of their own and their family's wellbeing.

Questions for reflection

- How do you reconcile these views with the self-confidence of the 'Special One' (see Box 3.2)?
- Pepe Guardiola was a successful football player and later a successful coach. Read Box 3.2. How can an unconfident coach be so successful? Is Guardiola an insecure overachiever?
- Is it possible to be self-confident *and* humble? To reflect on these questions, read Box 8.3 of Chapter 8 ('Exemplars of paradoxical humility').
- Is it possible to be perseverant and insecure? If so, in what conditions?

Do psychologically strong individuals make psychologically strong teams?[90]

PsyCap may develop at the team level through mechanisms such as ongoing inter-actions and coordinative dynamics, behaviour modelling,[91] social and emotional contagion,[92] social sharedness[93] and mental model convergence.[94] These mechanisms lead team members to develop similar perceptions, attitudes and beliefs that mutually reinforce sentiments and beliefs about team capacities.[95] Team PsyCap may be thus defined as 'a team's shared positive appraisal of their circumstances and probability for success under those circumstances based on their combined motivated effort and perseverance'[96] (see the difference between team PsyCap and other forms of collective

Table 3.4 Several forms of collective PsyCap

Form	Definition	Is high when
Team PsyCap	The team's shared appraisal of the team PsyCap.	The sum of the team members' perceptions about the team PsyCap is high.
Summated PsyCap	The total sum of team members' own PsyCap.	The sum of the individual PsyCap of all team members is high.
Assimilated PsyCap	Agreement among team members about their own (individual) PsyCap.	Team members agree about individual levels of PsyCap.
PsyCap strength	The degree of (in)consistency among team members' individual PsyCap.	Team members have a (dis)similar level of individual PsyCap.
Team PsyCap strength	The degree of (in)consistency among team member perceptions of team PsyCap.	Team members have (dis)similar perceptions about the level of team PsyCap.

PsyCap in Table 3.4). Team PsyCap develops from the interactions between team members and does not necessarily equate to the sum of the individuals' PsyCap. Imagine a team composed of modest self-confident individuals who, when working together (in a cooperative and cohesive way), believe that the team, as a whole, is able to set and pursue challenging goals. Conversely, imagine highly resilient team members who work for a non-resilient team (i.e., it may be necessary to be resilient to be able to work for a team that is weak in resilience).

There are several ways in which Team PsyCap contributes towards team performance[97] (see Chapter 7): (1) the team is better able to make use of the potential contained in the team's skills and competencies and to set challenging goals; (2) the team is more focussed on developing skills and more perseverant in achieving those goals; (3) as positive social/relational dynamics develop within the team, team members become more cooperative and mutually supportive in pursuing challenging goals, overcoming barriers as well as in facing opportunities and problems with individual and collective *grit*.[98]

In summary: with stronger PsyCap, a team is more likely to set challenging team goals, initiate individual and collective action and cooperatively maintain perseverance in pursuing goals, as the team feels confident in handling what it aims to achieve or what needs to be done.[99] To foster team PsyCap, it is not enough to select individuals with high PsyCap or develop individual PsyCap. Team dynamics must also be facilitated and developed, as the whole is greater than the sum of its parts. Psychologically strong individuals do not necessarily give rise to psychologically stronger team and vice-versa.

Final comments

While the previous chapter focussed on individual trait-like strengths (i.e., although being developable, they are relatively stable), this chapter has considered the four state-like HERO strengths that compose PsyCap: hope, efficacy, resilience and optimism. Trait-like strengths and state-like strengths interplay and may reinforce each other (see Box 3.5). PsyCap goes beyond other forms of capital (i.e., economic, human and social) and is therefore a source of competitive advantage. It is also a source of individuals' wellbeing, both within and beyond the workplace.[100] Leaders and organizations may develop employees' PsyCap by means of several policies and practices, which we have discussed here. It is important to note, however, that each component of PsyCap may also be considered a trait, or a trait-like characteristic. Individuals may *be* consistently more or less hopeful, efficacious, resilient or optimistic. But even those who *are* less hopeful, efficacious, resilient or optimistic may sometimes *experience high* levels of hopefulness, efficacy, resilience or optimism. If, over time, these experiences become frequent across different situations, PsyCap can become a trait-like characteristic within the individual.

Box 3.5　Negative in the positive: the interplay between grit and resilience

1 The collapse and recovery of a CEO

On November 2011, António Horta-Osório, after exactly eight months as CEO of Lloyds Banking Group ('the youngest CEO of a UK-listed bank by a country mile'[101]) was compelled, on medical advice, to take a break. The BBC reported that he 'has been told by his doctors that he is physically and mentally exhausted, as a result of the way he has immersed himself in running Lloyds Banking Group'. Jenkins and Goff explained in the *Financial Times* that the problem had been in part self-inflicted: 'Mr. Horta Osório's impatience to return the bank to health prompted him to launch a drastic restructuring shortly after his arrival'.[102] They also considered that while Horta-Osório

> is regarded in the industry as a talented and technical banker, some people close to him suggested that he had underestimated the step up from his previous position as head of Santander's UK arm. 'Working for a subsidiary means there is always someone you can phone when things get tough. As head of a large listed bank that just isn't the case,' says one.

Friends, colleagues and even rivals were shocked with the CEO's collapse. One former colleague said that Horta-Osório had 'never shown any sign of weakness before. He'd never failed at anything. He was the coolest man, a very proud man. He delegated stress, putting a lot of pressure on those who worked for him'.[103]

As a consequence of the breakdown, Lloyds' share price fell significantly. 'The big question' was, then, whether Horta-Osorio would ever come back: 'The issue for him and his family is whether he is capable of doing the Lloyds job in a way that reduces the stresses and pressures on himself'.[104] Some analysts believed that Lloyds would have to find a permanent replacement. Less than one year later, after Horta-Osório's return, Patrick Jenkins, the *Financial Times* banking editor, wrote about a tennis match between him and Horta-Osório:

> I was never as sceptical as some that a CEO could return to his job after a medical absence. [But] His determination is clearly his greatest weapon. Take the left-handed lob – that was honed along with a whole left-handed game after

breaking his right wrist, mid-game, on his 30th birthday. 'They told me I'd never play tennis again,' he says later. 'So I decided to learn as a left-hander. I played that way for two years.' Then he defied the medics and restarted as a right-hander, too. When he takes off his sweatband, the scars are still evident on both sides of his wrist. The drive is evident in the way he plays, too – he targets my weaker backhand side mercilessly until I move so far round to protect it that there is a gaping hole on my forehand side. There is talent as well, of course, but also a vital self-control.[105]

Questions for reflection

- Horta-Osório *lacked* (or had lost) resilience to face the pressures associated with his job as a CEO. Later, he demonstrated *being resilient* to recover from his illness and regained his reputation as a successful banker. What does this tell us about resilience? Is it a trait, a state, or a state-like? (read Chapter 2).
- What is the difference between resilience and grit? To answer this question, revisit Chapter 2 and take into account how Angela Duckworth replied to the question on the relationship between grit and resilience:

> The word resilience is used differently by different people. And to add to the confusion, the ways people use it often have a lot of overlap … What all those definitions of resilience have in common is the idea of a positive response to failure or adversity. Grit is related because part of what it means to be gritty is to be resilient in the face of failure or adversity. But that's not the only trait you need to be gritty … So grit is not just having resilience in the face of failure, but also having deep commitments that you remain loyal to over many years.[106]

2 Learning from adversity

Interestingly, in 2018, in a piece published in the *Guardian*, Horta-Osório himself defended the need for organizations to face the problems they contribute to create in terms of the health of their people. He wrote:[107]

> I have made mental health a big focus for my company as a result of my personal experience. It is clear to me that the most important change needed is one of mindset. We must move to a way of thinking that recognises that we all have mental health just as we all have physical health. As with our physical health, all of us can experience periods of mental ill health when immediate treatment is needed, or we run the risk of developing long-term conditions that will need continuing support. When an employee breaks a leg or suffers an infection, we know how to respond. Mental health should be dealt with in the same way. With a culture of adequate support and sufficient time off, an employee can return to work with confidence and without embarrassment. This is the mindset we are adopting and embedding at

Lloyds ... I personally have been involved in a ground-breaking programme which we called 'optimal leadership resilience.' This is designed to help senior leaders at Lloyds to think about and put in place actions that help them build personal resilience and positive wellbeing. The programme covers nutrition, heart monitoring, sleep management, mindfulness, psychological testing and analysis.

Questions for reflection

- Why is 'time off' important for resilience?
- Would Horta-Osório have discovered the virtues of 'time off' if he had not experienced mental illness?
- What lessons for leadership may we extract from this conversion from 'impatience' into 'patience'?
- What should organizations do to preserve and develop employees' resilience?

Want more?

If you are less familiar with PsyCap you might want to start reading the book by Luthans, Youssef-Morgan and Avolio,[108] as well as a paper written by Luthans and Youssef.[109] Literature reviews and meta-analyses of PsyCap have also been written by Avey, Reichard, Luthans and Mhatre,[110] Dawkins, Martin, Scott and Sanderson,[111] Luthans and Youssef-Morgan,[112] Newman, Ucbasaran, Zhu and Hirst,[113] and Youssef and Luthans.[114]

Glossary

Appreciative inquiry (AI)   A strengths-based approach aimed at producing positive change in individuals, teams and organizations. AI involves the 4-D intervention cycle (Discovery, Dream, Design, Destiny)

HERO   Acronym reflecting the four components of PsyCap (hope, efficacy, resilience, optimism).

Hope   'A positive motivational state based on an interactively derived sense of successful (a) agency (goal-directed energy) and (b) pathways (planning to meet goals).'[115]

Imaginal experiences   Imagining oneself succeeding in effectively dealing with difficult situations and challenges.

Mastery experiences   Opportunities for experiencing success.

Optimism   'A positive explanatory style that attributes positive events to personal, permanent, and pervasive causes, and interprets negative events in terms of external, temporary, and situation-specific factors.'[116]

Pessimism   'A pessimistic explanatory style attributes positive events to external, temporary, and situation-specific causes, and negative events to personal, permanent, and pervasive ones.'[117]

Psychological capital (PsyCap)   A psychological state of development characterized by having self-efficacy, hope, optimism and resilience.

Resilience   'The capacity to rebound or bounce back from adversity, conflict, failure or even positive events, progress and increased responsibility.'[118]

Self-efficacy (as a state-like)   'The individual's conviction or confidence about his or her abilities to mobilize the motivation, cognitive resources or courses of action needed to successfully execute a specific task within a given context.'[119]

'Stepping'   Breaking down complex, difficult or long-term goals into manageable sub-goals.

Waypower   The pathways sub-component of hope.

Willpower   The agency (goal-directed energy) sub-component of hope.

Notes

1 Luthans (2002a, 2002b).
2 Luthans, Youssef-Morgan and Avolio (2015).
3 Luthans and Youssef-Morgan (2017, pp. 341–342).
4 Luthans, Youssef-Morgan and Avolio (2015) discussed other possible PsyCap dimensions: creativity, wisdom, well-being, flow and humour.
5 Luthans, Youssef-Morgan and Avolio (2015, p. 2).
6 Snyder, Irving and Anderson (1991, p. 287).
7 Snyder (1994, 2002).
8 Amabile (1997); Oldham and Cummings (1996); Shalley and Gilson (2004); Rego, Sousa, Marques and Cunha (2012a, 2012b); Snyder (2002).
9 Stajkovic and Luthans (1998, p. 66).
10 Bandura (1977); Luthans and Youssef (2004); Luthans, Youssef-Morgan and Avolio (2015).
11 Luthans (2002b, p. 702).
12 Luthans, Youssef and Avolio (2007, p. 123).
13 Tugade, Fredrickson and Barrett (2004).
14 Youssef and Luthans (2007); Giustiniano, Clegg, Cunha and Rego (2019).
15 Luthans and Youssef-Morgan (2017, p. 342).
16 Rego, Sousa, Marques and Cunha (2012a, 2012c).
17 Fredrickson (2001); Youssef and Luthans (2007).
18 Stajkovic (2006).
19 Luthans, Avolio, Avey and Norman (2007, p. 550).
20 Hobfoll (2002).
21 Luthans and Youssef-Morgan (2017, p. 343).
22 Stajkovic (2006, pp. 1211–1212).
23 Avey, Avolio and Luthans (2011); Bandura (1977); Luthans, Youssef-Morgan and Avolio (2015).
24 Luthans, Avolio, Avey and Norman (2007).
25 Luthans and Youssef-Morgan (2017); Newman, Ucbasaran, Zhu and Hirst (2014).
26 Luthans and Youssef-Morgan (2017, p. 346); see also: Luthans, Youssef-Morgan and Avolio (2015); www.mindgarden.com.
27 Avey, Avolio and Luthans (2011).
28 Harms and Luthans (2012); see also Harms, Vanhove and Luthans (2017).
29 McKenny, Short and Payne (2013).
30 Demerouti, van Eeuwijk, Snelder and Wild (2011).
31 Rego et al. (2019b).
32 Bolino, Long and Turnley (2016).
33 Dalal et al. (2015); Meyer, Dalal and Hermida (2010).
34 Wu, Tsui and Kinicki (2010).
35 De Dreu, Nijstad and van Knippenberg (2008); Harms and Spain (2014); Van Kleef, van den Berg and Heerdink (2015).
36 Reviews and syntheses in Dawkins, Martin, Scott and Sanderson (2013); Kleine, Rudolph and Zacher (2019); Luthans and Youssef-Morgan (2017); Newman, Ucbasaran, Zhu and Hirst (2014); Youssef and Luthans (2012).

37 Stajkovic (2006).
38 Stajkovic (2006).
39 Luthans and Youssef-Morgan (2017).
40 Fredrickson (2001).
41 Whitenay (2015).
42 In Press Association (2013).
43 In Press Association (2013).
44 In Marcus (2009).
45 Cowley (2015).
46 Retrieved from https://commons.wikimedia.org/wiki/File:CSKA-MU_2017_(4).jpg. This file is licensed under the Creative Commons Attribution-Share Alike 3.0 Unported license.
47 Fifield (2018).
48 www.espn.com/soccer/manchester-city/story/3435319/manchester-citys-pep-guardiola-neglects-medical-advice-bayern-munich-doctor.
49 Luthans, Youssef-Morgan and Avolio (2015).
50 Luthans and Youssef (2004).
51 Luthans and Youssef (2004, p. 155).
52 Caza and Milton (2012).
53 Margolis and Stoltz (2010).
54 Clair and Dufresne (2007).
55 Achor and Gielan (2016).
56 Luthans, Avey and Patera (2008); Luthans, Avey, Avolio, Norman and Combs (2006); Verleysen, Lambrechts and van Acker (2015).
57 Luthans and Youssef (2004); Luthans, Youssef-Morgan and Avolio (2015).
58 Luthans, Avey and Patera (2008); Luthans, Avey, Avolio and Peterson (2010); Luthans, Avey, Avolio, Norman and Combs (2006); Luthans, Luthans and Avey (2014).
59 To understand how neuroscience interventions may develop PsyCap, see Peterson, Balthazard, Waldman and Thatcher (2008).
60 Cooperrider and Godwin (2012); Cooperrider, Whitney and Stavros (2003).
61 Deci and Ryan (2000); Ryan and Deci (2000); Verleysen, Lambrechts and van Acker (2015).
62 Cooke, Wang, and Bartram (2019); Luthans, Norman, Avolio and Avey (2008).
63 Liu, Chang, Fu, Wang and Wang (2012); Wang, Liu, Wang and Wang (2012).
64 Gooty, Gavin, Johnson, Frazier and Snow (2009).
65 Peterson, Walumbwa, Avolio and Hannah (2012); Rego, Sousa, Marques and Cunha (2012a).
66 Bouckenooghe, Zafar and Raja (2015).
67 Liu (2013).
68 Story, Youssef, Luthans, Barbuto and Bovaird (2013).
69 Cooper and Sosik (2012); Fredrickson (2001); Wijewardena, Härtel and Samaratunge (2017).
70 Walumbwa, Peterson, Avolio and Hartnell (2010).
71 Rego, Marques, Leal, Sousa and Cunha (2010).
72 Schraeder, Becton and Portis (2007, p. 21).
73 Rego, Marques, Leal, Sousa and Cunha (2010, p. 1537).
74 Rego, Cunha, Reis Júnior and Anastácio (2018).
75 Herzberg, Glaesmer and Hoyer (2006); Robinson-Whelen, Kim, MacCallum and Kiecolt-Glaser (1997).
76 Rego, Cunha, Reis Júnior and Anastácio (2018).
77 Beshears and Gino (2015); Tugade and Fredrickson (2004).
78 Beshears and Gino (2015).
79 Day (2010, p. 42).
80 Lovallo and Kahneman (2003).
81 Gladwell (2009a, p. 26).
82 Malmendier and Tate (2015); Park, Kim, Chang, Lee and Sung (2018).
83 She bases her arguments mainly on *Confidence*, a book authored by Thomas Chamorro-Premuzic.
84 Kellaway (2013, p. 12).
85 Brooks (2014).
86 Kets de Vries (2012, p. 177).

87 See Braslow, Guerrettaz, Akin and Oleson (2012).
88 Based on *Leading Professionals*, authored by Laura Empson.
89 Hill (2017, p. 12).
90 See synthesis in Rego et al. (2017).
91 Bandura (1977).
92 Barsade (2002); Dawkins, Martin, Scott and Sanderson (2015).
93 Tindale and Kameda (2000).
94 Mathieu, Heffner, Goodwin, Sales and Cannon-Bowers (2000).
95 Biemann, Cole and Voelpel (2012); Dawkins, Martin, Scott and Sanderson (2015).
96 Peterson and Zhang (2011, p. 134).
97 Clapp-Smith, Vogelgesang and Avey (2009); Dawkins, Martin, Scott and Sanderson (2015); Heled, Somech and Waters (2016); Peterson and Zhang (2011); Rego et al. (2017), Rego et al. (2019a); West, Patera and Carsten (2009).
98 Duckworth, Peterson, Matthews and Kelly (2007).
99 Stajkovic (2006).
100 Youssef-Morgan and Luthans (2015).
101 Hume (2011).
102 Jenkins and Goff (2011, p. 18).
103 In Jenkins and Goff (2011, p. 18).
104 Peston (2011).
105 Jenkins (2012, p. 44).
106 In Perkins-Gough (2013, pp. 14–15).
107 Horta-Osório (2018).
108 Luthans, Youssef-Morgan and Avolio (2015).
109 Luthans and Youssef (2004).
110 Avey, Reichard, Luthans and Mhatre (2011).
111 Dawkins, Martin, Scott and Sanderson (2013).
112 Luthans and Youssef-Morgan (2017).
113 Newman, Ucbasaran, Zhu and Hirst (2014).
114 Youssef and Luthans (2012).
115 Snyder, Irving and Anderson (1991, p. 287).
116 Luthans and Youssef-Morgan (2017, p. 342).
117 Luthans and Youssef-Morgan (2017, p. 342).
118 Luthans (2002b, p. 702).
119 Stajkovic and Luthans (1998, p. 66).

References

Achor, S., & Gielan, M. (2016). Resilience is about how you recharge, not how you endure. *Harvard Business Review*, June 26 (https://hbr.org/2016/06/resilience-is-about-how-you-recharge-not-how-you-endure).

Amabile, T. M. (1997). Motivating creativity in organizations: On doing what you love and loving what you do. *California Management Review*, 40(1), 39–58.

Avey, J. B., Avolio, B. J., & Luthans, F. (2011). Experimentally analyzing the impact of leader positivity on follower positivity and performance. *The Leadership Quarterly*, 22(2), 282–294.

Avey, J. B., Reichard, R. J., Luthans, F., & Mhatre, K. H. (2011). Meta-analysis of the impact of positive psychological capital on employee attitudes, behaviors, and performance. *Human Resource Development Quarterly*, 22(2), 127–152.

Baltes, P. B., & Smith, J. (1990). Toward a psychology of wisdom and its ontogenesis. In R. J. Sternberg (Ed.), *Wisdom: Its nature, origins, and development* (pp. 87–120). Cambridge: Cambridge University Press.

Bandura, A. (1977). *Social learning theory*. Oxford, England: Prentice-Hall.

Barsade, S. G. (2002). The ripple effect: Emotional contagion and its influence on group behavior. *Administrative Science Quarterly*, 47, 644–675.

Beshears, J., & Gino, F. (2015). Leaders as decision architects. *Harvard Business Review*, May, 51–62.

Biemann, T., Cole, M. S., & Voelpel, S. (2012). Within-group agreement: On the use (and misuse) of rwg and rwg(J) in leadership research and some best practice guidelines. *The Leadership Quarterly*, 23(1), 66–80.

Bolino, M., Long, D., & Turnley, W. (2016). Impression management in organizations: Critical questions, answers, and areas for future research. *Annual Review of Organizational Psychology and Organizational Behavior*, 3, 377–406.

Bouckenooghe, D., Zafar, A., & Raja, U. (2015). How ethical leadership shapes employees' job performance: The mediating roles of goal congruence and psychological capital. *Journal of Business Ethics*, 129, 251–264.

Braslow, M. D., Guerrettaz, J., Akin, R. M., & Oleson, K. C. (2012). Self-doubt. *Social and Personality Psychology Compass*, 6(6), 470–482.

Brooks, D. (2014). The problem with confidence. *The New York Times*, May 13, A21.

Caza, B. B., & Milton, L. P. (2012). Resilience at work: Building capability in the face of adversity. In K. S. Cameron, & G. Spreitzer (Eds.), *The Oxford handbook of positive organizational scholarship* (pp. 895–908). Oxford, England: Oxford University Press.

Clair, J. A., & Dufresne, R. L. (2007). Changing poison into medicine: How companies can experience positive transformation from a crisis. *Organizational Dynamics*, 36(1), 63–77.

Clapp-Smith, R., Vogelgesang, G. R., & Avey, J. B. (2009). Authentic leadership and positive psychological capital: The mediating role of trust at the group level of analysis. *Journal of Leadership & Organizational Studies*, 15(3), 227–240.

Cooke, F. L., Wang, J., & Bartram, T. (2019). Can a supportive workplace impact employee resilience in a high pressure performance environment? An investigation of the Chinese banking industry. *Applied Psychology*, 68(4), 695–718.

Cooper, C. D., & Sosik, J. J. (2012). The laughter advantage: Cultivating high quality connections and workplace outcomes through humor. In K. S. Cameron, & G. Spreitzer (Eds.), *The Oxford handbook of positive organizational scholarship* (pp. 474–489). Oxford, England: Oxford University Press.

Cooperrider, D. L., & Godwin, L. (2012). Positive organization development: Innovation inspired change in an economy and ecology of strengths. In K. Cameron, & G. Spreitzer (Eds.), *The Oxford handbook of positive organizational scholarship* (pp. 737–750). New York: Oxford University Press.

Cooperrider, D. L., Whitney, D. K., & Stavros, J. M. (2003). *Appreciative inquiry handbook: The first in a series of AI workbooks for leaders of change* (Vol. 1). San Francisco, CA: Berrett-Koehler.

Cowley, J. (2015). NS Man of the year - Jose Mourinho. *New Statesman*, December 19 (www.news tatesman.com/node/163466).

Dalal, R. S., Meyer, R. D., Bradshaw, R. P., Green, J. P., Kelly, E. D., & Zhu, M. (2015). Personality strength and situational influences on behavior: A conceptual review and research agenda. *Journal of Management*, 41(1), 261–287.

Dawkins, S., Martin, A., Scott, J., & Sanderson, K. (2013). Building on the positives: A psychometric review and critical analysis of the construct of Psychological Capital. *Journal of Occupational and Organizational Psychology*, 86, 348–370.

Dawkins, S., Martin, A., Scott, J., & Sanderson, K. (2015). Advancing conceptualization and measurement of Psychological Capital as a collective construct. *Human Relations*, 68(6), 925–949.

Day, D. V. (2010). The difficulties of learning from experience and the need for deliberate practice. *Industrial and Organizational Psychology*, 3(1), 41–44.

De Dreu, C. K. W., Nijstad, B. A., & van Knippenberg, D. (2008). Motivated information processing in group judgment and decision-making. *Personality and Social Psychology Review*, 12(1), 22–49.

Deci, E. L., & Ryan, R. M. (2000). The "what" and" why" of goal pursuits: Human needs and the self-determination of behavior. *Psychological Inquiry*, 11(4), 227–268.

Demerouti, E., van Eeuwijk, E., Snelder, M., & Wild, U. (2011). Assessing the effects of a 'personal effectiveness' training on psychological capital, assertiveness and self-awareness using self-other agreement. *Career Development International*, 16, 60–81.

Duckworth, A. L., Peterson, C., Matthews, M. D., & Kelly, D. R. (2007). Grit: Perseverance and passion for long-term goals. *Journal of Personality and Social Psychology*, 92(6), 1087–1101.

Fifield, D. (2018). Pep Guardiola: Manchester City 'can be the best team in history'. *The Guardian*, April 29 (www.theguardian.com/football/2018/apr/29/pep-guardiola-manchester-city-can-be-best-team-in-history).

Fredrickson, B. L. (2001). The role of positive emotions in positive psychology: The broaden-and-build theory of positive emotions. *American Psychologist*, 56(3), 218–226.

Giustiniano, L., Clegg, S., Cunha, M. P., & Rego, A. (2019). *Elgar introduction to theories of organizational resilience*. Cheltenham: Edward Elgar.

Gladwell, M. (2009a). Cocksure: Banks, battles, and the psychology of overconfidence. *The New Yorker*, July 27, 24–28.

Gladwell, M. (2009b). *Outliers: The story of success*. New York: Penguin.

Gooty, J., Gavin, M., Johnson, P., Frazier, L., & Snow, D. (2009). In the eyes of the beholder: Transformational leadership, positive psychological capital and performance. *Journal of Leadership and Organization Studies*, 15, 353–357.

Harms, P. D., & Luthans, F. (2012). Measuring implicit psychological constructs in organizational behavior: An example using psychological capital. *Journal of Organizational Behavior*, 33, 589–594.

Harms, P. D., & Spain, S. M. (2014). Follower perceptions deserve a closer look. *Industrial and Organizational Psychology*, 7(2), 187–191.

Harms, P. D., Vanhove, A., & Luthans, F. (2017). Positive projections and health: An initial validation of the implicit psychological capital health measure. *Applied Psychology*, 66(1), 78–102.

Heled, E., Somech, A., & Waters, L. (2016). Psychological capital as a team phenomenon: Mediating the relationship between learning climate and outcomes at the individual and team levels. *The Journal of Positive Psychology*, 11(3), 303–314.

Herzberg, P. Y., Glaesmer, H., & Hoyer, J. (2006). Separating optimism and pessimism: A robust psychometric analysis of the Revised Life Orientation Test (LOT-R). *Psychological Assessment*, 18, 433–438.

Hill, A. (2017). Insecure overachiever? You are perfect for the job. *Financial Times*, October 2, 12.

Hobfoll, S. E. (2002). Social and psychological resources and adaptation. *Review of General Psychology*, 6(4), 307–324.

Horta-Osório, A. (2018). It's time to end the workplace taboo around mental health. *The Guardian*, May 1 (www.theguardian.com/commentisfree/2018/may/01/removeing-taboo-mental-health-work-lloyds-banking-group-antonio-horta-osorio).

Hume, N. (2011). Lloyds, de-helmed. *Financial Times*, November 2 (http://ftalphaville.ft.com/2011/11/02/721201/lloyds-de-helmed/).

Jenkins, P. (2012). Tennis with the FT: António Horta-Osório. *Financial Times*, July 27 (www.ft.com/intl/cms/s/2/f3a0c8e8-d6b9-11e1-ba60-00144feabdc0.html#axzz2WUsV1Tjm).

Jenkins, P., & Goff, S. (2011). Lloyds left to ponder chief's sick leave. *Financial Times*, November 3, 18.

Kellaway, L. (2013). Competence beats confidence every time at the office. *Financial Times*, October 14, 12.

Kets de Vries, M. (2012). Star performers: Paradoxes wrapped up in enigmas. *Organizational Dynamics*, 41, 173–182.

Kleine, A. K., Rudolph, C. W., & Zacher, H. (2019). Thriving at work: A meta-analysis.*Journal of Organizational Behavior*. doi: 10.1002/job.2375.

Liu, L., Chang, Y., Fu, J., Wang, J., & Wang, L. (2012). The mediating role of psychological capital on the association between occupational stress and depressive symptoms among Chinese physicians: A cross-sectional study. *BMC Public Health*, 12, 219–227.

Liu, Y. (2013). Moderating effect of positive psychological capital in Taiwan's life insurance industry. *Social Behavior and Personality*, 41, 109–112.

Lovallo, D., & Kahneman, D. (2003). Delusions of success. *Harvard Business Review*, 81(7), 56–63.

Luthans, B. C., Luthans, K. W., & Avey, J. B. (2014). Building the leaders of tomorrow: The development of academic psychological capital. *Journal of Leadership and Organizational Studies*, 21(2), 191–199.

Luthans, F. (2002a). Positive organizational behavior: Developing and managing psychological strenghts. *Academy of Management Executive*, 16(1), 57–72.

Luthans, F. (2002b). The need for and meaning of positive organizational behavior. *Journal of Organizational Behavior*, 23, 695–706.

Luthans, F., Avey, J. B., Avolio, B. J., Norman, S. M., & Combs, G. M. (2006). Psychological capital development: Toward a micro-intervention. *Journal of Organizational Behavior*, 27(3), 387–393.

Luthans, F., Avey, J. B., Avolio, B. J., & Peterson, S. J. (2010). The development and resulting performance impact of positive psychological capital. *Human Resource Development Quarterly*, 21(1), 41–67.

Luthans, F., Avey, J. B., & Patera, J. L. (2008). Experimental analysis of a web-based intervention to develop positive psychological capital. *Academy of Management Learning and Education*, 7(2), 209–221.

Luthans, F., Avolio, B. J., Avey, J. B., & Norman, S. M. (2007). Positive psychological capital: Measurement and relationship with performance and satisfaction. *Personnel Psychology*, 60(3), 541–572.

Luthans, F., Norman, S. M., Avolio, B. J., & Avey, J. A. (2008). The mediating role of psychological capital in the supportive organizational climate - employee performance relationship.. *Journal of Organizational Behavior*, 29(2), 219–238.

Luthans, F., & Youssef, C. (2004). Human, social, and now positive psychological capital management: Investing in people for competitive advantage. *Organizational Dynamics*, 33(2), 143–160.

Luthans, F., Youssef, C. M., & Avolio, B. J. (2007). *Psychological capital*. Oxford, England: Oxford University Press.

Luthans, F., Youssef-Morgan, C., & Avolio, B. J. (2015). *Psychological capital and beyond*. Oxford, England: Oxford University Press.

Luthans, F., & Youssef-Morgan, C. M. (2017). Psychological capital: An evidence-based positive approach. *Annual Review of Organizational Psychology and Organizational Behavior*, 4, 339–366.

Malmendier, U., & Tate, G. (2015). Behavioral CEOs: The role of managerial overconfidence. *Journal of Economic Perspectives*, 29(4), 37–60.

Marcus, J. (2009). Q. and A.: The Special One, José Mourinho. *The New York Times*, March 10 (https://goal.blogs.nytimes.com/2009/03/10/q-mourinho/).

Margolis, J. D., & Stoltz, P. G. (2010). How to bounce back from adversity. *Harvard Business Review*, January–February, 86–92.

Mathieu, J. E., Heffner, T. S., Goodwin, G. F., Sales, E., & Cannon-Bowers, J. A. (2000). The influence of shared mental models on team process and performance. *Journal of Applied Psychology*, 85(2), 273–283.

McKenny, A. F., Short, J. C., & Payne, T. (2013). Using computer-aided text analysis to elevate constructs: An illustration using psychological capital. *Organizational Research Methods*, 16, 152–184.

Meyer, R. D., Dalal, R. S., & Hermida, R. (2010). A review and synthesis of situational strength in the organizational sciences. *Journal of Organizational Behavior*, 36, 121–140.

Newman, A., Ucbasaran, D., Zhu, F., & Hirst, G. (2014). Psychological capital: A review and synthesis. *Journal of Organizational Behavior*, 35, S120–S138.

Oldham, G. R., & Cummings, A. (1996). Employee creativity: Personal and contextual factors at work. *Academy of Management Journal*, 39, 607–634.

Park, J. H., Kim, C., Chang, Y. K., Lee, D. H., & Sung, Y. D. (2018). CEO hubris and firm performance: Exploring the moderating roles of CEO power and board vigilance. *Journal of Business Ethics*, 47(4), 919–933.

Perkins-Gough, D. (2013). The significance of grit: A conversation with Angela Lee Duckworth. *Educational Leadership*, 71(1), 14–20.

Peston, R. (2011). Lloyd's boss flunks stress test. BBC News, 2 November (https://www.bbc.com/news/business-15551669).

Peterson, S. J., Balthazard, P. A., Waldman, D. A., & Thatcher, R. W. (2008). Neuroscientific implications of psychological capital: Are the brains of optimistic, hopeful, confident, and resilient leaders different? *Organizational Dynamics*, 37(4), 342–353.

Peterson, S. J., & Zhang, Z. (2011). Examining the relationships between top management team psychological characteristics, transformational leadership, and business unit performance. In M. A. Carpenter (Ed.), *Handbook of top management research* (pp. 127–149). New York: Edward Elgar.

Peterson, S. S., Walumbwa, F. O., Avolio, B. J., & Hannah, S. T. (2012). The relationship between authentic leadership and follower job performance: The mediating role of follower positivity in extreme contexts. *The Leadership Quarterly*, 23(3), 502–516.

Press Association. (2013). Chelsea's Frank Lampard says José Mourinho's management is second to none. *The Guardian*, 20 May (www.theguardian.com/football/2013/may/20/frank-lampard-jose-mourinho-sport).

Rego, A., Cunha, M. P., Reis Júnior, D., & Anastácio, C. Savagnago, M. (2018). The optimism-pessimism ratio as predictor of employee creativity: The promise of duality. *European Journal of Innovation Management,* 21(3), 423–442.

Rego, A., Marques, C., Leal, S., Sousa, F., & Cunha, M. P. (2010). Psychological capital and performance of civil servants: Exploring neutralizers in the context of an appraisal system. *International Journal of Human Resource Management*, 21(9), 1531–1552.

Rego, A., Owens, B., Leal, S., Melo, A., Cunha, M. P., Gonçalves, L., & Ribeiro, L. (2017). How leader humility helps teams to be humbler, psychologically stronger, and more effective: A moderated mediation model. *The Leadership Quarterly*, 28, 639–658.

Rego, A., Owens, B., Yam, K. C., Bluhm, D., Cunha, M. P., Silard, T., Gonçalves, L., Martins, M., Simpson, A. V., & Liu, W. (2019a). Leader humility and team performance: Exploring the mechanisms of team psychological capital and task allocation effectiveness, *Journal of Management*, 45(3), 1009–1033.

Rego, A., Sousa, F., Marques, S., & Cunha, M. P. (2012a). Authentic leadership promoting employees' psychological capital and creativity. *Journal of Business Research*, 65, 429–437.

Rego, A., Sousa, F., Marques, S., & Cunha, M. P. (2012b). Retail employees' self-efficacy and hope predicting their positive affect and creativity. *European Journal of Work and Organizational Psychology*, 21(6), 923–945.

Rego, A., Sousa, F., Marques, S., & Cunha, M. P. (2012c). Optimism predicting employees' creativity: The mediating role of positive affect and the positivity ratio. *European Journal of Work and Organizational Psychology*, 21(2), 244–270.

Rego, A., Yam, K. C., Owens, B., Story, J., Cunha, M. P., Bluhm, D., & Lopes, M. P. (2019b). Conveyed leader Psycap predicting leader effectiveness through positive energizing. *Journal of Management*, 45(4), 1689–1712.

Robinson-Whelen, S., Kim, C., MacCallum, R. C., & Kiecolt-Glaser, J. (1997). Distinguishing optimism from pessimism in older adults: Is it more important to be optimistic or not to be pessimistic? *Journal of Personality and Social Psychology*, 73(6), 1345–1353.

Ryan, R. M., & Deci, E. L. (2000). Self-determination theory and the facilitation of intrinsic motivation, social development and well-being. *American Psychologist*, 55(1), 68–78.

Schraeder, M., Becton, J. B., & Portis, R. (2007). A critical examination of performance appraisals: An organization's friend or foe? *Journal of Quality and Participation*, 30(1), 20–25.

Shalley, C. E., & Gilson, L. L. (2004). What leaders need to know: A review of social and contextual factors that can foster or hinder creativity. *The Leadership Quarterly*, 15(1), 33–53.

Snyder, C. R. (1994). *The psychology of hope: You can get there from here*. New York: Free Press.

Snyder, C. R. (2002). Hope theory: Rainbows in the mind. *Psychological Inquiry*, 13, 249–275.

Snyder, C. R., Irving, L., & Anderson, J. (1991). Hope and health: Measuring the will and the ways. In C. R. Snyder & D. R. Forsyth (Ed.), *Forsyth handbook of social and clinical psychology* (pp. 285–305). Elmsford, NY: Pergamon.

Stajkovic, A. D. (2006). Development of a core confidence higher-order construct. *Journal of Applied Psychology*, 91, 1208–1224.

Stajkovic, A. D., & Luthans, F. (1998). Social cognitive theory and self-efficacy: Going beyond traditional motivational and behavioral approaches. *Organizational Dynamics*, 26, 62–74.

Story, J., Youssef, C. M., Luthans, F., Barbuto, J. E., & Bovaird, J. (2013). Contagion effect of global leaders' positive psychological capital on followers: Does distance and quality of relationship matter? *The International Journal of Human Resource Management*, 24(13), 2534–2553.

Tindale, R. S., & Kameda, T. (2000). 'Social sharedness' as a unifying theme for information processing in groups. *Group Processes Intergroup Relations*, 3(2), 123–140.

Tugade, M. M., & Fredrickson, B. L. (2004). Resilient individuals use positive emotions to bounce back from negative emotional experiences. *Journal of Personality and Social Psychology*, 86(2), 320–333.

Tugade, M. M., Fredrickson, B. L., & Barrett, L. M. (2004). Psychological resilience and positive emotional granularity: Examining the benefits of positive emotions on coping and health. *Journal of Personality*, 72(6), 1161–1190.

van Kleef, G. A., van den Berg, H., & Heerdink, M. W. (2015). The persuasive power of emotions: Effects of emotional expressions on attitude formation and change. *Journal of Applied Psychology*, 100(4), 1124–1142.

Verleysen, B., Lambrechts, F., & van Acker, F. (2015). Building psychological capital with appreciative inquiry: Investigating the mediating role of basic psychological need satisfaction. *Journal of Applied Behavioral Science*, 51(1), 10–35.

Walumbwa, F. O., Peterson, S. J., Avolio, B. J., & Hartnell, C. A. (2010). An investigation of the relationship between leader and follower psychological capital, service climate and job performance. *Personnel Psychology*, 63, 977–1003.

Wang, Y., Liu, L., Wang, J., & Wang, L. (2012). Work–family conflict and burnout among Chinese doctors: The mediating role of psychological capital. *Journal of Occupational Health*, 54, 232–240.

West, B. J., Patera, J. L., & Carsten, M. K. (2009). Team level positivity: Investigating positive psychological capacities and team level outcomes. *Journal of Organizational Behavior*, 30(2), 249–267.

Whitenay, A. (2015). Frank Lampard talks Chelsea, Jose Mourinho and champions league in compelling interview. *90min.com*, May 17 (www.90min.com/posts/2170493-frank-lampard-talks-chelsea-jose-mourinho-and-champions-league-in-compelling-interview).

Wijewardena, N., Härtel, C. E., & Samaratunge, R. (2017). Using humor and boosting emotions: An affect-based study of managerial humor, employees' emotions and psychological capital. *Human Relations*, 70(11), 1316–1341.

Wu, J. B., Tsui, A. S., & Kinicki, A. J. (2010). Consequences of differentiated leadership in groups. *Academy of Management Journal*, 53(1), 90–106.

Youssef, C. M., & Luthans, F. (2007). Positive organizational behavior in the workplace: The impact of hope, optimism and resilience. *Journal of Management*, 33(5), 774–800.

Youssef, C. M., & Luthans, F. (2012). Positive global leadership. *Journal of World Business*, 47(4), 539–547.

Youssef-Morgan, C. M., & Luthans, F. (2015). Psychological capital and well-being. *Stress and Health*, 31(3), 180–188.

4 Emotions and happiness at work

This chapter discusses the emotional nature of individuals, teams and organizations. After clarifying related concepts (e.g., affect, mood, emotions, psychological wellbeing, subjective wellbeing and happiness), the chapter discusses the antecedents and consequences of happiness at work. Special attention is paid to the circumplex model as well as broaden-and-build theory. The relationship between leadership and affect is also discussed. We explore emotions at the collective level and discuss several processes (e.g., emotional contagion) that help individuals' emotions to converge in teams. The components and consequences of emotional intelligence (EI) are also considered, along with its limitations and dark side. Limitations and the dark side of EI are also considered. Although the chapter in mainly centred on positive emotions and happiness, a balanced perspective is adopted. Both positive and negative affect may produce negative and positive consequences, with individual and organizational functioning emerging from the interplay between the positive and the negative.

The assent of emotion in organizations

The past couple of decades has seen emotions within the workplace become a topic of growing interest for managers and researchers.[1] Considering that emotions have historically been unwelcome in the workplace, with employees being expected to enter work with their reason intact while leaving their emotions at the door, this growing interest constitutes a significant shift.[2] Emotions have traditionally been understood to cloud judgement and thereby undermine effectiveness. High organizational performance was thought to rely on cold, analytical intelligence.

Today, however, many organizations are governed in a manner that emphasizes emotion-related constructs such as subjective wellbeing, psychological wellbeing, happiness and emotional intelligence as factors critical to organizational success. A couple of organizations even have a position of Chief Happiness Officer (CHO) – aimed at ensuring workers are kept happy[3] (see Box 4.1).

The seeds of recognizing the importance of emotions within organizations were planted in organization theory in the 1930s with the emergence of the Human Relations Movement[4] as a reaction to Taylor's approach of 'Scientific Management',[5] albeit one that was equally as instrumental in its own way.[6] Taylor applied principles of mechanical engineering to address problems of managing people in organizations. His approach focussed on specialization and routinization as a means of achieving objectives of efficiency, productivity and profitability. With the appearance of the

Human Relations approach, psychological theories coexisted with those of engineers to enhance engineering means of exploitation and control with those premised on psychology.[7]

Box 4.1 Chief Happiness Officers (CHO) – hired or fired?

A CHO in a Saudi Investment Bank

A search (July 20, 2018) of CHO job positions posted in LinkedIn found offers from organizations such as The Saudi Investment Bank, isahit, Agorastore, Groupe Karavel – Promovacances and the Ministry of Higher Education, Research, Science and Technology of Québec. The job description for the Saudi Investment Bank was as follows:[8]

> The Chief Happiness Officer's main role is to ensure the happiness of employees in the workplace. By setting a new way of thinking, acting, empowering staff, a way of changing the culture for the better from within, enabling happiness to grow from the inside. Happy employees are better employees!

The main tasks in that job description were making sure employees feel valued, guaranteeing basic principles, listening to employees, valuing day-to-day work, supporting growth, creating a positive work environment, encouraging teamwork and empowering employees. Of course, given what we know about the context of Saudi society as extremely autocratic and highly gendered, one might wonder how effective such as officer might be.

Might unhappiness be a good thing?

'Fire your Chief Happiness Officer' is the title of an article authored by Tomas Chamorro-Premuzic (Professor of Business Psychology at Columbia University & UCL), published in *Fast Company*.[9] The author argues that one may be happy and disengaged at work and that some level of unhappiness is necessary to be motivated to change the 'state of affairs'. According to the author,

> anyone who's entirely contented is unlikely to innovate. With no imbalance to address, they grow complacent … It's not hard to imagine happy work environments where employees are having way too much fun to be productive; too much getting along can inhibit getting ahead.

In his view, the goal of individuals being happy at work may backfire: 'Work has always been a poor vehicle for self-actualization, which is why very few people would do it for free. And pretending otherwise adds heaps of unfair pressure on the average employee to find their "dream job"'. Creating job positions like CHO and investing in employees' happiness may also backfire: 'Many scientific studies have shown that trying to coax people into being happy usually generates the opposite result. In other words, happiness may or may not emerge as the *product* of the work you do but the work you do will invariably either drive or diminish how happy you already are – that's why psychologists consider happiness a "collateral symptom." It's just as possible to do great work and be unhappy as it is to be happy without doing any great work, but organizations are much more interested in the former than the latter'.

Is the CHO position antithetical to the concept of workplace happiness?

Critical perspectives about the CHO job position are also discussed in an article authored by Leah Messinger, published in the *Guardian*.[10] Richard Sheridan, CEO and chief storyteller at Menlo Innovations, pointed out that: 'If anything, we want a chief happiness officer mentality in the company, rather than a chief happiness officer person in the company'. Charles D. Kearns, a professor of behavioural science at Pepperdine University's business school, argued that 'assigning companywide happiness to a bureaucrat is antithetical to the concept of workplace happiness'. In his view,

> the top management team and all of the managers and supervisors, and for that matter all of the organization's employees, should have built into their job description to increase happier high performance, starting with themselves … How can you legislate that with a chief happiness officer?

Questions for reflection

- What are the strengths and limitations of appointing a CHO?
- Do the limitations outweigh the strengths or vice versa?

A leading theorist of the Human Relations movement was Elton Mayo. Failed clinician turned organizational theorist, Mayo became famous for explaining the result of the Hawthorne experiment as highlighting the importance of social relations of empathy over mechanical determination.[11] Mayo directed managers to communicate with employees in a manner that mimicked psychotherapy techniques of empathic listening without judgement, practically simulating non-directive therapy where the therapist rephrases the concerns described.[12] Cynically, the manager didn't have to change things within the organization as a result of listening to employee grievances – just listen. In accordance with therapy, simply having an opportunity to share concerns with an authority figure would, in most cases, it was thought, be enough to resolve employee distress. Mayo was steeped in the same objectives as Taylorism.[13] With Mayo, we find emphasis on the human needs of employees in the interests of increasing control, efficiency and productivity via the agency of the 'science of organizational behaviour' (for a 'human–Tayloristic' approach adopted nowadays in some organizations, consult Box 4.2).

In the 1980s emotions became fully embraced within the organizational domain. Academically, it was the work of Hochschild, studying the way flight attendants were trained to express emotionality, that was instrumental in bringing the issues to research attention.[14] As Western nations battled reduced international competitiveness within their manufacturing sectors and as government debts climbed, managers shifted their approach from bureaucracy to an approach that has come to be known as post-bureaucracy.[15] Bureaucracy was characterized by conformity with rules and commands delivered from the top of the organization and communicated through the organizational hierarchy to achieve maximum efficiency and productivity. Post-bureaucracy, in contrast, gave much more importance to employees' and customers' emotional experience, emphasizing dialogue and consensus in decision-making, horizontal communication networks, organizational culture, total quality and customer service.[16]

Box 4.2 The positive in the negative or the negative in the positive? Big Brother is watching your emotions

Deayea, a technology company in Shanghai, is producing brain-monitoring caps that are being worn by workers across China.[17] Train drivers working on the Beijing–Shanghai high-speed rail line wear the devices to monitor mental states such as fatigue and stress. When the device detects dozing it sends an alarm to the cabin to wake up the driver. The driver's supervisor handles the detection of too much stress in the worker's brain through the redesign of work schedules. The organization defends the use of these devices on the grounds that they protect public safety by preventing mistakes resulting from fatigue or other emotionally dangerous states on the world's busiest train route.

The wearing of these devices is not restricted to train drivers. Production line workers wear the brainwave-monitoring caps at Hangzhou Zhongheng Electric. The data is streamed to central computers used to identify spikes in anxiety, rage or depression. Management use the data to redesign workflows including the pace of production, as well as the length and frequency of breaks. Cheng Jingzhou, a Hanzhou Zhongeng Electric official, claims that since its rollout in 2014, the company's emotional surveillance programme has boosted profits by about 2 billion yuan (US\$315 million). Discussions are underway to introduce the use of these brain-monitoring devices into other industries, including Chinese airlines to determine a pilot's fitness to fly before take-off.

Questions for reflection

- Think about the utopian and dystopian possibilities raised by this technology. Would you recommend its use? Why?
- The use of such devices is grounded in the belief that they are accurate in assessing emotions. Is such a belief realistic? If not, what may be the consequences of their use?

There were macro-economic corollaries to the new organizational emphases. Neo-liberal governments elected in 1979, led by President Ronald Reagan in the USA and Prime Minister Margaret Thatcher in the UK, sought to reform what they branded as the 'inefficient' public welfare system, which they characterized as 'stifling' government regulation and as staffed by 'interfering' unions. Public organizations such as hospitals, universities and government enterprises were to be reorganized for greater efficiency, productivity and profitability.[18] In parallel with these organizational and social reforms, employee subjectivity was also reframed with the emphasis being given to values of individual autonomy, motivation, entrepreneurship, self-fulfilment and self-actualization, in a desire to create 'entrepreneurial subjects'.[19]

Rugged individualism had a paternalist edge, however. Tom Peters and Robert Waterman argued in their 1982 book *In Search of Excellence* that the new entrepreneurial management style required a duty of care by leaders to employees as a corollary (see Box 4.3). The intensity of such care was held to be a crucial factor distinguishing America's most productive businesses from less successful organizations. Providing such care would facilitate employees' natural human tendencies to seek meaning, responsibility, fulfilment, purpose and success at work, enabling enhanced 'productivity through people'.[20]

Box 4.3 Positively wonderful stories based on faked data.

In Search of Excellence was a bestseller (more than three million copies sold in the first four years): 'the case can be made that it is the most influential management book not only in these last three decades, but perhaps ever'.[21] Several limitations were soon pointed out, however, including criticisms of the method: 'the book failed to look at unsuccessful companies that may have embodied some or all of the eight characteristics, risking survivor bias'.[22] Moreover, in the ensuing years, some of the 'excellent' companies weren't as successful as Peters and Waterman suggested. Finally, Tom Peters himself admitted, in an interview, to having faked the data to support a story: 'I confess: We faked the data'.[23]

These criticisms do not imply that the core ideas contained in the book were not relevant but they do suggest that, even within the pseudo-rational corporate world and its less than disinterested observers (Peters and Waterman were McKinsey consultants, shaping 'excellence' consulting), positive wonderful stories are attractive, irrespective of their veracity.

The popularity of such programmes facilitated the emergence of employee subjectivities centred on the 'care of the self' that increasingly became framed within a discourse of self-help and popular psychology in alignment with organizational and governmental programmes of productivity and efficiency.[24] Summing up Peters and Waterman's arguments, McCoy held that they advocated a culture of empowerment built upon self-directed teams, open structures, shared information and flexible work hours.[25]

Feminist values also played their part: much as the contributions of women had mostly been absent in the organization and management literature so had the stress on feminine values.[26] Robert Solomon challenged the dominant masculine portrayals of organization as calculating, self-interested, cutthroat and profit-focussed as a matter of interpretation that acted as a self-fulfilling prophecy.[27] Female executives 'breaking through the "glass ceiling"', he argued, were precipitating a 'serious shift in values and the "feminization" of attitudes in the corporation'.[28] Solomon called for recognition of the softer side of organizations as communities, where 'caring and compassion is what we all in fact expect and demand in our various jobs and positions'.[29]

Significantly, 1998 marked a momentous demographic shift in the US with records indicating that, for the first time, there were more adults over the age of 40 than below. Wolfe argues that this change shifted the 'psychological center of gravity' towards 'kinder and gentler' midlife values.[30] For John Mackey and Raj Sisodia, the birth of the Internet, changing demography and the general adoption of midlife values has significant implications for business with stakeholders demanding more 'caring and compassion, a greater desire for meaning and purpose, and concern for one's community'.[31]

Because of these and other reasons, emotions also emerged as central among both scholars and practitioners. Barsade and Gibson wrote in 2007 that, 'In the last 30 years, an "affective revolution" has taken place, in which academics and managers alike have begun to appreciate how an organizational lens that integrates employee affect provides a perspective missing from earlier views'.[32] This chapter discusses, both at the conceptual and empirical level, some important aspects of such a revolution.

We will start by clarifying concepts (e.g., affect, mood, emotions, psychological wellbeing, subjective wellbeing and happiness) and then discuss consequences and antecedents of happiness at work. The circumplex model and the broaden–and–build theory of positive emotions are also explained. After considering relationships between leadership and affect, we explore happiness at the collective level. Next, we discuss emotional intelligence (EI), mainly its components and consequences. Limitations and the dark side of EI are also considered.

Affect, moods and emotions

Before proceeding, it is important to make some conceptual clarifications. First, the relationship between affect and emotion should be clarified. Affect is an 'umbrella term encompassing a broad range of feelings that individuals experience, including feeling states, such as moods and discrete emotions, as well as traits, such as positive and negative affectivity'.[33] While (discrete) emotions tend to be generally of short duration and are associated with a specific stimulus, moods are more enduring, diffuse and less related to specific stimuli.[34] However, Gable and Harmon-Jones[35] state that '[a]lthough moods may be different from emotions, past research has found that positive moods and positive emotions have identical effects on broadening of cognition and attention'. In this chapter, we use the term 'emotions' in a broader sense, including both emotions and moods.

Second, *affect* may be considered both as a state or as a trait disposition. One individual may *experience* happiness today (a state), although he/she may tend to *be* sad on most days (a trait). Dispositional affect is the 'overall personality tendency to respond to situations in stable, predictable ways'.[36] Individuals characterized by positive affectivity are those that 'tend to be cheerful and energetic, and who experience positive moods, such as pleasure or well-being, across a variety of situations as compared to people who tend to be low energy and sluggish or melancholy'.[37] Conversely, individuals characterized by negative affectivity 'tend to be distressed and upset, and have a negative view of self over time and across situations, as compared to people who are more calm, serene and relaxed'.[38] Literature suggests that employees' positive affectivity has a significant relationship with several indicators of performance (e.g., personal initiative and proactive behaviours), although the relationship is probably nonlinear: after a threshold is reached, the relationship is negative.[39] As Lam et al. argued and demonstrated empirically:[40]

> Although employees experiencing high levels of positive affect at work experience broadened cognitions, enhanced action tendencies, and increased resources, they are also more likely to perceive that things are going well and there is little need to be proactive to initiate changes in the workplace. The higher levels of positive affect may create a kind of contentment or even complacency.

Such evidence shows that too much of a good thing is a bad thing and why negative affectivity may engender positive consequences, at least if combined with positive affectivity. We discuss this issue in other parts of this chapter (see 'Grappling with complexity: the value of negative emotions' below).

A third important clarification relates to how emotions (in the broader sense) are contagious, in that they transfer between individuals. Emotional contagion is the process that allows 'the sharing or transferring of emotions from one individual to other group members; the tendency to mimic the nonverbal behaviour of others, to "synchronize facial expressions, vocalizations, postures, and movements" with others, and in turn, to converge emotionally'.[41] Emotional contagion helps explain why the positive and negative emotions of team members tend to converge and thus give rise to group affective tone.[42]

Classifying emotions: the circumplex model

Every human being experiences a wide range of emotions, both positive and negative, across his/her life and even within a single day. How should these be classified? The circumplex model, developed by James Russell, holds that emotions arise from two neurophysiological systems: one, a continuum of positive–negative affect, the other, a continuum of high–low activation, arousal or attention.[43] Circumplex theorists hold that all affective experiences are generated from the intersection between varying degrees of the positive–negative and high–low activation dimensions. The fact that people have difficulty in discerning and describing their personal emotions is taken as suggesting that emotions are not experienced as discrete and isolated but as overlapping and ambiguous.[44] Like the colour spectrum where there are no discrete borders differentiating colours, similarly there appear to be no discrete borders between emotions.[45] People rarely describe feeling a single positive emotion without additionally describing others.[46]

Support for the circumplex model is found in sophisticated statistical analyses of emotional intercorrelations, emotional words and facial expressions that consistently yield two-dimensional models of affective experiences,[47] (1) positive–negative affect and (2) high–low activation. In the circumplex model high–low activation is positioned as the vertical axis, while positive–negative affect is represented as the horizontal axis. Different emotions are interpreted as being represented at various positions within the circumplex (Figure 4.1). For example, positive feelings of calmness and contentedness represent lower level activation (bottom right quadrant) as compared with feelings of happiness, engagement, excitement or enthusiasm (top right quadrant). Similarly, negative emotions may range from feeling tired or gloomy (bottom left quadrant) to feeling agitated, hostile and tense (top left quadrant).

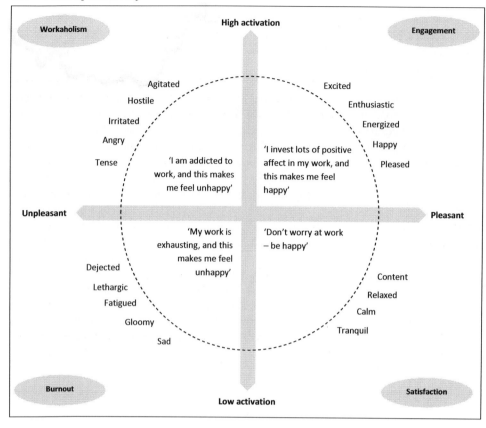

Figure 4.1 The circumplex model of affect applied to the organizational context.[49]

Bakker and Oerlemans have considered the organizational implications of the circumplex model.[48] They associate the top right-hand quadrant, indicating highly activated positive affect, with workplace engagement. Low activated pleasant affect in the bottom right hand quadrant is associated with job satisfaction. The bottom left quadrant, representing low activated negative emotion, is associated with workplace burnout. Finally, the quadrant involving highly activated negative affect, represented in the top left-hand quadrant, is associated with workaholism.

The broaden-and-build theory

Emotions as evolutionary resources

The value of positive emotions for survival advantage was not articulated until as recently as the early 1990s with the introduction of the broaden-and-build theory,[50] which has been described as providing a theoretical underpinning for positive psychology.[51] Broaden-and-build theory posits that humans adopted positive emotions through evolutionary processes to fulfil the important survival mechanism of broadening-and-building Palaeolithic humans' thought-action repertoires. The broadening-and-building of physical, psychological, intellectual and social repertoires provided resources in times of safety that could be later drawn upon for survival advantage in times of threat.

Fredrickson accordingly posits that expression of positive emotions in times when Palaeolithic humans were not under threat *broadened* their cognitive awareness and *built* physical, intellectual, social and emotional resources (Figure 4.2).[52] The broaden-and-build effect of positive emotions accordingly equipped the Palaeolithic human with survival advantages beyond mere physical strength that could be used to outwit predators and competitors. Positive expressions of joy broadened to activities of play and creativity building physical, relational, psychological and intellectual resources. Similarly, other emotions, such as interest, broadened to behaviours of exploration and learning, while contentment led to activities of savouring and information sharing. Intellectual resources included information learning and problem-solving skills. Social resources included those for forming and nurturing bonds. Physical resources included strength, coordination and cardiovascular health. Psychological resources included identity, goal orientation as well as resilience and optimism. The personal resources were enduring, outlasting the transient positive emotional states leading to their acquisition. Fredrickson explains:[53]

> The broaden-and-build theory suggests that positive emotions broaden people's modes of thinking and action, which over time builds their enduring personal and social resources. The resources, in turn, function as reserves that can be drawn on later to help people to survive and thrive.

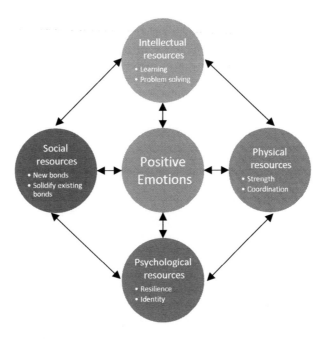

Figure 4.2 Positive emotions broaden and build four types of resources contributing to survival advantage.

At the group or organizational level, broaden-and-build theory holds that positive emotions do not merely benefit individuals but may also benefit groups within organizations or communities, creating positive upward spirals.[54] Such an effect is seen when a kind act by one person inspires similar responsive behaviours in others, generating flow-on effects.[55] Fredrickson writes on the applicability of this theory to the organizational level:

> Because an individual's experiences of positive emotions can reverberate through other organizational members and across interpersonal transactions with customers, positive emotions may also fuel optimal organizational functioning, helping organizations to thrive as well.

Testing broaden-and-build theory

Fredrickson specifically tested her broaden-and-build theory by measuring participants' thought–action repertoires immediately after viewing films selected to evoke what were classified as emotions of either joy, contentment, fear or anger, as well as a neutral condition.[56] After viewing the films, participants were asked to imagine themselves in another situation where those emotions arose and to list all the things they would like to do. Participants in the positive conditions identified more things they would like to do than those in the negative and neutral conditions. Further, those in the neutral condition identified more activities than those in the negative conditions.

An implicit correlate of the broaden-and-build model is the undoing hypothesis, which describes a process whereby the effects of negative emotions are undone by the nurturing of positive emotions.[57] While negative emotions such as anger and fear incite the 'flight-fight' response of the sympathetic nervous system, the predominance of positive emotions of appreciation, compassion and love *undo* these stress responses by activating the 'rest and digest' response of the parasympathetic nervous system, thereby reverting energized systems to normality and relaxation.[58]

Support for the undoing hypothesis is provided by a number of studies linking positive emotions with parasympathetic autonomic activity of lowering cortisol, blood pressure, neuroendocrine and cardiovascular risk and stress responses.[59] One study involved exposing participants to a film designed to induce negative emotions, increasing their level of cardiovascular activation.[60] Randomly assigned viewing of one of four film conditions each designed to induce amusement, contentment, sadness or neutrality was designed. Those exposed to the positive films demonstrated quicker returns to pre-stimuli levels of cardiovascular activation in comparison with those who viewed the sad and neutral films, which the authors suggest has important implications for stress levels and overall wellbeing within the workplace context. Other studies have found that when participants imagined hurtful memories and nursed grudges it prompts higher skin conductance, heart rate and blood pressure changes from baseline.[61] Conversely, when they imagined empathetic perspective taking and the granting of forgiveness, it prompted greater perceived control and comparatively lower physiological stress responses.

Is happiness more than experiencing positive emotions?

The term 'happiness' is often used in a broad sense (see, for example, the *World Happiness Report* 2015),[62] and may represent different things for different people, even among scholars. Sometimes, happiness is equated with simply experiencing satisfaction or positive emotions. At other times, happiness is equated with experiencing positive emotions as much as possible and negative emotions as infrequently as possible. However, happiness represents more than 'merely' experiencing emotions. In this section, we discuss happiness as subjective wellbeing (SWB) or as psychological wellbeing (PWB). We acknowledge, however, that 'happiness at work' is a big umbrella under which many related and overlapping constructs are housed (Table 4.1). The most central and frequently used of these constructs is job satisfaction.[63]

Subjective wellbeing (SWB)

Subjective wellbeing is defined as 'a person's cognitive and affective evaluations of his or her life'.[65] The cognitive element refers to how the individual thinks about his/her life satisfaction, both in global terms (i.e., life as a whole) and in specific domains (e.g., at work, in relationships). The affective component refers to emotions, moods and feelings. Affect is positive when the emotions, moods and feelings experienced are pleasant (e.g. joy, pleasure, excitement, contentment, etc.). Affect is negative when the emotions, moods and feelings experienced are unpleasant (e.g., guilt, anger, shame, etc.). Having a high level of SWB (i.e., being happy) thus means having a high level of life satisfaction, experiencing greater positive affect and little or less negative affect. The concept of SWB is aligned with the 'hedonic' perspective (see Chapter 1), which considers wellbeing or happiness as resulting mainly from maximizing pleasure and avoiding or minimizing pain. The hedonic perspective differs from the eudemonic perspective (see Chapter 1), which considers happiness as living according to one's 'true self' by experiencing meaning in life and self-realization.

Table 4.1 Happiness-related constructs in the workplace, as suggested by Fisher (2010)[64]

Transient level (i.e., momentary; short-lived moods and emotions that individuals experience at work)	Individual level (answers the question: why are some employees happier or unhappier than others?)	Collective level (i.e., happiness of collectives such as teams, work units or organizations)
• State job satisfaction • Momentary affect • Flow state • Momentary mood at work • State engagement • Task enjoyment • Emotion at work • State intrinsic motivation	• Job satisfaction • Dispositional affect • Affective organizational commitment • Job involvement • Typical mood at work • Engagement (i.e., vigour and learning) • Thriving • Vigour • Flourishing • Affective wellbeing at work	• Morale/collective job satisfaction • Group affective tone • Group mood • Unit-level engagement • Group task satisfaction

---

Box 4.4 Negative in the positive, positive in the negative: job satisfaction

Job satisfaction is the component of 'happiness' at work that has been most studied, possibly based on the assumption that a satisfied worker is a productive worker.[66] Interestingly this assumption does not hold as strongly as one would imagine. Job satisfaction has been defined as a 'pleasurable emotional state resulting from the appraisal of one's job',[67] and can be contrasted with engagement where employees additionally present with high-level activation. In other words, work engagement is a more positive workplace assessment than job satisfaction. Although employees who indicate high job satisfaction may experience high positive affect, they may have low work-related aspirations or energy.[68] The satisfaction they feel towards their jobs may in fact dampen their levels of aspiration.[69] Or, employees with high satisfaction, as indicated by low activation and high positive affect, may appreciate that the job they have, while not ideal, could be a lot worse.

Applied to the workplace, a person has high work-related SWB if he/she (a) is satisfied with their job (cognitive evaluation), and (b) experiences more frequent positive emotions than negative ones (affective experience).[70] Such a person would likely experience high work engagement (top right quadrant of the circumplex model). Conversely, someone with low work-related SWB, having negative cognitive evaluations of their job satisfaction and experiencing more negative emotions, may be suffering from workaholism (top left quadrant) or burnout (bottom left quadrant of the circumplex model).

Psychological wellbeing (PWB)

Subjective wellbeing and psychological wellbeing are sometimes spoken of interchangeably; however, they differ.[71] The literature is unclear on how they differ but a possible distinction considers that while SWB represents hedonic happiness, PWB represents eudemonic happiness. One of the most important models of PWB was proposed by Ryff,[72] viewing wellbeing as not just feeling good but having positive life evaluations across six dimensions: (1) purpose in life, (2) personal growth, (3) environmental mastery, (4) positive relationships, (5) autonomy and (6), self-acceptance (Figure 4.3).[73] While SWB and PWB are highly correlated and represent a general factor of global wellbeing, they represent distinct aspects of positive psychological functioning.[74] Both SWB and PWB are further used interchangeably with happiness, which is regarded as a less precise lay or colloquial term. Having pointed out these academic distinctions, for the rest of this chapter we will treat these terms interchangeably, following lay conventions.

Consequences of (un)happiness at work

People's happiness is strongly associated with or even causes positive life outcomes such as physical health, mental health, longevity, strong relationships, cognitive clarity and greater work productivity. As Lyubomirsky and colleagues have argued, numerous studies have shown that individuals with high levels of PWB or happiness are successful across multiple life domains, including marriage, friendship, income, health, work performance and career success.[75] In the following section we focus primarily on the workplace implications of happiness for work engagement, workplace relationships, work performance and creativity.[76]

Work engagement

Happier employees demonstrate higher levels of work engagement, frequently defined as 'a positive, fulfilling, work-related state of mind that is characterized by vigor, dedication, and absorption'.[77] Vigour is indicated by energy and enthusiasm even in the face of setbacks, contrasting with the slow emptiness and burnout that sometimes characterize people's lived experience. Dedication suggests high involvement and investment in work activities, going 'above and beyond' to achieve goals that provide a sense of meaning and purpose. Absorption is indicated through strong interest and deep concentration when performing work activities.

Engaged workers have high energy, are self-sufficient and command a strong sense of control over the events influencing their lives.[78] They further demonstrate independence in creating positive feedback loops for themselves, giving and receiving recognition and appreciation.[79] Unlike workaholics, engaged employees also have high levels of energy and enthusiasm for activities beyond the workplace, such as athletic pursuits, volunteering and hobbies.[80] Even when feeling exhausted at the conclusion of a hard day's work, engaged employees tend to view their being tired as something pleasant, associating it with meaningful achievements. Work engagement is positively associated with organizational commitment, performance and health and negatively associated with turnover intentions.[81] Such a happy and engaged workforce thereby contributes to higher levels of organizational performance.[82]

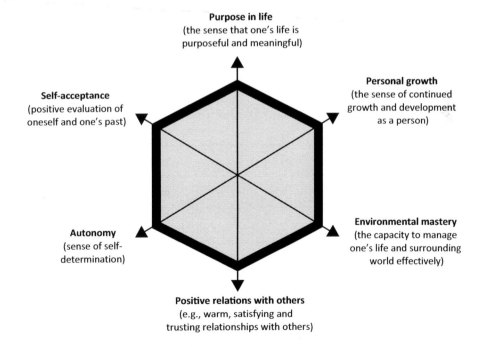

Figure 4.3 The six-factor model of PWB (by Carol Ryff).

Positive workplace relationships

The association between positive emotional states and positive relationships has been established in the literature for some time.[83] Within the organizational context, positive interpersonal relationships are one of the most important predictors of employee wellbeing,[84] regardless of gender and working time (full-time versus part-time). Positive interpersonal workplace relationships have been identified by research as an important predictor of work performance (see Chapter 6). In one study participants were given measures of positive affect before completing a series of job-related group tasks, where performance was rated by peer and professional staff in terms of interpersonal behaviour.[85] Peers judged those with higher levels of positive affect as making greater contributions towards group performance. Staff observers also rated the participation and leadership of people with high positive affect more highly than those with low or medium positive affect. Similarly, high positive affect individuals were also rated highly for their knowledge of the information required to persuasively present their cases. Interestingly, there were no significant effects of positive affect on the measures for social compliance, politeness or being critical. The researchers suggest that what 'this pattern of data seems to show is that positive affect is not necessarily responsible for people being just nice or accommodating but, rather, more effective interpersonally'.[86] Furthermore the researchers suggest that these findings rule out the possibility of the study results being accounted for by halo effects:

> If halo or liking accounted for all the interpersonal effects, one would have expected the strongest results to have been manifested on affectively toned items. Yet, there were no significant effects on the items such as being critical, social compliance, and politeness. Instead, the strongest results were evidenced on the performance related measures.[87]

One more reason given by the researchers for ruling out the halo effect was that the ratings provided by peers or professionally trained staff consistently rated those with high positive affect as being more competent in interpersonal relations than those with low or medium affect, with no significant difference between the peer and staff ratings.

It should be noted that the association between positive emotional states and interpersonal relationships does not mean, per se, that it is positive emotions that *cause* more positive socioemotional relationships. Literature suggests that it can be the other way around as well (see also Chapter 6), as we discuss below (section on 'Antecedents of individual happiness'). The reciprocal causality (happiness →positive social relationships →happiness) illustrates the notion of positive upward spirals at work.[88]

Cognitive processing and creativity

The 'happy but dumb' or 'sad but wise' view is disputed by a vast amount of research supporting a positive relationship between positive affect and creativity.[89] A longitudinal study of 222 employees assessed daily creativity from self-report, other-report and daily diary entries across seven organizations to ascertain if positive affect was associated with enhanced creativity.[90] The findings indicated a strong linear association between high positive mood and organizational creativity. Another study, undertaken within the knitwear industry, found that positive mood plays a mediating role in facilitating the support provided to employees performing creative work, which enhances their creative performance.[91] Note, however, that some research suggests that it is the interplay between positive and negative emotions, rather than positive emotions alone, that explain creativity, an issue we discuss below.

Work performance

While it might not be surprising that research also indicates that people rated with more positive emotions are also more satisfied with their jobs, it is interesting to note that they also tend to be evaluated more highly in productivity reports by their supervisors and have higher incomes. Staw, Sutton and Pelled measured 272 employees using various emotion scales and followed their job performance over an 18-month period.[92] Their study found that employees with more positive emotions received better supervisor evaluations, higher pay and received greater social support than their less happy peers.

In another study participants took measures of affective disposition before completing various simulations of workplace decision-making care and accuracy.[93] Participants with high levels of positive affect were significantly more accurate in their decisions, providing more accurate responses than those with either low or mid-level affect. Those with high positive affect further appeared to perform more effectively on the processes supporting effective decision-making. For example, when the data informing the decisions was insufficient those with high positive affect were more likely to request more information. Participants with high positive affect also demonstrated a tendency towards recognizing contextual contingencies, such as when a particular decision would have an adverse effect over other decisions. Within the context of sales, research has also found that salespeople's positive affect towards their clients is a significant predictor of sales performance.[94]

In attempting to discern whether positive emotion or productivity comes first, research methodologies that involve inducing positive states by offering rewards and then evaluating performance have found that when people are put into a positive mood they choose higher goals, show more endurance and perform better.[95] Positive affect may also lead to higher levels of work performance because people with higher levels of optimism and more positive perspectives on the world tend to bring more resilience, persistence and energy to their work.[96] Further, they may be friendlier and more engaging in their dealings with customers and colleagues.[97] High positive affect people may also expect the world to be benevolent on the basis of previous positive experiences with success, reinforcing a cycle of positive affect–expectation–performance. Emotional contagion also appears to play a role. As an illustration, a bank teller's positive mood has been identified as having a positive emotional contagion effect on clients, showing a positive linear relationship with high ratings of service quality from customers.[98] It may also be that the positive-affect/high-performance relationship is a general tendency that also depends upon the type of job. In some jobs, such as tax collection, more frequent displays of negative affect lead to higher performance. This leads us to discuss 'another side of the coin': the positive value of negative affect.

Box 4.5 The happy:grumpy ratio in a bank with a 'sad' ethical record

Consider the use of a happy:grumpy ratio at a bank in the USA:

> At Wells Fargo, managers have dreamt up a new ratio to track alongside such bank-ing stalwarts as provision coverage and capital adequacy. It is called the happy:grumpy ratio and measures the number of cheery staff the bank employs for every curmudgeon. The point of this exercise, executives told the *Wall Street Journal* ... was that happy employees are more likely to do the right thing than unhappy ones. Financial regulators, who have recently been exercising themselves about the nasty culture of banks, will no doubt be impressed. And they will be even more so when they see how this ratio is moving at the San Francisco bank. Only five years ago happy bankers (measured by their own assessment) outnumbered the grumpy ones by 3.8 to 1; by last year there were eight times as many Pollyannas at Wells Fargo as there were miserable sods. (*Lucy Kellaway doubts the data and sounds a sceptical note.*)
>
> When I first read about the happy:grumpy ratio, I thought it sounded so good it should become compulsory in the industry ... Even its premise is dubious. Are workers who claim to be happy really less likely to do bad things? There are no numbers to prove it; neither is there any obvious reason it should be so ... As for the numbers themselves, they look too good to be true. I don't believe for a moment that the happy outnumber the grumpy by eight to one among Wells Fargo's 260,000 people, nor is it likely that a ratio could double in such a short time ... If Wells Fargo produced such a statistic, I doubt if it would tell the regula-tor whether a scandal was round the corner.[99]

Questions for reflection

- Shortly after the sarcastic comment of Lucy Kellaway, Wells Fargo was caught in a scandal involving fake accounts and other unethical practices,[100] which resulted from a 'pressure-cooker sales culture'[101] and an aggressive management by objectives system.[102] How do you interpret the company's behaviour?
- Explore the case and reflect on how workers' 'happiness' may be used manipulatively by organizations. How do you interpret the criticism that some organizations and leaders aim to foster positivity simply to get more efforts from satisfied employees on an analogy with those contented cows that allegedly produce more milk?[103]

Grappling with complexity: the value of negative emotions

The arguments presented thus far might appear to be quite binary in nature, suggesting that positive emotions are good and negative emotions are bad. Such a conclusion, however, is overly simplistic. Indeed, positive psychology has been criticized for being 'negative about negativity'.[104] While there is substantial evidence concerning the dele-terious effects of negative emotions, individually[105] and organizationally,[106] negative emotions also play an important role in human survival – providing warnings about potential threats and the need to take action. There is a body of evidence suggesting that a combination of both positive and negative emotions supports optimum functioning. Two main theories may explain the relevance of such interplay: the broaden-and-build theory (discussed above) and the affect-as-information theory.[107]

According to the broaden-and-build theory, positive emotions enhance flexible thinking and encourage employees to focus on new possibilities and opportunities rather than problems and constraints. Broadening of employees' cognition and action tendencies can be cumulative and help them to build cognitive, psychological and social resources over time. On the other hand, negative affect has adaptive functions in problematic situations. Therefore, negativity may help the employee to focus on handling problems and threats. More specifically, while negative affect impels individuals to focus on 'threatening' situations, positive emotions *broaden* the employee's momentary thought-action repertoire and promote the discovery of novel and creative actions for dealing with such 'threats'. It is the interplay between the two *forces* that makes employees find not only *new* but also *useful* ideas to handle problems and opportunities.

The affect-as-information theory[108] suggests that individuals use emotions as information about how to respond to their environment and pursue goal attainment: positive emotions signal that all is well, while negative emotions signal that something needs to be changed, repaired, corrected or improved. Therefore, employees may stop working on tasks when they experience positive emotions, while they will continue to strive when they experience negative ones. If employees use negative affect to determine how they feel about their level of goal attainment, they will work more and persevere in trying to solve problems and overcome obstacles, including the search for creative solutions.

Consistent with this reasoning, a cross-sectional study of 595 retail employees in Portugal found an inverted-U relation between employees' positivity ratio and supervisor ratings of creativity[109] (see Box 4.6). This supports Amabile and colleagues' observation that, 'simultaneously experiencing positive and negative emotions may serve to activate a greater number of memory nodes, thereby increasing both cognitive variability and creativity'.[110] These scholars also found that some individuals who experienced frustration by repeated failures to solve a complex problem developed, as a consequence, more creative thought. They suggested that, by experiencing frustration, the employees may have increased motivation to triumph, thus allocating more time and effort to deal with the problem and come up with creative solutions. Negative emotions can also play an important role in drawing attention to organizational injustice and unfairness,[111] awareness of power dynamics,[112] as well as contributing towards better negotiation outcomes.[113]

Box 4.6 Positive in the negative, negative in the positive: emotions, stress and ratios

1 The positive side of 'getting mad'

As we discuss in this chapter, while positive emotions are beneficial, negative emotions can also play a role in organizations. Even anger, the quintessential negative emotion, can be positive. Anger can lead bosses to manage better. It can be a source of action against injustice. It can be an appropriate reaction to wrongdoing. As Geddes, Callister and Gibson argued, there are important messages to consider when employees get mad.[114]

2 The role of stress in optimum performance

To understand the significance of negative emotion let us consider stress, associated with negative emotions of fear, anxiety and anger, which exhibits a two-way inter-actional effect where too much stress increases negative emotion and where too much negative emotion also causes stress.[115] Even physiologically, too much stress is destructive, increasing the risk of strokes, ulcers, heart attack and mental illness. Too little stress, however, can have a dampening effect on positive emotion associated with boredom and a lack of motivation, optimism and hope. Between the extremes of too little and too much stress, then, lies the optimum ratio of positive and negative emotions that contributes to peak performance.

Research with some 200 hospital patients exposed to high levels of stress found that those with optimum levels of functioning demonstrated a 3:1 ratio, expressing three positive emotions for every negative emotion.[116] In the happiness literature, including within the workplace context, the balance between the stress induced by a challenging task and confidence in one's skill level to meet the challenge is understood to produce an enjoyable flow state of being in the zone, where complete absorption in the moment while performing a task causes time to just fly.[117]

3 Criticizing critical positivity ratios

One should note that positivity ratio theory has been strongly criticized by some authors.[118] However, even admitting that the theory is wrong and that 'there is no empirical evidence for critical positivity ratios',[119] the benefits of positive/negative emotion combinations should not be underestimated,[120] including predicting creativity. Fong[121] found that emotional ambivalence (i.e., the simultaneous experiences of positive and negative emotions) facilitated creativity. George and Zhou[122] found that, under some conditions, negative affect actually had a positive relation with creativity. Another study[123] found that employees were more creative when both positive and negative affects were high and when supervisors built a supportive context.

Antecedents of employees' happiness

Where does happiness come from?

Everyone experiences happiness and unhappiness, at least sometimes. But some people tend to be consistently (un)happier than others. A possible explanation is that chronic happiness levels in individuals have a genetic source. For example, a cheerful baby will potentially present with a happy disposition in their teen years, midlife and old age.

Based on studies with identical twins raised apart, scholars have concluded that genetics accounts for about 50 per cent of a person's chronic level of happiness.[124] The other two components are the environmental context and voluntary thoughts and behaviours. Surprisingly, research suggests that environmental factors such as wealth, beauty, education, age, gender, place of residence, job type, etc., account for only 10 per cent of a person's chronic level of happiness. This is surprising considering the energy we invest into improving our environments as a way of enhancing our experience of life, particularly happiness. The remaining 40 per cent of our emotional experience is informed by voluntary thoughts and behaviours.

The 'half empty glass' perspective would lead us to conclude that happiness is mostly determined by genetics, such that few things can be made to change the individual's chronic happiness level. However, the 'half full glass' leads to a different conclusion: happiness is significantly malleable. In fact, an important implication of the empirical evidence is that by choosing to do more of the things that research demonstrates do make a difference we can significantly influence our happiness.[125] Important factors that make a difference here include a healthy diet, regular exercise, rich relational-social interactions and engagement in hobbies or interests that provide a sense of meaning. Relevant to promoting engagement and meaning (or eudemonia) is the cultivation of virtuous responses to our past, present and future life experiences.[126]

Antecedents of employees' happiness

As the above discussion suggests, a significant portion of employees' happiness comes from their personal dispositions. For example, employees high on dispositional positive affectivity and core self-evaluations (see Chapter 2) tend to be happier at work.[127] However, the working context, including leaders' behaviours, interpersonal relationships and organizational policies and practices, also play a crucial role in people's happiness.[128] As Gavin and Mason[129] point out:

> It seems clear that if there is any hope for people to find general happiness in their lives today, they must be happy at work. Work by itself, of course, cannot make a person happy, but a person cannot be genuinely happy if he or she is unhappy at work.

De Neve also stated:[130]

> Work and employment play a central role in most people's lives. In OECD countries, for example, people spend around a third of their waking hours engaging in paid work. We not only spend considerable amounts of our time at work, employment and workplace quality also rank among the most important drivers of happiness.

Therefore, promoting employees' happiness is intrinsically beneficial and also a good way to promote individual and organizational performance.[131] The literature on the organizational antecedents of employees' happiness is abundant, which is why we present only a sample of relevant studies. Authentizotic organizational climates (e.g., cultures characterized by high levels of spirit of camaraderie, trust and credibility of the leader, open and frank communication with the leader,

opportunities for learning and personal development, fairness and work-family conciliation) are important predictors of employees' happiness[132] (see Chapter 9). Such
climates, together with providing employees with feelings of being respected,[133]
help employees to find support in fulfilling seven human needs or 'senses of' purpose, self-determination, impact, competence, belonging, meaning and enjoyment.
These senses meet two motivational needs of individuals that are of particular
interest for life in organizations: attachment/affiliation and exploration/assertion.[134]
These findings are consistent with studies suggesting that positive interpersonal
workplace relationships are one of the most important predictors of employee happiness (see Table 4.2). Feeney and Collins[135] suggested 'close and caring relationships are undeniably linked to health and well-being at all stages in the life span'.
The relationships between managers and employees are more relevant than relationships with co-workers. A significant number of individuals who leave their
organizations do so in order to get away from their bosses.[136] Studies have also
suggested that job/task characteristics are important predictors of employees' happiness. Illustrative factors are[137] work-scheduling autonomy, decision-making autonomy, task significance, task identity, task variety, feedback from the job and from
others, social support and supportive supervision, physical security and fairness.

It is important to point out that employee happiness emerges from the interplay
between individual and contextual/job/organizational characteristics. Different individuals react differently to a specific contextual factor. For example, individuals with
a stronger need for autonomy will react more positively to work-scheduling autonomy
and decision-making autonomy than employees who value such job features less.
Feedback from the job and from others is more important for individuals with high
achievement motivation and social support is probably more important for employees
with stronger affiliation needs.

Jan-Emmanuel de Neve[138] provided a global perspective about 'work and wellbeing' that is useful. He looked at job satisfaction as the happiness outcome of interest,
focussing on 12 domains of workplace quality. Table 4.2 presents those components,
ranking their importance. Again, positive interpersonal workplace relationships emerge
as one of the most important predictors of employee wellbeing,[139] regardless of
gender and working time (full-time versus part-time).

Fisher[141] adopted a broader approach (i.e., focussing on more than 'mere' job
satisfaction) and discussed two main routes to increase happiness at work. First,
employees may adopt individual actions such as practicing gratitude, nurturing relationships, finding activities adjusted to their individual characteristics and motivations in which they may experience flow, adjusting expectations to match reality,
finding another job that suits them better, adopting job crafting activities (see
Chapter 5), discovering their personal strengths and design or looking for jobs
where they can cultivate such strengths. Second, organizations may adopt the following actions:

- Creating a fair, respectful and supportive organizational culture.
- Supplying competent leadership (i.e., competent, supportive, respectful and devel-
  opmental) at all levels.
- Providing fair treatment (at the distributive, procedural and interactional levels)
  and security, and recognizing employees' efforts and contributions.
- Designing jobs that are interesting, challenging, autonomous and rich in feedback.

Table 4.2 Components of workplace quality that predict job satisfaction (by ranking of importance)[140]

1. Interpersonal relationships (i.e., contact with other people in general; subjective assessment of employees' relationship with management and co-workers)
2. Interesting job
3. Pay (the actual income of employees, and their subjective assessment of whether that income is high)
4. Work-life balance (i.e., work interfering with the family; difficulty of taking time off on short notice when needed; working on weekends)
5. Difficulty, stress, danger (i.e., physically taxing work; stressful work)
6. Job security
7. Opportunities for advancement
8. Independence (e.g., possibility to work with autonomy, including at home; daily work flexible vs. fixed; working hours flexible vs. fixed; job crafting)
9. Skills match (i.e., match between the skills the employee has and those necessary to perform the job)
10. Usefulness (i.e., doing something that is beneficial for other people or is useful for society)
11. Working hours mismatch (i.e., mismatch between the actual and the desired number of working hours)
12. (Number of) working hours

- Facilitating employees' skill development.
- Selecting for person–job and person–organization fit and enhancing such fit through using realistic job previews and appropriate socialization practices.
- Avoiding unrealistically positive 'promises' to employees and persuading them to reframe a current less-than-ideal work environment as acceptable.
- Adopting high performance work practices (i.e., high involvement and high commitment approaches, such as redesigning work to be performed by autonomous teams, being selective in employment, offering job security, investing in training and development, sharing information with employees and empowering them, adopting flat structures, rewarding for organizational performance).

Note the significant overlap between Fisher and De Neve's organizational factors affecting employees' performance. Careful attention shows that at least two main topics emerge: (1) job content richness (mainly in terms of intrinsic motivation and opportunities for development and growth) and (2) respectful interpersonal relationships. Positive social relationships are especially worth mentioning here because they have emerged as crucial for happiness across several domains and probably have a neurobiological base. In the *World Happiness Report* 2015, Richard Davidson and Brianna Schuyler wrote:[142]

One of the strongest predictors of well-being is the quality of an individual's social relationships. In fact, when individuals are made to experience social isolation many of the same brain regions become active that are active in the experience of physical pain. Behavior that increases social bonds (altruism and pro-social behavior) reliably increases well-being in children and adults and appears to be consistent across cultures.

Leadership and affect

Leadership is inherently an emotional process.[143] The relationship between affect and leadership is complex and multidimensional, one that may be approached from several perspectives. Do leaders' affective displays shape followers' affect and leadership effectiveness? How and why? Which mechanisms (e.g., emotional contagion and cognitive interpretation) explain the impact of leaders' affect on followers? Are happier leaders more affective? How do leaders' emotions affect their own judgements, attitudes and behaviours? How do leaders' emotions become contagious for team members and vice-versa? How are leaders' emotions conveyed via their facial expressions, body movements, their pitch and tone of voice? Which conditions moderate the relationship between leaders' affective displays and followers' affective, motivational and behavioural reactions?

A growing body of research has suggested that leaders' behaviours influence followers' affect; that the leaders' emotional displays influence followers' attitudes, cognitions, affective states and behaviours, although such influence is neither universal nor direct or linear.[144] The literature is so prolix that any synthesis would be insufficient to capture the richness of the topic. Therefore, we highlight a couple of highly relevant issues:[145]

- Leaders use emotional labour to regulate and gain control of their own emotions and to manage the followers' moods, job attitudes and performance.[146] For example, 'when times are tough, followers need to have confidence in their leaders, and followers cannot feel confident if their leaders are expressing fear, anxiety, and other confidence-sapping emotion'.[147]
- Leaders' behaviours influence followers' affect. For example, one study[148] suggests that supportive leadership fosters positive mood in followers leading to higher follower creativity. Another study[149] found that authentic leadership predicts employees' positive affect, which in turn predicts employee hope and creativity. These and other effects are likely contingent on some conditions. For example, a study[150] found that followers' affect is more negative under conditions of autocratic leadership *and* low distributive fairness (e.g., the relationship between leader distributive justice and followers' negative emotions was significant when the leadership style was low in autocratic behaviour). Another study[151] found that the leader's procedural fairness (i.e., 'giving' voice, versus 'not giving' voice to followers) interacts with followers' need to belong, in predicting followers' positive emotions: followers' emotions are more positive under conditions of voice but only for individuals with a higher need to belong. A possible explanation is that having voice helps satisfy the need to belong of those who are high in that need.
- Leaders' happiness may also affect followers' reactions, both at the individual and collective levels. A study[152] found that leaders who experience more pleasantness at work are rated by their subordinates as more transformational, a relationship partially mediated by leaders' affective organizational commitment (i.e., a happy leader will be more affectively committed and this leads followers to consider him/her as more transformational). Evidence[153] further suggests that the leader's happiness enhances team performance, both directly and through two mediators. Specifically, happy leaders (1) are more likely to engage in transformational leadership and also (2), foster positive group affective tone (see the section 'Emotions

at the collective level', next). As a consequence, team goal commitment, team satisfaction and team helping behaviours increase, which in turn leads to higher team performance.

• The leader's displays of positive affect may motivate followers either because his/ her positivity is motivating or because the leader's affect is contagious and produces positive affective states in followers that are motivating and lead them to be more effective. However, some evidence also suggests that the leader's negative affective displays contribute to their motivational effectiveness (e.g., the leader's negative mood leads to greater effort).[154] The effectiveness of leader displays of positive as compared with negative affect may depend on the leadership effectiveness criterion in question:[155] the leader's displays of happiness enhance follower creative performance, while a leader's displays of unhappiness enhance follower analytical performance.

• The match or similarity between leader affective displays and follower affect may also influence follower performance, this being higher when the valence of the leader's affective display is more in line with the level of follower positive affect.[156] A study[157] found that teams composed of individuals with lower agreeableness perform better when their leader expresses anger, whereas teams composed of participants with a higher level of agreeableness perform better when the leader expresses happiness.

Overall,[158] the research suggests that the leader's emotions influence leadership effectiveness. That influence is not direct, neither is it universal. It is not direct in that the influence occurs through several mechanisms, including the following two:[159] (1) emotional contagion and (2) cognitive interpretation of leader affect (e.g., followers make inferences about the leader's personality by interpreting the leader's emotional displays). The influence is not universal in that it is contingent on several conditions. For example, the influence is stronger when followers are more susceptible to emotional contagion.

The general pattern emerging from research, according to Koning and Van Kleef,[160] is that: (a) 'expressions of happiness enhance followers' task performance to the degree that the expressions elicit positive affective reactions (i.e., positive emotions, increased liking) in followers'; (b) 'leaders' expressions of happiness undermine followers' performance to the degree that followers infer from the leader's happiness that no additional effort is needed to meet organizational goals'; (c) leaders' expressions of anger 'enhance followers' performance to the degree that followers deduce from the leader's anger that their performance was insufficient'; (d) 'leaders' expressions of anger undermine followers' performance to the degree that they elicit negative affective reactions (i.e., negative emotions, reduced liking) in followers'.

Emotions at the collective level

Group affective tone

In recent years, research has shown that affect may be a collective phenomenon. Group affective tone is one the most important constructs in this regard. As argued above, although affective states are influenced by dispositional factors, they are also shaped by outside influences. For example, in teams, the individuals' affective states are influenced by the affective states and dispositions of other team members.[161]

Consequently, affect converges between individuals, thus giving rise to group affective tone,[162] which is defined as the 'consistent or homogeneous affective reactions within a group'.[163] Consistency is definitionally central in that 'if affective reactions are not consistent within groups, then it is meaningless to speak of an affective tone of the groups'.[164]

Several processes that explain group affective tone include: emotional contagion,[165] behavioural entrainment,[166] empathy,[167] attraction-selection-attrition,[168] socialization to group affective norms[169] and exposure to common affective events.[170] Affective convergence at the collective level may also occur indirectly through spillover (i.e., simply witnessing affective interactions between other team members).[171] These processes, in turn, are affected by several individual and team factors.[172] For example, in teams composed of individuals characterized by high emotional contagion susceptibility and by a high level of emotional intelligence (see the section about this topic below), affective convergence and the development of group affective tone are more likely. Exposure to common affective events also makes affective convergence and the development of group affective tone more likely.

Group affective tone and performance

It is generally assumed that a higher group positive affective tone is more beneficial for team functioning and performance than a lower group positive affective tone, and that a higher group negative affective tone will produce less beneficial outcomes than a lower group negative affective tone.[173] For example, high levels of negative affective tone may give rise to more problematic conflicts and less prosocial behaviours, distracting members from task completion. In contrast, the broaden-and-build perspective, discussed above, suggests that group positive affect can lead to higher team performance through increasing the amount of information shared between team members, fostering goal commitment.[174] Some research has supported such a prediction: group positive affective tone associates with higher team performance.[175] However, group positive affective tone may be less positive than is often assumed. Group positive affective tone may lead to a single-shared reality, to a higher motivation toward conformity, hindering performance in complex tasks that require diverse perspectives about reality. As a consequence, the team may develop less effort and be more complacent. Therefore, it is likely that the positive effect of the group positive affective tone on performance depends on the team tasks and on team characteristics. For example, a high group positive affective tone can be detrimental for team performance in creative tasks when there is a high amount of trust in the team:[176] when both positive tone and intra-team trust are higher, team members are less likely to express differing opinions and to explore different routes to handle problems and opportunities, leading to less creativity.

Other research has shown that the effect of group positive affective tone on team performance depends on team emotional skills (a kind of team emotional intelligence). Emotional skills at the team level are conceptualized

> as the average of individual member emotional skills, based on the notion of emotional skills as a 'resource that team members draw on and that members of the team can pool their abilities to share and compensate for one another'.
>
> (Elfenbein, 2006, p. 170)[177]

Examples of team emotional skills are team members being aware of their emotions (e.g., recognizing their positive or negative feelings) and managing not only their but also others' emotions (e.g., downplaying both positivity and negativity when necessary). Such emotional skills moderate the relationship between positive affective tone and performance because of the following:

- Positive affective tone facilitates increased information sharing and goal commitment toward team goals when teams have high levels of collective emotional skills.
- Positive affective tone hinders team performance when the level of collective emotional skills is low, because low emotional skills lead to groupthink (see Chapter 7) and task complacency.

Research by Collins and colleagues suggests, 'that positive affective tone is not universally helpful to team performance'.[178] Complex tasks of decision-making or idea generation entail that a team's potential for managing collective emotions will be important in ensuring optimal team outcomes are achieved from a positive affective tone.

In short, both positive and negative affective tone may have positive and negative consequences for team functioning and performance, depending on team conditions and circumstances. Moreover, as George[179] argued with her dual-tuning perspective, 'researchers should consider the combined effects of positive and negative affect. Both positive and negative affect are adaptive for different reasons and it is through their combined effects that effective functioning results in and outside of organizations'.

Emotional intelligence

Emotional intelligence is defined as individual competency in recognizing emotions, in one's self and others, differentiating between and appropriately labelling various feelings, drawing upon emotional information to guide thoughts and behaviours, and managing emotions in changing environments or goal achievement.[180] Research on emotional intelligence (EI) in organizations started after the publication of seminal theoretical articles by Salovey and Mayer.[181] It was Daniel Goleman, however, who popularized EI through his 1995 *New York Times* bestselling book *Emotional Intelligence: Why it can matter more than IQ*.[182] In the book, the Intelligence Quotient (IQ), often used as a predictor for academic success, is contrasted with an Emotional Intelligence Quotient (E-IQ), believed necessary for success in life outside the classroom, including in the workplace (see Box 4.7).

People with sophisticated EI find that it acts as a touchstone for enhanced personal performance, including influence over others, group collaboration and workplace excellence. According to Goleman, personality characteristics accompanying high IQ typically include critical and condescending attitudes, sensual discomfort, inhibition and emotional blandness. In contrast, those associated with high EI include poise, gregariousness, confidence, as well as commitment to causes and people, caring and sympathy. Goleman's ideas quickly attracted a 'flood of interest from the business community' prompting him to write *Working with Emotional Intelligence*, which is about the application of EI in the organizational context.[183] The promising message of this work is that teaching EI in the workplace will lead to reduced bullying with greater caring, compassion and cooperation.

Box 4.7 The Big Bang Theory: who is the smartest character?

Who is the smartest of the six main characters in the popular sitcom *The Big Bang Theory?* Well, it depends on how you define smart. In terms of IQ and broad reading Sheldon has the highest IQ and an eidetic memory. On this basis the order would probably be Sheldon, Raj, Leonard, Howard, Amy, Bernadette, with Penny last. But is Sheldon really that smart? Most of the time he seems quite ignorant. Due to a lack of empathy, he interprets conversational language too literally. His inability to understand the language of feelings conveyed through irony, sarcasm and humour and his general lack of social skills become the cause of ongoing social awkwardness. Sheldon lacks EI.

In terms of social skills and common sense, the order of intelligence gets reversed: Penny, Bernadette, Leonard, Howard, Raj, Amy, Sheldon. Yes, Penny is the most emotionally intelligent of all the characters! Penny may be less educated but she is not unintelligent: there is a big difference between the gloss of education and the ability to act intelligently. Contrasting extreme characterizations of academic and emotional intelligence creates comic effect, which is the winning formula that has made *The Big Bang Theory* one of the world's most loved TV shows.

Can you think of any other TV shows where the main plot draws on contrasting the attitudes of characters epitomizing academic and emotional intelligence?

Emotional intelligence has 'important implications for selecting employees and managing their performance' (see Box 4.8).[184] It also has implications for transformational leadership.[185] EI may also develop at the team/group level,[186] although high emotionally intelligent individuals do not necessarily give rise to a high emotionally intelligent team. In this chapter, we focus on individual EI although we do consider some organizational implications.

Box 4.8 Clarifying terms related to EI

1 Different scholars use the expression 'emotional intelligence' to mean different things.[187] EI has been considered as a set of cognitive abilities (ability model), while other approaches combine abilities with a broad range of personality traits (mixed models).[188] Both the ability and the mixed models have strengths and limitations,[189] although Côté has suggested that 'to avoid committing the jingle fallacy, researchers should instead select ability models of EI'.[190] The most popular mixed model was proposed by Goleman[191] and includes 25 competencies grouped into five categories (see Table 4.2).

2 Emotional regulation may be considered as a dimension of EI. It represents the individual's attempts to 'influence which emotions they have, when they have them, how they experience and express these emotions'.[192] Emotional labour is the process of emotional regulation for pursuing organizational goals.[193] Emotional labour 'refers to the process by which workers are expected to manage their feelings in accordance with organizationally defined rules and guidelines' and is 'typically measured by observing workers' interactions with customers in natural settings'.[194] Emotional labour involves both deep acting (modifying feelings) and surface acting (modifying expressions of feelings, i.e., expressing a 'fake' feeling). Surface acting may lead to emotional exhaustion.[195] Highly emotionally intelligent individuals are likely more effective in performing emotional labour.[196]

Dimensions of EI

Different definitions and dimensions of EI have been proposed. For example, Salovey and Mayer defined EI as 'The ability to monitor one's own and others' feelings, to discriminate among them, and to use this information to guide one's thinking and action'.[197] Later, these authors[198] refined this definition and considered EI as composed of four abilities: perceiving, using, understanding and managing emotions.[199] In contrast, Goleman's emotional competence framework comprises five categories, three being personal competencies (self-awareness, self-regulation and motivation) and two being social competencies (empathy, social skills). Classified under the five categories are 25 additional emotional competencies that are learned capabilities rather than innate talents (Table 4.2). General EI is thought to determine individual potential for learning emotional competencies.[200]

The dark side and limits of EI

While the initial theorizing and research on EI seemed to suggest that by teaching EI in schools, workplaces and hospitals we would have more caring communities and healthier and more effective individuals and organizations, enthusiasm for EI has been tempered in recent times. Two main issues mitigate such enthusiasm.

First, although research has suggested that EI at work may produce several desirable effects (e.g., emotionally intelligent leaders are more effective[201] and emotionally intelligent workers denote higher performance),[202] the relationship is contingent on several factors and conditions.[203] For example, it is likely that the relationship between EI and job performance is stronger in jobs with higher emotional labour demands than in jobs with lower emotional labour demands. High emotional regulation has a mixed scorecard as a predictor of high performance depending upon the nature of the profession.[204] High emotional intelligence is found to be an asset facilitating stress management and enhanced performance in professions requiring emotional sensitivity, such as sales, real estate, call-centre work and counselling. In work with lower emotional demands, however, EI is a performance inhibitor. For accountants, scientists and mechanics, high emotional intelligence can be a liability.

The second point relates to the dark side of EI. A new body of evidence indicates that people can consciously develop their emotional skills not just as a force for good but also as a tool for manipulation.[205] Machiavellians tend to be highly emotionally aware and practice emotion regulation to hide their true feelings and fabricate favourable impressions. They sometimes use knowledge of what others feel to influence them in acting against their own personal interests. Sensitivity towards others can also be directed towards demeaning and embarrassing others for personal gain. Kilduff,

Chiaburu and Menges provide a poker analogy: 'a poker player with high EI can detect the emotions of other players around the table and use that information to advantage, while simultaneously controlling and regulating self-emotional display'.[206]

Empathy, one crucial dimension of EI, may lead to other negative consequences. As Waytz argued,[207] empathy 'takes us mentally and emotionally, it's not an infinite resource, and it can even impair our ethical judgment'. For example, an empathic leader may close his/her eyes to unethical behaviours of other organizational members because he/she anticipates that those perpetrators will suffer if they are accused of wrongdoing. Empathy may inhibit whistleblowing and lead individuals to lie, cheat or steal to benefit the person with whom they empathize. At worst, empathy may lead to racism and violence:[208] empathizing with some people can lead us to be unreasonably cruel to others. For this reason, as Gjersoe writes, Paul Bloom recommended adopting reasoned compassion instead of empathy:[209]

> He argues that reasoned compassion, utilitarian cost-benefit calculations and sticking to moral principles are much fairer and more reliable guides to moral behaviour. Compassion and empathy may seem to be inextricably intertwined but imaging studies reveal that they activate different areas of the brain. Furthermore, in these studies empathy training frequently led to empathetic distress, a precursor to emotional burnout, inactivity and lack of engagement with those in distress. Compassion training, by contrast, not only predicted moral behaviour on subsequent tasks but also boosted resilience which in turn fostered better coping in stressful situations.

The negative in positive is illustrated below (see Box 4.9).

Box 4.9 The negative in positive

EI as an inhibitor of work performance

We have seen that high emotional intelligence can be considered a liability for roles believed to require a detached engagement with data.

1 Do you choose fairness or empathy?

Imagine the following scenario:[210]

> Sheri Summers is a bright ten-year-old girl who is suffering from a life-threatening condition which has already paralyzed her. Unless she receives treatment soon it is likely that she will die. If she receives the treatment the condition can be reversed. However, the treatment that could help her is only available via private healthcare and her family cannot afford it. They have joined a children's charity that helps families to pay for expensive treatments for life-threatening diseases but she is far down the waiting list. You have the option of moving her to the top of the waiting list but doing so will mean that other children who are higher on the list due to earlier application, greater need or shorter life expectancy will have to wait longer.

Questions for reflection

- Imagine that you had met Sheri and have realized how much she was suffering. Would you choose to move her to the top of the waiting list?
- Imagine now that you hadn't met Sheri and you realized that, by benefiting her, we would put other suffering children in danger. What would you do?

Final comments

Individuals (including leaders), teams, organizations and all collective action involve not only rational and relational entities but also emotional ones. However, it wasn't until the economic restructuring of the advanced economies in the 1980s away from a manufacturing economy towards a services economy that management began purposefully and strategically to turn attention to human emotions in designing a dedicated organizational culture emphasizing specific values, attitudes and purposes. Research has tried to answer questions such as: (a) Are happy employees more effective? (b) Are emotionally intelligent leaders more effective? (c) What is the role played by negative emotions in individual and collective performance? (e) Does 'happiness' develop at the team and organizational levels (i.e., does it make sense to consider teams and organizations as being more or less happy?).

This chapter provides some tentative answers to these and other questions. The main 'answer' is that positive affect and happiness, although important for individual and collective functioning and health, must be approached through a realistic and balanced perspective. Both positive and negative emotions are important, with both producing possible positive and negative consequences. Even EI, once considered as a kind of 'medicine' for leadership and organizational maladies, has a dark side, with its effects being limited.

Therefore, if you, the reader, want to experience and foster positivity around you, including in your workplace, be realistic and prepared for the fruits of the interplay between positive and negative emotions. In your search for creating happy employees and positive teams, you may end up being manipulative and producing misery. If you wish to be happy at work, don't be too idealistic: in your search for personal happiness you may end up very unhappy.[211] As Mauss et al. argued,[212] valuing happiness 'could be self-defeating, because the more people value happiness, the more likely they will feel disappointed. This should apply particularly in positive situations, in which people have every reason to be happy'. As the great philosopher, John Stuart Mill, once wrote,[213] 'those only are happy who have their minds fixed on some object other than their own happiness'. A similar effect may be found for organizations and this explains why some have suggested (see Box 4.1) that Chief Happiness Officers should be retired.

Want more?

For a critical review of the emergence of emotion within organizations (with a specific focus on organizational compassion) read Simpson, Clegg and Pitsis' article '"I used to care but things have changed": A genealogy of compassion in organizations'.[214] In reconstructing the history of managerial use of compassion as a technology of power, the authors demonstrate how compassion has been repeatedly re-defined in accordance with changing needs of different economic imperatives.

Barbara Frederickson has written numerous publications on her *broaden-and-build* theory. A great summary of this work with a specific organizational focus is a chapter Frederickson wrote for the *Handbook of Positive Organizational Scholarship* titled 'Positive emotions and upward spirals in organizations'.[215]

Important works about the relevance of happiness at work are, e.g., Boehm and Lyubomirsky, De Neve, Fisher, and Lyubomirsky, King and Diener.[216] To reflect on the 'happiness traps' and how 'we sabotage ourselves at work', read McKee,[217] as well as Fitz et al.[218] and Mauss et al.[219]

For the relationship between leadership and affect, three papers may be particularly helpful: Gooty et al., Kaplan et al. and Van Knippenberg and Van Kleef.[220]

If you are interested in learning more about emotional intelligence within the organizational context then Goleman's groundbreaking text *Emotional Intelligence and why it can matter more than IQ* is still one of the best resources.[221] Although published more than two decades ago, the book is packed with practical examples of how to develop your emotional intelligence and apply it for greater effectiveness in your relationships, work and personal health. To understand the relevance of EI in organizations, Côté's review is also very helpful.[222] A critical perspective may be found in the paper 'Emotional Intelligence: sine qua non of leadership or folderol?'[223] by Walter et al.

Glossary

Affect   'Umbrella term encompassing a broad range of feelings that individuals experience, including feeling states, such as moods and discrete emotions, and traits, such as trait positive and negative affectivity.'[224]

Autonomic nervous system   A bodily control system that functions largely automatically in regulating heart rate, respiratory rate, digestion, pupillary response, urination, sexual arousal and other bodily functions. The two branches of the autonomic nervous system are the sympathetic nervous system or the 'fight or flight' response and the parasympathetic nervous system or the 'rest and digest' response.

Broaden-and-build theory   A theory which posits that humans adapted positive emotions through evolutionary processes to fulfil the important survival mechanism of broadening-and-building Palaeolithic humans' thought-action physical, psychological, intellectual and social repertoires that could be later drawn upon for survival-advantage in times of threat.

Circumplex model of emotion   The circumplex model holds that emotions arise from two neurophysiological systems, one concerned with a continuum of positive-negative affect, the other concerned with a continuum of how-low activation, arousal or attention.

Dispositional (trait) affect 'Overall personality tendency to respond to situations in stable, predictable ways. A person's "affective lens" on the world'.[225] It can be positive (positive affectivity trait) and negative (negative affectivity trait).

Emotional contagion The process that allows 'the sharing or transferring of emotions from one individual to other group members; the tendency to mimic the nonverbal behavior of others, to "synchronize facial expressions, vocalizations, postures, and movements" with others, and in turn, to converge emotionally'.[226]

Emotional convergence The tendency for the emotions within teams to change in convergent ways. Convergence unfolds as a consequence of several processes (e.g., emotional contagion, empathy, attraction-selection-attrition, socialization to group affective norms, as well as exposure to common affective events and spillover effects).

Emotional labour 'Refers to the process by which workers are expected to manage their feelings in accordance with organizationally defined rules and guidelines.'[227]

Emotional regulation The individuals' attempts to 'influence which emotions they have, when they have them, and how they experience and express these emotions.'[228]

Engagement 'A positive, fulfilling, work-related state of mind that is characterized by vigor, dedication, and absorption.'[229]

Flight or fight response A state of hyper arousal associated with the emotions of fear and anger in response to a perceived threat. Activated by the sympathetic nervous system with the secretion of stress hormones, the response is symptomized by physiological reactions of quickened heart rate, paling or flushing, slower digestion, tense muscles, dilation of pupils, bladder relaxation, inhibition of erection, hearing loss, tunnel vision and shaking.

Group affective tone 'Consistent or homogeneous affective reactions within a group'[230] (see 'emotional contagion' and 'emotional convergence' in this table).

Happiness A lay term represented in the constructs of SWB and PWB. A possible distinction considers that while SWB represents hedonic happiness, PWB represents eudemonic happiness.

Human relations movement An approach to management emphasizing employee group climate related to the fulfilment of emotional and social needs in contributing to organizational productivity.

Job satisfaction A 'pleasurable emotional state resulting from the appraisal of one's job'.[231]

Mood 'Generally takes the form of a global positive (pleasant) or negative (unpleasant) feeling; tend to be diffuse – not focused on a specific cause – and often not realized by the perceiver of the mood; medium duration (from a few moments to as long as a few weeks or more).'[232]

Subjective wellbeing (SWB) 'A person's cognitive and affective evaluations of his or her life.'[233]

Psychological wellbeing (PWB) PWB, such as proposed by Ryff, includes six dimensions: (1) purpose in life, (2) personal growth, (3) environmental mastery, (4) positive relationships, (5) autonomy and (6), self-acceptance.[234]

Notes

1   Ashkanasy and Daus (2002).
2   Rose (1989).
3   Knowles (2015); Messinger (2015).
4   Mayo (1949/2003).
5   Taylor (1911).
6   Hassard (2012).
7   Jacques (1996).
8   www.linkedin.com/jobs/view/744917441/.
9   Chamorro-Premuzic (2017). All quotes are from this article.

10   Messinger (2015). All quotes are from this article.
11   Mayo (1949/2003).
12   Miller and Rose (1994).
13   O'Connor (1999).
14   Hochschild (1983).
15   Blanksby (1987); Cowland (1989); Josserand, Teo and Clegg (2006).
16   Kelemen (2000, 2002).
17   Chen (2018).
18   Fournier and Grey (2000).
19   Du Gay (2008).
20   Peters and Waterman (1982, p. 235).
21   Hoban (2012).
22   Featherston (2018); see also Rosenzweig (2014).
23   Peters (2001).
24   Rose (1985).
25   McCoy (2007).
26   Kelan (2008).
27   Solomon (1997, 1998).
28   Solomon (1998, p. 518).
29   Solomon (1998, p. 531).
30   Solomon (1998, p. 16).
31   Mackey and Sisodia (2013, pp. 28–29).
32   Barsade and Gibson (2017, p. 36).
33   Barsade and Gibson (2007, p. 38).
34   Frijda (1994).
35   Gable and Harmon-Jones (2008, p. 476).
36   Barsade and Gibson (2007, p. 38).
37   Barsade and Gibson (2007, p. 38).
38   Barsade and Gibson (2007, p. 38).
39   Lam, Spreitzer and Fritz (2014).
40   Lam, Spreitzer and Fritz (2014, p. 532).
41   Barsade and Gibson (2007, p. 38); see also Hatfield, Cacioppo and Rapson (1994).
42   Barsade (2002); Lehmann-Willenbrock, Chiu, Lei and Kauffeld (2017).
43   Russell (1980).
44   Saarm (1999).
45   Russell and Fehr (1994).
46   Watson and Clark (1992).
47   Lang, Bradley and Cuthbert (1998); Larsen and Diener (1992); Russell (1980).
48   Bakker & Orlemans (2012).
49   Model modified from BusiRhee and Yoon's (2012) adaptation of Russell's (1980) Circumplex
      Model to the organizational context.
50   Fredrickson (1998).
51   Cabiria (2008); Roepke (2013).
52   Fredrickson (1998).
53   Fredrickson (2003, p. 164).
54   Fredrickson and Levenson (1998).
55   vanOyen Witvliet, Ludwig and Vander Laan (2001).
56   Fredrickson and Branigan (2005).
57   Heaphy and Dutton (2008).
58   Ekman, Levenson and Friesen (1983); Todaro, Shen, Niaura, Spiro and Ward (2003).
59   Lawler et al. (2003); Oman, Thoresen and McMahon (1999); Post (2005); Wilson and
      Musick (1999).
60   Heaphy and Dutton (2008).
61   Berry, Benson and Klemchuk (1974); Morris and Maisto (2005); Newberg and Iversen
      (2003).
62   Helliwell, Layard and Sachs (2015).
63   Fisher (2010).

64   Adapted from Fisher (2010, p. 385).
65   Diener, Lucas and Oishi (2002, p. 63).
66   BusiRhee and Yoon (2012); Fisher (2010).
67   Locke (1969, p. 317).
68   Grebner, Semmer and Elfering (2005).
69   Büssing, Bissels, Fuchs and Perrar (1999).
70   BusiRhee and Yoon (2012).
71   Chen, Jing, Hayes and Lee (2013).
72   Ryff (1989); Ryff and Keyes (1995); Ryff and Singer (2006, 2008).
73   The six-factor model was criticized by Springer, Hauser and Freese (2006).
74   Chen, Jing, Hayes and Lee (2013).
75   See, e.g., Boehm and Lyubomirsky (2008) and Lyubomirsky, King and Diener (2005).
76   See Fisher (2010) for distinguishing consequences of happiness at different levels: transient/ momentary happiness, person-level happiness, and collective-level happiness.
77   Schaufeli, Salanova, González-Romá and Bakker (2002, p. 74).
78   Schaufeli et al. (2001).
79   Bakker and Xanthopoulou (2009).
80   Schaufeli, Taris and Bakker (2006).
81   Halbesleben (2010).
82   Schneider, Yost, Kropp, Kind and Lam (2018).
83   Harker and Keltner (2001).
84   De Neve (2018).
85   Staw and Barsade (1993).
86   Staw and Barsade (1993, p. 321).
87   Staw and Barsade (1993, p. 321).
88   Fredrickson (2013); Lehmann-Willenbrock, Chiu, Lei and Kauffeld (2017); BusiRhee and Yoon (2012); Walter and Bruch (2008).
89   Amabile, Barsade, Mueller and Staw (2005); Staw and Barsade (1993); Vosburg (1998).
90   Amabile, Barsade, Mueller and Staw (2005).
91   Madjar, Oldham and Pratt (2002).
92   Staw, Sutton and Pelled (1994).
93   Staw and Barsade (1993).
94   Sharma and Levy (2003).
95   Hom and Arbuckle (1988).
96   Seligman and Schulman (1986).
97   Rafaeli and Sutton (1989).
98   Pugh (2001).
99   Kellaway (2015, p. 10).
100   Kouchaki (2016); Ochs (2016).
101   Reckard (2013).
102   Independent Directors of the Board of Wells Fargo & Company (2017).
103   Catlette and Hadden (2012).
104   Held (2004, p. 18).
105   Miner, Glomb and Hulin (2005).
106   Aquino, Douglas and Martinko (2004).
107   Synthesis in Lam, Spreitzer and Fritz (2014).
108   Schwarz and Clore (2003).
109   Rego, Sousa, Marques and Cunha (2012).
110   Amabile, Barsade, Mueller and Staw (2005, p. 372).
111   George (2000).
112   Tiedens (2001).
113   van Kleef, De Dreu and Manstead (2004).
114   Geddes & Callister (2007).
115   Mroczek and Almeida (2004).
116   Shrira et al. (2011).
117   Csikszentmihalyi (1990).
118   Brown, Sokal and Friedman (2014); Nickerson (2018).

119   Nickerson (2018, p. 284).
120   Anderson, Potocnik and Zhou (2014).
121   Fong (2006).
122   George and Zhou (2002).
123   George and Zhou (2007).
124   Lyubomirsky, Sheldon and Schkade (2005).
125   Sheldon and Lyubomirsky (2006a, 2006b).
126   Sandvik, Diener and Seidlitz (1993); Otake, Shimai, Tanaka-Matsumi, Otsui and Fredrickson (2006).
127   See synthesis on Fisher (2010).
128   De Neve (2018).
129   Gavin and Mason (2004, p. 381).
130   De Neve (2018, p. 76).
131   Daniels and Harris (2000); Wright and Cropanzano (2000); Wright and Cropanzano (2004); Wright, Cropanzano, Denney and Moline (2002); Rego and Cunha (2008).
132   Rego and Cunha (2008).
133   Rogers (2018); Rogers and Ashford (2017).
134   Ketsde Vries (2001).
135   Feeney and Collins (2015, p. 113).
136   Harter and Adkins (2015).
137   From Fisher's (2010) literature review.
138   De Neve (2018).
139   De Neve (2018).
140   Built from De Neve (2018).
141   Fisher (2010).
142   Davidson and Schuyler (2015, p. 96). Sources to support the argument are provided by Davidson and Schuyler.
143   Humphrey, Burch and Adams (2016).
144   Koning and Van Kleef (2015); Van Knippenberg and Van Kleef (2016).
145   A comprehensive approach to the relationship between leadership and affect may be found in Van Knippenberg and Van Kleef (2016).
146   Humphrey (2012).
147   Humphrey (2012).
148   Madjar, Oldham and Pratt (2002).
149   Rego, Sousa, Marques and Pina E Cunha (2014).
150   De Cremer (2007).
151   De Cremer and Alberts (2004).
152   Jin et al. (2016).
153   Chi, Chung and Tsai (2011).
154   Van Knippenberg and Van Kleef (2016).
155   Visser, van Knippenberg, van Kleef and Wisse (2013).
156   Damen, van Knippenberg and van Knippenberg (2008).
157   Van Kleef, Homan, Beersma and van Knippenberg (2010).
158   Van Knippenberg and Van Kleef (2016).
159   Van Kleef (2009).
160   Koning and Van Kleef (2015, p. 491).
161   Collins, Lawrence, Troth and Jordan (2013), (2016); George (1990); Sy and Choi (2013); Sy, Côté and Saavedra (2005).
162   For a review see Collins, Lawrence, Troth and Jordan (2013).
163   George (1990, p. 108).
164   George (1990, p. 108).
165   Hatfield, Cacioppo and Rapson (1994).
166   Kelly (1988).
167   De Vignemont and Singer (2006).
168   George (1990); Schneider, Goldstein and Smith (1995). The ASA framework suggests that, through attraction, selection and attrition processes, groups/organizations can be composed of employees with highly similar personalities.

169   Morrison (1993).
170   Westman (2002).
171   Felps, Mitchell and Byington (2006).
172   See Collins, Lawrence, Troth and Jordan (2013) review.
173   See Collins, Lawrence, Troth and Jordan (2013) review.
174   See Collins, Jordan, Lawrence and Troth (2016).
175   For a review, see Collins, Jordan, Lawrence and Troth (2016).
176   Tsai, Chi, Grandey and Fung (2012).
177   Elfbein 2006 as cited in Collins, Jordan, Lawrence and Troth (2016, p. 169).
178   Collins, Jordan, Lawrence and Troth (2016, p. 179).
179   George (2011, p. 158).
180   Colman (2015).
181   Mayer and Salovey (1997); Salovey and Mayer (1990). See Côté (2014).
182   Goleman (1995).
183   Goleman (1998, p. 4).
184   Ashkanasy and Daus (2002).
185   Brown and Reilly (2008).
186   Druskate and Wolff (2001).
187   Côté (2014).
188   Three streams of EI research are explained in Ashkanasy and Daus (2005) and Walter, Cole and Humphrey (2011).
189   Caruso, Mayer and Salovey (2001).
190   Côté (2014, p. 462).
191   Goleman (1995, 1998).
192   Gross (1998, p. 275); see also Barsade and Gibson (2007, p. 38).
193   Côté (2014).
194   Wharton (2009, p. 147, p. 156).
195   See Côté (2014) for the consequences of emotional labour.
196   Daus and Ashkanasy (2005).
197   Salovey and Mayer (1990, p. 189).
198   Mayer and Salovey (1997).
199   See also Salovey and Grewal (2005).
200   Boyatzis, Goleman and Rhee (2000).
201   For example, Wong and Law (2002). See the Walter, Cole and Humphrey (2011) review (specifically Table 4 for a summary of studies linking EI and leader effectiveness).
202   For example, O'Boyle, Humphrey, Pollack, Hawver and Story (2011).
203   See Côté (2014) for a review.
204   Joseph and Newman (2010).
205   Kilduff, Chiaburu and Menges (2010).
206   Côté, DeCelles, McCarthy, van Kleef and Hideg (2011, p. 130).
207   Waytz (2016, p. 71).
208   Bloom (2017); Gjersoe (2017).
209   Gjersoe (2017).
210   Adapted from Batson, Klein, Highberger and Shaw (1995) by Gjersoe (2017).
211   See Fritz and Lyubomirsky (in press) to understand 'When, how, and why might positive activities undermine well-being'. See also Mauss, Tamir, Anderson and Savino (2011); Mauss et al. (2012).
212   Mauss, Tamir, Anderson and Savino (2011, p. 807).
213   In Grant (2015).
214   Simpson, Clegg and Pitsis (2014a).
215   Fredrickson (2003).
216   Boehm and Lyubomirsky (2008); De Neve (2018); Fisher (2010); Lyubomirsky, King and Diener (2005).
217   McKee (2017).
218   Fritz and Lyubomirsky (in press).
219   Mauss, Tamir, Anderson and Savino (2011), Mauss et al. (2012).

220   Gooty et al. (2010); Kaplan, Cortina, Ruark, LaPort and Nicolaides (2014); Van Knippenberg and Van Kleef (2016).
221   Goleman (1995).
222   Côté (2014).
223   Walter, Cole and Humphrey (2011).
224   Barsade and Gibson (2007, p. 38).
225   Barsade and Gibson (2007, p. 38).
226   Barsade and Gibson (2007, p. 38); see also Hatfield, Cacioppo and Rapson (1994).
227   Wharton (2009, p. 147, 156).
228   Gross (1998, p. 275); see also Barsade and Gibson (2007, p. 38).
229   Schaufeli, Salanova, González-Romá and Bakker (2002, p. 74).
230   George (1990, p. 108).
231   Locke (1969, p. 317).
232   Barsade and Gibson (2007, p. 38).
233   Diener, Lucas and Oishi (2002, p. 63).
234   Ryff (1989); Ryff and Keyes (1995); Ryff and Singer (2006, 2008).

References

Amabile, T. M., Barsade, S. G., Mueller, J. S., & Staw, B. M. (2005). Affect and creativity at work. *Administrative Science Quarterly*, 50(3), 367–403.

Anderson, N., Potocnik, K., & Zhou, J. (2014). Innovation and creativity in organizations: A state-of-the-science review, prospective commentary, and guiding framework. *Journal of Management*, 40(5), 1297–1333.

Aquino, K., Douglas, S., & Martinko, M. J. (2004). Overt anger in response to victimization: Attributional style and organizational norms as moderators. *Journal of Occupational Health Psychology*, 9(2), 152.

Ashkanasy, N. M., & Daus, C. S. (2002). Emotion in the workplace: The new challenge for managers. *Academy of Management Perspectives*, 16(1), 76–86.

Ashkanasy, N. M., & Daus, C. S. (2005). Rumors of the death of emotional intelligence in organizational behavior are vastly exaggerated. *Journal of Organizational Behavior*, 26, 441–452.

Bakker, A. B., & Oerlemans, W. (2011). Subjective well-being in organizations. In K. Cameron & G. Spreitzer (Eds.), *The Oxford handbook of positive organizational scholarship* (pp. 178–189). Oxford: Oxford University Press.

Bakker, A. B., & Xanthopoulou, D. (2009). The crossover of daily work engagement: Test of an actor–Partner interdependence model. *Journal of Applied Psychology*, 94(6), 1562.

Barsade, S. G. (2002). The ripple effect: Emotional contagion and its influence on group behavior. *Administrative Science Quarterly*, 47, 644–675.

Barsade, S. G., & Gibson, D. E. (2007). Why does affect matter in organizations? *Academy of Management Perspectives*, 21(1), 36–59.

Batson, C. D., Klein, T. R., Highberger, L., & Shaw, L. L. (1995). Immorality from empathy-induced altruism: When compassion and justice conflict. *Journal of Personality and Social Psychology*, 68(6), 1042–1054.

Berry, J. F., Benson, H., & Klemchuk, H. P. (1974). A simple psychophysiologic technique which elicits the hypometabolic changes of the relaxation response. *Psychomsomatic Medicine*, 36(4), 115–120.

Blanksby, M. (1987). Changing a bureaucracy into an open organisation. *Journal of European Industrial Training*, 11(6), 21–27.

Bloom, P. (2017). *Against empathy: The case for rational compassion*. New York: Random House.

Boehm, J. K., & Lyubomirsky, S. (2008). Does happiness promote career success? *Journal of Career Assessment*, 16(19), 101–116.

Bono, J. E., & Vey, M. A. (2005). Toward understanding emotional management at work: A quantitative review of emotional labor research. In C. E. J. Hartel, W. J. Zerbe, & N. M. Ashkanasy (Eds.) *Emotions in organizational behaviour* (pp. 213–233). Mahwah, NJ: Lawrence Erlbaum Associates.

Boyatzis, R., Goleman, D., & Rhee, K. (2000). Clustering competence in emotional intelligence: Insights from the emotional competence inventory (ECI). In R. Bar-On, & J. D. A. Parker (Eds.), *Handbook of emotional intelligence* (pp.343–362). San Francisco, CA: Jossey-Bass.

Brown, F. W., & Reilly, M. D. (2008). Emotional intelligence, transformational leadership and gender: Correlation and interaction possibilities. *The Journal of International Management Studies*, 3(2), 1–9.

Brown, N. J. L., Sokal, A. D., & Friedman, H. L. (2014). The persistence of wishful thinking: Response to "Updated thinking on positivity ratios". *American Psychologist*, 69, 629–632.

BusiRhee, S., & Yoon, H. J. (2012). Shared positive affect in workgroups. In K. S. Cameron, & G. Spreitzer (Eds.), *The Oxford handbook of positive organizational scholarship* (pp.215–227). Oxford: Oxford University Press.

Büssing, A., Bissels, T., Fuchs, V., & Perrar, K. M. (1999). A dynamic model of work satisfaction: Qualitative approaches. *Human Relations*, 52(8), 999–1028.

Cabiria, J. (2008). Virtual world and real world permeability: Transference of positive benefits for marginalized gay and lesbian populations. *Journal for Virtual Worlds Research*, 1(1), 1–13.

Catlette, B., & Hadden, R. (2012). *Contented cows still give better milk, revised and expanded: The plain truth about employee engagement and your bottom line*. New York: John Wiley & Sons.

Chamorro-Premuzic, T. (2017). Fire your chief happiness officer. *Fast Company*, 12 June (www.fastcompany.com/40429336/fire-your-chief-happiness-officer).

Chen, F. F., Jing, Y., Hayes, A., & Lee, J. M. (2013). Two concepts or two approaches? A bifactor analysis of psychological and subjective well-being. *Journal of Happiness Studies*, 14(3), 1033–1068.

Chen, S. (2018). 'Forget the Facebook leak': China is mining data directly from workers' brains on an industrial scale. *South China Moining Post*, 29 April (www.scmp.com/news/china/society/article/2143899/forget-facebook-leak-china-mining-data-directly-workers-brains).

Chi, N.-W., Chung, -Y.-Y., & Tsai, W.-C. (2011). How do happy leaders enhance team success? The mediating roles of transformational leadership, group affective tone, and team processes. *Journal of Applied Social Psychology*, 41(6), 1421–1454.

Collins, A. L., Jordan, P. J., Lawrence, S. A., & Troth, A. C. (2016). Positive affective tone and team performance: The moderating role of collective emotional skills. *Cognition and Emotion*, 30(1), 167–182.

Collins, A. L., Lawrence, S. A., Troth, A. C., & Jordan, P. J. (2013). Group affective tone: A review and future research directions. *Journal of Organizational Behavior*, 34(S1), S43–S62.

Colman, A. M. (2015). *A dictionary of psychology*. Oxford: Oxford University Press.

Côté, S. (2014). Emotional intelligence in organizations. *Annual Review of Organizational Psychology and Organizational Behavior*, 1, 459–488.

Côté, S., DeCelles, K. A., McCarthy, J. M., van Kleef, G. A., & Hideg, I. (2011). The Jekyll and Hyde of emotional intelligence: Emotion-regulation knowledge facilitates both prosocial and interpersonally deviant behavior. *Psychological Science*, 22(8), 1073–1080.

Cowland, J. (1989). Big need not be bureaucratic. *Education and Training*, 31(6), 8–9.

Csikszentmihalyi, M. (1990). *Flow*. New York: Harper & Row.

Damen, F. J. A., van Knippenberg, D., & van Knippenberg, B. (2008). Leader affective displays and attributions of charisma: The role of arousal. *Journal of Applied Social Psychology*, 38(10), 2594–2614.

Daniels, K., & Harris, C. (2000). Work, well-being and performance. *Occupational Medicine*, 50, 304–309.

Daus, C. S., & Ashkanasy, N. M. (2005). The case for the ability-based model of emotional intelligence in organizational behavior. *Journal of Organizational Behavior*, 26(4), 453–466.

Davidson, R. J., & Schuyler, B. S. (2015). Neuroscience of happiness. In J. Helliwell, R. Layard, & J. Sachs (Eds.), *World happiness report 2015* (pp. 88–105). New York: Sustainable Development Solutions Network.

De Cremer, D. (2007). Emotional effects of distributive justice as a function of autocratic leader behavior. *Journal of Applied Social Psychology*, 37, 1385–1404.

De Cremer, D., & Alberts, H. J. E. M. (2004). When procedural fairness does not influence how positive I feel: The effects of voice and leader selection as a function of belongingness need. *European Journal of Social Psychology*, 34, 333–344.

De Neve, J.-E. (2018). Work and well-being: A global perspective. In *Global happiness policy report 2018* (pp. 74–111). Global Happiness Council.

De Vignemont, F., & Singer, T. (2006). The empathic brain: How, when and why? *Trends in Cognitive Sciences*, 10(10), 435–441.

Diener, E., Lucas, R. E., & Oishi, S. (2002). Subjective well-being: The science of happiness and life satisfaction. In C. R. Snyder & S. J. Lopez (Eds.), *Handbook of positive psychology* (pp. 63–73). Oxford and New York: Oxford University Press.

Druskate, V. U., & Wolff, S. B. (2001). Building emotional intelligence of groups. *Harvard Business Review*, March, 79(3), 81–90.

Du Gay, P. (2008). "Without affection or enthusiasm": Problems of involvement and attachment in "responsive" public management. *Organization*, 15(3), 335–353.

Elfenbein, H. A. (2006). Team emotional intelligence: What it can mean and how it can affect performance. In V. U. Druskat, F. Sala, & G. Mount (Eds.), *Linking emotional intelligence and performance at work: Current research evidence with individuals and groups* (pp. 165–184). Mahwah, NJ: Lawrence Erlbaum.

Featherston, O. (2018). In search of excellence: Is the book still relevant 36 years on? *CEO Magazine*, 20 March (www.theceomagazine.com/business/management-leadership/search-excellence-book-still-relevant-36-years/).

Feeney, B. C., & Collins, N. L. (2015). A new look at social support: A theoretical perspective on thriving through relationships. *Personality and Social Psychology Review*, 19(2), 113–147.

Felps, W., Mitchell, T. R., & Byington, E. (2006). How, when, and why bad apples spoil the barrel: Negative group members and dysfunctional groups. *Research in Organizational Behavior*, 27, 175–222.

Fisher, C. D. (2010). Happiness at work. *International Journal of Management Reviews*, 12, 384–412.

Fong, C. T. (2006). The effects of emotional ambivalence on creativity. *Academy of Management Journal*, 49, 1016–1030.

Fournier, V., & Grey, C. (2000). At the critical moment: Conditions and prospects for critical management studies. *Human Relations*, 53(1), 7–32.

Fredrickson, B. L. (1998). What good are positive emotions. *Review of General Psychology*, 2(3), 300–319.

Fredrickson, B. L. (2003). Positive emotions and upward spirals in organizations. In K. S. Cameron, J. E. Dutton, & R. E. Quinn (Eds.), *Positive organizational scholarship* (pp.163–175). San Francisco, CA: Berrett-Khoeler.

Fredrickson, B. L. (2013). Positive emotions broaden and build. In P. Devine, & A. Plant (Eds.), *Advances in experimental social psychology*, Vol. 47, 1–53.

Fredrickson, B. L., & Branigan, C. (2005). Positive emotions broaden the scope of attention and thought, action repertoires. *Cognition & Emotion*, 19(3), 313–332.

Fredrickson, B. L., & Levenson, R. W. (1998). Positive emotions speed recovery from the cardiovascular sequelae of negative emotions. *Cognition and Emotion*, 12(2), 191–220.

Frijda, N. H. (1993). Moods, emotion episodes, and emotions. In M. Lewis & J. M. Haviland (Eds.), Handbook of emotions (p. 381–403). Guilford Press.

Fritz, M. M., & Lyubomirsky, S. (2018). Whither happiness? When, how, and why might positive activities undermine well-being. In J. P. Forgas, & R. F. Baumeister (Eds), *The social psychology of living well* (pp. 101–115). New York: Psychology Press.

Gable, P. A., & Harmon-Jones, E. (2008). Approach-motivated positive affect reduces breadth of attention. *Psychological Science*, 19, 476–482.

Gavin, J. H., & Mason, R. O. (2004). The virtuous organization: The value of happiness in the workplace. *Organizational Dynamics*, 33(4), 379–392.

Geddes, D., & Callister, R. R. (2007). Crossing the line (s): A dual threshold model of anger in organizations. *Academy of Management Review*, 32(3), 721–746.

George, J. M. (1990). Personality, affect, and behavior in groups. *Journal of Applied Psychology*, 75(2), 107–116.

George, J. M. (2000). Emotions and leadership: The role of emotional intelligence. *Human Relations*, 53(8), 1027–1055.

George, J. M. (2011). Dual tuning: A minimum condition for understanding affect in organizations? *Organizational Psychology Review*, 1(2), 147–164.

George, J. M., & Zhou, J. (2002). Understanding when bad moods foster creativity and good ones don't: The role of context and clarity of feelings. *Journal of Applied Psychology*, 87, 687–697.

George, J. M., & Zhou, J. (2007). Dual tuning in a supportive context: Joint contributions of positive mood, negative mood, and supervisory behaviors to employee creativity. *Academy of Management Journal*, 50, 605–622.

Gjersoe, N. (2017). Empathy is crucial to being a good person, right? Think again. *The Guardian*, 7 February (https://www.theguardian.com/science/head-quarters/2017/feb/07/empathy-is-crucial-to-being-a-good-person-right-think-again).

Goleman, D. (1995). *Emotional intelligence: Why it can matter more than IQ*. New York: Bantam.

Goleman, D. (1998). *Working with emotional intelligence*. New York: Bantam.

Goleman, D. (2013). The focused leader. *Harvard Business Review*, December, 91(12), 50–60.

Gooty, J., Connelly, S., Griffith, J., & Gupta, A. (2010). Leadership, affect and emotions: A state of the science review. *The Leadership Quarterly*, 21, 979–1004.

Grant, A. (2015). Does trying to be happy make us unhappy? *Psychology Today*, 14 May (www.psychologytoday.com/blog/give-and-take/201305/does-trying-be-happy-make-us-unhappy).

Grebner, S., Semmer, N. K., & Elfering, A. (2005). Working conditions and three types of well-being: A longitudinal study with self-report and rating data. *Journal of Occupational Health Psychology*, 10(1), 31–43.

Gross, J. J. (1998). The emerging field of emotion regulation: An integrative review. *Review of General Psychology*, 2(3), 271.

Halbesleben, J. R. B. (2010). A meta-analysis of work engagement: Relationships with burnout, demands, resources, and consequences. In A. B. Bakker & M. L. Leiter (Eds.), *Work engagement: A handbook of essential theory and research* (pp.102–117). Hove and New York: Psychology Press.

Hallowell, E. M. (1999). The human moment at work. *Harvard Business Review*, January–February, 77(1), 1–8.

Harker, L., & Keltner, D. (2001). Expressions of positive emotion in women's college yearbook pictures and their relationship to personality and life outcomes across adulthood. *Journal of Personality and Social Psychology*, 80(1), 112–124.

Harter, J., & Adkins, A. (2015). Employees want a lot more from their managers. *Gallup Business Journal*, 8 April (http://news.gallup.com/businessjournal/182321/employees-lot-managers.aspx).

Hassard, J. S. (2012). Rethinking the Hawthorne studies: The Western electric research in its social, political and historical context. *Human Relations*, 65(11), 1431–1461.

Hatfield, E., Cacioppo, J., & Rapson, R. (1994). *Emotional contagion*. New York: Cambridge University Press.

Heaphy, E. D., & Dutton, J. E. (2008). Positive social interactions and the human body at work: Linking organisations and physiology. *Academy of Management Review*, 33(1), 137–162.

Held, B. S. (2004). The negative side of positive psychology. *Journal of Humanistic Psychology*, 44(1), 9–46.

Helliwell, J., Layard, R., & Sachs, J. (Eds.), (2015). *World happiness report 2015*. New York: Sustainable Development Solutions Network.

Hoban, M. (2012). The most influential business book of the last 30 years? *Fast Company*, 6 February. (www.fastcompany.com/1813817/most-influential-business-book-last-30-years).

Hochschild, A. R. (1983). *The managed heart*. Berkeley, CA: University of California Press.

Hom, H. L., & Arbuckle, B. (1988). Mood induction effects upon goal setting and performance in young children. *Motivation and Emotion*, 12(2), 113–122.

Humphrey, R. H. (2012). How do leaders use emotional labor? *Journal of Organizational Behavior*, 33(5), 740–744.

Humphrey, R. H., Burch, G. F., & Adams, L. L. (2016). The benefits of merging leadership research and emotions research. *Frontiers in Psychology*, 7, 1022.

Independent Directors of the Board of Wells Fargo & Company. (2017). *Sales practices investigation report*. 10 April.

Jacques, R. (1996). *Manufacturing the employee: Management knowledge from the 19th to 21st centuries*. Thousand Oaks, CA: Sage.

Jin, S., Seo, M. G., & Shapiro, D. L. (2016). Do happy leaders lead better? Affective and attitudinal antecedents of transformational leadership. *The Leadership Quarterly*, 27(1), 64–84.

Joseph, D. L., & Newman, D. A. (2010). Emotional intelligence: An integrative meta-analysis and cascading model. *Journal of Applied Psychology*, 95(1), 54–78.

Josserand, E., Teo, S., & Clegg, S. R. (2006). From bureaucratic to post-bureaucratic: The difficulties of transition. *Journal of Organizational Change Management*, 19(1), 54–64.

Kaplan, S., Cortina, J., Ruark, G., LaPort, K., & Nicolaides, V. (2014). The role of organizational leaders in employee emotion management: A theoretical model. *The Leadership Quarterly*, 25(3), 563–580.

Kelan, E. K. (2008). The discursive construction of gender in contemporary management literature. *Journal of Business Ethics*, 81(2), 427–445.

Kelemen, M. (2000). Too much or too little ambiguity: The language of total quality management. *Journal of Management Studies*, 37(4), 483–498.

Kelemen, M. (2002). *Managing quality*. London: Sage.

Kellaway, L. (2015). Wells Fargo's happy: Grumpyratio is no way to audit staff. *Financial Times Europe*, 9(February), 10.

Kelly, J. R. (1988). Entrainment in individual and group behavior. In J. E. McGrath (Ed.), *The social psychology of time: New perspectives* (pp.89–110). Newbury Park, CA: Sage.

Ketsde Vries, M. F. R. (2001). Creating authentizotic organizations: Well-functioning individuals in vibrant companies. *Human Relations*, 54(1), 101–111.

Kilduff, M., Chiaburu, D. S., & Menges, J. I. (2010). Strategic use of emotional intelligence in organizational settings: Exploring the dark side. *Research in Organizational Behavior*, 30, 129–152.

Knowles, V. (2015). If you're happy and you know it … become a chief happiness officer. *The Guardian*, 13 July (www.theguardian.com/careers/2015/jul/13/if-youre-happy-and-you-know-it-become-a-chief-happiness-officer).

Koning, L. F., & Van Kleef, G. A. (2015). How leaders' emotional displays shape followers' organizational citizenship behavior. *The Leadership Quarterly*, 26(4), 489–501.

Kouchaki, M. (2016). How Wells Fargo's fake accounts scandal got so bad. *Fortune*, 15 September (http://fortune.com/2016/09/15/wells-fargo-scandal/).

Lam, C. F., Spreitzer, G., & Fritz, C. (2014). Too much of a good thing: Curvilinear effect of positive affect on proactive behaviors. *Journal of Organizational Behavior*, 35, 530–546.

Lang, P. J., Bradley, M. M., & Cuthbert, B. N. (1998). Emotion, motivation, and anxiety: Brain mechanisms and psychophysiology. *Biological Psychiatry*, 44(12), 1248–1263.

Larsen, R. J., & Diener, E. (1992). Promises and problems with the circumplex model of emotion. In M. S. Clark (Ed.), *Review of personality and social psychology* (Vol. 13, pp. 25–59). Newbury Park, CA: Sage.

Lawler, K. A., Younger, J. W., Piferi, R. L., Billington, E., Jobe, R., Edmondson, K., & Jones, W. H. (2003). A change of heart: Cardiovascular correlates of forgiveness in response to interpersonal conflict. *Journal of Behavioral Medicine*, 26(5), 373–393.

Lehmann-Willenbrock, N., Chiu, M. M., Lei, Z., & Kauffeld, S. (2017). Understanding positivity within dynamic team interactions: A statistical discourse analysis. *Group & Organization Management*, 42(1), 39–78.

Levenson, R. W., Ekman, P., & Friesen, W. V. (1990). Voluntary facial action generates emotion-specific autonomic nervous system activity. *Psychophysiology*, 27(4), 363–384.

Locke, E. A. (1969). What is job satisfaction? Organizational behavior and human light at the end of the tunnel. *Psychological Science*, 1(4), 309–336.

Lyubomirsky, S., King, L., & Diener, E. (2005). The benefits of frequent positive affect: Does happiness lead to success? *Psychological Bulletin*, 131(6), 803–855.

Lyubomirsky, S., Sheldon, K. M., & Schkade, D. (2005). Pursuing happiness: The architecture of sustainable change. *Review of General Psychology*, 9(2), 111–131.

Mackey, J., & Sisodia, R. S. (2013). *Conscious capitalism: Liberating the heroic spirit of business*. Boston, MA: Harvard Business Review Press.

Madjar, N., Oldham, G. R., & Pratt, M. G. (2002). There's no place like home? The contributions of work and nonwork creativity support to employees' creative performance. *Academy of Management Journal*, 45, 757–767.

Mauss, I. B., Savino, N. S., Anderson, C. L., Weisbuch, M., Tamir, M., & Laudenslager, M. L. (2012). The pursuit of happiness can be lonely. *Emotion*, 12(5), 908–912.

Mauss, I. B., Tamir, M., Anderson, C. L., & Savino, N. S. (2011). Can seeking happiness make people unhappy? Paradoxical effects of valuing happiness. *Emotion*, 11(4), 807–815.

Mayer, J. D., & Salovey, P. (1997). What is emotional intelligence? In P. Salovey & D. Sluyter (Eds.), *Emotional development and emotional intelligence: Implications for educators* (pp.3–31). New York: Basic Books.

Mayer, J. D., Salovey, P., & Caruso, D. R. (2004). Emotional Intelligence: Theory, Findings, and Implications. *Psychological inquiry*, 15(3), 197–215.

Mayo, E. (1949/2003). *The social problems of an industrial civilization*. London: Routledge.

McCoy, B. H. (2007). *Living into leadership: A journey in ethics*. Stanford, CA: Stanford University Press.

McKee, A. (2017). Happiness traps: How we sabotage ourselves at work. *Harvard Business Review*, September–October, 95(5), 66–73.

Messinger, L. (2015). Is a chief happiness officer really the best way to increase workplace happiness? *The Guardian*, 26 August (www.theguardian.com/sustainable-business/2015/aug/26/chief-happiness-officer-cho-employee-workplace-woohoo-google).

Miller, P., & Rose, N. (1994). On therapeutic authority: Psychoanalytical expertise under advanced liberalism. *History of the Human Sciences*, 7(3), 29–64.

Miner, A. G., Glomb, T. M., & Hulin, C. (2005). Experience sampling mood and its correlates at work. *Journal of Occupational and Organizational Psychology*, 78(2), 171–193.

Morris, C. G., & Maisto, A. A. (2005). *Psychology: An introduction* (12th ed.). Upper Saddle River, NJ: Prentice-Hall.

Morrison, E. W. (1993). Newcomer information seeking: Exploring types, modes, sources, and outcomes. *Academy of Management Journal*, 36(3), 557–589.

Mroczek, D. K., & Almeida, D. M. (2004). The effect of daily stress, personality, and age on daily negative affect. *Journal of Personality*, 72(2), 355–378.

Newberg, A. B., & Iversen, J. (2003). The neural basis of the complex mental task of meditation: Neurotransmitter and neurochemical considerations. *Medical Hypotheses*, 61(2), 282–291.

Nickerson, C. A. (2018). There is no empirical evidence for critical positivity ratios: Comment on Fredrickson (2013). *Journal of Humanistic Psychology*, 58(3), 284–312.

O'Boyle, E. H., Jr, Humphrey, R. H., Pollack, J. M., Hawver, T. H., & Story, P. A. (2011). The relation between emotional intelligence and job performance: A meta-analysis. *Journal of Organizational Behavior*, 32(5), 788–818.

O'Connor, E. S. (1999). The politics of management thought: A case study of the Harvard Business School and the Human Relations School. *Academy of Management Review*, 24(1), 117–131.

Ochs, S. M. (2016). In Wells Fargo scandal, the buck stopped well short. *The New York Times*, 15 September, A27.

Oman, D., Thoresen, C. E., & McMahon, K. (1999). Volunteerism and mortality among the community-dwelling elderly. *Journal of Health Psychology*, 4(3), 301–316.

Otake, K., Shimai, S., Tanaka-Matsumi, J., Otsui, K., & Fredrickson, B. L. (2006). Happy people become happier through kindness: A counting kindnesses intervention. *Journal of Happiness Studies*, 7(3), 361–375.

Peters, T. J. (2001). Tom Peters's true confessions. *Fast Company*, 30 January (www.fastcompany.com/44077/tom-peterss-true-confessions)

Peters, T. J., & Waterman, R. H. (1982). *In search of excellence: Lessons from American's best-run companies*. New York: Harper & Row.

Post, S. G. (2005). Altruism, happiness, and health: It's good to be good. *International Journal of Behaviour*, 12(2), 66–77.

Pugh, S. D. (2001). Service with a smile: Emotional contagion in the service encounter. *Academy of Management*, 26(1), 59–78.

Rafaeli, A., & Sutton, R. I. (1989). The expression of emotion in organizational life. *Research in Organizational Behavior*, 11(1), 1–42.

Reckard, E. S. (2013). Wells Fargo's pressure-cooker sales culture comes at a cost. *Los Angeles Times*, 21 December (www.latimes.com/business/la-fi-wells-fargo-sale-pressure-20131222-story.html).

Rego, A., & Cunha, M. P. (2008). Authentizotic climates and employee happiness: Pathways to individual performance? *Journal of Business Research*, 61(7), 739–752.

Rego, A., Sousa, F., Marques, C., & Cunha, M. P. (2012). Optimism predicting employees' creativity: The mediating role of positive affect and the positivity ratio. *European Journal of Work and Organizational Psychology*, 21(2), 244–270.

Rego, A., Sousa, F., Marques, C., & Pina E Cunha, M. (2014). Hope and positive affect mediating the authentic leadership and creativity relationship. *Journal of Business Research*, 67, 200f.

Roepke, A. M. (2013). Gains without pains? Growth after positive events. *The Journal of Positive Psychology*, 8(4), 280–291.

Rogers, K. (2018). Do your employees feel respected? *Harvard Business Review*, 96(4), 63–70.

Rogers, K. M., & Ashford, B. E. (2017). Respect in organizations: Feeling valued as "We" and "Me". *Journal of Management*, 43(5), 1578–1608.

Rose, N. (1985). *The psychological complex: Psychology, politics, and society in England, 1869-1939.* London: Routledge & Kegan Paul.

Rose, N. (1989). *Governing the soul.* London: Routledge.

Rosenzweig, P. (2014). *The halo effect … and the eight other business delusions that deceive managers.* New York: Simon and Schuster.

Russell, J. A. (1980). A circumplex model of affect. *Journal of Personality and Social Psychology*, 39(6), 1161.

Russell, J. A., & Fehr, B. (1994). Fuzzy concepts in a fuzzy hierarchy: Varieties of anger. *Journal of Personality and Social Psychology*, 67(2), 186.

Ryff, C. D. (1989). Happiness is everything, or is it? Explorations on the meaning of psychological wellbeing. *Journal of Personality and Social Psychology*, 57, 1069–1081.

Ryff, C. D., & Keyes, C. L. M. (1995). The structure of psychological well-being revisited. *Journal of Personality and Social Psychology*, 69, 719–727.

Ryff, C. D., & Singer, B. H. (2006). Best news yet on the six-factor model of well-being. *Social Science Research*, 35, 1103–1119.

Ryff, C. D., & Singer, B. H. (2008). Know thyself and become what you are: A eudaimonic approach to psychological well-being. *Journal of Happiness Studies*, 9, 13–39.

Saarm, C. (1999). *The development of emotional competence.* New York: Guilford.

Salovey, P., & Grewal, D. (2005). The science of emotional intelligence. *Current Directions in Psychological Science*, 14(6), 281–285.

Salovey, P., & Mayer, J. D. (1990). Emotional intelligence. *Imagination, Cognition and Personality*, 9(3), 185–211.

Sandvik, E., Diener, E., & Seidlitz, L. (1993). Subjective well-being: The convergence and stability of self-report and non-self-report measures. *Journal of Personality*, 61(3), 317–342.

Schaufeli, W. B., Salanova, M., González-Romá, V., & Bakker, A. B. (2002). The measurement of engagement and burnout: A two sample confirmatory factor analytic approach. *Journal of Happiness Studies*, 3(1), 71–92.

Schaufeli, W. B., Taris, T. W., & Bakker, A. B. (2006). Dr. Jeckyll or Mr. Hyde: On the differences between work engagement and workaholism. In R. J. Burke (Ed.), *Research companion to working time and work addiction* (pp.193–217). Cheltenham Glos: Edward Elgar.

Schaufeli, W. B., Taris, T. W., Le Blanc, P., Peeters, M., Bakker, A. B., & De Jonge, J. (2001). Maakt arbeid gezond? Op zoek naar de bevlogen werknemer [Does work make happy? In search of the engaged worker]. *De Psycholoog*, 36, 422–428.

Schneider, B., Goldstein, H. W., & Smith, D. B. (1995). The ASA framework: An update. *Personnel Psychology*, 48, 747–779.

Schneider, B., Yost, A. B., Kropp, A., Kind, C., & Lam, H. (2018). Workforce engagement: What it is, what drives it, and why it matters for organizational performance. *Journal of Organizational Behavior*, 39(4), 462–480.

Schwarz, N., & Clore, G. L. (2003). Mood as information: 20 years later. *Psychological Inquiry: An International Journal for the Advancement of Psychological Theory*, 14(3–4), 296–303.

Seligman, M. E., & Schulman, P. (1986). Explanatory style as a predictor of productivity and quitting among life insurance sales agents. *Journal of Personality and Social Psychology*, 50(4), 832.

Sharma, A. &., & Levy, M. (2003). Salespeople's affect toward their customers: Why should it matter for retailers. *Journal of Business Research*, 56(7), 523–528.

Sheldon, K. M., & Lyubomirsky, S. (2006a). Achieving sustainable gains in happiness: Change your actions, not your circumstances. *Journal of Happiness Studies*, 7, 55–86.

Sheldon, K. M., & Lyubomirsky, S. (2006b). How to increase and sustain positive emotion: The effects of expressing gratitude and visualizing best possible selves. *The Journal of Positive Psychology*, 1(2), 73–82.

Shrira, A., Palgi, Y., Wolf, J. J., Haber, Y., Goldray, O., Shacham-Shmueli, E., & Ben-Ezra, M. (2011). The positivity ratio and functioning under stress. *Stress and Health*, 27(4), 265–271.

Simpson, A. V., Clegg, S., & Pitsis, T. (2014a). I used to care but things have changed": A genealogy of compassion in organizational theory. *Journal of Management Inquiry*, 23(4), 347–359.

Solomon, R. C. (1997). Competition, care, and compassion: Toward a nonchauvinist view of the corporation. In A. Larson & R. E. Freeman (Eds.), *Women's studies and business ethics: Toward a new conversation* (pp.144–173). New York: Oxford University Press.

Solomon, R. C. (1998). The moral psychology of business: Care and compassion in the corporation. *Business Ethics Quarterly*, 8(3), 515–534.

Springer, K. W., Hauser, R. M., & Freese, J. (2006). Bad news indeed for Ryff's six-factor model of well-being. *Social Science Research*, 35(4), 1120–1131.

Staw, B. M., & Barsade, S. G. (1993). Affect and managerial performance: A test of the sadder-but-wiser vs. happier-and-smarter hypotheses. *Administrative Science Quarterly*, 38(2), 304–331.

Staw, B. M., Sutton, R. I., & Pelled, L. H. (1994). Employee positive emotion and favorable outcomes at the workplace. *Organization Science*, 5(1), 51–71.

Sy, T., & Choi, J. N. (2013). Contagious leaders and followers: Exploring multi-stage mood contagion in a leader activation and member propagation (LAMP) model. *Organizational Behavior and Human Decision Processes*, 122(2), 127–140.

Sy, T., Côté, S., & Saavedra, R. (2005). The contagious leader: Impact of the leader's mood on the mood of group members, group affective tone, and group processes. *Journal of Applied Psychology*, 90(2), 295.

Taylor, F. W. (1911). *The principles of scientific management*. New York: Harper.

Tiedens, L. Z. (2001). Anger and advancement versus sadness and subjugation: The effect of negative emotion expressions on social status conferral. *Journal of Personality and Social Psychology*, 80(1), 86–94.

Todaro, J. F., Shen, B. J., Niaura, R., Spiro, A., III, & Ward, K. D. (2003). Effect of negative emotions on frequency of cronary heart disease. *The American Journal of Cariology*, 92(15 October), 901–990.

Tsai, W.-C., Chi, N.-W., Grandey, A. A., & Fung, S.-C. (2012). Positive group affective tone and team creativity: Negative group affective tone and team trust as boundary conditions. *Journal of Organizational Behavior*, 33(5), 638–656.

Van Kleef, G. A., De Dreu, C. K. W. and Manstead, A. S. R. (2004). The interpersonal effects of anger and happiness in negotiations. *Journal of Personality and Social Psychology*, 2004, Vol. 86, No. 1, 57–76.

Van Kleef, G. A. (2009). How emotions regulate social life: The emotions as social information (ESASI) model. *Current Directions in Psychological Science*, 18(3), 184–188.

Van Kleef, G. A., Homan, A. C., Beersma, B., & van Knippenberg, D. (2010). On angry leaders and agreeable followers: How leader emotion and follower personality shape motivation and team performance. *Psychological Science*, 21, 1827–1834.

Van Knippenberg, D., & Van Kleef, G. A. (2016). Leadership and affect: Moving the hearts and minds of followers. *The Academy of Management Annals*, 10(1), 1–42.

vanOyen Witvliet, C., Ludwig, T. E., & Vander Laan, K. L. (2001). Granting forgiveness or harboring grudges: Implications for emotion, physiology, and health. *Psychological Science*, 12(2), 117–123.

Visser, V. A., van Knippenberg, D., van Kleef, G., & Wisse, B. (2013). How leader displays of happiness and sadness influence follower performance: Emotional contagion and creative versus analytical performance. *The Leadership Quarterly*, 24, 172–188.

Vosburg, S. K. (1998). The effects of positive and negative mood on divergent-thinking performance. *Creativity Research Journal*, 11(2), 165–172.

Walter, F., & Bruch, H. (2008). The positive group affect spiral: A dynamic model of the emergence of positive affective similarity in work groups. *Journal of Organizational Behavior*, 29, 239–261.

Walter, F., Cole, M., & Humphrey, R. (2011). Emotional intelligence: Sine qua non of leadership or folderol? *The Academy of Management Perspectives*, 25(1), 45–59.

Watson, D., & Clark, L. A. (1992). On traits and temperament: General and specific factors of emotional experience and their relation to the five-factor model. *Journal of Personality*, 60(2), 441–476.

Waytz, A. (2016). The limits of empathy. *Harvard Business Review*, 94(1), 68–73.

Westman, M. (2002). Crossover of stress and strain in the family and workplace. In P. L. Perrewé & D. C. Ganster (Eds.), *Research in occupational stress and well being* (Vol. 2, pp. 143–181). Greenwich, CT: JAI Press.

Wilson, J., & Musick, M. A. (1999). The effects of volunteering on the volunteer. *Law and Contemporary Problems*, 62(4), 141–168.

Wong, C., & Law, K. S. (2002). The effects of leader and follower emotional intelligence on performance and attitude: An exploratory study. *The Leadership Quarterly*, 13, 243–274.

Wright, T. A., & Cropanzano, R. (2000). Psychological well-being and job satisfaction as predictors of job performance. *Journal of Occupational Health Psychology*, 5, 84–94.

Wright, T. A., & Cropanzano, R. (2004). The role of psychological well-being in job performance. *Organizational Dynamics*, 33(4), 338–351.

Wright, T. A., Cropanzano, R., Denney, P. J., & Moline, G. L. (2002). When a happy worker is a productive worker: A preliminary examination of three models. *Canadian Journal of Behavioral Science*, 34, 146–150.

5 Designing work for meaning, learning and health

Summary and objectives

This chapter discusses the conditions that turn work into a source of flourishing and how and when work acts as an enabler of positive employee development. We start by discussing top-down models of job design and complement them with more recent bottom-up perspectives. We explore concepts such as work as a calling, job crafting and pro-social sources of motivation. We also distinguish intrinsic and extrinsic sources of motivation and offer ideas for the practical design of intrinsically rich jobs.

Work: torture or meaning?

Work constitutes such a central feature of modern life that a significant part of a person's waking hours, for a significant number of people, is dedicated to work. Accordingly, it seems important that work should represent a positive dimension of one's life. Empirics, however, suggest otherwise. A study reported that in Europe:[1]

- 33 per cent of workers have poor quality work designs, with low job discretion and low job complexity, sometimes combined with related time constraints;
- 28 per cent reported jobs of moderate quality, combining teamwork and repetitive tasks with a moderate amount of job discretion;
- 39 per cent of workers considered their work as high quality, with high job discretion and task complexity.

Analyses of large datasets in Asia, Australia and the US point in the same direction, suggesting that low quality jobs are prevalent – consider Gallup's survey on the state of the global workplace.[2] Evidence also indicates that in the US and Europe, over the last two decades, work and physical loads have intensified, while job discretion and cognitive demands have declined.[3] The findings can be helpful in explaining why different people doing different jobs have different types of attitudes to work. For some, work is exhilarating and fun; for others, work is a daily grind (see Box 5.1 on 'Tripalium'). This would not constitute a major problem if people worked for mainly extrinsic reasons, such as a salary. Research suggests, however, that external rewards such as a monetary bonus produce limited motivational effects. Motivational strategies that focus primarily on extrinsic rewards are ineffective: 'individuals whose commitments and motivation are external depend on their managers to give them the incentive to work'.[4] Evidence also suggests that motivated persistence, psychological wellbeing and higher performance have been associated with intrinsic motivation.[5] Therefore, organizations should pay close attention to defining strategies aimed at increasing their employees' intrinsic motivation. The way jobs are designed is critical in this regard.

Box 5.1 'Tripalium' or work as torture

In an influential book titled *Working*, oral historian Studs Terkel notes that 'working is about a search for daily meaning as well as daily bread, for recognition as well as cash, for astonishment rather than torpor; in short, for a sort of life rather than a Monday through Friday sort of dying'.[6] Meaningful work has been defended by some authors as a fundamental human need,[7] as we discuss in this chapter. But in some cases it might be better described as a 'sort of dying', a daily form of torture.

Interestingly, the root of the word 'work', in several Latin languages, is 'tripalium', which denotes three stakes or poles (see Figure 5.1) used as an instrument of torture. Recognition that the words *trabajo* (Spanish), *travail* (French) and *trabalho* (Portuguese) derive from the Latin 'tripalium' is in itself inconsequential but is also a genealogy too telling to ignore. Expelled from the gardens of Eden, where he was to be God's idle gardener, Adam and all his descendants were condemned to a 'tripalium',[8] a punishment for original sin.

Figure 5.1 A tripalium.

In this chapter, we discuss how to turn work into a positive experience. We do so by focussing on developing work that is a source of motivation, a facilitator of learning, as well as a creator of personal health and wellbeing. This is not to say, of course, that work can be free from hassles, challenges and difficulties. Unrealistic ideals of positivity at work may even be a source of frustration. But research gives clear indications about how to design jobs in a way that makes the work experience richer, more meaningful and more productive. From a positive perspective, organizations have an obligation to provide decent work.

The changing nature of work and workers

The evolution of jobs is shaped by wider societal forces, namely in the domains of technology and social organization. These result in changes in work and in workers, the primary topics discussed in this section. It is now widely accepted that work will be revolutionized in the near future as the fourth industrial evolution unfolds (see Box 5.2).

Box 5.2 The bright and the dark sides of the fourth industrial revolution

Is no office job safe?

The *Financial Times* 2015 book of the year was Martin Ford's *The Rise of the Robots*. Robots, artificial intelligence (AI), the Internet of things, cloud computing: these are some of the expressions of a coming revolution, billed by some as 'the fourth industrial revolution',[9] a broad term encompassing a constellation of technological advances that is altering the nature of work and organization. The first industrial revolution mechanized work with water and steam power; the second saw electric power used to drive mass production; the third automated work with electronics and information technologies. The coming fourth industrial revolution is seen as the result of a combination of AI, autonomous vehicles, 3D printing, quantum computing and probably other innovations yet to be seen.

The incoming revolution will produce important consequences, permitting cyber-physical systems to cooperate with each other and with humans in real time via the Internet of services and the Internet of things. The impact of this change is already visible in some sectors but it will probably increase the importance of acquiring, developing and retaining talent, a critical factor for competition.

The challenges will be immense. At the societal level, the rise of inequality is a major risk, as are job losses for the less educated. AI technologies have revolutionized the way computers learn and solve problems. Machine learning is no longer limited to variations of prompts from human-generated code. Now, AI chips mimic human cognitive functions wherein exposure to millions of images enhances the breadth and depth of the schema categories used as a reference to process and make sense of new impressions. Important approaches in this process include probabilistic inference, neural reference simulation, decision trees and pattern analysis.

AI is currently being integrated into systems to provide all kinds of services, including those that are mundane, along with those previously only provided by highly trained specialists. For example, AI robots are now deployed in screening customer calls, proposing insurance premium options, driving automated vehicles, executing military operations, diagnosing cancer, even in selecting embryos for assisted pregnancy. Automated cars, for example, will potentially recreate a number of industries, including manufacturing, trucking, retail and parking. Individually, the effects will not be negligible. Sebastian Thrun, an expert in AI, explained that 'No office job is safe', a declaration that led Simon Kuper, a journalist at the *Financial Times*, to write a column under the theme 'How to cope when robots take your job'.[10] Organizations will also have to adapt, and positive leadership can be viewed as a management philosophy more aligned with the management of organizations that expect more than repetitive execution from members. In this digital age, repetitive tasks will be performed by machines: people will have to use different skills, which will require different forms of management.

With regards to work design, one thing seems clear: the characteristics of well-designed jobs are not fixed but constructed in relation to specific social and technical systems. Consequently, instead of seeing some model as the Holy Grail of job design, it seems critical to consider that job designs will necessarily have to accommodate change in the sociotechnical domain.

Luminaries warning about the dark side of AI

Warnings by luminaries like Elon Musk and Nick Bostrom about 'the singularity' – when machines become smarter than humans – have attracted millions of dollars and spawned a multitude of conferences. But this hand-wringing is a distraction from the very real problems with artificial intelligence today, which may already be exacerbating inequality in the workplace, at home and in our legal and judicial systems. Sexism, racism and other forms of discrimination are being built into the machine-learning algorithms that underlie the technology behind many 'intelligent' systems that shape how we are categorized and advertised to.

Take a small example from last year: Users discovered that Google's photo app, which applies automatic labels to pictures in digital photo albums, was classifying images of black people as gorillas. Google apologized; it was unintentional. But similar errors have emerged in Nikon's camera software, which misread images of Asian people as blinking, and in Hewlett-Packard's web camera software, which had difficulty recognizing people with dark skin tones.[11]

Question for reflection

• Think about possible applications of AI for people management practices such as recruitment, selection, training and performance management. Be creative and inventive! Then, reflect on the possible advantages and problems of each application. Discuss your thoughts with other people.

From 'solid' stability to liquid modernity

Changes in the nature of work result from a number of forces, some of them quite broad, called the *omnibus* context. This 'big' context is composed of a number of important social and technological forces operating at several levels. Technological developments in fields such as AI, the Internet of things and 3-D printing are feeding the processes of the fourth industrial revolution. At the same time, globalization allows production to be geographically dispersed and flattened organizational structures have implications for leadership processes and empowerment. The notion of the *omnibus* context is important because it helps in understanding why and how jobs change: to some extent they change because the context of work changes.

Traditional job design approaches, especially the most traditional ones, were the product of their time. Careers were different in the past, jobs were relatively stable and organizations were more hierarchical. Organizations, however, are changing. They are less vertical and increasingly based on projects. Consider the following description:

> Now individuals may telecommute rather than come to the office or plant every morning. They may be responsible for balancing among several different activities and responsibilities, none of which is defined as their main job. They may work in temporary teams whose membership shifts as work requirements change. They may be independent contractors, managing simultaneously temporary or semi-permanent relationships with multiple enterprises. They may serve on a project team whose other members come from different organizations – suppliers, clients or organizational partners. They may be required to market their services within their own organizations, with no single boss, no home organizational unit, and no assurance of long-term employment.[12]

This depiction corresponds to what sociologist Zygmunt Bauman called liquid modernity. In the 'liquid' world as envisaged by Bauman, organizations are seen more as projects than vertical hierarchies or pyramids. This means that people will move from project to project rather than from hierarchy to hierarchy. Organizations subcontract work and operate as integrated networks. In some cases, 'creative' employees subcontract their own work: a programmer in the US recently outsourced his job to a worker in China for a fraction of the cost. This programmer was rated by his respective supervisor as one of the highest-performing professionals in the unit.[13] The case illustrates the challenges implied in the management of a highly autonomous workforce in liquid times.

The implications of these changes for the design of jobs are significant. For example, people will become partly responsible for the management of their careers. They will negotiate individualized deals that make sense for them (see discussion on I-Deals below). Careers will be defined by progression in terms of competence rather than by progression in a hierarchy. Teaming skills will become more important: the capacity to work with others without a common past or a predictable future (see Chapter 7). These organizations will be defined more by cooperation and mutual adjustment than by hierarchical integration, which will require more sophisticated self-leadership skills.[14]

Fluidity

For some people, employment relationships are becoming more fluid and precarious than they used to be. Work is sometimes conducted in flattened, project-based organizations, in cross-organizational teams, in interim jobs, as temporary workers who work in one agency but who are formally employees of another organization. Bauman's 'liquid' metaphor captures these new relational settings, in which what used to be a solid relationship becomes more temporary and unstable, as in the case of the gig economy (Box 5.3).

Box 5.3 Does the changing world of work have consequences for employee happiness?

The so-called gig economy is changing the workplaces of many: employees are transformed into freelancers with minimal benefits and the gig economy disrupting traditional industries that do offer stable work and benefits – Uber vs traditional taxis, Airbnb vs the hotel industry, Amazon vs the retail industry. The overall end result is more wealth going to the haves and taken from the have nots.[15] Some pioneering research[16] suggests that the gig economy has a number of positive dimensions: it offers autonomy and freedom, countering the alienating dimension of working for a boss. In other words, it can be presented as a source of emancipation. On the other hand, the gig economy creates a *precariat*, a class of people characterized by the lack of stability and protection. Therefore, the gig economy offers a paradoxical mix of 'agony and ecstasy'.[17] Jeffrey Sachs considers the broader implications of technology on business and society in the *Global Happiness Policy Report 2018*:[18]

> One of the key challenges facing every society is to benefit from the rapid advances of digital technologies, including artificial intelligence … Every economy will be affected. Most recently, these technological advances have favored a few of the Digital giants, Amazon, Apple, Alphabet (Google), Facebook, and Microsoft, making these five companies the most highly capitalized corporations in the world, with a combined market valuation in December 2017 of $3.3 trillion dollars. These companies have pioneered new services and business models, but the evidence is also growing that these business models threaten personal privacy, the faith in our electoral systems, and the exacerbation of inequalities of wealth and income.

Question for reflection

What are the consequences of AI for employee happiness? To reflect on this issue take into account the following argument of Jeffrey Sachs:[19]

> We know well that decent work is one of the most important underpinnings of happiness … Yet the digital revolution will almost surely cause a labor force upheaval in the years ahead. Many existing jobs will be rapidly replaced by smart machines; millions of individuals will struggle to find a viable livelihood, and often will have to accept a much lower wage. Happiness, in short, will be threatened unless societies find creative new ways to ensure basic livelihoods and dignity for all those who seek work.

Do you agree that happiness may be threatened by advances in AI? Why?

In liquid times, relationships between people and their organizations become more variable and the traditional expressions of loyalty lose meaning. Organizations grant employability rather than stable employment. Careers need to be redefined as protean, i.e., defined by the person, not the organization. People will reinvent their careers and will own them, instead of letting the organizations decide the shape of their careers for them. Despite the promise of flatness, these environments can become extremely panoptical. Translated into the corporate context, the panopticon, Jeremy Bentham's hexagonal architectural design, meant that the overseer, located in a tower at the centre, could observe all those working in the six cells radiating from the central tower without being watched. Organizations that adopt this and similar designs based on surveillance could control employees without actually being seen to do so, creating a context in which those under surveillance are always aware of the possibility that they are being watched. Being aware creates a form of psychic subjection to the norm of surveillance being enacted in conformance with managerial behavioural expectations. More autonomous employees will be controlled more subtly, by cultural norms, key performance indicators, teamwork, performance management practices, and so on. Today electronic and digital surveillance is pervasive, supplementing architectural with electronic panopticism.

Polarization of job quality

In parallel with the above movements, jobs have become more polarized. There are more good jobs and more bad jobs, with these two extremes becoming more differentiated than in the past.[20] Many jobs are McJobs (Box 5.4) or 'dead-ends'.[21] For the core organizational membership, organizations design enriched and enriching jobs to create solid 'employee brands'. Employee brands are critical to attract and retain so-called 'talent'. For core talent, organizations offer every type of perk that escalates commitment and presenteeism, especially in resource-rich organizations (from cafeterias catering to several types of dietary preferences, to sleeping pods, to pet-friendly policies). Other employees are viewed as human resources, hired and fired according to need and in coordination with efficiency criteria.

Service economy

As economies become more service-oriented, the nature of jobs is changing. Service jobs have a strong human component, rendering the so-called soft skills more important than in the past. The high contact involved in service work implies that social impact is more important than in traditional manufacturing jobs. When work is intensely interactional, the quality of interactions matters.[22] Where organizations are flattening[23] (i.e., reducing the number of intermediary levels between top and base) such that employees are, in some cases, less (explicitly) supervised than in the past, self-management, lateral skills and teamwork acquire increasing importance: it is harder to cheat yourself or your work mates than a supervisor.[24]

Gamification

Work gamification refers to the application of principles of digital and computer games to the work context. The expectation is that the transference of some principles found in the context of games will make work more interesting and exciting.[25] It is sometimes conceived as a new approach to job design.[26] Gamification could help to achieve two important goals simultaneously: to make jobs more enjoyable and to improve performance. Among the most important features of work gamification is the availability of feedback-enabling technologies that will offer real-time feedback to employees. The availability of real-time performance information, in turn, will stimulate people to improve. The process is expected to introduce important affective and informational benefits.

The process of gamification is, however, too recent to be considered a solid foundation for work design. It can be more useful for some tasks than others. For example, tasks that require intense cooperation may be less prone to being gamified. Gamification can create the risk of feedback overload.[27] It can apply particularly to individuals with a more competitive orientation. Furthermore, it can increase short-termism and action without reflection on the consequences of work. It can also contribute to creating the notion that work should be fun, which may be the case, but not necessarily. Work does not have to be a 'tripalium', a torture, but it may not be a game that will be interesting and fun. Gamification may also have negative consequence for performance and learning. Consider the following illustration and argument by Herminia Ibarra:[28]

> Combining social media, fitness tracking and gamification, the BetterWorks product allows people to set long- and short-term goals, log their progress on a digital dashboard that others in the company can see and comment on, and get instant feedback in the form of 'cheers' or 'nudges' from colleagues … London-based executive coach Gwenllian Williams tells me that transparent, tech-enhanced goal tracking raises performance, including her own. The cheering and nudging put in play the psychological principle in which a combination of peer pressure and social reinforcement pushes people to redouble their efforts. Also, the gaming aspects add fun and sustain attention, which encourages people to stick with it. However, critics worry that the less measurable but equally crucial tasks will be ignored. Because targets focus attention, they reduce people's awareness of other things that may be important even if they are not included in the tracking system … Enthusiasts and sceptics do agree, however, that goal-setting can impede learning, which requires apparently non-productive time. As psychologist Carol Dweck has shown, people who are being driven along by performance goals want to impress others with their achievements. Employees prefer tasks that will help them look good, rather than tasks that help them learn new ways of doing things.

Box 5.4 The McJob and the McDonaldization thesis

Sociologist George Ritzer coined the McDonaldization thesis, referring to the fact that many things in the world are becoming as similarly standardized as that fast food outlet's routines. Retail outlets and shopping malls are becoming ever more homogenous. The world is being shaped by the same brands and stores, with each one becoming more indistinguishable as they become standardized, often on the McDonald's model of inflexible systems, limited offerings and junk jobs. One of the characteristics of the McDonaldized world is the McJob, a term first used by Amitai Etzioni, an eminent sociologist, in an article published in *The Washington Post* in 1986. The idea entered the dictionaries, meaning low-skilled jobs, with low pay levels and limited career opportunities. Etzioni vehemently defended that McJobs are 'uneducational' in several ways, as they do not promote self-supervision, entrepreneurship or self-discipline given the fact that they are 'highly routinized'.[29] Although derived from the name of the global fast food chain, which protested at being signified in this way, it is widely used to refer to this job type in general. The McJob refers to precarious, poorly-designed jobs, often occupied by students and 'temps' (temporary workers) who are paid low salaries.

The McJob has been presented by critics as a professional dead-end, with no real opportunities. The McDonald's corporation responded by stating that it gives people an opportunity to get a job as students. The McJob, metaphorically speaking, represents jobs devoid of real opportunities for progress and personal growth, the epitome of Tayloristic scientific-management-designed jobs and the main vestige of primitive modernity in the present.

Changes in workers

Changes in work evolve side by side with changes in workers. Increasing levels of formal education have led more qualified people to see themselves as owners of human capital and as volunteers in their organizations.[30] These people expect their organizations to appreciate (rather than to deprecate and depreciate) their human capital. When organizations do act appreciatively, they are able to attempt more valuable organizational projects, becoming better able to appreciate the human capital they can attract.

Organizations are also now more aware than in the past about cross-generational differences. In the same organization, different generations will work together: Veterans (1925–1942), Baby Boomers (1943–1960), Generation X (1961–1976), Generation Y or Millennials (1977–1994)[31] and Generation Z (1995–2012).[32] Different generations bring diverse expectations to the workplace. Changes in worker expectations invite organizations to design work flexibly to meet different types of expectations. On the one hand, they have to tailor work to the specifics of each generation. For example, some research indicates that Generation Y gives less importance to intrinsic motivational factors but attributes more value to work–life balance than previous generations.[33] This suggests that Generation Y may respond less to job design than previous generations.

The (timeless) search for decent work

Despite all the changes in work and organizations, for millions of people the right to decent work is still a mirage. In the modern world, there are still a considerable number of people (estimated at about 27 million) whose work is executed in conditions of modern slavery.[34] Even respected, supposedly well-managed organizations submit their workers to unbearable working conditions that in some cases have culminated in waves of work-related suicides[35] (see Box 5.5).

Box 5.5 Perverse consequences of 'ever-expanding ambitions'

1 A very successful 'Bruising Workplace'

On 16 August 2015, *The New York Times* published an article titled 'Inside Amazon: Wrestling Big Ideas in a Bruising Workplace'. It was argued than the company was 'conducting an experiment in how far it can push white collar workers to get them to achieve its ever-expanding ambitions'.[36] Read the article or, at least, the following excerpts:

- 'At Amazon, workers are encouraged to tear apart one another's ideas in meetings, toil long and late (emails arrive past midnight, followed by text messages asking why they were not answered), and held to standards that the company boasts are 'unreasonably high.' The internal phone directory instructs colleagues on how to send secret feedback to one another's bosses. Employees say it is frequently used to sabotage others. (The tool offers sample texts, including this: 'I felt concerned about his inflexibility and openly complaining about minor tasks.')'.
- 'Some workers who suffered from cancer, miscarriages and other personal crises said they had been evaluated unfairly or edged out rather than given time to recover.'
- 'In Amazon warehouses, employees are monitored by sophisticated electronic systems to ensure they are packing enough boxes every hour. (Amazon came under fire in 2011 when workers in an eastern Pennsylvania warehouse toiled in more than 100-degree heat with ambulances waiting outside, taking away laborers as they fell. After an investigation by the local newspaper, the company installed air-conditioning.)'
- 'Motherhood can also be a liability. Michelle Williamson, a 41-year-old parent of three who helped build Amazon's restaurant supply business, said her boss, Shahrul Ladue, had told her that raising children would most likely prevent her from success at a higher level because of the long hours required. Mr. Ladue, who confirmed her account, said that Ms. Williamson had been directly competing with younger colleagues with fewer commitments, so he suggested she find a less demanding job at Amazon. (Both he and Ms. Williamson left the company.) He added that he usually worked 85 or more hours a week and rarely took a vacation.'
- 'A woman who had breast cancer was told that she was put on a 'performance improvement plan' – Amazon code for 'you're in danger of being fired' – because 'difficulties' in her 'personal life' had interfered with fulfilling her work goals. Their accounts echoed others from workers who had suffered health crises and felt they had also been judged harshly instead of being given time to recover.'

Jeff Bezos responded to this story by sending an email[37] to Amazon employees stating that he didn't 'recognize the company described in the article', and requesting:

> But if you know of any stories like those reported, I want you to escalate to HR. You can also email me directly at jeff@amazon.com. Even if it's rare or isolated, our tolerance for any such lack of empathy needs to be zero.

Shortly after, Joe Nocera wrote in *The New York Times*:[38]

Even when Bezos sent around an email last weekend about the *Times* story, he didn't exactly apologize. He said that he didn't recognize the Amazon *The Times* wrote about, and that some of the incidents were so callous they should have been reported to the human resources department. But he didn't say they weren't true. That's because they are true. The real issue Amazon's work culture raises – for blue- and white-collar employees alike – is: How disposable are people?

2 What is the right thing to do?

Questions for reflection

- How do you interpret the success of Amazon.com in light of the picture above?
- Revisit the Box I.2, in the Introduction, about Jeffrey Pfeffer's argument that 'The leaders we admire aren't always that admirable' and that 'People participate in and rationalize their own subjugation'. Do you agree with this argument? Why?

In the 2005 World Summit of the United Nations General Assembly, the heads of state of more than 150 countries committed to implement an agenda facilitating 'decent work for all, including women and young children'. The International Labour Organization was involved in the coordination of a Decent Work Agenda, which defends the proposition that people should not only have jobs but also that these jobs should respect the principles of high-quality work, providing opportunities for flourishing and empowerment.[39] Decent work is characterized by:

> conditions of freedom, equity, security and human dignity. Decent work involves opportunities for work that is productive and delivers a fair income; provides security in the workplace and social protection for workers and their families; offers better prospects for personal development and encourages social integration; gives people the freedom to express their concerns, to organize and participate in decisions that affect their lives; and guarantees equal opportunities and equal treatment for all.[40]

What is important about the Decent Work Agenda is the fact that it transforms work design, broadly understood, into a societal and political issue, rather than it being a purely organizational choice. This change in perspective is supported by the fact that the choices organizations make have implications for society at large. As will be discussed below, managerial choices have an impact on the lives of employees as well as healthcare expenses. The Decent Work Agenda indicates that these costs should not be simply 'externalized' to taxpayers and that organizations have a responsibility for designing work that is balanced and minimizes the costs of poor work design, including ill health, mental and physical, that can result from careless and inconsiderate design. Pfeffer has similarly argued:

> There is no reason why building sustainable companies should focus only on the physical and not on the social environment. It is not just the natural world that is at risk from harmful business practices. We should care as much about people as

we do about polar bears – or the environmental savings from using better milk jugs – and also understand the causes and consequences of how we focus our research and policy attention.[41]

Work design matters for several reasons: several are central and discussed in this chapter and they are motivation and learning, as well as health and wellbeing. In fact, research indicates that well-designed jobs bring a number of important organizational and individual advantages, in terms of performance and satisfaction as well as wellbeing. Good job design is not a silver bullet for high performance but it has been associated with a number of desirable organizational outcomes. Stated differently, poor job designs and negative leadership practices may have consequences in terms of employees' health, morbidity and mortality.[42]

What is my work: a job? A career? A calling?

Naturally, how organizations and their leaders behave has consequences for how employees perceive their jobs and how they experience hedonic or eudemonic wellbeing (see below). The fact is that the work can be perceived variously by different people. It is often perceived as if work is objective: a job, is a job, is a job. The same job, however, can be approached by different people in highly distinct ways (see Box 5.6).

Box 5.6 Turning a career into a calling

We all go into professions for many reasons: money, status, security. But some people have experiences that turn a career into a calling. These experiences quiet the self. All that matters is living up to the standard of excellence inherent in their craft. Frances Perkins was a young woman who was an activist for progressive causes at the start of the 20th century. She was polite and a bit genteel. But one day she stumbled across the Triangle Shirtwaist factory fire, and watched dozens of garment workers hurl themselves to their deaths rather than be burned alive. That experience shamed her moral sense and purified her ambition. It was her call within a call. After that, she turned herself into an instrument for the cause of workers' rights. She was willing to work with anybody, compromise with anybody, push through hesitation. She even changed her appearance so she could become a more effective instrument for the movement. She became the first woman in a United States cabinet, under Franklin D. Roosevelt, and emerged as one of the great civic figures of the 20th century.[43]

Questions for reflection

- Think about the triggers that made leaders such as Mandela and Lincoln respond to 'calls'.
- What kind of triggers may unfold in organizations that make individuals find their calling?

Work orientations

The manner in which people make sense of their jobs can transform the nature of work itself. Stanford University Professor Amy Wrzesniewski and colleagues refer to different attitudes towards work as related to one's work orientation.[44] For some, work is a job; others see it as a career; some approach work as a calling.[45] For people who orient towards their work as a *job* — it is a means for some material advantage, namely a salary. Someone with a job orientation is motivated to work solely for extrinsic, immediate, material financial rewards. The relation is fundamentally transactional and the attitude instrumental.[46] People work '9 to 5' and receive their salary, to support their families, pay their rent or mortgage and to fund their leisure activities. Individual interests are not expressed through work but motivation can be managed (e.g., family motivation) as a source of meaning and energy. When intrinsic motivation is lacking, the family can be activated as a source of psychological energy and a facilitator of high performance.[47]

When seen as a *career*, work has a different meaning. A person with a career orientation is motivated by opportunities for achieving prestige, power, recognition and advancement. A career involves a sense of progress and advancement in an organization's professional structure. With such progress come more material benefits, social prestige, increased power and behavioural latitude as well as possible benefits in terms of the self, such as sense of success and self-worth.

In both of the cases, job and career orientations, the work is approached as a means towards achieving something else held to be meaningful. Someone with a calling, in contrast, works for the sake of the work itself, viewing the work as intrinsically motivating and inherently fulfilling, for which the classical reference is Max Weber's analysis of 'Science as a vocation'.[48] Here, work is a central part of life, a central dimension of the self, an end in itself, an expression of the social contribution one makes. Money and advancement are not the sole or sometimes not even the main motivators, because accomplishing work provides a sense of fulfilment. These people aim to 'make a difference'; sometimes they are highly trained professionals such as scientists and doctors; sometimes they can be found in dangerous sites, including war theatres, where doctors are working as rear-located medics, where the professional ethos and the care for those in extreme danger is melded.[49]

Next time you go to an organization (say a coffee shop, a supermarket, a bank), take a close look at the employees' behaviour. Try to associate their attitude to work: does it appear to be a job, career or calling? Can you identify people who see work as a mere job? Have you noticed behaviours typical of a sense of calling? Have you noticed organizations that stimulate a disproportional amount of engaged behaviours? How would you explain this?

Some research indicates that people with a sense of calling tend to be viewed by others as more trustworthy.[50] The word 'calling' originally comes from the religious vocabulary, where it refers to a sense of being 'called' by God to do something socially and morally meaningful, for which, once again, Weber provides the classic reference in his analysis of the 'protestant ethic'.[51] Work becomes an end in itself, which does not mean that the activities involved need to be intrinsically pleasurable. But being 'called' implies significant challenges for the chosen (see Box 5.7).

Box 5.7 The positive in the negative, and the negative in the positive

1 Finding a call in a 'poor' job

You might think that only people working in caring professions such as doctors, dentists or teachers can realistically expect to be oriented to a calling. Could we expect a calling orientation of someone working in low-paying work such as, for example, a supermarket cashier? Research suggests that the three orientations (job, career and calling) can be found across professions, it depends not only on the type of work but also the employees' interpretation of the work. Wrzesniewski and Dutton found, for example, that in a hospital, whereas most cleaners had a job orientation towards their work that included having to clean excrement and vomit off oncology ward floors, some had a calling orientation. These cleaners saw their work as critical in contributing to the patients' healing. Building on our earlier supermarket example, the US supermarket chain Wholefoods has a policy of recruiting employees with a calling orientation to ensure they fit with the organization's conscious culture and its stated purpose, which is: 'to nourish people and the planet'. People with a calling orientation tend to find a higher level of meaning and purpose in their work than those with job or career orientations. They achieve this sense of meaning by engaging in what Wrzesniewski and colleagues refer to as job crafting (discussed later in this chapter).

2 The dark side of calls

A calling is generally portrayed as a positive source of meaning and intrinsic motivation. The called are presented as passionate people who deeply care about their work. The calling orientation has been correlated with happiness, engagement, fulfilment. Calling has been associated with four characteristics: passion for the work; enjoyment of the work; a sense of obligation; the need to make a prosocial difference.

A calling can also have negative effects. For example, supervisors may adopt an opportunistic approach against employees whose work is lived as a calling. A zookeeper said 'I would not tell them [how committed I am] because they can get a strong hold on you that way. If management knows you love your job, they'll try to do things to undercut your pay and stuff like that'. Other possible negative effects are fatigue and perceptions of ideological violation. These negative effects can be explained differently. People with a sense of calling can, for example, develop unrealistic expectations about the nature of the work involved in the pursuit of their calls. They can subsequently feel disappointed because reality is less beautiful than they anticipated. Or they can overinvest, sacrificing their wellbeing for the cause.

Seeing work as a calling reveals the presence of intrinsic motivation, which in turn is one of the predictors of the state called flow, wherein people feel so absorbed by an activity that their concentration is complete (Figure 5.2).[52] Flow has been associated with peak performance, and emerges when perceived ability matches the challenge. The opposite of flow at work is when people develop a 'job myopia' approach (the so-called 'that's not my job' syndrome) and restrict their contribution to what is strictly predicted in formal terms.[53] In other words, work can stimulate both optimal and aversive experiences.

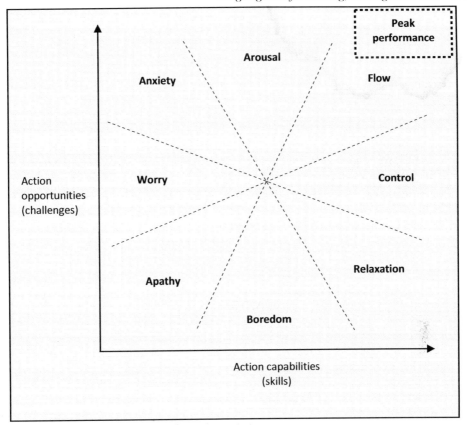

Figure 5.2 The optimal experience of flow.[54]

Eudemonic and hedonic wellbeing

Different approaches to work help to distinguish the two components of psychological well-being normally delineated by psychologists and already introduced in Chapter 1: a hedonic component and a eudemonic component. The hedonic dimension, in the organizational context, refers to the subjective evaluation of the work experience in terms of the pleasure and the positive (and negative) thoughts and feelings it evokes. The more satisfied an employee is, the higher his/her degree of hedonic wellbeing. As will be discussed, organizations have managed this dimension via work design: they try to structure jobs in such a way that people see their work as a source of positive feelings and attitudes.

Feeling positive about one's work is obviously positive but some authors claim that this sort of approach to organization represents a state of passive contentment. As observed by Grant and his colleagues, sometimes this state is described with bovine metaphors: people in this state are akin to 'contented cows', in a state of 'bovine contentment'.[55] This state, according to the critics, is closer to a state of passivity than to genuine happiness. This view is consistent with the search for work designs conducive to obedience and compliance. In this approach, what can be critically represented as bovine passivity may be, in fact, a functional response to work design.

In humanistic organization theory, satisfaction has been perceived as one of the fundamental outcomes of people management, a positive attitude with a number of desirable consequences, such as low turnover, higher productivity, more expressions of citizenship. In this sense, developing employees with an overall positive attitude about work and organization, one with a clear hedonic resonance, was an important organizational requirement. Scholars are now emphasizing the need to combine hedonic with eudemonic wellbeing. This refers to fulfilment and pursuing meaningful purpose. In organizations, it refers to the extent to which individuals see their work as a source of purpose and personal fulfilment. In this sense, work should generate more than passive contentment: it should be designed to allow people to accomplish something significant. For example, staffers at Wegman's grocery chain explain that doing fulfilling work offers them a sense of purpose. The company's mission, 'helping people live healthier, better lives through food', is part of the explanation.[56]

In practical terms, this approach of emphasizing meaning and purpose in work represents a path that differs, markedly, from the pursuit of hedonic work goals. When organizations assume the challenge of investing in eudemonic wellbeing, they have to find ways to raise intrinsic motivation. In this case, motivation is not something that comes from the outside (such as a well-designed job, adequate rewards) but from the inner search for some meaningful orientation, a purpose. This involves the definition of purpose and a vision that subsumes such purpose – employees not only complete their tasks; they know *why* they are accomplishing them. NASA's purpose of advancing knowledge by landing a man on the moon provides perhaps the ultimate example of the power of ultimate goals. Knowing *why* work needs to be done is a powerful way of explaining to oneself why one's daily tasks are worth caring about. Leaders play a fundamental role in this process, framing purpose in a way that is credible and aspirational.[57] Furthermore, if people represent their work as meaningful, they will potentially be able to act as crafters rather than as mere receivers of tasks designed by others. This can increase the adjustment of work to the needs of the customer – internal or external.

Research has shown that the effects of external sources of motivation, such as pay, should not be overestimated. Pay is important of course (it signals success, confers social prestige, facilitates the acquisition of necessary or desired goods), but its motivational effects are limited.[58] Job characteristics are better predictors of satisfaction than pay. The implications are clear for both individuals and organizations. Organizations should not consider pay as the yellow brick road to motivation and meaning. Investing in good leadership, purpose, positive relationships and well-designed jobs is an important complement of fair pay. For organizations, it means that defining purpose and clarifying the management practices that support such a purpose can offer competitive advantage (Box 5.8). The creation of corporate volunteering is a way of mobilizing people for their organization's cause. Corporate volunteering practices foster a sense of collective pride even for those employees who do not volunteer, having a positive impact on affective commitment with the organization.[59]

In aligning a stated purpose with clear practice, it is necessary for that purpose to be credible and practical: declarations of purpose in the absence of supportive examples limit their credibility,[60] sooner or later. At Wells Fargo, managers showed bankers videos of people describing how low-interest loans rescued them from severe debt. This practice allegedly 'aimed to remind bankers that they are striving to serve their customers, not their managers'.[61] Shortly afterwards, however, the company was caught in a scandal of fake accounts and other unethical behaviours,[62] as a consequence of a 'pressure-cooker sales culture'.[63]

Box 5.8 Purpose: in search of why

In some cases, people know *why* they have to do their work because they have spontaneously grasped it. They have found meaning at work because they have the joy of doing their dream jobs (say the jobs they envisioned when they were children). For example, people with a passion for animals may see zoo-keeping as intrinsically motivating work.[64] Of course, other people may take it as simply dirty, dangerous, meaningless work.

Most people, however, are less fortunate and have to do something other than their dream jobs. But they can learn to like their work. One powerful way to do so consists in answering why their work is meaningful and important. In some companies, practices have been developed to instil a sense of learning. One example is constituted by the so-called Patient Days at Medtronic, a company specialized in medical technologies. In order to clarify its sense of purpose, the company introduced an initiative which consists of inviting people whose lives have been positively touched by the company's products to explain why and how their lives are better because of Medtronic and its people. One of the authors once met a Medtronic worker who confessed that it was normal, during these events, to see people crying, given the highly emotional content of the sessions. It can be emotionally touching to see the impact that one's everyday work might be having.

In other cases, some people spontaneously change their jobs (craft them, as we will explain next) to increase their content. In Lisbon, Portugal, Samuel, an employee on the toll of the 25th of April bridge, enriched his work by making it more high contact. He sells tickets but has learned to manage 'his' customers in a personalized way. He became so popular that a Facebook page was dedicated to him, with more than 12,000 'likes'. People some of the authors have met, customers of his, confess that Samuel makes their day seem better.

The recent focus on eudemonic wellbeing (see Chapters 1 and 4), translated into the notion of purpose, indicates that it is necessary to broaden the understanding of work design so that it is perceived not as something that managers do so much as a process of articulating an organizational purpose that provides people with local potentialities for self-management and discretion. Instead of seeing workers as passive receivers of black-boxed tasks, organizations need to design work as a source of learning and adaptation. Historically, in work design, classical models were top-down indications of what to do, whereas more recent approaches represent people as active builders of their jobs.

Managing through work design: from the top down to bottom up

Substantial research indicates that it is feasible to imagine and design work with positive consequences for individuals and organizations. Work design refers to 'the content and

Table 5.1 Approaches to job design: a comparison[66]

Dimensions	Job redesign	I-Deals	Job crafting
Who starts the change	Management	Managers and employees, by negotiation	The employee
How implementation proceeds	Through planning	Through employee–management negotiation	Via employee discretion
Permission	Formal	Negotiated and within the organization's policies	Informal
Employee's role	Recipient, mainly	Actor and recipient	Agent
Focus	Classes of jobs	Individual jobs	Individual jobs
Primary goal	Increase in intrinsic motivation and performance	Mutual benefits	Personal needs or motivations, aligned with work
Design content	Work characteristics	The employment relation	Tasks and interactions
Results expected	Objective changes in tasks	Objective, contractual changes	Objective or non-objective (cognitive reinterpretation) changes
Process	Episodic, rare	Intermittent	Process, ongoing
Organizational mindset	Top down	Both	Bottom up

organization of one's tasks, activities, relationships and responsibilities'.[65] The more traditional notion of 'job design', which instead refers to a set of prescribed, more or less fixed tasks within a job, is now less relevant. As discussed in this chapter, this top–down approach to the design of work is now complemented with the view that work is also sculptured in a proactive, emergent and bottom–up way by workers (Table 5.1).

'One best way'

One of the earliest modern approaches to job design from the late 1890s was Frederick Taylor's 'scientific management' (Figure 5.3). By experimenting with different uses of time and motion, industrial engineers sought to create the 'one best way' to do a given job. Discovery of the best way was aimed at simplifying and standardizing work to the point that one worker could be replaced by another, as if the organization constituted a big machine. It is no coincidence that Taylor was himself a mechanical engineer.

Taylor's goal was to prevent the waste of human effort and to create efficient and reliable organizations. 'Scientific management', as he called it, created several dysfunctions, however, that to some extent neutralized the efficiency that the approach sought to achieve. Scientific management can be explained as a management philosophy that assigns mental work to managers and manual work to employees.[68] This was achieved through job fragmentation and simplification. The impact was tremendous in terms of efficiency but strikes, absenteeism and turnover, as well as a sense of alienation from work, were unanticipated consequences. The introduction of Fordism, based on the moving production line, only made the alienation worse as basic work cycles could be as little as 15 seconds, repeated at a pace dictated by the speed of the line.[69] The fruits of this

Figure 5.3 Frederic Taylor (1856–1915) named his approach 'scientific management'.[67]

philosophy are satirized in Charlie Chaplin's movie *Modern Times*, particularly in a famous segment where the worker on a Fordist production line acts as if he were a robot, repeating the same gesture even after completing his shift, because the production line had become embodied in his everyday being at work (Figure 5.4). Today, car factories use robots designed to replace people rather than designing people to be robots.

Figure 5.4 Original poster for Chaplin's 1936 film *Modern Times*.[70]

In extreme cases of Tayloristic implementation, such as in some automobile factories, people simply sabotaged the system,[71] for example by damaging the cars they were themselves producing:

> [In the GM Fremont plant, around 1980] Workers intentionally sabotaged many vehicles. For example, empty cola bottle caps were left in the doors with the sole purpose to annoy the customer through its clanking sound. Or worse, half-eaten

tuna sandwiches were welded in.[72] Cars were intentionally scratched. Screws on safety-critical parts were deliberately left loose. The employees wanted to hurt the company by hurting the customer.[73]

Taylorism also had an upside. In addition to significant efficiency gains, it contributed to the creation of what the so-called Nobel Prize for Economics[74] winner Daniel Kahneman and his colleagues called 'noise-free' jobs[75] (i.e., jobs such as that of a clerk at a bank or post office, where their occupants are supposed to follow strict rules in order to perform their jobs in the same way). Tasks can be complex while their execution is predictable. This, in principle, produces highly consistent and reliable organizations. Even these highly scripted jobs can be made 'noisy', as is now known. The philosophy is clear: 'scientifically designed' jobs will create genuine machine-like organizations – for better and for worse. Such jobs may be reliable and predictable in how what is being done is accomplished but they will also be monotonous for those acting like cogs in the big organizational machinery. As Weber presciently remarked at the turn of the 20th century (see also Box 5.9):

> It is horrible to think that the world could one day be filled with nothing but those little cogs, little men clinging to little jobs and striving towards bigger ones – a state of affairs which is to be seen once more, as in the Egyptian records, playing an ever-increasing part in the spirit of our present administrative system, and especially of its offspring, the students. This passion for bureaucracy ... Is enough to drive one to despair. It is as if in politics ... We were deliberately to become men who need 'order' and nothing but order, become nervous and cowardly if for one moment this order wavers, and helpless if they are torn away from their total incorporation in it. That the world should know no men but these: it is such an evolution that we are already caught up, and the great question is, therefore, not how we can promote and hasten it, but what can we oppose to this machinery in order to keep a portion of mankind free from this parcelling-out of the soul, from this supreme mastery of the bureaucratic way of life.[76]

Box 5.9 Still Taylorist after all these years?

It is easy and comforting to think that Taylorist work is a relic of a past long gone, an echo of a black and white organizational movie, similar to Chaplin's *Modern Times*. But consider the following passage from an essay by David Courpasson:[77]

> nothing has really changed since Taylor: the Google factory may be more outwardly smiling, more connected, and its offices more colourful too, but it is still designed to constrain bodies to be at work all the time, by mixing up leisure and work, by tying people physically to their workplace. This nicely oppressive factory reproduces a view of the adequate worker as being physically resilient for supporting the long hours that s/he spends at work, which is the exact spitting image of the corporeal Taylorian discipline.

Some researchers argue that top managers still maintain a Taylorist mindset as an 'enduring cultural frame'.[78] This cultural frame may represent a naive inclination in terms of designing jobs: simplification and its supposed resultant efficiency may inform the dominant logic of work design as demonstrated in a study with MBA students playing the role of naïve job designers.[79] Is it possible that even a century after Taylor, we still represent Taylorism as the template for good job design?

Questions for reflection

- Could there be a post-modern, digital-age version of Taylorism?
- Do the new forms of positive management function as a colourful version of Taylorism for the 21st century?

By the 1960s and 1970s, the limits of such an approach to job design were well known. In Japan, Toyota maintained a Taylorist ethos of repetition and standardization but invited employees to improve their jobs and the organization's processes.[80] Under the logic of *kaizen*, or continuous improvement, every employee is a designer (i.e., thinker) and an executant.

Frederick Herzberg presented a radically different approach to job design, suggesting that jobs should be enriched, not simplified, and that job enrichment is crucial for creating a motivated and high-performing workforce. Herzberg distinguished hygiene and motivating factors. Hygiene factors, if poorly handled, would lead to dissatisfaction but could not be used to motivate, as motivation would result from factors related to growing competence, responsibility and recognition. Herzberg's work attracted significant attention and was the origin of the job characteristics model, further developed by Hackman and Oldham (see also Box 5.10).

Box 5.10 Job design and the promotion of initiative[81]

One way of enriching work is allowing individuals to take the initiative and improve both their work and the organizational processes with which they are involved. Parker qualified this approach as a combination of a 'can do', 'reason to' and 'energized to' motivational states. If one's organization provides space for people to develop a sense of power and mastery, they will develop self-efficacy beliefs that, in turn, will stimulate people to reflect as they practice and to be enthusiastic about their work. As individuals feel involved, the improvement initiatives will support organizational learning on an ongoing basis. The combination of perceptions of job control and social support predict proactive work behaviour.[82] The above, in turn, will allow individuals to develop a perception of control of 'variance at the source' to immediately gather feedback about their actions. By understanding the effects of their actions and feeling in control of their work, employees develop sophisticated mental models of work and an anticipatory understanding of consequences, allowing them to prevent process problems and deficiencies.[83] Research suggests that work design promotes learning, as it facilitates attention control through psychological flexibility.

The job characteristics model

The influential job characteristics model (JCM) was introduced by Hackman and Oldham in 1975. According to this model, five core characteristics define the motivational richness of a job: task identity, task significance, skill variety, feedback and autonomy. For decades, the job characteristics model was the dominant approach to job design.[84] The model suggests that organizations can enrich work by investing in jobs rich in the five enunciated characteristics:

- **Task identity** refers to 'the degree to which the job requires completion of a "whole" and identifiable piece of work – that is, doing a job from beginning to end with a visible outcome'.[85] Task identity matters because if one contributes only a tiny fraction to a larger process without any sense of completion, work is hardly reflected in one's identity. Doing something beginning to end, as a solitary craft worker, such as a painter or an artist working alone in some other medium, has desirable consequences for one's identity. Two trends, the adoption of leaner, flattened hierarchies[86] and the necessities imposed by teamwork, stimulate the merging of previously distinct jobs. Some research confirms that the change in the direction of assigning jobs as wholes rather than parts increases task identity.[87] In addition, the move towards a service economy, one in which workers complete a set of tasks to provide a complete service to a customer, may have increased the perception of task identity.
- **Task significance** describes 'the degree to which the job has substantial impact on the lives or work of other people – whether in the immediate organization or in an external environment'.[88]
- **Skill variety** refers to 'the degree to which the job requires a variety of different activities in carrying out the work, involving the use of a number of different skills and talents of the person'.[89]
- **Job-based feedback** describes 'the degree to which carrying out the work activities required by the job provides the individual with direct and clear information about the effectiveness of his or her performance'.[90]
- **Autonomy** is 'the degree to which the job provides substantial freedom, independence and discretion to the individual in scheduling the work and in determining the procedures to be used carrying it out'.[91]

Together, identity, significance and variety will in principle contribute to the meaningfulness experienced on the job. Autonomy will contribute to a sense of felt responsibility and feedback will contribute to the direct knowledge of results. These three critical psychological states – perceiving one's work as meaningful, feeling individually responsible for the outcomes of work and knowing the results of one's efforts – lead to internal motivation and superior performance.

The model is predicted to apply to the majority of people, with the authors considering two individual differences: growth needs strength as well as knowledge and skill. 'Growth needs strength' refers to the degree to which one person sees the opportunity to grow as positive. The idea is that people may be more or less responsive to challenging jobs. Job-related knowledge and skill are also important because even people highly responsive to challenge will lose their motivation if they lack important skills and therefore fail, more than they succeed, in getting the work done. Naturally, specific job characteristics may motivate individuals with diverse needs and motivations differently. For example, a job characterized by high autonomy is more motivating for an employee characterized by a high level of autonomy needs than one who has a lower need for autonomy.

The job characteristics model has been highly successful in showing that it is an organization's responsibility to design work in such a way that jobs constitute a source of intrinsic motivation for their occupants. The JCM's important contribution notwithstanding, it (1) focusses on the job itself, paying less attention to the social context in which it takes place and (2), constitutes a top-down approach to job design: it represents job enrichment as a process managed by the organization in an effort to make a class of jobs more intrinsically motivating. Abundant research attests to the power of the JCM, including meta-analytical work.[92]

The JCM assumes a sort of 'passive contentment'[93] in terms of how people approach work, which certainly describes some but not all people. The top-down approach fails to explain the way individuals can change how and what they do at work on their own initiative or how people *craft* their jobs. The JCM is also not necessarily sensitive to temporal dynamics: individual motivations may change over time as individuals accumulate 'on the job' experience. Different individuals may react differently: some may start crafting their work (those with a calling orientation), others may feel frustrated with the lack of stimulation (those with a career orientation), whereas others may accept things as they are and look for excitement outside of work (those with a job orientation).[94] Not everybody has the same expectations and because of this organizations started to develop idiosyncratic deals with their employees.

I-Deals: designing jobs idiosyncratically

Another powerful expression of partly bottom-up job design is known as idiosyncratic deals or, briefly, I-Deals. I-Deals are 'voluntary, personalized agreements of a nonstandard nature negotiated between individual employees and their employers regarding terms that benefit each party'.[95] I-Deals have four defining characteristics. First, employees negotiate personalized individual contractual arrangements with their organizations. These individualized terms may be initiated by the employee or the organization. Second, the bargains result in different individual terms that may confront teams with fairness issues. Third, I-Deals are expected to benefit the two parties. The employee can satisfy some personal need by designing contracts idiosyncratically. The employers will possibly gain in terms of attracting or retaining employees. Fourth, because of their very nature, I-Deals may vary significantly inside the same organization. In some cases, the deal may be fairly standardized with some idiosyncrasies, whereas in other cases the contract may be much more singular.

From a positive perspective, I-Deals are expected to be beneficial because employees are supposed to reciprocate the organization's willingness to fit the context to individual needs and motivations. From the organization's part, reciprocation may result from the fact that the organization recognizes the unique contributions and characteristics of individuals.[96]

Job crafting: designing motivating jobs bottom up

Traditional approaches represented jobs as 'black boxes', designed at the top. Job design studied 'how people fit with their jobs'.[97] Organizations with this approach knew what to expect from workers. As Argyris put it, 'Years ago, when organizations still wanted employees who did only what they were told',[98] they designed jobs in order to elicit the behaviours they wanted. Recently, however, some organizations have begun to accept that they cannot plan for every contingency in a rapidly changing market landscape. They therefore need employees who not only do what they're told but also do what they have to do to achieve organizational objectives.

Bottom-up job design (i.e., job design initiated by workers themselves) is gaining traction in a service economy in which employees can tailor work, for intrinsic and extrinsic reasons, making it a better 'fit' with their expectations. Freedom to craft helps people 'learn to like' their jobs.[99] Intrinsically, crafting can adjust work to individual motivations. One of the established concepts in terms of bottom-up job design is known as *job crafting*, comprising processes of sculpting one's job to make it more suitable to personal and/or client needs.

Developed by researchers at the University of Michigan Center for Positive Organizations, job crafting involves consciously or unconsciously assessing and altering core work practices or orientations to experience a greater sense of meaning. As described by three central proponents of job crafting theory, Wrzesniewski, Berg and Dutton, when employees engage in job crafting, they turn the jobs they have into the jobs they want.[100]

Workers do not necessarily passively accept their work as a given, as crystalized in some job description. While some so-called job-myopic employees[101] actually do stay within the bounds of their formal roles, doing what they are supposed to do, others instead respond to what they perceive as necessary measures for getting the job done and responding to customer needs via the exercise of proactive behaviour, a category of actions that includes job crafting, expressions of voice, role expansion and task revision.[102] Job crafting has been defined as 'the physical and cognitive changes individuals make in their task or relational boundaries'.[103] Wrzesniewski and Dutton point out that through job crafting, individuals alter the boundaries of their work.[104] Three core boundary conditions that are the focus areas for job crafting are:

- *The task* boundaries – the tasks themselves, be they in the number of operations.
- *The relationship* boundaries – the way people interact with others in their work environment.
- *The cognitive* boundaries – the way the job is perceived by its incumbents.

People can adjust the boundaries of their work tasks, by taking more or fewer responsibilities, by extending or minimizing the scope of the tasks they perform, or by reviewing how tasks are performed. Relationships can make work more meaningful through efforts to enhance the quality of workplace human interactions. Finally, and possibly most importantly, perceptions can make work more meaningful by adjusting personal views concerning the purpose of certain aspects of one's work or reframing perceptions of one's work as a whole.

Evangelia Demerouti[105] has advanced three related practical dimensions of crafting: through crafting, people may engage in resource seeking (asking a colleague or a superior for feedback or advice), challenge seeking (autonomy maximization) and demands reduction (for example, eliminating some physical or emotional demands). Job crafting is important for organizations because it can make jobs more meaningful, more engaging and more satisfying. It constitutes a form of proactive work behaviour in which employees initiate changes in terms of job demands or job resources to make them more gratifying or responsive to change. Job crafting has been predicted to increase adaptivity and engagement. Employees, in other words, spontaneously introduce modifications in their jobs that are unsupervised, in the sense that they are not sanctioned by their organizations. The organizational context influences the expression of crafting. Some contexts, more supportive of change and proactivity, are more conducive to crafting than others (see Box 5.11). In other words, crafting is a bottom-up strategy in which the way organizations communicate their norms influences positively or negatively the adoption of crafting.[106] Personality and hierarchical position also influence the inclination to craft one's work.[107]

Box 5.11 Crafting your job by hiring your next supervisor

Inside organizations, people often need support to craft their jobs. Managers can play a major role in designing motivating, meaningful jobs. The best go out of their way to help people do work they enjoy – even if it means rotating them out of roles where they're excelling. A few years ago, one of Facebook's directors, Cynthia, was leading a large team of HR business partners. She realized that she wasn't spending her time doing what she enjoyed most: solving problems with her clients. She had taken on more responsibilities managing a large team because of her strength as a trusted adviser to some of Facebook's key leaders. But once she was in the job, she realized it meant doing less of the work that energized her. With her manager's support, Cynthia hired someone new onto the team, with the long-term vision of asking her to run the team and then moving back to an individual contributor role. Cynthia wasn't just hiring a direct report; she was hiring her future boss. Once the new hire was ramped up, and it was clear that she enjoyed the organizational and people management elements of her job, she and Cynthia made the switch. Cynthia is now thriving, solving problems with the clients she loves so much, and her new hire is leading the team. Keeping Cynthia at Facebook was much more important to her manager than keeping her in a particular role.[108]

Questions for reflection

- What would have happened if Cynthia hadn't had support from her manager?
- Can an employee craft his/her job if he/she doesn't have supervisor support? How?

As an illustration of job crafting, think back to the example provided earlier in Box 5.7 describing hospital cleaners who developed a calling orientation.[109] These cleaning staff realized, as they learned about their work, that the job had relational impact, with opportunities to interact with patients in ways that differ from those of the medics and nurses: ways that are more human, more personal, less cold and professional. The more they experimented with this form of self-initiated enrichment, the more they felt gratified by the experience. Even though they did not receive formal recognition from the organization they worked for, through practices of (a) adding new tasks to their jobs, making them less routine, (b) adding meaningful relationships with patients and their families, and (c) giving a touch of comfort and humanity to the place, they reframed their role as more expansive and important than formally established.

Once when one of the authors of this book was teaching an executive course and mentioned this case, a participant shared that, in a recent hospitalization, she waited anxiously every day for the cleaning lady. With her, she said, 'I could be a person rather than a patient for a few minutes'. The case also resonates with research by Jane Dutton and her colleagues who concluded that the sense of worth of one's job and its impact over the lives of others may not be appreciated by external observers.[110] For example, a member of the cleaning staff may be 'invisible' to the healthcare professionals, yet highly visible and relevant for the patients themselves. In an organization staffed by busy professionals they may be able to take the time to deal with the patient not as an object of clinical practice but as someone that they have known personally, if only for a short while. Their human touch can make all the difference.[111]

Antecedents and consequences of job crafting

The notion of job crafting departs from the acceptance of the idea that people are passive receivers of their 'environment', in this case in the form of formally defined jobs. Organizations and leaders may affect job crafting in that they differ in the degree to which they give autonomy to employees and support employees in their search for meaningful work. Employee personality and motivation also affect job crafting: while some people may be more willing to accept the job as it comes, others have more proactive personalities (i.e., they express a tendency to initiate change in their environment; see also Box 5.12).[112]

Job crafting provides a sense of control and a more positive sense of self (see Boxes 5.13–5.16). It potentially fulfils the basic human need of connection to other people and it allows people to alter their jobs in forms that better suit their motivations. Job crafting has been associated with work engagement, the 'positive, fulfilling, work-related state of mind that is characterized by vigor, dedication, and absorption'.[113] Engagement is a concept that captures the way workers perceive and experience their work. Three dimensions are significant mediators of the relationship between work and engagement:

- **vigour** refers to the perception that the work is a stimulating and energetic force, something to which it is worth devoting time and effort;
- **dedication** measures the degree to which work is perceived as meaningful;
- **absorption** describes the degree of concentration it involves.

Engaged employees have been found to be energetic, self-efficacious and involved in deciding what happens to them.[114] Further, when workers change their work environment to make it more resourceful and more challenging, they become more engaged. Therefore, self-initiated engagement via crafting can produce a number of positive effects. Other research, however, indicates that organizations can create higher levels of engagement via the adoption of micro-practices that will change the relationship of people and their jobs.

Box 5.12 Pause and reflect! Enjoy your traffic jam or how to craft your commute[115]

Gino, Staats, Jachimowicz, Lee and Menges discussed the importance of approaching the commute between work and home as positively as possible. Before reading the paper, consider the following:

- Can your commute be improved by applying principles of job crafting?
- How can commuting be redesigned in such a way that it can be used more positively?
- Next, read the paper and compare your interpretation with that of the authors.

A well-known case of workers adopting micro-practices that positively changed their relationship with their jobs has been presented by Wagner and Harter.[116] Research has further verified the idea that engaging with one's job facilitates the cultivation of eagerness for self-development.[117] A study by Bakker and his colleagues explains the cycle:[118] a proactive orientation leads individuals to craft and to introduce changes in the work environment to make it more meaningful. They mobilize psychological and physical resources to effect this change. By crafting their jobs, they increase their engagement. This, in turn, stimulates higher levels of in-role performance as measured by colleagues.

Box 5.13 Positive in the negative: job crafting entrepreneurs and mental disorders[119]

Job crafting has mostly been associated with the introduction of changes in a formal job in a pre-existing organization. Some research is opening up another fascinating possibility. People with some mental disorders may have an entrepreneurial advantage because they fit less with typical organizational jobs. The alternative: forming their own companies and adapting their work to themselves. Because what is functional and dysfunctional is sometimes defined by context, some conditions can be beneficial in some contexts: dyslexia can promote creative thinking; ADHD (Attention Deficit Hyperactivity Disorder) with sensation seeking, bipolar disorder with perseverance. All these characteristics have been associated with entrepreneurial success. Now reflect: can you recognize differences in some successful entrepreneurs of the present and the past?

Stimulating learning through work design

Well-designed work may constitute a valuable tool for organizational learning. Designing work to assist learning means that jobs are not necessarily 'given' to employees as black boxes, i.e., as finished sets of tasks. Deskilled jobs involve not only negative implications for learning but also, potentially, moral issues. The 'not my job' role orientation at work reduces self-efficacy but also perspective taking[120] and empathy with customers. Coercive forms of bureaucracy[121] not only narrow scope and responsibility; they also facilitate the diffusion of responsibility, meaning that people do not feel themselves to be the owners of their work. The way organizations are designed has important consequences for the amount of on-the-job learning they stimulate. A sense of learning contributes to wellbeing. When growth is seen as a cultural resource, the organization may be more willing to adopt learning-oriented work designs.[122]

Box 5.14 The negative in the positive: the dangers of autonomy

Autonomy is a core characteristic of a well-designed job. Coercive forms of bureaucracy stimulate the 'not my job' type of thinking. Can autonomy be dangerous? Research suggests so, at least in some circumstances. When, for some reason, individuals are motivated to behave unethically (e.g., in order to reach stretch goals), autonomy can be problematic. This seems to be the case with rogue traders,[123] whose autonomy gives them the latitude to pursue their finalities with some freedom.

Complacency may look similar to empowerment and autonomy in cases such as that of the famous trader of Barings Bank Singapore who precipitated the collapse of the venerable institution. In short: autonomy has limits and should be complemented with rigorous control systems. For further illustration, consider reading a paper by Roberts and Bea, 'When systems fail'[124] or watching the movie *Rogue Trader*.

Goals and learning

Goal setting is a powerful form of motivation. More than 1,000 studies have tested the theory.[125] Goal setting establishes three major tenets: first, defining a challenging goal leads to higher performance than setting an easy goal. Second, the higher the goal the higher the performance (the goal should not be overwhelming, however, as that will lead to a sense of hopelessness – see below). Third, participation and knowledge of results improves performance if they result in the acceptance of a difficult and specific goal.

The above three relationships hold when four boundary conditions are observed:[126] first, people need to have the abilities required to get the job done. Second, they need the right situational resources, such as technological and financial resources. Third, people need to be committed, i.e., they must want to reach the goal. Finally, people must receive objective feedback with regards to goal attainment. Latham and his colleagues described the importance of abundant, real-time feedback with the case of videogames: these are addictive because they give players immediate information about progress. Goals are effective because they allow people to prioritize, to focus, to persist and to compose strategies that will allow them to reach a goal.

Types of goals

There are three types of goals: behavioural, performance and learning goals. *Perform-ance* goals refer to the achievement of some outcome. Most organizations refer to this type of goal when they manage by objectives. Performance goals can refer to sales in a given period, cost reduction, market share, etc. *Behavioural* goals describe the adoption of some specific conduct, such as greeting a customer, inquiring rather than assessing an employee, and so on. In this chapter, without denying the import-ance of the first two types (behavioural and performance), we focus on the third: learning.

Learning goals are adopted to stimulate change (i.e., more varied individual and team repertoires of action). Research indicates that a focus on performance goals in the absence of learning objectives can produce more organizational harm than good. For example, goals can go 'wild', meaning that people can ignore limits and ethical common sense to reach a goal. Additionally, performance goals can stimulate people to repeat their behav-iours with more effort as goals are re-set and raised, rather than considering how to do things differently and to do different things. In a world of change, continued repetition is problematic and even routine actions have to be improved.

Adopting learning goals

How can organizations stimulate the adoption of learning goals? Two sets of evidence are critical to answer this question: first, research indicates that learning unfolds more consistently when the challenge occurs within a person's 'zone of proximal develop-ment' rather than when a 'sink-or-swim' approach is adopted.[127] Goals that challenge but that are perceived as realistic are interesting. On the contrary, stretch goals often involve a sink-or-swim approach, especially when organizations face difficult situations and are willing to assume risks. In these circumstances, however, stretch goals often lead to failure, as stretching tends to work better when organizations are winning (rather than losing) and when resources are abundant.[128]

Goals with moderate amounts of difficulty allow the progressive accumulation of knowledge, thus building self-confidence incrementally. Combined with abundant, rich feedback, and the right organizational infrastructure, they allow individuals to fail safely. The sink-or-swim approach promises high rewards coupled with significant risks. More often than not, stretch goals can lead to failure as they apply to a limited range of situations.[129] Only in the rare cases where organizations combine sufficient slack resources with strong recent performance can stretch goals help to build up self-confidence. Therefore, organizations should use goal setting with a clear awareness of both its advantages and limits.

Box 5.15 The negative of the positive: too much of a good thing?

Stretched or over-stretched?

A number of companies have recently been attracted by the power of stretch goals. These include some success stories, such as that of Southwest Airlines, as well as some flagrant organizational disasters such as the case of Wells Fargo.[130] Watch the movie *Everest* and consider how the pursuit of a target at any cost produced a number of tragic consequences that nobody wished for. Consider the following about the Wells Fargo scandal:[131] 'Bankers across Wells Fargo's giant branch system were tacitly encouraged to meet their sales goals by committing fraud; opening unwanted or unneeded accounts in customers' names; and, sometimes, moving money into and out of the sham accounts'.

Always available![132]

Over the last years, some organizations have cultivated a culture of permanent availability. Because work is important and/or thrilling, employees sometimes find themselves in work situations that demand complete availability and the subordination of all non-work aspects of life. Extreme devotion to work, be it authentic or fake, has a number of dysfunctional consequences. Work becomes so important that all other dimensions can lead to psychological fragility. Family and friends are important sources of happiness that can be jeopardized if not well-tended. In addition, people whose self is tied mostly to the professional self (i.e., whose identity mainly comes from work) fail to develop a 'multifaceted identity', which is critical to living a healthy, well-rounded life. For these and other reasons, organizations should approach 24/7 cultures with care. What seems positive can, at the end, be highly dysfunctional.

An emphasis on learning and development in goal achievement is consistent with a second line of research that indicates how to adopt learning goals: Carol Dweck's studies on mindsets (discussed in Chapters 1 and 2).[133] Gary Latham, one of the main proponents of goal setting theory, argues that a learning orientation is positive even for individuals with a dispositional inclination towards a focus on performance. As they put it, 'state trumps trait'.[134] How can organizations stimulate the adoption of learning goals? Several possibilities can be considered:

- Make challenge desirable.
- Create cultures of feedback.
- Instil a culture of psychological safety (see Chapter 7).
- Frame failures as steps to progress and opportunities for learning.
- Create cultures of celebration.

Box 5.16 Reflection: a growth mindset at Microsoft[135]

As CEO of Microsoft, Satya Nadella initiated a change process with a goal, not of introducing an organizational shake up but of initiating a cultural change aimed at challenging the 'respect for old category definitions'. Nadella explained that he was trying to embed in the organization a new 'cultural meme' that could make it more flexible. He called this 'meme' a 'growth mindset', explicitly crediting Carol Dweck for the idea. Such cultural change was presented by Nadella as 'the existential thing' that could determine the company's future.

Questions for reflection

- How can a growth mindset be used to change an organization's culture?
- How can a manager design an intervention geared to adopting a growth mindset?
- What obstacles can obstruct the process?
- How can the success of such an initiative be measured?

Designing work to preserve health and wellbeing

Some organizations try to create contexts that engage employees and that increase job satisfaction or employee wellbeing. An association between wellbeing and workplace performance has been found empirically, suggesting that managing to increase employee wellbeing may generate positive organizational performance effects.[136] Paradoxically, some organizations are so successful in designing interesting jobs that the psychological gains associated with work, combined with organizational cultures of availability (i.e., those that value being there for long hours), stimulate people to overwork.

Work should be managed with care, as increases in job satisfaction and engagement can be accompanied by negative consequences in terms of health. Enriched jobs, competitive contexts and stretch goals together can undermine health, as challenges often lead to fatigue, strain and work overload.[137] The effects of these practices are not always visible as they are unfolding: 'we can see machinery break down, we notice broken arms and legs. We do not see broken minds – until it is too late'[138] (revisit Box 3.5 on the case of António Horta-Osório).

Given the popularity of stretch goals and the discourse of hyper-competition, organizations can be expected to adopt managerial practices that turn work into a 'radical' practice, an extreme sport, one that, even when approached with commitment and enthusiasm, produces serious consequences for individuals, organizations and society, including lack of balance between different life spheres and a decrease in health and wellbeing. These highly challenging, highly engaging forms of work design have been labelled 'over-enriched work'.[139]

Naturally, stress is not only produced by 'positive' stimulating contexts. Rather, it is caused more often by challenging work environments. Recent research indicates that the risks associated with how work is designed and how organizations are managed is significant. Highly challenging jobs have been associated with an increase of the risk of cardiovascular disease.[140] Evidence collected by Goh and his colleagues[141] considers the influence of ten workplace stressors (Table 5.2). While there could be more, this list itself is revealing.

The authors empirically tested and confirmed a model showing that these factors are associated with lower health and wellbeing, and higher mortality. Lack of health insurance produces stress, directly and indirectly. Directly because it can impede access to adequate medical care, including prevention; indirectly because it is a source of financial distress. In the US, a portion of cases of personal bankruptcy is associated with healthcare costs. A second cause of stress is unemployment and layoffs. The explanations for this are intuitive: a lack of income and its consequences for the person and his/her family as well as diminished social status and personal identity. Research indicates that job loss increases the

Table 5.2 Ten causes of workplace stress[142]

Source of stress	Explanation and illustrations	How it can be tackled
Lack of health insurance	The lack of health insurance increases financial distress.	Provide healthcare insurance to workers.
Unemployment and layoffs	Increases financial and identity losses as individuals lose their financial means and sever their ties with the profession.	Conceive layoffs and downsizing as a solution of last resort. If inevitable, provide support to those affected.
Job insecurity	Increases stress.	Establish policies supportive of job security. Represent the organization as a community of work.
Long work hours	Some organizations have developed cultures of permanent availability. People spend most of their time working – voluntarily or involuntarily, due to pressure. In extreme cases, this leads to death. In Japan, a word was coined to explain this: *karoshi*, death by excessive work.	To combat the 'fetish of overwork'[143] companies may adopt rules for telework and adopt policies that protect non-work time.
Shift work	Causes pernicious effects resulting from poor quality of sleep, stress and possible work–family conflicts.	Find tactics to minimize the hassles of shift work, namely by providing medical and social support to employees and their families.
Work–family conflict	Jobs may have important spillover in the family domain. This causes stress.	Design family-supportive policies.
Low job control	The lack of control over one's job constitutes an important source of stress.	Design jobs so that they incorporate a dimension of control.
Excessive job demands	Some tough organizational cultures turn excess into the norm. Japan's biggest advertising agency Dentsu is a case in point. The staff was stretched to recover business but the result was overbilling hundreds of clients as well as death by overwork of a 24-year-old trainee. The resigning president, Tadashi Ishii, explained: 'Everything about this … was excessive'.[144]	Develop and sustain cultures of balance. At Dentsu the excessive cultural principles were known as 'the devil's 10 principles'. One of them read 'Never give up on a task till you reach your goal, even if you die in the process'.[145] .
Lack of social support	A cause of stress; it also depletes resilience (see Chapter 3).	Organizations can adopt policies favourable to the creation of positive relationships at work (see Chapter 6). They can institutionalize cultures favourable to helping behaviours.
Organizational injustice	Perceptions of unfairness are an important source of stress.	Delineate and enforce policies promotive of justice (e.g., clear rules, mechanisms of appeal, transparency, ethicality).

risk of depression. It is better for your health to live and work in a social democracy with a flourishing welfare state that funds health, unemployment and other benefits, rather than in a liberal democracy which leaves funding provision up to the individual and what they can or cannot afford.

Stress is also caused by job insecurity. It is not only job loss but also the prospects of it that function as a source of stress. Job insecurity has been associated both with psychological (sickness absence) and physical problems (myocardial infarction). Work hours and shift work are sources of stress because they harm the quality of sleep, the capacity to manage work–non-work balance and they stimulate unhealthy behaviours. Not only can the number of hours worked be excessive but new technologies, such as smartphones and email, create a culture of 24/7 availability. This has led to the introduction of legally established limits to work activities. In a number of countries in the European Union (e.g., France, Spain, Portugal) legislation has been approved under the banner of the 'right to disconnect', which establishes the right of employees not to answer email messages after working hours.[146] In Germany, Volkswagen pioneered the adoption of counter-exhaustion measures such as the blocking of the company's email access between 18:15 and 07:00.[147] Yet, in other contexts, pressure for long work schedules is still enforced and sleep deprivation damages individuals' wellbeing, health, decision-making and performance, and impairs leadership effectiveness[148] (see Table 5.3 about possible organizational policies and practices aimed at dealing with the problem). As we were finishing this book, in 2018, boutique investment bank Moelis & Co received media attention because a mid-level banker sent a 12:30 a.m. email to junior professionals explaining that in the bank's competitive environment, 'the only way I can think of to differentiate among you is to see who is in the office in the wee hours of the morning'.[149]

Table 5.3 Company policies and practices to reduce risks associated with insufficient sleep[150]

- Implement training programmes teaching the importance of sleep.
- Encourage flexibility in travel (e.g., allow employees to take an earlier plane, rather than an overnight 'red eye' flight, to get a good night's sleep before important meetings).
- Be careful regarding scheduling team working (e.g., be mindful of local times and the time preferences of team members involved when scheduling global calls).
- Impose 'blackout times' on work emails.
- Set work-time limits.
- Implement mandatory work-free vacations (in contexts where they are not mandatory by law).
- Encourage 'predictable time off' policies.
- Adopt sleep pods and nap rooms.
- Consider supplying (or at least informing employees about) gadgets and tools designed to improve sleep management.

Work–family conflict has been associated with substance abuse and psychological problems. The lack of job control and excessive job demands impair health conditions by leading to strain and cardiovascular risk. Social support, or the lack of it, causes health problems. Social support buffers people from some negative effects of stress, evidencing the importance of good relationships (see Chapter 6). Poor relationships, or toxic climates, thus increase vulnerability. Finally, organizational injustice is a source of stress as it reduces predictability and counters the expectations of fairness that most people hold about work and life in general.

It is important to consider that some factors, per se, are not necessarily nefarious. For example, working long hours may not be as problematic for engaged workers as it is for the disengaged, as engagement provides people with resources that help them handle job demands.[151] In this sense, increasing engagement can be beneficial for psychological as well as for physical reasons. As Pfeffer notes in a critical response to the study, there are limits and a maximum of engagement does not substitute for rest.[152]

Organizations have a responsibility to provide safe workplaces, a responsibility that falls above all upon management. Yet, evidence collected by Goh and his colleagues concluded that 120,000 deaths per year in the US can be associated with bad management practices. Their findings suggest that mortality associated with work-related practices compares with the fourth and fifth causes of death in the US, namely cerebrovascular diseases and accidents. The implications of the study are important. In order to design work that helps people flourish, organizations should avoid bad practices or, when these seem to be unavoidable, mitigate their effects.

The articulation between work design and health and wellbeing is important because organizations cannot simply externalize the social consequences of poor practices, as they might do with other social considerations. The discussion of the policy implications of work-related stress is beyond the scope of this chapter[153] but a few points are important to this discussion. We consider that the voluntary adherence to good design practices: (1) is first and foremost a moral responsibility, (2) is also a legal responsibility, avoiding legal and reputational costs associated with being a 'social pollutant'[154] and (3) contributes towards creating the sort of workplace that attracts and retains human talent.

The trade-offs of work design

The creation of work contexts conducive to flourishing is desirable but difficult because there are trade-offs among the different goals of work design: motivation, learning and wellbeing. For example, research has shown that when people are given more autonomy, they develop a higher sense of satisfaction (psychological wellbeing) in the short term. In the long run, however, greater autonomy has been shown to lead to increased fatigue and strain, lowering physical wellbeing.[155] This tension is not the only one involved in job design. Nor is it the exception. Organizational life is rich in tension and contradiction, with some scholars claiming that contradiction is constitutive of organization[156] and that, consequently, managing can be partly equated with the tackling of contradictions.[157]

The process of work design is no exception. In this section, we advance three trade-offs involved in job design to sensitize you to the tension between promise and peril. We have discussed job crafting as an approach rich with possibility. Through crafting, employees can personalize their jobs, making them more idiosyncratic and thus more compatible with their motivations and dispositions, which is potentially good. However, it is possible that people craft their jobs in ways that are not aligned with the organization's policies or goals. Because crafting is highly informal and non-sanctioned, it is also possible that deviations will go unnoticed. In this sense, a good thing can turn out to be bad, creating inconsistencies between employees and the organization's standards. Therefore, even something that started as a positive approach to work may end up being problematic.

Second, I-Deals have been presented as a form of negotiation between workers and their organizations. I-Deals are seen to be promising as they facilitate the personalization of contracts and the mutual adjustment between people and their organizations. If people are different, they should be treated differently. This seems fair and can even be theoretically approached with the lens of equity theory. The fact is that, in practice, I-Deals can become problematic. The bargaining power of different people can be distinct, and some people can take more advantage of I-Deals than others. For example, new hires can be in a better position to define better deals. Employees who marketize themselves more aggressively may have a bargaining edge. The organization may unwittingly stimulate people to be less rather than more loyal, as the loyalists lose bargaining power. Ironically, then, a tool that was intended to increase attraction and retention may cause unintended effects.

Finally, with regards to health, organizations can be so successful in terms of developing interesting work that they alienate their people or work them to death. Hewlett and Luce's view of work as a radical experience is demonstrative: some jobs are so fulfilling and rewarding that they distract people from other facets of their lives, especially if these facets are not entirely satisfactory.[158] Engaging more with work may mean engaging less with family. In some circumstances, this can be perceived as a positive option. Overworking can also be perceived as a sign of dedication, an important resource in face of overall greater job insecurity.[159] However, at the end, this can be just another manifestation of the 'too much of a good thing' syndrome. By investing too much in one dimension of life, one invests less in others. A life well lived, however, must be balanced.

Final comments

The world is changing with the world of work changing accordingly. This chapter discussed some of the central dimensions of the process. First, it is known that good job design provokes a number of positive outcomes. Yet, bad job designs persistently prevail. We have discussed different approaches to job design: top down and bottom up. Traditionally, jobs were designed by management representatives. More recently, it has been assumed that jobs can be co-designed (I-Deals) or partly designed by the employees themselves, the process known as job crafting. Work can be designed to facilitate learning as when organizations adopt a growth mindset. Instead of focussing on talent as fixed, they can create contexts where talent is viewed as expandable through positive approaches to talent. Finally, we discussed the implications of job design for health and wellbeing. Recent research is exploring the health impacts of management practices.

Overall, in a time of change, the capacity of organizations to create fulfilling work and positive talent-expansion environments represents a path towards the creation of attractive employer brands and customized workplaces. This can be beneficial for the organization as well as for individuals themselves. By persisting in the implementation of poor designs, organizations deprive their members of the capacity to see the workplace as a source of personal flourishing and help to understand why work does not have to be a 'tripalium'.

Want more?

In case you want to continue exploring the challenges involved in the design of good jobs, there are several important sources. Studs Terkel's[160] *Working* offers a good introduction to how people see work. To explore work design, the book *Job and Work Design* by Parker and Wall[161] is recommended reading. In terms of seeing work as a source of learning, Dweck's[162] *Mindset* is a crucial reference. Pfeffer and Goh have conducted important work on the impact of management and work practices on health, which was summarized by Pfeffer[163] in his book *Dying for a Paycheck*. The discussion of Gallup's 12 practices can be found in Wagner and Harter's[164] *12: The Elements of Great Managing*, as well as in Gallup.[165]

Glossary

Adaptivity   The extent to which employees respond to changes interfering with their roles as organizational members.[166]

Calling   'Meaningful beckoning toward activities that are morally, socially, and personally significant, involving work that is an end in itself.'[167]

Corporate volunteering programmes   Policies and practices, both formal and informal, devised by organizations to stimulate people to donate some of their time to external volunteering initiatives.[168]

Decent work agenda   An agenda launched by the UN to create decent work for all.

Engagement   A psychological state of positive fulfilment marked by vigour, dedication, and absorption.[169]

Flow   A psychological state of complete absorption by an activity.

Gamification   The transference of digital gaming features to non-game contexts.

I-deals   'Voluntary, personalized agreements of a nonstandard nature negotiated between individual employees and their employers regarding terms that benefit each party.'[170]

Job crafting   Changes spontaneously introduced in the job by individuals in an expression of bottom-up job (re)design. People can change the task, the relationships involved in doing it or the way they think about it.

Job design   The structural characteristics of a job performed by employees.

Meaningful work   The consideration that quotidian responsibilities have a broader level of significance.[171]

Proactivity   Extra-role behaviours initiated by employees to change themselves or their work environments.[172]

Protean careers   Careers that are mainly driven by individuals rather than by the organization. People can thus reinvent or change their careers as their life stages change. The name is inspired by Proteus, a Greek god, who had the capacity to change shape depending on his will.[173]

Purpose   'The pursuit of a goal that transcends measurable financial benefits, and whose outcome may not be realized during the planning horizons of the principal and the agent.'[174]

Scientific management   A pioneering management theory that split design and execution, fragmenting and simplifying work in order to achieve high levels of efficiency.

Stretch goals   Organizational goals that are extremely difficult to achieve given an organization's present competencies.

Work engagement   A worker's positive state of mind that denotes the three characteristics of vigour, dedication and absorption.

Work orientation   Amy Wrzesniewski's research describes meaningful work and intrinsic vs extrinsic motivation around three work orientations: job, career and calling. A job orientation is motivation to work for the extrinsic, immediate, material and financial rewards it offers. A career orientation is motivated by opportunities for achieving prestige, power, recognition and advancement. A calling orientation views work as intrinsically motivating and inherently fulfilling.

Notes

1 Lorenz and Valeyre (2005).
2 Gallup (2013, 2017).
3 Parker, Van Den Broeck and Holman (2017).
4 Argyris (1994, p. 84).
5 Deci, Koestner and Ryan (1999).
6 Terkel (2011, p. 1).
7 Yeoman (2014).
8 Mendes (2008).
9 Schwab (2015).
10 Kuper (2016).
11 Crawford (2016).
12 Oldham and Hackman (2010, p. 466).
13 Wegman, Hoffman, Carter, Twenge and Guenole (2016).
14 Cunha, Pacheco, Castanheira and Rego (2017).
15 Rhodes (2018).
16 Petriglieri, Ashford and Wrzesniewski (2018a).
17 Petriglieri, Ashford and Wrzesniewski (2018b).
18 Sachs (2018, p. 7).
19 Sachs (2018, p. 8).
20 Kalleberg (2011).
21 Davis (2010).
22 Wegman, Hoffman, Carter, Twenge and Guenole (2016).
23 Rajan and Wulf (2006).
24 Barker (1993).
25 Cardador, Northcraft and Whicker (2017).
26 Cardador, Northcraft and Whicker (2017).
27 Wegman, Hoffman, Carter, Twenge and Guenole (2016).
28 Ibarra (2015, p. 8).
29 Etzioni (1986).
30 Gratton and Ghoshal (2003).
31 Oldham and Fried (2016).
32 Note that the dates for each generation are indicative: different people define different boundaries for each generation.
33 Twenge, Campbell, Hoffman and Lance (2010).
34 Crane (2013).
35 Clegg, Cunha and Rego (2016).
36 Kantor and Streitfeld (2015).
37 See Cook (2015).
38 Nocera (2015, p. A17).
39 www.ilo.org.
40 International Labour Organization (2007, p. vi).
41 Pfeffer (2010, p. 439).

42 Goh, Pfeffer and Zenios (2015, 2016).
43 Brooks (2015, SR1).
44 Fried, Grant, Levi, Hadani and Slowik (2007).
45 Wrzesniewski, McCauley, Rozin and Schwartz (2001).
46 Goldthorpe, Lockwood, Bechhofer and Platt (1969).
47 Menges, Tussing, Wihler and Grant (2017).
48 Weber (1958).
49 De Rond and Lok (2016).
50 Pratt, Lepisto and Dane (2018).
51 Weber (2013).
52 Csikszentmihalyi (1990); Nakamura and Csikszentmihalyi (2014).
53 Parker (2007).
54 Adapted from: Csikszentmihalyi (1990); Nakamura and Csikszentmihalyi (2014).
55 Grant, Christianson and Price (2007, p. 53).
56 Bush and Lewis-Kulin (2018, p. 26).
57 Carton (2017).
58 Judge, Piccolo, Podsakoff, Shaw and Rich (2010).
59 Rodell, Booth, Lynch and Zipay (2017).
60 Gartenberg, Prat and Serafeim (2016).
61 Grant (2011).
62 Independent Directors of the Board of Wells Fargo & Company (2017).
63 Reckard (2013).
64 Bunderson and Thompson (2009).
65 Parker (2014).
66 Adapted, with small changes, from Hornung, Rousseau, Glaser, Angerer and Weigl (2010, p. 188).
67 Source: anonymous (https://commons.wikimedia.org/wiki/File:Frederick_Winslow_Taylor_crop.jpg), 'Frederick Winslow Taylor crop', marked as public domain, details on Wikimedia Commons: https://commons.wikimedia.org/wiki/Template: PD-old.
68 Parker (2014); Braverman (1974).
69 Gramsci (1971).
70 Retrieved from https://commons.wikimedia.org/wiki/File:Modern_Times_poster.jpg. Work in the public domain.
71 Duhigg (2016).
72 Childress (2013, p. 219).
73 Roser (2016, p. 1).
74 So-called because it is not a Nobel Prize endowed by the estate of Nobel; instead it is funded by the *Sveriges Riksbank* as a prize established in honour of Alfred Nobel, as a legitimating device for the profession of economics.
75 Kahneman, Rosenfield, Gandhi and Blaser (2016).
76 Weber, in Mayer (1943, pp. 127–128).
77 Courpasson (2016, p. 1095).
78 Vidal (2013, p. 604).
79 Campion and Stevens (1991).
80 Takeuchi, Osono and Shimizu (2008).
81 Sources: Parker (2014).
82 Tornay and Frese (2013).
83 Leach, Wall and Jackson (2003).
84 Grant, Gino and Hoffman (2011, p. 421).
85 Hackman and Oldham (1975, p. 161).
86 Rajan and Wulf (2006).
87 Wegman, Hoffman, Carter, Twenge and Guenole (2016).
88 Hackman and Oldham (1975, p. 161).
89 Oldham and Hackman (2010, p. 464).
90 Oldham and Hackman (2010, p. 464).
91 Oldham and Hackman (2010, p. 464).
92 Humphrey, Nahrgang and Morgeson (2007).

93 Parker (2014, p. 667).
94 Fried, Grant, Levi, Hadani and Slowik (2007).
95 Rousseau et al. (2006, p. 978).
96 Liao, Wayne and Rousseau (2016).
97 Mitchell (2018, p. 16).
98 Argyris (1994, p. 77).
99 Nishi (2011).
100 Wrzesniewski, Berg and Dutton (2010).
101 Parker (2007).
102 Grant and Ashford (2008).
103 Bakker, Tims and Derks (2012, p. 1361).
104 Wrzesniewski and Dutton (2001).
105 Demerouti (2014).
106 Petrou, Demerouti and Schaufeli (2018).
107 Berg, Wrzesniewski and Dutton (2010).
108 Goler, Gale, Harrington and Grant (2018).
109 Wrzesniewski and Dutton (2001).
110 Dutton, Debebe and Wrzesniewski (2016).
111 Frost (2007).
112 Bateman and Crant (1993).
113 Schaufeli, Salanova and Bakker (2002).
114 Schaufeli et al. (2002, p. 74).
115 Gino, Staats, Jachimowicz, Lee and Menges (2017).
116 Source: Wagner and Harter (2006).
117 Hyvonen, Feldt, Salmela-Aro, Kinnunen and Makikangas (2009).
118 Bakker, Tims and Derks (2012).
119 Source: Wiklund, Hatak, Patzelt and Shepherd (2018).
120 Parker (2014).
121 Adler and Borys (1996).
122 Sonenshein, Dutton, Grant, Spreitzer and Sutcliffe (2013).
123 Parker (2014).
124 Roberts and Bea (2001).
125 Latham, Seijts and Slocum (2016).
126 Latham, Seijts and Slocum (2016).
127 Day, Harrison and Halpin (2009).
128 Sitkin, Miller and See (2017).
129 Sitkin, See, Miller, Lawless and Carton (2011).
130 Independent Directors of the Board of Wells Fargo & Company (2017).
131 Cowley and Kingson (2017, p. A1).
132 Reid and Ramarajan (2016).
133 Dweck (2006).
134 Latham, Seijts and Slocum (2016, p. 3 do artigo).
135 Source: Waters (2016, p. 9).
136 Bryson, Forth and Stokes (2017).
137 Grant, Christianson and Price (2007).
138 Heffernan (2016, p. 11).
139 Johns (2010).
140 Melamed, Shirom, Toker, Berliner and Shapira (2006).
141 Goh, Pfeffer and Zenios (2015, 2016).
142 Built from Goh, Pfeffer and Zenios (2016).
143 Heffernan (2016, p. 11).
144 Lewis and Inagaki (2016, p. 16).
145 Lewis and Inagaki (2016, p. 16).
146 Martins (2017).
147 Faria (2017).
148 Barnes, Lucianetti, Bhave and Christian (2015); van Dam and van der Helm (2016a, 2016b).
149 In Masters (2018, p. 9).

150 As suggested van Dam and van der Helm (2016a, 2016b).
151 Ten Brummelhuis, Rothbard and Uhrich (2017).
152 Pfeffer (2018b).
153 See Goh, Pfeffer and Zenios (2015).
154 Pfeffer (2018a).
155 Campion and McClelland (1991, 1993).
156 Putnam et al. (2016).
157 Cunha and Clegg (2018).
158 Hewlett and Luce (2006).
159 Davis (2010).
160 Terkel (1974).
161 Parker and Wall (1998).
162 Dweck (2006).
163 Pfeffer, J (2018).
164 Wagner and Harter (2006).
165 Gallup (2013, 2017).
166 Griffin, Neal and Parker (2007).
167 Schabram and Maitlis (2017, p. 584).
168 Rodell, Booth, Lynch and Zipay (2017).
169 Schaufeli, Bakker and Salanova (2006).
170 Rousseau, Ho and Greenberg (2006, p. 978).
171 Carton (2017).
172 Grant and Ashford (2008).
173 Hall (1996).
174 Thakor and Quinn (2013).

References

Adler, P. S., & Borys, B. (1996). Two types of bureaucracy: Enabling and coercive. *Administrative Science Quarterly*, 41, 61–89.

Argyris, C. (1994). Good communication that blocks learning. *Harvard Business Review*, July–August, 77–85.

Bakker, A. B., Tims, M., & Derks, D. (2012). Proactive personality and job performance: The role of job crafting and work engagement. *Human Relations*, 65(10), 1359–1378.

Barker, J. R. (1993). Tightening the iron cage: Concertive control in self-managing teams. *Administrative Science Quarterly*, 38(3), 408–437.

Barnes, C. M., Lucianetti, L., Bhave, D. P., & Christian, M. S. (2015). "You wouldn't like me when I'm sleepy": Leaders's sleep, daily abuse supervision, and work unit engagement. *Academy of Management Journal*, 58(5), 1419–1427.

Bateman, T. S., & Crant, M. J. (1993). The proactive component of organizational behavior: A measure and correlates summary. *Journal of Organizational Behavior*, 14, 103–119.

Berg, J. M., Wrzesniewski, A., & Dutton, J. E. (2010). Perceiving and responding to challenges in job crafting at different ranks: When proactivity requires adaptivity. *Journal of Organizational Behavior*, 31, 158–186.

Braverman, H. (1974). *Labor and monopoly capital*. New York: Monthly Review.

Brooks, D. (2015). The moral bucket list. *The New York Times*, April 12, SR 1.

Bryson, A., Forth, J., & Stokes, L. (2017). Does employees' subjective wellbeing affect workplace performance? *Human Relations*, 70(8), 1017–1037.

Bunderson, J. S., & Thompson, J. (2009). The call of the wild: Zookeepers, callings, and the double-edged sword of deeply meaningful work. *Administrative Science Quarterly*, 54(1), 32–57.

Bush, M. C., & Lewis-Kulin, S. (2018). 100 best companies to work for 2018. *Fortune*, March, 21–23.

Campion, M. A., & McClelland, C. L. (1991). Interdisciplinary examination of the costs and benefits of enlarged jobs: A job design quasi-experiment. *Journal of Applied Psychology*, 76(2), 186–198.

Campion, M. A., & McClelland, C. L. (1993). Follow-up and extension of the interdisciplinary costs and benefits of enlarged jobs. *Journal of Applied Psychology*, 78(3), 339–351.

Campion, M. A., & Stevens, M. J. (1991). Neglected questions in job design: How people design jobs, task-job predictability, and influence of training. *Journal of Business and Psychology*, 6, 169–191.

Cardador, M. T., Northcraft, G. B., & Whicker, J. (2017). A theory of work gamification: Something old, something new, something borrowed, something cool? *Human Resource Management Review*, 27 (2), 353–365.

Carton, A. (2017). "I'm not mopping the floors, I'm putting a man on the moon": How NASA leaders enhanced the meaningfulness of work by changing the meaning of work. *Administrative Science Quarterly*, 63(2), 323–369.

Clegg, S., Cunha, M. P., & Rego, A. (2016). Explaining suicide in organizations. Durkheim revisited. *Business & Society Review*, 121(3), 391–414.

Cohan, J. A. (2002). "I didn't know" and "I was only doing my job": Has corporate governance careened out of control? A case study of Enron's information myopia. *Journal of Business Ethics*, 40(3), 275–299.

Cook, J. (2015). Full memo: Jeff Bezos responds to brutal NYT story, says it doesn't represent the Amazon he leads. *GeekWire*, August 16 (https://geekwire.com/2015/full-memo-jeff-bezos-responds-to-cutting-nyt-expose-says-tolerance-for-lack-of-empathy-needs-to-be-zero/)

Courpasson, D. (2016). Looking away? Civilized indifference and the carnal relationships of the contemporary workplace. *Journal of Management Studies*, 53(6), 1094–1100.

Cowley, S., & Kingson, J. A. (2017). Wells Fargo says 2 ex-leaders owe $75 million more. *The New York Times*, April 11, A1.

Crane, A. (2013). Modern slavery as a management practice: Exploring the conditions and capabilities for human exploitation. *Academy of Management Review*, 38(1), 49–69.

Crawford, K. (2016). A.I.'s white guy problem. *The New York Times*, June 26, SR1.

Csikszentmihalyi, M. (1990). *Flow: The psychology of optimal experience*. New York: Harper & Row.

Cunha, M. P., & Clegg, S. (2018). Persistence in paradox. In M. Farjoun, W. K. Smith, A. Langley, & H. Tsoukas (Eds.), *Perspectives on process organization studies: Dualities, dialectics and paradoxes in organizational life* (Vol. 8, pp. 14–34). Oxford: Oxford University Press.

Cunha, M. P., Pacheco, M., Castanheira, F., & Rego, A. (2017). Reflexive work and the duality of self-leadership. *Leadership*, 13(4), 472–495.

Davis, G. F. (2010). Job design meets organizational sociology. *Journal of Organizational Behavior*, 31, 302–308.

Day, D. V., Harrison, M. M., & Halpin, S. (2009). *An integrative approach to leader development: Connecting adult development, identity, and expertise*. New York: Routledge.

De Neve, J.-E. (2018). Work and wellbeing: A global perspective. In *Global Happiness Policy Report 2018* (pp. 74–111). Paris: Global Happiness Council.

De Rond, M., & Lok, J. (2016). Some things can never be unseen: The role of context in psychological injury at war. *Academy of Management Journal*, 59(6), 1965–1993.

Deci, E. L., Koestner, R., & Ryan, R. M. (1999). A meta-analytic review of experiments examining the effects of extrinsic rewards on intrinsic motivation. *Psychological Bulletin*, 125(6), 627–668.

Demerouti, E. (2014). Design your own job through job crafting. *European Psychologist*, 19(4), 237–247.

Duhigg, C. (2016). *Smarter faster better: The secrets of being productive*. New York: Random House.

Dutton, J. E., Debebe, G., & Wrzesniewski, A. (2016). Being valued and devalued at work: A social valuing perspective. In B. Bechky, & K. Elsbach (Eds.), *Qualitative organizational research: Best papers from the Davis Conference on Qualitative Research* (Vol. 3, pp. 9–52). Charlotte, NC: Information Age Publishing.

Dweck, C. (2006). *Mindset: The new psychology of success*. New York: Ballantine.

Etzioni, A. (1986). The fast-food factories: McJobs are bad for kids. *The Washington Post*, August 24 (https://washingtonpost.com/archive/opinions/1986/08/24/the-fast-food-factories-mcjobs-are-bad-for-kids/b3d7bbeb-5e9a-4335-afdd-2030cb7bc775/?noredirect=on&utm_term=.5e7e894a8292).

Faria, N. (2017). França, Alemanha e Japão adotaram medidas. *Público*, January 6, 3.

Fried, Y., Grant, A. M., Levi, A. S., Hadani, M., & Slowik, L. H. (2007). Job design in temporal context: A career dynamics perspective. *Journal of Organizational Behavior*, 28, 911–927.

Frost, P. J. (2007). *Toxic emotions at work and what you can do about them*. Boston, MA: Harvard Business School Press.

Gallup. (2013). *State of the global workplace: Employee engagement insights for business leaders worldwide*. Washington, DC: Gallup.

Gallup. (2017). *State of the American workplace*. Washington, DC: Gallup.

Gartenberg, C., Prat, A., & Serafeim, G. (2016). Corporate purpose and financial performance. Harvard Business School, Working paper 17–23.

Gino, F., Staats, B., Jachimowicz, J., Lee, J., & Menges, J. (2017). Reclaim your commute. *Harvard Business Review*, May–June, 149–153.

Goh, J., Pfeffer, J., & Zenios, S. A. (2015). Workplace stressors and health outcomes. *Behavioral Science & Policy*, 1(1), 43–52.

Goh, J., Pfeffer, J., & Zenios, S. A. (2016). The relationship between workplace stressors and mortality and health in the United States. *Management Science*, 62(2), 608–628.

Goldthorpe, J. H., Lockwood, D., Bechhofer, F., & Platt, J. (1969). *The affluent worker in the class structure*. Vol. 3, Cambridge, MA: Cambridge University Press.

Goler, L., Gale, J., Harrington, B., & Grant, A. (2018). Why people really quit their jobs. *Harvard Business Review*, January 11 (https://hbr.org/2018/01/why-people-really-quit-their-jobs).

Gramsci, A. (1971). *Selections from the prison notebooks*. London: Lawrence and Wishart.

Grant, A. (2011). How customers can rally your troops. *Harvard Business Review*, 89(6), 96–103.

Grant, A. M., & Ashford, S. J. (2008). The dynamics of proactivity at work. *Research in Organizational Behavior*, 28, 3–34.

Grant, A. M., Christianson, M. K., & Price, R. H. (2007). Happiness, health, or relationships? Managerial practices and employee wellbeing tradeoffs. *Academy of Management Perspectives*, August, 21(3), 51–63.

Grant, A. M., Gino, F., & Hoffman, D. A. (2011). Reversing the extraverted leadership advantage: The role of employee proactivity. *Academy of Management Journal*, 54(3), 528–550.

Gratton, L., & Ghoshal, S. (2003). Managing personal human capital: New Ethos for the volunteer' employee. *European Management Journal*, 21(1), 1–10.

Griffin, M. A., Neal, A., & Parker, S. K. (2007). A new model work role performance positive behavior in uncertain and interdependent contexts. *Academy of Management Journal*, 50, 327–347.

Hackman, J. R., & Oldham, G. R. (1975). Development of the job diagnostic survey. *Journal of Applied Psychology*, 60, 159–170.

Hall, D. T. (1996). Protean careers of the 21st century. *The Academy of Management Executive*, 10(4), 8–16.

Heffernan, M. (2016). Making a fetish of overwork is bad for productivity. *Financial Times*, October 25, 11.

Hewlett, S. A., & Luce, C. B. (2006). Extreme jobs: The dangerous allure of the 70-hour workweek. *Harvard Business Review*, 84(12), 49–59.

Hornung, S., Rousseau, D. M., Glaser, J., Angerer, P., & Weigl, M. (2010). Beyond top–down and bottom–up work redesign: Customizing job content through idiosyncratic deals. *Journal of Organizational Behavior*, 31, 187–215.

Humphrey, S. E., Nahrgang, J. D., & Morgeson, F. P. (2007). Integrating motivational, social and contextual work design features: A meta-analytic summary and theoretical extension of the work design literature. *Journal of Applied Psychology*, 92, 1332–1356.

Hyvonen, K., Feldt, T., Salmela-Aro, K., Kinnunen, U., & Makikangas, A. (2009). Young managers' drive to thrive: A personal work goal approach to burnout and work engagement. *Journal of Vocational Behavior*, 75, 183–196.

Ibarra, H. (2015). Tech tools that track how we perform need monitoring too. *Financial Times*, April 14, 8.

Independent Directors of the Board of Wells Fargo & Company. (2017). Sales practices investigation report. April 10.

International Labour Organization. (2007). *Toolkit for mainstreaming employment and decent work* (2nd ed.). Geneva: ILO.

Johns, G. (2010). Some unintended consequences of job design. *Journal of Organizational Behavior*, 31, 361–369.

Judge, T. A., Piccolo, R. F., Podsakoff, N. A., Shaw, J. C., & Rich, B. L. (2010). The relationship between pay and job satisfaction: A meta –analysis. *Journal of Vocational Behavior*, 77, 157–167.

Kahneman, D., Rosenfield, A. M., Gandhi, L., & Blaser, T. (2016). Noise. *Harvard Business Review*, October, 38–46.

Kalleberg, A. L. (2011). *Good jobs, bad jobs: The rise of polarized and precarious employment systems in the United States, 1970s to 2000s*. New York: Russell Sage.

Kantor, J., & Streitfeld, D. (2015). Inside Amazon: Wrestling big ideas in a bruising workplace. *The New York Times*, August 16, A1.

Kuper, S. (2016). How to cope when robots take your job. *Financial Times Life & Arts*, October 8–9, 2.

Latham, G., Seijts, G., & Slocum, J. (2016). The goal setting and goal orientation labyrinth: Effective ways for increasing employee performance. *Organizational Dynamics*, 45(4), 271–277.

Leach, D. J., Wall, T. D., & Jackson, P. R. (2003). The effect of empowerment on job knowledge: An empirical test involving operators of complex technology. *Journal of Occupational and Organizational Psychology*, 76, 27–52.

Lewis, L., & Inagaki, K. (2016). Culture of excess catches up with Dentsu. *Financial Times*, December 30, 16.

Liao, C., Wayne, S. J., & Rousseau, D. M. (2016). Idiosyncratic deals in contemporary organizations: A qualitative and meta-analytical review. *Journal of Organizational Behavior*, 37, S9–S29.

Lorenz, E., & Valeyre, A. (2005). Organizational innovation, human resource management and labour market structure: A comparison of the EU-15. *The Journal of Industrial Relations*, 47(4), 424–442.

Martins, R. (2017). Devemos ter o "direito a desligar" do trabalho? Governo abre debate. *Público*, January 6, 2–3.

Masters, B. (2018). Wall street still has lessons to learn about overwork. *Financial Times*, April 18, 9.

Mayer, J. P. (1943). *Max Weber and German politics*. London: Faber & Faber.

Melamed, S., Shirom, A., Toker, S., Berliner, S., & Shapira, I. (2006). Burnout and risk of cardiovascular disease: Evidence, possible causal paths, and promising research directions. *Psychological Bulletin*, 132(3), 327–353.

Mendes, J. M. (2008). O trabalho: Punição divina e libertação prometaica. *Janus*, 11, 118–119.

Menges, J. I., Tussing, D. V., Wihler, A., & Grant, A. M. (2017). When job performance is all relative: How family motivation energizes effort and compensates for intrinsic motivation. *Academy of Management Journal*, 80(2), 695–719.

Mitchell, T. R. (2018). A dynamic, inclusive, and affective evolutionary view of organizational behavior. *Annual Review of Organizational Psychology and Organizational Behavior*, 5, 1–19.

Nakamura, J., & Csikszentmihalyi, M. (2014). The concept of flow. In M. Csikszentmihalyi (Ed.), *Flow and the foundations of positive psychology* (pp. 239–263). Dordrecht: Springer.

Nishi, D. (2011). How to learn to like your job. *The Wall Street Journal*, June 9, 29.

Nocera, J. (2015). Jeff Bezos and the Amazon way. *The New York Times*, August 22, A17 (http://nytimes.com/2015/08/22/opinion/joe-nocera-jeff-bezos-and-the-amazon-way.html?_r=0)

Oldham, G. R., & Fried, Y. (2016). Job design and theory: Past, present and future. *Organizational Behavior and Human Decision Processes*, 136, 20–35.

Oldham, G. R., & Hackman, J. R. (2010). Not what it was and not what it will be: The future of job design research. *Journal of Organizational Behavior*, 31, 463–479.

Parker, S., & Wall, T. D. (1998). *Job and work design: Organizing work to promote wellbeing and effectiveness*. Thousand Oaks, CA: Sage.

Parker, S. K. (2007). 'That is my job': How employees' role orientation affects job performance. *Human Relations*, 60(3), 403–434.

Parker, S. K. (2014). Beyond motivation: Job and work design for development, health, ambidexterity, and more. *Annual Review of Psychology*, 65, 661–691.

Parker, S. K., Van Den Broeck, A., & Holman, D. (2017). Work design influences: A synthesis of multi-level factors that affect the design of work. *Academy of Management Annals*, 11(1), 267–308.

Petriglieri, G., Ashford, S., & Wrzesniewski, A. (2018a). Thriving in the gig economy. *Harvard Business Review*, March–April, 140–143.

Petriglieri, G., Ashford, S., & Wrzesniewski, A. (2018b). Agony and ecstasy in the gig economy: Cultivating holding environments for precarious and personalized work identities. *Administrative Science Quarterly*, doi: 10.1177/0001839218759646.

Petrou, P., Demerouti, E., & Schaufeli, W. B. (2018). Crafting the change: The role of employee job crafting behaviors for successful organizational change. *Journal of Management*, 44(5), 1766–1792.

Pfeffer, J. (2010). Building sustainable organizations: The human factor. *Academy of Management Perspectives*, 24(1), 34–45.

Pfeffer, J. (2018b). Work hours and health: A comment on "Beyond nine to five". *Academy of Management Discoveries*, 4(1), 94–96.

Pfeffer, J (2018a). *Dying for a paycheck: How modern management harms employee health and company performance – and what we can do about it*. New York: Harper.

Pratt, M. G., Lepisto, D. A., & Dane, E. (2018).The hidden side of trust: Supporting and sustaining leaps of faith among firefighters. *Administrative Science Quarterly*. doi: 10.1177/0001839218769252.

Rajan, R. G., & Wulf, J. (2006). The flattening firm: Evidence from panel data on the changing nature of corporate hierarchies. *Review of Economics and Statistics*, 88(4), 759–773.

Reckard, E. S. (2013). Wells Fargo's pressure-cooker sales culture comes at a cost. *Los Angeles Times*, December 21 (http://.latimes.com/business/la-fi-wells-fargo-sale-pressure-20131222-story.html)

Reid, E., & Ramarajan, L. (2016). Managing the high intensity workplace. *Harvard Business Review*, June, 85–90.

Rhodes, C. (2018). The future of work is under threat, but it's not robots we need to fear. *ABC News*, March 21 (www.abc.net.au/news/2018-03-22/future-of-work-not-robots-we-need-to-fear/9567112)

Roberts, K. H., & Bea, R. G. (2001). When systems fail. *Organizational Dynamics*, 29(3), 179–191.

Rodell, J. B., Booth, J. E., Lynch, J. W., & Zipay, K. P. (2017). Corporate volunteering climate: Mobilizing employee passion for societal causes and inspiring future charitable action. *Academy of Management Journal*, 60(5), 1662–1681.

Roser, C. (2016). *"Faster, Better, Cheaper" in the history of manufacturing: From the stone age to lean manufacturing and beyond*. Boca Raton, FL: CRC Press.

Rousseau, D. M., Ho, V. T., & Greenberg, J. (2006). I-deals: Idiosyncratic terms in employment relationships. *Academy of Management Review*, 31, 977–994.

Sachs, J. (2018). Good governance in the 21st century. In *Global Happiness Policy Report 2018* (pp. 3–10). Paris: Global Happiness Council.

Schabram, K., & Maitlis, S. (2017). Negotiating the challenges of a calling: Emotion and enacted sensemaking in animal shelter work. *Academy of Management Journal*, 60(2), 584–609.

Schaufeli, W. B., Bakker, A. B., & Salanova, M. (2006). The measurement of work engagement with a short questionnaire: A cross-national study. *Educational and Psychological Measurement*, 66, 701–716.

Schaufeli, W. B., Salanova, M. G.-R., & Bakker, A. B. (2002). The measurement of engagement and burnout: A two sample confirmatory factor analytic approach. *Journal of Happiness Studies*, 3, 71–92.

Schwab, K. (2015). The fourth industrial revolution: What it means and how to respond. *Foreign Affairs*, December 12.

Sitkin, S. B., Miller, C. C., & See, K. E. (2017). The stretch goal paradox. *Harvard Business Review*, January–February, 93–99.

Sitkin, S. B., See, K. E., Miller, C. C., Lawless, M. W., & Carton, A. M. (2011). The paradox of stretch goals: Organizations in pursuit of the seemingly impossible. *Academy of Management Review*, 36(3), 544–566.

Smith, W. K., & Lewis, M. W. (2011). Toward a theory of paradox: A dynamic equilibrium model of organizing. *Academy of management Review*, 36(2), 381–403.

Sonenshein, S., Dutton, J. E., Grant, A. M., Spreitzer, G. M., & Sutcliffe, K. M. (2013). Growing at work: Employees' interpretations of progressive self-change in organizations. *Organization Science*, 24(2), 552–570.

Takeuchi, H., Osono, E., & Shimizu, N. (2008). The contradictions that drive Toyota's success. *Harvard Business Review*, June, 96–104.

Taylor, F. (1911). *The principles of scientific management*. New York: WW Norton.

Ten Brummelhuis, L. L., Rothbard, N. P., & Uhrich, B. (2017). Beyond nine to five: Is working to excess bad for health? *Academy of Management Discoveries*, 3, 262–283.

Terkel, S. (2011). *Working: People talk about what they do all day and how they feel about what they do*. New York: The New Press.

Thakor, A. V., & Quinn, R. E. (2013). The economics of higher purpose. European Corporate Governance Institute, Working paper 395.

Tornay, K., & Frese, M. (2013). Construct clean-up in proactivity research: A meta-analysis on the nomological net of work-related proactivity constructs and their incremental validities. *Applied Psychology*, 62(1), 44–96.

Twenge, J. M., Campbell, S. M., Hoffman, B. J., & Lance, C. E. (2010). Generational differences in work values: Leisure and extrinsic values increasing, social and intrinsic values decreasing. *Journal of Management*, 36, 1117–1142.

van Dam, N., & van der Helm, E. (2016a). There's a proven link between effective leadership and getting enough sleep. *Harvard Business Review*, February 16 (https://hbr.org/2016/02/theres-a-proven-link-between-effective-leadership-and-getting-enough-sleep)

van Dam, N., & van der Helm, E. (2016b). The organizational cost of insufficient sleep. *McKinsey Quarterly*, February (https://mckinsey.com/business-functions/organization/our-insights/the-organizational-cost-of-insufficient-sleep#0)

Vidal, M. (2013). Low-autonomy work and bad jobs in post-Fordist capitalism. *Human Relations*, 66, 587–612.

Wagner, R., & Harter, J. K. (2006). *12 elements of great managing*. New York: Gallup Press.

Waters, R. (2016). Targeting the 'next big thing'. *Financial Times*, November 29, 9.

Weber, M. (1958). Science as a vocation. *Daedalus*, 87(1), 111–134.

Weber, M. (2013). *The protestant ethic and the spirit of capitalism*. London: Routledge.

Wegman, L. A., Hoffman, B. J., Carter, N. T., Twenge, J. M., & Guenole, N. (2016). Placing job characteristics in context: Cross-temporal meta-analysis of changes in job characteristics since 1975. *Journal of Management*, 44(1), 35–386.

Wiklund, J., Hatak, I., Patzelt, H., & Shepherd, D. A. (2018). Mental disorders in the entrepreneurship context: When being different can be an advantage. *Academy of Management Perspectives*, 32(2), 182–206.

Wrzesniewski, A., Berg, J. M., & Dutton, J. E. (2010). Managing yourself: Turn the job you have into the job you want. *Harvard Business Review*, June, 114–117.

Wrzesniewski, A., & Dutton, J. M. (2001). Crafting a job: Revisioning employees as active crafters of their work. *Academy of Management Review*, 26, 179–201.

Wrzesniewski, A., McCauley, C., Rozin, P., & Schwartz, B. (2001). Jobs, careers, and callings: People's relations to their work. *Journal of Research in Personality*, 31, 21–33.

Yeoman, R. (2014). Conceptualising meaningful work as a fundamental human need. *Journal of Business Ethics*, 125(2), 235–251.

Part III

Positivity in collectives

6   Generative interactions in organizations

Summary and objectives

Abundant psychological energy, or motivation, is a fundamental characteristic of well-functioning organizations. In this chapter we discuss some of the main ways of building energy, emphasizing interactions as the building blocks of organizing and highlighting the importance of positive interactions in the construction of great organizations. We discuss the fundamental characteristics of generative interactions – respectful engagement, task enabling and trust; consider the role of conversations in the creation of positive organizations and explore the importance of engaging in difficult conversations to avoid difficult problems. Finally, we also highlight three virtues that facilitate organizational relational processes, contributing to higher levels of employee engagement, wellbeing and performance.

Organizations as relational productions

Relationships matter in organizations. Instead of seeing organizations as comprised of individuals, it is possible to represent them as processes articulating people in order to solve needs and create value. Whole Foods issued a mission statement titled 'Declaration of Interdependence', defining the organization as 'a community working together to create value for other people'[1] (for more information on B Corps declarations of interdependence, consult Chapter 11). At Valve, a company founded by former Microsoft employees, the so-called rule of three has been enacted: when three company employees consider that an idea, an initiative or a project deserves to be considered, they have the right to explore it. The organization is trying to take advantage of the wisdom of the crowds to create renewal initiatives that necessarily escape the attention of top managers. The Valve rule of three takes relationships seriously in several ways: it forces employees to test the validity of their ideas with their peers; it presents leadership as a dispersed relational process and it signals that not every important relationship must be validated by the hierarchs.[2]

It is common to define organizations as groups of people working together to reach shared goals. The focus on people as the unit of organizational analysis is understandable, yet limiting: organizations are relational productions and performances, outcomes of human interdependence rather than the (sum of) projects of independent individuals.[3] Relationality, the perspective that people are part of networks rather than separate entities, independent from one another does not deny that people are individuals; instead, it assumes that we are both separate and connected to one another and that relating corresponds to a constitutive feature of human agency.[4] Interactions that matter are not only those that evolve into deep relationships – even brief interactions can be significant in their influence.

A study conducted at Google found that '*who* is on a team matters less than how the team members interact, structure their work and view their contributions'.[5] Research on the organizational recovery after the 9/11 attacks by firms directly affected, found that speedier recovery was facilitated by the presence of rich personal ties, lateral self-organization and non-hierarchical relations,[6] as well as by relationships characterized by compassion.[7] Organizations can thus be viewed not so much as made up of people as entities and more by people in terms of their relations, i.e., organizations as 'ongoing relational processes'.[8]

The growing importance of relationality is reflected in the fact that employment and wage growth in the US is strongest in jobs that demand cognitive *and* social skill. Deming explains the importance of social skills as associated with the fact that social skills reduce coordination costs.[9] The richness of social skills allows workers to adjust collectively to changing circumstances, to work as real teams, to share knowledge, to develop synergies, to perform a greater variety of tasks interdependently. In a world of fast change, where collective adaption and improvised moves gain prominence,[10] work, in summary, becomes more relational and driven by reciprocity than used to be the case.[11] Relations, relational coordination and relational identification become important organizational assets; relational work practices facilitate collective coping.[12] Individuals work better and identify with the organization as a function of the quality of the interactions developed and nurtured at work.

Despite the above observations, 'low quality connections infect most organizations'.[13] In some cases, low-quality HRM practices and connections are created by design, as happens in the case of Ryanair. In this low-cost airline, employees are represented only as 'resources' and the organization adopts a 'low road' approach to people management. In the European summer of 2018 there were many cancelled flights as Ryanair pilots withdrew their labour in strike action or failed to meet the excessive rostering that the airline practiced.[14] In contrast, at Southwest Airlines, a competitor, a 'high road' approach is adopted.[15] The organization, instead of representing people as expendable resources, treats them as crucial to defending quality and values.

This chapter discusses the relational dimension of organizations. It assumes that organizations are relational accomplishments rather than individual constructions. Its premise is that the way people interact ends up establishing and stabilizing relational patterns that define the organization. When colleagues treat each other respectfully and with consideration, they will develop a relationship that differs from that established between situations where members see themselves mostly as rivals. When employees in high-risk systems make collective sense, they create more robust units than when they fail to do so.[16]

As relational systems, organizations may end up as being spaces in which collaboration prevails – or, alternatively, as collectives dominated by competition for scarce resources and, subsequently, largely by zero-sum politically motivated behaviours.[17] All organizations preserve spaces for collaboration and competition but established practices may lead to more or less of each. In the end, organizations may create what Positive Organizational Scholars and relational experts Monica Worline and Jane Dutton call relational ecosystems or egosystems (see Table 6.1).[18] In relational

Table 6.1 Relational egosystems and ecosystems[19]

Relational egosystems	Relational ecosystems
Individuals see each other as independent beings	Individuals see each other as interdependent and as relational beings
People prioritize self-promotion	People prioritize collaboration
Gains are individual	Gains are mutually beneficial
Assumptions of individual merit	Assumptions of shared humanity
Compassion is irrelevant	Compassion competence matters

ecosystems, people assume that good work and organizational success are collective accomplishments; in egosystems, individual competence rules and connections are not equivalently appreciated.

Organizational leaders promote ecosystems or egosystems in great part through the function of the everyday behaviours that form their role modelling. Leaders' influence results more from the example they provide than from the direct influence they exert upon others. In this sense, the way they conduct their interactions inclines the organization to emphasize egos or to channel talents towards some supra-ordained objective.[20] An illustration of the difference between the organization as a sum of individual talent or as a collective can be achieved with a simple exercise: 11 talented soccer players do not compose a competent soccer team. In a sense, the team is not in the individuals themselves but in the space between them, i.e., in their interactions and the way they stabilize and perform as a team rather than as 11 talented individuals.

Individual talent is, of course, important, but interactions make or break the team. In this chapter, we discuss organizations as interactional phenomena and explain how rich interconnectivity builds organizations that transcend the competences of their members. Rich interconnectivity, as explained by Uhl-Bien and Arena, refers to the creation of organizations in which the interactions between members change the employees and the organization in emergent, unexpected ways.[21] This means that organizations become less controlled but also nimbler and more responsive to changing environments.

Given the importance of interactions for coordination, learning, knowledge creation and diffusion, wellbeing and morale, organizations should take relationships seriously.[22] We start by discussing the nature of relationships and particularly positive relationships. We then focus on the reasons why interactions matter. The following section is dedicated to positive relationships. In this case we distinguish traditionally studied functions and emergent functions. We finally discuss how organizations can create positive relational contexts.

Organizations as relational phenomena

Evolutionary psychologist David Buss noted that 'Humans are perhaps the most complexly social of all animals'[23] (see Box 6.1). Humans live in groups and spend a significant part of their time interacting with others. The organizational literatures increasingly recognize that these interpersonal relationships matter in an emerging body of research that shows that positive relationships at work produce a number of important consequences.[24] Organizations are increasingly portrayed as relational phenomena. Yet, relationships are rarely at the forefront of managerial attention.

Box 6.1 Sleep your way to success

Humans are complex social animals. But still they are animals. This obvious observation helps us to understand the very simple fact that primary biological needs affect the quality of relationships and hence the quality of an organization. The quality of sleep and recovery positively impacts the quality of relationships and engagement in the workplace. McGrath and colleagues who have studied the relationship between sleep and human relations explain: 'Multilevel analyses revealed that sleep quality predicted morning positive affect, which in turn predicted work engagement directly and indirectly through having positive interactions with colleagues'.[25]

Leaders' good sleep improves their emotional reactions to others, facilitates their socioemotional processing and fosters trusted relationships, thus increasing leadership effectiveness.[26] On the other hand, leaders' sleep deprivation leads them to adopt abusive behaviours against employees, which in turn decreases employees' work engagement.[27] Robert Sutton argued: 'Sleep deprivation, for example, is one of the most reliable ways to become an asshole. If you're tired and in a hurry, you're likely to be an asshole'.[28]

Simon Kuper defended the thesis that 'good or bad nights can shape careers. I suspect that the key to success – at least in middle age – isn't talent, luck, nepotism or even showing up. It's getting enough sleep'.[29] A possible explanation for the importance of sleep is simple: it keeps one awake. Short sleepers, like President Macron of France, may have an advantage but the pressure on employers to design work, namely shift work, in a way that promotes sleep, is increasing.[30] In summary, to protect relationships and even performance, it is important to allow people a balanced life: good sleep is a source of competitive advantage. Barnes and Spreitzer argued that sleep is a 'strategic resource'.[31] Ariana Huffington argued that 'a sleep revolution will allow us to better solve the world's problems'.[32] And the *Financial Times* dedicated a special report to the issue (May 19, 2014).

At the micro level, individuals are obviously more salient than 'the space between' them, i.e., the interactions among them. At the macro organizational level, this has important implications for design. To manage scalability and deal with the challenges associated with growth, managers have devised bureaucratic structures that permit scalable growth, replicability and sustainability.[33] These bureaucracies, however, lack some important sources of organizational competitiveness, such as caring environments and timely response skills. In order to grow without losing the capacity to cultivate rich relationships, some organizations have experimented with the creation of rich relational infrastructures. The challenge consists of maintaining the capacity to grow and compete without becoming a cold and humanly indifferent organization. The implication is that managers that seek to be positive will provide a vision and cede control over relationships, letting them flow spontaneously, a challenge often faced with managerial reluctance given habitual dispositions gained through prior experience.[34]

To obtain a synthesis of the control provided by bureaucracy and caring resulting from relational organizing, some organizations are combining the best of bureaucracy (scalability, replicability, sustainability) with the best of relational forms (connectedness, empowerment, mutuality). The integration of these results in what has been called the 'relational bureaucracy', a higher-order hybrid form that seeks to avoid the rule tropism[35] of bureaucracy, where rules are followed slavishly irrespective of their appropriateness or functionality, as well as the pressures for emotional conformity and emotional cloning that can result in emotional fatigue where relationality is over-stressed.[36] How is a relational bureaucracy composed? We discuss this in more detail below but can illustrate the answer to the question here through the use of some examples. Companies such as carmakers and airlines are necessarily bureaucratic but not necessarily typical Kafkaesque bureaucracies in which rule tropism combines with arbitrariness and opacity (see Box 6.2); they might be relational bureaucracies. Toyota with its kaizen-based philosophy of continuous improvement would be an example, although the pressure to improve continuously can be quite intrusive. As researchers discovered over a lengthy period of investigation, employees at Toyota work in a culture in which they constantly grapple with challenges and problems and *must* come up with fresh ideas; the pressure is on each employee to do so.[37] Gulati has written about companies that provide freedom within a framework, such as Southwest.[38] Good rules are enabling: they are important but they do not constitute the ultimate goal of the organization, as in bureaucracies in which rule tropism is rife. A complex array of rules is not, per se, a source of mindlessness but it very easily can be when used defensively by employees to protect their interest in being seen to be compliant rather than creative.

Box 6.2 The Kafkaesque bureaucracy

The adjective 'Kafkaesque' is derived from the name of Franz Kafka, an important European writer born in Prague (Figure 6.1). Kafka's fictional work has had a lasting influence on organizational literature. Inspired by his lived experience as a petty bureaucrat, Kafka's writing highlights the dystopian effects of labyrinthine bureaucratic rules that, instead of serving a purpose, constitute a closed loop. The effect is the creation of an oppressive environment, leading to alienation, loneliness and marginalization.[39] Kafka thereby creates a 'counter-mythology' of organizational life, contradicting managerialist assumptions of organizational rationality.[40] Here are a couple of examples from his now classic works *The Castle* and *The Trial*:

Figure 6.1 Franz Kafka.[43]

In *The Castle*, Kafka describes a desperate father trying to obtain pardon after his daughter had been unjustly disgraced for resisting a powerful and corrupt government bureaucrat: 'He wasn't so much concerned with winning back her honour as with being forgiven. But to be forgiven he must first establish his guilt, and that very thing was denied him in the offices'.[41]

In *The Trial*, Kafka provides the following dialogue between the main protagonist and a priest: '"At least for the moment they think your guilt is proven." "But I'm not guilty," said K., "it's a mistake. How can a person be guilty anyway? We're all human, every single one of us." "That is correct," said the priest, "but that's the way guilty people talk".'[42]

The main characters in Kafka's stories are people lost within organizations that they cannot understand. We encourage our readers to explore the Kafkaesque organization by reflecting on personal experiences with Kafka-like bureaucracies, reading a paper that we have written on this theme[44] as well as papers by other authors on similar themes and enjoy the mastery of Kafka through his writings.

Characterizing high-quality connections

From a relational perspective, connections constitute the very fabric of human life in general. Medical evidence shows that loneliness increases the risk of cardiovascular disease, and that good relationships with family and friends are fundamental for happiness rather than luxuries.[45]

There are several types of relations and they can matter for different reasons. A connection is the 'dynamic, living tissue ... that exists between two people when there is some contact between them, involving mutual awareness and social interaction'.[46] A positive relationship is one that reoccurs and that is perceived by participants as mutually beneficial.[47] Connections do not, as per this definition, involve any form of recurring, enduring or intimate form of relationship. Yet, they too, like relationships, are important and exist in various forms. We treat relationships and connections as referring to the same broad processes, even while recognizing that relationships have different temporal horizons and deeper personal bonds. High-quality connections and relationships are both characterized by three features:[48]

- **positive regard** refers to the orientation of seeing the best in the other;
- **mutuality** means that the relationship is defined by responsiveness from the other;
- **vitality** expresses the elevated sense of energy created by the interaction.

As we will discuss, these apparently normal characteristics need to be actively managed to unfold in organizations if only because relations are no less important in organizational than in everyday life lived outside work. Relationships with organizational significance do not have to be sustained in the long term. The fact that these relational qualities seem trivial will not necessarily mean that they will simply emerge in the absence of managerial care. To explore the process of making them real, we next describe high-quality connections (Table 6.2). These satisfy three criteria[49]:

- A high-quality connection has high **emotional carrying capacity** (i.e., it assumes an ample spectrum of emotions, positive and negative). For example, when people feel afraid to communicate something negative, they are not forming a high-quality connection.
- They are rich in **tensility**. High-quality connections can shape themselves according to circumstances. The dyad or the team adjusts itself to circumstances in such a way that it expresses different behaviours in the face of differing circumstances. Tensile relations can sometimes be stretched but their elasticity helps the system recover. They are important for assuring resilience (see Chapter 3).
- They are high on **connectivity**. This characteristic reflects the generativity and openness to new ideas, as well as the capacity to avoid stimuli that will limit generativity. Interactions with this characteristic increase the organization's potential for innovation, because people are receptive to difference.

These three characteristics are important because they assure that interactions do not block organizational questioning and learning in the name of superficially good communication. In some contexts, in order to be a good team worker, to protect morale or in respect of some other equally positive objective, people can end up silencing their voice, not being a metaphorical 'tall poppy' or a 'nail that sticks out'. As a result, learning does not unfold and falsely positive communication is protected but at the cost of certain issues not being raised because there is the expectation that they would not be welcome by significant others. When people feel tempted to pretend they agree, especially when they don't, the organizational unit (dyad, team, board) lacks emotional carrying capacity.[50] People become defensive and defensive communication is '*anti*learning'.[51] In the name of being positive, organizations become negative. To learn,

Table 6.2 How to evaluate the quality of connections

Characteristic	Explanation	Illustration
Emotional carrying capacity	The unit comports a full range of emotions. It is adequate to express one's genuine thoughts. This should be done with respect for other people's emotions.	Coach K, i.e., Mike Krzyzewski, coach of the US basketball Olympic team, explained: 'We've created a jealous-free zone … we look each other in the eye. We tell the truth. And we trust each other'.[55]
Tensility	The system is tensile, meaning that relationships are able to adjust to circumstances. Seen in different moments, the same relationship can look different, as members adapt to a range of circumstances.	In certain moments a team looks very formal, in subsequent moments the same team appears very informal. The circumstances elicit different types of relational expressions.
Connectivity	Refers to the openness of connections to new ideas and influences, thereby moulding the receptivity to innovations.	A manager is open for feedback from her team even when team members counter her own ideas. Ideas can come from anywhere not just from hierarchy.

organizations need to encourage open conversations in order to produce change and to expand competencies, as competencies tend to focus on what is already well done.[52] Open conversations combined with a sense of connectivity and interpersonal trust are critical to stimulate exploration and improvisations in the direction of uncertain futures.[53] Innovative and creative organizations thrive because of polyphony; an organization without dissent, characterized by consensus that is falsely attributed to its deliberations, will be an emotional and relational autocracy.[54]

When connections exhibit the three characteristics above, they originate intersubjective experiences marked by feelings of vitality and aliveness, a positive regard, perceptions of mutuality. Feelings of *vitality and aliveness* mean that people feel energized. For people in this condition, work is a source of energy and enthusiasm. In the presence of their colleagues, people feel exhilarated and consider their team as a source of energy.[56] High-quality connections also mean that people see their organizations as a *source of recognition and love*[57] (for a critical view, see Box 6.3). Being loved, in this sense, has no romantic implications but is the platonic state of feeling fulfilled by the wisdom and virtue of relations with significant others. Organizationally, it characterizes the manifestation of authentic relationships in which people feel known, appreciated and cared for. It derives from the perception that the organization provides a sense of care and operates as a community of work, with sound values and individual consideration.[58] The third dimension of a high-quality connection refers to *mutuality*, the fact that the relation results from the active engagement of the participants and that the organization is governed by norms of reciprocity, to revive a term that a classic statement established.[59]

Box 6.3 Love in organizations: realism instead of 'corporate idiocy'

1 Don't be naïve

This chapter explores the importance of cultivating good connections. But it is important not to be naïve: good connections should not be taken as meaning that everyone in a team or organization likes everybody else. That is simply impossible. Most individuals do not have the luxury of working only with people they like nor do most leaders have the liberty to compose their teams, which means that they will have to work with people they do not necessarily like. Realistically, some critical relationships will simply have to work, regardless of one's feelings about the counterpart. Establishing a workable relationship is, in some cases, as positive as it gets.

2 Do respect, not love

When the head of Tesco in the UK said he wanted staff to love customers, Lucy Kellaway wrote sarcastically in the *Financial Times* that she followed up by visiting her local store[60]:

> 'I fixed my gaze on Niraj's red shirt, not daring to meet his dark eyes. "Do you love me?" I asked. He put the Vanish stain remover into a plastic bag, acting as if I hadn't said anything. After a pause he enquired: "Do you have a Clubcard?" I said no, I didn't have a Clubcard, and repeated my question, this time looking at him straight on.

"Do you love me?" A look of worry crossed his face. "Excuse me?" he asked. I told him I was following up on something his boss had said. Richard Brasher, the new head of Tesco in the UK, had just been quoted in the *The Times* saying: "What I want to do is embrace the staff, love the staff, so that they in turn will love the customers".

... In 2003 Jimmy Lee, a vice-chairman of JPMorgan, wrote to his underlings in corporate finance ordering them to "Take the time today to call a client and tell them you love them." Back then I wrote a column declaring this to be the high watermark of corporate idiocy. I decided that it was explicable – if not excusable – on the grounds that bankers were so high on vanity and money that they felt like God, and God loves everyone.

... What Mr. Brasher should have said was that he wanted to show respect for his employees, so that they would show respect for customers. By talking incontinently about love, he invites cynicism and looks like a fool to his staff – or would do if many of them a) read *The Times* or b) had any idea who he was.'

3 Suicides and pseudo–love[61]

Foxconn is a large subcontract manufacturer working for many household names, of which Apple is one of the best known. Between January and November 2010, 18 company employees attempted suicide, with 14 deaths. Most died by jumping from the dormitory. Suicide notes and survivors described a workplace characterized by 'immense stress, long workdays and harsh managers who were prone to humiliate workers for mistakes, of unfair fines and unkept promises of benefits'.[62] The suicides drew wide media attention to employment practices at the company. In 2017, an employee commented:[63] 'It wouldn't be Foxconn without people dying ... Every year people kill themselves. They take it as a normal thing'. Now read the following excerpt from Foxconn's (2010) 'Corporate Social & Environmental Responsibility annual report, which includes the word 'love' 13 times:

> In 2010, Foxconn IE Academy and the Shenzhen Labor Union jointly hosted a total of 90 workshops with more than 8,700 attendees to improve employees' personal qualities and abilities. In addition, Foxconn set up various speech and debate competition shows on the topic of "I love the company, the company loves me," and a happy mothers' forum (p. 23) ... In 2010, Foxconn organized 12 major volunteer programs and more than 200 major and midsize activities to "help the weak and the disabled, give love and support, and promote sanitation." Foxconn's Volunteer Team encouraged volunteers to make a difference by way of numerous forms of charitable functions. In 2011, Foxconn intends to initiate a "Foxconn Volunteer Network" to bring hope and love to those in crisis and to work together for a better society.

Creating high-quality connections

How can good connections be created in organizations? What is the process that leads to them? Seppälä and Cameron[64] responded to this question in an article published in the *Harvard Business Review*. They argued that a positive workplace culture 'boils down to six essential characteristics:

- Caring for, being interested in and maintaining responsibility for colleagues as friends.
- Providing support for one another, including offering kindness and compassion when others are struggling.
- Avoiding blame and forgive mistakes.
- Inspiring one another at work.
- Emphasizing the meaningfulness of the work.
- Treating one another with respect, gratitude, trust, and integrity'.

Seppälä and Cameron make the case that leaders can have a significant impact in creating such positive relational cultures by adopting four practices: (1) fostering social connections, (2) showing empathy, (3) going out of your way to help and (4) encouraging people to talk to you – especially about their problems.

Table 6.3 Four characteristics of high-quality connections

Characteristic	Explanation	Illustration
Respectful engagement	People see, appreciate and approach others with a sense of worth, dignity and respect, by acknowledging their presence and being present to them with authenticity and affirmation.	The members of one organization accept that everyone in the organization is important: doctors in a hospital appreciate the importance of the cleaning staff not only for their job of keeping the facilities hygienic.
Task enabling	People represent their work as including a dimension of help: it is my job to help others do their jobs through teaching, designing solutions, advocating, accommodating needs and nurturing.	People help each other. There is a sense of interdependence: 'If my colleague is in need, it is my duty to help'.
Trust	People accept that being vulnerable in the face of others is acceptable, as others will not take advantage of their vulnerability. Positive trust-building activities include providing access, sharing resources, delegating responsibility, seeking suggestions, maintaining openness, and 'walking the talk'. Actions undermining trust include: excessive control and monitoring, accusations of bad intentions, ignoring suggestions and offering inconsistent directions.	People admit their mistakes and see mistakes as opportunities for learning rather than for eliminating a rival.
Play	Play energizes human connections. It can be both formal (scheduled) and informal (spontaneous).	The organization conducts playful teambuilding exercises, provides opportunities for volunteering and makes available play equipment such as table tennis, pool tables and basketball courts.

University of Michigan researcher and positive organizational scholar Jane Dutton has been researching high-quality connections for decades. In her 2003 book titled *Energize Your Workplace: How to Create and Sustain High-Quality Connections at Work*, she explains that high-quality connections depend on the presence of three process elements: respectful engagement, task enabling and trust. Later she was to add a fourth element: play.[65] Each of these processes is described next (see Table 6.3).

Respectful engagement

Respect can be defined as being considered and valued by others. Rogers distinguished owed respect, which is supposed to be expressed with regards to every member of a given unit, from earned respect, which recognizes qualities or values displayed by specific individuals.[66] Each of the two forms is important because the lack of either one of them raises potential organizational problems (see Figure 6.2).

As the figure suggests, an organization that fails to appreciate extraordinary contributions risks being perceived as unfair or lacking an appreciation for merit and contribution. Conversely, an organization that appreciates stars rather more than other members potentially creates a Darwinian work environment, alienating the majority of its workforce.

Respect constitutes an important element in organizational life and is highly prized by individuals, often mattering the most for individuals in their relationship with the organization.[68] It 'is critical to both the functioning of collectives and the well-being of individuals', although organizational members 'rarely report adequately receiving it'.[69]

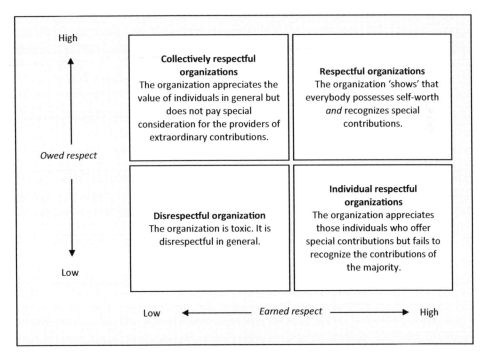

Figure 6.2 Respect and organizational profiles.[67]

The need for respect, perhaps, sounds obvious; nonetheless, it does not necessarily characterize everyday practice in many organizations. As an example, for many employees of Wells Fargo's Community Bank, disrespectful reactions, including career-hindering criticism and extra pressure, were expected by employees as a given if goals were not met.[70] Even the President of the United States can be exposed sometimes[71]: President Trump's tweets are particularly disrespectful of the many people who have, for a variety of reasons, left his administration. The lack of respect paid to those that went before is hardly likely to embolden those who come after; instead, it instils a culture of fearful compliance with a narcissistic, arrogant egotism that assumes authority provides the privilege to demean and diminish all slights, imagined or real, to that authority.

The implication seems clear: *practice a culture of respect – daily*. Respectful engagement with others facilitates relational information processing and promotes psychological safety (Chapter 7), which in turn positively impacts team learning and organizational functioning.[72] Respect stimulates mutual empowerment and allows people to grow together. The promotion of cultures of respect critically depends on how the organization signals, through its leaders, the worth of its members. To engage respectfully with others, organizational members can convey presence to others, be genuine and communicate affirmation[73]:

- **Conveying presence** begins with acknowledging the existence of another. When the Ritz Carlton hotel chain communicates that 'We are ladies and gentlemen serving ladies and gentlemen', it projects the idea that, regardless of what you do, you are an important member of the organization for whom and of whom mutual respect is expected. On the contrary, when the upper castes in an organizational system do not acknowledge the presence of others (as some doctors did to cleaning staff in the hospital studied by Dutton and her colleagues), they express disrespect. In general, signals of hierarchical segregation convey the message that some employees are more important than others. Presence also involves being there physically and psychologically. Such presence is conveyed through eye contact, body language and actions of disconnecting from other distractions such as the phone or computer while interacting with another. Being available to people when they need support is another way of conveying presence.
- **Being genuine** requires removing pretence and acting from a place of authenticity. Although we may not consciously know how or when we are being perceived as inauthentic, detractors will often sense it. Honesty is critical. A perceived lack of honesty is often the basis for undermining any effort to communicate genuineness, as a basis for high-quality connections.
- **Communicating affirmation** necessitates more than just presence. It requires an ongoing search for the positive core in the other. Multiple pathways are available for communicating affirmation and particularly critical among them are effective listening and communicating supportively. Effective listening involves listening both with empathy and active engagement (see Box 6.4). Empathy is communicated when the listener attends not just to the speakers' words but also to their feelings and meanings. Active listening articulates paraphrasing, summarizing and clarifying what you understand the speaker to have said. Supportive communication contrasts with communication that creates barriers to understanding, generating defensiveness against sarcasm, threats and negative comparisons. Supportive communication is enacted by (a) avoiding evaluative judgemental language but

remaining descriptive ('you are lazy' vs 'you didn't get the report in on time'), (b) being specific rather than abstract in expressing concerns ('you need to be more careful about punctuality' vs 'your end-of-the-month report is already three days late, and this is the second time this has happened in the past three months'), and (3) explaining one's requests rather than making demands ('I am concerned about getting our reports in on time each month, therefore I wonder if you can commit to giving me updates at the end of each week' vs 'I need you to keep me regularly updated').

Box 6.4 'Listening without an agenda'.

Adam Bryant, from *The New York Times*, asked Joel Peterson, chairman of JetBlue Airways and Professor at Stanford Graduate School of Business, 'What did you do to make people trust you?' He replied[74]:

> For me, a lot of it is listening. I'm a really good listener. It's not a technique – I'm really interested in what people have to say. But it does develop trust as a byproduct. If you're authentic, open, you call things as they are, you really are direct and you listen well, that develops trust. And you can't have an agenda. When you have your own agenda when you're listening to someone, what you're doing is you're formulating your response rather than processing what the other person is saying. You have to really be at home with yourself. If you have these driving needs to show off or be heard or whatever, then that kind of overwhelms the process. If you're really grounded and at home with yourself, then you can actually get in the other person's world, and I think that builds trust.

Task-enabling

Organizations develop superior relationships when individuals enable the others to conduct their tasks better. Leaders are task-enabling when they act as mentors or coaches; peers enable others to do their work when they create conditions for others to do a good job. They fail to enable others when they refuse help on the grounds that 'it is not my job'. Hence the importance for organizations of givers, people with a propensity to help others. Givers create an atmosphere of good will that turns employees into organizational citizens, interested in improving the organization even when there are no rewards involved (see Box 6.5). By being generous and helpful, givers develop trustful relationships and are more likely to promote in others the willingness to reciprocate – unless others are takers aiming at extracting the most from the givers.

There are numerous ways that high-quality connections can be nurtured in the workplace through task-enabling, both officially and unofficially. Five powerful approaches described by Jane Dutton include[75]: (1) *teaching* helpful information and insights; (2) *designing* new processes or systems to help another succeed in their job; (2) *advocating* to help another navigate the organization's political landscape; (4) *accommodating* another's needs or concerns in their job performance and delivery and (5), *nurturing* another person to facilitate their success.

Box 6.5 Givers and takers.[76]

In workplaces, givers are generous employees that contribute to others without seeking anything in return. They share knowledge and assist other team members. By acting generously, givers are also likely to benefit from the reciprocation behaviours adopted by other team members. In this way, positive upward spirals develop within the team. Teams and organizations have interest in selecting givers and fostering generous behaviours because giving increases cooperation, quality improvement and commitment to collective goals.

Takers are those who tend to get the most possible from others without giving anything in exchange – unless such an exchange is instrumental to extract. They are less inclined to share knowledge, to assist others and to cooperate. When other team members become aware about the 'extractive' orientation of a taker, it is likely they are less willing to help and assist him/her. Takers undermine team learning and flourishing. Are givers more effective than takers? It depends on how wise and prudent the givers are. They are more likely to flourish, both as individuals and team members, if they adopt behaviours such as the following: (1) they are generous but also ask for help; (2) they avoid dropping everything when someone asks for a favour; rather, they carve out time and space for uninterrupted work; (3) they are selective as to whom they help, and they may act as matchers (i.e., they help takers only if takers reciprocate).

Trust

At its essence, trust is about 'being vulnerable and relying on another person to follow through on their commitments'.[77] You trust the other if you believe that the other doesn't unduly use your vulnerability – you don't trust the other if you are afraid that the other will act opportunistically towards your vulnerability. Trust is communicated both by what you *do* say and do, as well as by what you do *not* say or do. Positive trust-building activities include providing access, sharing resources, delegating responsibility, seeking suggestions and maintaining openness. Actions that do *not* build trust but rather undermine it include: excessive control and monitoring, accusations of bad intentions, ignoring suggestions and offering inconsistent directions.

Contrasting examples of high- and low-trust organizations are found in Southwest Airlines and American Airlines. While both have cognitive cultures characterized by an outcome orientation, they have distinct emotional cultures: Southwest is often dubbed the LUV airline (LUV also being the code under which the company is traded on the New York Stock Exchange), whereas American has been referred to as the 'stainless steel' airline. At Southwest, employees are given significant amounts of autonomy in decision-making and are encouraged to express their authentic emotions, whereas at American employees are expected to transmit emotional restraint.[78] Organizations can thus communicate trust and stimulate connections that support positive emotions, or communicate a lack of trust through high levels of emotional control (for potential negative effects of trust see Box 6.6). The dimensions of trust, social support and reciprocity, quality of exchange, cooperation, coordination and integration define these relationships.[79]

Box 6.6 The potential negative side of a social lubricant

Kenneth Arrow (joint winner of the so-called Nobel Prize in Economic Sciences with John Hicks, 1972) referred to trust as an 'important lubricant of a social system'.[80] Interpersonal trust 'is a psychological state comprising the intention to accept vulnerability based upon positive expectations of the intentions or behavior of another'.[81] Intrateam trust refers to the 'aggregate levels of trust that team members have in their fellow teammates'.[82] Research has suggested that team trust contributes to team performance.[83] Trust helps team members to suspend uncertainty about and vulnerability towards each other, thus enabling them to work together more cooperatively and to allocate their energy and skills to pursue team goals. By contrast, a lack of trust leads team members to adopt defensive actions to protect themselves against possible harm by others. Cooperation efforts in the pursuit of common goals decrease.

Team trust has, however, a potential 'dark side',[84] mainly if trust is not accompanied by other team characteristics. An excess of proximity may make it more difficult to uncover unethical decisions and behaviours and may make team members lack discernment and 'close their eyes' regarding problematic behaviours. A possible way to overcome these risks is through vigilant trust. As Greenleaf, the proponent of servant leadership (see Chapter 8), argued, 'somewhere between blind trust and distrust there is an optimum of trust that supports leadership that moves toward what is richer, more honest, more fundamentally right'.[85] Psychological safety represents a good ground for such a 'vigilant trust' in that team members feel safe to raise concerns and speak up.

Play

The importance of play in building connections is often overlooked in the organizational context.[86] Play is more widely recognized and valued for facilitating creativity and innovation. Moments of play facilitate interaction, exploration and the development of new knowledge. They also give rise to positive emotions, facilitating openness to new creative ideas and innovative approaches. Less considered, however, is that play also has great importance in energizing human connections. Play can be both formal (scheduled play activities) and informal (spontaneous playfulness in meetings and other venues). Ways of institutionalizing play, even informally, in the organizational context include teambuilding exercises, volunteering opportunities and providing play equipment such as table tennis, pool tables and basketball courts. Play is a low-cost means of promoting high-quality connections. James March proposed a model of decision-making – by individuals, organizations, social and cultural systems – based on release from the logic of reason and through the use of sensible foolishness. Playfulness and playful behaviour are at the heart of the 'technology of foolishness', a method that allows for experimentation, acting unintelligently, irrationally and foolishly. A playful strategy can contribute to the transformation of people and organizations, suggests March.[87] March argues that hosting opportunities for a playful strategy allows organizations to experience new things and different perspectives, enabling organizational members to experiment and discover, with explicit permission to be less goal-oriented.[88] Sometimes actions need to precede purpose; plans need to be suspended or bracketed and ambiguity and fluidity of action encouraged, as opposed to insisting on consistency and prediction. Organizations need to relax the primacy of functional rationality, temporarily suspend logic, reason and intentionality in order to promote an openness to new actions, objectives and understandings.

Why interactions matter

From a relational perspective, organizing happens in the interaction. We say organizing with reason: organizing is active, a verb. Thinking always of organization orients us to something already fabricated, structured and designed: the solidity of nouns disguises the fluidity and process of actions and interactions. Actions and interactions are critical for a number of reasons. They coordinate people and activities; bond and provide a feeling of belongingness; support knowledge transfer and creation and become a source of social wellbeing.[89] Seppälä and Cameron discussed the consequences of positive social connections as follows[90]:

> A large number of empirical studies confirm that positive social connections at work produce highly desirable results. For example, people get sick less often, recover twice as fast from surgery, experience less depression, learn faster and remember longer, tolerate pain and discomfort better, display more mental acuity, and perform better on the job. Conversely, research by Sarah Pressman at the University of California, Irvine, found that the probability of dying early is 20% higher for obese people, 30% higher for excessive drinkers, 50% higher for smokers, but a whopping 70% higher for people with poor social relationships. Toxic, stress-filled workplaces affect social relationships and, consequently, life expectancy.

People develop connections for several reasons. Dutton and Heaphy highlight four: exchange, identity, growth and knowledge. First, people interact for *exchange* reasons. Exchange is based on the fact that, via their interactions, people trade resources and rewards. This happens because we all have resources (intellectual, emotional, social) that are relevant to others. Leaders have resources that are important to subordinates but subordinate engagement is critical for leader success. When the relationship works well, leaders provide their subordinates with empowerment, coaching and protection, whereas subordinates express stronger levels of commitment and motivation. Over time, the relationship can create its own resources, namely, mutual trust that stimulates people to invest more and exchange more valuable resources.

Second, connections are critical in defining *identity*. As individuals we can represent ourselves as 'a work in progress'.[91] The way we compose our identity is to some extent the product of our interactions. Our professional identity comes not only from our training and educational background but also from the relationships with those around us. If an organization projects, culturally, a positive meaning about what it does and if it treats its individual employees as important in and of themselves, it shapes identities in a given way. If it treats some as more important than others, it triggers a different view of identity. If an organization invites its members to fit to some cultural mould, rather than accepting people as they are, it creates different sorts of 'works in progress'. By genuinely stimulating diversity, organizations can become more tolerant of difference and more open to change. Such practices of organizing tend to be perceived as creating better places to work (see Chapter 9).[92] If, on the contrary, they value cultural 'strength' built upon a strong conception of identity embedded in the noun of the organization they will stimulate very different forms of connection.

Third, interactions are important for *growth* and development purposes. From an *independence* perspective, growth and development are processes that individuals undergo. From an *interdependence* perspective, however, they are a collaborative process, one that unfolds in interactions. In terms of organizing, when others are involved as coaches or mentors growth is more likely. Cultures of caring and fluid interactions facilitate growth because people feel that they belong to a collective that actively participates in a *process*. In this perspective, the process does not happen to individuals but occurs in actions and interactions between them (see Box 6.7).

Box 6.7 Transferring knowledge: learning-by-living.

1 The importance of educating children

Recent evidence suggests we can learn about organizations by looking at other sources of knowledge. When it comes to growth as a collaborative process, the most obvious example comes from parenting or from family life in general.[93] A powerful source of leadership learning consists in reflecting about one's life in several domains. In this way, the experiences of everyday life can be used as a source of personal reflection, growth and development. For example, the experience of educating children can be illuminating with regards to the importance of caring *and* being demanding. Learning from life can thus be a powerful source of personal development.

2 Do daughters 'teach' their parents to be more socially responsible CEOs?

Research with some of the largest public companies in the US has shown that firms whose CEO has a daughter rate better in terms of corporate social responsibility.[94] A possible explanation is that they tend to exhibit stronger other-regarding preferences. As parents may internalize the preferences of their children, CEOs parenting daughters may develop preferences more similar to those of females. And these preferences may involve the CEOs' increased concerns about diversity, environment, employee relations and other aspects of corporate social responsibility. As the sample included a small number of female CEOs, it is difficult to compare the effects on male versus female CEOs. But Henrik Cronqvist, the first author of the paper, commented in an interview[95]:

> We suspect that a CEO's own gender matters even more than the gender of his or her children. By our calculation, having a male CEO with a daughter produces slightly less than a third of the effect of having a female CEO. Comparisons of the data on congressmen and judges yielded similar numbers. So you could hypothesize that, on average, any man behaves one-third more 'female' when he parents a girl.

Finally, connections matter because they support *learning*. Learning is exhilarating but involves risks. For someone to evolve to the next level, it requires unlearning to facilitate further learning. Before one acquires new levels of proficiency, one will be less competent than before. In other words: before one becomes competent at a higher level, one will be less competent than before. This has been called the paradox of competence: to become more competent in the long run one needs to be willing to be less competent in the short run. The willingness to unlearn previous competences is dependent on relations and mainly upon the experience of psychological safety (see Chapter 7). In psychologically safe places, individuals perceive that it is safe to speak up, to ask questions, to voice concerns, to seek help, and to assume responsibility and learn from mistakes. A culture of honest questioning opens space for learning and promotes interpersonal bonding.[96] Additionally, high-quality connections make the absorption of knowledge faster and more effective, which facilitates the creation of new knowledge.

Why does relational competence matter?

Competence is often equated with being technically adept. Work by Tiziana Casciaro of the University of Toronto and Miguel Sousa Lobo of INSEAD has departed from equating competence with technical skill and proposed that people express different types of competences. Their simple but illustrative approach classifies people according to their technical and social competences – or likability. The combination of these two dimensions forms the conceptual matrix presented in Figure 6.3.

The matrix delineates four types. Some people express competences at the two levels. Casciaro and Lobo call these the lovable stars. In an ideal world, most of us would work with these stars. However, some people are more competent in one rather than the other dimension. Some people excel in the technical dimension but not at the social,

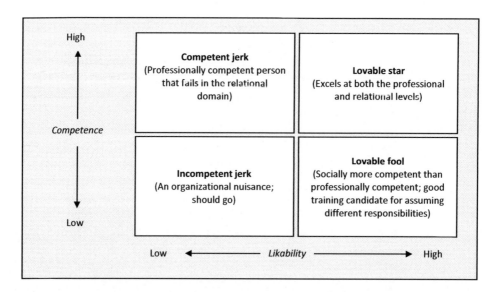

Figure 6.3 Combining social and technical competences.[98]

interpersonal level. These are the competent jerks. A competent jerk is someone who knows how to get things done with a social cost. Lovable fools present the opposite combination: they are interpersonally skilled but lack the technical savvy to shine. Finally, some people are incompetent in the two dimensions. They are the incompetent jerks. The authors observed that, even though rationally one might defend the opposite, people tend to avoid the competent jerk more than the lovable fool. In fact, they will try to extract 'every little bit of competence'[97] that likable people have to offer, while trying to avoid the penalty of working with someone who is unpleasant.

The implications for the management of relationships are clear: if organizations consider that the important dimension of competence refers only to the technical one, they are missing an important part of the picture: relational competences do matter. Hence the question: what can organizations do to nurture the right social competences?

First, organizations can recruit people with a relational edge. Instead of looking mainly to technical characteristics, they can consider social skills and an orientation for teamwork. The German carmaker BMW rigorously screens new hires 'for their ability to thrive as part of a team'.[99] Managers can coach employees to enact desired behaviours. As a leadership orientation, coaching refers to the process of stimulating behaviours that will help people to express their competences more fully and more productively.[100] By acting as coaches, managers help people self-regulate. Coaching can be supported by rich feedback, which can be a powerful stimulus for reflection when considering positives and negatives.

Box 6.8 Stars shine in different ways

Figure 6.3 indicated that stardom potentially involves a relational dimension. But do stars exist in one shape only? Research suggests otherwise. Rebecca Kehoe and Scott Bentley of Rutgers University, along with David Lepak of the University of Massachusetts Amherst, identified three types of star employees: universal stars, performance stars and status stars.[101]

Universal stars are those who combine exceptional task performance and have gained considerable external status. Performance stars obtain exceptional levels of performance and gain considerable status inside the organization – but not outside. Status stars demonstrate moderately high although not exceptional task performance but hold broad status among strategically relevant stakeholders. They can be critical for securing access to relevant external resources. Status stars can be affiliation-based (for example, due to personal associations with elite persons or institutions), former universal stars (universal stars whose task performance declined but who maintained their influence) and networking stars (those whose personal attributes as networkers make them critical to allow others access to relevant external resources).

What is interesting in this classification is the fact that stardom involves an element of connection. It is more than exceptional task performance. Its element of status inevitably involves a relational component. Stars help others by coaching, bringing prestige, facilitating access to networks and resources, oiling connections. The implication seems to be clear: exceptional task performers with no relational competencies are hardly viewed as stars.

Expressions of relationality

People in organizations interact for many reasons. In this section we discuss some of the most important, although not necessarily unique forms of relational expression in organizations. A team of scholars comprising Amy Colbert at the University of Iowa, Joyce Bono from the University of Florida and Radostina Purvanova from Drake University distinguish between traditional and emerging forms of work relationships.[102]

Traditional relationships involve task assistance, career advancement and emotional support:

- Task assistance is important because most tasks end up requiring some form of assistance. Assistance may be necessary because of peaks of excess work or because the task involves challenges that have not emerged before and require support from the leader or a more experienced colleague. These relationships are important as they help reduce stress and support development.
- Career advancement is also a well-established type of relationship. Relationships are used to facilitate access to new opportunities inside or outside an organization. Cultivating one's network is crucial for this matter. Career advancement can also result from the work of a mentor who helps the person reflect on his/her prospects.
- Emotional facilitation is another important relational resource. Leaders are expected to support and protect their subordinates, for example via the provision of human moments.[103] Listening, protecting and providing feedback are important relational resources.

Emerging relationships identified by Colbert and her colleagues include characteristics of facilitating personal growth, friendships and opportunity to give to others. *Personal growth* refers to facilitating the development of someone as a human being. In the past, this relationship was felt less intensely because the boundaries between work and non-work roles were better drawn. And, as employees, people did not necessarily expect to be treated as integral collaborators and owners of human capital to be appreciated. Rather, as employees, they saw their role as executing tasks which they expected to be managed by traditional control mechanisms (hierarchical, bureaucratic).

As organizations changed in the direction of softer forms of power, they charged their leaders with developing emotional intelligence, to approach their people holistically. For example, at Google, the profile of a good manager includes being a good coach, being a good communicator (listening and sharing information), showing concern for team members' success and wellbeing – in short, paying attention to employees as persons[104] (see Box 6.9). Increasingly, leaders are expected to act as coaches of their collaborators. Managers see their role sets extended, and they are expected to contribute towards retaining talent by expressing superior leadership skills. Leadership is thus increasingly perceived as relational.[105]

Box 6.9 Great managers: lessons from Google

Google is mostly a company of engineers. At some point it conducted an experiment: could it be possible to get rid of managers and yet keep the capacity to function? The practical answer was no. The company needed managers. Accepting that managers are necessary, Google then conducted a study, Project Oxygen, to identify the characteristics of the best managers at Google. Ten characteristics stood out. For Google, a good manager[106]:

- Is a good coach.
- Empowers the team – avoids micromanagement.
- Shows concern for team members' success and wellbeing.
- Is productive and results-oriented.
- Is a good communicator – listens and shares information.
- Supports team members' career development and discusses performance.
- Has a clear vision/strategy for the team.
- Has key technical skills that help him/her to advise the team.
- Collaborates across the company.
- Is a strong decision-maker.

Leaders are also expected to be *friends or companions*. The reasoning is simple; if people spend more time working together they probably will benefit from cultivating close relationships, getting along. Finally, relationships should involve an element of *giving to others*. This is expressed in roles supportive of development and acting in the other person's interests. This can be done, sometimes, behind the scenes, as when the leader secures a development opportunity for a subordinate.

Overall, these roles, traditional and emerging, have consequences and are indicative of a number of changes. First, in terms of consequences, research illustrates the fact that different roles have diverse types of impact. For example, task assistance increases job satisfaction, while giving to others is associated with work meaningfulness and companionship with positive emotions. Overall, the work of Colbert and colleagues indicates that work relationships are fundamental in the promotion of flourishing at and through work. On the other hand, managing relationships requires significant soft skills and challenges managers with a number of important trade-offs. For example, the role of being a friend is a double-edged sword. Managers have to make work-related decisions and these decisions are not always easy to frame inside a friendship perspective. Can a friend fire a friend? Can a friend give a negative performance appraisal? In this as in other cases, proximity may be good *or* bad.

Relating through communication

How can organizations nurture high-quality communication (particularly conversation) and translate it into good management practices?

Relational coordination

Organizations can strengthen the quality of relationships to facilitate relational coordination in highly interdependent work processes. Quality relationships can foster social capital, i.e., competitive advantage that is created based on the way an individual is connected to others, which partly substitutes the need for bureaucracy and other formal means of coordination. Traditional, Taylorist forms of coordination restrict communication among employees. Indeed, workstations were often designed to minimize the possibility. Post-bureaucratic forms, on the contrary, stimulate coordination and assume that each person has responsibility for the functioning and the success of the whole.[107] Jody Gittell has dedicated herself to the study of models of communication and coordination, concluding that the basis of effective communication is relational.[108]

Her theorizing on relational coordination, defined as a 'mutually reinforcing process of communicating and relating for the purpose of task integration',[109] alerted scholars to the existence of relational bureaucracies. Bureaucratic rules are not incompatible with communication richness. The two components of the relational coordination model are: high-quality connections and high-quality communication. The three principles of high-quality connections are: shared goals (for the work process), shared knowledge (of each other's tasks) and mutual respect (for other participants in the work process).

The four principles of high-quality communication are: frequent communication (which breeds familiarity through repetition), timely communication (ensures the information is up-to-date), accurate communication (the information must be precise) and problem-solving communication (instead of blaming and avoidance communication). Gittell's relational coordination model has been studied across numerous contexts in collaboration with various research teams, concluding that mechanisms of high-quality connections, supported by high-quality communication, have positive outcomes in terms of efficiency and quality.[110] These mechanisms, when applied cross-sectionally, generate synergistic effects that are highly beneficial with regards to performance outcomes. Gittell holds that the relational ties that facilitate effective communication are between roles rather than personal, which in turn indicates that organizations can be designed to take advantage of boundary spanners in different professional roles, even in the absence of previously existing personal connections.

Good conversations

Organizations are the product of conversations. Organizing is often achieved discursively; indeed, organizing consists of communication, written, spoken, web-based, etc. Lynda Gratton and Sumantra Ghoshal have presented a map of conversations at work which helps us to understand how good conversations contribute to create good organizations. These researchers framed a typology of conversations around two axes. Some conversations are marked, above all, by analytical rationality; others are rich in emotional content or, as they call it, emotional authenticity. Rationality is about structure and decomposition. Emotion is about meaning and holism. The two axes result in four types of conversations (Figure 6.4).

Many conversations in organizations consist of *dehydrated talk*. They are mostly ritual and do not carry important emotional or informational content. These conversations follow well-defined institutional norms. They correspond to what is established as adequate in the social life of the organization and fulfil mostly ritualized functions. Interestingly, part of the information passed in these interactions is already known at the receiving end.

Disciplined debates are a different sort of conversation. They are perceived as rational approaches to technical matters. To the extent that the debate refers to technical issues, information is shared and goals converge; this is the type of debate that helps people

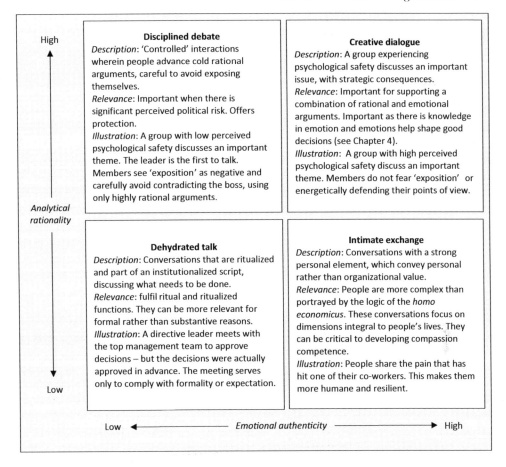

Figure 6.4 Different types of conversations in organizations.[111]

evolve in the direction of rational, objective solutions. When ambiguity enters the debate, the type of conversation can evolve to become more political and emotional.

A third type of conversation is the *intimate exchange*. These conversations are highly emotional in tone and have low rational content. They fulfil important functions in organizations as they give people the opportunity to be authentic and provide their interpretation of the organization. These conversations are important because when conducted with a boss and a supervisor, they signal the availability of the top brass to listen. They also play cathartic roles. The fact that people speak about the events that worry them is important in itself. Idealized roles of managers at Google imply an interest for the person rather than simply for the worker. Conversations with high emotional content satisfy this requirement, expressing personalized attention.

When managers avoid this type of conversation because they can elicit negative emotionality, they may paradoxically be encouraging the accumulation of negative emotions. When negative emotions arise and are handled properly, they contribute towards strengthening emotional carrying capacity, therefore playing a positive rather than a negative role. In fact, they signal the legitimacy of expressing negative emotions in a positive context. Their existence also reveals that people in the organization know how to speak to each other in mature ways, both when emotions are positive as well as when they are negative.

Finally, some conversations are high on reason *and* emotion. They correspond to what Gratton and Ghoshal call *creative dialogues*. These are difficult to balance because they involve reason and emotion that frequently become opposites and are difficult to integrate. However, it is important that, at some points, creative dialogues are adopted. Creative dialogues help provide meaning to structure and structure to meaning. They potentially synthesize and transcend what people know, bringing their thoughts to a higher level. They can be rare but are meaningful when they do occur. They do not deal with day-to-day business and organizational issues; they bring to the table topics that are relevant to individuals. For them to occur people need to be actively engaged with the topic, as the type of frankness they require is vulnerable to cynicism or indifference.

The four types of conversations fulfil distinct roles. They all matter. Scripted and highly ritualized conversations with peers or colleagues are important per se. They contribute towards the creation of a civilized workplace. In this sense, organizations should promote their existence. They can do so through several means. They can culturally legitimize practices of expressing doubt and speaking up. In other words, people should believe that the organization gives them a voice. They can assume that there is space for ignorance as the twin of wisdom.[112] In this sense, organizations cultivate positive interactions by accepting ignorance as a condition for wisdom rather than as a stain to be removed.

Good conversations take time. As such, managers should save time for this function. This is not wasted time; it is actually an investment in the organization's social capital. Sometimes these conversations can be short but, even so, as with all conversations, they have implicit rules. Psychiatrist Edward Hallowell argues that conversations should be perceived as corresponding to human moments. These moments have two requisites: (1) people must be physically present and (2) they must be intellectually and emotionally attentive to one another.[113] The provision of human moments facilitates true communication which in turn stimulates trust and respect.

Managers can also combine the formal and the informal: 'listening tours' are important but they do not replace the institutional and human value of town hall meetings, in which a large group of people are exposed to the same set of information and share the same emotions. The manager of a company described by Hallowell organized a Thursday free pizza lunch in the office. People just sat together in the manager's office to eat pizza and talk – no agenda. The weekly pizza lunch stimulated human moments. Organizing is sharing and organizing the sharing is important to the organizing. Communication rituals play such a sharing function. Space also matters. At a distinct level, authorities are well aware of the power of spaces where people share their emotions. Public spaces can be conducive for expressing intense, widely shared emotions, as studied by Stanford University scholars Rao and Dutta,[114] and witnessed, for example, in Egypt's Tahrir Square.

Listening tours

One way of promoting interactions consists of conducting listening tours.[115] These can be done with a specific project (e.g., the preparation of a new project) or as a routine. They provide opportunities for managers to interact with their teams without the formality of special moments and help create cultures of proximity that are important for letting interactions flow (see also Box 6.10).

Box 6.10 Good listeners – are they sponges or trampolines?

What do great listeners actually do? Zenger and Folkman[116] answered this question after analyzing data describing the behaviour of 3,492 participants in a development programme:

- Good listeners are not simply silent while the other person talks. Rather, they periodically ask questions 'that promote discovery and insight. These questions gently challenge old assumptions, but do so in a constructive way'.
- Good listeners build the other person's self-esteem. They make the conversation a positive experience for the other person, who feels supported and experiences a safe environment in which issues and differences are discussed openly.
- Good listeners make the moment a cooperative conversation. Feedback flows smoothly, supportively and respectfully in both directions.
- Good listeners tend to make suggestions in a way the other accepts and that open up alternative paths to consider.

The authors summarized:

> While many of us have thought of being a good listener being like a sponge that accurately absorbs what the other person is saying, instead, what these findings show is that good listeners are like trampolines. They are someone you can bounce ideas off of – and rather than absorbing your ideas and energy, they amplify, energize, and clarify your thinking. They make you feel better not merely passively absorbing, but by actively supporting. This lets you gain energy and height, just like someone jumping on a trampoline.

Relating through virtue

In Chapter 2 we discussed cultivating virtue strengths. Some virtues are particularly relational in nature: compassion, forgiveness and gratitude, for example. These virtues are relational in that they are often: (1) enacted between people and (2) they foster positive relations and even buffer them against negative setbacks. Cameron, Bright and Caza's study of organizations across 16 industry groups found that organizations that scored highest in fostering three categories of virtue performed significantly higher in different measures of performance than did other organizations in the same industry groups.[117] Organizations that collectively fostered compassion for members during their times of suffering, forgiveness for mistakes made and expressions of gratitude for positive opportunities and experiences, performed higher in terms of profitability, productivity, customer satisfaction and employee retention. In the remainder of this section we consider the positive relational effects of cultivating organizational virtues of compassion, forgiveness and gratitude.

Compassion

Organizational compassion is defined as a four-part collective process of: (1) **N**oticing the suffering of a workplace colleague, (2) **E**mpathizing with their pain, (3) **A**ssessing the causes of their suffering and (4), **R**esponding in a manner that is appropriate to the context and matches the needs of the person who suffers (i.e., NEAR).[118] Stressors that cause suffering within organizations include bullying and harassment, overwork and tight deadlines, workplace accidents, natural disasters, terrorist attacks and personal grief due to personal or family issues. Recognition of the negative effects of workplace stress and other forms of suffering in limiting organizational performance has seen a corresponding rise in awareness of compassion as an effective means of reducing organizational suffering.[119]

Research has identified factors that inhibit a collective organizational capacity for compassionate responding: these include productivity pressures, high control and higher power distances. Pressures of productivity and efficiency reduce the likelihood of employees recognizing a colleague's suffering due to limitations on their ability to connect and be present to learn more about a suffering colleague's concerns.[120] Formal control and bureaucracy also inhibit organizational compassion responding as it limits employees' ability to self-organize a compassionate workplace response to suffering due to employees being granted limited freedom and autonomy.[121] Organizational hierarchy can inhibit organizational compassion as it creates distances that limit individuals' abilities to see themselves in other people's suffering, instead casting those who suffer as 'the other' due to perceived hierarchical differences.[122]

Organizational practices facilitating organizational compassion include flexible organizational structures that provide employees with autonomy in interpreting their roles and a pro-social organizational identity concerned with human wellbeing[123]; a culture emphasizing care as a general mode of organizational practice[124] and recognizing and rewarding individual compassionate behaviours.[125] Other facilitators of organizational compassion include interdependent team relations, with quality interactions, diversity and caring leadership.[126] Organizations with these characteristics are better equipped to provide compassion to employees, almost automatically responding to employee suffering with empathetic communication, the bending of bureaucracy where necessary, as well as providing practical and financial support. See Box 6.11 for a more systematic description of organizational competencies and social architecture that research demonstrates are fundamental to organizing compassion.

Box 6.11 Organizational compassion competencies and social architecture

Research by Dutton, Worline and colleagues has identified that workplace compassion is greatly enhanced through organizing that involves four competencies and six principles of social architecture.[127]

Four organizational compassion competencies

Speed: Compassionate organizations are quick to respond to employee suffering. In contrast, non-compassionate organizations delay the providing of care.

Scope: High compassion organizations are able to access a vast array of resources to address an employee's suffering. In contrast, organizations with low compassion capabilities are limited in their resourcing of compassion responding.

Magnitude: Compassionate organizations are able to address employee suffering across many instances in a continual process. In contrast, low compassion organizations might provide compassion as a rare episode rather than as a general mode of practice.

Customization: High compassion organizations are able to customize their care according to the unique situation and needs of the employee who is suffering. In contrast, low compassion organizations might generate a standard response that applies to all, regardless of the suffering employee's actual needs.

Six principles of social architecture

Social networks: Organizations with high compassion are characterized by many clusters of people who share high-quality connections and know one another well. In contrast, low compassion organizations are limited in the number of high-quality connections.

Culture: Compassionate organizations put a high emphasis on values that promote prioritizing people above efficiency and profits. In contrast, low compassion organizations tend to treat people as expendable human resources.

Roles: In high compassion organizations, people have autonomy and see caring for one another as part of their role regardless of their job titles. In low compassion organizations, people tend to view caring for co-workers as the job of a designated supervisor, or care giver.

Routines: In high compassion organizations routine practices of hiring, training, development, performance reviewing and rewarding all incorporate values of caring and compassion. In low compassion organizations, care is not integrated within the organization's day-to-day routines.

Leadership: High compassion organizations are led by people who regularly highlight the importance of care and compassion for employees, both within their words and in their actions. In low compassion organizations, the leader does not put a value on compassion and is not a role model of compassionate practices.

Stories told: In compassionate organizations it is easy to recount stories of compassion that are widely known by the members. In low compassion organizations such stories are difficult to recall.

The benefits that ensue from cultivating organizational compassion are not limited to decreasing human suffering (see, however, Box 6.12). Research suggests additional benefits in a number of areas including enhancing organizational performance,[128] relationships, positive emotions and commitment,[129] as well as bolstering perceived leadership effectiveness and employees' sense of human dignity.[130]

Box 6.12 Negative in the positive – when compassion hurts

Scholars point out that, as a social process, organizational compassion involves power dynamics and is not necessarily positive in its effects.[131] It is therefore important not to assume that support will always be appreciated or even have beneficial effects, particularly when it is provided due to public pressure, public relations, legal concerns or to engender indebtedness and obligations in the receiver. Sincere goodwill on the part of both the giver and receiver are important in the different stages of the compassion process[132] and when mistakes are made it is important to say sorry and ask for forgiveness.

Forgiveness

Forgiveness is relevant to organizations, not only within the context of one-to-one interpersonal relations but also within the context of hurtful policy decisions such as cutbacks, downsizing, accidents and union negotiations.[133] Closing down plants, laying off employees and unethical practices erode trust and nor is it whether the offences are minor or major, the grudges, resentment and animosity that ensue can act as a millstone, weighing down individual and organizational progress.

Two forms of organizational forgiveness are interpersonal workplace forgiveness and the existence of a forgiveness climate. Interpersonal workplace forgiveness is described as a process where:

> an employee who perceives himself or herself to have been the target of a morally injurious offense deliberately attempts to (a) overcome negative emotions (e.g., resentment, anger, hostility) toward his or her offender and (b) refrain from causing the offender harm even when he or she believes it is morally justifiable to do so.[134]

A forgiveness climate is a shared belief amongst employees in the value of forgiveness, more specifically defined as 'the shared perception that empathic, benevolent responses to conflict from victims and offenders are rewarded, supported, and expected in the organization'.[135]

Cameron summarizes the findings of numerous studies of organizational forgiveness to articulate five specific leadership practices that facilitate these forms of organizational forgiveness:

- acknowledging the pain and suffering organizational members have experienced;
- associating the organization's activity with a higher social purpose that gives meaning to the sacrifices made by members;
- maintaining standards of integrity and virtue and clearly communicating that forgiveness does not correspond with tolerance of offences but rather enables moving on from the negative;
- providing support to members who suffer and feel harmed;
- paying careful attention to ensure that the language of care, compassion, courage and humility are present in the organizational lexicon, thereby legitimizing forgiveness as a valid response to pain.[136]

A major objection against granting forgiveness is that it can be perceived as unjust or unfair to the victim, blocking the natural revenge instinct. Everett Worthington is at pains to explain that forgiveness is not about forgetting, condoning or excusing offenses nor is it an obligation to reconcile or release an offender from legal accountability.[137] Rather it is about a deliberate decision to release feelings of resentment, anger and vengeance toward a person or group that has caused harm.

Evidence suggests that amongst the few organizations that flourish rather than significantly deteriorate after downsizing, organizational forgiveness functions as a significant enabler.[138] Researchers Aquino, Grover, Goldman and Folger accordingly argue that 'Forgiveness should be an important concern of both organizational theorists and practicing managers because it is a way for individuals to repair damaged workplace relationships and overcome debilitating thoughts and emotions resulting from interpersonal injury'.[139] Similarly, Struthers, Dupuis and Eaton's research concluded that, in the context of workplace interpersonal relationships where conflicts sometimes damage relationships, forgiveness has the restorative power to promote workplace wellbeing.[140]

Box 6.13 Nelson Mandela discussed in the organizational literature as an exemplar of forgiveness in leadership

Leadership plays an important legitimizing role for the practice of virtues such as forgiveness in organizations. Within this context, Nelson Mandela is sometimes presented as a striking leadership exemplar of forgiveness (Figure 6.5). While this is an example of forgiveness at individual and national levels, scholars such as Cameron and Caza have noted that it has workplace implications. South Africa's black population endured more than four decades of injustice and suffering under a racist apartheid policy, during which time freedom fighter Nelson Mandela was imprisoned for 27 years. His release in 1990 was brought about by international pressure, increasing condemnation of the South African Government and a realization by that government that its position was increasingly practically untenable.

Figure 6.5 Nelson Mandela, anti-apartheid revolutionary who served as President of South Africa from 1994–1999, is frequently referenced as a leader who promoted collective forgiveness.[141]

Once released, Mandela worked with the minority white government to hold a multiracial general election in 1994, which saw him elected as President of South Africa. Once in power, rather than pursuing a policy of revenge and retribution as the world had expected would happen, he promoted a policy of reconciliation and healing. Cameron and Caza observe: 'The forgiveness exemplified by Mandela helped transform an entire nation'.[142] When applied to the organizational context, Madsen, Gygi,

Hammond and Plowman note: 'This remarkable example of how forgiveness could change a whole nation has implications for the value of forgiveness in a corporation, particularly when large problems such as downsizing can affect the lives of many employees and their families'.[143]

Gratitude

Gratitude within the organizational context is defined by Kim Cameron as 'gratitude that is culturally embedded within the organization, through its people, policies and practices, such that thankfulness and appreciation are customary features of daily work life'.[144] Gratitude is practiced in organizations by offering thanks to one another.[145] Research has found that when volunteers working with HIV/AIDS patients receive appreciation and thanks from patients and managers, it buffers the care-worker from burnout.[146]

Choosing to focus on benefits rather than limitations through gratitude also promotes an abundance mentality (see positive assumptions in Chapter 1). Not surprisingly then, gratitude is also associated with pro-social behaviours such as helping out a friend or colleague by loaning money or taking time to offer sympathy and compassion to a colleague in distress. Such behaviours also contribute to better relationships.[147]

Research within the organizational context, specifically the educational environment, in which teachers often burnout due to the pressures of dealing with disruptive students, demonstrates an inverse relationship between keeping gratitude lists and teacher burnout.[148] In a study, teachers compiled weekly gratitude lists and practiced Naiken meditation at home over an eight-week period, with significant improvements in their overall life satisfaction and positive affect, including reduced work-related burnout. Another organizational study, also in the educational environment, saw teachers across two schools forming year-long gratitude groups that met in the staffroom each week to discuss and explore gratitude.[149] This qualitative research identified enhanced wellbeing and relationships as the outcome of the year-long gratitude practice.

Another study has found a positive relationship between high levels of gratitude among a sample of 308 white–collar employees and high levels of corporate social responsibility expressed as a greater level of concern for employees and for broader society.[150] Furthermore, a positive relationship has also been demonstrated between gratitude and job satisfaction.[151] Research also associates gratitude with authentic leadership, suggesting that leaders who recognize and are grateful for the support they receive from employees in successfully leading an organization are more likely to be recognized as virtuous, fair, having integrity and as treating others with respect and dignity.[152] Robert Emmons suggests that gratitude is relevant to the organizational context in other ways as well, including: an antidote to toxic workplace emotions and as a component of the organizational process of Appreciative Inquiry (see Chapter 3).[153]

Further organizational considerations

As suggested in the previous sections, rich relationships at work are not merely the prerogative of individuals. There are organizational factors that facilitate relationally rich human expressions, including leadership behaviours, the values that are emphasized in policies, recruitment and the rewarding of performance, the architecture and layout of the work space, as well as the organization's routines. We consider some of these factors next.

Role models

If leaders offer a good example of high quality human relations, it is difficult for others not to try to follow them. Research indicates that humble leaders even model their followers' behaviours and, in doing so, demonstrate to their followers how to cultivate growth. Such behaviours communicate that throughout one's development trajectory, feelings of uncertainty are legitimate. By maintaining their humility throughout their growth trajectories, both the leaders and followers become 'models of learning'.[154] On the contrary, if leaders conceal their doubts, they discourage others from doing the same. Getting help in such contexts is a dangerous choice.

Cultures of helping

In a number of organizational contexts, asking for help is perceived as inappropriate. In these organizations, getting help can be interpreted as a manifestation of weakness. People may also be reluctant to ask for help because they may expect others to be not inclined to help. Research indicates that this can be a mistake: people tend to be more willing to help than one might expect.[155]

IDEO, the design company, established helping as an espoused organizational value. Based on this policy, employees are expected to deploy 'collaborative generosity'.[156] Cultures of helping are natural when people are selected, trained and rewarded for expressing trust and accessibility. In these cultures, people feel that interdependence is more cherished than independence, which creates a culture of psychological safety. To a great extent, cultures of help are a result of leadership example. Companies that extol the importance of collective achievements and celebrate those that have indeed offered their help, stimulate others to do the same. Mindtree, an IT company based in Bangalore, India, invited its employees to use paper stars available throughout the company to praise and appreciate their colleagues. Similarly, Adam Grant, of the Wharton School, describes a company that reserved a space for people to post *Love Messages* to those colleagues who helped them.[157]

Measure collaboration

Performance metrics, associated with compensation or not, tend to drive human behaviour, particularly when the goals are highly salient. Organizations seeking to promote better human relations can measure forms facilitative of rich connections. For example, IDEO measures helping behaviours amongst its employees. And a company studied by one of the authors of this book has developed what it calls a 'trust barometer', aimed at stimulating the collaboration between its various business units.

Facilitate serendipitous encounters

Some organizations design their working spaces in such a way that they facilitate random encounters: 'Facebook has made its fortune connecting people, and its open plan layout, in theory, gives employees more opportunities to meet each other and interact'.[158] Unexpected encounters will in principle favour the creation of social capital, as they will densify the organization's social networks. For this reason, Steve Jobs toyed with the idea of having only one toilet at Pixar in order to increase unexpected, serendipitous encounters.[159] When he was at Pixar, 'he [also] required an office space with a huge atrium that everyone had to pass through',[160] thus making employees see each other every day (Figure 6.6). The same concerns were present in the design of the new Apple Campus:

> Once derided as a 'retrograde cocoon,' the facility was designed with painstaking attention to detail to maximize opportunities for creativity and collaboration and to capture founder Steve Jobs' complex vision for the space … Every detail has been carefully scrutinized, creating an end product that Apple hopes will foster even greater innovation … It's hoped that by housing so many employees in one facility, workers will be more likely to build relationships with those outside of their team, share ideas with co-workers with different specialties and learn about opportunities to collaborate.[161]

The new campus of Google was also designed to maximize serendipitous personal encounters.[163] Jon Fredrik Baksaas, the former CEO of Telenor, considered the company's headquarters 'not as real estate but as a communication tool' to promote interactions and accelerate decision-making.[164] BMW also designed its new Leipzig facility in order to stimulate conversations. The company's culture, together with its physical layout, produces a combination of 'togetherness and openness [that] sparks impromptu encounters among line workers, logistics engineers, and quality experts. They meet simply because their paths cross naturally … And they say "Ah, glad I ran into you, I have an idea"'.[165] An increasing number of companies are adopting flexible and open office space in order to promote diverse forms of interaction, including unplanned ones. Others adopt pet policies to redraw interactions within the space (Box 6.14).

It should be noted that space per se does not define the quality of interactions. A culture that discourages collaboration does not metamorphose into one of collaboration just because of changes in the physical workplace.[166] Moreover, spaces may be designed with panoptic surveillance motivations and thus kill, or prevent, high-quality connections.[167] Even when open spaces are designed with positive motivations (e.g.,

Figure 6.6 Pixar Animation Studios atrium, 19 November 2009.[162]

to foster fun, spontaneity and creativity), actual perverse effects may unfold. As Korn-berger and Clegg argued, the idea that open space enhances social relations may be a 'preconception of office interior designers' rather than a 'social fact'.[168] Sometimes, 'open spaces' don't turn into 'open minds'[169]:

> [An open-space design may work as] a decentralized form of panoptic control where everybody controls everybody through the internalization of peer surveillance as 'autosurveillance.' In a place where employees are defined in terms of seeing and being seen, not being seen is more conspicuously noticeable than in a setting where employees typically work in separate offices.

Box 6.14 Field work: can dogs (and turtles) stimulate positive interactions?

What if organizations could consider dogs as facilitators of better work relationships? The question may sound strange but some companies, including Google, have adopted pet-friendly policies in order to boost morale and to create more positive working climates. Robert Sherman, former US ambassador to Portugal, explained how his dog Zoe helped him in his ambassadorial work:

> We did a big event with the Portuguese airline TAP, which is establishing new routes to the US. There were some contentious negotiations beforehand but when we did the announcement ... Zoe walked in chewing an airplane toy. Everybody laughed and relaxed.[170]

To learn more about this, ask amongst the people you know about any stories they have involving dogs in organizations. The authors of this book did the same and they were surprised by the frequency of cases in which dogs played relevant relational roles in organizations. You can inspect the result in an article on the topic.[171]

A case in point is the Center for Positive Organizations where much of the positive organizational studies research discussed in this book has been undertaken. In the main reception of the Center is a turtle named Rosa, who has become the Center's unofficial mascot and even has her own Facebook page. 'Seeing Rosa' provides a perfect excuse for students and scholars interested in the Center's work to drop by unannounced and interact with the staff and scholars located there. Students can even earn a Rosa sticker for voluntarily showing up and attending book club sessions dedicated to newly published works exploring POS-related topics.

Sustaining or improving already existing positive interactions

Jane Dutton and Emily Heaphy have identified eight practices that can sustain or improve already existing connections[172]:

1   Create groups to informally discuss relevant issues – over lunchtime or after work hours.

2 Find self-created opportunities for learning.
3 Define learning goals and invite peers to work as your coaches throughout the process.
4 Create a task-force to tackle a relevant organizational issue, in parallel with the goal of creating a high-quality connection.
5 Learn from the experience of co-workers who have engaged in a high-quality relationship.
6 Stimulate mutual help.
7 Share stories.
8 Stretch the boundaries to engage the community.

These tactics will help people to learn and grow together with a sense of perceived organizational support. However, as Dutton and Heaphy point out, these practices will not work with low-quality connections.

Organizations can also nurture positive relationships by having people who act as toxic handlers (see Box 6.15). Toxic handlers are those employees who help others to manage their negative emotions. This eases pain and contributes to avoiding the accumulation and escalation of negative emotions. Repeated exposure to negative emotions is detrimental and toxin handlers are important because they reduce the toxicity inside the system.[173] Research indicates that when the role of toxic handling is formally incorporated into the job of HR managers, it is done more effectively and generates lower levels of emotional exhaustion.[174] The fact that the task is formally assigned reduces ambiguity and increases legitimacy of the role. Managers operate as toxic handlers when they reframe messages from the upper levels in a way that mitigates its negative effects, when they work behind the scenes to solve individual issues, and when they reduce stress in the organization. Toxic handling is critical for maintaining a positive relational environment.

Box 6.15 Negative in the positive

The role of a toxic handler is greatly beneficial in reducing the toxicity of negative emotions within an organization. Unfortunately, acting as a buffer between a toxic system and distressed employees can take its toll on the handler. Whether the role is one that is officially recognized or unofficially played, the effects of taking on and absorbing toxicity from both the system and the employees can negatively affect not only the handler's emotions but their physical health and wellbeing as well. Toxic handling is a form of emotional labour that is often unrecognized and unrewarded within organizational settings but critical to their functioning.

Think about your own experience within organizations. Was there a person who played the role of toxic handler for you or your peers? Is it something that they have been able to endure for the long term? Was this person younger or older? Male or female?

Outbound connections as a source of external social capital

Organizations and teams are not islands, their survival and development depending on how they are able to develop fruitful relationships with external stakeholders – including other organizations or other teams within the organization. Organizations are progressively embracing a knowledge-based economy, one in which knowledge creation and usage represents a fundamental source of competitive advantage. In this environment, external links can be as significant as internal ones. Establishing fruitful relationships with external stakeholders can offer new sources of knowledge, new interpretative angles and new mechanisms for revitalization. This is called *external social capital*, the relationships established with people outside one's unit, for example, or one's organization.[175] Organizations, in this view, are taken as part of larger collaborative communities which try to build synergistic relationships. In the section below, we discuss three facets of outbound-looking organizations, i.e., organizations that extend their vital relationships to their external environment.[176]

Extension to family

Organizations demand a significant period of the time of their employees, but they are not necessarily ranked above other dimensions of the life of their people. In this sense, the development of loyalty depends on how the organization supports a good work–family balance (see Box 6.16). To engender a sense of dedication from employees, organizations need to demonstrate that they genuinely care about their employees as whole persons. This consideration is put to the test when facing some crisis or critical personal event. In a study conducted in Brisbane, Australia, it was found that organizations who cared about their employees as caretakers of their families were able to develop a more positive relationship with their employees.[177] Practices of genuine organizational compassion therefore have a buffering effect that extends beyond the organization's borders to the wider community, providing a window into the true nature of the organization. Therefore, the creation of rich interactions incorporates other dimensions of life, including the family.

Box 6.16 Children and spouses putting executives in the hot seat

1 'Can you be a good father if you are running a business?'

The sentence above is the title of an article that the entrepreneur Luke Johnson wrote in the *Financial Times* about the poor relationships between successful entrepreneurs and their children. He shared his own experience as follows[178]:

> Recently I told my nine-year-old daughter that I would be unable to come and watch her netball match, owing to business commitments. Then I read an interview with the former boss of Pimco, Mohamed El-Erian, explaining why he resigned his $100m-a-year job. His 10-year-old daughter gave him a written list of 22 milestones he had missed because of work – including the first day of school, a parent-teacher meeting and a Halloween parade. Even though he had

legitimate excuses for every absence, he realized that actually none of the pressing meetings, travelling and so forth really mattered in the long run. So I cancelled my business meeting and attended the netball match – and it was great. Unfortunately, many successful men, especially entrepreneurs, have terrible relationships with their children.

2 Should companies provide marriage counselling to CEOs?

Considering the impact of 'high-profile divorce cases' on boardrooms, Gary Silverman wrote about 'The case for C-suite marriage counseling'.[179] Read the following excerpt:

> If you ask me, today's super-rich chief executives require marriage counseling – professional advice on maintaining domestic tranquility before turmoil at home becomes an issue not only in the bedroom, but in the boardroom, as well … To be sure, providing such marriage counseling services would require significant changes in the culture of the modern corporation. Today's 24/7 enterprises are good at many things, but helping people stay married is not one of them. I don't know about you, but I can't recall ever receiving a late-night email or phone call from a boss or a colleague urging me to pay more attention to my wife or get in touch with my emotions. The emphasis is invariably elsewhere. But the Hamm case suggests that the time has come to help corporate leaders manage their relationships with their domestic partners in the interest of all shareholders. We need not wait until a failure to remember an anniversary or an unfortunate night in Las Vegas leads to a change of control at a listed entity.

Questions for reflection

- How and why do divorces affect boardroom decisions?
- Should organizations provide marriage counselling, not only to the C-suite managers but also to all employees?
- What risks, if any, do you identify in such kind of counselling?

Extension to clients

Organizations can also use high-quality connections as levers for developing positive links with the outside, namely with clients. A study by Barsade and O'Neill in a long-term care setting found that cultures of companionate love were positively associated with outcomes of better patient mood and quality of life, higher satisfaction and a reduced need to use the emergency room.[180] The study suggests that good internal relations can positively impact the development of positive outside effects. Teams, for example, are highly sensitive to the quality of connections but they are also dependent upon some degree of porosity with their environments. Insulated teams become vulnerable to the threat of groupthink (see Chapter 7).

Box 6.17 The negative of the positive and organizational context

The nature and adequacy of emotions necessarily depends upon the organizational context. Barsade and O'Neil found that emotions focussed on companionate love were beneficial in healthcare contexts. But they added that, in other settings, such as sales and investment banking, it might happen that other emotions will prove more adequate as such organizations can be moved more by pride and enthusiasm. The implication: the meaning of high-quality relationships, although possibly involving some universals such as mutual respect and an amount of trust, might have different expressions in distinct organizational contexts.

Cohesive but porous teams

Traditional forms of organizing favoured group cohesion over network brokerage. In other words, people were supposed to be loyal members of their self-contained teams. As we discuss in Chapter 7, this understanding of teams has a number of advantages but also important limitations. Research indicates that organizations should aim to create the necessary amount of group cohesion to facilitate knowledge diffusion but also network brokerage to keep teams open to new information coming from other teams. Cohesion refers to the type of connection inside the team, whereas brokerage defines the bridges between teams. Both are fundamental for the development of adaptive organizations as, when people connect with members of other teams, they increase the chances of identifying new ideas, an expression of connectivity.[181]

Final comments

The organizational literature has been influenced by an 'affective revolution' that triggered attention to the role of emotions (see Chapter 4) and for relationships.[182] As Dutton and Heaphy have summarized, 'high-quality connections literally and figuratively enliven people'.[183] High-quality connections help people to learn together via the absorption of more knowledge, to build resilience, to broaden their action repertoires. Work relationships can thus be sources of meaning, pleasure and personal identity. But they can also be painful and debilitating when marked by bullying and incivility. In this case, connections lead to defensiveness, feelings of inadequacy and protection against the organization.

In this chapter we discussed the importance of positive relationships in the workplace. Organizations can be represented as constituted by relationships rather than by individuals. Given the constitutive nature of relationships, they need to be managed with care. We accordingly discussed multiple possibilities for creating organizations with high relational quality. Organizations should consider that relational competence is more than technical competence. The acquisition and development of relational competence can accordingly be viewed as a dimension of competitive advantage through people. Organizations should train people to prefer interactions that have high generative power. They can also design connective workspaces and promote organizational virtues that foster positive workplace relations: compassion, forgiveness and gratitude.

Want more?

In case you want to explore relationships in more detail, a good start is Jane Dutton's *Energize Your Workplace*. Dutton is a pioneer in the study of human relations at work and the book is a great entry point into the role of relationships at work. The paper by Rogers and Ashford[184] is an interesting academic approach to respect in organizations. *Awakening Compassion at Work*, by Monica Worline and Jane Dutton, explores the importance of compassion as an organizational capability. Organizing compassion leads to the creation of more humane organizations with better workplace relations. However, most organizations are poor at institutionalizing compassion, as Sherryl Sandberg and Adam Grant discuss in *Plan B*. Grant's *Give and Take* is another important book on how organizations critically need the generosity of givers.

Glossary

Ambiguity   Refers to the quality of something that is equivocal. The existing information may have several interpretations. Can be reduced through rich media or by developing a shared interpretation.[185]

Brokerage   The flow of resources from one actor to another via an intermediary.[186] The intermediary is habitually necessary when the actors lack access or trust in one another.

Compassion (organizational compassion) as NEAR   Organizational compassion is defined as a four-part process of collective **N**oticing of suffering, **E**mpathizing and feeling the focal actor's pain, **A**ssessing the causes of suffering and the appropriate response and **R**esponding in a manner that is appropriate to the context and matches the needs of the focal actor.

Connectivity   The level of openness to new ideas and influences expressed by the connections in an organization.[187]

Coordination   The process of smoothing interdependencies between tasks or functions in organizations.[188]

Cultures of companionate love   Emotional organizational cultures marked by 'feelings of affection, compassion, caring, and tenderness for others'.[189]

Forgiveness   A deliberate decision to release feelings of resentment, anger and vengeance toward a person or group that has caused harm. Workplace forgiveness has been described as a process where: 'an employee who perceives himself or herself to have been the target of a morally injurious offense deliberately attempts to (a) overcome negative emotions (e.g., resentment, anger, hostility) toward his or her offender and (b) refrain from causing the offender harm even when he or she believes it is morally justifiable to do so'.[190]

Gratitude   Organizational gratitude is 'gratitude that is culturally embedded within the organization, through its people, policies and practices, such that thankfulness and appreciation are customary features of daily work life'.[191]

Happiness   The personal sense of psychological wellbeing.

High quality connections   Short-term connections in which both people experience vitality, positive regard and mutuality.[192]

High road approach to people management   An approach to managing people that is inclusive and based on the logics of commitment and partnership.[193]

Human moments Interactions in which two people communicate authentically in the same shared physical space.

Interactions Moments of exchange between people, typically with a short time duration. Their quality defines the quality of the organization.

Kindness The intention to support the flourishing of someone in a voluntary and proactive way.[194]

Knowledge economy An economy defined by the prevalence of intellectual and social competences rather than by physical inputs.[195]

Love Authentic relationships in which people feel known, appreciated and cared for.

Low road approach to people management An approach to managing people that is adversative and based on the logics of control and avoidance.[196]

Organizing The social order that people actively create and sustain when they 'solve the dynamic problems of aligning goals and coordinating action'.[197]

Positive relationships Positive relationships at work can be defined as 'connections between people that are sustained over time and are characterized by mutual benefit'.[198]

Relationality An approach that represents 'the world as a complex network of active connections rather than visibly independent and identifiable forms and objects'.[199]

Relational coordination Forms of communication and interpersonal relating conducted for the benefit of work integration.[200]

Respect The state of being seen and valued.[201]

Rule tropism Following rules for the sake of being seen to follow rules without regard for consequences, as 'conditioned reflexes'.[202]

Social capital Relationships that constitute organizational resources. It is so important that elite individuals have been defined as those combining high levels of human and social capital.[203]

Social capital in organizations The 'competitive advantage that is created based on the way an individual is connected to others'.[204]

Social wellbeing The quality of one's relationships with others and with the surrounding communities.[205]

Speak up Voicing one's ideas to some organizational member with the power, real or perceived, to tackle the issue in question.

Star employees Employees who have demonstrated an exceptional level of productivity and enjoyed considerable external visibility.

Uncertainty 'An individual's perceived inability to predict something accurately.'[206] Can be reduced via the acquisition of additional information.

Voice A communicative act of challenge that aims to construct rather than simply to criticize. Voicers try to accomplish a difficult combination: to be critical *and* constructive.[207]

Notes

1 In Hamel (2007, p. 75).
2 Felin (2017).
3 Feldman and Worline (2016).
4 Cooper (2005).
5 Rozovsky (2015), italics in the original.
6 Kelly and Stark (2002).
7 Dutton, Frost, Worline, Lilius and Kanov (2002).
8 Bakken and Hernes (2006, p. 1607).
9 Deming (2015).
10 Cunha, Miner and Antonacopolou (2017).
11 Sluss and Ashford (2008).
12 Gittell (2008).

13 Dutton (2003, p. xvii).
14 Calder (2018).
15 Gittell (2010).
16 Berthod and Muller-Seitz (2018).
17 Wiedner, Barrett and Oborn (2017).
18 Worline and Dutton (2017).
19 Built from Worline and Dutton (2017, p. 120).
20 Brown, Treviño and Harrison (2005).
21 Uhl-Bien and Arena (2017).
22 Carmeli (2007).
23 Buss (1990, p. 265).
24 Dutton and Heaphy (2003).
25 McGrath, Cooper-Thomas, Garrosa, Sanz-Vergel and Cheung (2017).
26 Van Dam and van der Helm (2016a, 2016b).
27 Barnes, Lucianetti, Bhave and Christian (2015).
28 In Illing (2018).
29 Kuper (2018).
30 Cornish (2018).
31 Barnes and Spreitzer (2015).
32 Huffington (2015).
33 Gittell and Douglass (2012).
34 Gardner (2017).
35 Merton (1936), Gouldner (1957, 1958).
36 Thomas, Sugiyama, Rochford, Stephens and Kanov (2018).
37 Osono, Shimizu, Takeuchi and Dorton (2008).
38 Gulati (2018).
39 Warner (2007).
40 Munro and Huber (2012).
41 Kafka (2009 [1926], p. 187).
42 Kafka (2009 [1925], pp. 151–152).
43 Retrieved: Atelier Jacobi: Sigismund Jacobi (1860–1935) (https://commons.wikimedia.org/wiki/File:
    Kafka1906_cropped.jpg), 'Kafka1906 cropped', marked as public domain, more details on Wikimedia
    Commons: https://commons.wikimedia.org/wiki/Template:PD-1923.
44 Clegg, Cunha, Munro, Rego and Sousa (2016).
45 Ornish (2005).
46 Dutton and Heaphy (2003, p. 264).
47 Ragins and Dutton (2007).
48 Dutton and Heaphy (2016).
49 Stephens, Heaphy and Dutton (2012).
50 Argyris (2010).
51 Argyris (2010).
52 Harrison (2017).
53 Cunha, Miner and Antonacopolou (2017).
54 Kornberger, Carter and Clegg (2006).
55 Knights (2016, p. 11).
56 Cross and Parker (2004).
57 Barsade and O'Neill (2014).
58 Cunha et al. (2017).
59 Gouldner (1960).
60 Kellaway (2011, p. 12).
61 Based on Clegg, Cunha and Rego (2016).
62 Merchant (2017).
63 In Merchant (2017).
64 Seppälä and Cameron (2015).
65 Dutton (2014).
66 Rogers (2018).
67 Built on the basis of Rogers (2018).

68 Rogers (2018).
69 Rogers and Ashford (2017, p. 1578).
70 Independent Directors of the Board of Wells Fargo & Company (2017).
71 'Even the President of the United States sometimes must have to stand naked' (Dylan, 1965).
72 Carmeli, Dutton and Hardin (2015), Rogers and Ashford (2017).
73 Dutton (2003).
74 In Bryant (2015).
75 Dutton (2003).
76 Based on Grant (2013a, 2013b).
77 Dutton (2014).
78 Barsade and O'Neill (2014).
79 Grant, Christianson and Price (2007).
80 Arrow (1974, p. 23).
81 Rousseau, Sitkin, Burt and Camerer (1998, p. 395).
82 De Jong, Dirks and Gillespie (2016).
83 De Jong, Dirks and Gillespie (2016).
84 Skinner, Dietz and Weibel (2014).
85 Greenleaf (1996, p. 336).
86 Dutton (2014).
87 March (1988).
88 March (2006).
89 Grant, Christianson and Price (2007), Keyes (1998).
90 Seppälä and Cameron (2015, online).
91 Dutton and Heaphy (2003, p. 270).
92 Goffee and Jones (2013).
93 Sturm, Vera and Crossan (2017).
94 Cronqvist and Yu (2017).
95 In Beard (2015).
96 Brooks and John (2018).
97 Casciaro and Lobo (2005).
98 Adapted from Casciaro and Lobo (2005, p. 96).
99 Edmondson (2006).
100 Waldroop and Butler (1996); Ibarra and Scoular (2019).
101 Kehoe, Lepak and Bentley (2018).
102 Colbert, Bono and Purvanova (2016).
103 Hallowell (1999).
104 Garvin (2013), Harrell and Barbato (2018).
105 Uhl-Bien and Arena (2017).
106 Garvin (2013), Harrell and Barbato (2018).
107 Heckscher (1994).
108 Gittell (2001).
109 Gittell (2002b, p. 300).
110 Gittell, Seidner and Wimbush (2010).
111 Source: Gratton and Ghoshal (2002), with adaptations.
112 Rodrigues, Cunha, Rego and Clegg (2017).
113 Hallowell (1999).
114 Rao and Dutta (2012).
115 Gardner (2017).
116 Zenger and Folkman (2016).
117 Cameron, Bright and Caza (2004).
118 Dutton, Workman and Hardin (2014), Simpson et al. (2014).
119 Dutton, Worline, Frost and Lilius (2006), Lilius, Kanov, Dutton, Worline and Maitlis (2012), Simpson, Clegg and Pitsis (2014), Worline and Dutton (2017).
120 Hallowell (1999).
121 Dutton, Worline, Frost and Lilius (2006).
122 van Kleef et al. (2008).
123 Grant, Dutton and Rosso (2008).

124 Simpson, Clegg and Cunha (2013).
125 McLelland (2010).
126 Madden, Duchon, Madden and Plowman (2012).
127 Dutton, Worline, Frost and Lilius (2006), Worline and Dutton (2017).
128 Cameron, Bright and Caza (2004).
129 Frost, Dutton, Worline and Wilson (2000).
130 Dutton, Frost, Worline, Lilius and Kanov (2002).
131 Simpson, Cunha and Clegg (2015).
132 Simpson et al. (2014), Simpson, Clegg and Pitsis (2014).
133 Cameron (2008).
134 Aquino, Grover, Goldman and Folger (2003, p. 212).
135 Fehr and Gelfand (2012, p. 666).
136 Cameron (2008).
137 Worthington (2000).
138 Cameron and Caza (2002).
139 Aquino, Grover, Goldman and Folger (2003, p. 210).
140 Struthers, Dupuis and Eaton (2005).
141 Image source: South Africa The Good News/www.sagoodnews.co.za (https://commons.wiki
     media.org/wiki/File:Nelson_Mandela-2008_(edit).jpg), 'Nelson Mandela-2008 (edit)', https://
     creativecommons.org/licenses/by/2.0/legalcode.
142 Cameron and Caza (2002, p. 43).
143 Madsen, Gygi, Hammond and Plowman (2009, p. 253).
144 Cameron (2012).
145 Cameron, Mora, Leutscher and Calarco (2011).
146 Bennett, Ross and Sunderland (1996).
147 Emmons (2003).
148 Chan (2010).
149 Howells (2012).
150 Andersson, Giacalone and Jurkiewicz (2007).
151 Waters (2012).
152 Michie (2009), Michie and Gooty (2005).
153 Emmons (2003).
154 Owens and Hekman (2012).
155 Newark, Bohns and Flynn (2017).
156 Amabile, Fisher and Pillemer (2014).
157 Grant (2013a).
158 Suich (2016, p. 35).
159 D'Onfro (2015).
160 Wasik (2016).
161 Hess (2017).
162 Author: Jason Pratt. Retrieved from: https://commons.wikimedia.org/wiki/File:Pixar_Animation
     Studios_Atrium.jpg. This file is licensed under the Creative Commons Attribution 2.0 Generic
     license.
163 Waber, Magnolfi and Lindsay (2014).
164 Waber, Magnolfi and Lindsay (2014, p. 72).
165 In Edmondson (2006, p. 78).
166 Von Krogh and Geilinger (2014), Berti, Simpson and Clegg (2017).
167 Ahmed (2018).
168 Kornberger and Clegg (2004, p. 1100).
169 Thanem, Varlander and Cummings (2011).
170 Monocle (2016, p. 65).
171 Cunha, Rego and Munro (2019).
172 Dutton and Heaphy (2016).
173 Frost (2003).
174 Kulik, Cregan, Metz and Brown (2009).
175 Carmeli (2007).
176 Felin, Zenger and Tomsik (2009).

177 Simpson, Clegg and Cunha (2013).
178 Johnson (2014, p. 10).
179 Silverman (2014, p. 11).
180 Barsade and O'Neill (2014).
181 Lovas and Ghoshal (2000), Uhl-Bien and Arena (2017).
182 Barsade, Brief and Spataro (2003).
183 Dutton and Heaphy (2003, p. 275).
184 Rogers and Ashford (2017).
185 Daft and Lengel (1986).
186 Gould and Fernandez (1989).
187 Stephens, Heaphy and Dutton (2012).
188 For example, Gittell (2002a).
189 Barsade and O'Neill (2014, p. 551).
190 Aquino, Grover, Goldman and Folger (2003, p. 212).
191 Cameron (2012).
192 Dutton (2014).
193 Gittell and Bamber (2010).
194 Worline and Dutton (2017, p. 5).
195 Powell and Snellman (2004).
196 Gittell and Bamber (2010).
197 Heath and Sitkin (2001).
198 Tenney, Poole and Dieber (2016, p. 36).
199 Cooper (2005, p. 1704).
200 Gittell (2008).
201 Carmeli, Dutton and Hardin (2015, p. 1023).
202 Merton (1936, p. 896).
203 Eberhart, Eesley and Eisenhardt (2017).
204 Arena and Uhl-Bien (2016).
205 Keyes (1998).
206 Milliken (1987, p. 136).
207 Ashford, Sutcliffe and Christianson (2009).

References

Ahmed, S. (2018). Panopticism and totalitarian space. *Theory in Action*, 11(1), 1–16.

Amabile, T., Fisher, C. M., & Pillemer, J. (2014). IDEO's culture of helping. *Harvard Business Review*, 92(1–2), 54–61.

Andersson, L. M., Giacalone, R. A., & Jurkiewicz, C. L. (2007). On the relationship of hope and gratitude to corporate social responsibility. *Journal of Business Ethics*, 70(4), 401–409.

Aquino, K., Grover, S. L., Goldman, B., & Folger, R. (2003). When push doesn't come to shove: Interpersonal forgiveness in workplace relationships. *Journal of Management Inquiry*, 12(3), 209–216.

Arena, M. J., & Uhl-Bien, M. (2016). Complexity leadership theory: Shifting from human capital to social capital. *People + Strategy*, 39(2), 22–27.

Argyris, C. (2010). *Organizational traps: Leadership, culture, organizational design*. Oxford University Press: Oxford.

Arrow, K. (1974). Kenneth Arrow on capitalism and society. *Business and Society Review/Innovation*, 10, 22–27.

Ashford, S. J., Sutcliffe, K. M., & Christianson, M. K. (2009). Speaking up and speaking out: The leadership dynamics of voice in organizations. In J. Greenberg, & M. Edwards (Eds.), *Voice and silence in organizations* (pp. 175–201). Bingley: Emerald.

Bakken, T., & Hernes, T. (2006). Organizing is both a verb and a noun: Weick meets whitehead. *Organization Studies*, 27(11), 1599–1616.

Barnes, C. M., Lucianetti, L., Bhave, D. P., & Christian, M. S. (2015). "You wouldn't like me when I'm sleepy": Leaders's sleep, daily abuse supervision, and work unit engagement. *Academy of Management Journal*, 58(5), 1419–1427.

Barnes, C. M., & Spreitzer, G. (2015). Why sleep is a strategic resource. *MIT Sloan Management*, 56(2), 19–21.

Barsade, S., Brief, A. P., & Spataro, S. E. (2003). The affective revolution in organizational behavior: The emergence of a paradigm. In J. Greenberg (Ed.), *Organizational behavior: The state of the science* (2nd ed., pp. 3–52). Mawah, NJ: Lawrence Earlbaum.

Barsade, S., & O'Neill, O. (2014). What's love got to do with it? A longitudinal study of the culture of companionate love and employee and client outcomes in the long term care setting. *Administrative Science Quarterly*, 59(4), 551–598.

Beard, A. (2015). CEOs with daughters run more socially responsible firms: An interview with Henrik Cronqvist. *Harvard Business Review*, November, 34–35.

Bennett, L., Ross, M. W., & Sunderland, R. (1996). The relationship between recognition, rewards and burnout in AIDS caring. *Aids Care*, 8(2), 145–154.

Berthod, O., & Muller-Seitz, G. (2018). Making sense in pitch darkness: An exploration of the socio-materiality of sensemaking in crises. *Journal of Management Inquiry*, 27(1), 52–68.

Berti, M., Simpson, A. V., & Clegg, S. R. (2017). Making a place out of space: The social imaginaries and realities of a Business School as a designed space. *Management Learning*, 49(2), 168–186.

Brooks, A. W., & John, L. K. (2018). The surprising power of questions. *Harvard Business Review*, May–June, 60–67.

Brown, M. E., Treviño, L. K., & Harrison, D. A. (2005). Ethical leadership: A social learning perspective for construct development and testing. *Organizational Behavior and Human Decision Processes*, 97(2), 117–134.

Bryant, A. (2015). Joel Peterson of JetBlue on listening without an agenda. *The New York Times*, May 9 (www.nytimes.com/2015/05/10/business/joel-peterson-of-jetblue-on-listening-without-an-agenda. html?_r=0).

Buss, D. M. (1990). Evolutionary social psychology: Prospects and pitfalls. *Motivation and Emotion*, 14(4), 265–286.

Calder, S. (2018). Holiday Hell for thousandsas walkouts and storms leave them stranded. *The Independent* (www.independent.co.uk/travel/news-and-advice/flight-chaos-thunderstorms-rya nair-strike-british-airways-easyjet-a8487406.html), accessed August 14, 2018.

Cameron, K. (2012). *Positive leadership: Strategies for extraordinary performance*. San Francisco, CA: Berrett-Koehler.

Cameron, K., Mora, C., Leutscher, T., & Calarco, M. (2011). Effects of positive practices on organizational effectiveness. *The Journal of Applied Behavioral Science*, 47(3), 266–308.

Cameron, K. S. (2008). *Positive leadership: Strategies for extraordinary performance*. San Francisco, CA: Berrett-Koehler.

Cameron, K. S., Bright, D., & Caza, A. (2004). Exploring the relationships between organizational virtuousness and performance. *American Behavioral Scientist,* 47(6), 766–790.

Cameron, K. S., & Caza, A. (2002). Organizational and leadership virtues and the role of forgiveness. *Journal of Leadership & Organizational Studies*, 9(1), 33–48.

Carmeli, A. (2007). Social capital, psychological safety and learning behaviours from failure in organisations. *Long Range Planning*, 40, 30–44.

Carmeli, A., Dutton, J. E., & Hardin, A. E. (2015). Respect as an engine for new ideas: Linking respectful engagement, relational information processing and creativity among employees and teams. *Human Relations*, 68(6), 1021–1047.

Casciaro, T., & Lobo, M. S. (2005). Competent jerks, lovable fools, and the formation of social networks. *Harvard Business Review*, 83(6), 92–99.

Chan, D. W. (2010). Gratitude, gratitude intervention and subjective well-being among Chinese school teachers in Hong Kong. *Educational Psychology*, 30(2), 139–153.

Clegg, S., Cunha, M. P., Munro, I., Rego, A., & Sousa, M. O. (2016). Kafkaesque power and bureaucracy. *Journal of Political Power*, 9(2), 157–181.

Clegg, S., Cunha, M. P., & Rego, A. (2016). Explaining suicide in organizations: Durkheim revisited. *Business and Society Review*, 121, 391–414.

Colbert, A. E., Bono, J. E., & Purvanova, R. K. (2016). Flourishing via workplace relationships: Moving beyond instrumental support. *Academy of Management Journal*, 59(4), 1199–1223.

Cooper, R. (2005). Relationality. *Organization Studies*, 26(11), 999–1017.

Cornish, C. (2018). Night shift. *Financial Times Life & Arts*, 26–27(May), 18–19.

Cronqvist, H., & Yu, F. (2017). Shaped by their daughters: Executives, female socialization, and corporate social responsibility. *Journal of Financial Economics*, 126, 543–562.

Cross, R., & Parker, A. (2004). *The hidden power of social networks: Understanding how work really gets done in organizations*. Boston, MA: Harvard Business School Press.

Cunha, M. P., Clegg, S. R., Costa, C., Leite, A. P., Rego, A., Simpson, A. V., Sousa, M. O., & Sousa, M. (2017). Gemeinschaft in the midst of Gesellschaft? Love as an organizational virtue. *Journal of Management, Spirituality & Religion*, 14(1), 3–21.

Cunha, M. P., Miner, A. S., & Antonacopolou, E. (2017). Improvisation processes in organizations. In H. Tsoukas, & A. Langley (Eds.), *The Sage handbook of process organization studies* (pp. 559–573). Los Angeles, CA: Sage.

Cunha, M. P., Rego, A., & Munro, I. (2019). Dogs in organizations. *Human Relations*, 72(4), 778–800.

Daft, R. L., & Lengel, R. H. (1986). Organizational information requirements, media richness and structural design. *Management Science*, 32(5), 554–571.

De Jong, B. A., Dirks, K. T., & Gillespie, N. (2016). Trust and team performance: A meta-analysis of main effects, moderators, and covariates. *Journal of Applied Psychology*, 101(8), 1134–1150.

Deming, D. J. (2015). *The growing importance of social skills in the labor market*. CESifo Area Conferences. Munich: CESifo.

D'Onfro, J. (2015). Steve Jobs had a crazy idea for Pixar's office to force people to talk more. *Business Insider*, March 21 (www.businessinsider.com.au/steve-jobs-designing-pixar-office-2015-3).

Dutton, J. E. (2003). *Energize your workplace*. San Francisco, CA: Jossey-Bass.

Dutton, J. E. (2014). Build high-quality connections. In J. E. Dutton, & G. Spreitzer (Eds.), *How to be a positive leader: Insights from leading thinkers on positive organizations* (pp. 11–21). San Francisco, CA: Berrett-Koehler.

Dutton, J. E., Frost, P., Worline, M. C., Lilius, J. M., & Kanov, J. M. (2002). Leading in times of trauma. *Harvard Business Review*, 80(1), 54–61.

Dutton, J. E., & Heaphy, E. (2016). We lean more when we learn together. *Harvard Business Review*, January 12 (https://hbr.org/2016/01/we-learn-more-when-we-learn-together).

Dutton, J. E., & Heaphy, E. D. (2003). The power of high-quality connections. In K. S. Cameron, J. E. Dutton, & R. E. Quinn (Eds.), *Positive organizational scholarship: Foundations of a new discipline* (pp. 263–278). San Francisco, CA: Berrett-Koehler.

Dutton, J. E., Workman, K. M., & Hardin, A. E. (2014). Compassion at work. *Annual Review of Organizational Psychology and Organizational Behavior*, 1, 277–304.

Dutton, J. E., Worline, M. C., Frost, P. J., & Lilius, J. (2006). Explaining compassion organizing. *Administrative Science Quarterly*, 51(1), 59–96.

Dylan, B. (1965). Its alright ma (I'm only bleeding). *Bringing It All Back Home*. New York: Columbia.

Eberhart, R. N., Eesley, C. E., & Eisenhardt, K. M. (2017). Failing is an option: Institutional change, entrepreneurial risk and new form growth. *Organization Science*, 28(1), 93–112.

Edmondson, G. (2006). BMW's dream factory. *BusinessWeek*, October 16, 71–80.

Emmons, R. (2003). Acts of gratitude in organizations. In K. M. Cameron, J. E. Dutton, & R. E. Quinn (Eds.), *Positive organizational scholarship: Foundations of a new discipline* (pp. 81–93). San Francisco, CA: Berrett-Koehler.

Fehr, R., & Gelfand, M. J. (2012). The forgiving organization: A multilevel model of forgiveness at work. *Academy of Management Review*, 37(4), 664–688.

Feldman, M., & Worline, M. (2016). The practicality of practice theory. *Academy of Management Learning and Education*, 15(2), 304–324.

Felin, T. (2017). Quando a estratégia sai porta fora. *Executive Digest*, Janeiro, 40–43.

Felin, T., Zenger, T. R., & Tomsik, J. (2009). The knowledge economy: Emerging organizational forms, missing microfoundations, and key considerations for managing human capital. *Human Resource Management*, 48(4), 555–570.

Frost, P. J. (2003). *Toxic emotions at work*. Boston, MA: Harvard Business School Press.

Frost, P. J., Dutton, J. E., Worline, M. C., & Wilson, A. (2000). Narratives of compassion in organizations. In S. Fineman (Ed.), *Emotions in organizations* (pp. 25–45). London: Sage.

Gardner, H. K. (2017). Getting your stars to collaborate. Harvard Business Review, 95(1), 100–108.

Garvin, D. A. (2013). How Google sold its engineers on management. *Harvard Business Review*, December, 74–82.

Gittell, J. H. (2001). Supervisory span, relational coordination and flight departure performance: A reassessment of postbureaucracy theory. *Organization Science*, 12(4), 468–483.

Gittell, J. H. (2002a). Coordinating mechanisms in care provider groups: Relational coordination as a mediator and input uncertainty as a moderator of performance effects. *Organization Science*, 48(11), 1408–1426.

Gittell, J. H. (2002b). Relationships between service providers and their impact on customers. *Journal of Service Research*, 4(4), 299–311.

Gittell, J. H. (2008). Relationships and resilience: Care provider responses to pressures from managed care. *Journal of Applied Behavioral Science*, 44(1), 25–47.

Gittell, J. H., & Bamber, G. J. (2010). High-and low-road strategies for competing on costs and their implications for employment relations: International studies in the airline industry. *The International Journal of Human Resource Management*, 21(2), 165–179.

Gittell, J. H., & Douglass, A. (2012). Relational bureaucracy: Structuring reciprocal relationships into roles. *Academy of Management Review*, 37(4), 709–733.

Gittell, J. H., Seidner, R., & Wimbush, J. (2010). A relational model of how high-performance work systems work. *Organization Science*, 21(2), 490–506.

Goffee, R., & Jones, G. (2013). Creating the best workplace on earth. *Harvard Business Review*, May, 98–106.

Gould, R. V., & Fernandez, R. M. (1989). Structures of mediation: A formal approach to brokerage in transaction networks. *Sociological Methodology*, 19, 89–126.

Gouldner, A. W. (1957). Cosmopolitans and locals: Toward an analysis of latent social roles. I. *Administrative Science Quarterly*, 2, 281–306.

Gouldner, A. W. (1958). Cosmopolitans and locals: Toward an analysis of latent social roles. II. *Administrative Science Quarterly*, 2, 444–480.

Gouldner, A. W. (1960). The norm of reciprocity: A preliminary statement. *American Sociological Review*, 25, 161–178.

Grant, A. M. (2013a). In the company of givers and takers. *Harvard Business Review*, 91(4), 90–97.

Grant, A. M. (2013b). *Give and take: A revolutionary approach to success*. New York. Penguin.

Grant, A. M., Christianson, M. K., & Price, R. H. (2007). Happiness, health, or relationships? Managerial practices and employee well-being tradeoffs. *Academy of Management Perspectives*, August, 51–63.

Grant, A. M., Dutton, J. E., & Rosso, B. D. (2008). Giving commitment: Employee support programs and the prosocial sensemaking process. *Academy of Management Journal*, 51(5), 898–918.

Gratton, L., & Ghoshal, S. (2002). Improving the quality of conversations. *Organizational Dynamics*, 31(3), 209–223.

Greenleaf, R. K. (1996). *On becoming a servant leader*. San Francisco, CA: Jossey-Bass.

Gulati, R. (2018). Structure that's not stifling. *Harvard Business Review*, May–June, 70–79.

Hallowell, E. M. (1999). The human moment at work. *Harvard Business Review*, January–February, 1–8.

Hamel, G. (2007). *The future of management*. Boston, MA: Harvard Business School Press.

Harrell, M., & Barbato, L. (2018). Great managers still matter: The evolution of Google's Project Oxygen. *re: Work*, February 27 (https://rework.withgoogle.com/blog/the-evolution-of-project-oxygen/).

Harrison, R. T. (2017). Leadership, leadership development and all that jazz. *Leadership*, 13(1), 81–99.

Heath, C., & Sitkin, S. (2001). Big-B versus Big-O: What is organizational about organizational behavior? *Journal of Organizational Behavior*, 22, 43–58.

Heckscher, C. (1994). Defining the post-bureaucratic type. In C. Heckscher, & A. Donnellon (Eds.), *The post-bureaucratic organization* (pp. 98–106). Thousand Oaks, CA: Sage.

Helliwell, J. F. (2018). Global happiness policy synthesis 2018. In Sachs, J. D. (Ed.) *Global happiness policy report 2018* (pp. 10–25). New York: Global Happiness Council.

Hess, A. (2017). The science and design behind Apple's innovation-obsessed new workspace. *CNBC*, September 14 (www.cnbc.com/2017/09/13/the-science-and-design-behind-apples-innovation-obsessed-new-workspace.html).

Howells, K. (2012). *Gratitude in education: A radical view*. Rotterdam: Sense Publishers.

Huffington, A. (2015). A sleep revolution will allow us to better solve the world's problems. *The Huffington Post*, December 16 (www.huffingtonpost.com/arianna-huffington/a-sleep-revolution-will-allow-us-to-better-solve-the-worlds-problems_b_8818656.html?utm_hp_ref=sleep–wellness).

Ibarra, H., & Scoular, A. (2019). The Leader as Coach. *Harvard Business Review, 97*(6), available at https://hbr.org/2019/11/the-leader-as-coach, accessed 28.11.19.

Illing, S. (2018). A Stanford psychologist on the art of avoiding assholes. *Vox*, April 3 (www.vox.com/conversations/2017/9/26/16345476/stanford-psychologist-art-of-avoiding-assholes).

Independent Directors of the Board of Wells Fargo & Company (2017). *Sales practice investigation report.* San Francisco, CA: Wells Fargo & Company.

Johnson, L. (2014). Can you be a good father if you are running a business? *Financial Times Europe*, October 8, 10.

Kafka, F. (2009 [1925]). *The trial.* Translated by: Mitchell, M. Oxford: Oxford World Classics.

Kafka, F. (2009 [1926]). *The castle.* Translated by: Bell, A. Oxford: Oxford University Press.

Kehoe, R. R., Lepak, D. P., & Bentley, F. S. (2018). Let's call a star a star: Task performance, external status, and exceptional contributors in organizations. *Journal of Management, 44*(5), 1848–1872.

Kellaway, L. (2011). Unrequited love and journeys into corporate idiocy. *Financial Times*, July 11, 12.

Kelly, J., & Stark, D. (2002). Crisis, recovery, innovation: Responsive organization after September 11. *Environment and Planning A*, 34, 1523–1533.

Kets de Vries, M. F. (2012). Star performers: Paradoxes wrapped up in enigmas. *Organizational Dynamics*, 41(3), 173–182.

Keyes, C. L. M. (1998). Social well-being. *Social Psychology Quarterly*, 61(2), 121–140.

Knights, R. (2016). Basketball coach brings fame and money to class. *Financial Times*, October 31, 11.

Kornberger, M., Carter, C., & Clegg, S. R. (2006). Rethinking the polyphonic organization: Managing as discursive practice. *Scandinavian Journal of Management*, 22, 3–30.

Kornberger, M., & Clegg, S. R. (2004). Bringing space back in: Organizing the generative building. *Organization Studies*, 25(7), 1095–1114.

Kulik, C. T., Cregan, C., Metz, I., & Brown, M. (2009). HR managers as toxin handlers: The buggering effect of formalizing toxin handling responsibilities. *Human Resource Management*, 48(5), 695–716.

Kuper, S. (2018). How to get ahead? An office bed. *Financial Times Life & Arts*, May 26–27, 19.

Lilius, J. M., Kanov, J. M., Dutton, J. E., Worline, M. C. and Maitlis, S. (2012) 'Compassion revealed: What we know about compassion at work (and where we need to know more)', in Cameron, K.S. and Spreitzer, G. (eds.) *The Oxford Handbook of Positive Organizational Scholarship*. Oxford: Oxford University Press, pp. 273–287.

Lovas, B., & Ghoshal, S. (2000). Strategy as guided evolution. *Strategic Management Journal*, 21, 875–896.

Madden, L. T., Duchon, D., Madden, T. M., & Plowman, D. A. (2012). Emergent organizational capacity for compassion. *Academy of Management Review*, 37(4), 689–708.

Madsen, S. R., Gygi, J., Hammond, S. C., & Plowman, S. F. (2009). Forgiveness as a workplace intervention: The literature and a proposed framework. *Journal of Behavioral and Applied Management*, 10(2), 246–262.

March, J. G. (1988). The technology of foolishness. In J. March (Ed.), *Decisions and organizations* pp. (253–265). Oxford: Blackwell.

March, J. G. (2006). Rationality, foolishness, and adaptive intelligence. Strategic management journal, 27(3), 201–214.

McGrath, E., Cooper-Thomas, H. D., Garrosa, E., Sanz-Vergel, A. I., & Cheung, G. W. (2017). Rested, friendly, and engaged: The role of daily positive collegial interactions at work. *Journal of Organizational Behavior*, 38(8), 1213–1226.

McLelland, L. (2010). From compassion to client satisfaction: Examining the relationship between routines that facilitate compassion and quality of service (Doctoral dissertation, Emory University).

Merchant, B. (2017). Life and death in Apple's forbidden city. *The Guardian*, June 18 (www.theguar dian.com/technology/2017/jun/18/foxconn-life-death-forbidden-city-longhua-suicide-apple-iphone-brian-merchant-one-device-extract).

Merton, R. K. (1936). The unanticipated consequences of purposive social action. *American Sociological Review*, 1(6), 894–904.

Michie, S. (2009). Pride and gratitude: How positive emotions influence the prosocial behaviors of organizational leaders. *Journal of Leadership & Organizational Studies*, 15(4), 393–403.

Michie, S., & Gooty, J. (2005). Values, emotions, and authenticity: Will the real leader please stand up? *The Leadership Quarterly*, 16(3), 441–457.

Milliken, F. J. (1987). Three types of perceived uncertainty about the environment: State, effect, and response uncertainty. *Academy of Management Review*, 12(1), 133–143.

Monocle (2016). Political pooches. May, 63–65.

Munro, I. and Huber, C. (2012). 'Kafka's mythology: Organization, bureaucracy and the limits of sensemaking', *Human Relations*, 65(4), pp. 523–543.

Newark, D. A., Bohns, V. K., & Flynn, F. J. (2017). A helping hand is hard at work: Help-seekers' underestimation of helpers' effort. *Organizational Behavior and Human Decision Processes*, 139, 18–29.

Ornish, D. (2005). Love is real medicine. *Newsweek*, October 17, 43.

Osono, E., Shimizu, N., Takeuchi, H., & Dorton, J. K. (2008). *Extreme Toyota: Radical contradictions that drive success at the world's best manufacturer*. New York: John Wiley & Sons.

Owens, B. P., & Hekman, D. R. (2012). Modeling how to grow: An inductive examination of humble leader behaviors, contingencies, and outcomes. *Academy of Management Journal*, 55(4), 787–818.

Powell, W. W., & Snellman, K. (2004). The knowledge economy. *Annual Review of Sociology*, 30, 199–221.

Ragins, B. R., & Dutton, J. M. (2007). Positive relationships at work: An introduction and invitation. In J. M. Dutton & B. R. Ragins (Eds.), *Exploring positive relationships at work* (pp. 3–25). Mahwah, NJ: Lawrence Earlbaum.

Rao, H., & Dutta, S. (2012). Free spaces as organizational weapons of the weak: Religious festivals and regimental mutinies in the 1857 Bengal Native Army. Administrative Science Quarterly, 57(4), 625–668.

Rodrigues, F. R., Cunha, M. P., Rego, A., & Clegg, S. (2017). The seven pillars of paradoxical wisdom: On the use of paradox to synthesize knowledge and ignorance. In W. Kupers & O. Gunnlaugson (Eds.), *Wisdom learning: Perspectives on wising-up business and management education* (pp. 98–116). Abingdon: Routledge.

Rogers, K. M. (2018). Do your employees feel respected? *Harvard Business Review*, July–August, 63–70.

Rogers, K. M., & Ashford, B. E. (2017). Respect in organizations: Feeling valued as "we" and "me". *Journal of Management*, 43(5), 1578–1608.

Rousseau, D. M., Sitkin, S. B., Burt, R. S., & Camerer, C. (1998). Not so different after all: A cross-discipline view of trust. *Academy of Management Review*, 23, 393–404.

Rozovsky, J. (2015). The five keys to a successful Google team. *Re:work* (rework.withgoogle.com).

Seppälä, E., & Cameron, K. (2015). Proof that positive work cultures are more productive. *Harvard Business Review*, December 1 (https://hbr.org/2015/12/proof-that-positive-work-cultures-are-more-productive).

Silverman, G. (2014). The case for C-suite marriage counselling. *Financial Times Europe*, Novermber 15–16, 11.

Simpson, A. V., Clegg, S., & Cunha, M. P. (2013). Expressing compassion in the face of crisis: Organizational practices in the aftermath of the Brisbane floods of 2011. *Journal of Contingencies and Crisis Management*, 21(2), 115–124.

Simpson, A. V., Clegg, S., Lopez, M. P., Cunha, M. P., Rego, A., & Pitsis, T. (2014). Doing compassion or doing discipline? Power relations and the Magdalene Laundries. *Journal of Political Power*, 7(2), 253–274.

Simpson, A. V., Clegg, S., & Pitsis, T. (2014). Normal compassion: A framework for compassionate decision making. *Journal of Business Ethics*, 119(4), 473–491.

Skinner, D., Dietz, G., & Weibel, A. (2014). The dark side of trust: When trust becomes a "poisoned chalice". *Organization*, 21(2), 206–224.

Sluss, D. M., & Ashforth, B. E. (2008). How relational and organizational identification converge: Processes and conditions. *Organization Science*, 19(6), 807–823.

Stephens, J. P., Heaphy, E., & Dutton, J. (2012). High quality connections. In K. S. Cameron & G. M. Spreitzer (Eds.), *The Oxford handbook of positive organizational scholarship* (pp. 385–399). Oxford: Oxford University Press.

Struthers, C. W., Dupuis, R., & Eaton, J. (2005). Promoting forgiveness among co- workers following a workplace transgression: The effects of social motivation training. *Canadian Journal of Behavioral Science*, 37(4), 299–308.

Sturm, R. E., Vera, D., & Crossan, M. (2017). The entanglement of leader character and leader competence and its impact on performance. *The Leadership Quarterly*, 28(3), 349–366.

Suich, A. (2016). Versailles in the valley. *The Economist/1843*, April/May, 33–35.

Tenney, E. R., Poole, J. R., & Dieber, E. (2016). Does positivity enhance work performance? Why, when, and what we don't know. *Research in Organizational Behavior*, 36, 27–46.

Thanem, T., Varlander, S., & Cummings, S. (2011). Open space = open minds? The ambiguities of pro-creative office design. *International Journal of Work Organisation and Emotion*, 4(1), 78–98.

Thomas, N. K., Sugiyama, K., Rochford, K. C., Stephens, J. P., & Kanov, J. (2018). Experiential organizing: Pursuing relational and bureaucratic goals through symbolically – and experientially – oriented work. *Academy of Management Review*. doi:10.5465/amr.2016.0348.

Uhl-Bien, M., & Arena, M. (2017). Complexity leadership: Enabling people and organizations for adaptability. *Organizational Dynamics*, 46(1), 9–20.

van Dam, N., & van der Helm, E. (2016a). The organizational cost of insufficient sleep. *McKinsey Quarterly*, February (www.mckinsey.com/business-functions/organization/our-insights/the-organizational-cost-of-insufficient-sleep#0).

van Dam, N., & van der Helm, E. (2016b). There's a proven link between effective leadership and getting enough sleep. *Harvard Business Review*, February 16 (https://hbr.org/2016/02/theres-a-proven-link-between-effective-leadership-and-getting-enough-sleep).

van Kleef, G. A., Oveis, C., Van der Lowe, I., LuoKogan, A., Goetz, J., & Keltner, D. (2008). Power, distress, and compassion. *Psychological Science*, 19(12), 1315–1322.

Von Krogh, G., & Geilinger, N. (2014). Knowledge creation in the eco-system: Research imperatives. *European Management Journal*, 32(1), 155–163.

Waber, B., Magnolfi, J., & Lindsay, G. (2014). Workplaces that move people. *Harvard Business Review*, October, 69–77.

Waldroop, J., & Butler, T. (1996). The executive as coach. *Harvard Business Review*, November–December, 111–117.

Warner, M. (2007). 'Kafka, Weber and organization theory', *Human Relations*, 60(7), pp. 1019–1038.

Wasik, J. (2016). Apple innovation rules: Steve Jobs's secrets. *Forbes*, May 20 (www.forbes.com/sites/johnwasik/2016/05/20/apple-innovation-rules-steve-jobss-secrets/#2b705c763a4b).

Waters, L. (2012). Predicting job satisfaction: Contributions of individual gratitude and institutionalized gratitude. *Psychology*, 3(12), 1174.

Wiedner, R., Barrett, M., & Oborn, E. (2017). The emergence of change in unexpected places: Resourcing across organizational practices in strategic change. *Academy of Management Journal*, 60(3), 823–854.

Worline, M., & Dutton, J. (2017). *Awakening compassion at work*. Oakland, CA: Berrett-Koehler.

Worthington, E. L., Jr. (2000). Forgiving usually takes time: A lesson learned by studying interventions to promote forgiveness. *Journal of Psychology and Theology*, 28(1), 3–20.

Zenger, J., & Folkman, J. (2016). What great listeners actually do. *Harvard Business Review*, July 14 (https://hbr.org/2016/07/what-great-listeners-actually-do).

7 Real teams

Supporting learning and change

Summary and objectives

The rate of change in political climates, economic conditions, social trends, technological advances and legal regulations and environmental challenges has been growing exponentially since the Industrial Revolution and with the advance of globalization. For example, the top ten in-demand jobs in 2014 did not exist in 2008;[1] whereas today there are 3.5 billion Google searches per day, in 2010 there were not even 1 billion searches for the entire year;[2] and whereas it took radio 38 years to reach a market audience of 50 million, it took TV only 13 years, computers four years, the iPad three years, Facebook two years and YouTube just nine months![3] Today we have five times as many words in the English language as we had during the time of Shakespeare and the amount of technical information available is being doubled each year. All of these changes mean organizations have to develop ways for their members to be quick learners, constantly innovating and adapting to keep pace. Those organizations (and their members) that fail to learn are left behind. Organizations can no longer afford the slow process of relying on a single decision-making authority at the top of a many-tiered command structure. Stable, hierarchical bureaucratic structures are becoming in many instances akin to post-bureaucratic team-based network structures that facilitate learning, creativity and agility. This chapter discusses the role of teams in stimulating organizational renewal through learning. Critical dimensions and processes explaining team functioning and effectiveness are explored. We analyze Edmondson's research on combinations of psychological safety and accountability, challenge and support, as engines of deep learning. Communicational and relational patterns that foster and destroy collective intelligence are also considered. Teams are not simply the context where individual actors operate – they are also indispensable in pursuing organizational goals.

Teams are everywhere

The word 'team' is often associated with groups with high visibility in the media, such as Real Madrid, Manchester United, All Blacks, Springboks, the US 'Dream Team' and the 'Redeem Team', and even the US Navy SEALs. In fact, 'teams are involved in many facets of society, from military operations and healthcare systems to research groups and private companies'.[4] As Kozlowski and Ilgen have argued,[5] 'teams of people working together for a common purpose have been a centerpiece of human social organization ever since our ancient ancestors first banded together to hunt game, raise families, and defend their communities'.

In teams, individuals accomplish work through united efforts and interdependent actions in the direction of a common goal.[6] Increasingly, organizations are adopting team-based structures to deal with the growing complexities and uncertainties of the environments in which they operate. As Anderson and colleagues explain, organizations 'have moved inexorably to more team-based structures and will often be reliant upon teams'.[7] Teams are created for many different purposes:

- Lego established a self-managed team to create 'an entirely new business system, emphasizing speed to market, alliances with carefully selected partners, high annual novelty share, a close relationship and interaction with the consumer, and lean, globally centralized operations'.[8] Lego Mindstorms ('a programmable robotics construction set that gives you the power to build, program and command your own LEGO robots')[9] emerged from such a process.
- Cheetah teams (cheetahs are the fastest animals on Earth) have been created to deal, in high speed and ad-hoc ways, with unanticipated problems. The most significant feature of a cheetah team 'is that it is *never planned in advance*'.[10]
- Virtual teams, composed of geographically dispersed members, are created to work around-the-clock, to congregate skills and competencies, to produce creative outputs, to develop software.
- Cross-boundary teams, within and across organizations, are used to pursue innovation strategies. The construction of the Water Cube for the Beijing Olympics (see, later in this chapter, the section about 'teaming') was the outcome of several fluid teams, consisting of individuals from different countries and backgrounds.[11]

Several advantages have been attributed to teams, including increased productivity, flexibility, innovation and employee satisfaction, as well as decreased costs, turnover and absenteeism.[12] In teams, performance may exceed the sum of their parts, with the world of sport hosting many examples of such synergy.[13] These positive outcomes develop when teams facilitate team task coordination and interpersonal bonding, produce synergistic gains and minimize process losses.[14] Therefore, teams may be a source of positivity for team members, the organization where the team operates and for external stakeholders. But teams are not a panacea for handling all organizational problems. Team failures are frequent and teams may embark on problematic processes that mark the whole as less than the sum of its parts (e.g., groupthink; see Box 7.1). Hence, the old question of 'why groups often fail to out-perform their best member'.[15]

Box 7.1 The negative in the positive: groupthink

Imagine that you are a member of a cohesive team. The team leader is charismatic. The team has to make a critical decision under time pressure. The leader starts the meeting with strong self-confidence, arguing in favour of a specific course of action. You have doubts about the merits of such a proposal. However, you look around and realize that nobody questions the suggestion. When a team member expresses doubts, other people react by supporting the leader's view and arguing that 'there is no time' to discuss 'irrelevant issues'. Before the meeting, you had read a document that would recommend caution. But you prefer not to share such information in the meeting because you anticipate negative reactions from other team members. Above all, you see yourself as a 'good team member' and don't want to jeopardize collective harmony. Moreover, you believe in the wisdom of your leader. The meeting ends with a unanimous vote in favour of the leader's proposal.

A few minutes after the meeting, you talk informally with other team members. It is then that you realize that many of them had the same doubts – and hid them, as you did! Unanimity was illusory. The team was caught up in groupthink: a psychological phenomenon that emerges when the members of a group are 'dominated' by the desire for harmony or conformity, which leads the group to embark on irrational or dysfunctional decision-making processes and outcomes.[16] As a consequence, the group does not critically assess alternative viewpoints, actively suppresses dissenting perspectives and isolates itself from outside influences (to unconsciously protect itself from inconvenient truths that would lead to rethinking the preferred decision). Some of the symptoms of this phenomenon are the following:

- Illusion of invulnerability.
- Belief in the inherent morality of the group.
- Stereotypes about the out-groups ('our enemy').
- Pressures toward conformity and uniformity with pressures on dissenters (the 'black sheep').
- Self-censorship (team members avoid expressing disagreements with the aim to preserve internal harmony).
- Illusion of unanimity.
- Incomplete assessment of alternatives (i.e., the group chooses a decision outcome and then rationalizes this choice and neglects alternatives).
- Failure to examine the risks of the preferred choice and to reappraise initially rejected alternatives.
- Poor information search (only information that supports the preferred alternative is considered).

The phenomenon is more likely to emerge when the team is cohesive, the team leader is traditionally not impartial, team members share similar backgrounds and values, and the team experiences high stress from external threats. Tragic accidents such as the Challenger Space Shuttle explosion occurred in part under the influence of groupthink.[17]

Questions for reflection

- How may groupthink be prevented? What do you think team leaders should do to prevent it?
- Might cohesion be a facilitator of groupthink? Why?
- Adam Grant wrote:[18] 'For our society to remain free and open, kids need to learn the value of open disagreement. It turns out that highly creative adults

often grow up in families full of tension. Not fistfights or personal insults, but real disagreements'. In your view, why do 'real disagreements' matter for creativity and for preventing groupthink?

As a further recommendation watch the movie *12 Angry Men* (1957) directed by Sidney Lumet. What lessons do you take? Why is minority dissent important in producing better decisions?

This chapter discusses the main factors and processes that contribute to team functioning, learning and effectiveness. We start by clarifying the notions of team and teamwork, and discussing some criteria and dimensions of team effectiveness. Particular attention is paid to team creativity. Next, we focus on the dynamic nature of teams and discuss the 'hardware' and 'software' that supports effective teaming. Then, we concentrate specifically on how team psychological safety *and* team accountability represent the crucibles of team learning and performance, contributing to organizational renewal and change. Finally, we explore how communication patterns may build or destroy collective intelligence. The chapter is strongly grounded in the notion of 'positive teams' from a perspective adopted by Pentland to define high-performing teams: 'those blessed with the energy, creativity, and shared commitment to far surpass other teams'.[19]

Teams and teamwork

What is a team?

Different researchers have defined teams differently. For Salas and colleagues, a team is 'a distinguishable set of two or more people who interact dynamically, interdependently, and adaptively towards a common and valued goal/objective/mission'.[20] In a similar vein, Kozlowski and Ilgen defined a team as:[21]

(a) two or more individuals who (b) socially interact (face-to-face or, increasingly, virtually); (c) possess one or more common goals; (d) are brought together to perform organizationally relevant tasks; (e) exhibit interdependencies with respect to workflow, goals, and outcomes; (f) have different roles and responsibilities; and (g) are together embedded in an encompassing organizational system, with boundaries and linkages to the broader system context and task environment.

These definitions[22] consider that a dyad may be a team. However, some scholars distinguish dyads from teams made up of three or more people. Even Kozlowski and Ilgen recognize that, although 'many two-person teams (e.g., aircrews) exhibit the same basic work processes underlying team effectiveness in larger teams', teams of three or more members 'enable coalitions and related interpersonal interaction complexities that are absent in dyads'.[23] In this chapter, even though we acknowledge that a dyad may operate as a team, we consider that most phenomena that typify a team emerge from interdependent interactions between three or more individuals (Figure 7.1).

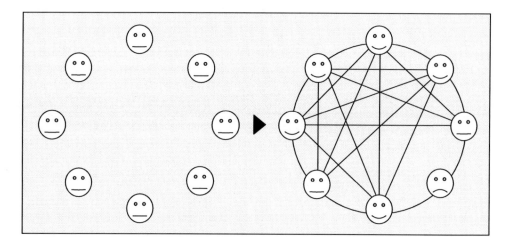

Figure 7.1 The team is in the relationships.

Teams and groups – are they different?

While some scholars distinguish teams from groups, others use both terms interchangeably.[24] For example, some researchers consider teams and groups as the polar ends of a continuum of task interdependence. From a similar perspective, while groups are characterized by low-role differentiation and low-task differentiation, teams are characterized by distributed expertise and high levels of role differentiation, task differentiation and task interdependence.[25] Biemann and colleagues acknowledge that teams and groups have potential differences but argue that both may be seen as 'a clustering of individuals who are interdependent based on a set of common expectations or hierarchical structuring and who interact with one another as if they are a group'.[26]

For simplicity, we use the terms teams and groups interchangeably, considering teams as social entities in which members share – implicitly or explicitly – a common identity and pursue some collective goal, interdependently. In a *real* team it is the relationships that make the team, not the individuals as entities that compose them. Real teams form relational ties that allow the team to be more competent than its members: the whole is more competent than the parts composing it. Real teams develop a 'spirit', i.e., a shared identity that allows them to deal productively with the tensions associated with teamworking, such as individual vs shared identity, learning from wins and from losses, proximity and individuality, etc.[27] As such, teams express paradoxical tensions that can make or break them.

The primary components of a team are multiple individuals, interdependency between them, together with shared objectives.[28] Interdependence is, perhaps, the most important component distinguishing 'teams' from mere collectives of individuals (see Figures 7.2a and 7.2b). A group of marathon runners who represent a country in the Olympics might not be a team: if they were working together to position one team member in a winning position they would be; if they were competing against each other individually they would not. Conversely, a group of diplomats, who campaign, in a coordinated and interdependent way, in different countries, in favour of their candidate for the post of Secretary-General of the United Nations, may be considered a temporary team.

Figure 7.2a A group: telephone operators, Seattle, Washington, US, 1952.[29]

Figure 7.2b A team: ABBA live at the Northlands Coliseum in Edmonton, Canada, September 13, 1979.[30]

Taskwork and teamwork: critical dimensions of team effectiveness

Two interrelated dimensions critical for successful team performance are taskwork and teamwork.[31] Taskwork represents the specific tasks (e.g., kicking the ball, playing violin, administrating anaesthesia before surgery, presenting ideas during a board meeting) aimed at achieving team goals. Teamwork (Figure 7.3) involves the shared attitudes (what team members *feel* or *believe*), cognitions (what team members *think* or *know*) and behaviours (what team members *do*) that are necessary for the team to accomplish taskwork, to function effectively and thus achieve team goals.[32] The members of an orchestra play instruments, the members of a football team play football and the members of a surgical team perform several operational tasks from pre-operative patient preparation to post-operative recovery. They engage in teamwork when they communicate with each other (through verbal and nonverbal messages) and coordinate their work to achieve team goals more effectively.

Team effectiveness depends on the successful interplay of taskwork and teamwork. It is teamwork that guides the execution of taskwork and makes a team more (or less) than the sum of its parts.[33] A group of five experts with extensive knowledge does not constitute an effective team if they do not share knowledge, do not communicate appropriately, do not coordinate behaviours, cooperate with and trust one another. A collective of highly self-effective individuals does not compose a highly self-effective team if team members do not trust each other, do not cooperate and, in consequence, do not believe that the team, as a whole, will be effective in pursuing its goals.[34] In a similar vein, team creativity is not the mere aggregation of novel and useful ideas generated by individual members; 'rather, it involves team members collectively processing information, considering disparate views, and eventually producing creative outcomes'[35] (see the section on creativity, below). In fact, individual creativity may give rise to different levels of team creativity as a result of distinct socioemotional processes within teams.

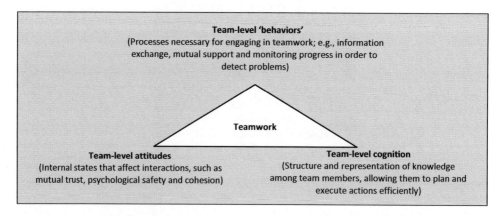

Figure 7.3 Components of teamwork.[36]

What is team effectiveness?

Criteria for measuring team effectiveness

It might be said that a team is effective if it is successful in reaching its collective goals. While simple and straightforward, this definition raises a number of difficulties. First, goals are not fixed, they change over time; moreover, team members do not necessarily agree about the goals the team must pursue. Second, many teams do not produce outputs that may be assessed from a purely objective perspective. Although it is easy to assess the effectiveness of a soccer team at the end of the match (the outcome of team performance is clear: a win, a loss or a draw),[37] it is more complicated to assess the effectiveness of an orchestra or of an executive board. Third, for many teams, effectiveness is a multidimensional phenomenon. As such, the team may be more effective in some dimensions but less effective in others. For example, a sales team may be very effective in increasing sales volume but less effective with respect to return on sales. Fourth, different constituencies use different lenses and criteria to assess team effectiveness. For example, for team members themselves, wellbeing and positive social relationships may be of paramount importance. Internal and external customers are likely to assess team effectiveness in terms of efficiency, service and product quality, costs, timeliness and productivity. Fifth, different time horizons used to assess team effectiveness may lead to varying conclusions, even when objective measures are considered. A sales team may be effective in the short term through aggressive sales strategies that jeopardize longer-term results. Sixth, the criteria for measuring team effectiveness must include not only the *ends* (i.e., the output) but also the *means*, including the social interactions between team members that have consequences for how the team learns and develops in the long run. For these and other reasons, it makes sense to use the following three criteria, in tandem, to assess team effectiveness:[38]

- **Productive output**. This criterion represents how the product, service or decision meets or exceeds standards of quantity, quality and client timeliness. The 'clients' may be internal 'customers' (e.g., the information technology unit and the HR team serve other departments and the entire organization), some external customers (e.g., a sales team), or both internal and external customers (e.g., a Medical Affairs team in a pharmaceutical company interacting with both external stakeholders, such as physicians and other healthcare professionals, and internal stakeholders).
- **Social processes used in carrying out work (team viability)**. This criterion represents team processes that enhance members' capabilities for working together interdependently in the future ('We define as effective only teams that are more capable as performing units when a piece of work is finished than they were when it was begun').[39] Over time, effective teams are able to detect and correct errors, to notice and exploit emerging opportunities, to develop their strengths (both at the individual and collective levels) as well as learn, improve and flourish.
- **Quality of group experience (team member satisfaction)**. This dimension represents the extent to which the team's collective experience contributes positively to the learning and wellbeing of team members ('We do not count as effective any team for which the net impact of the group experience on members' learning and well-being is more negative than positive').[40]

A team may produce and deliver a high-quality product or service in a timely and effective way. However, in the long run, team effectiveness may be jeopardized if the team does not learn and improve or if it is socially and emotionally toxic, thus impairing future team processes, interactions and learning, with negative consequences for team survival and prosperity. This holistic perspective, accounting for the interaction between three categories of criteria, does not suggest that there is a standard set of measures for evaluating team effectiveness. Mathieu and colleagues, who advocated a multilevel, multiple constituencies' framework to measure team effectiveness, noted that:[41]

> It is safe to say that there is not a standard set of criteria measures for team research – nor should there be. Team effectiveness is context specific, and although at an abstract level we may be able to refer to the efficiencies of airline cockpit, surgical, knowledge management, pharmaceutical sales, forensic accounting, and college basketball teams, clearly the manifestations and indicators of those efficiencies vary markedly across settings.

The I-P-O and the IMOI models

Over several decades the prevalent conceptualization of team effectiveness was the input-process-outcome (I-P-O) framework.[42] This framework considers that team processes (e.g., coordination, conflict management and affect management) are the mediating mechanisms linking inputs (e.g., team member characteristics, team composition, team diversity and resources) with outcomes (e.g., productivity, customers' satisfaction). Team processes are 'members' interdependent acts that convert inputs to outcomes via cognitive, verbal and behavioral activities directed toward organizing taskwork to achieve collective goals'.[43]

Although the framework was developed to organize the research literature on small groups and not as a theory or a formal causal model of team effectiveness, it has been frequently interpreted as a causal model to be tested.[44] Such a perspective neglects two important interrelated points: first, teams are dynamic entities that evolve over time (in dynamic contexts), sometimes following a positive path, other times declining. Second, input, processes and outcomes influence each other dynamically. As argued by Ilgen and colleagues,

> over time and contexts, teams and their members continually cycle and recycle. They interact among themselves and with other persons in contexts. These interactions change the teams, team members, and their environments in ways more complex than is captured by simple cause and effect perspectives.[45]

As a consequence of these limitations, Ilgen and colleagues proposed the IMOI (input-mediator-output-input) framework,[46] with mediators acting as mechanisms linking inputs to outcomes. These mediators include not only team processes but also team emergent states. Emergent states are 'properties of the team that are typically dynamic in nature and vary as a function of team context, inputs, processes, and outcomes'.[47] While team processes are the means by which individuals work interdependently to utilize various resources (e.g., knowledge, skills, equipment, money) to yield meaningful outcomes (e.g., product development, service, team creativity, satisfaction), emergent states are the cognitive, motivational and affective *states* of teams.

Emergent states are both products of team experiences (including team processes) and inputs to subsequent processes and outcomes.

The last 'I' in the model represents the presence of feedback loops, in which 'outputs' (including team performance) are inputs to future team process and emergent states. Ilgen and colleagues also point out the existence of several interactions between inputs and processes, between various processes, and between processes and emergent states. Moreover, the effects of a component on other components is affected by boundary conditions. For example, a high level of team diversity and cultural heterogeneity within the team may in some circumstances not only produce positive effects on team creativity but also negative ones in terms of team coordination and team conflict.

Critical dimensions of team effectiveness

Considering the dynamic and complex interplay between inputs, mediators and outcomes, Ilgen and colleagues identified processes and emerging states with potential effects on team effectiveness that could be targets for interventions to improve team functioning. They suggest two main categories:[48] (1) team cognitive processes and structures (i.e., unit and team climate, team mental models and transactive memory, team learning; see Box 7.2) and (2) team interpersonal, motivational and affective processes as well as emergent states (i.e., team cohesion, team efficacy and group potency, affect, mood and emotion, and team conflict).

Box 7.2 Do teams know, memorize, reflect and learn?

Team learning is fundamentally based on individual learning, in that teams learn only if team members learn. Team learning is not the mere sum of what team members learn, however. If team members learn something but do not share their learning with other team members, team learning as a whole is diminished. If a doctor in a medical team experiences a failure or makes a mistake but is too afraid to share such a setback with other doctors, the other team members and the team as whole are less likely to learn how to avoid making the same mistake or failure. This explains why 'Etsy engineers send company-wide emails confessing mistakes they made' (see Box 7.8). As Kozlowski and Ilgen argue,[49] team learning

> is fundamentally based on individual learning, but when viewed as more than a mere pooling of individual knowledge it can be distinguished as a team-level property that captures the collective knowledge pool, potential synergies among team members, and unique individual contributions.

Team learning thus refers to the 'acquisition of knowledge, skills, and performance capabilities of an interdependent set of individuals through interaction and experience'.[50] To understand how team learning unfolds, it is important to understand three other 'processes' and team states: team mental models, team transactive memory and team reflexivity. 'Team mental models and transactive memory both refer to cognitive structures or knowledge representations that enable team members to organize and acquire information necessary to anticipate and execute actions.'[51] While team mental models refer to shared understandings (i.e., knowledge) about task requirements, procedures and role responsibilities, transactive memory[52] refers to shared understandings about 'who knows what' (i.e., where particular knowledge is located among team members) and how such particular knowledge can help to handle specific problems and opportunities. Team reflexivity is 'the extent to which teams collectively reflect upon and adapt their working methods and functioning'.[53]

How do these four 'processes' interrelate? A possible answer is that team mental models, team transactive memory and team reflexivity are causes as well as consequences of team learning.[54] They nourish each other. For example, team reflexivity enables team learning – and learning helps the team reflect upon current processes. Transactive memory is a source of knowledge that may help the team learn and learning helps the team to develop its transactive memory. The three team processes/states are dynamic (i.e., developing and changing over time).

Recently, Salas and colleagues[55] considered 'nine critical considerations' for team effectiveness (Table 7.1). Six factors (cooperation, coordination, cognition, conflict, coaching and communication) represent core emergent states and processes. The other three components (context, composition and culture) are influencing conditions, representing factors that may affect both directly and indirectly (i.e., via the six core processes and emergent states) team outcomes. While the core emergent states and processes represent attitudes, cognitions and behaviours that occur *within* the team (i.e., teamwork), the influencing conditions shape how teams engage in teamwork.

These factors have important consequences for team functioning and performance. For example, the team sense of collective efficacy, intrateam trust and psychological safety (indicators of cooperation) predict team performance as well as other relevant attitudes and behaviours for the individual and the team functioning.[56] Within-team coordination is associated with higher team performance.[57] Coaching behaviours associate positively with perceived team learning, team performance, follower job satisfaction, leadership effectiveness and satisfaction with the leader.[58] Information sharing positively affects team performance.[59]

The nine factors should be considered holistically as they dynamically influence each other. For example, while collective efficacy influences team effectiveness, the reverse effect is also plausible: teams that are more effective develop higher confidence in their capacity to be effective in the future. A team characterized by high psychological safety will potentially solve conflicts in a more constructive and healthier way. Constructive conflict also builds psychological safety as it conveys the message that disagreement and dissonance are welcome and contribute to better decision-making. Actions aimed at fostering a specific factor may produce ripple and recursive effects upon other factors. For example, by promoting psychological safety[64] aimed at fostering constructive conflict, the team leader also affects communication flows, coordination behaviours, team cognitions and, in the long run, the team culture – and vice-versa.

Considering this dynamic and holistic perspective, Mathieu and colleagues[65] propose a framework composed of simultaneous and interrelated relationships between factors associated with team and individual outcomes. The framework includes three general

Table 7.1 Nine critical factors for teamwork and collaboration[60]

Critical factor	Definition	Illustrative indicators that are critical for each factor and team effectiveness
Macro-dimension: core processes and emergent states		
Cooperation	Represents the motivational drivers necessary for effective teamwork. Comprises team members attitudes, beliefs and feelings that drive behavioural action.	• Collective efficacy. • Trust. • Cohesion. • Team/collective orientation. • Team learning orientation. • Goal commitment. • Psychological safety.
Conflict	The perceived incompatibilities between the interests, values, beliefs, motivations and views held by one or more team members.	• Task conflict (i.e., differences in opinions about how team members should execute tasks). • Relationship conflict (i.e., interpersonal differences that spark tension among individuals). • Process conflict (i.e., conflict about the division and delegation of tasks and responsibilities among team members).
Coordination	'Orchestrating the sequence and timing of interdependent actions'.[61] Involves team-level strategies to align knowledge and actions to achieve team goals.	• Explicit coordination (e.g., team members intentionally adopt mechanisms, such as planning and communication, to manage interdependencies). • Implicit coordination (team members anticipate team needs and adjust their behaviours accordingly, without having to be instructed).
Communication	A reciprocal process through which team members send and receive information that shapes and is shaped by team's attitudes, behaviours and cognitions.	• Open and frank interpersonal communication. • Information sharing. • Openness of information in virtual environments.
Coaching (leadership)	'The enactment of leadership behaviors to establish goals and set direction that leads to the successful accomplishment of these goals'.[62] Coaching may come from either or both internal and external leaders, whether they are formal or informal.	• Recognizing and helping to correct vital team errors or problems. • Providing guidance in challenging situations. • Fostering team members and team's development. • Role modelling.

(Continued)

Table 7.1 (Cont.)

Critical factor	Definition	Illustrative indicators that are critical for each factor and team effectiveness
Cognition (team knowledge)	A shared understanding among team members about the team's situation (i.e., objectives, roles, expertise and operational procedures).	• A shared mental model (individuals are able to describe, explain and predict the behaviour of others). • Transactive memory, i.e., shared memory of a group (*internal*: what team members know personally; *external*: what individuals know can be retrieved from other sources, including from other team members). • Knowledge of roles and responsibilities. • Knowledge of the team mission objectives and norms. • Knowledge about the situation within which the team operates. • Familiarity with teammate knowledge, skills and abilities.
	Macro-dimension: influencing conditions	
Composition	Attributes (e.g., personality, skills, abilities, expertise and experience) of team members relevant to team performance.	• Characteristics of a 'good team member' (e.g., strong team orientation). • The best configuration of team member characteristics (knowledge, skills, abilities, attitudes and other characteristics). • The role of diversity (in terms of ethnicity, gender, age, culture, background, occupation, beliefs).
Context	'Situational characteristics or events that influence the occurrence and meaning of behavior, as well as the manner and degree to which various factors impact team outcomes.'[63]	• Organizational climate (i.e., shared perceptions of formal and informal organizational policies, practices and procedures). • Task context (e.g., manner of work to be performed; team or individual autonomy; uncertainty; accountability; resources available). • Physical context (e.g., tools, work spaces, information display, shift work, work pace, machine controls, location). • Technology (e.g., the one supporting virtual teams).

(*Continued*)

Table 7.1 (Cont.)

Critical factor	Definition	Illustrative indicators that are critical for each factor and team effectiveness
Culture	Shared assumptions that team and organizational members hold about their relationships with each other and their environment, manifest in individual values, beliefs, norms for social behaviour and artifacts.	• External threats, time pressure and stress (e.g., in fire and rescue squads, flight crews and military units). • Values, beliefs and norms regarding, e.g., individualism–collectivism, power distance and long-term/short-term orientation. • Degree of cultural homogeneity/heterogeneity within the team.

categories (team tasks and structure, members' characteristics, composition, processes and emergent states), which 'are all dynamic entities with likely reciprocal relationships with one another and team outcomes over time'.[66] Edmondson and Harvey,[67] considering that cross-boundary teaming, within and across organizations, is increasingly frequent (consider the section on teaming later in the chapter), propose a dynamic and complex cross-boundary model that includes knowledge attributes, emergent (individual and collective) states, team–member interactions and contextual factors. In summary: team effectiveness is the consequence (and the antecedent) of a complex and dynamic interplay between several team and contextual factors (see Figure 7.4). Next, we discuss such an interplay to explain how team creativity unfolds.

Team creativity as an indicator of team effectiveness

Creativity as a collective phenomenon

Creativity, defined as 'the production of ideas concerning products, practices, services, or procedures that are novel or original and potentially useful to the organization',[69] has been considered a 'key driver of organizational innovation and success'.[70] As organizations have evolved towards team-based structures, they have become more reliant on teams for developing creative and innovative solutions to problems and opportunities.[71]

Team creativity partially projects the creativity of its individual members. However, team creativity 'is not simply the aggregation of ideas generated by individual members; rather, it involves team members collectively processing information, considering disparate views, and eventually producing creative outcomes'.[72] Individual creativity may give rise to different levels of team creativity as a result of distinct socioemotional processes within teams.[73] Considering that creativity is challenging and risky, team members with highly creative ideas may refrain from sharing them with other individuals if they are risk averse.[74] Depending on team processes, the creative contributions of some individuals may be undervalued (or even underutilized or discarded) or overvalued, regardless of their effective potential.[75] For example, in a team characterized

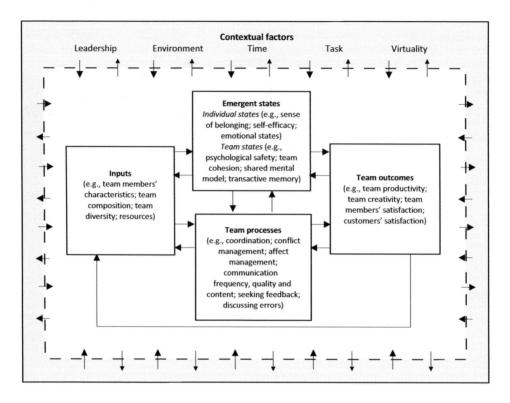

Figure 7.4 A systemic and dynamic model of team effectiveness.[68]

by conformity towards individuals with high power status, a highly creative solution from a low-power-status individual may be neglected in favour of a less creative solution from a high-power-status individual.[76]

Additionally, knowing about a creative idea from a colleague has the potential to stimulate other team members into being more creative, enabling a synergistic effect. Such a benefit can, however, be severely hampered depending on team processes. For example, in a team with low psychological safety (more on this topic below), in which members are afraid to speak up, even highly creative individuals may be unable to make effective use of their individual creative resources to benefit the team. In sum, individual creativity contributes to team creativity but that contribution can be significantly influenced by a variety of team processes, including leadership behaviours.

Teams as contexts for individual creativity

Teams may be seen as the *context* where individual creativity emerges – or fails to emerge. Some individuals are more creative than others (e.g., individuals with higher PsyCap[77] and those with stronger creative self-efficacy tend to be creative)[78] but several team features (e.g., team climate and team leadership) may magnify or diminish the expression of creative capacity. Individual creativity demands a supportive context, including an atmosphere of psychological safety in which team members feel free 'to engage in some of the risky behaviors involved in creativity'[79] and to 'propose new ideas and solutions without being judged or criticized'.[80] If people face emotional threats and experience low psychological safety, they are more likely to suppress the expression of creativity at work.[81]

Task characteristics also matter: some tasks and jobs allow, require, facilitate or demand more creativity than others. Individual creativity therefore emerges from the interplay between individual characteristics, task characteristics and the team context:[82]

- An individual may express different levels of creativity depending upon various team contexts and the varied nature of the tasks (with tasks that foster intrinsic motivation known to be more likely to stimulate individual creativity).
- A potentially creative individual may refrain from expressing such creativity if the team climate or the team leader 'kills' the creative drive.
- Some team contexts (e.g., peers and leader support, transformational leadership) may nourish the creativity of individuals who are not dispositionally creative. Studies suggest that 'even individuals or teams that are not predisposed or inclined to be creative may do so to a larger extent given certain facilitative conditions'.[83]

George and Zhou illustrate the effect of the interplay between individual characteristics, task characteristics and the team context.[84] They found that employees adopted more creative behaviours when they were highly open to experiences (an individual characteristic), received positive feedback (from the supervisor, a contextual factor) and worked on tasks with unclear means or ends (task characteristics).[85]

Team as the actor producing creativity

Teams may also be considered as the *actor* producing team creativity through several processes, with the outcome also dependent on the interplay between individual and collective conditions. Teams whose members have creative personalities and characteristics (e.g., PsyCap; see Chapter 3) are potentially more creative. However, the team context (including team leadership; see Chapter 8) may inhibit or facilitate the expression of team-level creative potential. Furthermore, even while the team context may potentially favour team creativity, realization of that potential may further depend on the team member characteristics or other features of the team context (e.g., team leadership style). For example, as different team members contribute distinct knowledge, expertise and experiences, the diversity of perspectives could inspire creative synergies and make the team more creative. The corollary would be that greater diversity in a team should lead to greater creativity (see the section on team diversity below). However, this expectation does not hold up to scrutiny, as reported by van Knippenberg and Hoever, 'the accumulated evidence speaks overwhelmingly against a robust main effect of team diversity on team creativity'.[86] A possible explanation is that realization of the benefits of team diversity on team creativity depends on other factors. For example, team diversity may produce higher team creativity only if team members have open mindsets, experience a sense of psychological safety and have positive perceptions of a highly inclusive climate. Knippenberg and Hoever[87] further note, 'the range of effects for the diversity-creativity relationship suggest that organizations seeking creativity from teamwork cannot simply rely on diverse team composition – they will also have to create the conditions conducive to reaping the benefits of diversity in team creativity'.

Team creativity thus emerges from the interplay between individual characteristics, team task context, team social context and team leadership. Zhou and Hoever argued that 'certain team leadership characteristics and styles are necessary to bring out the positive potential inherent in a team's informational resources, which otherwise remain without effect'.[88] Another study[89] found that transformational leadership moderated the effect of educational specialization heterogeneity (a team characteristic) on team creativity. More specifically, educational specialization heterogeneity had a positive effect on team creative self-efficacy and creativity when transformational leadership was high rather than low. In a different study[90] a team learning goal and team performance approach goal positively relate to both individual creativity and team creativity through the mediation of team information exchange. Furthermore, an indirect relationship was found to be moderated by a relationship of trust with the team leader: when the trust was stronger, the indirect positive relationship with team creativity and individual creativity was stronger for team's learning goals but weaker for team performance approach goals. Average individual creativity within the team was also positively associated with team creativity via the mediating factor of a supportive climate for creativity. It is possible that if team members are individually creative, a team climate favourable to creativity develops and this climate facilitates team creativity.

Teaming: the fluidity of new teams

Dynamic processes

Teams are dynamic human processes. A team's composition, boundaries and processes evolve over time. Cross-boundary, temporary and flexible teams are increasingly used to pursue innovation strategies within and across organizations: teams are changing from structures with bounded membership to spaces of dynamic participation.[91] For example, professionals from IT services at Fujitsu worked with specialists from Tech-Shop to develop several projects, including the first ever mobile makerspace for schools and other community members.[92] The Water Cube for the Beijing Olympics (formally the Beijing National Aquatics Centre; see Figure 7.5) emerged from a global complex collaboration between dozens of people from many disciplines and four countries that collaborated in fluid groupings over several years.[93]

The process involved in the creation, development and leadership of fluid teams is called 'teaming'.[95] Across the process, temporary teams are built and dismantled, team composition changes to handle emergent needs, with the interconnection between different teams evolving in fluid ways. Teaming may be observed in different fields, including aviation manufacturing (Box 7.3), educational settings and healthcare. For example, clinicians in an emergency room have to convene quickly to solve a specific patient problem and then move on to care, with different colleagues, for other patients. The success of their mission depends more on the effective teaming than on the stability of teams adopting stable processes and procedures.[96] Companies are also increasingly challenged to accomplish things that have not been done before and might not be done again, outcomes typically not achievable with traditional stable teams:[97]

Figure 7.5 Beijing National Aquatics Centre, January 8, 2007.[94] Output of complex teaming.

It's just not possible to identify the right skills and knowledge in advance and to trust that circumstances will not change. Under those conditions, a leader's emphasis has to shift from composing and managing teams to inspiring and enabling teaming.

Box 7.3 Teaming at GE aviation

Effective teaming is relevant not only for temporary cross-boundary teams; it is also important on more traditional and stable teams. First, the more 'traditional' teams are less stable than it is sometimes supposed. Teams are open systems and team diversity may decline or, more probably, expand: 'Dynamic team diversity theory expands the focus of team diversity research from teams being more diverse than others to teams becoming more diverse than before'.[98] Second, traditional teams have to continuously handle new challenges amidst uncertainty and changing circumstances. Consider the following excerpts from an article published on teaming in an aviation manufacturing facility of General Electric (GE):[99]

> 'Teaming' is what GE calls its management system of working groups who decide for themselves how work should be done. At Bromont, workers don't have supervisors, they have 'coaches', and they aren't given directions, they're given goals. Traditional supervisor tasks such as production planning and scheduling, policies about overtime and vacation, and improvements to manufacturing processes are managed by the teams themselves. Members from each team also sit on 'councils' with representatives from leadership and human resources to make decisions that affect the whole plant. Councils also weigh in on decisions such as when to cut overtime, whom to fire, and whom to promote. The principle is simple: The people closest to the work know best how to do it.

Questions for reflection

- If workers do not have supervisors, who supervises them? Is teaming possible without supervision? If so, who can build the hardware and software necessary for successful teaming?
- What skills and competencies do team members need to possess to work effectively toward team goals?
- Are those skills and competencies equally relevant for manufacturing teams and teams like those who projected and built the Water Cube? Why?

Increasingly employees in a multitude of organizations from different sectors, working on different projects (e.g., product design, product development, patient care, strategy development, pharmaceutical research, creative solutions, rescue operations) work within several fluid teams that change over time in terms of goals, composition, process and boundaries. Solutions for handling problems and opportunities can emerge from anywhere, the challenge being to identify and 'team' individuals with the pertinent background, knowledge, skills and expertise. The temporary and fluid nature of these teams may give rise to conflicts that would not emerge in stable traditional teams, where people know and trust each other, in which it is more comfortable to speak up and interact fluidly.

The complexity of teaming is increased when it involves individuals from different time zones communicating electronically as a virtual team. It is necessary to accommodate and manage differences and tensions in productive ways (see the section about virtual teams below). Team psychological safety is particularly critical for the development of collective intelligence.[100] Differences need to be respected, with constructive conflicts approached as opportunities for contributing to team learning and effectiveness.

Hardware and software

Effective teaming involves technical and interpersonal challenges that leaders need to articulate. Harvard Business School professor Amy Edmondson holds that leaders must operate both on the teaming hardware and software. The hardware represents the technical component of teaming and encompasses scoping, structuring and sorting:

- **Scoping out the challenge** means identifying the team challenge in a flexible way, determining what expertise is needed, tapping collaborators who possess the relevant expertise, outlining roles and responsibilities, continuously figuring out what resources are necessary to facilitate, nourish and develop the team's collective intelligence.
- **Structuring the boundaries** is akin to 'scaffolding' – a temporary structure that supports the team process (e.g., a list of team members describing pertinent biographical and professional information, a communication platform, visits to teammates' facilities or temporary shared office space).

- **Sorting tasks for execution** involves prioritizing work according to the degree (and type, pooled, sequential, reciprocal) of interdependence among team members.

The teaming software represents the social-relational features of teamwork that impel team members to act as if they trust one another, to cooperate toward a common purpose, to manage conflict in constructive ways, and to learn from mistakes and failures. Leaders use four tools to develop teaming software:

- **Emphasizing purpose**. Purpose is the ultimate goal of the team and is built around shared values. Team members must have a clear notion of their purpose, which should be emphasized frequently by the team leader. This does not mean that the purpose is static and rigid. The rescue of 33 Chilean miners trapped in the collapse of the San José Mine, in 2010, is illustrative[101] (see Figure 7.6). The purpose as articulated by the team leaders was to bring the miners home alive. From the very beginning the purpose was explicitly framed so that it could shift, however, in anticipation of the worst scenario, to returning the bodies to their families. Across the entire mission, André Sougarret, the rescue leader, often highlighted the team's purpose – a powerful energizer to pursue a clear mission in a tough context (the Atacama Desert), with a low probability of success (experts had estimated the probability of locating and rescuing the missing miners alive as less than 1%).[102]
- **Building psychological safety**. Psychological safety, the team members' sense that they can be 'themselves', is crucial for team learning (including from failures, setbacks and errors) and flourishing. Accordingly, this chapter dedicates a specific section to the topic of psychological safety (see below). Team leaders may foster it by encouraging team members to speak up,[103] acknowledging ignorance about a topic or area of expertise, assuming fallibility, admitting mistakes and failures and behaving with humility[104] (see Chapter 8).
- **Embracing failures and mistakes**. In pursuing a purpose with specific goals, teams need to explore new ways of doing things, in circumstances that are not predictable. Failures and mistakes are therefore likely and the most effective way of handling them is to learn from them – instead of playing a 'blame game'. Embracing failure with a learning approach requires psychological safety and a sense of individual and collective humility.[105]
- **Putting conflict to work**. When individuals have different backgrounds, come from different cultures and espouse different values and beliefs, conflict is more likely. Managed in appropriate ways, conflict may provide an antidote to groupthink, help manage cross-disciplinary problems and contribute to better decisions. Different perspectives may help team members reframe a problem or opportunity from various angles of vision and find more creative solutions. A team leader may foster constructive conflict by promoting psychological safety and mutual respect, helping members to reflect on their personal values and biases.

Teaming hardware and software are tightly intertwined. The complex and fruitful interplay between them underpins quality interactions (see Chapter 6). Furthermore, it supports five behaviours for successful teaming:

Figure 7.6 The team that rescued 33 trapped miners at the San José mine, Chile, and the Minister of Mining, Laurence Golborne, at a press conference the day after the rescue, October 13, 2010.[106]

- **Speaking up** – team members communicate openly and honestly with others (by asking questions, assuming errors and failures, raising issues, sharing information, explaining ideas).
- **Experimenting** – team members recognize the novelty and uncertainty inherent in the interactions and the whole context, remaining open to new possibilities and plans.
- **Reflecting** – team members observe, question, discuss processes and outcomes, in order to rethink the ways things are done.
- **Listening actively and intently** – team members pay active attention to what others know, think, say and do.
- **Integrating** – team members, individually and collectively, synthesize different views, approaches and facts to create new possibilities.

These five behaviours influence each other. For example, team members are less likely to speak up if others, including the leaders, do not listen actively. Speaking-up behaviours help the team to reflect. Reflecting is necessary for integrating different perspectives and creating new possibilities.

Teaming virtual teams

Norm rather than exception

Effective teaming is more relevant with virtual teams than with any other work arrangement. Virtual teams are those where 'members use technology to varying degrees in working across locational, temporal, and relational boundaries to accomplish an interdependent task'.[107] Virtual teams are becoming commonplace (examples in Box 7.4) as a result of various factors:[108] distributed expertise in a globalized world, organizations' need for rapid product development and innovation, and more effective networking and collaboration technologies that support e-collaboration. Jimenez and colleagues observe that 'working across boundaries has become the norm, rather than an exception, with members of such teams being not just full-time or part-time employees but also freelancers, contractors, suppliers, and other collaborators'.[109] According to these authors:

> More recent studies report that between 50 and 70% of all white-collar workers in OECD countries at least occasionally work on projects that require some form of virtual collaboration, and of those 20 to 35% involve collaborations across national borders – and the number of such interactions is increasing.[110]

Box 7.4 Global virtual teams

Consider the following five examples of global virtual teams (beginning with our own):

1   The authors of this textbook (from three different locations across two different countries) worked as a true global virtual team during the writing process. Over the course of about two years, three of us never met face to face, and the fourth met face to face with the other three on only two or three occasions. Each of us wrote some parts of the book while working abroad. On the whole, five countries were 'involved' in the writing process (Portugal, Australia, USA, Colombia, Italy). The job was facilitated by face-to-face encounters and mutual trust developed before the book writing was initiated. But two of the authors had never met face to face before or during the process of writing the book – this happened only after having submitted the book.

2   'A multinational engineering firm seeking to develop a product ... assigns the relevant internationally located employees to complete the task as a global virtual team. The senior project manager is located in the firm's London office, the project manager is in Shanghai and the project leader is located in Boston.'[111]

3   'The marketing team of a multinational pharmaceutical company had 17 members in different locations [Moscow, Singapore, Tokyo, London, Boston].'[112]

4   Individuals from 16 organizations (including multinational corporations, local government agencies and startups) formed a consortium, led by Bouygues Immobilier, to develop a run-down Paris suburb into an ecologically and technologically 'smart' (ecologically viable, high-tech, liveable) neighbourhood.[113]

5   The editors of a special issue of the *Journal of International Management*, on global virtual teams, wrote: 'the editors of this special issue are based in North America, Europe and Australia: we have never met face-to-face in preparing this special issue, nor have we been in one same location while working on it'.[114]

The composition, size, boundaries and purposes of virtual teams are diverse. Some may have a stable composition in the pursuit of a specific and short- or medium-term goal (e.g., the authorial team of this book). Conversely, others may have a very fluid composition and pursue a longer-term goal (e.g., designing and building the Water Cube for the Beijing 2008 Olympic Games).[115] They may be composed (a) by individuals from the same organization working in different locations or (b) by individuals from different organizations via outsourcing, supply chains, distributions networks or joint ventures. Although, by definition, a virtual team may be composed of individuals working in different locations within the same country and time zone, increasing numbers of virtual teams are composed of individuals working in different countries and time zones. Those teams are named 'global virtual teams',[116] their complexity emerging from the interplay between three dimensions: location, distance and time (Figure 7.7).

Advantages and benefits

Virtual teams, in their global format, provide several advantages, opportunities and benefits to organizations and team members,[118] including the following:

- Virtual teams can be composed of the more qualified and skilled individuals for the task, regardless of their physical or organizational location.
- By offering remote working options, organizations are better able to attract and retain valuable employees that are not willing to move abroad or commute frequently.
- Dispersing team members around the globe allows for a 24-hour relay workflow, i.e., working around the clock: 'members located in Asia and Australia work on the project during their business hours, pass it on to their colleagues in Europe/Africa for further processing during their business hours, and then on to the colleagues in Americas, who can work on it while their Eastern team members are

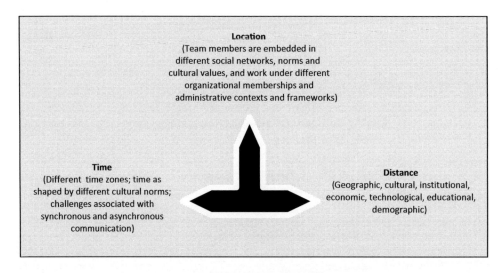

Figure 7.7 The three-dimensional nature of global virtual teams.[117]

asleep, and then back on to the team members in Asia in Australia when their new day starts. This can dramatically speed up project completion time'.[119]

- Virtual teams provide an 'effective structural mechanism for handling increased travel, time, coordination, and costs associated with bringing together geographically, temporally, and functionally dispersed employees to work on a common task'.[120]

- Cultural diversity and diverse backgrounds may provide a greater diversity of perspectives and a wider range of information, knowledge and cognitive sources, with potential positive consequences for adaptability, creativity and problem solving.

- Considering the challenges associated with virtual teams and the greater autonomy of their members, it is possible that individuals experience higher levels of motivation and job satisfaction.

Problems and difficulties

Virtual teams have advantages but also pose problems and difficulties (see examples in Box 7.5) that may jeopardize potential benefits:[121]

- Time-zone differences may make it more difficult to maintain a healthy work–life balance. A Spanish team member may have to interact with an Australian member when it is 16:00 in Madrid but 24:00 in Sydney.

- Communications may be delayed. An email message sent from Madrid at 16:00 may be received in Australia nine hours later, when the Australian arrives at the office in the morning. Scheduling a virtual meeting, through a live teleconference or videoconference, at a reasonable time for all team members may be difficult.

- The absence of face-to-face communication and interactions in the same physical space may complicate the coordination and passage of tacit knowledge. It is more difficult to develop transactive memory ('who knows what'), which is highly dependent on shared experiences within a common context[122] (e.g., distance between members make them less aware of cues signalling different views, thus leading to a false sense of agreement).

- Differences in native languages and proficiency levels of team members in the working language may make style more difficult, the differences giving rise to unbalanced teamwork contributions.

- Different cultural values, beliefs and assumptions may give rise to conflicts. For example, communicational assertiveness, so highly prized by Americans, may collide with the face-saving preferences of Asian members,[123] leading Asian team members to conclude that their American colleagues are aggressive, while the latter may think that their Asian colleagues are unforthcoming with opinions and advice.

- Team dispersion creates social distance, making it more difficult to detect and manage conflict among team members. Moreover, cultural and background differences may even produce dormant fault lines (more on this below).

- With team members representing different organizations, or at least different offices in the same organization, incompatible rules, procedures, protocols, goals, careers and performance appraisal systems may originate conflicts and coordination problems, and even aggravate fault lines.

- Non-verbal communication (e.g., gestures, voice tone, facial expressions) is absent in several electronic media channels (mainly email). Although videoconference technology has developed significantly, it cannot fully replace face-to-face contact, so important for building interpersonal trust, commitment and cohesion.
- The complex interplay between the difficulties and challenges mentioned above makes it more difficult to build trust. This difficulty is aggravated by the short life span of many virtual teams, 'as it is harder for members to gain the knowledge and shared experiences required for trust development'.[124] Difficulties in building trust give rise to a paradoxical challenge: considering the 'distance' between team members, trust is more necessary for lubricating the team processes and improving team effectiveness.[125] Trust is accordingly 'the glue of the global workplace'.[126]

Another potential problem, reinforcing and reinforced by those discussed above, relates to perceptions of power relations:[127]

> If most team members are located in Germany, for instance, with two or three in the United States and in South Africa, there may be a sense that the German members have more power. This imbalance sets up a negative dynamic. People in the larger (majority) group may feel resentment toward the minority group, believing that the latter will try to get away with contributing less than its fair share. Meanwhile, those in the minority group may believe that the majority is usurping what little power and voice they have. The situation is exacerbated when the leader is at the site with the most people or the one closest to company headquarters: team members at that site tend to ignore the needs and contributions of their colleagues at other locations.

Perceptions of power imbalance may even operate within teams whose members work at different locations within the same country. The emerging ingroups and outgroups can give rise to fault lines.

Box 7.5 Disconnects here and there

'Clearly, there is a disconnect here'

Cultural differences between members of virtual teams recommend that team leaders develop cross-cultural skills. Note what the *Virtual Teams Survey Report, 2016* stated about this issue:[128]

> It appears that team leaders believe they are better prepared to lead intercultural teams than do those who are members of their teams. For example, 58% of respondents (who are participants on teams) indicate that global team leaders are *not* adequately prepared to lead multicultural teams. But when we asked respondents who self-identified as leaders of teams to rate *their own* ability to lead effectively across countries and cultures, nearly all of them (96%) rated themselves as either effective or highly effective! Moreover, 98% of respondents

said they are comfortable leading multicultural teams (vs. local teams). Almost the same percentage (96%) said they are comfortable leading virtual teams (vs. leading collocated teams) ... While 98% of self-identified global team leaders were happy with their intercultural leadership skills, only 19% of team members felt that the great majority of their team leaders were well prepared for the challenge ... Clearly, there is a disconnect here.

What does it mean to be a 'rounded individual'?

While working in China, Jennifer Cable had a conversation with colleagues about being a rounded individual. 'They genuinely thought I was encouraging them to eat more,' recalls Ms. Cable, a talent management expert at PA Consulting. When working virtually, the potential for such mix-ups is magnified, she says. 'When we communicate, so much is picked up from body language'.[129]

Leadership challenges

Considering the advantages and difficulties mentioned above, monitoring, managing and leading virtual teams is significantly more challenging than managing traditional face-to-face teams.[130] Leaders must be particularly effective in developing the hardware and software of teaming. Several leadership behaviours that can help this process include (for a practitioner perspective consult Box 7.6): (a) improving the frequency and the quality of communication between team members, (b) providing guidance and coaching, and developing shared leadership, (c) facilitating knowledge sharing and enhancing interactions among team members (i.e., fostering team shared mental models and transactive memory; see Box 7.2), (d) investing time in developing coordinated efforts, (e) managing conflict, (f) showing professional respect and supporting each team member, and (g) building trust. Cross-cultural skills are additionally important for handling cultural differences between team members. Surprisingly, evidence suggests that many leaders are unaware of such a challenge.

Box 7.6 Nine key recommendations to lead virtual teams: a practitioner's perspective[131]

1 **Team charter.** One of the first activities of the team should be creating rules, structures and guidelines for team interaction (regarding, e.g., how meeting times are scheduled, expectations about participation and debate, and rules for expressing disagreements).
2 **Agenda.** An agenda should be circulated beforehand so that team members have the necessary time to formulate their thoughts and questions.

3   **Summary notes**. After each meeting, a short recap must be distributed so team members understand what happened.

4   **Time–zone rotation**. To accommodate participants' schedules in different time zones, it is also important to vary the time of meetings. In this way, the inconvenience of attending meetings is spread more fairly.

5   **Trust**. Individuals should adhere to their commitments and invest in relationships with other individuals.

6   **Relationships**. Developing relationships may be facilitated by procedures such as allowing time to share some personal information (e.g., hobbies, vacations, interests).

7   **Participation**. Efforts must be made for all team members to participate in discussions.

8   **Language difficulties**. It is crucial to create an environment where team members can ask questions for clarification, and thereby minimize misunderstandings emerging for language differences.

9   **Offline discussions**. It is important 'to set aside particularly challenging situations and negative feedback for a separate, private discussion, at which time it can be addressed more appropriately'.[132]

Psychological safety

Beyond interpersonal trust

The notion of psychological safety has been popularized by Amy Edmondson whose interest in the topic developed when a graduate student. At the time she was studying hospital teams, seeking to identify the factors that characterize high performance. She hypothesized that the highest performing teams would make the least amount of medical mistakes. Her data, however, suggested the opposite – the best performing teams made significantly more mistakes than the poor performing teams. Further analysis revealed why, as reported by Lebowitz in *Business Insider*:[133]

> It wasn't that the best teams were making the most errors, but that the best teams were admitting to errors and discussing them more often than other groups did. In other words, what distinguished the best performing teams was psychological safety, which facilitated a 'climate of openness'.

Team psychological safety is the best predictor of team performance.[134] Team psychological safety reflects the 'shared belief' that it is safe for team members to take interpersonal risks within the team,[135] which occurs when team members 'both trust and respect each other, and it produces a sense of confidence that the group won't embarrass, reject or punish someone for speaking up'.[136] Consequently, psychological safety not only involves but also goes beyond interpersonal trust (see Chapter 6).

Within psychologically safe environments, team members are more likely to ask for help and advice, to seek information from other team members to introduce change, to speak up to test assumptions about issues under discussion, to invite people from outside the team to present information, to offer constructive suggestions, to share ideas, knowledge and experiences, to discuss improvement possibilities, to acknowledge mistakes (thus preventing others from making the same mistakes), to experiment and learn from errors and failures.[137] Edmondson and Lei observed that 'a psychologically safe environment … motivates engagement in exploratory and exploitative learning',[138] critical for learning and the unfolding of organizational change. Team psychological safety improves decision quality, fostering information sharing, team learning, team creativity and innovation, as well as team performance.[139] In support of Edmondson's findings, Google has similarly recently concluded that its highest-performing teams have one thing in common: psychological safety (Box 7.7).[140]

Box 7.7 Project Aristotle

A Google project code-named Project Aristotle (a tribute to Aristotle's quote, 'the whole is greater than the sum of its parts')[141] sought to identify the characteristics of effective teams. Over two years, Google conducted more than 200 interviews with its employees and looked at more than 250 attributes of more than 180 active Google teams. According to a company report, the analysis showed that '*Who* is on a team matters less than how the team members interact, structure their work, and view their contributions'.[142] The five key dynamics that set successful teams apart from other teams at Google were identified as:

- **Psychological safety**: Team members feel safe to take risks and be vulnerable in front of each other.
- **Dependability**: Team members get things done on time and meet Google's high bar for excellence.
- **Structure & clarity**: Team members have clear roles, plans, and goals.
- **Meaning**: Work is personally important to team members.
- **Impact**: Team members think their work matters and creates change.

The Google report also stated that psychological safety 'was far and away the most important of the five dynamics we found – it's the underpinning of the other four'. Amit Singh, president of Google for Work, explained:[143]

> Diversity of thought is actually the most invaluable thing in a business community. If we're always agreeing with each other, then we haven't gone down paths of debate that allow new ideas to emerge. Some of the best discussions are passionate but respectful, so that you leave a meeting without feeling like you've lost something, even though your point of view may not have been the one that was adopted. That is what fosters innovation in a company – a clash of ideas, but a respectful clash.

How to promote team psychological safety

Team members with some specific personality attributes (e.g., higher levels of proactive personality, emotional stability, openness to experience, learning orientation)[144] are more likely to experience psychological safety. Organizations and teams may thus increase team psychological safety by selecting team members who possess such attributes. Several contextual characteristics, such as work design (e.g., characterized by high autonomy, interdependence and role clarity[145] which are also discussed in Chapter 5), a supportive work context and high-quality relationships (see Chapter 6) also facilitate team psychological safety. Leadership is also particularly relevant (Table 7.2). As Edmondson noted,

> the most important influence on psychological safety is the nearest boss. Signals sent by people in power are critical to employees' ability and willingness to offer their ideas and observations. This means that levels of psychological safety vary strikingly from department to department and work group to work group, even in organizations known for having a powerful corporate culture. [146]

Table 7.2 Promoting team psychological safety: guidelines for leaders[147]

• Frame work as a learning challenge, not as merely an execution one.	• Foster a team atmosphere where errors and failures are assumed and taken as opportunities for learning.
• Be humble: acknowledge your fallibility, and respect and value the talents and contributions of others.	• Foster a team climate characterized by 'healthy disrespect' (between team members and between them and you).[148] Respect those who disagree with your opinions and views.
• Be trustworthy.	• Coach your team. Share information and knowledge.
• Practice active listening.	• Approach conflict with a win–win stance, not as a zero-sum game.
• Model curiosity and ask lots of questions.	• Treat team members as human adults who have needs such as respect, competence, social status and autonomy.
• Walk the talk.	• Ask for feedback on how you deliver your messages.
• Don't kill the messenger of bad news.	• Soften power cues (e.g., your grandiose office or desk) that make people fear to speak up.
• Welcome speaking-up behaviours. With your behaviours, send a message to your team: 'Please speak up'.	• Do not assume that silence from team members represents assent or agreement. They may fear the consequences of speaking up or experience a sense of futility. ('No matter how open you are as a manager, our research shows, many of your people are more likely to keep mum than to question initiatives or suggest new ideas at work'.[149])
• Don't punish honest mistakes.	• Don't assume that your genuine desire to foster speaking up in your organization is replicated at all levels.
• Replace blame and criticism with curiosity – be factual, engage individuals in an exploration and ask them for solutions.	• Measure psychological safety. Don't take it for granted.

Team learning = team psychological safety multiplied by accountability

In a knowledge-based economy, a focus only on efficient execution inhibits team members' ability to learn and innovate.[150] Within such a strict task-oriented atmosphere, team members avoid experimentation and reflection, which are vital to continuous team learning and sustainable performance. Competition, markets and customers change continuously, today success, tomorrow nothing. A team risks being efficient in creating products and services with diminishing appeal to customers.

A mindset focussed on efficient execution may lead to counterproductive behaviours. Critical information and ideas fail to rise to upper levels where decisions are made: when team members 'get the message that speed, efficiency, and results are what matter, they become exceedingly reluctant to risk taking up managers' time with anything but the most certain and positive inputs'.[151] Because adopting new approaches and practices can give rise to errors and lower performance in the short run, team members don't have enough time to reflect upon and question the current processes, to experiment, to change and to learn.

Such an approach is particularly problematic because sustainable performance is increasingly determined by factors that cannot be controlled, such as intelligent experimentation, ingenuity, learning from error, resilience in the face of failures (see Box 7.8), obstacles and adversity. Therefore, organizations and teams must focus more on *execution-as-learning* rather than simply on *efficient execution*. Such an approach provides several benefits:[152]

- Team members, individually and collectively, use the best knowledge to make the best decisions when addressing problems and opportunities.
- Team members cooperate by making information available when and where it is needed. They share knowledge, information and ideas, thus fostering, on an ongoing basis, both a productive mental model and a rich transactive memory (see Box 7.2).
- Team members routinely reflect and capture process data to discover how work is being done, using those data to identify ways for improving processes, introducing change and sustaining performance.

Box 7.8 Learning from failures: reported evidence on the positive of the negative

The following quotes are statements from different organizations about their positive orientations towards mistakes:

Fail fast, fail cheap. At OutSystems errors are acceptable. How are you going to learn if you don't make mistakes? Just make sure that you learn from those mistakes and that those mistakes do not end up being a major crisis. Fail fast and fail cheaply, but don't be afraid of trying. Be proactive.[153]

'**Fostering greater creativity by celebrating failure**. After experiencing his own epic professional stumble, Tor Myhren vowed to foster creativity by banishing fear of failure.'[154]

'**This process requires employees to be able to make mistakes without fear**' (Ed Catmul, Pixar's co-founder, on 'Pixar's formula for creativity').[155]

'Why Etsy engineers send company-wide emails confessing mistakes they made' ... Fear of failure is often baked into workplace culture in a way that makes people either unwilling to take risks, inclined towards hiding mistakes, or too ready to blame others. Etsy, the recently public craft-focused e-commerce site, has made a concerted effort to change that. In a conversation ... with *Quartz* editor-in-chief Kevin Delaney, Etsy CEO Chad Dickerson revealed that people at the company are encouraged to document their mistakes and how they happened, in public emails. 'It's called a PSA and people will send out an email to the company or a list of people saying I made this mistake, here's how I made that mistake, don't you make this mistake,' Dickerson said. 'So that's proactive and I think really demonstrates that the culture is self-perpetuating' ... The company also gives out an annual award – a real three-armed sweater – to an employee who's made an error. This demonstrates that accidents are seen as a source of data, not something embarrassing to shy away from, according to Allspaw. The sweater goes to whomever who made the most surprising error, not the worst one, as a reminder to examine the gap between how things are expected to happen and how they actually do.[156]

A crucial requisite of team learning is psychological safety.[157] However, team learning and effectiveness also require a strong sense of accountability (Figure 7.8). In highly effective teams, team leaders generate psychological safety (Table 7.2) but also demand and set high performance expectations:[158]

- They establish standard processes aimed at facilitating both efficiency and learning. For example, the design firm IDEO adheres to a standard process for developing its innovative products, with even the value of interpersonal help supported through formal processes and explicit roles.[159]
- They foster conditions that enable team members to cooperate in real time, i.e., to make cooperative decisions in response to unforeseen, novel, and complex problems and opportunities.
- They invite team members who deviate from process guidelines to inform the system, thus helping the whole team to learn and to become more effective in pursuing team goals.
- They institutionalize disciplined reflection by assuring that the team actually dissects what is going right and what is going wrong, thereby learning from mistakes, improving processes, thus preventing some future failures.

Should teams fear speaking up?

One of best ways to understand why psychological safety is crucial for team learning and organizational change is to pay attention to the tragic consequences of its absence. There is evidence to suggest that the Volkswagen emissions scandal was associated with low levels of psychological safety and employees' fear of speaking up.[161] Wells Fargo's fake accounts scandal may also be explained, at least partially, by a fear of

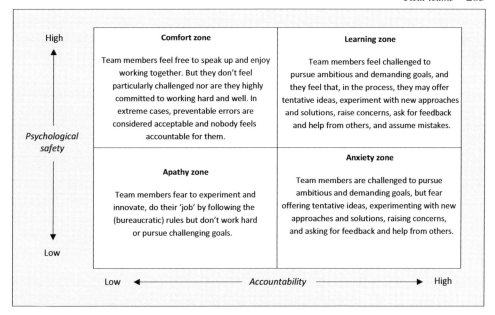

Figure 7.8 Psychological safety x accountability = team learning.[160]

speaking up. Maryam Kouchaki wrote in *Fortune* that 'whatever the sources of the scandalous Wells Fargo behaviour, the news raises the issue of *moral "muteness"*, or people's reluctance to communicate their moral concerns and speak up about unethical behaviors in the workplace'.[162]

On January 16, 1977, a McDonnell Douglas DC-8-62AF, operated by Japan Air Lines (JAL 8054), departed from Anchorage International Airport, Alaska, US. The destination was Tokyo-Haneda, Japan. Shortly after take off, the aircraft crashed. The three crewmembers and the two cargo handlers aboard the aircraft died in the accident. The accident report summarized the event as follows[163] (see Box 7.9):

> The National Transportation Safety Board determines that the probable cause of the accident was a stall that resulted from the pilot's control inputs aggravated by airframe icing while the pilot was under the influence of alcohol. Contributing to the cause of this accident was the failure of the other flight crew members to prevent the captain from attempting the flight.

This tragic consequence epitomizes how a low level of psychological safety to challenge authority figures may undermine team functioning and effectiveness. It is noteworthy that there have been other air crashes involving flight crews from high power-distance cultures (e.g., Korea and Colombia),[164] where deference toward authority figures is socially valued and a lack of will to challenge their decisions[165] has been found at least partially responsible.

Box 7.9 A drunken pilot who was not challenged by the crew

The pilot condition before and after the crash of Japan Air Lines 8054 on January 13, 1977 and the behaviour of the other crewmembers were reported as follows:[166]

> The taxicab driver who brought the outbound crew to the airport stated that he became concerned by the captain's actions in the taxi and called his dispatcher to report his impressions. About 04:50 the taxi dispatcher called the operations agent for the contract maintenance company and reported that one of her drivers had taken an 'intoxicated' JAL captain to the airport. The operations agent stated that ' … it seemed logical that JAL would detect anything unusual and act accordingly.' He further stated that at 06:20, he notified his line manager of the conversation with the taxi dispatcher and that 'I felt that if the captain was intoxicated JAL OPS … or his first officer would have stopped the flight immediately.' The JAL dispatch personnel and the inbound JAL crew stated that they noted nothing unusual about the outbound crew.
>
> The initial blood alcohol level of the captain was 298 mgs percent and a vitreous alcohol level of 310 mgs percent recorded in test conducted 12 hours after the accident by the Alaska Medical Laboratory. A blood alcohol level of 100 mgs percent is considered to be legally intoxicating for drivers in the state of Alaska … Of the 13 persons interviewed regarding the captain's activities before reporting to the airport, 5 close acquaintances said that he showed no signs of drinking or that he had not had a drink in their presence. Six persons who were not closely acquainted with the captain stated that he had been drinking or showed signs of being under the influence of alcohol within the 12 hours before the scheduled flight.
>
> The captain's physical and mental states were such that he could not effectively control the aircraft. The amount of alcohol in his system would have severely hampered his reactions, coordination and reasoning ability. It is extremely difficult for crewmembers to challenge a captain even when the captain offers a threat to the safety of the flight. The concept of command authority and its inviolate nature, except in the case of incapacitation, has become a practice without exception. As a result, second-in-command pilots react indifferently in circumstances where they should be more assertive.

Contrary to what is often assumed, most air crashes are the consequence of human errors (e.g., problems in coordination and interpersonal communication within the cockpit, an inability to challenge poor decisions made by the commander, excessive deference toward authority).[167] Over the years, several procedures and measures have been adopted to improve the relationships within the cockpit and between them and crew members. Consequently, the number of air crashes has significantly decreased over the last decades.[168] 'Crew resource management' (CRM) is one such measure aimed at reducing the power imbalance among crew members, increasing information fluidity and improving communication and decision-making processes[169] (see Figure 7.9).

Figure 7.9 The aircrew conducting CRM training at the Naval Air Station in Sigonella, Sicily (May 6, 2003).[173]

CRM is a process focussed on developing team spirit, communication fluidity and information sharing without the constraints of the command-and-control traditionally practiced by the pilots. CRM training therefore aims at developing a leadership process characterized by two crucial interrelated components:[170]

- Authority with participation: the captain exerts authority but is open to listen to other crew members and to accept being contradicted by any team member.
- Assertiveness with respect: the other crew members, while respecting the captain, communicate openly and frankly and confront him/her with possible mistakes he/she is committing.

The CRM philosophy is nowadays applied to other fields (emergency rooms in hospitals, medical surgery teams, merchant navy, offshore oil and gas industry, nuclear power industry)[171] and is valuable for all kinds of organizations.[172]

Building and destroying collective intelligence

The 'c factor'

Whether some teams are more intelligent than others was a question posed by *The New York Times*.[174] The response, supported by research in scientific journals,[175] concluded that:

> Individual intelligence, as psychologists measure it, is defined by its generality: People with good vocabularies, for instance, also tend to have good math skills, even though we often think of those abilities as distinct. The results of our studies

showed that this same kind of general intelligence ['c factor'[176]] also exists for teams. On average, the groups that did well on one task did well on the others, too. In other words, some teams were simply smarter than others.

Does this mean that teams whose members have higher IQ are smarter? The answer is negative. According to the authors, the teams with a higher collective intelligence or 'c factor' can be distinguished by three characteristics (see also Box 7.10). First, their members contributed more equally to the team's discussions. Contributions were balanced. Second, in smarter teams, members scored higher on a test called, 'Reading the mind in the eyes'. This test measures how individuals are able to read complex emotional states from images of faces with only the eyes visible. Third, teams with more women outperformed teams with more men. This effect was partially explained by the fact that women tended to score higher on the mindreading test.

In another study,[177] the authors tested whether groups that work online still express collective intelligence, and whether social ability also matters for them. They found[178] that 'online and off, some teams consistently worked smarter than others. More surprisingly, the most important ingredients for a smart team remained constant regardless of the medium of interaction: members who communicated a lot participated equally and possessed good emotion-reading skills'. The authors concluded:[179]

> What makes teams smart must be not just the ability to read facial expressions, but a more general ability, known as 'Theory of Mind', to consider and keep track of what other people feel, know and believe.

Box 7.10 Building collective intelligence: are team members like human sensors?

Tony Hsieh, Zappos' CEO, explained the meaning and relevance of collective intelligence in the following way:[180]

> I don't watch a lot of sports – except the Super Bowl – but even if I don't know who's playing, I do know that the sports-betting market, more than any other method that I'm aware of, does an amazing job of telling you what the right odds are. It does that by using the collective intelligence of the group. To harness collective intelligence, we think of every single employee as a human sensor. Everyone senses different things, and you want a way to process all of that input. An airplane is one analogy. There are all of these different sensors. Some sensors, like the altimeter, are probably more important than others, but you want to be aware of all of them. Even if the altimeter looks fine, and most of the other sensors look fine, that doesn't mean it's OK to ignore the low-voltage warning light when it turns on. You don't allow the other sensors to outvote the low-voltage warning light and ignore it, yet the analogous thing happens all the time in organizations.

Questions for reflection

- How does team psychological safety contribute to team collective intelligence?
- Imagine a team whose members act as human sensors to collect information and, at the same time, do not share that information with other team members. What team and leadership conditions are necessary for the collected information to be shared and used in the service of more effective decisions?
- Revisit Box 7.1 on 'groupthink'. Is groupthink a consequence of weak collective intelligence? What happens to the human sensors when groupthink develops within the team?

The '3e' approach: energy, engagement and exploration

Research carried out by Pentland[181] at MIT's Human Dynamics Laboratory corroborates the relevance of team communication patterns for team performance. The findings showed that successful teams shared the following characteristics:

- Team members contributed equally to the team's discussions, by talking and listening in roughly equal measure. Nobody, including the leader, dominates the communicational flow.
- Contributions were 'short and sweet',[182] i.e., communication was assertive *and* respectful (e.g., individuals actively and attentively listen and do not cut others off).
- Face-to-face communication prevailed over digital messages, with verbal and non-verbal communication being more energetic.
- Team members communicated directly with one another, not just through the leader. They did this during both work and in non-working hours.
- Team members carried on back channel or side conversations within the team.
- Team members periodically made a break, went exploring outside the team, bringing back new information.

These communication behaviours are the foundations for three key communication elements (Figure 7.10): energy, engagement and exploration. Energy represents the number and nature (e.g., face to face versus online) of exchanges for each team member. Energy is high when the team members frequently communicate with others face to face. Engagement represents the distribution of energy among team members. It is stronger when all members share an equally high level of energy with all others. Exploration represents the energy that team members share with members from other teams. Considering that energy is 'a finite resource',[183] embarking on both engagement and exploration may be problematic: the more energy the team members devote to their own team members (i.e., engagement), the less energy they have to communicate with members of other teams (i.e., exploration). Successful teams balance both: they *explore outside* the team for discovering ideas and *engage within* the team for integrating those ideas. This oscillation is crucial for team creativity.

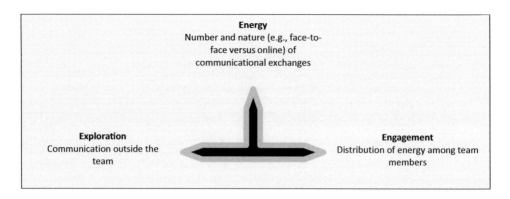

Figure 7.10 Three key elements of communication, according to Pentland.[184]

Team diversity: bright and dark

Collective intelligence develops, in part, because team members are diverse and such diversity is supported and channelled through positive communication patterns to improve team creativity, change, learning and performance. 'Diversity' represents 'the distribution of differences among the members of a unit with respect to a common attribute X, such as tenure, ethnicity, conscientiousness, task attitude, or pay'.[185] Three types of diversity may be considered: separation, variety and disparity:[186]

- **Separation** describes differences in opinions, beliefs, values and attitudes among team members (see Box 7.11).
- **Variety** represents differences in kind or category (e.g., information, knowledge, content expertise, functional background, network ties or experience) among team members.
- **Disparity** characterizes differences in concentration of valued social assets or resources such as pay, income, prestige, status, authority and power among team members.[187]

Does team diversity contribute to better team functioning and performance? The evidence is ambiguous, inconsistent and sometimes contradictory.[188] Diversity may enrich the array of knowledge and skills available within the team and thus contribute to better decisions and to prevent groupthink. Diversity may also contribute to creative and innovative solutions and therefore to instilling change in the system. However, diversity may also contribute to communication problems, misunderstandings, conflicts and cooperation problems. Moreover, the effects of diversity may be contingent on factors such as task characteristics, leadership styles, team member attitudes toward diversity and the competitive environment.[189] For example, diversity is more positively associated with team performance when the task and the competitive environment are volatile, complex or uncertain.[190] Diversity provides the team with the

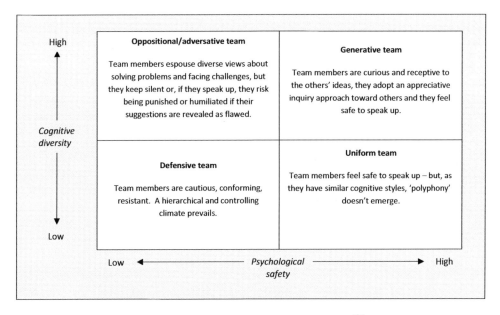

Figure 7.11 Cognitive diversity x psychological safety = generative teams.[194]

variety and flexibility necessary for dealing with such circumstances. Team diversity is also more positively related to performance when team members are interdependent, collocated and engaged in frequent decentralized information exchange and productive discussions.[191]

Therefore, team diversity, per se, is not enough. Psychological safety is also necessary for building generative teams.[192] When a team is cognitively diverse[193] (e.g., team members differ in how they process information) but characterized by low psychological safety, the team turns into an oppositional and adversarial arena (see Figure 7.11). In those teams, individuals espouse different approaches to solve problems and face challenges – but they keep silent or, if they speak up, they risk being punished or humiliated if their suggestions are revealed as flawed. If the team members are cognitively homogeneous and psychological safety is low, the team turns into a defensive arena.

The effect of diversity also depends on the *type* of diversity, as different types affect different processes and outcomes.[195] While separation and variety may lead to better creative outcomes, disparity may damage cooperation. It is also important to stress that, although the literature tends to treat diversity as an 'objective condition' of teams, *perceived* diversity (i.e., the members' awareness of differences) may be more relevant for team functioning than objective diversity,[196] as individuals react on the basis of their perception of reality rather than on reality itself. Finally, considering that team boundaries are fluid, team diversity is not static.[197] Therefore, team variety, team separation and team disparity evolve over time, as a consequence of team membership additions, substitutions and subtractions.[198]

Box 7.11 Which kind of team member are you – driver, guardian, integrator or pioneer?

Different team members have diverse work styles. Four main styles can be considered.[199]

- **Drivers** (results-oriented) are logical, focussed, competitive and deeply curious. They feel energized by solving problems, directness and winning. They are de-energized by indecision, inefficiency and lack of focus.
- **Guardians** (process-oriented) are methodical, reserved, detail-oriented and structured. They feel energized by predictability and consistency, clear procedures and detailed plans. They dislike disorder, time pressure and ambiguity and uncertainty.
- **Integrators** (people-oriented) are empathic, relationship-oriented and non-confrontational. They feel energized by collaboration, trust and respect. They feel alienated by politics and conflict.
- **Pioneers** (ideas-oriented) are spontaneous, adaptable and imaginative. They feel energized by brainstorming, trying new things and creative and innovative endeavours. They dislike rules and structures and detailed procedures.

Are these differences within a team problematic for team functioning and effectiveness? Vickerg and Christfort[200] argue that gaps and tensions created by differences, if not managed appropriately, may be a source of creativity and innovation. They recommend:[201] 'To foster productive friction, leaders should pull opposite types closer, seek input from people with nondominant styles, and pay attention to sensitive introverts, who risk being drowned out but have essential contributions to make'. In sum: differences between team members may be either problematic or healthy depending on how they are managed. A shared sense of psychological safety is especially important for team diversity contributing towards 'generative teams' (see Figure 7.11).

Do fault lines impair collective intelligence?

To overcome the inconclusive and even contradictory findings on the effects of team diversity, some researchers have focussed not on specific diversity features, but on the impact of several diversity attribute configurations.[202] This idea is captured in the construct of team fault lines, defined as 'hypothetical dividing lines that split a group into two or more subgroups based on the alignment of one or more individual attributes and have been found to influence group processes, performance outcomes, and affective outcomes'.[203] This definition represents *dormant* fault lines, which differ from *actual* fault lines in that the latter are actually perceived by team members.[204] This distinction 'is similar to that made in the diversity literature between objective (e.g., actual) diversity and perceived diversity'.[205] Dormant and active fault lines are highly correlated. And although active fault lines are more inhibiting to team functioning and performance, dormant fault lines have consequences for the team functioning even when they are not activated, i.e., perceived.[206] Dormant fault lines may become active via triggers, events or situations that make team members perceive the existence of subgroups (Box 7.12).

Box 7.12 Can a penalty be a trigger of a dormant fault line?

In 2017, Paris Saint-Germain (PSG), a successful French football team, hired Neymar, a Brazilian superstar (who until then had been a Barcelona player) for €222m. At the time this represented the most expensive transfer in the history of football. Neymar pledged to 'conquer the titles' for PSG and PSG's president, Nasser Al-Khelaifi, who was delighted to get the star, noted: 'Today, with the arrival of Neymar, I am convinced that we will come even closer, with the support of our faithful fans, to realising our greatest dreams'.[207]

Neymar's arrival at PSG, however, created discomfort among some players. A dormant fault line started to unfold. On September 17, 2017, a trigger transformed the dormant fault line into an active one. During a match between PSG and Lyon, when Cavani (the penalty taker in the 2016/2017 season) was carefully placing the ball on the spot, Neymar suddenly blocked him and sour words were exchanged. In the following hours and days, TV images reporting the event spread all over the football world. The *Guardian* explained:[208]

> Within hours of the final whistle, the rumours were already swirling as newspaper reports suggested that the pair had to be separated by team-mates in the dressing room after the match, with Cavani then eschewing his press duties in the mixed zone and sneaking out of a back entrance less than 20 minutes after the match had ended … As the days passed, more rumours began to emerge of the incident's destabilising effect on the PSG squad. The Catalonia-based newspaper *Sport* even went as far to suggest that Neymar informed Khelaifi 'that his coexistence with Cavani is totally impossible and he has asked for the transfer of the Uruguayan striker'.

Dani Alves, another PSG player, trying to calm things down, organized a dinner for the whole squad at an exclusive restaurant. However, it was claimed that the dinner 'had been "as animated as a funeral wake", with the majority of the squad said to have sided firmly with Cavani since Neymar's arrival in Paris'.[209]

On January 17, 2018, the crowd booed Neymar. Reason: he had impeded Cavani from scoring a penalty that would have allowed him to break a personal record.[210] PSG fans chanted 'Cavani, Cavani' as the Brazilian superstar took the penalty. The fault line was described by White and Devin in the *Guardian* as follows:[211]

> At a time when Cavani's standing in the team, at least internally, is already under fire after Thiago Silva offered some harsh words on his late return from holidays – saying that Cavani would 'have to work hard to earn his spot back' – could this be further evidence of a rift? And, if so, could it hinder their lofty ambitions this season, particularly in Europe?

In contrast with the main body of team diversity research, fault lines simultaneously capture the configuration of several diversity attributes. Two teams within the same level of diversity with regard to, for example, age, tenure, gender and background, may differ significantly in terms of the subgroups that emerge in each one (see Box 7.13).

Apparently, some fault lines emerge around a single attribute. For example, a gender fault line may divide team members into male and female subgroups.[212] Marital diversity may give rise to married and singles.[213] An age-based fault line may divide older and young workers.[214] A chronotype fault line may divide individuals who differ in terms of their biological predispositions toward the optimal timing for daily periods of activity and rest,[215] a difference that may give rise to three subgroups: morning, evening or intermediate chronotypes. However, those subgroups tend to differ along several other dimensions. For example, gender may be just the 'tip of the iceberg', and the real fault line may divide younger, less-experienced men from older and very experienced women.[216] The married and single subgroups might differ not just in terms of marital status but also in terms of age, values and attitudes about work. The chronotype subgroups may differ in terms of background, personality, life styles and attitudes toward work. Therefore, the strongest fault lines develop as the consequence of alignments around several attributes or issues.[217]

Box 7.13 The same level of diversity – different fault lines

Meyer and Glenz[218] provided an interesting illustration of how two eight-member medical teams that are equally diverse may develop different fault lines:

> [In a team], there are three young Black scrub nurses, three older Asian surgeons, and two Caucasian middle-aged anaesthesiologists. Compare this team to another medical team of the same size with a young Black, a middle-aged Asian, and an older Caucasian scrub nurse; a young Caucasian, a middle-aged Asian, and an older Black surgeon; and a young Black and an older Asian anaesthesiologist. If we look at the diversity attributes functional background, ethnicity, and age separately, these two teams are equally diverse (three older members, three younger members, and two middle-aged members; three nurses, three surgeons, and two anaesthesiologists; three Blacks, three Asians, two Caucasians). However, these teams differ with regard to the distribution of these diversity attributes, that is, with regard to the hypothetical split of the team. The first team has three homogeneous hypothetical subgroups based on age, ethnicity, and functional background and is thus characterized by a strong fault line that splits these subgroups. In contrast, the second team is what is called a crosscut team, where the hypothetical subgroups that are created by functional background are less homogeneous than in the first team, since age and race vary within functional background.

Thatcher and Patel[219] provided another illustration of how it is necessary to distinguish diversity from fault lines, and why strong fault lines may impede team functioning and effectiveness:

Two teams in a large engineering firm had been working productively together for a number of months. Team A was composed of three experienced male engineers and three relatively new female marketers. The six members of Team B had the same overall demographic makeup as Team A, but the distribution of the demographic attributes differed. The engineers consisted of one experienced female, one experienced male, and one new female. The marketers were composed of one experienced male, one new female, and one new male. Although both teams consist of three engineers, three marketers, three females, three males, three experienced workers, and three new workers, Team A contains a strong dormant fault line and Team B does not. Team A has a strong fault line because the alignment of the demographic characteristics (functional area, gender, experience) creates two relatively homogenous subgroups. Both teams experienced conflict but were generally productive. However, when the issue of bonus allocation among team members came up, everyone was surprised at how quickly Team A degenerated into two squabbling subgroups. The previously dormant fault line became active as a result of a fault line trigger (the bonus allocation decision). What was previously a relatively productive team now experienced increased levels of conflict and mistrust that decreased satisfaction and performance.

Meta-analytic evidence[220] suggests that strong fault lines are associated with perverse consequences for team performance, team organizational citizenship behaviours, creativity, learning, overall team satisfaction, cohesion, trust and respect, even if the fractures are not perceived by team members.[221] These relationships may be mitigated or reinforced by moderators. For example, a transformational leader may mitigate the negative effect of age-based fault lines on team performance.[222] The negative relationships between knowledge-based top management team (TMT) fault lines and team performance may be mitigated when the leader (i.e., the CEO): (a) socio-demographically resembles incumbent executives, (b) possesses a diverse career background, and (c) shares common socialization experiences with other TMT members.[223] Conversely, the salience of subgroup differences may reinforce the negative effect of fault lines.[224] Research has also suggested that the relationship between fault lines and team performance is curvilinear, in that team performance is higher when the strength of fault lines is moderate.[225]

Final comments

Teams are fundamental to many facets of society, from military operations and healthcare systems to research groups, sports franchises and business firms. In these dynamic social-relational bodies, individuals accomplish work through united efforts and interdependent actions towards realizing common goals. The collective outcome may be superior to the sum of individuals' outcomes, provided that the teams pursue a significant purpose, facilitate task coordination and interpersonal bonding, produce synergistic gains and create a higher level of collective intelligence. However, when communication patterns are poor and unbalanced and faults manifest with a fear of speaking up taking reign, then the collective outcome may be worse than the sum of individuals' potential and outcomes. The result can even be tragic, as in the Volkswagen diesel-emissions scandal and in air crashes that result from a pilot's 'male mentality' contributing to low states of psychological safety. This chapter discussed how to build collective intelligence to support team learning and effectiveness.

Want more?

For an overall understanding of how research about teams evolved over the last century, consult Mathieu, Hollenbeck, van Knippenberg and Ilgen.[226] Teaming is discussed in Edmondson[227] and the relevance of cross-boundary teaming for innovation is debated in Edmondson and Harvey.[228] The importance of psychological safety for team learning and performance is discussed in Edmondon, Edmondson and Lei, as well as in Frazier et al.[229] The book *Confronting Mistakes: Lessons from the Aviation Industry when Dealing with Error*[230] provides a rich understanding about the importance of psychological safety, speaking up and learning from mistakes. The relationship between trust and team performance is meta-analyzed by De Jong, Dirks and Gillespie.[231] Paulus and Kenworthy provide an overview of team creativity and innovation.[232] For the relationship between team diversity and team creativity see Knippenberg and Hoever.[233] A scholarly perspective on global virtuous teams may be found in Jimenez et al.[234] and Neeley[235] provides a practitioner view about the topic. Liao[236] discusses challenges associated with leadership in virtual teams. *Leading Teams*[237] provides a whole perspective about team leadership. For a more academic perspective see Van Knippenberg.[238]

Glossary

Collective intelligence   'The ability of a group to perform more effectively than any individual alone.'[239]

Fault lines   'Hypothetical dividing lines that split a group into two or more subgroups based on the alignment of one or more individual attributes and have been found to influence group processes, performance outcomes, and affective outcomes.'[240]

Groupthink   'A mode of thinking that people engage in when they are deeply involved in a cohesive in-group, when the members' strivings for unanimity override their motivation to realistically appraise alternative courses of action.'[241]

Interpersonal trust   'A psychological state comprising the intention to accept vulnerability based upon positive expectations of the intentions or behavior of another.'[242]

Intrateam trust   'Aggregate levels of trust that team members have in their fellow teammates.'[243]

Speaking up   A frank and direct manner of communication between individuals (mainly between/from subordinates to supervisors), including asking questions, seeking feedback, raising concerns and pointing out mistakes and failures.

Team   Collectives of three or more people with a formed identity that cooperate to achieve some common goal.

Team creativity 'The production of novel and useful ideas concerning products, services, processes, and procedures by a team of employees working together.'[244]

Team diversity 'Variation among team members on any attribute on which individuals may differ – demographic background, functional or educational background, personality, etc.'[245]

Team learning 'Acquisition of knowledge, skills, and performance capabilities of an interdependent set of individuals through interaction and experience.'[246]

Team mental models Shared understandings about task requirements, procedures and role responsibilities.

Team psychological safety The shared belief that it is safe for team members to take interpersonal risks within the team.

Team reflexivity 'The extent to which teams collectively reflect upon and adapt their working methods and functioning.'[247]

Team transactive memory Shared understandings about who knows what.

Teaming 'Teaming is flexible teamwork. It's a way to gather experts from far-flung divisions and disciplines into temporary groups to tackle unexpected problems and identify emerging opportunities. It's happening now in nearly every industry and type of company.'[248]

Teamwork Shared attitudes, cognitions and behaviours that are necessary for the team to accomplish taskwork, function effectively and thus achieve team goals.

Virtual teams 'Teams whose members use technology to varying degrees in working across locational, temporal, and relational boundaries to accomplish an interdependent task.'[249]

Notes

1 Murthy (2014).
2 Google search statistics: www.internetlivestats.com/google-search-statistics/.
3 Interactive Schools (2018).
4 Dinh and Salas (2017, p. 15).
5 Kozlowski and Ilgen (2006, p. 77).
6 Marks, Mathieu and Zaccaro (2001).
7 Anderson, Potocnik and Zhou (2014, p. 1309).
8 Oliver and Roos (2003, p. 1062).
9 www.lego.com/en-us/mindstorms/support.
10 Engwall and Svensson (2004, p. 297; italics in the original).
11 Edmondson (2012b, p. 74); see also Pentland (2012).
12 Aubé and Rousseau (2005).
13 Webster, Hardy and Hardy (2017).
14 Hu and Liden (2015); Marks, Mathieu and Zaccaro (2001).
15 Mathieu, Hollenbeck, van Knippenberg and Ilgen (2017, p. 456).
16 Esser (1998); Janis (1982).
17 Armenakis (2002).
18 Grant (2017).
19 Pentland (2012, p. 62).
20 Salas, Dickinson, Converse and Tannenbaum (1992, p. 4).
21 Kozlowski and Ilgen (2006, p. 79).
22 See also Aubé and Rousseau (2005).
23 Kozlowski and Ilgen (2006, p. 79).
24 Kozlowski and Ilgen (2006).
25 Chan (1998).
26 Biemann, Cole and Voelpel (2012, p. 67).
27 Silva et al. (2014).
28 Salas, Shuffler, Thayer, Bedwell and Lazzara (2015).

29 Source: Telephone operators, 1952. Author: Seattle Municipal Archives from Seattle, WA. Retrieved from: https://commons.wikimedia.org/wiki/File:Telephone_operators,_1952.jpg. This file is licensed under the Creative Commons Attribution 2.0 Generic license.

30 Source: www.mynewsdesk.com/se/abba-the-museum/images/abba-the-museum-the-choir-250208. Author: Anders Hanser. Retrieved from: https://commons.wikimedia.org/wiki/File: ABBA_Edmonton_1979_001.jpg. This file is licensed under the Creative Commons Attribution 3.0 Unported license.

31 Dinh and Salas (2017); Salas, Shuffler, Thayer, Bedwell and Lazzara (2015).

32 Dinh and Salas (2017); Salas, Shuffler, Thayer, Bedwell and Lazzara (2015).

33 Marks, Mathieu and Zaccaro (2001).

34 Rego et al. (2017, 2019).

35 Dong, Bartol, Zhang and Li (2017, p. 444).

36 Built from Salas, Shuffler, Thayer, Bedwell and Lazzara (2015).

37 Webster, Hardy and Hardy (2017).

38 Hackman (1987, 2002); Hackman and Wageman (2005); Wageman, Hackman and Lehman (2005).

39 Wageman, Hackman and Lehman (2005, p. 376).

40 Hackman and Wageman (2005, p. 272).

41 Mathieu, Hollenbeck, van Knippenberg and Ilgen (2017, p. 455).

42 See Kozlowski and Ilgen (2006); Marks, Mathieu and Zaccaro (2001). The I-P-O framework was used by Martins, Gilson and Maynard (2004) and by Dulebohn and Hoch (2017) to discuss the effectiveness of virtual teams (see the section about the issue below).

43 Marks, Mathieu and Zaccaro (2001, p. 357).

44 Kozlowski and Ilgen (2006).

45 Ilgen, Hollenbeck, Johnson and Jundt (2005, p. 519).

46 Marlow, Lacerenza and Salas (2017) adopted the IMOI framework to explain communication processes in virtual teams (see section about this topic below).

47 Marks, Mathieu and Zaccaro (2001, p. 357).

48 Ilgen, Hollenbeck, Johnson and Jundt (2005).

49 Kozlowski and Ilgen (2006, p. 86).

50 Kozlowski and Ilgen (2006, p. 86).

51 Ilgen, Hollenbeck, Johnson and Jundt (2005, p. 83).

52 Wegner, Giuliano and Hertel (1985).

53 Schippers, West and Dawson (2015, p. 769).

54 Kozlowski and Ilgen (2006).

55 Salas, Shuffler, Thayer, Bedwell and Lazzara (2015).

56 Costa, Fulmer and Anderson (2018); De Jong, Dirks and Gillespie (2016); Edmondson and Lei (2014); Frazier, Fainshmidt, Klinger, Pezeshkan and Vracheva (2017).

57 Stewart (2006).

58 Burke, Sims, Lazzara and Salas (2007); DeRue, Nahrgang, Wellman and Humphrey (2011).

59 Mesmer-Magnus and DeChurch (2009).

60 Adapted from: Dinh and Salas (2017); Salas, Shuffler, Thayer, Bedwell and Lazzara (2015).

61 Marks, Mathieu and Zaccaro (2001, p. 363).

62 Salas, Shuffler, Thayer, Bedwell and Lazzara (2015, p. 10).

63 Salas, Shuffler, Thayer, Bedwell and Lazzara (2015, p. 5).

64 Edmondson (1999); Edmondson and Lei (2014).

65 Mathieu, Hollenbeck, van Knippenberg and Ilgen (2017).

66 Mathieu, Hollenbeck, van Knippenberg and Ilgen (2017, p. 455).

67 Edmondson and Harvey (2017).

68 Built from: Dulebohn and Hoch (2017); Edmondson and Harvey (2017); Ilgen, Hollenbeck, Johnson and Jundt (2005); Marlow, Lacerenza and Salas (2017); Marks, Mathieu and Zaccaro (2001).

69 Oldham and Baer (2012, p. 388).

70 Zhou and Hoever (2014, p. 333). We approach creativity as an outcome, rather than a process. The creative process represents the dynamic actions involving (1) identifying a problem or opportunity, gathering information and resources, generating ideas and evaluating, modifying and selecting ideas (Gilson, Lim, Litchfield & Gilson, 2015). Such a process may not lead to a

creative outcome: 'a team that collectively identifies problems, generates ideas, and tries out new solutions only to select an off-the-shelf remedy for a problem may not have a creative outcome'; Gilson, Lim, Litchfield and Gilson 2015, p. 179).

71 Anderson, Potocnik and Zhou (2014); van Knippenberg and Hoever (2017).
72 Dong, Bartol, Zhang and Li (2017, p. 444).
73 Dong, Bartol, Zhang and Li (2017); Pirola-Merlo and Mann (2004).
74 van Knippenberg (2017).
75 Paulus, Dzindolet and Kohn (2012); Pirola-Merlo and Mann (2004).
76 Gilson, Lim, Litchfield and Gilson (2015).
77 See Chapter 3.
78 Zhou and Hoever (2014).
79 Paulus, Dzindolet and Kohn (2012, p. 349).
80 Anderson, Potocnik and Zhou (2014).
81 Paulus, Dzindolet and Kohn (2012, p. 337).
82 Zhou and Hoever (2014).
83 Synthesis on Zhou and Hoever (2014, p. 345).
84 George and Zhou (2001).
85 George and Zhou (2001).
86 van Knippenberg and Hoever (2017, p. 41).
87 van Knippenberg and Hoever (2017, p. 53).
88 Zhou and Hoever (2014, p. 344).
89 Shin and Zhou (2007).
90 Gong, Kim, Lee and Zhu (2013).
91 Mortensen and Haas (2018).
92 Edmondson and Harvey (2016, 2017).
93 Edmondson (2012b).
94 Source: CN-Peking-Swimming Centre 2008-05-12.01.07. Author: Angus. Retrieved from https://commons.wikimedia.org/wiki/File:Beijing_National_Aquatics_Centre_2.jpg. The file is licensed under the Creative Commons Attribution 2.0 Generic license.
95 Edmondson (2012a, 2012b).
96 Edmondson and Harvey (2017).
97 Edmondson (2012b, p. 74).
98 Li, Meyer, Shemla and Wegge (2018).
99 Kessler (2017).
100 Woolley, Chabris, Pentland, Hashmi and Malone (2010); Woolley, Malone and Chabris (2015).
101 Edmondson (2016); Rashi, Edmondson and Leonard (2013); Useem, Jordan and Koljatic (2011).
102 Rashi, Edmondson and Leonard (2013).
103 Cunha, Simpson, Clegg and Rego (2019).
104 Hu, Erdogan, Jiang, Bauer and Liu (2018); Owens, Johnson and Mitchell (2013); Rego et al. (2019).
105 Owens and Hekman (2016); Rego et al. (2017).
106 Author: Secretaria de Comunicaciones, Chile. Attribution: Hugo Infante/Government of Chile. Retrieved from: https://commons.wikimedia.org/wiki/File:Last_rescuers_press_conference_ (5081900186).jpg. This file is licensed under the Creative Commons Attribution 2.0 Generic license.
107 Martins, Gilson and Maynard (2004, p. 808). Some researchers consider that the expression 'virtual team' refers to teams whose members interact *only* through electronic media. In contrast, other researchers allow for some face-to-face communication while the majority of interactions occur electronically. However, nowadays 'pure' virtual teams are almost nonexistent, with teams differing in the extent to which they use electronic communication.
108 Dulebohn and Hoch (2017).
109 Jimenez, Boehe, Taras and Caprar (2017, p. 341).
110 Jimenez, Boehe, Taras and Caprar (2017, p. 342).
111 http://lexicon.ft.com/Term?term=global-virtual-teams.
112 Neeley (2015, p. 76).
113 Edmondson and Harvey (2017); Edmondson, Moingeon, Bai and Harvey (2016).

114 Jimenez, Boehe, Taras and Caprar (2017, p. 342).
115 Edmondson (2012b).
116 Jimenez, Boehe, Taras and Caprar (2017).
117 Adapted from Jimenez, Boehe, Taras and Caprar (2017, p. 345).
118 Dulebohn and Hoch (2017); Jimenez, Boehe, Taras and Caprar (2017); Liao (2017); Martins, Gilson and Maynard (2004).
119 Jimenez, Boehe, Taras and Caprar (2017, p. 342).
120 Martins, Gilson and Maynard (2004, p. 807).
121 Jimenez, Boehe, Taras and Caprar (2017); Marlow, Lacerenza and Salas (2017); Neeley (2015).
122 Burke, Diaz Granados and Salas (2011).
123 House, Hanges, Javidan, Dorfman and Gupta (2004).
124 Burke, Diaz Granados and Salas (2011, p. 341).
125 De Jong, Dirks and Gillespie (2016), Marlow, Lacerenza and Salas (2017).
126 Kirkman, Rosen, Gibson, Tesluck and McPhers (2002, p. 69).
127 Neeley (2015, p. 77).
128 RW^3 Culture Wizard (2016, pp. 2, 3).
129 In Murray (2017, p. 11).
130 Laio (2017).
131 RW^3 Culture Wizard (2016).
132 RW^3 Culture Wizard (2016, p. 6).
133 Lebwitz (2015).
134 Edmondson (1999); Edmondson and Lei (2014).
135 Edmondson (1999).
136 Edmondson (2012b, p. 119).
137 Edmondson (1999); Edmondson and Lei (2014).
138 Edmondson and Lei (2014, p. 31).
139 Edmondson and Lei (2014); Frazier, Fainshmidt, Klinger, Pezeshkan and Vracheva (2017).
140 Delizonna (2017); Rokovsky (2015).
141 https://rework.withgoogle.com/guides/understanding-team-effectiveness/steps/introduction/.
142 Rokovsky (2015); italics in the original.
143 Bryant (2016, p. BU2).
144 Frazier, Fainshmidt, Klinger, Pezeshkan and Vracheva (2017).
145 Frazier, Fainshmidt, Klinger, Pezeshkan and Vracheva (2017).
146 Edmondson (2008, p. 65).
147 Sources: Cunha, Simpson, Clegg and Rego (2019); Delizonna (2017); Detert and Burris (2016); Edmondson (1999), Edmondson (2012a, 2012b); Frazier, Fainshmidt, Klinger, Pezeshkan and Vracheva (2017); Hu, Erdogan, Jiang, Bauer and Liu (2018).
148 Kets de Vries (2001).
149 Detert and Burris (2016, p. 82).
150 Edmondson (2008, 2012a, 2012b).
151 Edmondson (2008, p. 63).
152 Edmondson (2008).
153 Outsystems (2013, p. 12).
154 Title and subtitle of an article published in *Fast Company* (Moran, 2014).
155 In Garrahan (2014, p. 10).
156 Nisen (2016).
157 Sanner and Bunderson (2015) explain why psychological safety is more strongly associated with learning and performance in settings that involve complexity, creativity and sensemaking.
158 Edmondson (2008).
159 Amabile, Fisher and Pillemer (2014).
160 Adapted from Edmondson (2008, p. 64).
161 Ewing (2015); Jung and Park (2017).
162 Kouchaki (2016, italics in the original). See also Independent Directors of the Board of Wells Fargo & Company (2017).
163 US National Transportation Safety Board, Bureau of Accident Investigation (1979, p. 1). See also Hagen (2013).
164 Dinh and Salas (2017).

165 Hagen (2013).
166 See US National Transportation Safety Board, Bureau of Accident Investigation (1979), and parts of this accident report on www.aviationchief.com/japan-air-lines-8054.html.
167 Hagen (2013).
168 Hagen (2013); Salas, Wilson and Burke (2006).
169 Flin, O'Connor and Mearns (2002); Hagen (2013).
170 Hagen (2013).
171 Flin, O'Connor and Mearns (2002); Moffatt-Bruce et al. (2017); Salas, Wilson and Burke (2006).
172 Hagen (2013).
173 Author: U.S. Navy photo by Photographer's Mate 1st Class Matthew J. Thomas. Retrieved from: https://commons.wikimedia.org/wiki/File:US_Navy_030506-N-0020T-004_Aviation_Structural_Mechanic_1st_Class_James_Hale_prepares_for_engine_start_on_an_MH-53E_Sea_Dragon_helicopter_at_Naval_Air_Station_(NAS)_Sigonella.jpg. As a work of the U.S. federal government, the image is in the public domain in the United States.
174 Woolley, Malone and Chabris (2015, p. SR5).
175 Engel, Woolley, Jing, Chabris and Malone (2014); Woolley, Chabris, Pentland, Hashmi and Malone (2010).
176 Woolley, Chabris, Pentland, Hashmi and Malone (2010).
177 Engel, Woolley, Jing, Chabris and Malone (2014).
178 Woolley, Malone and Chabris (2015, p. SR5).
179 Woolley, Malone and Chabris (2015, p. SR5).
180 In De Smet and Gagnon (2017).
181 Pentland (2012).
182 Pentland (2012, p. 65).
183 Pentland (2012, p. 65).
184 Built from Pentland (2012).
185 Harrison and Klein (2007). For van Knippenberg and Hoever (2017, p. 43), team diversity 'is understood as variation among team members on any attribute on which individuals may differ – demographic background, functional or educational background, personality, etc.'.
186 Edmondson and Harvey (2017); Harrison and Klein (2007).
187 Bunderson and Van der Vegt (2018), focussing specifically on management teams, proposed a somewhat different perspective about team diversity. They distinguished diversity (i.e., horizontal differences) from inequality (i.e., vertical differences).
188 Bunderson and Van der Vegt (2018); Kunze and Bruch (2010); Meyer and Glenz (2013); Webber and Donahue (2001).
189 See Li, Meyer, Shemla and Wegge (2018).
190 Bunderson and Van der Vegt (2018).
191 See Bunderson and Van der Vegt (2018) for a synthesis.
192 Reynolds and Lewis (2018).
193 Reynolds and Lewis (2017).
194 Adapted from Reynolds and Lewis (2018).
195 Horwitz and Horwitz (2007).
196 Shemla, Meyer, Greer and Jehn (2016).
197 Li, Meyer, Shemla and Wegge (2018).
198 Li, Meyer, Shemla and Wegge (2018).
199 Vickerg and Christfort (2017).
200 Vickerg and Christfort (2017).
201 Vickerg and Christfort (2017, p. 53).
202 Meyer and Glenz (2013).
203 Thatcher and Patel (2012, p. 969).
204 Bezrukova, Jehn, Zanutto and Thatcher (2009); Jehn and Bezrukova (2010).
205 Thatcher and Patel (2012, p. 982).
206 Thatcher and Patel (2012).
207 In Lowe and Aarons (2017).
208 In Lowe and Aarons (2017).
209 In Lowe and Aarons (2017).

210 White and Devin (2018).
211 White and Devin (2018).
212 Lau and Murnighan (1998).
213 Jehn and Conlon (2018).
214 Kunze and Bruch (2010).
215 Volk, Pearsall, Christian and Becker (2017).
216 Kunze and Bruch (2010).
217 Bunderson and Van der Vegt (2018, p. 67).
218 Meyer and Glenz (2013, p. 395).
219 Thatcher and Patel (2012, p. 970).
220 Thatcher and Patel (2011, 2012); see also Meyer and Glenz (2013).
221 For a synthesis, see Thatcher and Patel (2012).
222 Kunze and Bruch (2010).
223 Georgakakis, Greve and Ruigrok (2017).
224 Meyer, Shemla and Schermuly (2011).
225 Chen, Wang, Zhou, Chen and Wu (2017).
226 Mathieu, Hollenbeck, van Knippenberg and Ilgen (2017).
227 Edmondson (2012a, 2012b).
228 Edmondson and Harvey (2017).
229 Edmondson (2008; 2018), Edmondson and Lei (2014) and Frazier, Fainshmidt, Klinger, Pezeshkan and Vracheva (2017) see also Newman, Donohue, and Eva (2017).
230 Hagen (2013).
231 De Jong, Dirks and Gillespie (2016).
232 Paulus and Kenworthy (2017).
233 Knippenberg and Hoever (2017).
234 Jimenez, Boehe, Taras and Caprar (2017).
235 Neeley (2015).
236 Liao (2017).
237 Hackman (2002).
238 van Knippenberg (2017).
239 Mann and Helbing (2017).
240 Thatcher and Patel (2012, p. 969).
241 Janis (1982, p. 8).
242 Rousseau, Sitkin, Burt and Camerer (1998, p. 395).
243 De Jong, Dirks and Gillespie (2016).
244 Shin and Zhou (2007, p. 1715).
245 Knippenberg and Hoever (2017, p. 43).
246 Kozlowski and Ilgen (2006, p. 86).
247 Schippers, West and Dawson (2015, p. 769).
248 Edmondson (2012b, p. 75).
249 Martins, Gilson and Maynard (2004, p. 808).

References

Amabile, T., Fisher, C. M., & Pillemer, J. (2014). IDEO's culture of helping. *Harvard Business Review*, January–February, 54–61.

Anderson, N., Potocnik, K., & Zhou, J. (2014). Innovation and creativity in organizations: A state-of-the-science review, prospective commentary, and guiding framework. *Journal of Management*, 40(5), 1297–1333.

Armenakis, A. A. (2002). Boisjoly on ethics: An interview with Roger M. Boisjoly. *Journal of Management Inquiry*, 11(3), 274–281.

Aubé, C., & Rousseau, V. (2005). Team goal commitment and team effectiveness: The role of task interdependence and supportive behaviors. *Group Dynamics: Theory, Research, and Practice*, 9(3), 189–204.

Bezrukova, K., Jehn, K. A., Zanutto, E. L., & Thatcher, S. (2009). Do workgroup fault lines help or hurt? A moderated model of fault lines, team identification, and group performance. *Organization Science*, 20, 35–50.

Biemann, T., Cole, M. S., & Voelpel, S. (2012). Within-group agreement: On the use (and misuse) of rwg and rwg(J) in leadership research and some best practice guidelines. *Leadership Quarterly*, 23(1), 66–80.

Bryant, A. (2016). Amit Singh of Google for work: A respectful clash of ideas. *The New York Times*, January 24, BU2.

Bunderson, J. S., & Van der Vegt, G. S. (2018). Diversity and inequality in management teams: A review and integration of research on vertical and horizontal member differences. *Annual Review of Organizational Psychology and Organizational Behavior*, 5, 47–73.

Burke, C. S., Diaz Granados, D., & Salas, E. (2011). Team leadership: A review and look ahead. In A. Bryman, D. Collinson, K. Grint, B. Jackson, & M. Uhl-Bien (Eds.), *The Sage handbook of leadership* (pp. 338–351). London: Sage.

Burke, C. S., Sims, D. E., Lazzara, E. H., & Salas, E. (2007). Trust in leadership: A multi-level review and integration. The Leadership Quarterly, 18(6), 606–632.

Chan, D. (1998). Functional relations among constructs in the same content domain at different levels of analysis: A typology of composition models. *The Journal of Applied Psychology*, 83, 234–246.

Chen, S., Wang, D., Zhou, Y., Chen, Z., & Wu, D. (2017). When too little or too much hurts: Evidence for a curvilinear relationship between team fault lines and performance. *Asia Pacific Journal of Management*, 34(4), 931–950.

Costa, A. C., Fulmer, C. A., & Anderson, N. R. (2018). Trust in work teams: An integrative review, multilevel model, and future directions. *Journal of Organizational Behavior*, 39(2), 169–184.

Cunha, M. P., Simpson, A. V., Clegg, S., & Rego, A. (2019). Speak! Paradoxical effects of a managerial culture of "speaking up". *British Journal of Management*, 30(4), 829–846.

De Jong, B. A., Dirks, K. T., & Gillespie, N. (2016). Trust and team performance: A meta-analysis of main effects, moderators, and covariates. *Journal of Applied Psychology*, 101(8), 1134–1150.

De Smet, A., & Gagnon, C. (2017). Safe enough to try: An interview with Zappos CEO Tony Hsieh. *McKinsey Quarterly*, October (www.mckinsey.com/business-functions/organization/our-insights/safe-enough-to-try-an-interview-with-zappos-ceo-tony-hsieh?cid=other-eml-alt-mkq-mck-oth-1710)

Delizonna, L. (2017). High-performing teams need psychological safety: Here's how to create it. *Harvard Business Review*, August 24 (https://hbr.org/2017/08/high-performing-teams-need-psychological-safety-heres-how-to-create-it).

DeRue, D. S., Nahrgang, J. D., Wellman, N., & Humphrey, S. E. (2011). Trait and behavioral theories of leadership: An integration and meta-analytic test of their relative validity. *Personnel Psychology*, 64(1), 7–52.

Detert, J. R., & Burris, E. R. (2016). Can your employees really speak freely? *Harvard Business Review*, 94(1), 80–87.

Dinh, J. V., & Salas, E. (2017). Factors that influence teamwork. In E. Salas, R. Rico, & J. Passmore (Eds.), *The Wiley Blackwell Handbook of teamwork and collaborative processes* (pp. 15–41). Chichester: Wiley Blackwell.

Dong, Y., Bartol, K. M., Zhang, Z. X., & Li, C. (2017). Enhancing employee creativity via individual skill development and team knowledge sharing: Influences of dual-focused transformational leadership. *Journal of Organizational Behavior*, 38(3), 439–458.

Dulebohn, J. H., & Hoch, J. E. (2017). Virtual teams in organizations. *Human Resource Management Review*, 27(4), 569–574.

Edmondson, A. C. (1999). Psychological safety and learning behavior in work teams. *Administrative Science Quarterly*, 44(2), 350–383.

Edmondson, A. C. (2008). The competitive imperative of learning. *Harvard Business Review*, July–August, 60–67.

Edmondson, A. C. (2018). *The fearless organization: Creating psychological safety in the workplace for learning, innovation, and growth*. John Wiley & Sons.

Edmondson, A. C. (2012a). *Teaming: How organizations learn, innovate, and compete in the knowledge economy*. Chichester: John Wiley & Sons.

Edmondson, A. C. (2012b). Teamwork on the fly. *Harvard Business Review*, 90(4), 72–80.

Edmondson, A. C. (2016). Wicked problem solvers: Lessons from successful cross-industry teams. *Harvard Business Review*, June, 52–59.

Edmondson, A. C., & Harvey, J. F. (2016). *Open innovation at Fujitsu (A)*. HBS Case No. 616-034.

Edmondson, A. C., & Harvey, J. F. (2017). Cross-boundary teaming for innovation: Integrating research on teams and knowledge in organizations. *Human Resource Management Review*.

Edmondson, A. C., & Lei, Z. (2014). Psychological safety: The history, renaissance, and future of an interpersonal construct. *Annual Review of Organizational Psychology and Organizational Behavior*, 1, 23–43.

Edmondson, A. C., Moingeon, B., Bai, G., & Harvey, J. F. (2016). *Building smart neighborhoods at Bouygues*. HBS Case No. 617-007.

Engel, D., Woolley, A. W., Jing, L. X., Chabris, C. F., & Malone, T. W. (2014). Reading the mind in the eyes or reading between the lines? Theory of mind predicts collective intelligence equally well online and face-to-face. *PLoS ONE*, 9(12), e115212.

Engwall, M., & Svensson, C. (2004). Cheetah teams in product development: The most extreme form of temporary organization? *Scandinavian Journal of Management*, 20, 287–317.

Esser, J. K. (1998). Alive and well after 25 years: A review of groupthink research. *Organizational Behavior and Human Decision Processes*, 73(2–3), 116–141.

Ewing, J. (2015). Volkswagen inquiry's focus to include managers who turned a blind eye. *The New York Times*, October 26, B3.

Flin, R., O'Connor, P., & Mearns, K. (2002). Crew resource management: Improving team work in high reliability industries. *Team Performance Management: An International Journal*, 8(3/4), 68–78.

Frazier, M. L., Fainshmidt, S., Klinger, R. L., Pezeshkan, A., & Vracheva, V. (2017). Psychological safety: A meta-analytic review and extension. *Personnel Psychology*, 70, 113–165.

Garrahan, M. (2014). Pixar's formula for creativity. *Financial Times*, June 26, 10.

Georgakakis, D., Greve, P., & Ruigrok, W. (2017). Top management team fault lines and firm performance: Examining the CEO-TMT interface. *The Leadership Quarterly*, 28(6), 741–758.

George, J. M., & Zhou, J. (2001). When openness to experience and conscientiousness are related to creative behavior: An interactional approach. *Journal of Applied Psychology*, 86(3), 513–524.

Gilson, L. L., Lim, H. S., Litchfield, R. C., & Gilson, P. W. (2015). Creativity in teams: A key building block for innovation and entrepreneurship. In C. Shalley, M. A. Hitt, & J. Zhou (Eds.), *The Oxford handbook of creativity, innovation, and entrepreneurship* (pp. 177–204). Oxford: Oxford University Press.

Gong, Y., Kim, T. Y., Lee, D. R., & Zhu, J. (2013). A multilevel model of team goal orientation, information exchange, and creativity. *Academy of Management Journal*, 56(3), 827–851.

Grant, A. (2017). Kids, would you please start fighting? *The New York Times*, November 5, SR7.

Grijalva, E., Maynes, T. D., Badura, K. L., & Whiting, S. W. W. (2019). Examining the "I" in team: A longitudinal investigation of the influence of team narcissism composition on team outcomes in the NBA. *Academy of Management Journal*, https://doi.org/10.5465/amj.2017.0218.

Hackman, J. R. (1987). The design of workteams. In J. W. Lorsch (Ed.), *Handbook of organizational behavior* (pp. 315–342). Englewood Cliffs, NJ: Prentice Hall.

Hackman, J. R. (2002). *Leading teams: Setting the stage for great performances*. Boston, MA: Harvard Business School Press.

Hackman, J. R., & Wageman, R. (2005). A theory of team coaching. *Academy of Management Review*, 30(2), 269–287.

Hagen, J. U. (2013). *Confronting mistakes: Lessons from the aviation industry when dealing with error*. New York: Palgrave Macmillan.

Harrison, D. A., & Klein, K. J. (2007). What's the difference? Diversity constructs as separation, variety, or disparity in organizations. *Academy of Management Review*, 32, 1199–1228.

Horwitz, S. K., & Horwitz, I. B. (2007). The effects of team diversity on team outcomes: A meta-analytic review of team demography. *Journal of Management*, 33(6), 987–1015.

House, R., Hanges, P., Javidan, M., Dorfman, P., & Gupta, V. (2004). *Culture, leadership, and organizations*. Thousand Oaks, CA: Sage.

Hu, J., Erdogan, B., Jiang, K., Bauer, T. N., & Liu, S. (2018). Leader humility and team creativity: The role of team information sharing, psychological safety, and power distance. *Journal of Applied Psychology*, 103(3), 313–323.

Hu, J., & Liden, R. C. (2015). Making a difference in the teamwork: Linking team prosocial motivation to team processes and effectiveness. *Academy of Management Journal*, 58(4), 1102–1127.

Ilgen, D. R., Hollenbeck, J. R., Johnson, M., & Jundt, D. (2005). Teams in organizations: From input-process-output models to IMOI models. *Annual Review of Psychology*, 56, 517–543.

Independent Directors of the Board of Wells Fargo & Company. (2017). *Sales practices investigation report*. April 10 (www08.wellsfargomedia.com/assets/pdf/about/investor-relations/presentations/2017/board-report.pdf).

Interactive Schools. (2018, February 8). 50 million users: How long does it take tech to reach this milestone? *Interactive Schools* (http://blog.interactiveschools.com/blog/50-million-users-how-long-does-it-take-tech-to-reach-this-milestone).

Janis, I. (1982). *Groupthink*. Boston, MA: Houghton Mifflin Company.

Jehn, K. A., & Bezrukova, K. (2010). The fault line activation process and the effects of activated fault lines oncoalition formation, conflict, and group outcomes. *Organizational Behavior and Human Decision Processes*, 112, 24–42.

Jehn, K. A., & Conlon, D. E. (2018). Are lifestyle differences beneficial? The effects of marital diversity on group outcomes. *Small Group Research*, 49(4), 429–451.

Jimenez, A., Boehe, D. M., Taras, V., & Caprar, D. V. (2017). Working across boundaries: Current and future perspectives on global virtual teams. *Journal of International Management*, 23(4), 341–349.

Jung, J. C., & Park, S. B. A. (2017). Volkswagen's diesel emissions scandal. *Thunderbird International Business Review*, 59(1), 127–137.

Kessler, S. (2017). GE has a version of self-management that is much like Zappos' Holacracy—And it works. *Quartz*, June 6 (https://qz.com/974188/ge-has-a-version-of-self-management-that-is-much-like-holacracy-and-it-works/).

Kets de Vries, M. F. R. (2001). *The leadership mystique*. London: Financial Times/Prentice Hall.

Kirkman, B. L., Rosen, B., Gibson, C. B., Tesluck, P. E., & McPherson, S. O. (2002). Five challenges to virtual team success: Lessons from Sabre, Inc. *Academy of Management Executive*, 16(3), 67–79.

Kouchaki, M. (2016). How Wells Fargo's fake accounts scandal got so bad. *Fortune*, September 15 (http://fortune.com/2016/09/15/wells-fargo-scandal/).

Kozlowski, S. W. J., & Ilgen, D. R. (2006). Enhancing the effectiveness of work groups and teams. *Psychological Science in the Public Interest*, 7(3), 77–124.

Kunze, F., & Bruch, H. (2010). Age-based fault lines and perceived productive energy: The moderation of transformational leadership. *Small Group Research*, 41(5), 593–620.

Lau, D. C., & Murnighan, J. K. (1998). Demographic diversity and faultlines: the compositional dynamics of organizational groups. *Academy of Management Review*, 23, 325–40.

Lebwitz, S. (2015). Google considers this to be the most critical trait of successful teams. *Business Insider*, November 21 (www.businessinsider.com.au/amy-edmondson-on-psychological-safety-2015-11?r=US&IR=T).

Li, J., Meyer, B., Shemla, M., & Wegge, J. (2018). From being diverse to becoming diverse: A dynamic team diversity theory. *Journal of Organizational Behavior*, 39(8), 956–970.

Liao, C. (2017). Leadership in virtual teams: A multilevel perspective. *Human Resource Management Review*, 27(4), 648–659.

Lowe, S., & Aarons, E. (2017). Neymar pledges to 'conquer the titles' for PSG after world record £198m move. *The Guardian*, August 3 (www.theguardian.com/football/2017/aug/03/psg-neymar-buy-out-rejected-la-liga-barcelona).

Mann, R. P., & Helbing, D. (2017). Optimal incentives for collective intelligence. *Proceedings of the National Academy of Sciences*, 114, 5077–5082.

Marks, M. A., Mathieu, J. E., & Zaccaro, S. J. (2001). A temporally based framework and taxonomy of team processes. *Academy of Management Review*, 26, 356–376.

Marlow, S. L., Lacerenza, C. N., & Salas, E. (2017). Communication in virtual teams: A conceptual framework and research agenda. *Human Resource Management Review*, 27(4), 575–589.

Martins, L. L., Gilson, L. L., & Maynard, M. T. (2004). Virtual teams: What do we know and where do we go from here? *Journal of Management*, 30(6), 805–835.

Mathieu, J. E., Hollenbeck, J. R., van Knippenberg, D., & Ilgen, D. R. (2017). A century of work teams in the Journal of Applied Psychology. *Journal of Applied Psychology*, 102(3), 452–467.

Mesmer-Magnus, J. R., & DeChurch, L. A. (2009). Information sharing and team performance: A meta-analysis. *Journal of Applied Psychology*, 94(2), 535–546.

Meyer, B., & Glenz, A. (2013). Team fault line measures: A computational comparison and a new approach to multiple subgroups. *Organizational Research Methods*, 16(3), 393–424.

Meyer, B., Shemla, M., & Schermuly, C. C. (2011). Social category salience moderates the effect of diversity fault lines on information elaboration. *Small Group Research*, 42, 257–282.

Moffatt-Bruce, S. D., Hefner, J. L., Mekhjian, H., McAlearney, J. S., Latimer, T., Ellison, C., & McAlearney, A. S. (2017). What is the return on investment for implementation of a crew resource management program at an academic medical center? *American Journal of Medical Quality*, 32(1), 5–11.

Moran, G. (2014). Fostering greater creativity by celebrating failure. *Fast Company*, April 4 (www.fastcompany.com/3028594/bottom-line/a-real-life-mad-man-on-fighting-fear-for-greater-creativity)

Mortensen, M., & Haas, M. R. (2018). Rethinking teams: From bounded membership to dynamic participation. *Organization Science*, 29(2), 341–355.

Murray, S. (2017). Global teams try to break communication barriers. *Financial Times*, FT Special Report, February 28, 11.

Murthy, S. (2014). Top 10 job titles that didn't exist 5 years ago. *Linkedin* (https://business.linkedin.com/talent-solutions/blog/2014/01/top-10-job-titles-that-didnt-exist-5-years-ago-infographic).

Neeley, T. (2015). Global teams that work. *Harvard Business Review*, 93(10), 74–81.

Newman, A., Donohue, R., & Eva, N. (2017). Psychological safety: A systematic review of the literature. *Human Resource Management Review*, 27(3), 521–535.

Nisen, M. (2016). Why Etsy engineers send company-wide emails confessing mistakes they made. *Quartz*, September 18 (http://qz.com/504661/why-etsy-engineers-send-company-wide-emails-confessing-mistakes-they-made/)

Oldham, G. R., & Baer, M. (2012). Creativity and the work context. In M. D. Mumford (Ed.), *Handbook of organizational creativity* (pp. 387–420). London: Academic Press.

Oliver, D., & Roos, J. (2003). Dealing with the unexpected: Critical incidents in the LEGO Mindstorms team. *Human Relations*, 56(9), 1057–1082.

Outsystems (2013). *The small book of the few rules.* (www.outsystems.com/the-small-book/).

Owens, B. P., & Hekman, D. R. (2016). How does leader humility influence team performance? Exploring the mechanisms of contagion and collective promotion focus. *Academy of Management Journal*, 58(3), 1088–1111.

Owens, B. P., Johnson, M. D., & Mitchell, T. R. (2013). Expressed humility in organizations: Implications for performance, teams, and leadership. *Organization Science*, 24(5), 1517–1538.

Paulus, P. B., Dzindolet, M., & Kohn, N. W. (2012). Collaborative creativity – Group creativity and team innovation. In M. Mumford (Ed.), *Handbook of organizational creativity* (pp. 295–326). London: Academic Press.

Paulus, P. B., and Kenworthy, J. B. (2017). Group and intergroup creativity. In L. Argote and J. M. Levine (Eds), *The Oxford Handbook of Group and Organizational Learning*. Oxford: Oxford University Press.

Pentland, A. S. (2012). The new science of building great teams. *Harvard Business Review*, 90(4), 60–70.

Pirola-Merlo, A., & Mann, L. (2004). The relationship between individual creativity and team creativity: Aggregating across people and time. *Journal of Organizational Behavior*, 25(2), 235–257.

Rashi, F., Edmondson, A. C., & Leonard, H. B. (2013). Leadership lessons from the Chilean mine rescue. *Harvard Business Review*, July–August, 113–119.

Rego, A., Owens, B., Leal, S., Melo, A., Cunha, M. P., Gonçalves, L., & Ribeiro, L. (2017). How leader humility helps teams to be humbler, psychologically stronger, and more effective: A moderated mediation model. *The Leadership Quarterly*, 28, 639–658.

Rego, A., Owens, B., Yam, K. C., Bluhm, D., Cunha, M. P., Silard, T., Gonçalves, L., Martins, M., Simpson, A. V., & Liu, W. (2019). Leader humility and team performance: Exploring the mechanisms of team psychological capital and task allocation effectiveness. *Journal of Management*. 45(3), 1009–1033.

Reynolds, A., & Lewis, D. (2017). Teams solve problems faster when they're more cognitively diverse. *Harvard Business Review*, March 30 (https://hbr.org/2017/03/teams-solve-problems-faster-when-theyre-more-cognitively-diverse).

Reynolds, A., & Lewis, D. (2018). The two traits of the best problem-solving teams. *Harvard Business Review*, April 2 (https://hbr.org/2018/04/the-two-traits-of-the-best-problem-solving-teams).

Rokovsky, J. (2015). The five keys to a successful Google team. *re:Work*. November 17 (https://rework.withgoogle.com/blog/five-keys-to-a-successful-google-team/).

Rousseau, D. M., Sitkin, S. B., Burt, R. S., & Camerer, C. (1998). Not so different after all: A cross-discipline view of trust. *Academy of Management Review*, 23, 393–404.

RW[3] Culture Wizard. (2016). *Trends in global virtual teams*. Culture Wizard. (http://cdn.culturewizard.com/PDF/Trends_in_VT_Report_4-17-2016.pdf).

Salas, E., Dickinson, T. L., Converse, S. A., & Tannenbaum, S. I. (1992). Toward an understanding of team performance and training. In: Swezey, R.W. and Salas, E., Eds., *Teams: Their Training and Performance*, Ablex, Norwood, 3–29.

Salas, E., Shuffler, M. L., Thayer, A. L., Bedwell, W. L., & Lazzara, E. H. (2015). Understanding and improving teamwork in organizations: A scientifically based practical guide. *Human Resource Management*, 54(4), 599–622.

Salas, E., Wilson, K. A., & Burke, C. S. (2006). Does crew resource management training work? An update, an extension, and some critical needs. *Human Factors*, 48(2), 392–412.

Sanner, B., & Bunderson, J. S. (2015). When feeling safe isn't enough: Contextualizing models of safety and learning in teams. *Organizational Psychology Review*, 5(3), 224–243.

Schippers, M. C., West, M. A., & Dawson, J. F. (2015). Team reflexivity and innovation: The moderating role of team context. *Journal of Management*, 41(3), 769–788.

Shemla, M., Meyer, B., Greer, L., & Jehn, K. A. (2016). A review of perceived diversity in teams: Does how members perceive their team's composition affect team processes and outcomes? *Journal of Organizational Behavior*, 37, S89–S106.

Shin, S. J., & Zhou, J. (2007). When is educational specialization heterogeneity related to creativity in research and development teams? Transformational leadership as a moderator. *Journal of Applied Psychology*, 92(6), 1709–1721.

Silva, T., Cunha, M. P., Clegg, S., Neves, P., Rego, A., & Rodrigues, R. (2014). Smells like team spirit: Opening a paradoxical black box. *Human Relations*, 67(3), 287–310.

Stewart, G. L. (2006). A meta-analytic review of relationships between team design features and team performance. *Journal of Management*, 32(1), 29–54.

Thatcher, S., & Patel, P. (2011). Demographic fault lines: A meta-analysis of the literature. *Journal of Applied Psychology*, 96, 1119–1139.

Thatcher, S., & Patel, P. (2012). Group fault lines: A review, integration, and guide to future research. *Journal of Management*, 38, 969–1009.

US National Transportation Safety Board, Bureau of Accident Investigation (1979). *Japan Air Lines Company, Ltd. McDonnell-Douglas DC-8-625, JA 8054, Anchorage, Alaska, January 13, 1977*. Washington, DC: National Transportation Safety Board. (www.ntsb.gov/investigations/AccidentReports/Reports/AAR7807.pdf).

Useem, M., Jordan, R., & Koljatic, M. (2011). How to lead during a crisis: Lessons from the rescue of the chilean miners. *MIT Sloan Management Review*, 53(1), 49–55.

van Knippenberg, D. (2017). Leadership and creativity in business. In M. D. Mumford & S. Hemlin (Eds.), *Handbook of research on leadership and creativity* (pp. 384–400). Cheltenham: Edward Elgar.

van Knippenberg, D., & Hoever, I. J. (2017). Team diversity and team creativity: A categorization-elaboration perspective. In R. Reiter-Palmon (Ed.), *Team creativity* (pp. 41–60). New York: Oxford University Press.

Vickerg, S. M. J., & Christfort, K. (2017). Pionners, drivers, integrators & guardians. *Harvard Business Review*, March–April, 50–57.

Volk, S., Pearsall, M. J., Christian, M. S., & Becker, W. J. (2017). Chronotype diversity in teams: Toward a theory of team energetic asynchrony. *Academy of Management Review*, 42(4), 683–702.

Wageman, R., Hackman, J. R., & Lehman, E. (2005). Team diagnostic survey: Development of an instrument. *Journal of Applied Behavioral Science*, 41, 373–398.

Webber, S. S., & Donahue, L. M. (2001). Impact of highly and less job-related diversity on work group cohesion and performance: A meta-analysis. *Journal of Management*, 27, 141–162.

Webster, L. V., Hardy, J., & Hardy, L. (2017). Big Hitters: Important factors characterizing team effectiveness in professional cricket. *Frontiers in Psychology*, 8, 1140.

Wegner, D. M., Giuliano, T., & Hertel, P. T. (1985). Cognitive interdependence in close relationships. In *Compatible and incompatible relationships* (pp. 253–276). Springer, New York, NY.

White, A., & Devin, E. (2018). Neymar was superb but PSG's 8-0 win raised more questions about unity. *The Guardian*, January 18 (www.theguardian.com/football/2018/jan/18/neymar-psg-dijon-edinson-cavani-penalty).

Woolley, A., Malone, T. W., & Chabris, C. F. (2015). Why some teams are smarter than others. *The New York Times*, January 18, SR5 (www.nytimes.com/2015/01/18/opinion/sunday/why-some-teams-are-smarter-than-others.html?_r=0).

Woolley, A. W., Chabris, C. F., Pentland, A., Hashmi, N., & Malone, T. W. (2010). Evidence for a collective intelligence factor in the performance of human groups. *Science*, 330(6004), 686–688.

Zhou, J., & Hoever, I. J. (2014). Research on workplace creativity: A review and redirection. *Annual Review of Organizational Psychology and Organizational Behavior*, 1, 333–359.

Part IV

Building contexts

8 Positive leadership

Humble, ethical, authentic and servant

Summary and objectives

This chapter discusses four main positive leadership approaches: humble leadership, ethical leadership, authentic leadership and servant leadership. For each approach, we discuss the meaning and leadership dimensions emphasized, as well as the impact of these leadership approaches on followers and team/organizational outcomes. Risks, dangers and problems of each style are also discussed. We also consider the conditions that facilitate the enactment of positive leadership approaches. The chapter helps with understanding that positive leadership is a valuable endeavour, albeit one that should be treated wisely, in case it becomes what David Collinson refers to as 'Prozac leadership', where being excessively positive leaves little space for critical and constructive dissonance in the face of the overwhelming positivity that is broadcast as leadership.[1]

Leaders shaping the positive

Leaders may shape the positive in organizations in two ways. First, by adopting and conveying *positive* leadership behaviours and attitudes. For example, by empowering employees, a leader fosters employee psychological strengths and potentially their performance. But leaders may shape the positive by adopting and conveying leadership behaviours and attitudes that, although not definitionally positive (i.e., negative or neutral), produce positive effects. For example, transactional leadership, a *neutral* style, may foster the employees' sense of justice/fairness and thus contribute to individual performance and wellbeing. This chapter adopts the first approach, assuming the following definition of positive leadership:[2]

> The systematic and integrated manifestation of leadership traits, processes, intentional behaviors and performance outcomes that are elevating, exceptional and affirmative of the strengths, capabilities and developmental potential of leaders, their followers and their organizations over time and across contexts.

Positive leaders act in accordance with the lines of positivity: they reach results; they act virtuously; they focus on what is strong and attractive. It is however important to acknowledge that the relationship between positive and negative is of the duality type. Therefore there can be *positive in the negative*, and *negative in the positive*.

The positive in negative leadership

There is a positive side to be seen in more traditional and negative leadership approaches characterized by traits such as narcissism, hubris, social dominance and Machiavellianism.[3] Narcissistic leaders, by favouring bold, aggressive and magnanimous actions, are more likely to draw attention to their vision and leadership. In this way, they may enroll others to such a vision, which may have positive implications for firm strategy and performance. Hubristic leaders are more likely to act with the confidence and commitment that tests the limits of their organization's productive capacity, with positive consequences for organizational innovation and competitiveness. Machiavellian behaviours may also produce positive results. At least in some circumstances, leaders may adopt a negative approach to reach positive consequences. Abraham Lincoln, nicknamed *Honest Abe*, 'hunted' for votes to pass the 13th amendment and thus abolish slavery.[4] One may question the means – but few except slavers would question the end. Would it have been possible to abolish slavery without such a questionable procedure? We don't know. We just know that Lincoln's actions contributed towards abolishing one of the most perverse human conditions in his country.

Authoritarian leadership provides further illustrations of how the positive may emerge from the negative. Although being autocratic is not the kind of leadership style one would normally recommend, in some circumstances an authoritarian approach may engender positive results. The authoritarian Lee Kuan Yew was described as having transformed Singapore into one of Asia's wealthiest and least corrupt countries, albeit at the expense of a democratic opposition that was suppressed using the law courts for libel actions against critics inside and outside parliament. Charismatic leadership, as its foremost analyst Max Weber realized, is not easily routinized after the passing of the charismatic leader[5] – and this view is remarkably valid for Lee Kuan Yew's successors, potential pretenders to being 'little Lee Kuan Yews'.[6]

In short, even when an autocratic leadership is rated negatively from a positively principled perspective, beneficial results can be acknowledged. Naturally, any assessment of consequences depends upon the principles, values and beliefs of the observer. For some, an autocratic and even abusive leader deserves to be 'forgiven' if favourable economic results are achieved for the organization. For others, such results should not be part of the equation; the autocratic style should be regarded as inherently perverse.[7]

Balancing the positive and the negative is a difficult exercise. It is impossible to ignore that some negative leadership may produce positive results, while it is always possible to argue that such results would have been better if the leader had adopted a positive stance. Regarding the alleged incivility of Jeff Bezos, the founder and CEO of Amazon, it makes sense to ask if he has been so successful *because* he is so nasty, or if he has been *successful* despite his extremely demanding management of Amazon employees[8] (see Box 5.5 in Chapter 5). Unpleasantness, indeed nastiness, may not have been necessary and hindered more than it helped.[9]

The negative of the positive

A simple Manichean view should not be adopted when assessing leadership. Accordingly, although this chapter focusses mainly on the positive effects of positive leadership, it is necessary to acknowledge that positive leadership behaviours, attitudes, emotions and traits may sometimes generate negative consequences. There can be a dark side to traits such as conscientiousness, agreeableness, emotional stability, openness to experience, core self-evaluations, intelligence and charisma.[10] Highly conscientious individuals may often be less willing to innovate or take risks. They may resist change and delay critical decisions. Leaders who enjoy good will may avoid interpersonal conflict. Moreover, by being especially sensitive to the feelings and desires of others, they may avoid decisions that put them at odds with others.

The list of positive attributes and behaviours that may produce negative results does not stop here. For example, empathy may make a leader unable to make a tough decision (e.g., disciplinary action) against individuals deserving of such a response.[11] Empathizing with an employee or colleague can be associated with being violent or cruel against others opposing that person.[12] Emotional intelligence may be used to manipulate others (see Chapter 4). Being dauntless and fearless can be liberating but it can also be dangerous because it makes a leader both complacent and overconfident.[13]

Approaches to positive leadership

Humble, ethical, authentic and servant leadership approaches are the main approaches considered in this chapter because there is now significant evidence suggesting that such 'styles' have substantial positive impacts on positive leaders' followers, teams and organizations. These leadership 'styles' also reflect several practitioners' perspectives. For example, according to a sample of 195 leaders in 15 countries, the top ten leadership competencies are recognizably positive; they are as follows:[14]

1   High ethical and moral standards.
2   Provides goals and objectives with loose guidelines/direction.
3   Communicates expectations clearly.
4   Flexible enough to change opinions.
5   Committed to ongoing training.
6   Communicates frequently and openly.
7   Being open to new ideas and approaches
8   Creates a feeling of succeeding and failing together.
9   Helps followers to grow into a next generation of leaders.
10 Provides safety for trial and error.

These competencies relate to several leadership dimensions that we will discuss in this chapter. For example, having high ethical and moral standards is a component of both ethical and authentic leadership. Providing goals and objectives with loose guidelines/direction represents empowerment, which is a component of servant leadership. Communicating expectations clearly represents the component of role clarification in ethical leadership. Having the flexibility to change opinions and being open to new ideas and approaches requires humility (servant leadership), power sharing (ethical leadership) and balanced processing (authentic leadership). Providing safety for trial and error demands interpersonal acceptance (servant leadership), as well as humility.

Project Oxygen at Google[15] (See Box 6.9 in Chapter 6) also identified ten behaviours of their best managers that, to a great extent, are associated with or reflect components of authentic, servant, ethical and humble leadership. Being a good coach may be instrumental in empowering and serving followers (servant leadership). Expressing interest in and concern for team members' success and personal wellbeing is related to ethical and servant leadership. Being a good communicator through listening and sharing information is associated with balanced processing (authentic leadership), humility, as well as empowerment and power sharing (servant and ethical leadership). Finally, empowering the team and not micromanaging are components of servant leadership.

In summary, humble, ethical, authentic and servant leadership are lenses through which specific aspects of positive leadership may be observed and learned. Furthermore, enactment of these positive leadership approaches may help leaders multiply, instead of diminish, positivity (see Table 1.6 in Chapter 1). When the leader invites people's best thinking and contributions, thus leading as a multiplier, followers make greater efforts, develop more mental and physical energy and contribute with more fresh ideas in the pursuit of long-term success.[16]

In the next sections, we explain the meanings, main components and general outcomes of each leadership approach. We also consider the negative sides and limitations of each approach. Although these leadership styles afford great potential for fostering positive outcomes, potential negative effects must not be ignored. Furthermore, the positive potential of these leadership approaches is realized only when the leader displays a cluster of characteristics/behaviours. This constellation sometimes involves paradoxical combinations, such as humility *and* fierce resolve, genuine authenticity *and* adaptive authenticity, ethicality and the capacity to accommodate moral compromises.

The remainder of the chapter is structured as follows. We discuss humility first because humility may encourage both ethical leadership[17] and authentic leadership.[18] Humility is also a component of several models of servant leadership. We then focus on ethical leadership because it represents, directly or indirectly, a component of the other leadership styles, including the authentic and servant forms of leadership. We discuss servant leadership after authentic leadership because of the holistic nature of the former, which includes components such as humility, authenticity and ethicality.

Humility in leaders

Conceptualization and dimensions

The word 'humility' comes from the Latin words *humus*, meaning 'earth' or 'ground', and *humilis*, meaning 'on the ground'.[19] Being humble means having a grounded view of oneself and others (to understand the differences between humility and other concepts such as modesty see Box 8.1). A grounded perspective enables humble individuals to acknowledge their personal strengths and weaknesses (as well as those of others). Humble individuals are able to acknowledge their personal strengths and weaknesses in relation to those of others without developing either a superiority or an inferiority complex.[20] Furthermore, they may be so humble that they under-report their own humility.[21] In contrast, unhumble individuals may brag about their humility: for instance, Donald Trump Tweeted on December 25, 2013:[22] 'The new Pope is a humble man, very much like me, which probably explains why I like him so much!' In reality, being humble means recognizing that one is not the centre of the universe and that 'something greater than the self exists'.[23]

Box 8.1 Modesty, false modesty and humblebragging

Humility ≠ modesty ≠ the opposite of narcissism

Modesty. To be modest means being unassuming or having a moderate estimation of oneself.[24] Differently, humility represents holding a balanced perspective about the self, acknowledging both strengths and limitations, not seeking to under- or over-represent the self. For some,[25] modesty means having an accurate view of oneself. From this perspective, modesty can be considered a dimension of humility but it does not embrace other dimensions such as an ability to learn or an appreciation of others' strengths.[26]

Narcissism. Humility is not the lack, or the opposite, of narcissism. Narcissism involves a strong desire for self-focus, attention and self-affirmation. However, humility is not merely a lack of displayed grandiosity or self-absorption (characteristics typical of narcissistic individuals) because it includes the ability to learn as well as an appreciation of others.[27] Morris et al. argue that 'The absence of narcissism does not necessarily imply self-awareness. At best, the absence of narcissism is a necessary but incomplete condition for humility'.[28] One of the best demonstrations that humility and narcissism are not opposites is found in research showing that a leader may be both humble and narcissistic, with most effective leaders actually being both.[29]

Humblebragging and false modesty

Leaders, like every human, aim to manage the impressions they make on others. Normally, they wish to be viewed positively – one possible tactic being self-promotion, which allows them to bring their good qualities to others' attention and thus impress others and elicit their sympathy. However, because modesty is a valued quality, self-promotion efforts, such as bragging about achievements, can backfire: people who brag may be perceived as presumptuous and cocky. Some individuals handle such a tension via humblebragging – bragging masked by a complaint or humility.[30] The *Oxford English Dictionary* defines humblebragging as 'an ostensibly modest or self-deprecating statement whose actual purpose is to draw attention to something of which one is proud'.[31] Illustrations of humblebragging are:[32] (a) 'Graduating from two universities means you get double the calls asking for money/donations. So pushy and annoying!' (complaint); (b) 'It's been ten years but I still feel uncomfortable with being recognized. Just a bit shy still I suppose' (humility); (c) 'Being the know-how person at work is so exhausting. People come to me first' (complaint); (d) 'I am so exhausted from getting elected to leadership positions all the time' (complaint).

Does humblebragging work? Research involving nine studies suggests that the tactic is ineffective. While perceived sincerity is crucial for the success of self-promotion, humblebraggers are seen as insincere and hypocrites. The research suggests that both forms of humblebragging (complaint-based or humility-based) reduce liking, perceived competence, compliance with requests and financial generosity toward the humblebragger, thus being less effective than bragging. Complaint-based humblebrags are less effective than humility-based humblebrags, and are even less effective than simply complaining. The moral: 'Humblebragging doesn't work. If you want to brag, just brag. Even better, just complain'.[33]

While defining humility as a grounded view of oneself and others has the strength of parsimony, it obscures the lack of consensus concerning the content and dimensions of humility.[34] Definitions abound ranging from three to thirteen dimensions.[35] Regarding humility in leaders, two main frameworks have been suggested:

- Owens et al.'s framework[36] (see Table 8.1), labelled *expressed* (i.e., behavioural) *humility*, embraces three dimensions: (a) a manifested willingness to view oneself accurately (i.e., without positive or negative exaggeration), (b) a displayed appreciation of others' strengths and contributions (i.e., viewing others in a positive and appreciative non-threatened way), and (c) teachability (i.e., showing openness to new ideas, advice, learning, and feedback).[37]
- Ou et al.'s framework includes these three dimensions plus three cognitive and motivational components: low self-focus, self-transcendent pursuit and transcendent self-concept.[38]

Table 8.1 Dimensions of humility

Dimensions (Owens, Johnson and Mitchell, 2013)	Definitions (Owens, Johnson and Mitchell, 2013)
Self-awareness	A manifested willingness to see the self accurately, through an ongoing process of achieving accurate self-awareness through interactions with others.
Appreciation of others	The capacity of a leader (i.e., a powerful figure) to transcend the tendency of devaluing the worth and contributions of others, thus expressing genuine appreciation and valuing the efforts, strength and abilities of these others.
Openness to feedback (teachability)	A manifested openness to learning, feedback and new ideas from others.
Other operationalizations and measures (illustrations)	*CEO humility*: Ou et al. (2014). Dimensions (the first three correspond with those of Owens et al., 2013): self-awareness; appreciation of others; openness to feedback; low self-focus; self-transcendent pursuit; transcendent self-concept. *Relational humility*: Davis et al. (2011). Dimensions: global humility; superiority; accurate view of self. *Intellectual humility* (self-reported): Leary et al. (2017). Unidimensional. *Intellectual humility* (self-reported): Alfano et al. (2017). Dimensions: openmindedness; intellectual modesty; corrigibility; engagement.

Considering that leadership is mainly relational (see also Chapter 7), most empirical studies on humility in leaders focus on the interpersonal (i.e., the expressed/behavioural) dimension of humility that emerges from the interactions between leaders and followers, both individually and collectively. Owens and Hekman argue that, although humility has been examined on the intrapersonal, cognitive level, 'our observable, social view of humility is appropriate since our purpose is to understand humility as it pertains to leadership influence processes and team member interaction patterns'.[39] In short, the intra-cognitive aspects of humility, such as transcendence, are less relevant to the expression of leaders' humility.[40]

Humility in leaders: virtue or vice?

Humility in leaders has been the target of heated debate and some controversy. Some authors extol the merits of humble leaders. Others express disdain for such a virtue and highlight the 'virtues' of arrogance and immodesty, calling for proud leaders who are successful and admired for their success. Next, we briefly discuss both perspectives.

Humility as weakness

Humility is often depreciated and considered a flaw. The *Oxford English Dictionary*[41] defines humility as the 'quality of having a modest or low view of one's importance'. Another source considers humility as synonymous with 'lowliness, meekness, submissiveness'.[42] As a consequence, humility is frequently considered an indicator of low self-esteem,[43] a disposition incompatible with the tough realities faced by leaders in modern organizations. Luke Johnson, a British entrepreneur, wrote in the *Financial Times*, shortly after the Virgin Galactic crash:

> We should not expect entrepreneurs to be humble, nor even apologetic when their grand designs come crashing down. By necessity they tend towards over-weening self-belief. But such pride and arrogance are required if the status quo is to be challenged with radical new ideas; after all, weak characters give up too soon – harried by regulators, safety obsessives and the overcautious.[44]

Jeffrey Pfeffer used Donald Trump to illustrate how humility is overrated as a useful leadership quality, arguing that self-promotion and assertiveness tend to produce better career results in the 'real world'.[45] However, timing is important. The arrogance of the leaders of Enron and other companies was assessed very differently before and after the company's collapse. After having been enthroned in business publications by their overconfidence and 'magical' skills, those leaders were later credited as the cause of the collapse of their organizations.[46] It was arrogant leadership that led these organizations to disaster.

Humility as strength

Misconduct by firms and the common emergence of corporate scandals attributed to hubris, overconfidence, greed and inflated egos have redirected fascination away from heroic leaders towards those endowed with qualities of character,[47] such as authenticity (a topic explored below) and humility.[48] *The Economist* has argued that (a) 'arrogance breeds mistakes'[49] and (b) 'If leadership has a secret sauce, it may well be humility'. A report by Oxford's Saïd Business School and Heidrick & Struggles,[50] involving more than 150 CEOs from around the world, concluded that humility is a critical requirement for next-generation CEOs. Howard Schultz, founder and executive chairman of Starbucks (CEO between January 2008 and April 2017), stated that the United States of America deserves a humble president.[51] Nonetheless, the next President of the United States of America was to be Donald J. Trump.

Vera and Rodriguez-Lopez consider humility as a critical strength for leaders and organizations.[52] They further suggest that humble leaders are more open to new paradigms, eager to learn from others, ready to acknowledge personal limitations, willing to make efforts to learn from mistakes, being ready to seek advice, offer respect, provide mentorship to subordinates and avoid self-complacency. Overall, these actions facilitate positive organizational effects of lower employee turnover, higher engagement, continuous adaptation and renewal, better team integration, greater innovation and higher productivity.[53] Humble leaders foster innovation because team members feel freer to adopt an open attitude toward experimentation and risk-taking when exploring new ideas. When facing problems, humble leaders do not deny them and rather deal with reality as it is and move forward.[54]

Humble leaders are also more likely to adopt a socialized power orientation,[55] fostering greater team effectiveness.[56] Furthermore, social exchange theory suggests that a humble leader's ability to develop strengthened social bonds with team members[57] will be reciprocated through higher team commitment and performance.[58] As argued by Weick, proclaiming that 'I don't know' (a feature of humble leaders) creates 'leader credibility in an unknowable world' and 'strengthens rather than weakens relationships'.[59] Conversely, a proud leader with minimal humility may exploit employees,[60] leading to counterproductive withdrawal behaviours, along with decreased engagement and citizenship behaviours.[61] Outside the corporate world, humility has been recognized and praised as a distinguishing quality in highly respected leaders such as Nelson Mandela,[62] Abraham Lincoln[63] and Pope Francis.[64]

Are humble leaders more effective?

Humility in leaders fosters a number of positive effects in leaders, followers, teams and organization. One study found that humble leaders are perceived as more effective because they adopt balanced processing behaviours (i.e., soliciting views, including those of subordinates and peers, that challenge deeply held personal beliefs, processing information that contradicts initial viewpoints).[65] Another study found that humble leaders foster employee engagement by facilitating stronger team-learning-goal orientations in employees.[66] Humble leaders send signals validating, accepting and promoting employees' learning and personal development, and also foster trust and openness, which promote a learning-goal orientation. The same study found that humble leaders promote higher job satisfaction in employees, contributing to decrease voluntary employee turnover. Another study indicated that leader humility fosters employee perspective taking (i.e., imagining the world from another's point of view, or putting oneself in another's shoes)[67] in this way, enhancing their creativity.[68]

At the team level, leader humility fosters team humility via social contagion among followers, thus producing an emergent state that fosters team performance.[69] Another study found that CEO humility is positively associated with empowering leadership behaviours, which in turn correlates with top management team (TMT) integration.[70] It was also found that TMT integration relates to middle managers' perception of having an empowering organizational climate, which is then associated with their work engagement, affective commitment and job performance. Another study found that humble team leaders foster team performance through the enhancement of team-shared leadership.[71] This happens because humble leaders, via modelling teachability, the capacity to learn as well as open-mindedness, encourage team members to listen to one another and to accept shared leadership. By recognizing and openly acknowledging their own limitations, humble leaders also reinforce the contributions and leadership capabilities of team members.

Cross-cultural research involving three studies conducted in China, Singapore and Portugal found that leader humility enhances team performance serially through increased team psychological capital and team task allocation effectiveness.[72] These effects happen because the three behavioural components of humility allow team members, both individually and collectively, to have mastery experiences that lead to higher self-efficacy. Humble leaders also make the team more adaptive and prepared to face risks resiliently, accept drawbacks and learn from failures. One study found that humble team leaders enhance team psychological capital (PsyCap) through facilitating greater team humility and that such an effect is stronger if all team members perceive the leaders as *consistently* humble.[73] It is possible that, by being consistently humble, those leaders develop team humility and team PsyCap in a more consistent way, with such consistency reinforcing the positive impact of team humility on team PsyCap. Conversely, when team members see the leader as *consistently* not humble, the team develops a conviction that the leader genuinely lacks humility, thus resulting in lower team humility and team PsyCap. Leaders who wish to develop team performance through team humility and team PsyCap must therefore express humility in a consistent way. At the organizational level, it has been found that CEO humility leads to higher TMT integration and negatively predicts TMT vertical pay disparity.[74] Both TMT integration and TMT vertical pay disparity indirectly influence overall firm performance. Overall, empirical research suggests the following:[75]

- Humility predicts perceived leader effectiveness, follower outcomes (e.g., engagement), team outcomes (e.g., team performance) and organizational outcomes (e.g., firm performance and firm innovation).
- These relationships are mediated by followers' attitudes (e.g., job satisfaction), leaders' behaviours (e.g., empowering leadership) and team characteristics (e.g., team learning orientation, team humility and team PsyCap).
- Some conditions (e.g., leader narcissism, strength of leader-expressed humility) moderate those relationships (more below). The relationship is stronger if the leader expresses humility in a consistent way toward the generality of team members.

Box 8.2 'Showing off by not showing off'

Countersignalling

Countersignalling may be defined as the behaviour of affluent individuals who invest less in proving their affluence than less affluent (or medium-type) individuals: 'Since medium types are signaling to differentiate themselves from low types, high types may choose to not signal, or 'countersignal,' to differentiate themselves from medium types'.[76] The website 'Conceptually' defines countersignalling,

> as showing off by not showing off … Imagine you are so rich that signaling your wealth is no longer worth the effort, so you don't splurge on fancy cars and extravagances. Your lack of signaling wealth is a way of countersignaling that you are wealthy.[77]

For example, tycoons of Silicon Valley such as Mark Zuckerberg (as did the late Steve Jobs) dress in a modest way and show frugality, perhaps to differentiate themselves from other people (Figure 8.1). Jeff Bezos continued to drive a Honda Accord long after becoming a billionaire and it has been argued that such focussed behaviour 'reveals why he's so successful'.[78]

Figure 8.1 US Secretary of State John Kerry and Facebook CEO Mark Zuckerberg at Facebook's headquarters in Menlo Park, California, June 23, 2016: is Zuckerberg's clothing a countersignal?[79]

Philip Delves Broughton[80] wrote in the *Financial Times* that 'shows of humility can be too much, even in Silicon Valley':

> In Silicon Valley, Steve Jobs was a master countersignaler, though this came with a large side order of Zen. For all his money, the Apple co-founder lived in a modest house in Palo Alto and wore Levi's and New Balance sneakers. The countersignal was that he was not a prisoner of his affluence. Mark Zuckerberg of Facebook followed, with his uniform of grey T-shirt and jeans, telling us he was focused on work not clothes. Tailored suits and silk pocket squares are for insecure guys on Wall Street. But towards the end of his life, Jobs ordered himself a lavish yacht designed by Philippe Starck. Two years ago Mr. Zuckerberg splurged on 700 acres of oceanfront Hawaii, which he has since hemmed in

with a 6ft wall. The self-imposed austerity of countersignaling can pall. Every now and again, even the most adroit countersignaller likes to channel his inner Russian billionaire and send up a gaudy flare to remind us who is king.

Was the founder of IKEA a humble man?

Ingvar Kamprad (1926–2018), founder of IKEA, was often described as modest, humble and thrifty. He personally portrayed those traits as the basis for Ikea's success. The narrative was that

> he drove an old Volvo, flew only economy class, stayed in budget hotels, ate cheap meals, shopped for bargains and insisted that his home was modest, that he had no real fortune and that Ikea was held by a charitable trust.[81]

Is this plausible? Robert McFadden[82] wrote in an obituary published in *The New York Times*:

> It was not exactly so, as reporters found. His home was a villa overlooking Lake Geneva, and he had an estate in Sweden and vineyards in Provence. He drove a Porsche as well as the Volvo. His cut-rate flights, hotels and meals were taken in part as an exemplar to his executives, who were expected to follow suit, to regard employment by Ikea as a life's commitment – and to write on both sides of a piece of paper ... He sought to control his work force, too.

Contingency factors

There are contingencies to discuss because they help explain why the impact of humble leaders on followers and teams is not always significant and positive. Certain contingencies that may be critical for realizing the potential of in leaders, in a broad sense, include follower and team characteristics, the cultural context, as well as the leader him/herself.[83] It is likely that followers who value humility and low power distance are more sensitive and respond more positively to leader humility.

Team characteristics and organizational conditions also matter. One study found that the indirect effect of leader humility on team performance through enhanced shared leadership was significant only when a team's proactive personality and performance capability were also high.[84] It is possible that leader humility is more effective under conditions that do not involve external threats or crisis and that allow for a learning culture,[85] including a culture of learning from mistakes. Humble leaders may also perform poorly if they fail to decide swiftly and act boldly in turbulent, problematic and urgent situations.[86]

The cultural context may be a relevant contingency. One study found that Singaporean versus Portuguese team members react *more negatively* to a leader characterized by low humility.[87] It is possible that, in contexts where the value of humility is strongly endorsed,[88] individuals are more sensitive to leaders who do not show humility.

Finally, leaders possess many attributes and the effect of one attribute such as humility is not independent of other attributes.[89] A study found that CEOs that are both humble *and* narcissistic have a socialized charisma, which leads them to cultivate an innovative culture and deliver innovative performance.[90] Humility alone is therefore not enough to produce the best outcomes. In a similar vein, narcissistic leaders can have positive effects on followers (in terms of perceptions of leader effectiveness, follower job engagement and subjective and objective follower job performance) when their narcissism is tempered by humility.[91] Steve Jobs was a paragon of such a paradoxical profile.[92] His narcissism was tempered with humility developed over the years, probably as a consequence of the 'humiliation' from having been 'fired' from 'his' Apple.

Jim Collins also pointed out that the most effective leaders have a paradoxical mixture of humility and fierce resolve, timidity and ferocity, shyness and fearlessness.[93] One may thus conclude that the most effective leaders combine paradoxical features (Box 8.3). They are humble *and* self-confident.

Box 8.3 Exemplars of paradoxical humility

Darwin Smith: 'shy, unpretentious, even awkward' and also stoic

Jim Collins described Darwin Smith, then at the helm of Kimberly-Clark, as follows:

> Darwin Smith seems to have come from Mars. Shy, unpretentious, even awkward, Smith shunned attention … But if you consider Smith soft or meek, you would be terribly mistaken. His lack of pretense was coupled with a fierce, even stoic, resolve toward life. Smith grew up on an Indiana farm and put himself through night school at Indiana University by working the day shift at International Harvester. One day, he lost a finger on the job. The story goes that he went to class that evening and returned to work the very next day. Eventually, this poor but determined Indiana farm boy earned admission to Harvard Law School. He showed the same iron will when he was at the helm of Kimberly-Clark. Indeed, two months after Smith became CEO, doctors diagnosed him with nose and throat cancer and told him he had less than a year to live. He duly informed the board of his illness but said he had no plans to die anytime soon. Smith held to his demanding work schedule while commuting weekly from Wisconsin to Houston for radiation therapy. He lived 25 more years, 20 of them as CEO.[94]

Abraham Lincoln: 'extremely self-confident but extremely humble'

Scholars and practitioners have praised the virtues of Abraham Lincoln (Figure 8.2). Nancy Koehn,[95] a historian at Harvard Business School, wrote an article for *The New York Times* on 'Lincoln's School of Management'. Howard Schultz, chief executive of Starbucks until 2017, argued 'Lincoln's presidency is a big, well-lit classroom for business leaders seeking to build successful, enduring organizations'.[96]

David Brooks explained Lincoln's legacy as follows:

Lincoln's temperament surpasses all explanation. His early experience of depression and suffering gave him a radical self-honesty. He had the double-minded personality that we need in all our leaders. He was involved in a bloody civil war, but he was an exceptionally poor hater. He was deeply engaged, but also able to step back; a passionate advocate, but also able to see his enemy's point of view; aware of his own power, but aware of when he was helpless in the hands of fate; extremely self-confident but extremely humble. Candidates who don't have a contradictory temperament have no way to check themselves and are thus dangerous.[97]

Figure 8.2 Abraham Lincoln, circa 1858.[98]

Ethical leadership

When ethics are missing

Scandals like those involving Enron (misreporting profits, hiding losses), Facebook/Cambridge Analytica (data appropriation), Uber's Trevor Kalanick (cultivation of a culture of sexual harassment), Volkswagen (manipulation of emissions) and Wells Fargo (fraud with customer accounts) have highlighted that organizations, their employees, the community and other stakeholders may be seriously damaged when unethical leadership contaminates teams and the whole organization. It can lead to a situation in which unethical behaviours are not only tolerated by their leaders but are also encouraged, and this may have happened at Wells Fargo[99] (see Box 8.4). It has been argued[100] that, at Volkswagen, the centralized management style and the neglect of outside voices may have contributed to the scandal. Over time, a process of normalization of deviance developed.[101]

Box 8.4 Do good codes mean good ethics?

Codes of ethics and leadership statements are sometimes used as backcourt curtains or PR actions aiming at diverting public attention from unethical behaviours. Consider, for example, the following leadership statement of Volkswagen: 'We aim to be the world's most successful, fascinating and sustainable automobile manufacturer'. Reflect also on the first paragraph of the former Wells Fargo Code of Ethics and Business Conduct:

> Wells Fargo expects its team members to adhere to the highest possible standards of ethics and business conduct with customers, team members, vendors, stockholders, other investors, and the communities it serves and to comply with all applicable laws, rules, and regulations that govern our businesses.[102]

Both organizations fell very short of the code. Kenneth Lay, then CEO and Chairman of Enron, released a memorandum addressed to all employees on July 1, 2000, under the subject heading 'Code of ethics'. The first sentence was: 'As officers and employees of Enron Corp., its subsidiaries, and its affiliated companies ... we are responsible for conducting the business affairs of the Company in accordance with all applicable laws and in a moral and honest manner'. One key extract from this code was: 'We are dedicated to conducting business according to all applicable local and international laws and regulations ... and with the highest and ethical standards'.[103] One year later, the company collapsed. It turned out Enron had been managed under toxic and unethical leadership for years. The feast of arrogance and unethicality ended in disaster.[104]

Concept and dimensions

Scandals like those discussed above have called attention, amongst scholars and practitioners, to the need for promoting ethical leadership. Researchers have started to consider ethical leadership as a distinctive leadership style, rather than considering ethics as the ethical component of other leadership styles. Ethical leadership has been defined 'as the demonstration of normatively appropriate conduct through personal actions and interpersonal relationships, and the promotion of such conduct to followers through two-way communication, reinforcement, and decision-making'.[105] An ethical leader behaves as a moral person and as a moral manager.[106] As a moral person, he/she reveals traits (e.g., honesty and integrity) and behaviours (e.g., concern, fairness, ethical decision making) that make followers see him/her as an 'authentically moral person'.[107] A moral manager actively influences followers (through communication, disciplinary actions and leading by example) to be ethically conscientious and encourages them to act ethically.

Several researchers have operationalized ethical leadership by developing reliable and validated instruments that measure its key dimensions. The Ethical Leadership Scale (ELS)[108] treats ethical leadership as a uni-dimensional construct. The Ethical

Table 8.2 Dimensions of ethical leadership

Dimensions (De Hoogh and Den Hartog, 2008)	Definitions (De Hoogh and Den Hartog, 2008, p. 298)
Morality and fairness	Being 'honest, trustworthy, fair and caring'.
Role clarification	'Transparency, engagement in open communication with followers and clarification of expectations and responsibilities so that employees are clear on what is expected from them.'
Power sharing	'Allowing followers a say in decision making and listening to their ideas and concerns.'
Other operationalizations and measures (illustrations)	*Ethical leadership*: Lu and Lin (2014). Unidimensional. *Ethical Leadership Scale*: Brown, Treviño and Harrison (2005). Unidimensional. *Ethical Leadership at Work Questionnaire* (Kalshoven, Den Hartog and De Hoogh, 2011). Dimensions: fairness; integrity; ethical guidance; people orientation; power sharing; role clarification; concern for sustainability.

Leadership at Work Questionnaire[109] embraces seven dimensions: fairness, integrity, ethical guidance, people orientation, power sharing, role clarification and concern for sustainability. A more parsimonious model[110] includes three dimensions: morality and fairness, empowerment and role clarification (Table 8.2). Ethical leaders act fairly toward employees (and other stakeholders), behaving honestly and taking responsibility for their own actions. They communicate in transparent and respectful ways, and clarify responsibilities, expectations and performance goals (i.e., they help employees understand what is expected from them). They share power by providing subordinates with voice, listening to them, asking for their input, inviting them to participate in decision-making. It has been argued that this was precisely the kind of ethical conduct that was absent from Volkswagen.[111]

Despite the variety of scales for measuring ethical leadership, the ELS[112] remains the most commonly used measure.[113] There are reasons, however, to use multidimensional models, considering that the antecedents and consequences of each dimension are not necessarily the same.

Outcomes of ethical leadership

Ethical leadership relates positively with several followers' attitudes and behaviours, such as commitment, satisfaction with the leader, trust, gratitude; satisfaction with the job, the leader and personal and family life; commitment, engagement, psychological wellbeing, role and extra-role performance and perceived leader effectiveness.[114] Moreover, ethical leaders, by setting clear standards of conduct, promote followers' moral reasoning and ethical conduct,[115] encourage them to speak up against unethical behaviour and to internally report wrongdoing.[116] Research has also found that ethical leadership by top managers has an indirect 'trickle down' effect on supervisors' ethical leadership, which increases team/organizational citizenship behaviours and performance.[117]

The impact of ethical leadership on followers and team/organizational outcomes is therefore not necessarily direct; rather it may be mediated.[118] For example, followers are more likely to report internal wrongdoing because ethical leaders promote psychological safety by genuinely supporting the practice of speaking up.[119] Followers of ethical leaders are happier at work and more committed and effective because ethical leaders foster positive psychological resources such as PsyCap[120] (see Chapter 3). Ethical leaders contribute to team/organizational performance and reputation because they:

1   Encourage a fair and ethical team/organizational climate.
2   Foster collective conscientiousness.
3   Promote team cohesion and voice.
4   Reduce workplace jealousy.
5   Operate as antidotes against perverse political manoeuvers and manipulations.

Ethical leaders, in summary, positively/ethically shape the context of work (see Box 8.5), producing spirals of justice and ethicality within the team/organization, creating more sustainable businesses. Several theoretical routes may explain such effects.[121] One is social learning theory, which suggests that followers learn the norms of appropriate conduct by observing how their leaders behave. Ethical leaders act as role models by demonstrating the type of behaviours they want to encourage and those that are not allowed. The other route is social exchange: when employees perceive the leader as caring and concerned about their wellbeing, they reciprocate by developing trust in the leaders, higher commitment and more organizational citizenship behaviours.

Box 8.5 What leads people to lead ethically?

The individual and the context

Two main factors may explain why leaders behave ethically.[122] First, individuals characterized by high conscientiousness, agreeableness, emotional stability and by a strong moral identity are more likely to lead ethically. Conversely, morally disengaged leaders tend to be less ethical. Second, both context and the situation matter. A mid-level leader may experience difficulties in being ethical if their supervisor is unethical and does not support an ethical style. As Zimbardo argued[123] (and demonstrated with the Stanford Prison Experiment), 'a vinegar barrel will always transform sweet cucumbers into sour pickles – regardless of the best intentions, resilience, and genetic nature of those cucumbers'. Conversely, ethical top managers and an ethical team/organizational climate encourage and facilitate ethical leadership at the intermediate and lower levels. The ASA (attraction, selection, attrition)[124] framework helps with understanding such an effect: ethical organizations attract and select ethical leaders (who also feel attracted to and select ethical organizations) and those leaders who do not fit such a context leave voluntarily or are 'pushed out'.

A similar process unfolds when the context is unethical. Socialization processes may also operate as facilitators or instigators of (un)ethical leadership. The process called 'Enronization'[125] is illustrative:

> Individuals with a risk-taking management style and competent trading talent were recruited, primarily from among top Harvard and Stanford business school graduates, lured by US$20,000 signing bonuses, US$80,000 salaries, and annual bonuses

of up to 100 percent. Once hired, they were 'Enronized' to compete fiercely among themselves and leave all other loyalties, including family, behind. Under Skilling, this 'best place to work in America' is, backstage, among the worst.

Attrition at Goldman Sachs

Greg Smith, then a Goldman Sachs executive director and head of the firm's United States equity derivatives business in Europe, the Middle East and Africa, explained in *The New York Times* why he was leaving the company:

> Today is my last day at Goldman Sachs. After almost 12 years at the firm – first as a summer intern while at Stanford, then in New York for 10 years, and now in London – I believe I have worked here long enough to understand the trajectory of its culture, its people and its identity. And I can honestly say that the environment now is as toxic and destructive as I have ever seen it … The culture was the secret sauce that made this place great and allowed us to earn our clients' trust for 143 years. It wasn't just about making money; this alone will not sustain a firm for so long. It had something to do with pride and belief in the organization. I am sad to say that I look around today and see virtually no trace of the culture that made me love working for this firm for many years. I no longer have the pride, or the belief … I knew it was time to leave when I realized I could no longer look students in the eye and tell them what a great place this was to work … How did we get here? The firm changed the way it thought about leadership. Leadership used to be about ideas, setting an example and doing the right thing. Today, if you make enough money for the firm (and are not currently an axe murderer) you will be promoted into a position of influence.[126]

Contingency factors

Several individual and contextual features condition the positive impact of ethical leaders on the followers and organizational outcomes.[127] The ethical orientation of a mid-level ethical leader may be undermined or neutralized by an unethical context or unethical top management. The followers' characteristics may also facilitate or neutralize the ethical efforts of the leader. For example, followers with stronger entity morality beliefs are more likely to see an ethical leader as their role model and thus respond positively. Conversely, followers with weaker moral beliefs may react less positively and may even boycott a leader's ethical actions.

Leader characteristics and behaviours other than ethics may also condition the effect of ethical leadership. Ethical leadership behaviours carried out by Machiavellian leaders may be received with distrust and suspicion – because followers suspect the authenticity of such 'ethical' behaviour. Conversely, ethical leadership may produce more positive effects in followers if leaders have a reputation of being technically competent. As discussed above, leaders express a plethora of attributes and the effect of ethical leadership is not independent of other attributes. Being ethical is not enough to be a positive leader.

Perverse consequences of ethical leadership

Despite the potential positive consequences of ethical leadership, the potential negative effects, both for the leaders and the followers, must not be neglected. Being an ethical leader may be mentally tiring,[128] lead to a sense of moral licensing,[129] or moral superiority,[130] ultimately leading to the adoption of unethical behaviours. Three interrelated mechanisms explain this paradox: mental fatigue, moral licensing and moral superiority.

Mental fatigue

Behaving ethically may imply following norms that are not aligned with the leader's natural – and often self-interested – tendencies. Abiding by such norms, incentivizing followers to act ethically, adopting disciplinary actions against followers who act unethically, and incorporating complex ethical issues (e.g., facing moral dilemmas and adopting moral compromises) in the decision-making process are all depleting activities that consume self-regulatory resources.[131] As a consequence, the leader feels depleted and low in willpower, thus being less able to suppress abusive and unethical behaviours, both in their self and in followers.[132]

Moral licensing

Moral licensing 'refers to the effect that when people initially behave in a moral way, they are later more likely to display behaviours that are immoral, unethical, or otherwise problematic'.[133] Therefore, having just behaved morally, a leader may feel entitled to perform morally questionable behaviour later.[134] One possible explanation is that after having established a moral image a leader may feel that an immoral action is allowed without losing the halo of that moral image. Such perceived permission may emerge because ethical behaviours accumulate *moral credits* and *moral credentials*.[135] First, when leaders feel that they have a surplus of these credits, they may use such an excess to 'purchase' the right to deviate from social and ethical norms. Second, ethical behaviours may make the leader develop a more favourable self-concept and consequently perceive actions that would otherwise be perceived as questionable to be legitimate or, at least, be less negative.[136] Moral licensing helps to explain why leaders such as Nelson Mandela and Martin Luther King[137] and other leaders with a long track record of good deeds were caught adopting questionable actions. The loyalty of Mandela to his successor Jacob Zuma (the fourth President of South Africa from 2009 to his resignation, on February 14, 2018, under accusations of corruption) 'seemed to have trumped his disgust of corruption and nepotism'.[138] Martin Luther King 'had his own personal demons: It is well chronicled that he was a serial adulterer'.[139]

Perceptions of moral superiority

Leaders strongly committed to a personal ethical philosophy can develop a sense of moral superiority.[140] Consequently, they may act unethically through silencing and delegitimizing followers who resist them or who do not espouse their ethical philosophy. Those leaders may also be unable to face ethical dilemmas with circumspection and moral compromising. Even when a leader does not develop an inner sense of moral superiority, followers may perceive the leader as having such a sense, from which unintended effects may emerge. Followers who consider the leader highly ethical may respond with less organizational citizenship behaviours.[141] Followers may perceive that the leader looks down upon their morality and considers them insufficiently moral (i.e., the leader is perceived as being ethically arrogant). Followers may reciprocate by reduced engagement in organizational citizenship behaviours. Conversely, a leader who forgives others' questionable behaviours may be more able to make an organization (or a country, like Mandela's South Africa) flourish.[142]

Authentic leadership

'Know Thyself'

The concept of authenticity has its roots in ancient Greek philosophy and is reflected in the aphorism 'Know Thyself' (inscribed in the Temple of Apollo at Delphi, see Figure 8.3).[143] The etymology of the word can be traced to the Greek *authenteo*, meaning 'to have full power over',[144] and reflects the notion of an authentic being as one who is 'the master of his or her own domain'.[145] Authenticity differs from sincerity, in that one can be sincere with others while not having an accurate perspective of one's own values, strengths and limitations; furthermore, they may lack understanding of others' perceptions of these personal capabilities. While sincerity is an intersubjective experience that depends upon the existence of an external 'other', authenticity contains a self-referential component[146] that does not require an explicit involvement or relationship with others.[147] One may be sincere (toward others) without being self-aware.

The concept of authenticity has been applied in different contexts, including leadership. Some practitioners have been especially vocal in extolling the virtues of leaders who 'are true to themselves'.[149] The fascination with authenticity is epitomized in Norma Hollis, 'Chief Authenticity Officer' of Authenticity U (allegedly 'The Company that Teaches Authenticity'),[150] and who describes herself as an 'Authority on Authenticity and Self-Awareness, Leadership and Communication'.[151] Authentic leaders, she argues,

> are a special breed of people. They know who they are and this self-awareness empowers them to transform their life and the lives of those they lead. Their authenticity builds loyalty, trust, collaboration, engagement and commitment. It forges positive change in their teams, their company, their community and their industry. They are the new, emerging force in an ever changing arena.[152]

Figure 8.3 'Gnōthi Sauton' (Know Thyself). Memento Mori (Latin: 'remember that you have to die') mosaic from excavations in the convent of San Gregorio, Via Appia, Rome, Italy. Now in the National Museum, Rome, Italy.[148]

Authentic leadership and its components

Harvard Business School Professor and former Medtronic CEO Bill George[153] has contributed towards developing interest in authentic leadership, not only amongst practitioners but also within the scholarly community.[154] The concomitant proliferation of practitioner and scholarly writings has given rise to competing conceptions of authentic leadership (AL), creating confusion about the construct.[155] Conceptualization and operationalization efforts have, however, been carried out to provide clarity. Although no agreed-upon definition of authentic leadership has been reached,[156] most researchers agree that AL is

> a pattern of leader behaviour that draws upon and promotes both positive psychological capacities and a positive ethical climate, to foster greater self-awareness, an internalized moral perspective, balanced processing of information, and relational transparency on the part of leaders working with followers, fostering positive self-development.[157]

Based on this definition, AL has been operationalized as a construct embracing four components (definitions on Table 8.3): self-awareness, relational transparency, balanced processing and internalized moral perspective.

Table 8.3 Dimensions of authentic leadership

Dimensions (Neider and Schriesheim, 2011; Walumbwa, Avolio, Gardner, Wernsing and Peterson, 2008)	Definitions (Rego, Sousa, Marques and Cunha, 2012a, p. 430; see also Gardner et al., 2005; Hannah, Avolio and Walumbwa, 2011 and Walumbwa, Avolio, Gardner, Wernsing and Peterson, 2008)
Self-awareness	'The degree to which the leader demonstrates an understanding of how (s)he derives and makes sense of the world and is aware of his or her strengths, limitations, how others see him or her, and how (s)he impacts others.'
Relational transparency	'The degree to which the leader presents his/her authentic self (as opposed to a false or distorted self) to others, openly shares information, and expresses his/her true thoughts and feelings, reinforcing a level of openness with others that provides them with an opportunity to be forthcoming with their ideas, challenges, and opinions.'
Balanced processing	'The degree to which the leader shows that (s)he objectively analyzes the relevant data before coming to a decision and solicits views that challenge deeply held positions.'
Internalized moral perspective	'The degree to which the leader sets a high standard for moral and ethical conduct, guides actions by internal moral standards and values (versus group, organizational, and societal pressures), and expresses decision making and behaviours that are consistent with such internalized values.'

(Continued)

Table 8.3 (Cont.)

Other operationalizations and measures (illustrations)	*ALQ, Authentic Leadership Questionnaire* (Walumbwa, Avolio, Gardner, Wernsing and Peterson, 2008). Dimensions: self-awareness; relational transparency; balanced processing; internalized moral perspective. *Leader Authenticity Inventory* (LAI; Henderson and Hoy, 1983). Three dimensions: acceptance of personal and organizational responsibility for action outcomes and mistakes; the non-manipulation of subordinates; the salience of the self over role requirements. *Authentic Leadership* (Tate, 2008). Dimensions (based on George, 2003): self-discipline and ethical standards; establishing positive relationships; passion for purpose. *AL-IQ, Authentic Leadership Integrated Questionnaire* (Levesque-Côté, Fernet, Austin and Morin, 2017). A combination of ALQ and ALI, with the same dimensions.

Authentic leadership theory is rooted in the concept of self-regulation,[158] a process through which leaders align their behaviours with their values and intentions, thus making their authentic selves transparent to others. The four dimensions mentioned above have a self-regulatory focus governed partially through the leader's internal standards and evaluations of their own behaviours.[159] Each separate component does not independently contribute to making a leader *authentic* – the four components are necessary together. Being relationally transparent (a form of sincerity) is not enough to consider someone authentic. Being authentic is far more than saying what pops up in the person's mind and a leader such as Donald Trump cannot be considered authentic just because he plays to the authentic racism and sexism of many of his base.[160]

Outcomes of authentic leadership

Authentic leadership theory has emphasized that, through processes such as positive role modelling, leaders help their followers achieve positive outcomes – and avoid negative ones.[161] Empirical evidence suggests that AL produces several positive outcomes, both at individual and collective levels. Specifically, it has been shown that authentic leadership is related to outcomes such as:

* Followers' job satisfaction (including satisfaction with the leader) and wellbeing, creativity, task performance, work engagement, affective commitment, organizational citizenship behaviours and other pro-social behaviours, and psychological capital.
* Team/group and organization performance, team potency.
* Rated leader effectiveness.[162]

These effects may be explained by multiple mechanisms (e.g., follower identification with the leader, trust in the leader, follower empowerment, social learning and positive role modelling, as well as positive follower states).[163] For example, employees led by an authentic leader develop higher PsyCap (e.g., when authentic leaders solicit views that challenge deeply held positions and openly share information with employees, employees become more self-confident) and this psychological resource drives them to be more creative.[164] The relationship between authentic leadership and followers' pro-social and ethical behaviours may emerge because authentic leaders foster followers' moral courage (i.e., 'the ability to use inner principles to do what is good for others, regardless of threat to self, as a matter of practice').[165] Specifically, through social learning and role modelling processes, the four components of authentic leadership foster followers' moral courage and make them more willing to face ethical challenges in more ethical and socially desirable (i.e., prosocial) ways.[166]

The process of team reflexivity may be explained by the relationship between authentic leadership and team performance[167] (see Box 7.2 in Chapter 7). The self-regulation process inherent to authentic leadership has a contagious effect on team members and thus manifests in team reflexivity, mainly through role-modelling and social information processing.[168] Team reflexivity fosters team performance because of several reasons. First, team members critically examine the appropriateness and alignment of their goals and processes. Second, they check that those goals and processes are sustainable and reflect their true intentions. Third, team members' knowledge and skills are more likely to be integrated and deployed. Fourth, individual and collective decisions are more informed and effective, thus yielding higher levels of performance.[169]

Authentic leadership may also have positive consequences for the leaders themselves (see Box 8.6 for a critical perspective). For example, authentic leaders experience better mental wellbeing.[170] By acting in accord with their true self and expressing themselves in ways that are consistent with their inner thoughts and feelings, authentic leaders are less prone to ego-depletion,[171] thus experiencing less job stress and developing stronger work engagement. This relationship is moderated by interactions with subordinates. More authentic leaders deplete less during subordinate interactions (i.e., through developing authentic followership, authentic leaders 'build reserves of relational trust that they are able to tap during difficult times'[172]). In contrast, less authentic leaders deplete more from subordinate interactions (more interactions *force* them to adopt faking and masking behavioural displays more often). Considering that leaders' mental wellbeing may influence both employees' wellbeing and leaders' effectiveness,[173] this empirical evidence indirectly suggests that authentic leadership promotes followers' wellbeing and leaders' effectiveness.

Box 8.6 Fighting the negative in the positive through dialogical pedagogy

Can individuals discover and develop their authentic potential by themselves, via a combination of self-awareness and self-narration, is a question Izhak Berkovic has explored.[174] In his view, the attempt to develop a coherent self-narrative through a retrospective perspective (i.e., reflecting on personal life stories[175]) can lead to false narratives and self-deception:

> Individuals often submit themselves – even unconsciously – to external expectations or social roles and act in a conformist manner ... It is no surprise, therefore, that authentic leaders frequently create stories portraying themselves in a positive light, as being humble, good-hearted, and selfless.[176] At present, authentic leadership

theory appears unwilling to acknowledge that pressures on leaders to be consistent with the dominating positive images of leadership can cause them to suppress or hide parts of their true selves.[177]

Berkovic also argues that encouraging leaders to develop their authentic leadership can inadvertently foster in them feelings of moral superiority, leading them to silence and delegitimize followers who resist them, thus harming interpersonal relations and individual and collective performance. Finally, he argues that the idea of developing an authentic harmonious self-concept, as a prerequisite to acting as a leader, is problematic. In his view, the notion of one's stable self is chimerical because life is a work in progress that raises continuous challenges. Therefore, the quest for authenticity is a dynamic and lifelong exploration. Consequently, he argues, two main didactic methods of AL development (i.e., narrative identity processing and dramaturgical enactment) are based on technical-functionalist premises that are worthy of questioning. He recommends an alternative method: dialogical pedagogy. This approach assumes that leader development is an intersubjective communication that occurs during the development interactions (e.g., between the leader and the facilitator, or between the leader and the followers). Dialogical pedagogy, supported in four communicational pillars (candor, inclusion, confirmation and presentness),[178] includes eight components: self-exposure, open-mindedness, empathy, care, respect, critical thinking, contact and mutuality.

Questions for reflection

- Identify the limitations of (a) narrative identity processing and (b) dramaturgical enactment as ways of developing authentic leadership.
- Suppose that, as mentor, you are invited to help a leader to develop his/her authentic leadership. Based on dialogical pedagogy, identify the main stages of the process you would adopt.

Dangers and challenges of authentic leadership

As Grant suggests, authenticity may be a dangerous route and 'be yourself' may be undesirable advice. People have thoughts and feelings that are fundamental to their lives and that, for that reason, must be left unspoken.[179] In no other field is this caution more relevant than in leadership. A true-to-oneself leader may become blind to others' selves and feelings, lose the respect of her/his followers and other stakeholders, thereby derailing her/himself as a leader. Such a leader may convince him/herself that the dysfunctional side of his/her authenticity is the inevitable price of being effective. And, assuming that authenticity is a positive quality regardless of the circumstances and the effects upon the others, one may become an 'authentic asshole'[180] who humiliates others (see Box 8.7).

Box 8.7 The negative in the positive: authentic idiots

Trump: an authentic idiot?

1   'Nixon was not acting authentically, where it can be argued, Trump was. As we can see, authenticity is not an unambiguously good concept … a person can be authentic about destructive characteristics of the self; an "authentic asshole".'[181]

2   'One of the reasons Donald Trump has become the Republican frontrunner in the US is because he says what he thinks, and he doesn't care if you disagree. Trump may be an idiot, but he's an authentic idiot.'[182]

Mrs Thatcher: a 'fucking stupid, petit bourgeois woman'?

Margaret Thatcher's first foreign secretary, Lord Carrington, classified her as a 'fucking stupid, petit bourgeois woman'.[183] Her 'natural' style made her unable to listen to her advisers and ended up threatening her position:

> She was capable of humiliating a staff member in public, she was a notoriously bad listener, and she believed that compromise was cowardice. As she became known to the world as the 'Iron Lady,' Thatcher grew more and more convinced of the rightness of her ideas and the necessity of her coercive methods. She could beat anyone into submission with the power of her rhetoric and conviction, and she only got better at it. Eventually, though, it was her undoing – she was ousted by her own cabinet.[184]

Being authentic is therefore not necessarily desirable.[185] Anthony Weiner, the congressman and New York mayoral candidate who sent pictures of his penis to women he met on the Internet, was 'authentic' in sharing his thoughts, needs and wants. In contrast, one of Pfeffer's colleagues, a senior-level college administrator whose daughter died from a drug overdose, adopted an inauthentic approach: he remained committed to his job, providing motivation and encouragement to followers, despite his grief and grieving. Pfeffer's scepticism about the alleged virtues of authentic leadership did not set aside the presumed authenticity of one its gurus: Bill George. According to an individual who knows him, the ideas in *True North*, his book, are closer to what Bill George currently believes than to the behaviour he engaged in while he was leading Medtronic.[186] The implication: being authentic is different from believing in the merits of authenticity.

Being true to the self the leader wants to become

Although authenticity is potentially beneficial for effective leadership, it contains risks, which raises an authenticity paradox: being true to oneself may have a negative impact on followers, while 'feeling like a fake can be a sign of growth'[187] (see Box 8.8). While going against natural inclinations can make the leader feel like an impostor, the inclination to obey one's true self may be an excuse for keeping doing what it is more comfortable, instead of doing what it is necessary to do to pursue valuable goals and be effective in new and challenging roles.[188]

Leaders facing changes in demands and expectations and new leadership roles (including in different cultural contexts) may require adopting attitudes and behaviours that are different from those required by former roles. A leader maintaining strict coherence between personal attitudes and behaviours, who furthermore discloses every personal thought and feeling, loses credibility and effectiveness (Box 8.8), especially if they have not yet proven their value as a leader. Therefore, being true to oneself may be a privilege of those leaders who have proven their credibility and effectiveness or who are financially successful.[189] For those who have no such a status, it is important that they see themselves as 'works in progress' and maintain the courage and love of learning to evolve and transform through experiencing new and more challenging roles. As Ibarra pointed out, although this 'adaptive approach to authenticity can make us feel like impostors, because it involves doing things that may not come naturally ... it's outside our comfort zones that we learn the most about leading effectively'.[190]

Box 8.8 The positive in the negative: the benefits of hiding feelings and emotions

It could be said that hiding feelings and emotions is inauthentic. But there are circumstances in which leaders must hide what's in their 'soul'. An illustration is US President Abraham Lincoln:[191]

> A sensitive man, Lincoln was sickened by the bloodshed of the Civil War. He often grew deeply distressed about the conflict, its carnage, and his own ability to keep doing what he believed he must as commander-in-chief. Some of his emotional anxiety took itself out on his appetite. He lost more than 30 pounds as president, weighing about 155 pounds when he died. He also had a great deal of trouble sleeping and spent many nights pacing the second-floor hallway of the White House. Despite his own distress, he rarely revealed his doubts and fears to anyone other than his closest confidants. He knew that if the president displayed such anxiety, it would quickly spread to his generals, his advisors, and the American people, and this contagion would damage his mission to save the Union. Throughout his presidency, Lincoln relied heavily on such emotional awareness and control.

Effective leaders are, therefore, paradoxically[192] both chameleons (i.e., high self-monitors) *and* people that are true to self (i.e., high self-monitors). They are able to develop new true-selves through experience and learning, experimenting with different identities according to the requirements of the situation.[193] In short, 'leading authentically does not make one a good leader', it simply makes the leader authentic (Box 8.9). To be effective, a leader must be 'adaptively authentic',[194] able to internalize their (new) roles into their self-concept.[195] Naturally, this 'adaptive' endeavour is more acceptable and effective for some authentic leadership dimensions (such as relational transparency and balanced processing) than for others (like the internal moral compass). It is difficult to envision how a chameleon leader, in terms of moral compass, may win credibility and respect from their followers and partners. Even in this regard, however, an authentic leader must be able to face ethical dilemmas (i.e., when different values compete) via moral compromises that represent the lesser of several evils.[196]

Box 8.9 'Leading authentically does not make one a good leader, it simply makes them authentic'

Susan Faircloth is a professor at the University of North Carolina Wilmington, whose research interests include Indigenous education. In a paper published in the journal *Advances in Developing Human Resources*, she shares her reflections on the conception of AL from an Indigenous scholar/leader perspective.[197] The paper is a self-narrative around her family and cultural origins, significant life events and turning points, and about her values and beliefs. She confesses that she applied for a leadership position in a university as department chair but, one year later, she made 'the heart-wrenching decision' to step down: 'My own personal and professional values and beliefs as an Indigenous female leader – values regarding relationships, respect, responsibility, and reciprocity – were not in sync with the environment in which I was tasked with leading'.[198]

Suggestions and questions for reflection

- Faircloth realized that 'one's ability to step away from an environment in which one cannot lead authentically may, in fact, be a sign of real leadership'.[199] Do you agree? What are the implications of such a leadership philosophy for the team or the organization from which the leader steps down?
- After acknowledging that a leader must take into account not only their own values but also those of the other people, Faircloth writes:[200] 'The challenge then becomes how to maintain one's sense of Indigeneity while also adopting or adapting non-Indigenous theories and practices. Herein lies the root of the messiness of leadership for me'. How do you relate this perspective with that of Herminia Ibarra about being 'adaptively authentic'?[201]
- In the last part of the paper, Faircloth asks and answers:[202] 'Can individuals be taught how to be authentic leaders in traditional Westernized institutions? Perhaps not'. Do you agree or disagree? Why? Under which conditions?
- Faircloth also states that 'leading authentically does not make one a good leader, it simply makes them authentic'.[203] How do you relate this argument with literature suggesting that authentic leaders are more effective?
- In which position could Faircloth have more impact in terms of defending her values and heritage – as the department chair or as a 'simple' professor?

Servant leadership

Influencing and serving

The notion of servant leadership contradicts the assumption of leadership as top down and considers instead that leadership can be both service *and* influence. Servant leadership is about exercising power as a *responsibility*, not as a *right* or a source of *freedom*.[204]

Robert Greenleaf (1904–1990) coined 'servant leadership'; he had worked for 40 years at AT&T. After retiring, he started exploring how institutions can better serve society. He characterized servant leadership as follows:

> The servant-leader is servant first ... It begins with the natural feeling that one wants to serve, to serve first. Then conscious choice brings one to aspire to lead. That person is sharply different from one who is leader first, perhaps because of the need to assuage an unusual power drive or to acquire material possessions ... The best test, and difficult to administer, is: Do those served grow as persons? Do they, while being served, become healthier, wiser, freer, more autonomous, more likely themselves to become servants? And, what is the effect on the least privileged in society? Will they benefit or at least not be further deprived?[205]

According to the Greenleaf Center for Servant Leadership (initially called 'The Center for Applied Ethics', founded in 1964), servant leadership 'is a philosophy and set of practices that enriches the lives of individuals, builds better organizations and ultimately creates a more just and caring world'.[206] Larry Spears[207] studied Greenleaf's original writings and identified ten critical characteristics of servant leadership:

1. Listening
2. Empathy
3. Healing
4. Awareness
5. Persuasion
6. Conceptualization
7. Foresight
8. Stewardship
9. Commitment to the growth of people
10. Building community.

Servant leadership was adopted as a guiding philosophy in companies including Herman Miller, ServiceMaster, Synovus Financial Corporation, Southwest Airlines and TDIndustries[208] (see Box 8.10). Howard Schultz advocated that the US was in desperate need of servant leaders.[209]

Box 8.10 The positive of the positive

TDIndustries positions itself on its website as supporting 'a culture of inclusion, a culture of ownership. We accomplish this through a Servant Leadership philosophy that puts others first'.[210] One of the company's values is 'Lead with a servant's heart', and is operationalized as follows:[211] 'Be humble and respectful. Listen to understand, not to respond. Teach, inspire and support others to be their best. Hold yourself and others accountable'. The company uses a number of techniques to ensure that its leaders do not exploit workers and, rather, enables them to flourish. Every year, employees evaluate whether their supervisor treats them fairly, offers appropriate training and includes them in their team. This feedback affects supervisors' salaries and promotions.[212]

Ingvar Kamprad (1926–2018; see Figure 8.4), founder of IKEA, told *Forbes* in 2000,

> I see my task as serving the majority of people. The question is, how do you find out what they want, how best to serve them? My answer is to stay close to ordinary people, because at heart I am one of them.[213]

Cheryl Polote-Williamson, who defines herself as a 'visionary, influencer, motivator'[214] and as aiming to help 'female entrepreneurs build business and personal relationships built on honesty, integrity, and trust',[215] wrote in *Forbes*:

> For as long as I can remember, I have had an extremely strong and uncommon desire to serve others. As I have grown and developed as a professional and leader, I have realized that my innate desire to serve has catapulted my career to astronomical heights; all because I have always followed my desire to serve *first*. A leader with a servant's heart is a truly invaluable asset, and everyone in a leadership position should seek to adopt this type of mentality. [Italics in the original.]

Self-reporting as a servant leader may be somewhat peculiar but the declaration points out that the topic attracts practitioner attention.

Components of servant leadership

Servant leadership has been accepted more as a leadership approach than as a theory. With the exception of an article by Graham[217] in the inaugural issue of *The Leadership Quarterly*, servant leadership attracted little interest from the academic community until the 2000s. Since then (mainly after the seminal work of Ehrhart, 2004), researchers have examined the conceptual underpinnings of servant leadership, developed theory and carried out a significant number of empirical studies. A central feature of servant leadership is that such a style places the good of the followers over the self-interest of the leader, focusses on follower development and de-emphasizes the glorification of the leader.[218] Several psychometrically sound instruments were also

Figure 8.4 Ingvar Kamprad lecturing a group of students at Växjö University in Sweden.[216]

developed to measure the core dimensions of servant leadership (see Table 8.4). Empirical research has demonstrated the increments to value of servant leadership in comparison with other leadership styles.[219]

It has been argued that servant leadership is particularly relevant in today's business world because servant leaders, through adopting behaviours that transcend their self-interest to serve the interests of all stakeholders, produce several positive consequences:[220] employees experience greater happiness, develop more positive attitudes and adopt a serving orientation that benefits the organization, its members and the greater community. The theory development suffers, however, from three main limitations.[221] First, there is no consensus about how servant leadership is defined.[222] Second, there is a lack of agreement among researchers about the components of servant leadership, as illustrated by Table 8.4. Although significant overlaps exist between the dimensions of these models, differences are also significant.[223] Third, researchers disagree about whether servant leadership is to be treated as a trait phenomenon or as a set of cognitive abilities and behavioural processes and demonstrations. As shown in Table 8.4, conceptualizations include as dimensions individual characteristics or traits such as humility, courage and conceptual skills but also behavioural processes such as empowerment, emotional healing and creating value for the community.

Are servant leaders more effective?

There is now a significant number of empirical studies suggesting that servant leadership may have a positive impact upon employees' attitudes and behaviours such as job satisfaction, wellbeing, organizational commitment, follower disengagement, reduced turnover intentions, creative behaviours and role and extra-role performance.[225] Servant leaders may also promote team and organizational performance[226] (see Box 8.11 for what impels someone to be a servant leader).

Several mechanisms are advanced to explain such effects. Followers of servant leaders are able to realize their full capabilities, develop higher self-efficacy, develop the sense of being fairly treated, feel psychologically safer to assume risks, experiment and innovate, thus becoming more identified with the leader, developing higher commitment and carrying out more organizational citizenship behaviours. One study[227] found that servant leadership contributes to followers' performance by helping them to fulfil their needs for autonomy, competence and relatedness. Additional research[228] has found that servant leadership promotes a fair workplace environment that promotes organizational citizenship behaviours. Researchers[229] have also discovered that a promotion focus (versus prevention) mediates the relationship between servant leadership and helping and creative behaviours.

Effects at the team level may also develop. One study[230] found that servant leadership fosters team performance through affect-based trust and increased team psychological safety (while transformational leadership operates via cognitive-based trust and increased team potency). Other researchers[231] have found that servant leadership propagates servant leadership behaviours among followers by creating a serving culture, which in turn influences unit performance and enhances individual attitudes and behaviours (job performance, creativity, customer service behaviour) directly and through the mediating influence of individuals' identification with the unit.

Another study[232] has found that servant leadership, as well as team-level goal and process clarity, enhanced team effectiveness through fostering team potency (i.e., the team members shared confidence that they could be effective as a team). The positive relationships

Table 8.4 Dimensions of servant leadership

Dimensions (van Dierendonck and Nuijten, 2011)	Definitions (van Dierendonck and Nuijten, 2011, pp. 251–252)
Empowerment	'A motivational concept focused on enabling people and encouraging personal development … Includes aspects like encouraging self-directed decision making, information sharing, and coaching for innovative performance.'
Standing back	'The extent to which a leader gives priority to the interest of others first and gives them the necessary support and credits.'
Accountability	'Holding people accountable for performance they can control … It ensures that people know what is expected of them.'
Interpersonal acceptance (includes empathy and forgiveness)	'The ability to understand and experience the feelings of others, understand where people come from (George, 2000), and the ability to let go of perceived wrongdoings and not carry a grudge into other situations.'
Courage	'Daring to take risks and trying out new approaches to old problems … Means strongly relying on values and convictions that govern one's actions.'
Authenticity	'Is about being true to oneself, accurately representing – privately and publicly – internal states, intentions, and commitments.'
Humility	'The ability to put one's own accomplishments and talents in a proper perspective.'
Stewardship	'The willingness to take responsibility for the larger institution and go for service instead of control and self-interest.'
Other operationalizations and measures (illustrations)	*Short measure of van Dierendonck and Nuijten (2011); Sousa and Van Dierendonck (2016).* Dimensions: empowerment, accountability, stewardship, humility. *Short measure of van Dierendonck and Nuijten (2011); Van Dierendonck et al. (2017).* Dimensions: empowerment, humility, standing back, stewardship, authenticity. *Liden, Wayne, Zhao, and Henderson (2008).* Dimensions: emotional healing, creating value for the community, conceptual skills, empowering, helping subordinates grow and succeed, putting subordinates first, behaving ethically. *Ehrhart (2004).* Dimensions: forming relationships with subordinates, empowering subordinates, helping subordinates grow and succeed, behaving ethically, having conceptual skills, putting subordinates first, creating value for those outside of the organization.[224] *Sendjaya et al. (2008).* Dimensions: voluntary subordination, authentic self, covenantal relationship, responsible morality, transcendental spirituality, transformational influence.

between both goal and process clarity and team potency were stronger in the presence of servant leadership. In the absence of servant leadership, the effect of goal and process clarity on team potency was no longer positive and could even become negative. One possible explanation is that, in the absence of servant leadership, followers feel frustrated: they know what the goal is but do not receive the support needed for its accomplishment.[233]

Box 8.11 What impels someone to be a servant leader?

The literature[234] suggests that individuals with (a) a motivational profile combining power motivation and *agape* love (the Greek term for moral love), (b) stronger servant identity, (c) higher/stronger self-determination, moral maturity, cognitive complexity, emotional intelligence, prosocial identity, core self-evaluation, and (d) lower narcissism, are more likely to adopt a servant leadership style. Individuals from cultures characterized by high humane orientation and low power distance are also more likely to adopt servant leadership. Psychological safety is another relevant contextual feature (see Chapter 7). Although servant leaders contribute towards creating psychological safety in their teams and organizations, it is also likely that individuals are more prone to adopt servant leadership behaviours if they perceive that the atmosphere in which they work is psychologically safer. Some life circumstances and events may also be triggers of servant leadership.[235] As Johnson[236] argued:

> Humanitarian leaders reflect on their life stories. They develop empathy for the needs of others through (1) role models (parents, teachers, religious leaders, friends) and positive values, such as caring for the poor or serving others; (2) a troubling awareness about a societal problem like sex abuse or lack of clean water; or (3) traumatic personal experiences, such as the death of parents or a cancer diagnosis.

Doris Goodwin[237] argued that it was Lincoln's familiarity with tragic loss, pain and personal disappointment that 'imbued him with a strength and understanding of human frailty' unavailable to the other members of his cabinet, which nourished his purpose of abolishing slavery and serving his citizens.

Contingency factors

The effects of servant leadership upon followers, both at individual and collective levels, are contingent on several conditions. One study[238] found that the impact of servant leadership on employees depends on the employees' motivational orientations (selfless versus self-serving motives). Specifically, the impact is higher for employees with selfless motivations. The authors concluded that the servant leadership style may not be appropriate for all followers, teams and organizations, and the impact of servant leadership on subordinate satisfaction is stronger when leaders' and subordinates' interests are aligned (i.e., both are selflessly motivated). The effect of servant leaders on followers' motivation and performance may also be contingent on the followers' proactive personality, core self–evaluations, as well as the servant leadership prototype:[239]

- Proactive employees select, create and influence work situations in ways that increase the likelihood of success.[240] They develop proactive behaviours and personal initiative in order to seize opportunities and to face problems and obstacles.

It is possible that servant leaders feel more comfortable with proactive followers and are thus more likely to empower and support them to grow and succeed.[241]

- Followers with stronger core self-evaluation (see Chapter 2) react more favourably to empowerment opportunities, and thus benefit more, in terms of performance, from a servant leader that helps them to grow and succeed. Conversely, it is possible that followers with weaker core self-evaluation react more positively to the emotional healing behaviours adopted by a servant leader, helping them deal with negative psychological wellbeing that can accompany their low self-esteem and self-efficacy.[242]

- It is possible that followers who espouse a prototype of an ideal leader that is consistent with the servant leadership style respond more favourably to servant leaders.[243] Such prototypes may be influenced not only by the idiosyncrasies of the followers but also by the culture in which they are immersed. Different cultures endorse servant leadership in different ways.[244] Not all followers value servant leaders in the same way, and servant leadership may be more effective with followers in cultures that endorse such a leadership style more strongly. The stronger the fit between servant leadership behaviour and the culture, the stronger the influence of servant leaders.[245] On the contrary, a mismatch between the followers' desire for servant leadership and actual leadership style may reduce followers' performance or OCB when servant leadership is adopted. In extreme cases, such a mismatch may even lead followers to not perceive the superior as a leader.[246]

Risks of being a servant leader

Servant leadership is not exempt from risk. Not all followers value servant leadership in the same way. Those that consider serving as atypical of a good leader may even respond negatively (i.e., not identifying with a servant leader and reducing their work engagement and commitment). Other risks may be involved.[247] First, servant leaders must balance the concerns and preferences of multiple stakeholders (e.g., supervisor, followers, community, family), which can be complex, sometimes impossible and emotionally taxing. Second, the behaviours of servant leaders (e.g., listening, empathizing, mentoring, helping, healing, empowering) are much more demanding, in terms of emotional labour costs, than 'directing and controlling'. Third, by attempting to serve all relevant 'others' first, servant leaders may experience role conflicts, not only at the professional level (e.g., conflict between the interests/demands of the supervisor and those from subordinates) but also between organizational and personal roles. Fourth, a servant leader may be susceptible to manipulation and exploitation by followers. To escape from such a trap, servant leaders must have a paradoxical combination of scepticism and naiveté (Box 8.12).

Box 8.12　Countering the negative in the positive: being 'wise as a serpent and innocent as a dove'

David Brooks discussed the paradoxical nature of Lincoln's leadership as follows:[248]

> People with good private morality are better at navigating for the long term. They genuinely love causes beyond themselves ... People with astute moral

sentiments have an early warning system. They don't have to think through the dangers of tit-for-tat favor-exchanges with billionaires. They have an aesthetic revulsion against people who seem icky and situations that are distasteful, which heads off a lot of trouble. Of course, private morality is not enough. You have to know how to react to unprincipled people who want to destroy you. But, historically, most effective leaders – like, say, George Washington, Theodore Roosevelt and Winston Churchill – had a dual consciousness. They had an earnest, inner moral voice capable of radical self-awareness, rectitude and great compassion. They also had a pragmatic, canny outer voice. These two voices were in constant conversation, checking each other, probing for synthesis, wise as a serpent and innocent as a dove.

Final comments

Positive leadership represents the ways 'in which leaders enable positively deviant performance, foster an affirmative orientation in organizations, and engender a focus on virtuousness and the best of the human condition'.[249] Humble leadership, ethical leadership, authentic leadership and servant leadership are different but they do share some commonalities (Table 8.5) as modes for enacting positive leadership. Other approaches

Table 8.5 Contrasting four types of positive leadership

	Humble leadership	*Ethical leadership*	*Authentic leadership*	*Servant leadership*
Core idea	Leaders may be more effective if they are self-aware of their own strengths and limitations, appreciate the others' strengths and contributions, and are willing to learn (including from their own mistakes).	Leaders may be more effective if they are honest, trustworthy, fair and caring.	Leaders are more effective if they are self-aware, relate with others in a transparent way, are willing to process information from different sources (even if such information colludes with the leader's view) and behave according to an internal compass.	Leaders are more effective (and builders of a better society) if they position themselves as servants before attending their own needs.
Unique features (sample)	One may be humble without being a servant.	One may be ethical without being humble or a servant.	One may be authentic without being humble or a servant.	The distinctive feature is leader as a servant. No other type includes serving.
Dimensions	Different models embrace different dimensions. The most common model (Owens	Different models embrace different dimensions. One of the most frequently used frameworks	The most important models include four dimensions: (1) self-awareness; (2) relational	Different models embrace different dimensions. One model (van Dierendonck and

(Continued)

Table 8.5 (Cont.)

	Humble leadership	Ethical leadership	Authentic leadership	Servant leadership
	et al., 2013) includes: (1) self-awareness; (2) appreciation of others; (3) openness to feedback (teachability).	(De Hoogh and Den Hartog, 2008) includes: (1) morality and fairness; (2) role clarification; (3) power sharing.	transparency; (3) balanced processing of information; (4) internalized moral perspective.	Nuijten, 2011) includes (1) empowerment, (2) standing back, (3) accountability, (4) internal acceptance, (5) courage, (6) authenticity, (7) humility and (8) stewardship.
Practical implications (sample)	Acknowledge that you are not the centre of the universe. Have a grounded and accurate view of yourself and others. Listen to others. Know yourself. Learn with your own mistakes and failures.	Be honest. Walk the talk. Share your power. Clarify what you expect from your followers. Act as an ethical role model.	Be self-aware. Listen to others. Express your true thoughts and feelings (but also be wise). Be objective when analyzing information and do not be biased toward others' views and your own. Follow your internal compass.	Serve followers before attending to your own needs. Act as a servant leader in all realms of life (work, home and community). Develop followers into servant leaders.

and styles could, however, be included under that umbrella: empowering leadership,[250] responsible leadership,[251] self-sacrificing leadership,[252] inspirational leadership,[253] spiritual leadership,[254] virtuous leadership,[255] engaging leadership[256] and (at least some dimensions of) transformational leadership.[257] By showing that positive leadership approaches also involve risks and dangers for leaders who adopt them, we consider that positive leadership must be interpreted as a lens to identify how leaders can be more effective and facilitate followers and team flourishing, without falling into the trap of 'Prozac leadership'.[258]

Want more?

Good reviews of authentic leadership may be found in Avolio and Mhatre,[259] Banks et al.[260] and Gardner et al.[261] Bill George's[262] books provide an interesting practitioner perspective. Gill and Caza[263] distinguish between personalized authentic leadership and generalized authentic leadership. For understanding the relevance of humility in leaders, see Nielsen and Marrone[264] and Owens et al.[265] Researchers Vera and Rodriguez-Lopez[266] also discuss 'humility as a source of competitive advantage' in a theoretical-practical way.[267] Collins discusses how the combination of humility and a 'fierce resolve' gives rise to 'Level 5 leadership'. For the paradoxical combination of humility and narcissism in leaders, consider Owens et al.[268] and Zhang et al.[269] For servant leadership, consult the literature reviews by Liden et al.[270] and van

Dierendonck.[271] To understand the thoughts of the 'founder' of servant leadership see Greenleaf.[272] For ethical leadership, see Brown and Treviño[273] and Ko et al.,[274] who present integrative reviews and outline a future research agenda. Bedi et al.[275] present a meta-analysis of servant leadership, while Eisenbeiss[276] provides a critical perspective. For an overall perspective about the virtuous/good leadership, see Newstead, Dawkins, Macklin, and Martin (2019a, 2019b).

Glossary

Authentic leadership   A pattern of leader behaviour that includes self-awareness, internalized moral perspective, balanced processing of information and relational transparency.

Authenticity   Being true to one's self and accurately representing – privately and publicly – internal states, intentions and commitments.

Balanced processing of information   Objectively analyzing the relevant data before coming to a decision and soliciting views that challenge deeply held positions.

Ethical leadership   Leading as a moral person and as a moral manager.

Humblebragging   Bragging masked by a complaint or humility.

Humility   Having a grounded view of oneself and others, enabling the individual to acknowledge his/her personal strengths and weaknesses (as well as those of others).

Internalized moral perspective   Setting a high standard for moral and ethical conduct, and behaving accordingly.

Interpersonal humility   Humility as expressed in interpersonal relationships.

Intrapersonal humility   Accurate view of oneself and an awareness of one's limitations.

Leader-expressed humility   An interpersonal characteristic involving '(a) a manifested willingness to view oneself accurately, (b) a displayed appreciation of others' strengths and contributions, and (c) teachability' (i.e., showing openness to new ideas, advice, learning and feedback).

Level 5 leadership   Combination of humility and a 'fierce resolve'.

Modesty   Being unassuming or having a moderate estimation of oneself.

Moral licensing   After having established a moral image of him/herself, developing the feeling that an immoral action is allowed without the fear of losing that moral image.

Moral superiority   A leader's sense that he/she is morally superior and thus has 'permission' to silence and delegitimize followers who resist them or who do not espouse their ethical philosophy.

Narcissism   A strong desire for self-focus, attention and self-affirmation.

Positive leadership   Umbrella for a wide range of leadership approaches and styles (e.g., humble leadership; ethical leadership; authentic leadership; servant leadership; responsible leadership; empowering leadership; virtuous leadership).

Relational transparency   Presenting oneself to others in a transparent/authentic way.

Role clarification   Clarification of expectations and responsibilities so that employees are clear on what is expected from them.

Role modelling   Influencing others through leading them to adopt our own behaviours.

Self-awareness   Willingness to see the self accurately.

Servant leadership   Leadership prioritization of serving followers before attending to one's own needs.

Sincerity   An intersubjective experience. Being sincere and transparent with others.

Stewardship   Willingness to take responsibility for the larger institution and go for service instead of control and self-interest.

Teachability   Openness to learning, feedback and new ideas from others.

Notes

1 Collinson (2012).
2 Youssef & Luthans (2012, p. 541).
3 Judge, Piccolo, and Kosalka (2009).
4 Goodwin (2005).
5 Weber (1978).
6 Denyer and Wan (2015).
7 Skapinker (2015).
8 Schwartz (2015b); *The New York Times* (2015).
9 In Schwartz (2015a).
10 Judge, Piccolo and Kosalka (2009).
11 Waytz (2016).
12 Bloom (2016).
13 Kellaway (2014).
14 Giles (2016).
15 Garvin (2013); Harrell and Barbato (2018).
16 Wiseman and McKeown (2010).
17 Wright and Quick (2011).
18 Rego, Cunha and Simpson (2018).
19 Argandoña (2015); Owens, Rowatt and Wilkins (2012).
20 Owens, Rowatt and Wilkins (2012).
21 Nielsen and Marrone (2018).
22 https://twitter.com/realdonaldtrump/status/415868924841189376.
23 Ou et al. (2014, p. 37).
24 Nielsen and Marrone (2018); Woodcock (2008).
25 Oc, Basshur, Daniels, Greguras and Diefendorff (2015).
26 Sezer, Gino and Norton (2018).
27 Ou et al. (2014); Owens, Johnson and Mitchell (2013).
28 Morris et al. (2005, p. 1335).
29 Owens, Walker and Waldman (2015); Zhang, Ou, Tsui and Wang (2017).
30 Sezer, Gino and Norton (2018).
31 https://en.oxforddictionaries.com/definition/humblebrag.
32 Sezer, Gino and Norton (2018).
33 Thompson (2015).
34 Ou et al. (2014).
35 Ou et al. (2014).
36 Owens, Johnson and Mitchell (2013).
37 Owens et al. (2013, p. 1518).
38 Ou et al. (2014).
39 Owens and Hekman (2016, p. 1090).
40 Nielsen and Marrone (2018).
41 *Oxford English Dictionary* (2010, p. 854).
42 http://dictionary.reference.com.
43 Ou et al. (2014).
44 Johnson (2014, p. 10). Johnson's self-characterization as an entrepreneur with flair suffered severe damage when one of his ventures, Patisserie Valerie, a chain of coffee and cake outlets, collapsed into receivership, the result of significant fraud in the business (in which Johnson was not implicated but for which he was ultimately responsible as Executive Chairman).
45 Pfeffer (2015, p. 78).
46 Feder and Sahibzada, 2014).

47 Kiel (2015).
48 Argandoña (2015); Collins (2001); Owens, Johnson and Mitchell (2013).
49 *The Economist* (2013, p. 59).
50 Saïd Business School and Heidrick and Struggles (2015).
51 Schultz (2015).
52 Vera and Rodriguez-Lopez (2004).
53 Vera and Rodriguez-Lopez (2004, p. 393).
54 Vera and Rodriguez-Lopez (2004).
55 Morris, Brotheridge and Urbanski (2005); Van Dierendonck (2011).
56 Vera and Rodriguez-Lopez (2004, p. 393).
57 Davis et al. (2013); Morris, Brotheridge and Urbanski (2005); Owens, Johnson and Mitchell (2013).
58 De Jong and Elfring (2010); Dirks and Ferrin (2002).
59 Weick (2001, pp. 101–102).
60 Cascio and Luthans (2014).
61 Van Dierendonck (2011).
62 Cascio and Luthans (2014).
63 Goodwin (2005).
64 Vallely (2013).
65 Rego, Cunha and Simpson (2018).
66 Owens, Johnson and Mitchell (2013).
67 Galinsky, Ku and Wang (2005).
68 The study suffers, however, from the limitation of measuring leader humility through self-report.
69 Owens and Hekman (2016).
70 Ou et al. (2014, 2018).
71 Nielsen and Marrone (2018).
72 Rego et al. (2019).
73 Rego et al. (2017).
74 Rego et al. (2019).
75 Nielsen and Marrone (2018).
76 Rego et al. (2017).
77 https://conceptually.org/concepts/signalling-and-countersignalling/.
78 Michaels (2018).
79 Author: U.S. Department of State. Image in the public domain. Retrieved from https://com mons.wikimedia.org/wiki/File:Secretary_Kerry_and_Facebook_CEO_Zuckerberg_Chat_A bout_Zuckerberg%27s_Broken_Arm_Before_Their_Meeting_at_Facebook%27s_Headquarters_ in_Menlo_Park_(27786875621).jpg.
80 Broughton (2016, p. 9).
81 McFadden (2018, p. A1).
82 McFadden (2018, p. A1).
83 Nielsen and Marrone (2018). See also: Lin, Chen, Herman, Wei, and Ma (2019); Wang, Li, and Yin (2019).
84 Chiu, Owens and Tesluk (2016).
85 Nielsen and Marrone, 2018).
86 Ou et al. (2014).
87 Rego et al. (2017a).
88 Nielsen and Marrone (2018).
89 Ou et al. (2014).
90 Zhang, Ou, Tsui and Wang (2017).
91 Out et al. (2014).
92 Owens and Hekman, 2016, p. 1023).
93 Collins (2001).
94 Collins (2001, p. 68).
95 Koehn (2013).
96 In Koehn (2013, p. BU1).
97 Brooks (2015, p. A23).

98 Carl Schurz, *Reminiscences*, Volume Two, McClure Publishing Co., 1907, facing p. 84. Retrieved from https://commons.wikimedia.org/wiki/File:Abraham_Lincoln_1858.png. The file is in the public domain in the US.

99 Kouchaki (2016); see also Independent Directors of the Board of Wells Fargo & Company (2017).

100 Jung and Park (2017).

101 Brooks (2015, p. A23).

102 The new code may be found at: www08.wellsfargomedia.com/assets/pdf/about/corporate/code-of-ethics.pdf.

103 Boje, Roslie, Durant and Luhman (2004).

104 Boje, Roslie, Durant and Luhman (2004).

105 Brown et al. (2005, p. 120).

106 Bedi, Alpaslan and Green (2016); Brown, Treviño and Harrison (2005).

107 Ko, Ma, Bartnik, Haney and Kang, 2018, p. 106).

108 Brown, Treviño and Harrison (2005).

109 Kalshoven, Den Hartog and De Hoogh (2011).

110 De Hoogh and Den Hartog (2008).

111 Ewing (2015).

112 Brown, Treviño and Harrison (2005).

113 Ko, Ma, Bartnik, Haney and Kang (2018).

114 See Bedi et al.'s (2016) meta-analysis, and Ko et al.'s (2018) review.

115 Lu and Lin (2014).

116 Bhal and Dadhich (2011); Cheng, Bai and Yang (2018).

117 Ko, Ma, Bartnik, Haney and Kang (2018).

118 For a synthesis, see Ko, Ma, Bartnik, Haney and Kang (2018).

119 Cunha, Simpson, Clegg and Rego (2019); Ko, Ma, Bartnik, Haney and Kang (2018).

120 Ko, Ma, Bartnik, Haney and Kang (2018).

121 Brown and Trevino (2006); Ko, Ma, Bartnik, Haney and Kang (2018).

122 Ko, Ma, Bartnik, Haney and Kang (2018).

123 Zimbardo (2004, p. 47).

124 Schneider, Goldstein and Smith (1995).

125 Boje et al. (2004, p. 759).

126 Smith (2012, p. A27).

127 Ko et al. (2018).

128 Lin, Ma and Johnson (2016).

129 Merritt, Effron and Monin (2010); Pffefer (2015).

130 Berkovich (2014).

131 Baumeister, Gailliot, DeWall and Oaten (2006).

132 Lin, Ma and Johnson (2016).

133 Blanken et al. (2015, p. 540).

134 Conversely, *moral cleansing* describes moral behaviours aimed at regaining some of the lost worth resulting from past unethical actions (Ayal and Gino, 2011; Sachdeva, Iliev and Medin, 2009).

135 Lin, Ma and Johnson (2016).

136 Sachdeva, Iliev and Medin (2009).

137 Pffefer (2015).

138 de Vos (2003).

139 Sorkin (2015, p. B1).

140 Berkovich (2014). Although moral licensing and moral superiority are interrelated, they differ. Moral superiority is the sense that one is morally superior to others, while moral licensing is the sense that one is licensed to adopt questionable behaviours. Naturally, the sense of moral superiority may lead to the sense of moral licensing.

141 Stouten, van Dijke, Mayer, De Cremer and Euwema (2013).

142 Kuper (2013).

143 Avolio and Gardner (2005); Gardner, Cogliser, Davis and Dickens (2011). See also Lehman, O'Connor, Kovacs, and Newman (2019).

144 Triillng (1972, p. 131). It may also mean to commit a murder.

145 Kernis and Goldman (2006).

146 Avolio and Gardner (2005).
147 Ford and Harding (2011).
148 Retrieved from https://commons.wikimedia.org/wiki/File:Roman-mosaic-know-thyself.jpg. Work in the public domain.
149 George (2003); George, Sims, McLean and Mayer (2007).
150 www.linkedin.com/in/normahollis/.
151 www.linkedin.com/in/normahollis/.
152 Hollis (2017).
153 George (2003); George and Sims (2007).
154 For example, Avolio, Wernsing and Gardner (2018); Banks et al. (2016); Gardner, Cogliser, Davis and Dickens (2011).
155 Gardner, Cogliser, Davis and Dickens (2011).
156 Berkovich (2014); Gill and Caza (2018); Spain and Kim (2017).
157 Walumbwa et al. (2008, p. 94).
158 Gardner, Cogliser, Davis and Dickens (2011).
159 Gardner, Cogliser, Davis and Dickens (2011); Lyubovnikova, Legood, Turner and Mamakouka (2017).
160 Talbot-Zorn (2016).
161 Levesque-Côté, Fernet, Austin and Morin (2018).
162 See the reviews of Banks et al. (2016) and Gardner, Cogliser, Davis and Dickens (2011).
163 Gills and Caza (2018).
164 Rego, Sousa, Marques and Cunha (2012a).
165 Rego, Sousa, Marques and Cunha (2012a).
166 Hannah, Avolio and Walumbwa (2011).
167 Lyubovnikova, Legood, Turner and Mamakouka (2017).
168 Salancik and Pfeffer (1977); Shamir and Eilam (2005).
169 Baumeister, Bratslavsky, Muraven and Tice (1998).
170 Weiss, Razinskas, Backmann and Hoegl (2018).
171 Baumeister, Bratslavsky, Muraven and Tice (1998).
172 Gardner et al. (2005, p. 365).
173 Rajah, Song and Arvey (2011); Weiss, Razinskas, Backmann and Hoegl (2018).
174 Berkovic (2014).
175 Shamir and Eilam (2005).
176 Shaw (2010).
177 Berkovic (2014, p. 246).
178 Buber (1958).
179 Grant (2016).
180 James (2016); Spain and Kim (2017).
181 Spain and Kim (2017, p. 170).
182 Edwards (2015).
183 Watt and Wintour (2013).
184 Ibarra (2015, p. 57).
185 Pffefer (2015).
186 Pffefer (2015, pp. 36–37).
187 Ibarrra (2015, p. 53).
188 Ibarra (2015).
189 Pfeffer (2016).
190 Ibarra (2015, p. 54).
191 Koehn (2016).
192 Smith, Lewis and Tushman (2016).
193 Goffee and Jones (2005).
194 Ibarra (2015).
195 Shamir and Eilam (2005).
196 Rego, Cunha and Clegg (2012b).
197 Faircloth (2017).
198 Faircloth (2017, p. 410).
199 Faircloth (2017, p. 411).

200 Faircloth (2017, p. 414).
201 Ibarra (2015).
202 Faircloth (2017, p. 415).
203 Faircloth (2017, p. 417).
204 Hutson (2017); Williams (2014).
205 Greenleaf (1970, p. 15).
206 www.greenleaf.org/what-is-servant-leadership/.
207 Spears (2002).
208 Spears (2002).
209 Schultz (2015, p. A27).
210 www.tdindustries.com/our-company/our-culture/.
211 www.tdindustries.com/our-company/our-culture/.
212 Hutson (2017).
213 Heller (2000).
214 www.cherylpwspeaks.com/.
215 Williamson (2017).
216 Photographer: Hasse Karlsson. Retrieved from https://commons.wikimedia.org/wiki/File:Kam
     pradlectur.jpg.
217 Graham (1991).
218 Hale and Fields (2007).
219 Liden et al. (2015, p. 254); see also Chiniara and Bentein (2016); Van Dierendonck, Stam,
     Boersma, De Windt and Alkema (2014).
220 Donia, Raja, Panaccio and Wang (2016).
221 Liden, Panaccio, Meuser, Hu and Wayne (2014a); Northouse (2016).
222 Liden et al. (2015).
223 Van Dierendonck (2011, Table 2, p. 1241) provides a synthesis of similarities and differences
     between different conceptualizations and dimensionalizations).
224 Psychometric properties are presented just for overall servant leadership.
225 Synthesis on Chiniara and Bentein (2016), and Donia, Raja, Panaccio and Wang (2016), and
     van Dierendonk (2011).
226 Hu and Liden (2011); Liden, Panaccio, Meuser, Hu and Wayne (2014a, 2014b); Peterson,
     Galvin and Lange (2012).
227 Chiniara and Bentein (2016).
228 Ehrhart (2004).
229 Neubert, Kacmar, Carlson, Chonko and Roberts (2008).
230 Schaubroeck, Lam and Peng (2011).
231 Liden, Wayne, Liao and Meuser (2014b).
232 Hu and Liden (2011).
233 Northouse (2016).
234 Liden, Panaccio, Meuser, Hu and Wayne (2014a); Sun (2013); Van Dierendonck (2011).
235 Sun (2013).
236 Johnson (2018, p. 81).
237 Goodwin (2005, p. 4).
238 Donia, Raja, Panaccio and Wang (2016).
239 Liden, Panaccio, Meuser, Hu and Wayne (2014a).
240 Seibert, Kraimer and Crant (2001).
241 Liden, Panaccio, Meuser, Hu and Wayne (2014a).
242 Liden, Panaccio, Meuser, Hu and Wayne (2014a).
243 Sendjaya and Cooper (2011).
244 Mittal and Dorfman (2012); Van Dierendonck (2011).
245 Mittal and Dorfman (2012); Van Dierendonck (2011).
246 Liden, Panaccio, Meuser, Hu and Wayne (2014a).
247 Liden, Panaccio, Meuser, Hu and Wayne (2014a); Van Dierendonck (2011).
248 Brooks (2015, p. A27).
249 Cameron (2012, p. 2).
250 Lee, Willis and Tian (2018).
251 Waldman and Balven (2014); Miska and Mendenhall (2018).

252 Choi and Mai-Dalton (1999); Choi and Yoon (2005).
253 Joshi, Lazarova and Liao (2009).
254 Fry (2008).
255 Wang and Hackett (2016).
256 Schaufeli (2015).
257 Bass (1999); Wang, Oh, Courtright and Colbert (2011). See also Bass and Steidlmeier (1999) and Kark, Shamir and Chen (2003) for a *less positive* perspective about transformational leadership.
258 Collinson (2012).
259 Avolio and Mhatre (2012).
260 Banks et al. (2018).
261 Gardner, Cogliser, Davis and Dickens (2011).
262 George (2003); George and Sims (2007).
263 Gill and Caza (2018).
264 Nielsen and Marrone (2018).
265 Owens et al. (2012, 2013).
266 Vera and Rodriguez-Lopez (2004).
267 Collins (2001).
268 Owens, Walker and Waldman (2015).
269 Zhang, Ou, Tsui and Wang (2017).
270 Liden, Panaccio, Meuser, Hu and Wayne (2014a).
271 Van Dierendonck (2011).
272 Greenleaf (1970).
273 Brown and Treviño (2006).
274 Ko, Ma, Bartnik, Haney and Kang (2018).
275 Bedi, Alpaslan and Green (2016).
276 Eisenbeiss (2012).

References

Alfano, M., Iurino, K., Stey, P., Robinson, B., Christen, M., Yu, F., & Lapsley, D. (2017). Development and validation of a multi-dimensional measure of intellectual humility. *PloS ONE*, 12(8), e0182950.

Argandoña, A. (2015). Humility in management. *Journal of Business Ethics*, 132, 63–71.

Avolio, B. J., & Gardner, W. (2005). Authentic leadership development: Getting to the root of positive forms of leadership. *The Leadership Quarterly*, 16(3), 315–338.

Avolio, B. J., & Mhatre, K. H. (2012). Advances in theory and research on authentic leadership. In K. S. Cameron, & G. Spreitzer (Eds.), *The Oxford handbook of positive organizational scholarship* (pp. 773–783). Oxford: Oxford University Press.

Avolio, B. J., Wernsing, T., & Gardner, W. L. (2018). Revisiting the development and validation of the Authentic Leadership Questionnaire: Analytical clarifications. *Journal of Management*, 44(2), 399–411.

Ayal, S., & Gino, F. (2011). Honest rationales for dishonest behaviour. In M. Mikulincer, & P. R. Shaver (Eds.), *The social psychology of morality: Exploring the causes of good and evil* (pp. 149–166). Washington, DC: American Psychological Association.

Banks, G. C., McCauley, K. D., Gardner, W. L., & Guler, C. E. (2016). A meta-analytic review of authentic and transformational leadership: A test for redundancy. *The Leadership Quarterly*, 27(4), 634–652.

Bass, B. M. (1999). Two decades of research and development in transformational leadership. *European Journal of Work and Organizational Psychology*, 8(1), 9–32.

Bass, B. M., & Steidlmeier, P. (1999). Ethics, character, and authentic transformational leadership behaviour. *The Leadership Quarterly*, 10(2), 181–217.

Baumeister, R. F., Bratslavsky, E., Muraven, M., & Tice, D. M. (1998). Ego depletion: Is the active self a limited resource? *Journal of Personality and Social Psychology*, 74(5), 1252–1265.

Baumeister, R. F., Gailliot, M., DeWall, C. N., & Oaten, M. (2006). Self-regulation and personality: How interventions increase regulatory success, and how depletion moderates the effects of traits on behaviour. *Journal of Personality*, 74, 1773–1802.

Bedi, A., Alpaslan, C. M., & Green, S. (2016). A meta-analytic review of ethical leadership outcomes and moderators. *Journal of Business Ethics*, 139(3), 517–536.

Berkovich, I. (2014). Between person and person: Dialogical pedagogy in authentic leadership development. *Academy of Management Learning & Education*, 13(2), 245–264.

Bhal, K. T., & Dadhich, A. (2011). Impact of ethical leadership and leader–member exchange on whistle blowing: The moderating impact of the moral intensity of the issue. *Journal of Business Ethics*, 103 (3), 485–496.

Blanken, I., van de Ven, N., & Zeelenberg, M. (2015). A meta-analytic review of moral licensing. *Personality and Social Psychology Bulletin*, 41(4), 540–558.

Bloom, P. (2016). *Against empathy: The case for rational compassion*. New York: Ecco.

Boje, D. M., Roslie, G. A., Durant, R. A., & Luhman, J. T. (2004). Enron spectacles: A critical dramaturgical analysis. *Organization Studies*, 25, 751–774.

Brooks, D. (2015). What candidates need. *The New York Times*, April 7, A23.

Broughton, D. (2016). Shows of humility can be too much, even in Silicon Valley. *Financial Times Europe*, July 9–10, 9.

Brown, M. E., & Treviño, L. K. (2006). Ethical leadership: A review and future directions. *The Leadership Quarterly*, 17(6), 595–616.

Brown, M. E., Treviño, L. K., & Harrison, D. A. (2005). Ethical leadership: A social learning perspective for construct development and testing. *Organizational Behaviour and Human Decision Processes*, 97(2), 117–134.

Buber, M. (1958). *I and thou* R. G. Smith (Trans.). New York: Scribner's.

Cameron, K. (2012). *Positive leadership: Strategies for extraordinary performance*. San Francisco, CA: Berrett-Koehler.

Cascio, W. F., & Luthans, F. (2014). Reflections on the metamorphosis at Robben Island: The role of institutional work and positive psychological capital. *Journal of Management Inquiry*, 23(1), 51–67.

Cheng, J., Bai, H., & Yang, X. (2018). Ethical leadership and internal whistleblowing: A mediated moderation model. *Journal of Business Ethics*, 39(3), 306–325.

Chiniara, M., & Bentein, K. (2016). Linking servant leadership to individual performance: Differentiating the mediating role of autonomy, competence and relatedness need satisfaction. *The Leadership Quarterly*, 27(1), 124–141.

Chiu, C.-Y., Owens, B., & Tesluk, P. E. (2016). Initiating and utilizing shared leadership in teams: The role of leader humility, team proactive personality, and team performance capability. *Journal of Applied Psychology*, 101(12), 1705–1720.

Choi, Y., & Mai-Dalton, R. R. (1999). The model of followers' responses to self-sacrificial leadership: An empirical test. *The Leadership Quarterly*, 10, 397–421.

Choi, Y., & Yoon, J. (2005). Effects of leaders' self-sacrificial behaviour and competency on followers' attribution of charismatic leadership among Americans and Koreans. *Current Research in Social Psychology*, 11, 51–69.

Collins, J. (2001). Level 5 leadership: The triumph of humility and fierce resolve. *Harvard Business Review*, (January), 79(1), 67–76.

Collinson, D. (2012). Prozac leadership and the limits of positive thinking. *Leadership*, 8(2), 87–107.

Cunha, M. P., Simpson, A. V., Clegg, S., & Rego, A. (2019). Speak! Paradoxical effects of a managerial culture of "speaking up". *British Journal of Management*, 30, 829–846.

Davis, D. E., Hook, J. N., Worthington, E. L., Jr., Van Tongeren, D. R., Gartner, A. L., Jennings, D. J. I. I., & Emmons, R. (2011). Relational humility: Conceptualizing and measuring humility as a personality judgment. *Journal of Personality Assessment*, 93(3), 225–234.

Davis, D. E., Worthington, E. L., Jr., Hook, J. N., Emmons, R. E., Hill, P. C., Bollinger, R. A., & Van Tongeren, D. R. (2013). Humility and the development and repair of social bonds: Two longitudinal studies. *Self and Identity*, 12(1), 58–77.

De Hoogh, A. H. B., & Den Hartog, D. N. (2008). Ethical and despotic leadership, relationships with leader's social responsibility, top management team effectiveness and subordinates' optimism: A multi-method study. *The Leadership Quarterly*, 19, 297–311.

De Jong, B. A., & Elfring, T. (2010). How does trust affect the performance of ongoing teams? The mediating role of reflexivity, monitoring, and effort. *Academy of Management Journal*, 53(3), 535–549.

de Vos, P. (2003). To call Mandela a saint is to dishonour his memory. *Daily Maverick*, December 6 (www.dailymaverick.co.za/opinionista/2013-12-06-to-call-mandela-a-saint-is-to-dishonour-his-memory/#.WtNlDS7wapo).

Denyer, S., & Wan, W. (2015). In China and West, contrasting views on legacy of Singapore's patriarch. *The Washington Post*, March 23 (www.washingtonpost.com/world/asia_pacific/in-china-and-west-contrasting-views-on-legacy-of-singapores-patriarch/2015/03/23/6b285de1-9e39-45de-ae15-1ef95c80792f_story.html?utm_term=.c965f6710a44).

Dirks, K. T., & Ferrin, D. L. (2002). Trust in leadership: Meta-analytic findings and implications for research and practice. *Journal of Applied Psychology*, 87(4), 611–628.

Donia, M. B., Raja, U., Panaccio, A., & Wang, Z. (2016). Servant leadership and employee outcomes: The moderating role of subordinates' motives. *European Journal of Work and Organizational Psychology*, 25(5), 722–734.

The Economist (2013). The global-leadership industry needs re-engineering. The Economist, January 26th, 59.

Edwards, J. (2015). Don't underestimate Jeremy Corbyn's hatred of the media – That's his secret weapon. *Business Insider*, September (http://uk.businessinsider.com/jeremy-corbyn-hatred-of-the-media-2015-9).

Ehrhart, M. G. (2004). Leadership and procedural justice climate as antecedents of unit-level organizational citizenship behaviour. *Personnel Psychology*, 57(1), 61–94.

Eisenbeiss, S. A. (2012). Re-thinking ethical leadership: An interdisciplinary integrative approach. *The Leadership Quarterly*, 23, 791–808.

Ewing, J. (2015). Volkswagen inquiry's focus to include managers who turned a blind eye. *The New York Times*, October 26, B3.

Faircloth, S. C. (2017). Reflections on the concept of authentic leadership: From an indigenous scholar/leader perspective. *Advances in Developing Human Resources*, 19(4), 407–419.

Feder, Z., & Sahibzada, K. (2014). Turns out, humility offers a competitive advantage. *Entrepreuner*, October 10 (www.entrepreneur.com/article/238328).

Ford, J., & Harding, N. (2011). The impossibility of the 'true self' of authentic leadership. *Leadership*, 7(4), 463–479.

Fry, L. W. (2008). Spiritual leadership: State-of-the-art and future directions for theory, research, and practice. In J. Biberman, & L. Tishler (Eds.), *Spirituality in business* (pp. 106–124). New York: Palgrave Macmillan.

Galinsky, A. D., Ku, G., & Wang, C. S. (2005). Perspective-taking and self-other overlap: Fostering social bonds and facilitating social coordination. *Group Processes & Intergroup Relations*, 8, 109–124.

Gardner, W. L., Avolio, B. J., Luthans, F., May, D. R. & Walumbwa, F. (2005). "Can you see the real me?" A self-based model of authentic leader and follower development. *The Leadership Quarterly*, 16, 343–372.

Gardner, W. L., Cogliser, C. C., Davis, K. M., & Dickens, M. P. (2011). Authentic leadership: A review of the literature and research agenda. *The Leadership Quarterly*, 22(6), 1120–1145.

Garvin, D. A. (2013). How Google sold its engineers on management. *Harvard Business Review*, December, 74–82.

George, B. (2003). *Authentic leadership: Rediscovering the secrets to creating lasting value*. San Francisco, CA: Jossey-Bass.

George, B., Sims, P., McLean, A. N., & Mayer, D. (2007). Discovering your authentic leadership. *Harvard Business Review*, February, 129–138.

George, J. M. (2000). Emotions and leadership: the role of emotional intelligence. *Human Relations*, 53(8): 1027–1055.

George, W., & Sims, P. (2007). *True north: Discover your authentic leadership*. San Francisco, CA: Jossey-Bass.

Giles, S. (2016). The most important leadership competencies, according to leaders around the world. *Harvard Business Review*, March 15 (https://hbr.org/2016/03/the-most-important-leadership-competencies-according-to-leaders-around-the-world).

Gill, C., & Caza, A. (2018). An investigation of authentic leadership's individual and group influences on follower responses. *Journal of Management*, 44(2), 530–554.

Goffee, R., & Jones, G. (2005). Managing authenticity: The paradox of great leadership. *Harvard Business Review*, December, 86–94.

Goodwin, D. K. (2005). *Team of rivals: The political genius of Abraham Lincoln*. New York: Simon & Schuster.

Graham, J. W. (1991). Servant-leader in organizations: Inspirational and moral. The *Leadership Quarterly*, 2, 105–119.

Grant, A. (2016). Unless you're Oprah, "be yourself" is terrible advice. *The New York Times*, June 5, SR6.

Greenleaf, R. (1970). *The servant as leader*. Indianapolis, IN: Robert K. Greenleaf Center.

Hale, J. R., & Fields, D. L. (2007). Exploring servant leadership across cultures: A study of followers in Ghana and the USA. *Leadership*, 3(4), 397–417.

Hannah, S. T., Avolio, B. J., & Walumbwa, F. O. (2011). Relationships between authentic leadership, moral courage, and ethical and pro-social behaviours. *Business Ethics Quarterly*, 21(4), 555–578.

Harrell, M. & Barbato, L. (2018). Great managers still matter: the evolution of Google's Project Oxygen. *re:Work*, February 27 (https://rework.withgoogle.com/blog/the-evolution-of-project-oxygen/).

Heller, R. (2000). The billionaire next door. *Forbes*, August 7 (www.forbes.com/global/2000/0807/0315036a.html#51465d364b69).

Henderson, J. E., & Hoy, W. K. (1983). Leader authenticity: The development and test of an operational measure. *Educational and Psychological Research*, 3(2), 63–75.

Hollis, N. (2017). Why we need authentic leaders. *Renaissance Executive Forums*, May 25 (www.executiveforums.com/single-post/2017/05/25/Why-We-Need-Authentic-Leaders).

Hu, J., & Liden, R. C. (2011). Antecedents of team potency and team effectiveness: An examination of goal and process clarity and servant leadership. *Journal of Applied Psychology*, 96(4), 851–862.

Hutson, M. (2017). When power doesn't corrupt. *The New York Times*, May 21, BU11.

Ibarra, H. (2015). The authenticity paradox. *Harvard Business Review*, 93(1/2), 52–59.

Independent Directors of the Board of Wells Fargo & Company. (2017). *Sales practices investigation report*. April 10.

James, A. (2016). *Assholes: A theory of Donald Trump*. New York: Penguin Random House.

Johnson, C. E. (2018). *Meeting the ethical challenges of leadership* (6th ed.). Los Angeles, CA: Sage.

Johnson, L. (2014). The Virgin Galactic crash and the need for risk-takers. *Financial Times Europe*, November 5, 10.

Joshi, A., Lazarova, M. B., & Liao, H. (2009). Getting everyone on board: The role of inspirational leadership in geographically dispersed teams. *Organization Science*, 20(1), 240–252.

Judge, T. A., Piccolo, R. F., & Kosalka, T. (2009). The bright and dark sides of leader traits: A review and theoretical extension of the leader trait paradigm. *The Leadership Quarterly*, 20, 855–875.

Jung, J. C., & Park, S. B. A. (2017). Volkswagen's diesel emissions scandal. *Thunderbird International Business Review*, 59(1), 127–137.

Kalshoven, K., Den Hartog, D. N., & De Hoogh, A. H. (2011). Ethical leadership at Work Questionnaire (ELW): Development and validation of a multidimensional measure. *The Leadership Quarterly*, 22(1), 51–69.

Kark, R., Shamir, B., & Chen, G. (2003). The two faces of transformational leadership: Empowerment and dependency. *Journal of Applied Psychology*, 88(2), 246–255.

Kellaway, L. (2014). Losing the fear can be liberating – and dangerous. *Financial Times Europe*, November 10, 12.

Kernis, M. H., & Goldman, B. M. (2006). A multicomponent conceptualization of authenticity: Theory and research. In M. P. Zanna (Ed.), *Advances in Experimental Social Psychology* (Vol. 38, pp. 283–357). San Diego, CA: Academic Press.

Kiel, F. (2015). *Return on character: The real reason leaders and their companies win*. Boston, MA: Harvard Business Review Press.

Ko, C., Ma, J., Bartnik, R., Haney, M. H., & Kang, M. (2018). Ethical leadership: An integrative review and future research agenda. *Ethics & Behavior*, 28(2), 104–132.

Koehn, N. F. (2013). Lincoln's School of Management. *The New York Times*, January 27, BU1.

Koehn, N. F. (2016). Why Lincoln hid his strongest feelings from the public. *Harvard Business Review*, October 10 (https://hbr.org/2016/10/why-lincoln-hid-his-strongest-feelings-from-the-public).

Kouchaki, M. (2016). How Wells Fargo's fake accounts scandal got so bad. *Fortune*, September 15 (http://fortune.com/2016/09/15/wells-fargo-scandal/).

Kuper, S. (2013). What Mandela taught us. *Financial Times*, December 5 (www.ft.com/content/a342e372-5c64-11e3-931e-00144feabdc0).

Leary, M. R., Diebels, K. J., Davisson, E. K., Jongman-Sereno, K. P., Isherwood, J. C., Raimi, K. T., … Hoyle, R. H. (2017). Cognitive and interpersonal features of intellectual humility. *Personality and Social Psychology Bulletin*, 43(6), 793–813.

Lee, A., Willis, S., & Tian, A. W. (2018). Empowering leadership: A meta-analytic examination of incremental contribution, mediation, and moderation. *Journal of Organizational Behaviour*, 39(3), 306–325.

Lehman, D. W., O'Connor, K., Kovacs, B., & Newman, G. E. (2019). Authenticity. *Academy of Management Annals*, 13(1), 1–42.

Levesque-Côté, J., Fernet, C., Austin, S., & Morin, A. J. (2018). New wine in a new bottle: Refining the assessment of authentic leadership using exploratory structural equation modeling (ESEM). *Journal of Business and Psychology*, 33(5), 611–628.

Liden, R. C., Panaccio, A., Meuser, J. D., Hu, J., & Wayne, S. (2014a). Servant leadership: Antecedents, processes, and outcomes. In D. V. Vay (Ed.), *The Oxford handbook of leadership and organizations* (pp. 357–379). New York: Oxford University Press.

Liden, R. C., Wayne, S. J., Liao, C., & Meuser, J. D. (2014b). Servant leadership and serving culture: Influence on individual and unit performance. *Academy of Management Journal*, 57, 1434–1452.

Liden, R. C., Wayne, S. J., Meuser, J. D., Hu, J., Wu, J., & Liao, C. (2015). Servant leadership: Validation of a short form of the SL-28. *The Leadership Quarterly*, 26(2), 254–269.

Liden, R. C., Wayne, S. J., Zhao, H., & Henderson, D. (2008). Servant leadership: Development of a multidimensional measure and multi-level assessment. *The Leadership Quarterly*, 19(2), 161–177.

Lin, S., Ma, J., & Johnson, R. E. (2016). When ethical leader behaviour breaks bad: How ethical leader behaviour can turn abusive via ego depletion and moral licensing. *Journal of Applied Psychology*, 101(6), 815–830.

Lin, X., Chen, Z. X., Herman, H. M., Wei, W., & Ma, C. (2019). Why and when employees like to speak up more under humble leaders? The roles of personal sense of power and power distance. *Journal of Business Ethics* 158(4), 937–950.

Lu, C.-S., & Lin, -C.-C. (2014). The effects of ethical leadership and ethical climate on employee ethical behaviour in the International Port Context. *Journal of Business Ethics*, 124, 209–223.

Lyubovnikova, J., Legood, A., Turner, N., & Mamakouka, A. (2017). How authentic leadership influences team performance: The mediating role of team reflexivity. *Journal of Business Ethics*, 141, 59–70.

McFadden, R. D. (2018). Ingvar Kamprad, founder of Ikea and creator of a global empire, dies at 91. *The New York Times*, January 29, A1.

Merritt, A. C., Effron, D. A., & Monin, B. (2010). Moral self-licensing: When being good frees us to be bad. *Social and Personality Psychology Compass*, 4, 344–357.

Michaels, M. (2018). Amazon's Jeff Bezos continued to drive a Honda long after becoming a billionaire — and it reveals why he's so successful. *Business Insider*, January 19 (www.businessinsider.com/jeff-bezos-honda-reveals-reveals-why-hes-so-successful-2018-1).

Miska, C., & Mendenhall, M. E. (2018). Responsible leadership: A mapping of extant research and future directions. *Journal of Business Ethics*, 148(1), 117–134.

Mittal, R., & Dorfman, P. W. (2012). Servant leadership across cultures. *Journal of World Business*, 47(4), 555–570.

Morris, J. A., Brotheridge, C. M., & Urbanski, J. C. (2005). Bringing humility to leadership: Antecedents and consequences of leader humility. *Human Relations*, 58(10), 1323–1350.

Neider, L. L., & Schriesheim, A. C. (2011). The Authentic Leadership Inventory (ALI): Development and empirical tests. *The Leadership Quarterly*, 22, 1146–1164.

Neubert, M. J., Kacmar, K. M., Carlson, D. S., Chonko, L. B., & Roberts, J. A. (2008). Regulatory focus as a mediator of the influence of initiating structure and servant leadership on employee behaviour. *Journal of Applied Psychology*, 93(6), 1220–1233.

Newstead, T., Dawkins, S., Macklin, R., & Martin, A. (2019a). We don't need more leaders–We need more good leaders. Advancing a virtues-based approach to leader (ship) development. *The Leadership Quarterly* . doi.org/10.1016/j.leaqua.2019.101312.

Newstead, T., Dawkins, S., Macklin, R., & Martin, A. (2019b). The virtues project: an approach to developing good leaders. *Journal of Business Ethics*, 1–18.

The New York Times (2015). Depiction of Amazon stirs a debate about work culture. August 18 (www.nytimes.com/2015/08/19/technology/amazon-workplace-reactions-comments.html?_r=1).

Nielsen, R., & Marrone, J. A. (2018). Humility: Our current understanding of the construct and its role in organizations. *The International Journal of Management Reviews*, 20, 805–824.

Northouse, P. G. (2016). *Leadership: Theory and practice* (pp. 225–256). Thousand Oaks, CA: Sage.

Oc, B., Basshur, M. R., Daniels, M. A., Greguras, G. J., & Diefendorff, J. M. (2015). Leader humility in Singapore. *The Leadership Quarterly*, 26, 68–80.

Ou, A. Y., Tsui, A. S., Kinicki, A. J., Wladman, D. A., Xiao, Z., & Song, L. J. (2014). Humble Chief Executive Officers' connections to top management team integration and middle managers' responses. *Administrative Science Quarterly*, 59(1), 34–72.

Ou, A. Y., Waldman, D. A., & Peterson, S. J. (2018). Do humble CEOs matter? An examination of CEO humility and firm outcomes. *Journal of Management*, 44(3), 1147–1173.

Owens, B. P., & Hekman, D. R. (2016). How does leader humility influence team performance? Exploring the mechanisms of contagion and collective promotion focus. *Academy of Management Journal*, 58(3), 1088–1111.

Owens, B. P., Johnson, M. D., & Mitchell, T. R. (2013). Expressed humility in organizations: Implications for performance, teams, and leadership. *Organization Science*, 24(5), 1517–1538.

Owens, B. P., Rowatt, W. C., & Wilkins, A. L. (2012). Exploring the relevance and implications of humility in organizations. In K. S. Cameron, & G. Spreitzer (Eds.), *The Oxford handbook of positive organizational scholarship* (pp. 260–272). Oxford: Oxford University Press.

Owens, B. P., Walker, A. S., & Waldman, D. A. (2015). Leader narcissism and follower outcomes: The counterbalancing effect of leader humility. *Journal of Applied Psychology*, 100(4), 1203–1213.

Peterson, S., Galvin, B. M., & Lange, D. (2012). CEO servant leadership: Exploring executive characteristics and firm performance. *Personnel Psychology*, 65, 565–596.

Pffefer, J. (2015). *Leadership BS*. New York: HarperCollins.

Pfeffer, J. (2016). Why the assholes are winning: Money Trumps all. *Journal of Managerial Studies*, 53(4), 663–669.

Rajah, R., Song, Z., & Arvey, R. D. (2011). Emotionality and leadership: Taking stock of the past decade of research. *The Leadership Quarterly*, 22(6), 1107–1119.

Rego, A., Cunha, M. P., & Clegg, S. (2012). *The virtues of leadership: Contemporary challenge for global managers*. Oxford: Oxford University Press.

Rego, A., Cunha, M. P., & Simpson, A. (2018). The perceived impact of leaders' humility on team effectiveness: An empirical study. *Journal of Business Ethics*, 48(1), 205–218.

Rego, A., Owens, B., Leal, S., Melo, A., Cunha, M. P., Gonçalves, L., & Ribeiro, L. (2017). How leader humility helps teams to be humbler, psychologically stronger, and more effective: A moderated mediation model. *The Leadership Quarterly*, 28, 639–658.

Rego, A., Owens, B., Yam, K. C., Bluhm, D., Cunha, M. P., Silard, T., Gonçalves, L., Martins, M., Simpson, A. V., & Liu, W. (2019). Leader humility and team performance: Exploring the mechanisms of team psychological capital and task allocation effectiveness. *Journal of Management*, 45(3), 1009–1033.

Rego, A., Sousa, F., Marques, S., & Cunha, M. P. C. (2012). Authentic leadership promoting employees' psychological capital and creativity. *Journal of Business Research*, 65, 429–437.

Sachdeva, S., Iliev, R., & Medin, D. L. (2009). Sinning saints and saintly sinners: The paradox of moral self-regulation. *Psychological Science*, 20(4), 523–528.

Saïd Business School & Heidrick & Struggles. (2015). *The CEO Report: Embracing the paradoxes of leadership and the power of doubt*. Oxford: Saïd Business School & Heidrick & Struggles.

Salancik, G. R., & Pfeffer, J. (1977). An examination of needs satisfaction models of job attitudes. *Administrative Science Quarterly*, 22(3), 427–456.

Schaubroeck, J., Lam, S. S. K., & Peng, A. C. (2011). Cognition-based and affect-based trust as mediators of leader behaviour influences on team performance. *Journal of Applied Psychology*, 96(4), 863–871.

Schaufeli, W. B. (2015). Engaging leadership in the job demands-resources model. *Career Development International*, 20(5), 446–463.

Schneider, B., Goldstein, H. W., & Smith, D. B. (1995). The ASA framework: An update. *Personnel Psychology*, 48, 747–779.

Schultz, H. (2015). We need a servant leader. *The New York Times*, August 6, A27.

Schwartz, T. (2015a). The bad behaviour of visionary leaders. *The New York Times*, June 26 (www.nytimes.com/2015/06/27/business/dealbook/the-bad-behaviour-of-visionary-leaders.html).

Schwartz, T. (2015b). Why Jeff Bezos should care more for Amazon's employees. *The New York Times*, August 21 (www.nytimes.com/2015/08/22/business/dealbook/why-jeff-bezos-should-care-more-for-amazons-employees.html).

Seibert, S. E., Kraimer, M. L., & Crant, J. M. (2001). What do proactive people do? A longitudinal model linking proactive personality and career success. *Personnel Psychology*, 54, 845–874.

Sendjaya, S., & Cooper, B. (2011). Servant Leadership Behaviour Scale: A hierarchical model and test of construct validity. *European Journal of Work and Organizational Psychology*, 20(3), 416–436.

Sendjaya, S., Sarros, J., & Santora, J. (2008). Defining and measuring servant leadership behaviour in organizations. *The Journal of Management Studies*, 45(2), 402–424.

Sezer, O., Gino, F., & Norton, M. I. (2018). Humblebragging: A distinct—and ineffective—self-presentation strategy. *Journal of Personality and Social Psychology*, 114(1), 52–74.

Shamir, B., & Eilam, G. (2005). "What's your story?" A life-stories approach to authentic leadership development. *The Leadership Quarterly*, 16(3), 395–417.

Shaw, J. 2010. Papering the cracks with discourse: The narrativeidentity of the authentic leader. *Leadership*, 6: 89–108.

Skapinker, M. (2015). Singapore's law sets it apart and makes it hard to imitate. *Financial Times Europe*, April 2, 8.

Smith, G. (2012). Why I am leaving Goldman Sachs. *The New York Times*, March 14, A27.

Smith, W. K., Lewis, M. W., & Tushman, M. L. (2016). "Both/and" leadership: Don't worry so much about being consistent. *Harvard Business Review*, May, 63–70.

Sorkin, A. R. (2015). Decoding Steve Jobs, in life and on film. *The New York Times*, September 8, B1.

Sousa, M., & Van Dierendonck, D. (2016). Introducing a short measure of shared servant leadership impacting team performance through team behavioural integration. *Frontiers in Psychology*, 6, 2002.

Spain, S. M., & Kim, J. (2017). Leadership, work careers, and self-concept clarity. In J. L. Smith, & K. G. DeMarree (Eds.), *Self-concept clarity* (pp. 165–176). Cham: Springer.

Spears, L. C. (2002). Introduction: Tracing the past, present, and future of servant-leadership. In L. C. Spears, & M. Lawrence (Eds.), *Focus on leadership: Servant-leadership for the twenty-first century* (pp. 1–16). New York: John Wiley & Sons.

Stevenson, A. (Ed.). (2010). Oxford dictionary of English. Oxford University Press, USA.

Stouten, J., van Dijke, M., Mayer, D. M., De Cremer, D., & Euwema, M. C. (2013). Can a leader be seen as too ethical? The curvilinear effects of ethical leadership. *The Leadership Quarterly*, 24(5), 680–695.

Sun, P. Y. (2013). The servant identity: Influences on the cognition and behaviour of servant leaders. *The Leadership Quarterly*, 24(4), 544–557.

Talbot-Zorn, J. (2016). Donald Trump is not "authentic" just because he says the bad things in his head. *Time*, October 10 (http://time.com/4519851/2016-election-authenticity/).

Tate, B. (2008). A longitudinal study of the relationships among self-monitoring, authentic leadership, and perceptions of leadership. *Journal of Leadership and Organizational Studies*, 15, 16–29.

Thompson, D. (2015). How to brag. *The Atlantic*, May 26 (www.theatlantic.com/entertainment/archive/2015/05/how-to-brag/394136/).

Trilling, L. *Sincerity and Authenticity*. Harvard University Press, 1972.

Vallely, P. (2013). *Pope Franscis: Untying the knots*. London: Bloomsbury.

Van Dierendonck, D. (2011). Servant leadership: A review and synthesis. *Journal of Management*, 37(4), 1228–1261.

van Dierendonck, D., & Nuijten, I. (2011). The servant leadership survey: Development and validation of a multidimensional measure. *Journal of Business and Psychology*, 26, 249–267.

van Dierendonck, D., Sousa, M., Gunnarsdóttir, S., Bobbio, A., Hakanen, J., Pircher Verdorfer, A., Duyan, E. C., & Rodriguez-Carvajal, R. (2017). The cross-cultural invariance of the Servant Leadership Survey: A comparative study across eight countries. *Administrative Sciences*, 7(2), 8. doi:10.3390/admsci7020008.

van Dierendonck, D., Stam, D., Boersma, P., De Windt, N., & Alkema, J. (2014). Same difference? Exploring the differential mechanisms linking servant leadership and transformational leadership to follower outcomes. *The Leadership Quarterly*, 25(3), 544–562.

Vera, D., & Rodriguez-Lopez, A. (2004). Strategic virtues: Humility as a source of competitive advantage. *Organizational Dynamics*, 33(4), 393–408.

Waldman, D. A., & Balven, R. M. (2014). Responsible leadership: Theoretical issues and research directions. *The Academy of Management Perspectives*, 28(3), 224–234.

Walumbwa, F. O., Avolio, B. J., Gardner, W. L., Wernsing, T. S., & Peterson, S. J. (2008). Authentic leadership: Development and validation of a theory-based measure. *Journal of Management*, 34, 89–126.

Wang, G., & Hackett, R. D. (2016). Conceptualization and measurement of virtuous leadership: Doing well by doing good. *Journal of Business Ethics*, 137(2), 321–345.

Wang, G., Oh, I., Courtright, S., & Colbert, A. (2011). Transformational leadership and performance across criteria and levels: A meta-analytic review of 25 years of research. *Group & Organization Management*, 36(2), 223–270.

Watt, N., & Wintour, P. (2013). Thatcher biography reveals adviser's early warnings. *The Guardian*, April 23 (www.theguardian.com/politics/2013/apr/23/margaret-thatcher-biography-adviser-early-warning).

Waytz, A. (2016). The limits of empathy. *Harvard Business Review*, January–February, 69–73.

Weber, M. (1978). Economy and society: An outline of interpretive sociology (Vol. 1). Oakland, CA: University of California Press.

Weick, K. E. (2001). Leadership as the legitimation of doubt. In W. Bennis, G. Spreitzer, & T. Cummings (Eds.), *The future of leadership: Today's top leadership thinkers speak to tomorrow's leaders* (pp. 91–102). San Francisco, CA: Jossey-Bass.

Weiss, M., Razinskas, S., Backmann, J., & Hoegl, M. (2018). Authentic leadership and leaders' mental wellbeing: An experience sampling study. *The Leadership Quarterly*, 29(2), 309–321.

Williams, M. J. (2014). Serving the self from the seat of power: Goals and threats predict leaders' self-interested behaviour. *Journal of Management*, 40(5), 1365–1395.

Williamson, C. (2017). The importance of humility in leadership. *Forbes*, September 14 (www.forbes.com/sites/forbescoachescouncil/2017/09/14/the-importance-of-humility-in-leadership/#13afc54b2253).

Wiseman, L., & McKeown, G. (2010). Bringing out the best in your people. *Harvard Business Review*, May, 117–121.

Woodcock, S. (2008). The social dimensions of modesty. *Canadian Journal of Philosophy*, 38, 1–29.

Wright, T. A., & Quick, J. C. (2011). The role of character in ethical leadership research. *The Leadership Quarterly*, 22(5), 975–978.

Youssef, C. M., & Luthans, F. (2012). Positive global leadership. *Journal of World Business*, 47(4), 539–547.

Zhang, H., Ou, A. Y., Tsui, A. S., & Wang, H. (2017). CEO humility, narcissism and firm innovation: A paradox perspective on CEO traits. *The Leadership Quarterly*, 28(5), 585–604.

Zimbardo, P. (2004). A situationist perspective on the psychology of evil: Understanding how good people are transformed into perpetrators. In A. Miller (Ed.), *The social psychology of good and evil: Understanding our capacity for kindness and cruelty* (pp. 21–50). New York: Guilford.

9 Great workplaces

Summary and objectives

Great workplaces are rare. We explore the characteristics of great workplaces and how they might be developed. We also discuss the importance of organizational culture, purpose and values and how positive cultures of abundance contribute to creating organizations that are perceived as positive. Great workplaces take into account employee wellbeing and the role of active design in supporting wellness.

Great places to work

What are the characteristics of a great workplace and which organizations most effectively deliver on those characteristics? These were the questions a New York editor posed to two business writers – Robert Levering and Milton Moskowitz – in 1981 as he commissioned them to write a book published in 1984 as *The 100 Best Companies to Work for in America*.[1] Their effort to identify America's top 100 companies did not end with the publication of their bestselling book in 1984 but began a decades-long research effort into identifying and developing great workplaces.

The key insight uncovered from Levering and Moskowitz's initial study of American workplaces was that a great workplace is not founded upon a prescriptive formula for calculating employee benefits or programmes but the quality of member relationships. The best workplaces are those characterized by high-quality relationships with high levels of trust, camaraderie and pride. Levering further developed the theme of trust in another book in 1988 titled *A Great Place to Work: What Makes Some Employers so Good (and Most so Bad)*.[2]

As organizations took notice, Levering and Moskowitz began receiving invitations to speak about their findings and to provide consulting services to organizations wanting to implement them. Eventually they founded the Great Places to Work Institute in 1991 to further develop models and survey methods for measuring and developing great workplaces. Since 1997 the Institute has partnered with *Fortune* magazine to publish a yearly global ranking of the *100 Best Companies to Work For* (see Table 9.1). The list is based on company scores from the Trust Index Employee Survey and a Culture Audit as rated by random groups of employees from each company. The Trust Index comprises questions relating to the credibility of management, job satisfaction and camaraderie within the firm. The Culture Audit comprises questions related to employee pay and perks (facilities and benefits), hiring practices, training and recognition, sense of meaning and purpose, inspirational leadership as well as internal communication and

Table 9.1 Fortune magazine Top Company to Work For from global rankings for the years 2008–2018

Year	Company
2008	Google
2009	NettApp
2010	SAS
2011	SAS
2013	Google
2014	Google
2015	Google
2016	Google
2017	Google
2018	Salesforce

diversity. Policies and strategies supporting these types of values include employee profit sharing and stock options, flat non-hierarchical structures, flexible work hours, casual dress codes and workspaces, benefits such as use of fitness facilities, onsite child care, generous health insurance and excellent cafes and dining options. Google has ranked first on the list six times out of ten in the years 2008–2018 (and eight times overall) (see Table 9.1). Today, the Great Places to Work Institute has offices around the world and publishes 100 Best Companies lists for 45 countries.

Are the great so great?

Idyllic perspectives about the 'greatness' of the 'greatest' need to be countered by realism. Otherwise the positive perspective turns into a view characterized by naivety. Two main issues are worth mentioning. The first is that *being included in a ranking* of the 'great workplaces' is not a guarantee of *being* a great workplace. Before it collapsed, Enron was widely recognized as one of the best places to work in America! Several explanations for the discrepancy between common perceptions and the reality of Enron's fraudulent and corrupt culture are possible. No one suggests, however, that a *good* Enron transformed into a *bad* one over the course of a few years. More plausible explanations highlight the biased participation of 'Enronized'[3] employees and deceptive PR efforts coordinated by hubristic and manipulative leaders.[4] The second point deserving of attention is that 'being a great workplace' is not a straightforward issue; even 'the great' may to some extent incorporate 'the bad'. The case of Google is illustrative.

A slide, or a fireman's pole, as alternatives for getting from one floor to the next (in addition to conventional stairs); hippy caravans, Indigenous First Nations tepees or dodgem cars as meeting spaces; hammocks or soundproofed 'sleep pods' for taking a nap while on the job – while all of this may sound like new-age foolery it constitutes reality for employees in Google workplaces around the world. Google assumes that attending to the health and happiness of employees will engender greater creativity, productivity and loyalty.[5]

Insider comments by former Google employees on social platforms such as Quora,[6] however, suggest that there is also a sinister dimension to the multi-billion-dollar company's strange and quirky campus designs and office perks. From surveillance of workers' weight and their children in company childcare facilities, to doing their laundry, cutting their hair and providing their meals, overarching paternalism blurs the boundaries of work–life balance.

Getting hired at Google is challenging. Job applicants endure five exacting interviews that include complex puzzles, all designed to identify top talent. New employees are called 'Nooglers', current employees 'Googlers', while former workers, of whom there are some 20,000 around the globe, are 'Xooglers'. A downside of recruiting such brilliant people is that many employees report experiencing the confidence-crushing 'imposter syndrome' of not feeling up to par with their peers. Ramajayam, a Googler, explains: 'It's an amazing feeling to be constantly surrounded by talented, accomplished people, but sometimes, it can sting'.[7] With so much invested in the hiring process, Google does not easily let go of staff. The Xoogler alumni network seeks to maintain close connections with former employees, frequently inviting them for presentations, mentoring and networking opportunities.

'People Operations', shortened to 'POPS', is the Google nomenclature for the human resources department whose 'People Analysts' tend to be significantly more involved with employees than a typical HR department. Employees are regularly required to take surveys and personality tests, which, combined with behavioural data, such as records of gym use and lunch preferences, are extracted to provide insights into employee ambition and productivity. The Ford Sociological Department, born in the first blush of Fordism in 1914, could fittingly claim to be echoed down the years in a legacy of moral surveillance that Google adopts.[8] The all-pervasive Google eye is not appreciated by everyone, with a former employee comparing it with Big Brother in George Orwell's *1984*. Some claim they were constrained from discussing their boss with their spouse or friends and remain restricted from disclosing their previous work during subsequent job interviews elsewhere.

Google workplaces around the world are famous for their perks: many are equipped with futuristic-looking 'sleep pods' manufactured by MetroNaps of New York, who claim their product enhances mood, learning and creativity, while also boosting productivity and alertness. The sleep pod is a reclining chair equipped with a head-fitting visor. Users select a 15- to 20-minute programme to shift the pod into a head down and feet raised 'zero-gravity position' while relaxing music plays. Users are awakened by a series of flashing lights and vibrations. Older Google workplaces not equipped with pods have nap rooms, featuring soundproof door locks. Employees do not always use the nap facilities as intended. Stories abound of oversleeping or employees taking their 40 winks too frequently. Marissa Mayer, Google's 20th employee and later CEO of Yahoo, explained, 'The nap rooms at Google were there because it was safer to stay in the office than walk to your car at 3am'.[9] For employees seeking to unwind in a different way, Google offices also feature 'wellness centres' equipped with saunas, gyms and massage facilities. Employees can reward one another for a job well done by gifting 'massage credits' that can be redeemed as a free hour-long session.

Pet owners working at Google have an option of bringing their dog to work, with frequent pet visitors being provided with a personal photographic pass. Not only is bringing your dog to work welcome, it is encouraged. The company's employee Code of Conduct states: 'Google's affection for our canine friends is an integral facet of our corporate culture'.[10] A former employee reports that the policy contributed towards his being more productive at work, helping him make new friends amongst his colleagues and getting him outdoors during lunchtime to take the dog for a walk.

Overall, the policy is said to enhance the job satisfaction of employees with dogs far more than it increases the dissatisfaction of those who are not dog owners.

Unfortunately for those with feline friends, bringing cats to work is discouraged. It is not that the company has anything against felines but that, with all of the dogs around, canine–feline encounters might well be disruptive and potentially dangerous for the animals. Google policy states: 'For the health and wellbeing of the cat, with so many dogs around, owners are discouraged from bringing cats, though Google does not discriminate against them'.

Keeping employees in the workplace appears to be a Google priority. The company provides onsite dentists, doctors, physiotherapists, legal advisors, hairdressers, beauticians and a shoeshine service. Many of these amenities are provided free of charge, as are the laundry facilities: employees can load their own dirty clothes into the workplace washing machines or drop them off for dry cleaning.

Food is also provided in abundance and quality: it is not regular workplace canteen fare but world cuisine – including fresh-baked patisserie or gelato made on site, all provided free of charge. When the company began in 1998 Google's co-founder, Sergey Brin, directed office designers and architects that 'no one should be more than 200 feet away from food' (Figure 9.1).[11]

Although employees love the free food, a questionable purpose in providing free breakfast and lunch is to ensure employees have no reason to leave the workplace. Joe Cannella, a former senior Google account manager over a nine-year period, reflects on how the company colonizes its employees' lives:

> Basically, you end up spending the majority of your life eating Google food, with Google coworkers, wearing Google gear, talking in Google acronyms, sending Google emails on Google phones, and you eventually start to lose sight of what it's like to be independent of the big G, and every corner of your life is set up to reinforce the idea that you would be absolutely insane to want to be anywhere else.[13]

Canteen queues are also intentionally kept long to encourage employee engagement. Dan Cobley, former managing director of Google UK, explained: 'We know people will chat while they're waiting. Chats become ideas, and ideas become projects'.[14] Free food has its challenges, with new employees often being informally alerted to

Figure 9.1 Staff outdoor dining facility at Googleplex, Mountainview California.[12]

'Google 15', referencing the 15 lb often gained by new recruits in their first few months at Google. Shakespeare's 'in jest there is truth' applies here. Not wanting an unhealthy workforce, in 2012 Google established practices to 'nudge' staff towards staying slim: serving food on smaller plates; giving salads prime position at the front of the serving area and relocating desserts to a less conspicuous position; placing complimentary sugary treats in opaque jars, while displaying nuts and fruits in clear jars throughout the workplace. Colour-coding food labels also helped: green for low-calorie options, yellow for moderate portions and red for desserts and pastas. Dining area signs were also put up reading 'people who take big plates tend to eat more'.[15] Within less than two months of introducing these healthy-eating initiatives, 2,000 employees in Google's New York office had a 3.1 million reduction in their calorie consumption.[16]

Google is unique in offering employee 'death benefits'. If an employee dies while working for the company, the surviving partner receives 50 per cent of their salary for a decade. There is no minimum term requirement for this benefit, an employee qualifies from their very first day on the job. The perks for new parents include five months' pay for mums on maternity leave and six weeks for new dads. 'Baby bonding money' is given for nappies and other expenses in the month following the baby's birth.

Google staff around the world often have a vast array of on-campus sporting choices, from rock-climbing walls, to ice-skating rinks, putting greens, running tracks, bowling alleys, basketball courts and Ping-Pong tables. There are also swimming pools, some with wave machines where staff can surf under the watchful eye of a lifeguard. The less athletic may find more excitement in mobile libraries that also offer training programmes and language courses. Employees with green fingers can also get onto a waiting list for a plot of land on campus to grow their own fruits, vegetables and herbs.

Google also arranges off-campus recreation. During their holidays many employees attend annual ski trips and summer picnics organized by the firm, so they end up vacationing with colleagues in their spare time. Google's emphasis on fun and games can create a sense of juvenile immaturity. 'It's like never-never land', says one employee, 'people never grow up. They drink at all hours, socialize constantly, play games and do little to no work'.[17]

Emphasis on playfulness is pervasive in Google's gimmicky interiors, particularly the meeting spaces. The London office features artificial beach huts, rooms designed as huge dice and dodgem cars; the Israel office has a fake beach with a slide, while in Amsterdam meetings are held inside Sixties caravans, with lawn chairs placed outside next to fake BBQ grills to complete the kitsch. On a slightly more serious note, Google also invites A-list speakers to deliver inspirational talks to staff, including at its annual 'Zeitgeist Conference'. Past speakers have included: entrepreneur Sir Richard Branson, Prince Charles, actor Will Smith, singer Lady Gaga, model Christy Turlington and former US President Barack Obama.

Considering the emphasis Google places on investing in employee wellbeing, fun and learning, it is not surprising that Google is consistently ranked as the best place to work on Earth! As we have pointed out throughout the book, the positive, however, coexists with the negative. This is illustrated in Table 9.2. With this in mind, we next discuss several frameworks that include the components of a great/positive workplace and their possible consequences.

Table 9.2 The negative of the positive: the bright and the dark of the Google workplace

Factor	Positive	Negative
Strict recruitment	• Brilliant employees	• Imposter syndrome
Alumni network	• Keeps former employees connected	• The company doesn't let go of former employees
Highly involved People Operations (HR) department	• Data–research–driven policies and practices	• Orwellian implications
Sleep pods	• Employees are more productive	• Employees are less productive
Free food	• Increases employee interaction	• Employees less likely to eat with family and friends who are not Googlers
		• Employees put on weight
Free laundry, hair-cuts, massages, sport activities and other perks	• Employees' wellbeing needs are addressed by the company	• Employees become dependent on the company, blurring boundaries between work and life (no life outside of Google)
Gimmicky interiors	• Promotes playfulness and creativity	• Promotes immaturity

Authentizotic organizations

Authenteekos and *zoteekos*

From the psychological perspective of subconscious motivational need systems theory, Manfred Kets de Vries,[18] Clinical Professor of Leadership Development at INSEAD Business School, argues that the organizations that appear in the top 100 lists produced by Great Places to Work and *Forbes* are unfortunately 'more the exception than the rule' and that, in reality, employees are facing increasing instability and uncertainty. With the rise of neoliberalism emphasizing the supremacy of maximizing shareholder value (see Box 9.1), the psychological contract between organizations and employees has been broken. Previously, Kets de Vries maintains, organizations were committed to providing long-term employment and accordingly employees gave their loyalty and commitment to the organization. Work was not just a job but also a source of stability and identity that facilitated coping with the turbulence of social and economic upheaval.

Stable employee security and identity has been undermined by the casualization of work and policies that pit employees against one another as they compete for bonuses or just recognition to maintain their jobs. In many countries showing increases in the number of jobs created, these jobs are frequently casual positions. Employees are hired as independent agents, working on an hourly rate with none of the traditional worker entitlements such as paid annual leave, sick leave, parental leave, health insurance or a retirement pension. Many of the entitlements that social activists and unions have fought hard to have enshrined into law as workers' rights are being eroded by this increasing trend towards casualization, zero-hours contracts and the gig economy in which, by having a larger workforce of casual employees who work fewer hours per week than long-term employees, organizations lower their operating expenses as well as their commitment to employee wellbeing.

Box 9.1 Shareholder value maximization – a 20th-century philosophy?

1 The 'mess' of shareholder value maximization

Martin Wolf, chief economics commentator at the *Financial Times*, wrote in a 2014 article that

> Almost nothing in economics is more important than thinking through how companies should be managed and for what ends. Unfortunately, we have made a mess of this. That mess has a name: it is 'shareholder value maximisation'. Operating companies in line with this belief not only leads to misbehaviour but may also militate against their true social aim, which is to generate greater prosperity.

Wolf continued:

> I am not the first person to worry about the joint-stock company. Adam Smith, founder of modern economics, argued: 'Negligence and profusion … must always prevail, more or less, in the management of the affairs of such a company.' His concern is over what we call the 'agency problem' – the difficulty of monitoring management. Others complain that companies behave like psychopaths: a company aiming at maximising shareholder value might conclude it would be profitable – and so perhaps even its duty – to pollute the air and water if allowed to do so. It might also use its resources to obstruct an appropriate regulatory response to such (mis)behaviour.

2 Are business schools still living in the 20th century?

More recently, Steve Denning wrote in *Forbes* magazine[19] that while

> the world undergoes a Fourth Industrial Revolution that is 'fundamentally altering the way we live, work, and relate to one another – in its scale, scope, and complexity, a transformation … unlike anything humankind has experienced before', many business schools continue to live in the 20th century: 'For the most part, today's business schools are busy teaching and researching 20th century management principles and, in effect, leading the parade towards yesterday'.

Denning concluded:

> The 'good' management of yesterday that [some] firms are practicing – profit maximization and a philosophy of controlism – is obsolete. It was a relatively good fit for much of the 20th century. But then the world changed, and 'good' management began to falter. It couldn't cope with the fast pace and complexity of a customer-driven marketplace. Yet this 'good management of yesterday' is, by and large, what is being taught in today's business schools.

3 Is profit maximization 'the error at the heart of corporate leadership'?

Bower and Paine, two Harvard Business School professors, wrote in the *Harvard Business Review* that profit maximization is 'the error at the heart of corporate leadership'. They argue:[20]

> The agency model's extreme version of shareholder centricity is flawed in its assumptions, confused as a matter of law, and damaging in practice. A better model would recognize the critical role of shareholders but also take seriously the idea that corporations are independent entities serving multiple purposes and endowed by law with the potential to endure over time. And it would acknowledge accepted legal principles holding that directors and managers have duties to the corporation as well as to shareholders. In other words, a better model would be more company centered.

Questions for reflection

1   What are the main perverse consequences of managing for profit maximization?
2   Read the Bower and Paine article and reflect on their eight propositions for 'a radically different and, we believe, more realistic foundation for corporate governance and shareholder engagement'.[21] How do these propositions change the way you see the role of corporations in society?
3   If the profit maximization mantra is a 'mess', why do many business schools continue stick with it?

Kets de Vries holds that it is not external factors of workplace perks and gimmicks that make for extraordinary organizational performance. Rather, it is the fulfillment of three deeper motivational needs that underpins what he describes as an *authentizotic* organization. Authentizotic is a term that derives from combining two Greek words: *authenteekos* and *zoteekos*. *Authenteekos* relates to authenticity, where there is alignment between rhetoric and practice, creating an environment of trustworthiness, reliability and accountability. Kets de Vries[22] explains:

> As a workplace label, *authenticity* implies that the organization has a compelling connective quality for its employees in its vision, mission, culture, and structure. The organization's leadership has communicated clearly and convincingly not only the *how* but also the *why*, revealing meaning in each person's task. These are the kinds of organizations where people find a sense of flow; where they feel complete and alive.

Zoteekos communicates zest, vigour and vitality. In organizations characterized by *zoteekos* employees feel a sense of enthusiasm, completeness and confidence. Kets de Vries[23] explains the effects of this quality:

> the human need for exploration, closely associated with cognition and learning, is met. The *zoteekos* element of this type of organization allows for self-assertion in the work place and produces a sense of effectiveness and competency, of autonomy, initiative, creativity, entrepreneurship, and industry.

Fulfilling human needs

Authentizotic organizations are characterized by the fulfillment of human needs, providing a sense of belonging, a sense of enjoyment, a sense of meaning. *A sense of belonging* derives from experiences of commitment and community within the organization that provides for human yearning for affiliation and attachment. These powerful drivers form the basis of mutually trusting and respectful relations (see Chapter 6). Designing the organizational social architecture with many small units in which each member is known to their colleagues is seen to count in meeting organizational objectives and enabling individuals to be recognized for their contributions and feel significant and valued. Coordinating frequent interpersonal interactions through gatherings and events can also facilitate the development of more intimate workplace relations that provide a greater sense of connectedness and belonging. Close identification with others in a community also generates greater empathy, helpfulness and compassion for colleagues. It can also contribute towards greater cohesiveness around common values, attitudes and objectives.

As trust grows between members and responsibilities are delegated to team members 'distributed leadership' emerges, where decision-making authority is dispersed across the organization as opposed to being concentrated in a single decision-making authority. Senior executives in such organizations act more as facilitators, mentors and coaches,[24] taking pride in the achievements of junior executives, which also facilitates leadership succession and continuity.

A *sense of enjoyment* facilitates imagination, risk taking and creativity. Organizational life need not be defined by zombie-like formality, rigidity and boredom, where members mindlessly follow orders without considering the consequences of 'just doing my job', constantly looking at a clock that seems to move ever so slowly for when they might be able to take a break or leave for the day. Rather, work can be creative, passionate and committed. Not only does joyfulness facilitate closer relations and enhanced creativity but it also strengthens resilience and wellbeing. When people are happy and playful, imagination soars and experimentation with new approaches becomes more common as people are not afraid of failing but regard mistakes as learning opportunities. Extraordinary institutions recognize the value of encouraging their members to have fun and enjoy their work as a way of cultivating an additional motivating human need, the need for learning, discovery and meaning.

Belonging and enjoyment are two personal human needs that contribute to making things meaningful; yet, there are other factors of meaning that transcend personal needs that can be promoted within an organization. A *sense of meaning* is experienced most profoundly in an organization that provides opportunities for engaging in activities that are bigger than ourselves by contributing towards helping other people, improving their quality of life or contributing towards improving greater social wellbeing. In some instances in organizations where people have a strong sense of meaning, work no longer feels like a *tripalium* (see Chapter 5) at all but becomes a personal mission and an opportunity to self-actualize. In these organizations members are more likely to stretch themselves, engaging their best talents in addressing meaningful challenges and, as a consequence, experiencing a sense of 'flow',[25] where they are so concentrated and invested in what they are doing that they lose track of time.

Kets de Vries holds that the cultivation of the three human needs described above will generate congruence between the needs of both the individual and the organization. The effect of such congruence will be the manifesting of positive individual outcomes of a greater sense of self-determination, a greater sense of impact, a greater sense of competence, all of which are also beneficial to the organization:[26]

> congruence will lead to a greater sense of *self-determination*. In other words, organizational participants will have a greater feeling of control over their lives; they will perceive (and rightly so) that they have a voice in what they are doing and where they are going. Such a sense of congruence will contribute to a sense of *impact*, a belief that each employee's actions make a difference in the organization and each person has the power to affect organizational performance. This is what empowerment is all about. In addition, leaders have the obligation to contribute to their people's sense of *competence*, helping them gain a feeling of personal growth and development, a feeling that they are learning new things.

To attract and retain quality talent, increasingly managers are being challenged to create organizations with authentizotic characteristics. There is a growing expectation that responsible organizations offer employees a workplace environment that facilitates fun, creativity and connection, supports health, wellbeing and thriving, and provides meaning, purpose and personal fulfillment (see Box 9.2). Despite providing all of these benefits, such organizations must also encourage employees in maintaining a healthy work–life balance on their own terms rather than those specified by a paternalistic panoptical apparatus.

Box 9.2 Three workplace factors endorsed as most important by hundreds of thousands of Facebook employees

For years, Facebook has been collecting data twice a year on what their employees rate as mattering most at work. In early 2018, an analysis of hundreds of thousands of repeat responses to these questions was published in the *Harvard Business Review*.[27] Three primary motivations were identified (two are identical to the primary human needs espoused by Kets de Vries):

* **Career** is described at Facebook as concerning people 'having a job that provides autonomy, allows you to use your strengths, and promotes your learning and development. It's at the heart of intrinsic motivation'.
* **Community** is concerned with employees 'feeling respected, cared about, and recognized by others', which 'drives our sense of connection and belongingness'.
* **Cause** is about meaning and purpose, with employees 'feeling that you make a meaningful impact, identifying with the organization's mission, and believing that it does some good in the world. It's a source of pride'.

Facebook HR personnel consider these three needs as the basis of a psychological contract comprising implicit employee–employer obligations and expectations. Upholding the contract inspires people to bring discretionary effort, enthusiasm and commitment to their workplace; breach the contract and people become demotivated and dissatisfied underperformers. Facebook HR holds that, whereas previously organizations could afford to build their cultures upon a single one of these three factors that make up the psychological contract, this data suggests that for most employees just one factor is insufficient. Over a quarter of Facebook employees rated as important all three: career, community and cause. More significantly, 90 per cent had a tie in importance between at least two of these factors.

Facebook also analyzed endorsement of these values by different age groups, performance levels, geographic location in the world and work function and, overall, they found that Facebook employees held these three factors as similarly important.

Now pause and reflect

- Considering the 2018 scandal that involved Facebook in the effort of Cambridge Analytica to manipulate electoral processes in several countries, including the UK and US,[28] what does this case say about positivity and meaning, authenticity and PR? Take into account the words of Campbell Brown, Facebook's head of news partnerships: 'The company has been too focused on the positive and not nearly vigilant [enough] about the negative and we've been caught flat-footed'.[29]
- *The Economist* described Facebook's culture as a meld of 'a ruthless pursuit of profit with a Panglossian and narcissistic belief in its own virtue'.[30] Is this culture exclusive to Facebook? How do companies end up creating this sort of culture? How do they believe their own virtues?

Authentizotic psychological climates

Inspired by Kets de Vries' authentizotic notion, Rego and colleagues[31] crafted and validated a quantitative psychometric scale for assessing authentizotic psychological climates (i.e., how the employee perceives the authentizotic nature of their workplaces). They found that six factors/components are relevant (see Table 9.3): spirit of camaraderie, trust/credibility of the leader, open and frank communication with the leader, opportunities for learning and personal development, fairness, and work–family conciliation.

Rego and Cunha[32] (yes the same first two authors of this textbook) tested how the perceptions of these authentizotic factors predict employee happiness and work performance. Their results suggest that authentizotic psychological climates matter. Particularly noteworthy were findings that employees are more stressed when they perceive their leaders as untrustworthy and when the organization does not provide the conditions required to balance both work and family commitments appropriately. In contrast, when employees observe a positive spirit of camaraderie they report greater comfort, pleasure and peacefulness within their work environment. They are also more likely to report that their organization enables them to: 'meet social needs, obtain social support for dealing with work difficulties, challenges and opportunities, experience fewer relationship conflicts and feel intrinsically motivated … being respected as human beings and not just as "resources"'.[33] Employees who report opportunities for personal development and learning are also more likely to express greater workplace enthusiasm, to perceive their work as intrinsically motivating and rewarding, to feel greater empowerment, and have a greater

Table 9.3 Psychological authentizotic climates – and the items measuring them

Spirit of camaraderie
 A sense of family exists among the employees.
 People show concerns for the wellbeing of the others.
 A great team spirit characterizes the organization.
 The organization atmosphere is friendly.
Trust and credibility of the leaders
 People trust in their leaders.
 Leaders fulfil their promises.
 People feel that the leaders are honest.
Open and frank communication with the leader
 People feel free to communicate frankly and openly with the leaders.
 People feel free to show discordances to their leaders.
 Talking with people placed at higher positions in the organization is easy.
Opportunities for learning and personal development
 People feel that they can learn continuously.
 People can place their creativity and imagination in benefit of the work and the organization.
 People feel that important responsibilities are assigned to them.
 People feel that they can develop their potential.
Fairness/justice
 When good outcomes are reached through the employee's efforts, the 'laurels' (e.g., compensation and praise) are distributed only to a few managers. (r)[34]
 People feel discriminated against. (r)
 Personal favouritism in the promotions exists. (r)
Work–family conciliation
 This organization helps employees to reconcile work and family life.
 The organization acts in order to allow people to conciliate work with their family responsibilities.
 For advancing in one's career, one needs to sacrifice family life. (r)
 The organization creates conditions so that people can maintain their children's instruction.

sense of making a contribution, of enjoyment, a sense of purpose and meaning and to experience a sense of fulfillment in their work lives.

 These findings additionally suggested a positive relationship between authentizotic psychological climates and self-reported individual performance. For example, when employees perceive good opportunities for learning and personal development they experience their work as more meaningful and are more likely to see it as an opportunity for developing their personal competencies and manifesting their potential. Another relationship between psychological climate and performance is indirect and mediated by wellbeing. Employees reporting experiences of greater affective wellbeing, particularly enthusiasm, vigour and peacefulness, are more likely to report higher levels of performance. Rego and Cunha conclude: 'enthusiastic, vigorous and "calm" employees express more commitment to work, apply their potential in performing the job, actively try to solve problems and take advantage of opportunities, and persevere calmly when facing obstacles'.[35]

Building workplaces from employees' DREAMS

'Dreams'

Robert Goffee and Gareth Jones agree that authentic organizations are fundamental for employee flourishing and thriving. Yet their research has led them to a slightly different, although related, model of what constitutes an authentic organization, as compared with the ideas discussed thus far in this chapter. Their book *Why Should Anybody Work Here: What It Takes to Create an Authentic Organization* reports on the findings of research that was guided by asking: 'how do you build the best workplace on Earth?'[36] Goffee and Jones' methodology dismissed attempts at answering this question by investigating organizations that are lauded for distinct cultures, high-performance track records or acclaimed brands. They also avoided a methodology of identifying causes of organizational disengagement or dysfunction. On the contrary, they took an approach of discovering people's positive dreams for their workplaces and the efforts they are making to design and deploy these visions as reality.

Goffee and Jones generalized their findings into six broad categories that make up the mnemonic DREAMS (see Box 9.3). These six attributes contrast with traditional organizational practices. They are also difficult to implement as there is tension between some of these attributes, their application requiring the balancing of competing values and interests along with reconsidering the allocation of resources. Seldom do organizations excel in all six attributes. We next consider each one of the six components in detail (as well as in summary, i.e., in Box 9.3).

Box 9.3 Organizational DREAMS: the six broad categories of Goffee and Jones' model[37]

Difference: 'I want to work in a place where I can be myself and express the ways in which I see things differently'.

Radical honesty: 'I want to know what's really going on'.

Extra value: 'I want to work in an organisation that magnifies my strengths and adds extra value for me and my personal development'.

Authenticity: 'I want to work in an organisation I'm proud of, one that truly stands for something'.

Meaning: 'I want my day-to-day work to be meaningful'.

Simple rules: 'I do not want to be hindered by stupid rules or rules that apply to some people but not others'.

Difference

'Creativity increases with diversity and declines with conformity' state Goffee and Jones.[38] In most organizations, difference is viewed as translating into diversity considerations, frequently classified according to categories of ethnicity, gender, age and religion. While these are important considerations, Goffee and Jones' research suggests there are subtler, more significant and difficult to implement considerations. These include differences in employee perspectives, mental habits, worldviews and deeply held assumptions. Great workplaces do not merely accommodate such differences but rather celebrate and leverage them to generate dividends of greater employee engagement, creativity and innovation.

Radical honesty

Organizations increasingly recognize the critical importance of internal and external communication; however, the more commonplace appointment of communications representatives into top organization committee positions is evidence of the growth of the communications industry rather than changed commitments. Unfortunately, communication is often superficial rather than authentic, frequently depriving stakeholders of critical information vital to performing their roles. Viewing information as power or spin as skill, old-world mindsets continue to undermine the messages disseminated and received. In a world defined and dominated by social media, over which companies have little control, organizations no longer monopolize information dissemination. Goffee and Jones argue: 'the imperative should be to tell the truth before someone else does. When you do, you will begin to build long standing organizational trust – both inside and outside of your firm'.[39]

Extra value

Top organizations invest in their people. Opportunity for further training and development is part of the agreement these organizations have with their employees. Goffee and Jones' research indicates that when employees view their work as an opportunity to grow, their performance grows as well. Recognition of the benefits of adding value to employees so that they add value to the organization is not as widespread as one would expect. Yet it is also not limited to knowledge economy organizations; for example, Starbucks also recognizes the importance of investing in training their people as vital for the success of their businesses.

Authenticity

Goffee and Jones take three indicators of an organization's authenticity into account. First, they consider if an organization is clear about its identity and if the association between this identity and the company's history is consistently rooted in its history. Second, they assess the relationship between an organization's espoused values and those reflected in its decisions and practices. Third, they seek to understand the commitment level of the organization's leadership towards products and services, stakeholders, history and vision. If the leaders are just there doing a job, employees will care little as well. If the leaders are personally invested and passionate about the company's mission, there is a greater likelihood that employees will get on board with what becomes a shared mission. Goffee and Jones acknowledge that achieving authenticity is easier said than done:

> in many organisations the task of building authenticity has collapsed into the industry of mission-statement writing. Some of the people we interviewed despaired that their company's mission statement had been rewritten four times in three years! Unsurprisingly, this produces not high performance but deep-rooted cynicism.[40]

Meaning

Three Cs that contribute to work being meaningful, according to Goffee and Jones, are connections, community and cause. First, people are inspired when they understand how the work they contribute connects with the contributions of others. Second, employees are looking for a work environment where they can feel a sense of community and belonging. Third, people become particularly motivated when they can see that their work efforts contribute towards the realization of longer-term goals related to wider social wellbeing. Organizations that fail to provide deeper senses of meaning will instead rely on faddish engagement to increase efforts, where any beneficial effects quickly fade.

Simple rules

Max Weber observed of bureaucratic organizational structure that rules provide predictability, discipline, structure and rationality. Weber acknowledged that rules can also lead to inefficiency and stifle innovation and creativity. Later Robert Merton identified the tendency of bureaucracies to 'rule tropism' where rules are followed for their own sake, forgetting the purpose they are meant to serve (revisit Box 6.2, Chapter 6, on Kafkaesque bureaucracy).[41] Simple rules have been associated with organizational success in fast-changing environments because those rules are 'virtuous' by way of being in the middle: between the rigidity resulting from too many rules and the confusion of too few rules.[42] In some organizations, such as Valve or Outsystems, rules are contained in booklets available on the Internet: *Handbook for New Employees*[43] and *The Small Book of the Few Big Rules* (see Box 9.4)[44] respectively.

Box 9.4 The rule of having few rules at Outsystems[45]

In the beginning we had a strict dress code (suit and tie) because we were dealing with enterprise customers. But after one of our engineers showed up at the office wearing orange shorts and sandals with socks, and was still able to command respect from the rest of the team, we decided to just ask people to exhibit common sense about what they wear, especially when meeting with customers. Since then we have tried to limit the number of rules we need to follow. We find that this freedom increases creativity, enabling us to come up with unique and possibly weird innovations that will help the company continue to be extremely competitive. So we don't have many rules here (you can wear sandals with socks if you want). But we do have some. Read on.

Here the rule is: enact rules that provide a framework; guidelines that preserve ample space for individual discretion or, as Gulati formulated it, freedom within a framework.[46] Creating flat structures where employees are empowered to make decisions on their own, with a loose network structure (as opposed to a bureaucratic hierarchy), is helpful for getting things done, rather than merely conforming to rules. Goffee and Jones hold that an

> ideal company is not a company without rules. It is a company with clear rules that make sense to the people who follow them, and remains ever vigilant about maintaining that clarity and simplicity – a much larger challenge with a far greater payoff.[47]

To sum up, the DREAMS attributes appear obvious at a surface level. Who would prefer a workplace with the opposite characteristics of enforcing conformity, lying to employees, worker exploitation, inconsistent values, stressful alienating work and a plethora of creativity-inhibiting bureaucratic rules? Yet few organizations exemplify even half of DREAMS attributes. Goffee and Jones' research suggests that even when organizations do attempt to address the negative workplace practices listed above, they do so reactively as an effort to put out fires, rather than addressing fundamental considerations underlying human wellbeing and flourishing.

Goffee and Jones see building better workplaces as a means of addressing the challenges of capitalism, whether they be in the forms of digital disruption and industry-redefining technologies, socio-political upheavals and cost pressures from cheaper alternatives, or ethical and sustainability conundrums. In their own words:

> The logic of capitalism is inevitable – so expect everything from disruptive new entrants and game-changing technologies to cheaper alternatives and pressures on costs. But, crucially, this is not a matter of either/or. Building better work places is not an alternative to, but rather a means of, responding to the new challenges of capitalism, for building productivity, unleashing creativity, and winning.[48]

Organizational cultures of abundance

Great workplaces depend, to a great extent, on employees' *shared* positive perceptions about how the organization and its members behave. Positive organizational cultures emerge from the interplay between organizational practices and policies, leadership traits, skills and behaviours, and employees' characteristics, attitudes and behaviours. If organizational practices and policies are inherently positive, yet employees share a cynical attitude toward those practices and policies, one cannot say the organization has a positive organizational culture. DREAMS turn into nightmares – particularly when the 'dream' is just a PR effort to milk employees as if they were contented cows.

Creating a positive organizational culture is an endeavour that requires consistent practices, policies and behaviours over the long run, in domains such as recruitment and selection, socialization, performance management, training and development, leadership selection and development, as well as in the relationships the organization establishes with the community and other external stakeholders. Before discussing positive organizational culture in more detail, let us briefly reflect on the notion of culture, which has in fact been borrowed by management from the field of anthropology. Later, we discuss several ways to foster a positive organizational culture – if at all possible, considering the doubts espoused by some scholars.

Do organizations have culture or are they cultures?

The assumption that organizations have culture is similar to the assumption that one has a particular suit of clothes one wears for work; as fashions change one discards that design for one more fashionable. By contrast, to say that organizations are cultures is to acknowledge that culture is much more than what one might see on the surface; it has depth, diversity and difference.

Management and organizational studies is a relatively new discipline; accordingly many ideas are appropriated from other fields. You will note that this book on POB borrows abundantly from psychology (as it is psychologists who are generally concerned with human behaviour) with some ideas drawn from sociology as well (particularly Chapter 11 on organizations as engines of social progress). For centuries, cultural anthropologists have studied the unique characteristics that define a specific group of people by observing characteristics of culture: shared patterns of knowledge and belief, communicated collectively through norms of behaviour, identity, deviance, language, symbols, artifacts, design and processes. These are often uniquely displayed in norms of food, dress, dance, music, ritual, worship and social relations.

A key difference in the ways managers and many management researchers treat culture from the way that anthropologists do is that, historically, cultural anthropologists have not sought to influence culture but merely to observe, record and describe it. Managers seek to design a unique and ideal organizational cultural identity to ensure greater organizational performance and many management researchers are happy to help them to do it. From an anthropological perspective, the notion of using culture as an instrument (i.e., as a tool of social control) and the assumption that it can be shaped according to managerial design (where all are bound by the same integrated values, beliefs and behaviours as dictated by a managerial authority) is both naïve and horrifying.[49] For an anthropologist, culture is something that *is*. From this view, people and communities do not have a *culture*, rather they *are cultures*. Similarly, organizations don't have cultures, they are cultures (see Box 9.5).[50] Moreover, anthropologists know that it is when a culture is under challenge or duress that there will most likely be attempts to assert it as an overarching singularity: strong cultures are more indicative of a failure to be open and innovative in the face of subcultural or opposing cultural challenges.

Box 9.5 Eight types of culture

Groysberg, Lee, Price and Chung have suggested a fruitful way to characterize organizational cultures that you, the reader, may enjoy learning about. They classify organizational cultures along two dimensions. The first refers to people interactions and coordination, the poles being highly independent employees vs highly interdependent employees. The second dimension refers to how the organization responds to change, the two poles being stability (i.e., prioritizing consistency, predictability, maintenance of the status quo) and flexibility (i.e., adaptability and receptiveness to change). Crossing these two dimensions gives rise to eight culture styles (see Figure 9.2):[51] caring, purpose, learning, enjoyment, results, authority, safety and order. According to this model, while Tesla has a learning culture (high flexibility and moderate independence), Huawei has an authority one (high stability, flexibility and moderate independence) and Disney has a caring culture (high interdependence and moderate flexibility).[52] Each culture is seen to have advantages and disadvantages. For example, a caring culture (which is warm, sincere and relational) fosters engagement, communication, trust, teamwork and a sense of belonging, but the emphasis on consensus building may reduce exploration behaviours, stifle competitiveness and slow decision-making. On the opposite side, a results-oriented culture has the advantages of improved execution, external focus, capability building and goal achievement, but it may lead to communication and collaboration problems and higher levels of stress and anxiety.

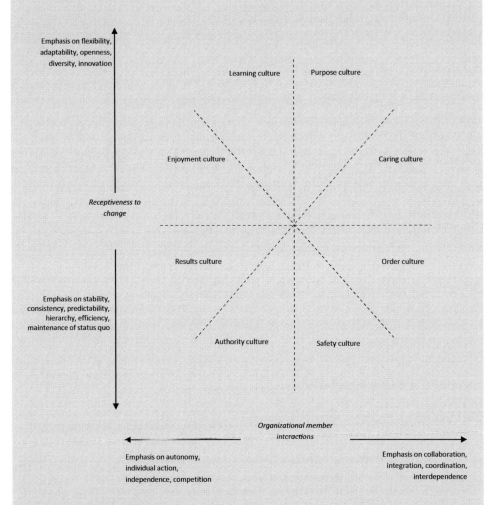

Figure 9.2 Cultural styles.

Suggestions for reflection

- After reading Groysberg, Lee, Price and Chung's paper, try to classify the culture of your organization – or another organization you are familiar with. For that, you may use the questionnaire provided by the authors (see p. 53 of the paper).
- Think about the positive and the negative sides of such a culture.
- Discuss the following provocative question with other people: is a great workplace one where all eight culture styles operate? Is this possible? Why and how?

The threat from Japanese organizations

The idea of organizational culture as something that organizations have and that managers can engineer achieved prominence in the 1980s at a time when economies in the developed world, particularly the US and the UK, were under considerable pressure. The US and the UK had dominated world markets with their manufactured goods – cars, TVs, washing machines and fridges – during the post-WWII period. By the late 1970s and early 1980s, as Western Europe and parts of Asia, particularly Japan, had recovered and rebuilt their infrastructure and industry that had been decimated by the war, US and UK dominance was seriously challenged, particularly because non-US manufactured goods were better quality.

One explanation for the poor quality of US-made goods was sabotage by employees, enacted as modes of resistance. The reality is that relationships between management and employees in these organizations were often toxic and adversarial – with little respect, trust or good will between them. Frequently, these organizations operated as the antithesis to a positive organizational culture of abundance. Managers kept workers under constant surveillance and control while on the shop floor; on the assumption that individual and organizational interests were necessarily incompatible these managers expected workers to act against the interests of the organization.

Workers accordingly took every opportunity to resist managerial control as a way of taking back some of their self-regard and autonomy. For example, at the General Motors factory at Fremont, California, where the Chevrolet Nova automobile was assembled, absenteeism averaged 20 per cent and employees walked off the job in wildcat strikes three or four times each year.[53] Employees sometimes deliberately sealed a part-eaten sandwich inside car door panels. Shortly after purchasing the vehicle, a customer would smell a disturbing stench and be unable to discern the source. Leaving loose screws inside a compartment of the metal car frame that was welded shut, so it would rattle the entire frame when the vehicle was driven, was another act of sabotage by employees. No wonder the goods produced in this plant received the lowest customer ratings for the entire company. It is also not surprising that, in the 1980s, sales were in decline at General Motors as customers opted for the cheaper but better quality Japanese imports. General Motors eventually closed the Fremont plant and laid-off all the factory workers.

As US manufacturers and academics sought to identify the factors that contributed to the poor quality of US manufacturing and the superiority of Japanese products in particular, an answer was found in the notion of culture. In part this was because of ignorance of other countries in many US Business Schools, and colleagues from the humanities and social science disciplines, for whom culture was their stock in trade, provided early explanations of the Japanese difference.[54] Japanese employees were perceived as having a much higher level of engagement, loyalty and trust towards their organizations as well as a sense of pride and ownership of the products produced in their firms. The positive attitude of the Japanese employee was explained by traditional Japanese cultural values of honour, pride and loyalty to the clan. Deeper analysis revealed that it was also associated with a different attitude from the managers who treated employees with honour, respect and dignity; almost as equal partners in a joint venture.[55] Culture quickly caught on as the key to organizational success although there was always more to the story than being Japanese, such as commitments to quality control, continuous improvement, lifelong employment and other related more specific practices.[56]

The Fremont plant was eventually reopened but as a joint venture between General Motors and the Japanese auto manufacturer Toyota. Japanese managers who ran the factory rehired many of the same workers who earlier had been laid off by General Motors. They achieved very different results using Toyota's operating principles, emphasizing a culture of employee empowerment, respect and trust. For example, workers were invited to choose their own job titles. An employee responsible for spot-welding and monitoring robots chose as his title 'Director of Welding Improvement'. Business cards with the new job titles printed on them were supplied to all workers. They were also paid a share of all the profits generated by the factory and were invited to provide input to improve the firm's operating procedures. Furthermore, they were trusted with cords to pull that stopped the conveyor belt, bringing the whole assembly line to a halt (costing tens of thousands of dollars per second) if they identified a fault during the manufacturing process.

These practices symbolize, according to Kim Cameron, a new culture of abundance.[57] The effect was that employees felt a greater sense of ownership and commitment. One employee (who was the source of the information about worker sabotage described above) recounted his new sense of identification with the organization, as follows:

> Now when I go to a San Francisco 49ers game or a Golden State Warriors game, or to a shopping mall I look for our cars on the parking lot. When I see one, I take out my business card and write on the back of it, 'I made your car. Any problems, call me.' I put my card under the windshield wiper of the car. I do it because I feel personally responsible for those cars.[58]

The turnaround of the Fremont auto manufacturing plant demonstrates that culture change in an organization is possible. Cameron writes in his book *Positive Leadership* that such a turnaround represents positive organizational change at the deepest level, that of deeply held assumptions (see Chapter 1):

> This example illustrates a fundamental culture change – gut level, values-centred, in the bones change in what is assumed to be right and acceptable. Employees adopted a different way to think about the company and their roles in it, with the result that productivity, quality, efficiency, and morality improved significantly. Ample empirical evidence confirms that an abundance culture and virtuous practices in organizations lead to dramatic positive impacts on performance and effectiveness.[59]

Arguments like this one are not, however, the final word. Despite prevailing managerial assumptions that management can change an organizational culture according to managerial design, there is provocative research suggesting that 90 per cent of culture change initiatives fail.[60] This is a challenging statistic for those concerned with creating a positive organizational culture of abundance. Is the statistic credible? If one considers culture as constituted mainly by unconscious assumptions (as large and ingrained in the organizational functioning as the submerged part of an iceberg; Figure 9.3) shared by organizational members, one has to recognize that changing and managing organizational culture is a massive challenge.

Figure 9.3 Iceberg in the Arctic[62] – where is the bigger portion?

The iceberg of organizational culture according to Schein

One of the most helpful models for understanding organizational culture was developed by former MIT professor Edgar Schein.[61] He described organizational culture in terms of three distinct levels: Level 1 includes artifacts, Level 2 includes espoused values and Level 3 includes basic assumptions. These three levels are compared with an iceberg.

Level 1 of organizational artifacts corresponds to the peak of the iceberg, visible above the ocean surface. These are the observable manifestations of culture that may be seen in:

- physical artifacts (e.g., buildings, furnishings, uniforms),
- symbolic artifacts (e.g., logo, branding, colours),
- language (type of language and industry-specific jargon), and
- myths (rites, rituals and founding stories).

Artifacts can be easily changed and are purposefully changed from time to time but the change remains only superficial if it is not supported at deeper levels. Changing an organization's culture at the level of artifacts (logos, buildings and uniforms) is also expensive.

Level 2, espoused values, corresponds to the place where the iceberg meets the sea. The word 'espouse' means to profess, support or adopt. In the organizational context, espoused values are the consistent beliefs in which the organization is emotionally invested. Organizational values are often expressed in a firm's mission statement, vision statement or statement of values. Many organizations have statements about their core mission and values listed on company websites or in brochures. A limitation of these statements is that they are at best aspirational. Frequently they are written by management, often advised by marketing consultants, so, while they may sound good on paper, they don't actually reflect the practices of the organization. They are not representative of the members' core values and beliefs. They may even be aligned with the artifacts of Level 1 but the acid test of their motivational strength is how they are consistent with the content of Level 3.

Level 3, representing shared basic assumptions, corresponds to the largest and most important but also least visible part of the iceberg, the part that sits beneath the water's surface. Basic assumptions are the intangible frames that subconsciously influence the manifestation of organizational values and artifacts. The organizational member's collective worldviews and beliefs about the nature of human relationships, human activity and justice, the nature of reality and truth and the organization's relationship with the natural environment are the core of organizational culture that unconsciously shapes the other levels. Basic assumptions are difficult to change, which would explain why most organizational change initiatives are unsuccessful. In his book *The Positive Organization*, Robert Quinn, Professor Emeritus at the University of Michigan, compares basic assumptions to mental maps:

> all of us have a set of assumptions or beliefs that help us navigate the world we live in. These beliefs are acquired over time from the people we live with and work with. We learn from these people what works and what doesn't. These assumptions and beliefs then become like maps in our minds that guide our responses to what we observe and experience around us … we take our beliefs as truth and seldom doubt them … The mental maps we hold influence our approach to, and our beliefs about culture in our organizations.[63]

Quinn suggests that the most effective way to positively transform a toxic organizational culture into a culture of abundance is by identifying positive exceptions. Seeking out, identifying and highlighting such cases of positive deviance within the organization challenges tightly held assumptions by exposing an alternative positive reality within an existing system – creating new frames of reference. Enacting change through identifying and highlighting positive deviance is what we discuss next.

Transforming organizational culture through appreciative inquiry

David Cooperrider and Suresh Srivastava have systematized the process of enacting positive change by seeking out existing strengths as cases of positive deviance.[64] Their approach, Appreciative Inquiry (AI), is a strength-based approach (see Chapter 3, mainly Box 3.3)[65] aimed at producing positive change at the individual, team and organizational levels. The process includes identifying an existing 'positive core' and then developing aligned organizational practices, policies and structures in a manner that heightens positive energy for change. Different from the traditional problem-solving change approaches, AI focusses on appreciative inquiry about current and potential strengths to identify and build a better future. Here organizational change is not thought of as problem solving but rather as possibility discovering. The process begins by framing an affirmative question. Rather than asking, for example, 'how can we minimize bullying within this workplace', the question would be framed instead to identify an existing 'positive core' by asking, 'how does kindness and compassion manifest in this workplace?' For organizational transformation, the entire organization is then engaged in a four-phase process (the 4-D cycle) in response to the affirmative question (See Box 3.3). Five philosophical principles provide the theoretical underpinning for AI:

- The **social constructionist** principle assumes that organizational realities are social constructions that individuals co-create through their relational processes (e.g., dialogues, storytelling).
- The **simultaneity** principle states that the process of inquiry is itself an intervention. When we inquire into a situation (appreciatively or depreciatively), we are changing that situation in the direction of the *inquiry*.
- The **poetic** principle considers that we can choose what we inquire into – we can choose to focus on what goes wrong (the repair-shop approach) or we can choose to focus on what gives life.
- The **anticipatory** principle holds that as we anticipate the future, we are changing our behaviours and social interactions in the direction of that future image. In that way, we co-create a new reality (i.e., as with the placebo effect, by anticipating cure, patients taking merely a sugar pill experience the anticipated effects of the 'medicine').
- The **positive** principle (or the heliotropic principle) is based on the notion that human systems are heliotropic: 'all living systems [are attracted] toward positive energy and away from negative energy, or toward that which is life giving and away from that which is life depleting'.[66]

Considering that organizational cultures should and can be changed is itself based on an assumption: cultures influence organizational performance. Is such an assumption realistic? The answer is not straightforward. Reality is often more complex than sometimes assumed. Ethical issues should also be included in the discussion because changing culture implies changing people's minds and not only their behaviours.

Perspectives on culture: integration, fragmentation, differentiation

Does integration integrate?

An example of a basic assumption subconsciously informing behaviour is the notion that a strong, unified and integrated culture leads to superior performance. On the basis of the assumptions that this integration perspective provides (one of three perspectives that will be considered in this section along with fragmentation and differentiation perspectives),[67] leaders may enact various policies of control and attempt to ensure a homogeneous and harmonious organizational culture. The leader's attempts to create such unity may, however, backfire, creating instead a culture of distrust and resentment amongst employees. It is therefore worth questioning if an integrated culture is in fact desirable, possible or even ethical.

Groupthink is one issue that makes a strong integrated culture undesirable (see Chapter 7). When all members think and act in the same way, as is the case with groupthink, the lack of counterfactual thinking and devil's advocacy may lead to poor decision making. A case in point is the influence of groupthink in ignoring safety concerns leading to the disaster of NASA's Space Shuttle Challenger on January 28, 1986.[68] Just 73 seconds after launching the shuttle exploded and broke apart, killing the seven astronauts on board. Groupthink also stifles innovation, creativity and adaptability. Pressures to conform have also played their part in the corporate scandals involving companies such as VW and Wells Fargo.

Another consideration is the ethic implicit in creating an integrated culture. If the core of an organization's culture is the deeply held subconscious attitudes, values and beliefs of its members, changing the culture of the organization requires attempting to change these. When an employment contract is signed between an employer and employee, the contract is for the employee's labour, performed as a particular type of work, over a certain time period each day. The employee is not providing authorization for the employer to attempt to change or influence their deeply held subconscious attitudes, values and beliefs. Historically, when strong leaders have attempted to create social integration and cohesion according to an idealized norm, it has been artificially propped up and maintained through high levels of secret monitoring and control. Individuals viewed as incompatible with the mandated values may well be branded as enemies of the state or firm, and duly ostracized, bullied and even murdered.[69]

Corporate examples pale in comparison but, as we have remarked earlier, the Ford Motor Company under Henry Ford, famous for its revolutionary policies of providing employees with above average wages and decent working conditions, also maintained a Sociological Department that paternalistically investigated the private lives of employees, visiting their homes to ensure they met the company's strict standards of the ideal employee.[70] The ideal Ford employee had to demonstrate character by cultivating qualities of self-regulation, personal hygiene and thrift. Immigrant employees also had to demonstrate their learning of the 'American Way', for example, by taking English classes. The Ford case demonstrates in clear relief the complex ethical implications of trying to create 'designer employees' that are 'corporate clones' of desired attitudes, values and beliefs. Aiming to create a 'happy workplace' does not change the ethical nature of the endeavour: think about an employee forced to be happy and positive even when they are in deep grief and stress about events in their personal life (see Box 9.6).

Box 9.6 'How do you know it is going to be okay?' – let me be sad, please!

Facebook CEO Sheryl Sandberg – excerpt from a Facebook post where she shared her feelings with the public, 30 days after her husband's death:[71]

A friend of mine with late-stage cancer told me that the worst thing people could say to him was 'It is going to be okay.' That voice in his head would scream, How do you know it is going to be okay? Do you not understand that I might die? I learned this past month what he was trying to teach me. Real empathy is sometimes not insisting that it will be okay but acknowledging that it is not. When people say to me, 'You and your children will find happiness again,' my heart tells me, Yes, I believe that, but I know I will never feel pure joy again. Those who have said, 'You will find a new normal, but it will never be as good' comfort me more because they know and speak the truth.

A fragmentation perspective

Even if creating a strong integrated culture were desirable and ethical, what makes an integrated culture difficult to establish or maintain is recognition that each individual is unique. The fragmentation perspective on organizational culture insists that inherent differences between people will always pose an obstacle to integration. It sees culture as fragmented, unstable and fluid, never clear but always muddled and opaque. The existence of unofficial cultures that seldom reflect the official culture of the organization is proof that creating an integrated culture is near impossible. Unofficial cultures are reflected in informal rules, subcultures and various forms of employee resistance. Disney is an interesting illustration of such a discrepancy between formal and informal cultures, as observed in the 1990s by John Van Maanen.[72]

The official Disney culture has been widely lauded for its creativity in crafting language that seeks to underpin a culture of expected employee behaviour and values. Disney employees are hired not by human resources but by 'central casting'. Employees are not workers but 'performers' or 'cast members'. They do not wear uniforms but 'costumes'. Their workplace is not an amusement park but 'Disneyland', divided into 'backstage', 'on stage' and 'staging' areas. While working employees are 'onstage', while relaxing they are 'offstage'. There are no customers or tourists but 'guests' and 'audience members'; no rides or stores but only 'attractions'; no police or law enforcement, only 'security hosts'; and no accidents, only 'incidents'. Employees are scripted in using this language and associated behaviours during their induction in the 'University of Disney'.

But Disney employees develop their own unofficial culture that new recruits learn on the job. This includes a parallel language used only when conversing amongst themselves, particularly in relation to obnoxious customers who act outside of their designated character as the nice 'guest' and instead insult, abuse or challenge one of the co-workers. These customers are referred to as 'duffesses', 'ducks' or, worse, 'a-holes'. Routine practices have developed for restoring a fellow employee's respect in such situations. Examples include the 'seatbelt squeeze' where a customer's required seatbelt is made so tight that they are left gasping for air during a ride; the 'seatbelt slap' where the customer receives a whack on the face with the seatbelt while entering or exiting a ride; and 'break up the party' where disturbing pairs are separated into separate units just before entering a ride, so they are made to sit with a stranger for the duration of a ride.

Van Maanen, while acknowledging the thoughtfulness, pervasiveness and effectiveness of Disney's integrated culture management through the use of powerful mental maps and positive language (see Figure 9.4), nonetheless concludes: 'not all of Disneyland is covered by the culture put forth by management. There are numerous pockets of resistance and various degrees of autonomy maintained by employees'.[73] Therefore, even when an organization aims at developing positivity as a consistent cultural feature of the organization, the tough realities of everyday and the employees' idiosyncrasies generate an unofficial (although real) culture that may, at worst, destroy the unifying cultural efforts.

Differentiation perspective

Fragmentation may develop at the group/unit level, forming subcultures that characterize the differentiation perspective. According to this view, in any organization the norm will likely involve many subcultures based on general differences such as gender,

Figure 9.4 Sleeping Beauty Castle, icon of Disneyland Park at Anaheim California, USA.[74]

age, nationality, ethnicity, profession, specialization, experience, seniority, religion and so on. Subcultures create diversity that may enrich organizational life – or not. These may be cultures of abundance that bring a wealth of perspectives, talents and experience, not only inspiring individual flourishing and wellbeing but also enhancing organizational decision-making, performance and profitability. At worst, however, fragmentation may create several fault lines (see Chapter 7) and even transform the organization into a collection of 'silos'.[75] The following observations by Gillian Tett about a GM scandal are relevant:[76]

> Last week Anton Valukas, a former federal prosecutor, released a 315-page report on the carmaker's scandalous failure to withdraw faulty ignition switches from several of its models, even though some employees knew about the technical problems for a decade. Before the report emerged, some observers expected that Mr Valukas would reveal dastardly villains … Mr Valukas, however, blamed events not on an evil plot, but on the 'silos' created by GM's profoundly fragmented structure. The group's culture and organisational matrix was so dysfunctional, he said, that employees failed to pass crucial information to each other or take responsibility for flaws. 'GM personnel's inability to address the ignition switch problem for over 11 years is a history of failures,' observed Mr Valukas.

Simultaneously managing unity in diversity, however, takes expertise – as we consider next.

Expanding mental maps to manifest positive organizational cultures of abundance

Quinn argues that the major obstacles to creating positive organizational cultures of abundance are rigid mental maps focussed on problem solving and task accomplishment. Mental maps are habitual and habituated dispositions and orientations to action. Quinn suggests cultures of abundance can begin to be developed by increasing awareness of existing maps and expanding them with an understanding that organizations are not static but rather dynamic. Humans tend to rely on binary categories to make sense of the world but no organizational culture is 100 per cent positive or negative. Even in organizations perceived as having predominantly negative cultures, good things may be taking place. Conversely, bad things happen in apparently positive organizations as indicated by the recent embroiling of the international charity Oxfam in sexual exploitation scandals (Box 9.7).

Box 9.7 The negative in the positive – exploring the positive and the negative in Oxfam

Founded in Oxford in 1942 by a group of academics, social activists and Quakers as the Oxford Committee for Famine Relief, today Oxfam International is a confederation of 20 independent charities focussed on alleviating global poverty.[77] In the 1960s, when the organization began establishing international chapters, these were registered with a name derived from the founding organization's telegraphic address OXFAM. In 1996, Oxfam International was registered as a non-profit foundation in the Hague, in the Netherlands.

Oxfam seeks to promote what it holds to be indivisible human rights (to life and security, being heard, identity, basic social services and a sustainable living) through three areas of focussed engagement: development work, humanitarian work and advocacy work. The development work has a mission of lifting disadvantaged people up from poverty by providing sustainable solutions based on identified community needs. Oxfam's humanitarian work focusses on providing immediate assistance to those negatively affected by disasters and conflicts, frequently leading to longer-term development work. The organization's advocacy work focusses on lobbying and campaigning at local, national and international levels to influence social change that alleviates conflict and poverty.

Despite the organization's high ideals and important achievements, over the years its governance has drawn criticism, including from other not-for-profit social organizations. For example, Oxfam Great Britain was criticized in 2005 for its closeness to the UK's then New Labour government.[78] In the same year, the *New Internationalist* magazine labelled Oxfam a BINGO, which is short for *Big International Non-Government Organization*, on account of its corporate style, lack of democratic process and acquiescence to neoliberal logics offering approaches focussed on alleviating the symptoms rather than the causes of international poverty.

In early 2018, Oxfam was also found to have mismanaged cases of sexual exploitation, the downloading of pornographic material, as well as intimidation and bullying at a premises paid for by Oxfam with donated funds.[79] When the abuses came to the attention of the international organization, none of the Oxfam employees involved were reported to police. Further, some of the higher-ranking employees were not even sacked but rather allowed to quietly resign to avoid embarrassment to the organization. Worst of all, for the highest ranking of these officers, the sexual misbehaviours were a repeat of activities perpetrated at an Oxfam team house in Chad in 2006.[80] At the time, another employee had taken the blame and been fired for the misbehaviour.

We tend to evaluate an organization's culture by assessing the ratio of positive and negative behaviours that simultaneously exist within the same organization. When we observe that patterns of positivity exceed conventional expectations, we may evaluate (with caution, prudence and 'vigilant trust') the organization as having a positive organizational culture. Quinn offers a list of 20 attributes that could form the basis of an abundant, positive organizational culture.[81] The first list is included in the left column of Table 9.4.

An organization that exemplifies these attributes would likely be progressive, productive and full of enthusiastic and accomplished people. However, deeper reflection on these attributes would also give rise to some apprehensions: too much of a focus on growth could lead to waste, while an achievement focus could cause exhaustion. As observed by Aristotle, too much of anything positive can become a vice (more in Chapters 2 and 12). Quinn states it this way: '*every* positive characteristic, without a competing positive value or characteristic, can become a negative'.[82] He then offers a second list of (counterbalanced) attributes, which are included in the right column of Table 9.4.

Table 9.4 Positive in the negative, negative in the positive – cultural values, even positive ones, create tensions that are inherent to organizing

First list	*Second list*
Growth focus: investing in the future, seeing possibility	Cost control: efficiency, preservation of assets
Self-organization: empowerment, spontaneity	Organizational predictability: stability, order
Creative action: responsive, learning organization	Procedural compliance: routines, policies
Intrinsic motivation: meaningful, fulfilling work	Managerial control: consistent, dependable performance
Positive contagion: positive motions, optimism, enthusiasm	Objective analysis: measurement, assessment
Full engagement: commitment, fully involved, loyal	Life balance: renewal, reenergizing
Individual accountability: responsibility, excellence	Cohesive teamwork: collaboration, belonging, positive peer pressure
Decisive action: speed, urgency	Group deliberation: participation, consensus
Achievement focus: accomplishment, success	Authentic relationships: caring, selfless service
Constructive confrontation: honesty, challenge	Appreciative expression: praise, celebration of others

Rather than being arbitrary, the second list counterbalances the first. Observe the contrasts. Growth counterbalances cost control; self-regulation is in tension with predictability; procedure contrasts with creativity, and so on. These are not oppositions in that each pair is not mutually exclusive; yet, exclusivity of terms is what most people would assume to be implied by these lists. These pairs are in fact most powerful when they exist simultaneously as growth and control, optimism and objectivity.

The mutual interdependence of contrasting tensions that are logical on their own but contradictory in relation to each other is what is called a paradox (discussed in more detail in Chapter 12). The successful integration of such tensions is called paradox transcendence. Scholars such as Wendy Smith and Marianne Lewis have described the ability to engage with such tensions and leverage them for extraordinary performance as the basis for exceptional leadership.[83] Quinn takes this idea further in suggesting that the ability to balance a whole system of many competing tensions within an organization at once, so that each attribute remains positive but doesn't become too extreme so as to become negative, is the underpinning of an extraordinary positive organizational culture. The tension between life–work balance and full engagement in work is a good example: too much of either is problematic, as is too little.

Quinn demonstrates this idea by taking the 20 positive characteristics listed in the table above and adding an additional list of 20 negative characteristics that develop when a positive attribute is over-emphasized. The author suggests that the tool in Figure 9.5 can be used to evaluate the strengths, weaknesses and

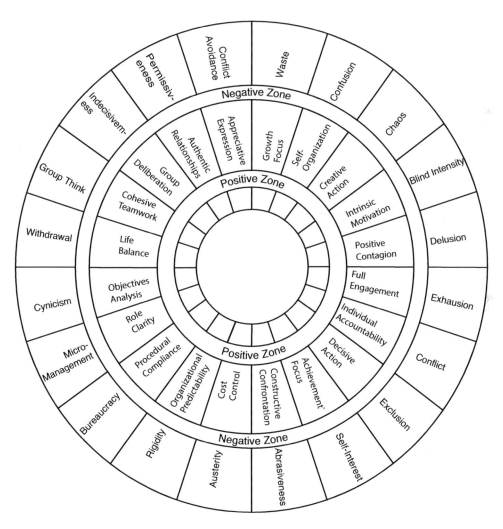

Figure 9.5 Framework of competing organizational values, with positive and negative zones.[84]

prominent tensions within the organization and thereby to cultivate thoughts and behaviours that are both more complex and positive. Look at the positive and negative attributes in the circle. Now either shade or circle the ones most reflective of your organization. The more positive characteristics identified, the healthier the organization. With the weaknesses identified in the negative zone, look to see their positive opposites and consider any changes that could generate positive tensions between two attributes. Now craft a strategic vision statement concerning what type of organization you would like to become and write some SMART goals concerning what specific actions will facilitate achieving that vision.

A positive culture might be thought of as something like the Goldilocks Zone astrophysicists refer to in relation to the Earth's distance from the Sun. The Earth's orbit of the Sun occurs in an arc that provides an incredibly narrow habitable zone in terms of proximity to the Sun. If the Earth were any closer, everything on our planet would be burnt and life could not be sustained; if it were any further away, everything would freeze and life would not be sustained.

The Earth is positioned at a distance that is 'just right', as in the story of Goldilocks and the three bears, where for Goldilocks to be satisfied the chair could be neither too big, nor too small; the porridge neither too hot nor too cold; the bed neither too hard nor too soft. The challenge for creating a positive culture of abundance, then, is not only of simultaneously cultivating opposite positive attributes, maintaining the organization within the positive zone, but also of not giving either competing value too much attention that it takes the organization into the negative zone.

The ability to engage in such paradoxical leadership in creating a positive differentiation culture of abundance is a rare talent. Some leaders are adept at analysis, control, efficiency and productivity but lack generative capabilities in creating cultures of respect, trust, connectivity, playfulness, purpose, learning and growth. Others are visionaries but struggle to maintain an organized system. It is rare to find a positive and abundant culture characterized both by stability and change, unity and diversity, playfulness and productivity, purpose and profit. Some of the examples presented in this chapter (and the textbook more broadly) suggest that it is possible but nonetheless it remains challenging to maintain balance.

In search of wellbeing at work

Organizational meaning and purpose

A critical aspect of a positive workplace where people are engaged and passionate about their work is that the organization has a clear sense of meaning and purpose beyond making profits (see Box 9.8 for a list of organizational statements from top companies, highlighting values that give the organization its purpose). Meaningful or purposeful work is experienced by employees as contributing towards something that is valuable and worthwhile for the individual or broader society.[85] When people feel that something is meaningful, they experience a sense of stability, energy and direction, even in challenging circumstances.

Box 9.8 Organizational statements highlighting values that give purpose[86]

- Disney: 'To use our imaginations to bring happiness to millions'.
- Johnson & Johnson: 'To alleviate pain & suffering'.
- Southwest Airlines: 'To give people the freedom to fly'.
- Pivot Leadership: 'Better leaders = Better world'.
- BMW: 'To enable people to experience the joy of driving'.
- Red Cross: 'Enabling the performance of extraordinary acts in the face of emergencies'.

There is a relationship between meaning or purpose, facts and values.[87] Although organizational decision making is always framed in terms of rationality, the reality is that decision making is not based purely on facts but on value priorities. Values are beliefs about what purposes or objectives are most important. For example, if as a business manager you had an opportunity to make a lot of money legally but through a method that would involve serious human rights violations, the choices you make will be based not just on facts but, more importantly, upon your and the organization's value priorities. If you value profits over people, you will take the deal and become very wealthy. If you value people over profit, you will walk away. The reality is that managers (and we as individuals) are making countless value judgements every day. That is, we are making judgements about what values are most important in every given situation.

Meaning at work can have different levels.[88] Work that has a low level of meaning tends to be concrete, immediate, specific and extrinsically rewarding. In contrast, work that has a high level of meaning tends to be abstract, broad, concerned with a longer time span and to be intrinsically rewarding. However, the same job may be associated with different levels of meaning (an issue we discussed in Chapter 5). Let's use an example for you as a student. Imagine the following two statements:

- 'If you put effort in your studies this term you will be rewarded with higher grades'. The underlying motivator is concrete, immediate and specific, and extrinsic.
- 'If you put a lot of energy into your education you will be able to make a much greater contribution to society'. The motivating force is abstract, broader, longer time span and intrinsic.

Which statement has more meaning? Almost nobody will doubt that the second statement is associated with a more meaningful purpose. Is it more motivating? Probably yes – but motivation also depends on the individual's values and purpose in life. Different students will react differently to the same 'purpose'. The same happens in organizations. Although more versus less meaningful organizational purposes are more likely to motivate employees, different employees may react differently to the same organizational purpose, and a specific organizational purpose may coexist with different purposes for different individuals. For example, while the Southwest Airlines purpose of 'connecting people to what's important in their lives with friendly and low-cost travel',[89] the main purpose of a specific employee may be to support his/her family, and for yet another it may be nourished by the purpose of becoming a servant leader – in Southwest Airlines or elsewhere.

A specific organizational statement of meaningful purpose may achieve the opposite effect in demotivating specific employees who don't identify with it. Furthermore, 'positive' and 'pious' purposes may give rise to cynicism and be interpreted as manipulating. Remember that Volkswagen highlighted its environmental 'purposes' while cheating on the emissions of its cars. The company won several environmental awards, including 'an international sustainability award by World Forum for Ethics in Business for responsible action in the environmental and social fields' in 2012:

> The World Forum for Ethics said that the reason for the award was the leadership of Volkswagen in the assumption of corporate social responsibility and the implementation of outstanding and innovative projects. The Forum also underlined that the Group made a positive contribution to society in many areas and set an example of universal values such as integrity, responsibility and respect for people and the environment through its various environmental and health projects.[90]

Another important consideration is that the stated purpose should be consistent with actual organizational practices and leadership behaviours. PepsiCo's motto 'Performance with purpose' ('PepsiCo is focused on delivering sustainable long-term growth while leaving a positive imprint on society and the environment')[91] has been criticized due to the nature of its products. Marion Nestle, a professor of food studies at New York University, has argued, 'The best thing PepsiCo could do for public health is go out of business'.[92] Therefore, in the end, an organization will more effectively motivate its employees when each employee feels able to follow their individual meaningful purpose. Manipulation and mere PR efforts are likely to invoke a backlash, at least in the medium or longer terms.

Workplace wellbeing

Employee wellbeing is multidimensional (see, e.g., Chapters 1 and 4). The possibility of performing meaningful work is an important dimension but other dimensions or components also matter. Increasingly, organizations are recognizing that they cannot claim to have a great organizational culture when their employees' wellbeing is harmed. Other important indicators of a positive organizational culture are employees' physical, emotional, material and even spiritual wellbeing. Recognizing this, organizations today are creating programmes to cultivate employee wellbeing (see the section about Google above; see also Box 9.9). The benefits of these programmes for the organizations that invest in them include: (1) reduced healthcare expenses due to having employees with less physical and emotional concerns; (2) enhanced productivity on account of having employees who are more focussed but less stressed; (3) enhanced recruitment and retention of top performing employees on account of increased work and life satisfaction.

Box 9.9 Seven principles for entrenching a workplace wellbeing programme

Dr Nate Klemp, cofounder of LIFE Cross Training (LIFE XT), which provides companies with tools for wellbeing training, offers 'seven core principles' for maximizing the effectiveness of a workplace wellbeing programme:[93]

1   **Communication** – Many workplace wellbeing programmes fail on account of poor communication. It is therefore critical to design an internal communication campaign about the benefits (see below) and practical logistics of the programmes on offer.

2   **Lead with benefits** – Rather than promoting practices such as learning meditation, yoga or mindfulness, instead promote the benefits of these practices: cultivating stress resilience, enhanced productivity and peak performance. The reality is that most people are not inspired by the idea of sitting and being aware of their breathing for five to ten minutes, but they would be interested in higher levels of focus, resilience and productivity.

3   **Create a physical space** – Designate a specific space as a wellbeing area. Having a distraction-free room for yoga, meditation or just to experience some rest or relaxation will increase the likelihood of employees finding time in their day to invest in their wellbeing.

4   **Build in permission** – Workers may have a sense of guilt for taking time out for health and wellbeing during work hours. This is particularly the case in high productivity cultures where people are under constant pressure to perform. It is therefore essential for leaders to explicitly endorse employees taking time out for their wellbeing and to model such behaviours themselves. Such formal and informal permission granting goes a long way towards encouraging employees to take advantage of an organization's workplace wellbeing programmes.

5   **Create company-wide routines** – Integrating positive wellbeing practices across the organization reminds employees that wellbeing is not just an individual commitment but one that the organization takes seriously. Examples of such rituals might include expressing gratitude at the beginning or end of company meetings, or of recognizing acts of compassion and kindness in internal newsletters.

6   **Identify a group of evangelists** – Finding people within the organization who are enthusiastic about the wellbeing programme and are willing to spread the word about its benefits can help generate internal excitement and enthusiasm for the programme, motivating others to participate.

7   **Make it opt-in** – Choice is of critical importance in creating a workplace wellbeing programme. If employees feel forced to engage, they will likely disengage from the programme as a form of resistance. To be successful, employees participating in the programme have to be actually driven by an inner motivation for change. Providing people with choice is one of the most effective ways for promoting the required intrinsic motivation.

A meta-study of the expenses and savings associated with 36 workplace wellbeing programmes conducted by a team of three scholars from Harvard University found that, for every dollar invested, medical expenses were reduced by around US $3.27 and absenteeism expenses were reduced by around US $2.73. These scholars concluded that, 'this return on investment suggests that the wider adoption of such programs could prove beneficial for budgets and productivity as well as health outcomes'.[94]

An important factor of worker wellbeing is the architecture of buildings where employees work. As Winston Churchill stated: 'We shape our buildings, and afterwards our buildings shape us'.[95] Architecture influences not only the material/physical component of wellbeing (e.g., indoor air quality and ventilation, thermal comfort, daylight and lighting) but also the emotional and interactional components. Unlike the work environments of our ancestors who mostly worked in outdoor agricultural environments, modern workplaces tend to be indoors. We accordingly spend most of our working lives inside company buildings. Unsurprisingly, then, there is a growing recognition that architecture plays an important role in facilitating employee workplace wellbeing. In fact, there is a growing understanding that workplace wellbeing programmes that are not supported by facilitative architecture are not as effective. A new wave of architectural design is therefore emerging that aims to translate the findings of health and wellbeing research into workplace design, thereby transforming typically sedentary workplace environments that promote obesity and a host of related illnesses into spaces that facilitate and encourage employee wellbeing. The case of Google, discussed above, is illustrative (see also Chapter 6). The case of the Nova School of Business and Economics campus, inaugurated in 2018, is also illustrative (see Figures 9.6a and 9.6b).

Figure 9.6a Nova SBE new Carcavelos campus, near Lisbon, Portugal: texting context. Credits by Francisco Nogueira.[96]

Figure 9.6b Nova SBE new Carcavelos campus, near Lisbon, Portugal.
Credits by Francisco Nogueira.

A nomenclature that has emerged to frame this philosophy is 'Active Design'.[97] A core principle underpinning this approach is the understanding that architecture that encourages movement throughout the course of the day is critical to promoting wellness and wellbeing. There are many architectural principles necessary for promoting a healthy and happy work environment. For example, providing lots of natural light supports the body's circadian rhythm and thereby promotes the body's need for rest and digestion. The Nova School of Business and Economics campus, inaugurated in 2018 (see Figure 9.6b), was designed to be a source of inspiration in itself, an architectural illustration of the search for what is clear and inspiring. Offering good clean air quality through ample ventilation and filtering of air mitigates irritation to the skin, eyes and respiratory system. The use of low toxin building materials and furnishings (such as carpets) is also important in this respect. A more comprehensive list of nine practices of Active Design based on the findings of a US-wide industry survey is provided in Box 9.10.

> **Box 9.10 Nine best practices of Active Design**
>
> An extensive survey of professionals from top US architecture and design firms as well as average office workers sought to identify the fundamental ways architecture can support workplace wellbeing. The report produced from the study titled *Understanding Active Design: The Rise of Human Sustainability* identified the nine best practices of Active Design listed below:[98]
>
> 1 **Incorporate daylight**. Strategies for increasing natural lighting include using lots of large windows, positioning offices within the centre of spaces as opposed to lining them along corridors, creating offices and meeting rooms with glass walls.
> 2 **Offer various workspace options**. There are many possibilities for doing office work that don't involve sitting at an office desk or workstation. Designers

can arrange a comparable quantity of seats in alternative configurations as lounge spaces, meeting areas, conference rooms and a café with dining tables.

3   **Facilitate face-to-face communication**. An open floor plan that facilitates face-to-face communication above electronic modes also promotes team-building. A simple way of promoting this practice is by positioning all employees on the very same floor where they can see one another with clear lines of vision. Being able to see a colleague increases the likelihood of talking to them rather than calling or sending an email.

4   **Provide healthy food options**. Offering healthy snacks in central work areas can encourage both employee movement, as well as better food choices. Vending machines with healthy options can be positioned in a central location, or a café and lounge space can be provided to not only facilitate healthier eating but also encourage employee engagement and interaction over meals.

5   **Encourage workplace movement**. Encouraging movement is what Active Design is all about. Some organizations are now providing walking paths in and around the workplace and encourage walking meetings, which apparently facilitate greater creativity.

6   **Design multi-use spaces**. Meeting rooms can be designed as flexible communal spaces that can be used for variety of uses. Rather than outfitting conference rooms and boardrooms with heavy tables and chairs, these spaces can be set up with movable furniture for more flexible additional use as studio space for yoga or Pilates or other wellness programmes.

7   **Inspire use of stairs**. Designing visually attractive and well-located staircases can subconsciously encourage employees to use the stairs rather than taking the elevator or an escalator.

8   **Provide height-adjustable desks**. Providing standing-height desks or, even better, height-adjustable desks, offers employees the option to change their position and work while standing for part of their workday.

9   **Offer outdoor workspaces**. Not yet widely used, there is a sense that organizations will increasingly be incorporating the outdoors as part of the workplace. Important considerations in creating an outdoor environment for employees to be in nature and feel refreshed at work will involve addressing glare and facilitating steady internet connectivity. Also, consideration of climatic variability is a key factor in appropriate design.

Final comments

Great workplaces integrate several dimensions of individuals and organizational flourishing. While they support employee wellbeing (at psychological, physical, emotional, relational and even spiritual levels), they are also effective at the economic and financial levels. An organization where employees are happy but that is not productive is not sustainable – and when the organization has to close its doors employees' happiness will be as naught. On the other hand, a productive workplace in which employees' wellbeing is neglected may be unable to sustain employee commitment and engagement in the medium and long run. An organization cannot claim to have a positive culture if, even though incredibly profitable, its employees suffer debilitating health problems due to high levels of anxiety and stress. This chapter highlighted several ways through which the synergies between individuals flourishing and organizational sustainable performance may be pursued. It also argues that the world's 'great workplaces' are sometimes not so great and that 'great' organizational features sometimes embody 'the bad'. Adopting a virtuous paradoxical approach is thus necessary for achieving positive synergies.

Want more?

A number of great resources have been cited in this chapter. Here are a few in particular that we recommend you follow up on if you are interested in the topics we covered. Goffee and Jones'[99] *Why Should Anyone Work Here?: What It Takes to Create an Authentic Organization* is worth reading in its entirety. In it they provide numerous practical examples and stories from global organizations for each of the six DREAMS principles, which are individually discussed in separate chapters. Kim Cameron's[100] *Positive Leadership: Strategies for Extraordinary Performance* derives from a wealth of research in organizational studies, medical research and psychology, which he supplements with real-world examples. Cameron's[101] follow up book *Practicing Positive Leadership: Tools and Techniques That Create Extraordinary Results* provides specific tactics for implementing the ideas discussed in the first. Robert Quinn's[102] *The Positive Organization: Breaking Free from Conventional Cultures, Constraints, and Beliefs* specifically focusses on building a positive organizational culture at the deepest level of unconscious beliefs and assumptions that inform organizational practices.

Glossary

Artifacts In Schein's three-level model of organizational culture, artifacts are level one, comprising observable manifestations of organizations' culture categorized as *physical* artifacts (buildings, furnishings, uniforms); *symbolic* artifacts (logo, branding, colours); *language* (type of language and industry-specific jargon) and *myths* (rites, rituals and founding stories).

Authentizotic A term that derives from combining two Greek words: *authenteekos* and *zoteekos*. An *authentizotic* organization is one that is authentic, where there is alignment between rhetoric and practice, creating an environment of trustworthiness, reliability and accountability. *Authentizotic* organizations are characterized by their fulfilment of human needs, providing a sense of belonging, a sense of enjoyment and a sense of meaning.

Basic assumptions In Schein's three-level model of organizational culture, basic assumptions are level three, comprising the intangible frames that subconsciously influence the manifestation of organizational values and artifacts. The organizational members' collective world views and beliefs about the nature of human relationships, human activity and justice, the nature of reality and truth and the organization's relationship with the natural environment are, in fact, the core of organizational culture that unconsciously shape the other levels.

Belonging   *A sense of belonging* at work, according to Goffee and Jones, derives from experiences of commitment and community within the organization that provides for human yearning for affiliation and attachment.

Culture   Shared patterns of knowledge and belief communicated collectively through norms of behaviour, identity, deviance, language, symbols, artifacts, design and processes. These are often uniquely assembled in a group's norms of food, dress, dance, music, ritual, worship and social relations.

DREAMS   Goffee and Jones' DREAMS mnemonic describes a great organization to work for: **D** stands for difference (where I can be myself), **R** for Radical honesty on the part of the organization, **E** is for the Extra Value employees get from working for the organization, **A** is the Authenticity perceptible in the organization's practices, **M** is for the Meaningfulness of the organization's services (beyond mere profits) and **S** is for Simple rules (as opposed to complicated ones that hold up organizational processes).

Enjoyment   *A sense of enjoyment* at work, according to Goffee and Jones, derives from having fun and enjoying one's work as a way of cultivating creativity, passion and commitment.

Espoused values   In Schein's three-level model of organizational culture, espoused values are level two, comprising the consistent beliefs in which the organization is emotionally invested. Organizational values are often expressed in a firm's mission statement, vision statement or statement of values.

Meaning   *A sense of meaning* at work, according to Goffee and Jones, is experienced most profoundly in an organization that provides opportunities for engaging in activities that are bigger than ourselves by contributing towards helping other people, improving their quality of life or contributing towards improving greater social wellbeing.

Organizational climate   'Employees' shared perceptions of the policies, procedures and practices that are rewarded, supported and expected in a given organizational environment'.[103] A cold organizational climate would suggest tense or chilly relationships with low enthusiasm, while a warm climate would indicate a supportive environment of positive relationships and high enthusiasm.

Organizational culture   'A set of *shared* values, normative beliefs, and underlying assumptions that characterize organizations and shape the way of doing things inside them.'[104]

Psychological climate   The individual perceptions about the organizational climate. While organizational climate is an organizational-level construct, psychological climate is an individual one.

Psychological contract   Implicit employee–employer obligations and expectations. Upholding the contract inspires people to bring discretionary effort, enthusiasm and commitment to their workplace; breach the contract and people become demotivated and dissatisfied underperformers.

Notes

1 Levering and Moskowitz (1984).
2 Levering (1988).
3 Boje, Roslie, Durant and Luhman (2004).
4 Eichenwald (2006).
5 Rainey (2017).
6 See comment on the Quora.com forum: www.quora.com/What-are-the-negatives-in-working-in-a-too-good-to-be-true-office-like-Google?redirected_qid=1080239&share=1.
7 Ramajayam, K. (2016) comment on the Quora.com forum, www.quora.com/What-are-the-negatives-in-working-in-a-too-good-to-be-true-office-like-Google#, accessed January 29, 2018.

8 Worstall (2012).

9 Chafkin (2016).

10 Google Code of Conduct, https://abc.xyz/investor/other/google-code-of-conduct.html, accessed January 29, 2018.

11 Burkus (2015).

12 Author: Drshaunakdas. Retrieved from: https://commons.wikimedia.org/wiki/File:Google_Campus_in_Googleplex.jpg. File licensed under the Creative Commons Attribution-Share Alike 4.0 International license.

13 Comment by Cannella from 2015 on www.quora.com/What-are-the-negatives-in-working-in-a-too-good-to-be-true-office-like-Google?redirected_qid=1080239&share=1, accessed January 29, 2018.

14 Walker (2013).

15 Chang and Marsh (2013).

16 Rainey (2017).

17 Anonymous comment from 2013 on the Quora.com forum: www.quora.com/What-are-the-negatives-in-working-in-a-too-good-to-be-true-office-like-Google/answers/2418330, that has since been deleted.

18 Kets de Vries (2001, p. 103).

19 Denning (2018).

20 Bower and Paine (2017, p. 52).

21 Bower and Paine (2017, p. 57).

22 Kets de Vries (2001, p. 110).

23 Kets de Vries (2001, p. 110).

24 Garvin (2013).

25 Csikszentmihalyi (1990).

26 Kets de Vries (1991, p. 198).

27 Goler, Gale, Harrington and Grant (2018).

28 Kuchler and Garrahan (2018).

29 Nicolaou, Edgecliffe-Johnson and Buck (2018, p. 11).

30 *The Economist* (2018, p. 9).

31 Rego and Souto (2004); Rego and Cunha (2008).

32 Rego and Cunha (2008).

33 Rego and Cunha (2008, p. 748).

34 (r) is a negative item and should be 'reverse scored' when tallying the results. In reverse scoring using a 5-point Likert scale, the numerical scale is applied in the opposite direction where strongly disagree is scored as 5, disagree is 4, neutral remains 3, agree is 2 and strongly agree is 1.

35 Rego and Cunha (2008, p. 749).

36 Goffee and Jones (2015b).

37 Based on Goffee and Jones (2015a, p. 10).

38 Goffee and Jones (2015a, p. 11).

39 Goffee and Jones (2015a, p. 11).

40 Goffee and Jones (2015a, p. 12).

41 Weber (1922/1978); Merton (1936).

42 Brown and Eisenhardt (1997).

43 https://steamcdn-a.akamaihd.net/apps/valve/Valve_NewEmployeeHandbook.pdf.

44 www.outsystems.com/the-small-book/.

45 www.outsystems.com/-/media/A49C3F1FB3BC4280904093BB45B151DC.ashx (see p. 2).

46 Gulati (2018).

47 Goffee and Jones (2015a, p. 12).

48 Goffee and Jones (2015a, p. 12).

49 Clegg, Kornberger and Pitsis (2011).

50 Smircich (1985).

51 Adapted from Groysberg, Lee, Price and Chung (2018, p. 48).

52 Something questioned in research by David Boje (1995).

53 Cameron and Quinn (2005).

54 Vogel (1979).

55 Adler (1993).

56 Clegg (1990).
57 Cameron (2013).
58 Cited in Cameron (2013, p. 24).
59 Cameron (2013, pp. 24–25).
60 Carr, Hard and Trahant (1996).
61 Schein (1984).
62 Source: AWeith (https://commons.wikimedia.org/wiki/File:Iceberg_in_the_Arctic_with_its_un
   derside_exposed.jpg), https://creativecommons.org/licenses/by-sa/4.0/legalcode.
63 Quinn (2015, pp. 7–8).
64 Cooperrider, Whitney, and Stavros (2008).
65 Cooperrider, Whitney and Stavros (2008).
66 Cameron, Mora, Leutscher and Calarco (2011, p. 288).
67 Martin (1992).
68 Dimitroff, Schmidt and Bond (2005).
69 Contemporary Presidents (of countries) still follow these practices: see Zelizer (2018) on Trump
   and his list of enemies of the state; Putin's Russia goes further than listing by assassinating such
   enemies, as Walton (2018) substantiates.
70 Worstall (2012).
71 www.facebook.com/sheryl/posts/10155617891025177:0.
72 Van Maanen (1996).
73 Van Maanen (1996, p. 217).
74 Retrieved from https://commons.wikimedia.org/wiki/File:Sleeping_Beauty_Castle_Disneyland_
   Anaheim_2013.jpg. File licensed under the Creative Commons Attribution-Share Alike 3.0
   Unported license.
75 Tett (2015).
76 Tett (2014, p. 7).
77 Oxfam Canada (n.d.).
78 Ransom (2005).
79 O'Neill (2018).
80 Ratcliffe and Quinn (2018).
81 Quinn (2015, p. 12).
82 Quinn (2015, p. 14, table used with permission).
83 Smith and Lewis (2012).
84 Quinn (2015, p. 15, figure used with permission).
85 Hackman and Oldham (1976).
86 Derived from Mackey and Sisodia (2013).
87 Riemer, Simon and Romance (2013).
88 Baumeister and Vohs (2002).
89 In Baldwin (2018, p. 90).
90 See www.csreurope.org/volkswagen-wins-international-sustainability-award#.Wy09BFVKipo.
91 www.pepsico.com/sustainability/performance-with-purpose.
92 In Bader (2015).
93 Klemp (2017).
94 Baicker, Cutler and Song (2010, p. 34).
95 In World Green Building Council (2014, p. 4).
96 See Naar and Clegg (2015) for more details of another innovative architectural design by Frank
   Gehry for the UTS Business School in Sydney which provides an architectural ethnography of
   the building as both a social and material construction.
97 Lee (2012).
98 Webb and Schneider (2015).
99 Goffee and Jones (2015a).
100 Cameron (2008).
101 Cameron (2013).
102 Quinn (2015).
103 González-Romá and Peiró (2014, p. 497).
104 González-Romá and Peiró (2014, p. 497).

References

Adler, P. S. (1993). The learning bureaucracy: New United Motor Manufacturing, Inc. In B. M. Staw, & L. L. Cummings (Eds.), *Research in organizational behavior* (Vol. 15, pp. 111–194). Greenwich, CT: JAI Press.

Bader, C. (2015). CEOs aren't as powerful as most people think. *The Atlantic*, 14 May (www.theatlantic.com/business/archive/2015/05/ceos-arent-as-powerful-as-most-people-think/392975/)

Baicker, K., Cutler, D., & Song, Z. (2010). Workplace wellness programs can generate savings. *Health Affairs*, 29(2), 304–311.

Baldwin, B. (2018). People, purpose, and performance. *Airliner World*, June, 88–96.

Baumeister, R. F., & Vohs, K. D. (2002). The pursuit of meaningfulness in life. In C. R. Snyder, & S. J. Lopez (Eds.), *Handbook of positive psychology* (pp. 608–618). London: Oxford University Press.

Boje, D. M. (1995). Stories of the storytelling organization: A postmodern analysis of Disney as "Tamara-Land". *Academy of Management Journal*, 38(4), 997–1035.

Boje, D. M., Roslie, G. A., Durant, R. A., & Luhman, J. T. (2004). Enron spectacles: A critical dramaturgical analysis. *Organization Studies*, 25, 751–774.

Bower, J. L., & Paine, L. S. (2017). The error at the heart of corporate leadership. *Harvard Business Review*, May-June, 50–60.

Brown, S. L., & Eisenhardt, K. M. (1997). The art of continuous change: Linking complexity theory and time-paced evolution in relentlessly shifting organizations. *Administrative Science Quarterly*, 42(1), 1–34.

Burkus, B. (2015). The real reason Google serves all of that free food. *Forbes*, 2 July (www.forbes.com/sites/davidburkus/2015/07/02/the-real-reason-google-serves-all-that-free-food/#7a20c61295f6)

Cameron, K. S. (2008). *Positive leadership: Strategies for extraordinary performance*. San Francisco, CA: Berrett-Koehler.

Cameron, K. S. (2013). *Practicing positive leadership: Tools and techniques that create extraordinary results*. San Francisco, CA: Berrett-Koehler Publishers.

Cameron, K. S., Mora, C., Leutscher, T. and Calarco, M. (2011). 'Effects of positive practices on organizational effectiveness', *The Journal of Applied Behavioral Science*, 47(3), pp. 266–308.

Cameron, K. S., & Quinn, R. E. (2005). *Diagnosing and changing organizational culture: Based on the competing values framework*. New York: John Wiley & Sons.

Canada, O. (n.d.). Oxfam history. (www.oxfam.ca/about/introduction)

Carr, D. K., Hard, K. J., & Trahant, W. J. (1996). *Managing the change process: A field book for change agents, consultants, team leaders, and reengineering managers*. New York: McGraw-Hill.

Chafkin, M. (2016). 'Yahoo's Marissa Mayer on selling a company while trying to turn It around', *Bloomberg Businessweek*, August 4th, p. Online. Available at: https://www.bloomberg.com/features/2016-marissa-mayer-interview-issue/.

Chang, J., & Marsh, M. (2013). The Google diet: Search giant overhauled its eating options to 'nudge' healthy choices. *ABC News*, 25 January (http://abcnews.go.com/Health/google-diet-search-giant-overhauled-eating-options-nudge/story?id=18241908)

Clegg, S. (1990). *Modern organizations: Organization studies in the postmodern world*. London: Sage.

Clegg, S. R., Kornberger, M., & Pitsis, T. (2011). *Managing and organizations: An introduction to theory and practice* (3rd ed.). London: Sage.

Cooperrider, D. L., Whitney, D. D. and Stavros, J. M. (2008). *The appreciative inquiry handbook: For leaders of change*. San Francisco, CA: Berrett-Koehler Publishers.

Csikszentmihalyi, M. (1990). *Flow*. New York: Harper & Row.

Denning, S. (2018). Why today's business schools teach yesterday's expertise. *Forbes*, May 27 (www.forbes.com/sites/stevedenning/2018/05/27/why-todays-business-schools-teach-yesterdays-expertise/)

Dimitroff, R. D., Schmidt, L., & Bond, T. (2005). Organizational behavior and disaster: A study of conflict at NASA. *Project Management Journal*, 36(2), 28–38.

The Economist. 2018). Epic fail. *Epic fail*, 9.

Eichenwald, K. (2006). Verdict on an era. *The New York Times*, May 26, C1.

Garvin, D. A. (2013). How Google sold its engineers on management. *Harvard Business Review*, 91(12), 74–82.

Goffee, R., & Jones, G. (2015a). Why should anyone work here? *London Business School Review*, 26(4), 10–12.

Goffee, R., & Jones, G. (2015b). *Why should anyone work here? What it takes to create an authentic organization*. Boston, MA: Harvard Business Review Press.

Goler, L., Gale, J., Harrington, B., & Grant, A. M. (2018). The 3 things employees really want: Career, community, cause. *Harvard Business Review*, 20 February (https://hbr.org/2018/02/people-want-3-things-from-work-but-most-companies-are-built-around-only-one)

González-Romá, V., & Peiró, J. M. (2014). Climate and culture strength. In B. Schneider, & K. Barbera (Eds.), *The Oxford handbook of organizational climate and culture* (pp. 496–531). New York: Oxford University Press.

Groysberg, B., Lee, J., Price, J., & Chung, Y. J. (2018). The leader's guide to corporate culture. *Harvard Business Review*, 96(1), 44–52.

Gulati, R. (2018). Structure that is not stifling. *Harvard Business Review*, May-June, 68–79).

Hackman, J. R., & Oldham, G. R. (1976). Motivation through the design of work: Test of a theory. *Organizational Behavior and Human Performance*, 16(2), 250–279.

Kets de Vries, M. F. (1991). Organizations on the couch: Clinical perspectives on organizational behavior and change. *European Management Journal*, 22(2), 183–200.

Kets de Vries, M. F. (2001). Creating authentizotic organizations: Well-functioning individuals in vibrant companies. *Human Relations*, 54(1), 101–111.

Klemp, N. (2017). Seven steps to creating a successful corporate wellness program. *Conscious Company*, *Jan/Feb 2017*, 44–45.

Kuchler, H., & Garrahan, M. (2018). Facebook feels the pressure over claims its data helped Trump win. *Financial Times*, 19 March.

Lee, K. K. (2012). Developing and implementing the active design guidelines in New York City. *Health & place*, 18(1), 5–7.

Levering, R. (1988). A great place to work: What makes some employers so good (and most so bad). New York: Random House New York.

Levering, R., & Moskowitz, M. (1984). *The 100 best companies to work for in America*. New York: Doubleday/Currency.

Mackey, J., & Sisodia, R. S. (2013). *Conscious capitalism: Liberating the heroic spirit of business*. Boston, MA: Harvard Business Press.

Martin, J. (1992). *Cultures in organizations: Three perspectives*. Oxford: Oxford University Press.

Merton, R. K. (1936). The unanticipated consequences of purposive social action. *American sociological review*, 1(6), 894–904.

Naar, L., & Clegg, S. R. (2015). *Gehry in Sydney*. Sydney: Images Press.

Nicolaou, A., Edgecliffe-Johnson, A., & Buck, T. (2018). Facebook admits to rough year after being "caught flat-footed" by data leak. *Financial Times*, 23 March, 11.

Quinn, R. E. (2015). *The positive organization: Breaking free from conventional cultures, constraints, and beliefs*. San Francisco, CA: Berrett-Koehler.

Rainey, S. (2017). Inside the worlds wackiest workplace. *The Daily Mail*, 5 July (www.dailymail.co.uk/news/article-4665838/World-s-wackiest-workplace-look-inside-Google-offices.html)

Ransom, D. (2005). The big charity bonanza. *New Internationalist*, 2 October (https://newint.org/features/2005/10/01/keynote)

Ratcliffe, R., & Quinn, B. (2018). Oxfam: Fresh claims that staff used prostitutes in Chad. *The Guardian*. (www.theguardian.com/world/2018/feb/10/oxfam-faces-allegations-staff-paid-prostitutes-in-chad)

Rego, A., & Cunha, M. P. E. (2008). Authentizotic climates and employee happiness: Pathways to individual performance? *Journal of Business Research*, 61(7), 739–752.

Rego, A., & Souto, S. (2004). Development and validation of an instrument for measuring authentizotic organizations. *International Journal of Psychology*, 39(5–6), 486.

Riemer, N., Simon, D. W., & Romance, J. (2013). *Challenge of politics.* Washington, DC: Sage.

Schein, E. H. (1984). Coming to a new awareness of organizational culture. *Sloan Management Review*, *25*(2), 3–16.

Smircich, L. (1985). Is the concept of culture a paradigm for understanding organizations and ourselves? In P. J. Frost, L. Moore, M. Louis, C. Lundberg, & J. Martin (Eds.), *Organizational culture: The meaning of life in the workplace* (pp. 55–72). Beverly Hills, CA: Sage.

Smith, W. K., & Lewis, M. W. (2012). Leadership skills for managing paradoxes. *Industrial and Organizational Psychology*, *5*(2), 227–231.

Tett, G. (2014). A fragmented corporate structure is the villain of the piece. *Financial Times Europe*, June 13, 7.

Tett, G. (2015). *The silo effect: The peril of expertise and the promise of breaking down barriers.* New York: Simon and Schuster.

Van Maanen, J. (1996). The smile factory. Sociology. Exploring the architecture of everyday life readings. 210–226.

Vogel, E. M. (1979). *Japan as number one: Lessons for America.* New York: Harper Colophon.

Walker, T. (2013). Perks for employees and how Google changed the way we work (while waiting in line). *The Independent*, 20 September (www.independent.co.uk/news/world/americas/perks-for-employees-and-how-google-changed-the-way-we-work-while-waiting-in-line-8830243.html)

Walton, C. (2018) Russia has a long history of eliminating 'enemies of the state'. *Washington Post*, 13 March (www.washingtonpost.com/news/monkey-cage/wp/2018/03/13/russia-has-a-long-history-of-eliminating-enemies-of-the-state/?noredirect=on&utm_term=.d9296168dfba) on September12, 2018.

Webb, J., & Schneider, A. (2015). *Understanding active design: The rise of human sustainability.* (www.ki.com/uploadedFiles/Docs/literature-samples/white-papers/KI99601_Active%20Design%20White%20Paper_Final.pdf)

Weber, M. (1922/1978). *Economy and society: An outline of interpretive sociology.* Berkeley, CA: University of California Press.

World Green Building Council. (2014). Health, wellbeing & productivity in offices. (www.jll.com/Research/Health_Wellbeing_Productivity.pdf)

Worstall, T. (2012). The story of Henry Ford's $5 a day wages: It's not what you think. *Forbes*, 4 March (www.forbes.com/sites/timworstall/2012/03/04/the-story-of-henry-fords-5-a-day-wages-its-not-what-you-think/#5cb6a303766d)

Zelizer, J. E. (2018) The new enemies list. *The Atlantic*, 19 August www.theatlantic.com/ideas/archive/2018/08/the-new-enemies-list/567874/ on September 12, 2018.

10 Powering positivity

Summary and objectives

Power is often perceived as a dark social and organizational force or as limited to hierarchical organizational positions of authority. In reality, power is a multidimensional construct that is a fundamental property of any system and is necessary for facilitating and enabling structures. In this chapter, we discuss power using a framework of four types of power relations: power over, power to, power with and power within. In discussing each of these types of power relations we draw on various theorists to discuss power as an indispensable source of social process – including organizational positivity. Positive power is viewed as generative, facilitative, empowering, collaborative, inclusive and polyphonic. We also distinguish between positive power relations that are voluntarily entered into as opposed to those that are imposed against a person's will. Resistance to power is also discussed.

Power hard and soft

Typically we think of power as a negative thing, as something external, hard and forceful, as, for instance, when we speak of the force of the law apprehending an individual. Several things are apparent in this example. Power relations invariably have a form of rule underlying them; in this case the rule of law. Second, it is these rules, rather than the acts of those enacting them, which assign power its legitimacy. Third, it is assumed that power is something done to individuals, against their will, and that it is a form of constraint. Fourth, it is assumed that power is a hard thing: once apprehended and tried one is either convicted as guilty or not; sharp and forceful justice determines guilt or lays it to the side given the benefit of the doubt. Power is presumed to be hard; guilt is deemed worthy of punishment; punishment should fit the crime.

Now let us consider another scenario. A small child is growing up: she is beautiful and much loved by her family. She is dressed in pretty clothes and has dolls galore with which to play. She knows she is loved and implicitly rewarded for her good behaviour in play and at home. She grows up knowing her femininity, her girlish appeal, which constant love and attention in the home have instilled in her disposition. On special occasions she gets her hair and her nails done by Mummy and Daddy always tells her how pretty she is when this is the case. Certain feminist authors would argue that a scenario such as this is a form of soft power, because the politics of the gendered self are being produced as a consequence of these social relations.[1] They see the power/knowledge relations entailed in socialization as a form of soft power, framing and shaping selfhood.

Table 10.1 Hard and soft forms of organizational power[2]

Hard power	Soft power
Power is based on coercion	Power is based on attraction
Based on traditional forms of control, such as hierarchy and bureaucracy	Based on new forms of power such as performance and culture management
Power is visible	Power is transparent
Power is concentrated	Power is distributed
Power is externally imposed	Power is socially constructed
Power is stable	Power is dynamic
Illustrations: the power of armies and hierarchies (e.g., the power of managers as structurally rooted)	Illustrations: the power of mission and purpose (e.g., Green social movements)

Just as social relations in the family may produce gendered selves so social relations in organizations may produce organized selves. We are all familiar with the hard power examples from too many Hollywood movies set in total institutions such as prisons or boot camps. There are rules; they are binary, you either follow them or are sanctioned. Soft power can also be organized. Just as soft power in the family works through the power/knowledge relations constituted in normal socialization so in organizations soft power can be developed, acculturated and actualized. One way of seeing this is in terms of the antimonies of hard and soft organizational power as in Table 10.1.

Power, organizations and positivity

Power is 'the central concept in the social sciences' and is at 'the core of organizational achievement'.[3] To inquire into organizations without addressing power relations is to miss everything that moulds the unfolding or inhibition of capabilities, choices and change. Power is not a thing with essential qualities but rather the dynamic of relations between people struggling for meaning.

The general perception of power is the negative view famously declared by Lord Acton – that it tends to corrupt. In reality, power can be used for negative or positive purposes. Negative power is manipulative, coercive, violent, dominating, constraining, antagonistic, destructive and inhibitive. Positive power, in contrast, is generative, empowering and facilitative (Table 10.2). Despite categorizations of positive and negative power, however, it should be noted that power is rarely just positive or negative. Most of the time it involves tensions producing shades of positivity and negativity. Power may be used negatively to pursue positive goals (e.g., a leader may use coercive power to fight negative forces and save the organization), and positive uses of power may give rise to negative results (empowering unethical employees may lead them to feel freer to adopt unethical behaviours).

Considering the positive and negative shades of power, organizational scholars tend to describe it as a process rather than as an outcome. Viewing power as an outcome – who wins – is to freeze analysis in the given moment, a moment that is static in the face of the embedded dynamics that frame any outcome. The reason for viewing power relations as a process is that outcomes are indeterminate and subject to revisions based upon the priorities, relevancies and connections made retrospectively and prospectively at a given moment in history. What appears as positive from one perspective, or in the short term,

Table 10.2 Notions of negative and
positive forms of power

Negative power	Positive power
Coercive	Voluntary
Domination	Authority
Fear	Love
Illegitimate	Legitimate
Manipulative	Authentic
Violent	Free
Opaque	Transparent
Constraining	Facilitative
Destructive	Generative

may be negative from another or in the longer term. When Chamberlain declared 'peace for our time' after meeting Hitler in a speech on September 30, 1938, what might have seemed to be an achievement became an illusion after Hitler's planned invasion of Poland, which occurred on September 3, 1939, was reported.[4] The invasion triggered the war.

Chamberlain never retrieved whatever reputation he had; no subsequent Prime Minister in the UK would regard him as a role model. His replacement, Winston Churchill, at least for his wartime leadership, has been a source of inspiration to many. He, in turn, had regard for certain leaders of the past. One of these was Abraham Lincoln (Box 10.1). Churchill wrote that Lincoln was

> anxious to keep the ship on an even keel and steer a steady course, he may lean all his weight now on one side and now on the other. His arguments in each case when contrasted can be shown to be not only very different in character, but contradictory in spirit and opposite in direction; yet his object will throughout have remained the same ... we cannot call this inconsistency. The only way a man can remain consistent amid changing circumstances is to change with them while preserving the same dominating purpose.

Box 10.1 How Abraham Lincoln interpreted and used power

Abraham Lincoln, the 16th President of the United States (1861–1865), continues to be one of the most admired US presidents. Some 15,000 books have been written about him.[5] Peter Baker wrote in *The New York Times* that Lincoln is 'the one President all of them want to be more like'.[6] In 2014 *The Washington Post* surveyed 162 members of the American Political Science Association's Presidents & Executive Politics section, asking them to rate the US presidents: Lincoln was ranked #1.[7] Gillian M. McCombs considers Lincoln a 'management guru'.[8] Howard Schultz, CEO of Starbucks, said 'Lincoln's presidency is a big, well-lit classroom for business leaders seeking to build successful, enduring organizations'.[9] Nancy Koehn wrote in *The New York Times* that Lincoln may be a source of knowledge and inspiration for business leaders. Considering this, read the following excerpts about 'Abraham Lincoln and Power':[10]

- 'Mr. Lincoln was also an idealist who believed that power must be exercised with principle.'
- 'Mr. Lincoln was very cognizant of the abuses of power – either by a mob or a dictator.'
- 'For Lincoln, power was inseparable from principle.'
- 'People were an essential ingredient in Lincoln's perception of power.'
- 'Lincoln understood the necessities of political patronage to reinforce his presidential power, and he understood it was sometimes more important to mollify his enemies than gratify his friends. Lincoln was also very conscious of the limits of his powers.'
- 'Lincoln understood that power was necessary to do good. Ambition was necessary to get power, as Lincoln himself acknowledged when he first campaigned for public office in 1832 … "Mr. Lincoln was an ambitious man, but he desired power less for the sake of prestige or authority than for the opportunities it presented of being useful and beneficent in its exercise," observed friend Ward Hill Lamon.'
- President Lincoln understood the power of his position, but he did not over-dramatize his importance. The position, not the occupant, was important to the nation.'

Questions for reflection

- To what extent is Lincoln's perspective of power relevant for business leaders?
- Do you agree that power is necessary for doing good? Why?
- Do you agree that the position, not the occupant, is more important for the organization? Why?
- How may a mob abuse power? Is this also possible in organizations?

Bearing in mind the centrality of power to organizational studies, it is surprising that scholars within the positive organizational scholarship community have devoted little attention to the topic of positive power within organizations. With this book we seek to right that wrong. As Pfeffer argues, 'If you are going to do good – for educational systems, public works, breast cancer, or shareholders – you are going to need to be in power. Otherwise, you won't be able to accomplish as much'.[11] We organize the material discussed in this chapter using a framework with four areas of analysis: (1) power over (2) power to, (3) power with and (4) power within (Table 10.3).[12]

Power over is the mode of power that is most commonly recognized. Associated with domination, it is theorized as the probability that actor A in a social relation can influence actor B to carry out their will. In this chapter four types of domination are discussed. Coercive power over is enacted by force and is therefore negative, whereas authoritative power over relies on voluntary submission and is therefore regarded as a more positive form of power over.

Power to is facilitative empowerment, supporting an individual's power to act and enact their will without interference. Power to is generally viewed as a mode of soft power that has the same objectives as hard power but sets about achieving them in a more benign and subtle manner. In this chapter we highlight culture management,

Table 10.3 Four modes of power relations

Power relation	Objective	Basis	Texture
Power over	Managerial control	Domination	Hard/soft
Power to	Managerial control	Domination	Soft
Power with	Shared interest	Collaboration	Soft
Power within	Autonomy	Self-respect	Soft/hard

the German governance model of *Mitbestimmung* or corporate co-determination and encouraging employees to raises their voices, as various modes of power to.

Power with facilitates personal development and growth through collaborative and democratic governance practices. Power with recognizes the importance of identifying common ground to cultivate collective strength. Within the management context, managers and workers cultivate power with by realizing that working together will enable each group to achieve shared mutual interests.

Power within relates to an individual's personal sense of self-worth and self-understanding. Included is the ability to be accountable for one's emotional responses and choices and thereby to live with a sense of inalienable freedom of will. It may additionally involve courageously speaking truth to power and resisting power over that violates human dignity, rights and ethics. When wise counsel is ignored, it may also involve sometimes taking a stand as an organizational whistleblower.

Power over: domination and authority

Domination as coercion and authority

Max Weber, a German scholar writing on organizational and management theory in the early 1900s, was possibly the first scholar to consider power within organizations using an explicit typological approach (Figure 10.1).[13] Weber offered various but related definitions of power, which he held to be the central concept of organized social engagement. One such definition holds power as 'the probability that one actor within a social relationship will be in a position to carry out his or her own will

Figure 10.1 Max Weber in 1894.[15]

despite resistance, regardless of the basis on which this probability rests'.[14] Weber was most interested in power as domination or power over.

Weber was less interested in power over as coercive power, one that is imposed, which is generally viewed as domination or negative power lacking legitimacy. His main focus was on analyzing authority relations, which he termed legitimate domination or authoritative power, where individuals consent to submit themselves to the will of another because they view the relation that ensues as legitimate in some respects. In his work *Economy and Society* Weber describes three types of legitimacy – charismatic, traditional and rational-legal:[16]

- Charismatic legitimacy attaches to power that relies on an individual's exceptional qualities of heroism, character or humanity, attracting followers towards them – sometimes with the appeal of a new vision, promises of ending different forms of suffering and achieving greater prosperity and wellbeing. From this perspective, leaders such as Gandhi, Martin Luther King, Nelson Mandela and the Dalai Lama are all widely recognized for their charisma. The power of their charisma legitimated their power in the eyes of their followers.
- Traditional power, in contrast, relies on the authority of culture, customs and conventions and belief in the sanctity of 'immortal' traditions. The power of a hereditary monarch such as Queen Elizabeth II of the British Royal Family is based upon the authority of tradition. Hereditary rule is not just an attribute of the monarchy: the dynastic Kim regime in North Korea operates, bizarrely, on the same principle in what is alleged to be a socialist republic.
- Finally, rational-legal authority is based upon belief in the legality of rules, policies and systems, organized in a rational manner towards the achievement of agreed-upon objectives, as well as in the legitimacy of the right to do so of those holding positions of authority from which commands emanate. An elected head of government such as a Prime Minister or President is an example of rational-legal authority. Once that elected official's term expires and they are voted out or dismissed from office, they no longer command the power of the office they once held.

Three additional points about charisma are particularly noteworthy (see also Box 10.2). First, even the most 'positive' charismatic leaders are not 'saints' (see Chapter 8) and sometimes use their power in negative ways. Second, charisma is not necessarily positive, and rather may be used for the pursuit of the leaders' self-interests or even perverse goals[17] – Hitler being, probably, the most dramatic case. John Potts, professor of media at Macquarie University in Australia, wrote about the charisma of political leaders:[18]

> The political biographer David Barnett has called charisma 'one of the most dangerous concepts in a democracy that you can find'. Charismatic leaders can inspire followers with soaring rhetoric – which can also prove divisive and damaging to a party's (or a nation's) fortunes. Political parties are generally content with popular, unthreatening, folksy leaders who appeal to ordinary people. In Australia, Paul Keating was a charismatic, visionary prime minister, but also a schismatic leader who alienated much of the Labour Party's traditional 'heartland' with his perceived arrogance. His successor, John Howard, was universally regarded as charisma-free, but his very ordinariness turned out to be his greatest asset: it was a reassuring rather than threatening style of leadership. Meanwhile in Italy, Silvio Berlusconi was

a populist leader whose tenure as prime minister was deleterious for democracy. The charismatic leader might be thrilling, even captivating, but the success of that leader might not leave a political party, or a democracy, in a healthy state.

Tomas Chamorro-Premuzic further notes:[19]

> Most people think charisma is as vital to leadership as it is to rock stars or TV presenters and, unfortunately, they are right. In the era of multimedia politics, leadership is commonly downgraded to just another form of entertainment and charisma is indispensable for keeping the audience engaged. However, the short-term benefits of charisma are often neutralized by its long-term consequences. In fact, there are big reasons for resisting charisma: 1. Charisma dilutes judgment ... 2. Charisma is addictive ... 3. Charisma disguises psychopaths ... 4. Charisma fosters collective narcissism ... Despite these dangers, the dark side of charm is commonly overlooked ... In brief, charisma distracts and destructs. Technology and science have enabled us to systematize many serendipitous practices (e.g., shopping, marketing, relationships, hiring, etc.). A more mature and evolved version of politics will require a charisma detox – leadership is not a game.

Third, as these statements suggest, charismatic leadership is more than the 'exceptional qualities' of an individual. It is a *process* of complex social relations involving leaders, followers and a specific situation of rule.[20] A leader may be charismatic towards some followers and uncharismatic with others. A charismatic relationship with followers may disappear as the situation changes. The relational and situational dynamism of charisma helps explain why some once charismatic and loved leaders ended up abandoned and hated: in recent history one thinks of Zimbabwe's Robert Mugabe or Nicaragua's Daniel Ortega.

Box 10.2 Three types of authority: charismatic, traditional and rational-based

Below you can see photos of several leaders (Figures 10.2a–f). Which of Weber's three types of authoritative power do they represent?

Figure 10.2a Gandhi, August 1942.[21]

Figure 10.2b Queen Elizabeth II, February 1953.[22]

Figure 10.2c Barack Obama, October 18, 2005.[23]

Figure 10.2d Hitler, April 20, 1937.[24]

Figure 10.2e Steve Jobs, January 11, 2015.[25]

Figure 10.2f Mother Teresa, December 10, 1985.[26]

Now reflect on how a leader may base his/her authority on different types of legitimacy. What are some strategies a leader may adopt for achieving power?

Systemic bureaucratic power as a mode of domination

Weber viewed the power of charismatic authority as the least stable mode of governance as it rests on the charisma of an extraordinary individual who makes decisions on
a case-by-case basis. These decisions are informed by the leader's (presumed) exceptional insights that might even be viewed by followers as 'revelations'. Traditional
authority is more stable, for while power is often concentrated in an individual, that
individual is guided by and bound to the authority of customary traditions, rules and
precedents handed down through generations of forbearers and buttressed by complex
protocols and procedures. When a charismatic leader dies, if their legacy is to endure
into the future as a mode of governmental authority it will need to be translated by

their followers either into traditional authority or a system of rational legality (see Box 10.3 for the difference between personalized and socialized charisma).

Box 10.3 Positive in the negative, negative in the positive – personalized and socialized charisma

You might be a little confused about charisma. A charismatic leader's sparkle may draw you in, only for you to be hurt once the shine and the sparkle wear off. What then distinguishes between different shades of charisma? Is there a way of discerning if a charismatic leader will help or harm you? Some research distinguishes between negative personalized charisma and positive socialized charisma:[27]

- Leaders with personalized charisma prioritize themselves, placing their own advantage ahead of their followers and the organizations they lead. Their sense is that their followers and organization exist for their own benefit. These leaders willingly perform activities that are adverse to their organization's interests, acting in a manner that is authoritarian, exploitative, narcissistic, self-aggrandizing and non-egalitarian. Consequently, followers of leaders who draw on personalized charisma most frequently experience negative outcomes.
- Leaders with socialized charisma direct their energy towards addressing the needs of their followers and the organization more broadly. In refocussing their personal sparkle towards their followers and organization by giving power and autonomy to their followers, these leaders demonstrate inclusiveness, egalitarianism and empowerment. Followers of leaders with socialized charisma, accordingly, mostly experience positive benefits.

Both charismatic styles can generate results, at least in the short term, but the critical issue is how they get results! Further, this analysis suggests that charisma itself is neither positive nor negative but rather it is how charisma is used that makes the critical difference. Despite these distinctions, however, Weber's criticism still holds: charisma is a weak and unstable form of power as compared with a rules-based bureaucratic system of power. Think of contemporary politics: are there any leaders that you can identify who seem to correspond to one or other of these charismatic styles?

Weber viewed rational legal power as the most stable and efficient type of authority, as it is based on systems of rational rules that transcend the authority of an individual. The rational-legal mode of power was what, according to Weber, underpinned the bureaucratic mode of organizing that emerged with the growth of the modern state, concurrently with maturing capitalism. In bureaucratic governance, all orders are written to ensure their rationality, universality and accountability. Weber devoted much attention to the topic of bureaucracy, inspired by his fascination with the newly formed modern Prussian (German) state and army – the envy of Europe at the time. Whereas military powers had traditionally depended on the strength and bravery of individual warriors, Weber observed that the effectiveness and efficiency of the modern Prussian military was based upon the monocratic force of many component parts operating in unison towards the achievement of a unified objective. The individual's role was essential but only as a component part of a greater system, as a cog in a greater organizational machine. The Prussian soldier did not have to be physically strong or even brave. They had to have a basic level of training in using their weapons and be drilled and disciplined to move as a unit when and as they were commanded.

Weber realized that the efficiency and effectiveness of the Prussian army was made possible through the development of a disciplined Prussian state as a rational-legal bureaucracy. Weber's description of bureaucratic organizing as a mode of power transforms the notion of power from (a) seeing it as a title or position held by an individual human or group of people who realize their will in social action, towards (b) understanding power as relational and systemic – embedded within the deep structures of an organization or broader society, influencing what people do or do not do.

Although Weber viewed rational legal power as the most stable and efficient type of authority, he observed both positive and negative effects of bureaucracy.[28] On the positive side, he appreciated the protection of civil liberty by limiting arbitrary power and social levelling in favour of technical competence. He also appreciated that rule following as a basis for organizing facilitated a right of appeal and accountability. The major negative Weber observed is that bureaucracy, as an impersonal machine (see Box 10.4), inhibits individuality. Power legitimated on the basis of policies creates uniformity but also depersonalization as all personnel become subject to impersonal bureaucratic control. In bureaucracies, rule abiding can become all-important, even at the expense of undermining the very purpose for which the rules were put in place. Such rule tropism, or following of rules for their own sake rather than as a means to an end, Weber observed, could crush the human spirit on account of a loss of freedom and personal meaning. A consequence is the so-called Kafkaesque organization (see Chapter 6).

Box 10.4 Chaplin's Modern Times, the worker as a cog in the bureaucratic machine

In the 1936 comedy film *Modern Times*, Charlie Chaplin portrays his iconic Little Tramp character struggling for survival as a factory worker in modern, bureaucratic, industrialized society.[29] Chaplin was greatly disturbed by the poverty he observed during the 1930s' Great Depression, and he wrote the film as a social commentary on the challenging financial and employment struggles people faced during this period, which he saw as rooted in the efficiencies caused by modern industrialization.

In the film, Chaplin gets a job as an assembly line factory worker where he must screw nuts onto machinery at an ever-accelerating rate as the boss orders the assembly line to be run at ever-faster speeds. One memorable moment has the factory worker fall into the machinery, providing visual imagery, as the worker passes through various cogs, of the factory worker as a literal cog in the bureaucratic machine. Eventually the factory worker has a nervous breakdown, running amok and causing mayhem on the factory floor. He is sent to hospital and, on his release, is wrongly arrested for instigating a Communist Party protest. In jail, he accidentally thwarts a jailbreak. As a reward for his heroism he is offered early release, which he unsuccessfully tries to argue against, preferring to remain in jail. For he finds jail more comfortable than factory work.

Now a free man, the factory worker observes an orphan girl Ellen running from the police who pursue her for stealing a loaf of bread. Wanting to return to jail and to protect Ellen, the factory worker confesses to the crime and is arrested. A witness, however, informs the police that the factory worker is innocent and he is again released. He thereafter goes to a restaurant and eats a huge amount of food that he cannot pay for and is successful in getting arrested again. His time in custody, how-ever, is short-lived. Ellen is also in the vehicle transporting them both to jail. When the car crashes Ellen convinces the factory worker to escape with her.

After many more such adventures of working, getting arrested and released, the film ends with the two fleeing from police once again. When Ellen expresses hopelessness in their struggles, the factory worker seeks to reassure her that somehow they will survive. The film closes with the two traversing a road into an uncertain but hopeful sunset.

Charlie Chaplin's biographer, Jeffery Vance, sees the film as even more relevant today than when it was released in the 1930s:[30]

> *Modern Times* is perhaps more meaningful now than at any time since its first release. The twentieth-century theme of the film, farsighted for its time – the struggle to eschew alienation and preserve humanity in a modern, mechanized world – pro-foundly reflects issues facing the twenty-first century. The Tramp's travails in *Modern Times* and the comedic mayhem that ensues should provide strength and comfort to all who feel like helpless cogs in a world beyond control. Through its universal themes and comic inventiveness, *Modern Times* remains one of Chaplin's greatest and most enduring works. Perhaps more important, it is the Tramp's finale, a tribute to Chaplin's most beloved character and the silent-film era he commanded for a generation.

Modern Times, Charlie Chaplin's satire on hyper rational-bureaucratic industrial organizations, remains as one of his most popular films and has been described as one of his crowning achievements.[31] (See also see Chapter 5.)

Power to: the power of empowerment

Is soft power more difficult than hard power?

Talcott Parsons, a researcher at Harvard University, was the person who introduced Weber to English-speaking audiences. Whereas Weber saw power relations as largely con-straining, Parsons viewed power as mostly positive and facilitative, in terms of *power to*.[32] Power to achieve outcomes, particularly at a system level, was a necessary capability of dynamic organization much as money was essential for a dynamic economy. Parsons asso-ciated power with authority *to* allocate resources for the attainment of collective goals. Like money, power's legitimacy is anchored in popular confidence in its currency. Such perceived legitimacy enables the deployment of power with the expectation that others will respect its injunctions. In this manner, power forms binding obligations, reproduces authority and maintains social norms. Parsons' critics have argued that while power may be positive and serves the collective goals of those so aligned, for those who do not share in the values and goals of the dominant majority, power remains *power over* and its authority lacks legitimacy.[33] The consensual basis of legitimacy and authority is mostly constructed through complexities that invariably precede collective goals and their attainment, relations that are embedded in law, custom and socialization.

The French historian of ideas Michel Foucault wrote of *power for architecture* to as a positive capacity rather than a negative relation constraining individuals' actions. Whereas domination generally relies on the hard power of coercive force to make another act in a manner they would not ordinarily do, positive power achieves the same by shaping and framing what others *want* to do. Foucault often wrote of 'power/knowledge' to capture the ways in which power is always constituted through regimes of knowledge, with specific regimes of truth.[34] Power/knowledge is a form of soft power because it is less obtrusive than those forms that seek to have people act against their own will. Such power is a much more efficient mode of domination as it normalizes power relations as a taken-for-granted reality in a manner that makes them hardly appear to be an external power at all. Surveillance is one fundamental mechanism for achieving this situation. Foucault conceptualized surveillance by rekindling interest in Jeremy Bentham's Panopticon design.[35]

Jeremy Bentham was one of the leading figures of late 18th- and 19th-century social philosophy in Britain. In 1786 and 1787 Bentham travelled to Krichev in modern Belarus to visit his brother Samuel, who managed various industrial and other projects for Prince Potemkin.[36] Samuel had conceived the idea of a circular building, a watchtower, at the hub of a larger compound that would allow a small number of managers to oversee the activities of a large and unskilled workforce. The watchtower would have narrow slits through which the overseers could exercise surveillance. Jeremy began to develop a model based on this idea, which was built for several purposes, including factories, libraries as well as imprisonment.

Bentham was concerned about repeat offending, the question of why people who commit crimes and are punished with a jail sentence often commit the same crime again once freed from jail. His response to this question was that while jail confined the prisoner's body, it did not reform their values, attitudes and beliefs. His objective, then, was to devise a prison design that would not just confine the prisoners' bodies but also reshape their values so they conformed with those of society. His proposed solution was a prison design referred to as the panopticon where prison cells would be arranged in a circular shape around a central watchtower (Figure 10.3).

The most important aspect of Bentham's design was that the guard was unseen by the prisoners who accordingly never knew when they were being watched – meaning the potential for their being watched was constant. The guard's ability to watch prisoners unseen would ensure that power functions automatically – permanently in effect, even if discontinuous in action. The mechanism of being the subject of inscrutable surveillance meant that the possibility of being watched was ever present in the consciousness of those arrayed in the panopticon. Such continuous surveillance would induce prisoners to internalize the demands of the system whose gaze they were subject to and to objectify themselves in terms of its judgements, ensuring that prisoners enacted self-discipline, self-control and self-regulation in accordance with the expectations of the surveilling system.

Foucault similarly suggested that the structures of modern society provide apparent freedom to the individual to be who and what they would be, yet through constant social

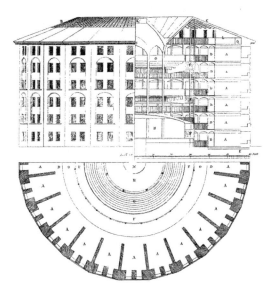

Figure 10.3 Elevation of Bentham's panopticon prison design, drawn by Reveley, 1791.[37]

observation amongst peers, in educational institutions, workplaces, recreational environments and every other sphere of social engagement, people internalize expectations that frame their ways of expressing their being in the world through the dominant forms of power/knowledge to which they are exposed. With the advance of technologies, such as the Internet and digital technologies that leave a trail of metadata, as well as more obvious social media technologies, one might suggest that constant observing surveillance has become much wider and its effect much deeper since the time that Foucault formulated his ideas in the 1970s and 1980s.

If we spend much of our formative years exposed to the soft power of the family we spend most of our mature years exposed to other forms of organized power. Institutions we have encountered on the path to maturity help to prepare our predispositions for the power relations we will encounter. Schooling is one obvious candidate but so also are the messages that we receive from the movies and television shows we watch, the video games we play and, perhaps most importantly, the organizations that we inhabit.

Soft power and culture management

Management scholars have drawn parallels between Foucault's ideas and the organizational context[38] where, since the 1970s and 1980s, managers have sought to engender greater commitment, loyalty and engagement through soft power relations fostered through the power/knowledge associated with culture management.[39] Weber's bureaucracy focussed on the regulation of the organization through the implementation of governance structures and policies as rational-legal structures of what we may call hard power. In contrast, culture management is concerned with defining, promoting and reinforcing specific values, attitudes and beliefs that define membership within a given organization, informing decision-making and behaviours that reinforce successful achievement of organizational objectives. (For more on organizational culture see Chapter 9.) The assumption is that if employees embody dominant organizational values such as initiative, creativity, engagement, responsibility and service, there will be no need to monitor and control their task performance. Through culture, managers will be able to control more by controlling less.

The culture management revolution of the 1970s and 1980s was coupled with a related initiative that has come to be known as post-bureaucracy. Post-bureaucracy rejects bureaucracy's hierarchy, top-down decision making, rigid adherence to processes outlined in policies and procedures, slow responsiveness and assumptions that employees are motivated solely by extrinsic rewards of the pay checks. A post-bureaucratic approach suggests an organization with decentralization of managerial decision making, a flatter network or team-based structure with less management levels and greater empowerment of employees who are expected to take the initiative and be motivated by intrinsic rewards residing in opportunities for personal development, prestige, fulfilment and even self-actualization through their work.[40] In post-bureaucracy, rules will ideally be flexibly interpreted for achieving organizational objectives. Such a post-bureaucratic approach, it is argued, is expected to contribute to greater organizational agility, creativity and innovation, so important in an increasingly disruptive environment in which political, economic, social demographic, technological and legal-legislative changes are taking place at an ever-increasing rate.

The empowerment of employees as responsible team members, decision makers and initiative takers that characterizes post-bureaucratic management can be seen as a mode of what Courpasson calls 'soft domination',[41] where the apparent freedoms and privileges actually create deeper obligations, commitments and conformity, along with added pressures, stresses and anxieties. An enhanced reliance on teams in post-bureaucratic organizing is seen to be a more effective mode of panoptical surveillance, where peer pressure and a desire to be liked by the team sees employees enact self-monitoring and self-regulation in conformity with expected organizational cultural attitudes, values and behaviours.[42] Management by workmates proves to be much more efficient and subtle than more intrusive supervision. From this viewpoint, post-bureaucratic management is more controlling – in such a way that the subject barely perceives how they are being controlled. Individuals are controlled because they are 'imprisoned' in a kind of normative power, as suggested by Etzioni.

Organizational power and employee commitment

Sociologist Amitai Etzioni of George Washington University further analyzes the notion of organizational *power to* as a means of engendering a greater level of employee commitment.[43] Etzioni's typology describes three modes of organizational power: coercive, instrumental and normative. Coercive power is enacted through the organization's ongoing potential to forcibly withhold privileges and impose punishments. Instrumental power is enacted through the control of material resources distributed as remuneration and other rewards. Finally, normative power derives from the organization's authority to manipulate, allocate and restrict the disbursement of benefits providing symbolic value through enhanced esteem and prestige. Etzioni suggests three ideal categories of employee commitment responses corresponding with these modes of organizational power: *coercive power* induces employee alienation from the organization; *normative power*

Table 10.4 Etzioni's forms of organizational power and employee commitment responses

Organizational power	Power mechanism	Employee commitment
Coercive	The organization's ongoing potential to forcibly withhold privileges and impose punishments.	Alienation from the organization.
Instrumental	The organization's control of material resources distributed as remuneration and other rewards.	Calculative commitment towards the organization.
Normative	The organization's authority to manipulate, allocate and restrict the disbursement of benefits providing symbolic value through enhanced esteem and prestige.	Sense of moral duty towards the organization.

induces moral involvement as a sense of responsibility or duty, whereas *instrumental power* induces calculative commitment (as per Table 10.4).[44]

Simpson, Clegg, and Freeder applied Ezioni's framework to analyze organizational responses towards their employees during floods that inundated the City of Brisbane, Australia, in 2011.[45] The findings revealed the following:

- Organizational responses of neglect (associated with Etzioni's coercive power) as perceived by employees (i.e., expecting employees to remain at work while the city was being evacuated, roads closed and public transport shut down, or to attend work when their homes were under water) induced employees to become distanced from the organization, diminishing their willingness to contribute extra effort by 'putting themselves out' for the organization in future. Thus, the total power available to the organizations decreased.
- Organizational responses of instrumental care (i.e., expressing concern in a manner that was delayed and appeared to be more legalistic than genuine, leading to conflicting and therefore confusing mixed messages of care while maintaining business-as-usual demands) induced employee responses of moralistic commitment, where employees were committed to the level demanded of their job description, neither less nor more.
- Employees who perceived their organization as providing compassionate care during the extraordinary flood event increased their social integration within the organization with a greater level of trust, loyalty and an expressed commitment to help the organization as best they can. Consequently, their commitment as more dependable employees deepened, increasing the total power available to the organization.

In terms of organizational strategy, this analysis of organizational responses to the Brisbane floods suggests that positive organizational practices such as cultivating organizational compassion can enhance (positive-sum) or minimize (zero-sum) the aggregate of systemic organizational power.[46] A note of warning should be taken against deploying compassion merely as a mode of soft power for the ends of creating more committed and compliant employees – this would likely be experienced by employees as Etzioni's instrumental power, generating a purely role-prescribed moral response towards the organization. Such an official-type response contrasts significantly with the deep loyalty, trust and engagement seen from those employees that experienced the compassionate support they received as an authentic expression of actual care (the response anticipated by Etzioni to normative organizational power). This analysis further suggests that organizations that cultivate negative power or zero-sum power over employees will be at a strategic disadvantage against positive-sum organizations which build enhanced system integration through the cultivation of *power with*, as discussed below.

Power with: the power of collaboration

Coactive power

The negative connotation of power tends to emerge from a power over perspective, one in which power is invariably theorized in terms of power over other people. Power, however, may be exercised *with* other people (see Box 10.5). Mary Parker Follett espoused this perspective (Figure 10.4). Follett is sometimes referred to as the mother of Organizational Studies or as a Prophet of Management (see also Chapter 1). Follett, writing at the turn of the 19th century and into the early years of the 20th century, was a person ahead of her time. Although she has been long ignored, in recent years she has gained increasing recognition. Her writings are to a certain extent foundational for the POS movement. Follett sought to harmonize power relations in the perennial conflict between labour (workers) and the owners of capital (shareholders and the managers employed to represent shareholder interests), through a project of democratizing power.[47] In her view, genuine power is not coercive power over but coactive *power with*. When managers and workers are on opposite sides and only one wins, both sides lose, she argues, because the whole has not been enriched.

According to Follett's circular theory of power, workers and managers influence one another in a web of social relations.[49] Circular power transforms perceived facts as the situation evolves, giving rise to new facts, new interpretations and experiences of facts over time. She further held that genuine power is a relational capacity rather than a 'thing' that can be wrenched from the powerful and seized by the powerless. The role

Figure 10.4 Mary Parker Follett, before 1933.[48]

of managers, then, is not to delegate but to facilitate workers in growing their capacities to act, while the aim of the organization is neither dominating employees through its power and control nor sharing power but increasing its circulation.

In summary, for Follett, genuine power is not the zero sum game of *power over* but the self-developing capacity of *power with* in democratic cooperative governance. Although she admitted that power over can never be eliminated, she advocated doing one's best to reduce its pernicious effects. Today, Follett's ideas about coactive power inform approaches to management that acknowledge stakeholder considerations, code-termination through worker representation on organizational boards, participative management in which management consults with workers' counsels on decisions relating to employee rights and status, profit sharing and encouraging polyphony through the expression of employee voice (for more information on Follett see Chapter 1).

Box 10.5 Power within team-based organizing, empowerment and benefits at Wholefoods

An example of employee co-determination is the empowerment of workplace teams at the US supermarket chain Wholefoods. This organization (recognized for its caring culture)[50] has given employees voting power in many areas related to team member hiring, composition and employee benefits.[51] Anyone hired at Wholefoods is hired into a specific team comprising six to 100 members and possibly a number of sub-teams. The initial hiring arrangement is probationary for a 30-to-90-day period, after which the recruit must receive a positive vote from two-thirds of the whole team before they can be hired as a full team member. The criteria for receiving a positive vote is that the other team members believe the new recruit is a good fit for the organization in terms of their alignment with the company's mission, values, work ethos and dealings with others: team members and customers.

We can see the power of organizational soft power at work in this feature. The leaders of each team form part of a store leadership team, with some members from the store leadership team also forming part of the regional leadership team with responsibilities to decide on produce and merchandise selection and logistical considerations. Every three years, Wholefoods team members vote on employee benefits. Company leadership assigns a percentage of total company income for employee benefits and provides employees with a list of potential benefits along with proposed percentage allocations for each benefit. Note where the initiative resides. All employees, or team members as they are referred to at Wholefoods, then vote by prioritizing which benefits they most desire. The benefits that reflect the desires and needs of the majority of members are those that are provided. Wholefoods also offers comprehensive health insurance and wellbeing programmes for employees. There is also a 20 per cent discount on all Wholefoods products that can be increased for employees who meet specific 'biometric criteria for cholesterol levels, body mass index, height-to-waist ratios, and blood pressure, along with being nicotine free'.[52] Again, the degree of surveillance required in monitoring these metrics is worth noting. Wholefoods are practicing a form of biopower, which literally deploys 'numerous and diverse techniques for achieving the subjugations of bodies and the control of populations'.[53]

Annually, a mobile lab is brought in to Wholefoods workplaces for voluntary testing paid for by the organization. The computed lab results are categorized according to four levels of bio performance (platinum, gold, silver and bronze), and inform the extent of additional store discounts made available to individual employees. Employees take pride in moving up to the higher levels through adopting diet and exercise regimes. The company also offers a Total Health Immersion programme for employees with conditions such as obesity, heart disease, high blood pressure or cholesterol and diabetes. Costing some $3,000 per employee and fully sponsored by Wholefoods, the programme offers a week-long medically supervised plan with intensive educational training, exercise and meal plans with demonstrated results that see sugar, weight, heart rate and cholesterol levels drop, providing employees with hope that they can control their health and wellbeing.

Compensation is also entirely transparent, with members being paid according to their position, and any member of the company being able to find out how much another member is being paid. Teams can also earn 'gain-sharing' bonuses through demonstrated higher productivity according to clearly defined criteria for determining and rewarding higher levels of team performance, rather than individual performance. The success of such collaborative coactive power sharing as demonstrated at Wholefoods is indicated by the low turnover rate of just 10 per cent against the industry average of 100 per cent.

The negative in positive

Looking at the case of Wholefoods through a Foucauldian lens, it presents as a prime example of the panopticon in action. Wholefoods team-member-based management structure, team-level incentives and individual incentives based upon health fitness criteria could be viewed as mechanisms of paternalistic domination. Wholefoods 'team membership' invokes constant self-surveillance and objectification both on and off the job. It requires submission to a regime of biopower that is, on the face of it, voluntary, but in the absence of participation material benefits will not flow the individual's way. Team members can vote on benefits – but can only do so for those that the organization prescribes: they have freedom of choice but within policed margins. In this way, the company makes employees adopt self-discipline, self-control and self-regulation to ensure their bodies and minds are shaped in accordance with company expectations.

Mitbestimmung – German corporate co-determination

One of the most impressive examples of organizational empowerment that goes beyond merely providing employees with decision-making authority within the narrow parameters of their task performance is the German model of *Mitbestimmung* or co-determination.[54] *Mitbestimmung* refers to the legal right of German workers to participate in decision making related to the governance of the companies in which they work. In

Germany, workers elect representatives (usually union representatives) to occupy nearly half of the positions of a company's board of directors for large companies of more than 2,000 members, and a third of the board positions on a smaller company of 500 to 2,000 members. German workers also have a right, on the basis of the industrial relations law *Betriebsverfassungsgesetz* first introduced in 1920 for businesses with more than 20 employees, to form work councils that oversee the procedures related to job perform-ance, job resourcing, personnel planning (hiring, training, development and firing) and role responsibilities. The objective of co-determination is to ensure that not only are organizational objectives of profit maximization taken into account but that equal emphasis is also given to employee needs for a safe and healthy work environment that upholds their dignity as humans above and beyond their work positions.

The process of enshrining co-determination in German law began as far back as 1848 when boundaries were imposed on corporate power through the establishment of work councils. While the Nazis abolished the works councils when they came to power in 1932, the works councils were reintroduced once WWII ended. Similar work councils were also experimented with for a period of time in the UK during the WWII effort as a way of generating greater engagement and cooperation from work-ers and increasing productivity. They were abolished shortly after the war ended, however, due to concerns about giving too much power to employees leading to too much workplace inefficiency. Interestingly, when the Global Financial Crisis saw most world economies go into recession, with leading financial institutions and even coun-tries going into bankruptcy and millions losing their jobs, homes and retirement sav-ings, Germany had one of the strongest and most resilient economies, despite its banks such as Deutsche Bank being as implicated in the crisis as those elsewhere. German industry quickly bounced back, while most of its trading partners have taken years to recover.[55] The constraints of the Eurozone have served German industry well.[56]

It is also noteworthy that comparisons of key economic, labour and manufacturing data between Germany, the USA, the UK and Australia (at the time of writing this textbook) show that Germany has a stronger Gross Domestic Product per person than the UK, as well as a lower unemployment rate and higher workforce participation rate than the other three countries.[57] German employees are less likely to be union members than employees from the UK, are just as likely to be unionized as employees from Australia and significantly more likely to be unionized than employees from the USA. Fascinatingly, German employees work about ten more hours per week than their counterparts from the other three countries; they do not have a fixed minimum wage across all industries but they are also significantly less likely to go on strike. These greater levels of workplace compliance from German employees offer support for Follett's arguments about co-active power as a way of generating greater employee engagement but also support concerns about domination being exercised through soft power as a more efficient and effective mode of organizational control.

Employee voice and polyphony

Another approach to employee empowerment is to encourage employees to express their voice and promote a polyphonic view of the organization. An underpinning principle of a free society is freedom of speech and freedom of the press, where the government pro-tects citizen's rights to express their views, including criticizing the government without fear of censorship or reprisal. The opposite case is where the government seeks to control the media and where citizens can be persecuted for voicing their views. In Russia, for example, according to the New-York-based Committee to Protect Journalists, between the years 1992–2017 82 Russian journalists have been murdered in their professional capacities covering topics related to: politics (22 murdered), corruption (21 murdered), war (20), crime (13), business (8), human rights (7) and culture (5).[58] Other types of intimidation experienced by Russian journalists include assaults, illegal layoffs, detention, legal harassment, evictions, censorship, confiscation of printed materials and interruptions to broadcasting.[59] Typically dictatorial regimes seek citizen conformity with a state-sanctioned ideology be it communism, nationalism or theocracy. An independent free press that voices opposing views, or just questions the assumptions of the prevailing dogma, is therefore viewed as a threat. In some places, such as the United States of the Trump Presidency, reporting the news can be dismissed as 'fake news' and journalists from specific media organizations are banned from rallies or ignored when asking questions.

While people living in 'the free world' with democratically elected government and a free press would likely question the legitimacy of state media control and restrictions on freedom of speech, it is interesting how infrequently people question the legitimacy of the assumption that employees are obliged to conform to organizationally sanctioned attitudes, values and culture. When they vote for a party in a democratic election they are free to choose the ideology that they support from those that are mobilized to seduce their interest; at work, however, one is expected to swallow hook, line and sinker whatever ideology is on offer, affording one less democratic freedoms in the workplace as an organizational citizen than one has as a member of civil society. One of the great myths of organization practice today is that an organization requires a homogeneous organizational voice where all people conform to the same managerially defined values, attitudes and behaviours for the organization to be successful.[60] People advocating such views forget what we know at the societal level: suppressing individual differences in the interests of creating a strong monoculture is more likely to produce unreflective conformity, often to inappropriate and even ethically questionable actions unilaterally dictated by an all-powerful leader. It can also lead to the branding of those who do not conform to the party line as troublemakers who are stigmatized as punishment for their non-conforming attitudes and behaviours.

Assumptions about the value of singular organizational voice supported by a strong organizational culture overlooks the problem of groupthink, where organizational members ignore important counterfactual information and make poor decisions in an effort to maintain group harmony (for a more extensive discussion on culture see Chapter 9).[61] The term groupthink was coined by Irving Janis who was seeking to understand how teams – even those that are well experienced, educated, of similar power and status – can make devastating decisions.[62] If the purpose of bringing people together to form a team is to benefit from the collective (and diverse) knowledge, experience, inclinations and contacts of all the members, then groupthink can certainly undermine that process.

Organizations can seek to avoid groupthink by encouraging not conformity but independence and individualism or 'unity in diversity' (for more information on groupthink see Chapter 7). Members can be encouraged to speak up and voice their views by providing forums for openly questioning and interrogating decision-making processes, demonstrating that dissenting voices are valued rather than punished for critiquing managerial decisions. Speaking up is seen as a way of articulating 'non-issues' to change the organizational agenda.[63] It represents the exercise of voice,[64] whether in challenging or supportive ways.[65] Voice expressed in challenging ways is, by definition, riskier for those expressing it than voice articulated in supportive ways. Some organizations encourage voice in humorous ways. Cirque du Soleil hired 'Madame Zazou', a clown, to work in its headquarters. Her job is to stage entertainments, to dispense popcorn and to play the role of court jester: she has 'full license', for example, to come into the executive committee meeting, do the introductions and make fun of the meeting participants.[66]

Managerially, especially in disruptive competitive environments, it is assumed that organizational learning, agility and adaptability can be enhanced when employees freely communicate observations and ideas.[67] Psychological safety (i.e., 'a shared belief held by members of a team that the team is safe for interpersonal risk taking'; see Chapter 7)[68] is seen in the managerial literature as a means of encouraging voice that is challenging rather than merely supportive of dominant assumptions. All communication is receiver-based, however; the level of psychological safety assumed to be prevailing managerially may differ widely from the sense that is made of managerial initiatives. Psychological safety, as an antecedent of a culture of speaking up, often clashes with the fragmented ways in which different people interpret what psychological safety and speaking up mean in practice.[69] One practical approach at the team level involves allocating the role of devil's advocate to one or two members tasked with actively questioning proposals in an objective manner.

The presence of conflicting and competing voices within an organizational context is referenced as polyphony, as compared with monophony, which describes a singular managerial voice. Much as the fabled Tower of Babel (Figure 10.5), where people spoke multiple languages inscrutable to one another, various forms of ethnic, gender and religious diversity amongst organizational members means that organizational life naturally comprises diverse cultures and subcultures, each with unique experiences, perspectives and voices, contributing to messy organization reality.[70] Rather than insisting on organizational members artificially conforming to a singular language, generating homogenized monotonic communication, leading ultimately to the death of creativity, scholars suggest that management must learn to acknowledge the value of polyphony.

Figure 10.5 Gustave Doré's depiction of the Tower of Babel and the confusion of the tongues.[71]

Boje draws upon the theatrical production *Tamaraland* as a metaphor for understanding organizations as polyphonic.[72] In the play *Tamaraland*, acts are performed simultaneously in various locations, with the audience freely moving between the acts. Depending upon the route taken, different members of the audience will encounter different acts and accordingly make various senses of the play. Notions of linearity are thereby disrupted on account of the audience potentially being able to have infinitely varied experiences of the performance contingent on the order in which they enter the various locations. Boje suggests that, like *Tamaraland*, organizations also present members with multiple experiences, meanings and outcomes. Despite the presence of well-crafted organizational scripts in the forms of mission statements, strategic plans and policy documents, with so many directors in the form of heads of marketing, finance and human resources, etc., there is little likelihood of a singular script being followed.

Accordingly, rather than perpetuating the myth of a singular organizational voice, justifying the silencing of those that differ from the official organization narrative, Boje holds that organizations should best be viewed as a meta-theatre. This is an organizational theatre comprising manifold simultaneous dramas, where sense-making unfolds through the process of creative engagement and learning, with various people making a variety of senses, expressed democratically as polyphony. A shared power with the approach of polyphony recognizes the reality of subcultures, reduces the potential for managerial groupthink and facilitates organizational agility, creativity and change. People's ability to enact positive *power with* also depends upon their sense of personal power or *power within*.

Power within: the power of the self

Nietzsche's will to power

A problem with the rational power of bureaucracy, observed by Max Weber, which is still relevant to many organizations, is that it can have the effect of crushing the human spirit, divesting the worker of personal agency, will and power. Karl Marx also wrote about this in his early work where he argued that the division of labour and relations of production in industrial capitalism produced alienation of the self from the organizational context; ultimately, he thought, this alienation of a consciousness in itself would fuse together in a collective consciousness of the oppressed proletarians who would rise up in resistance to the appalling work regimes of early capitalism.[73]

Marx held high hopes for the collective intelligence and political acumen of the working class movement that has never been realized. There are many possible reasons for the failure of Marx's scenario (other than in circumstances where a well-organized Party with a military capacity seizes power from a failed state, which was the situation with the Russian and Chinese revolutions) including: the growth of social insurance and the welfare state; the success of unionism in improving working conditions; the growth of social democracy placing limits on the exploitative capacities of rampant capitalism as well as the triumph of individualism over collectivism.

One of the great theorists of individual power, what has otherwise been termed as *power within*, is German philosopher Friedrich Nietzsche (1844–1900). Nietzsche's theory of *will to power* and of the *Übermensch* or superhuman sees all life as aiming for enhanced power – for its own sake.[74] Here Nietzsche is concerned with power as inner personal strength expressed through self-creation rather than through political power over others. For Nietzsche, the natural power-increasing instinct is an affirmation of life itself. Nietzsche assumed the will to power as the driving motiv-ational force of human behaviour. These ideas contrast with hedonistic assumptions that people are motivated by the pursuit of pleasure and avoidance of pain with the corresponding assumptions of utilitarian theory that ethical action is that which pro-vides the greatest pleasure or happiness for the greatest number.

Nietzsche viewed these hedonistic-utilitarian assumptions as vulgar and unsupported by an actual analysis of human behaviour through history. Humans frequently sacrifice pleasure and happiness for personal power through enhanced autonomy and the possibility of realiz-ing one's talents and abilities. Personal sacrifice of this sort is true of university students taking courses they don't necessarily appreciate, of workers doing jobs they don't enjoy, of soldiers heroically fighting wars they don't want to fight. Such behaviours, according to Nietzsche, are better explained by a will to power hypothesis than by the hypotheses of hedonism or utilitarianism. We don't just act for pleasure and we are not all that adverse to pain – we frequently take on all kinds of pain for the sake of thinking better of ourselves, elevating ourselves in the eyes of others, and for the sake of virtue. In contrast, Nietzsche sees weakness and giving in to the power of others as the denial or negation of life. He therefore controversially rejected traditional Christian virtues of humility, meekness and compassion in favour of more Homeric virtues of courage, valour, pride and honour.

Nietzsche's will to power is concerned with an individual affirming life, growth, strength, creativity and beauty. Nietzsche also rejected absolute notions of morality, valid for all people in all times and circumstances, insisting instead that an individual must understand what is right for him or herself, constructing one's own destiny within a given context and circumstances.[75] Becoming who you are and realizing your full potential through the will to power is regarded by Nietzsche as the basis of his 'master morality' of self-confidence and strength, saying 'yes' to one's life, both its pains and struggles as well as its joys and victories.[76] This he contrasted with the 'slave morality' or 'herd morality' of weakness, defensiveness, resentment and reaction – rather than action. While Nietzsche also spoke of power as the ability to overcome resistance and shape one's own environment, for the most part Nietzsche's emphasis on increasing power is directed internally through self-mastery, self-control and cultivating cultural excellence. Realizing values of self-mastery, excellence and fulfilment of personal potential, as espoused in Nietzsche's 'master morality', are the promises that are leveraged in post-bureaucratic organizing through power to initiatives such as culture management.[77]

Power to choose emotional responses

Existentialist philosopher and psychologist Victor Frankl also emphasized cultivating a type of power through developing an awareness of personal feelings and impulses and regulating those impulses to ensure they serve, rather than rule, the self.[78] Assuming control over one's own emotional responses and impulses is a way of expressing personal agency or choice and of affirming personal dignity. When you have strong self-regulation, your rational faculties are given time to moderate your impulsive feelings, enabling you to rise above petty jealousies, frustrations and arguments. You are thereby better able to handle stress and provide frequent and consistent communication. Fur-thermore, you are better equipped to intentionally choose your emotional and behav-ioural responses in different situations in different contexts. With such choice comes personal power and freedom, an inner power that is not dependent on things or titles and therefore one that cannot be taken from you, unless you let it go (see Box 10.6).

Our experience of a situation is further predicated on the meaning we choose to attribute to that event. Applying Frankl's ideas to the organizational context, Alex Pattakos and Elaine Dundon propose the following questions to help you identify and hold yourself accountable for personal responses to negativity within the workplace:

> How do you deal with negativity and complaining from others in your workplace or personal life? Are you a complainer? Why do you complain? What is the payoff from your complaining? Are you willing to change your attitude? If so, what steps can you take to change your attitude? How do you maintain a positive attitude in your personal life and at work?[79]

Pattacos and Dundon additionally propose the following questions for reflecting on the meaning you bring to your work, including workplace relationships, not least your relationship with yourself:

> What opportunities do you have on a daily basis to connect meaningfully with others? Can you describe your core essence or true nature? How would your work be different if you worked in alignment with your core essence? What energizes you at work? What depletes your energy? How could you feel more alive at work?[80]

Box 10.6 Victor Frankl on attaining freedom through enacting power-within

Victor Frankl (1905–1997), the Austrian psychiatrist and founder of Logo Therapy, was a Jewish Holocaust survivor (Figure 10.6). During World War II he was imprisoned in the death camps of Nazi Germany, where he lost his parents, wife and brother, all of whom were murdered in the gas chambers, their bodies incinerated. His sister was his only other family member to survive the death camp ordeal.

Figure 10.6 Victor Frankl.[81]

Frankl was personally tortured and made to endure innumerable indignities. He was never certain if he might be the next victim of Nazi murder or if he would be kept barely alive as one of the emaciated death camp workers, made to drag dead bodies from the gas chambers to the incinerators and later shovel out the ashes from the incinerators and dump them in to pits.

Once, while lying naked and alone in a small cell, Victor was struck by awareness of what he termed 'the last of the human freedoms – to choose one's attitude in any given set of circumstances'.[82] This was a freedom no Nazi captor could take from him. While they had control over his body and environment, they could not control how he would respond to their oppression. As a self-aware being with the power to observe and moderate his responses to his environment, Victor Frankl felt his essential identity was intact. He had the power to decide how his environmental circumstances would affect him.

Psychologist Aaron Beck, who founded cognitive therapy, promoted cultivating self-knowledge by attending to negative self-talk by questioning and disputing absoluteness, finality and universality.[83] Limiting beliefs, such as 'I will *never* be able to get a job' or '*everybody* hates me' can be disputed logically by questioning the absolute certainty of *never* and *everybody*. Similarly, the finality of disempowering beliefs such as 'I am *stupid*' or 'I am an *idiot*', often used as an explanation (or excuse) for failure, can be disputed by identifying contradictory evidence of competencies in areas where personal success has been demonstrated in the past. Weick has indicated the significance of a cognitive strategy of awareness of self-talk in arguing that 'organizations are presumed to talk to themselves'.[84] Other researchers have specifically tested the relationship between an individual's positive self-talk and work performance to make a case for positive self-talk as an effective tool for enhancing personal effectiveness.[85] In their review of this research Stewart, Courtwright and Manz summarize the findings as follows: 'Individuals who practice constructive self-talk feel more control over their work, have higher self-efficacy, and achieve higher performance'.[86]

Challenging limiting beliefs is liberating as it suggests the existence of alternative actions that might be undertaken to achieve a desired objective. For example, in disputing the explanation 'because I am stupid' as the reason for failing an exam, it might suggest a better explanation is that you just didn't properly prepare, with a liberating conclusion that with more preparation the exam can be re-taken and passed. Albert Ellis'[87] ABCDE method (see Box 10.7) is a powerful tool for training people to cultivate their power-within through heightened awareness of their Automatic Negative Thoughts (ANTS); practising to dispute them and replace them with more *empowering* alternatives. Positive Psychology founder Martin Seligman incorporated the ABCDE method into the 'building mental toughness' component of the Master Resilience Training programme he developed for the US military. He explained in an article published in the *Harvard Business Review*:[88]

It starts with Albert Ellis's ABCD model: C (emotional consequences) stem not directly from A (adversity) but from B (one's beliefs about adversity). The sergeants work through a series of A's (falling out of a three-mile run, for example) and learn to separate B's – heat-of-the-moment thoughts about the situation ('I'm a failure') – from C's, the emotions generated by those thoughts (such as feeling down for the rest of the day and thus performing poorly in the next training exercise). They then learn D – how to quickly and effectively dispel unrealistic beliefs about adversity.

Seligman argues that enhancing mental toughness using techniques such as the ABCDE method is one of the necessary 'core competencies for any successful manager'.[89]

Box 10.7 Albert Ellis' ABCDE method for challenging limiting beliefs

Albert Ellis taught an ABCDE method for challenging limiting, depressive thoughts, helping clients to regain their own sense of personal worth, esteem and power:

- A – identify the type of ***adversity*** where negative self-talk and depressing feelings are likely to arise.
- B – identify the negative ***beliefs*** underpinning the negative self-talk and emotional response.
- C – consider the ***consequences*** of holding onto those negative beliefs (i.e., the negative emotional reaction and the disempowerment that follows from it).
- D – ***dispute*** the negative belief by holding it up to scrutiny, asking 'what is the evidence', 'are there alternative explanations?'
- E – become ***energized*** on account of identifying more empowering beliefs.

In concluding this section, consider these techniques that can be used for cultivating power within through self-understanding and self-regulation:

- Be accountable and own your emotional responses to different situations.
- Listen to your self-talk and reframe negative impulses as challenging opportunities.
- Identify your emotional triggers so you can learn to manage them.
- Wait a few seconds, minutes, hours or even days before responding to emotionally charged situations, conflicts or decisions.
- Learn to accept uncertainty, disappointments and frustrations as part of life. Rather than becoming overwhelmed and hopeless, seek to reframe the context by identifying alternative perspectives and even opportunities.

Positive power and resistance

'Where there is power, there is resistance' said Michael Foucault.[90] Resistance involves opposing initiatives imposed from above against the will of those who will be affected by the imposed initiative.[91] If imposed power over infringes on individual freedoms and liberties and minimizes personal power within, then resistance to such domination might be seen as a type of positive power. Management tends to frame any resistance encountered as necessarily illegitimate as it is unauthorized. Yet, as argued by philosopher John Locke, there are natural human rights that even the government does not have a right to violate. These include individual rights to life, liberty and property, which demand that 'no one ought to harm another in his life, health, liberty, or possessions'.[92] While individuals give up some of their liberties to an organization, the organization nonetheless has a responsibility to protect the employees' human dignity by abiding by social rules, laws and ethics. When authority figures act beyond the parameters of their social contract in a manner that is not responsible, then the employees have a moral right and even an obligation to rise up and resist. Such resistance is positive even if not officially sectioned. Resistance can be of two types: (1) resistance by omission: passive efforts to undermine illegitimate organizational actions through withholding consent or support; (2) resistance by commission: active efforts to block, thwart or sabotage illegitimate organizational actions.

Resistance can be a force for good that cannot only benefit the organization but society more broadly. A historic case where resistance was absent was the classic case of the Ford Pinto, a car manufactured between 1971–1980. The car had a design fault with the fuel tank positioned in the rear of the vehicle, a safety hazard for rear-end collisions. When Ford became aware of the fault they used National Highway Traffic Safety estimates to do a cost-benefit analysis: accounting for 180 deaths which they converted to $200,000 each in compensation costs (the estimated cost of a human life), 180 injuries costing $67,000 each, with additional costs for the repair of 12,100 cars at an average cost of $700 each, they concluded it would be cheaper to absorb these costs (total $49.5 million), rather than recall the 12,500,000 cars sold and on the road to modify the tank at a cost of merely $11 each (the cheapest of the options considered), which they calculated would cost $137 million (12.5 million vehicles × $11).[93] Anand, Ashforth and Joshi reflect on the fundamental flaw in Ford's rational, legal but immoral conclusion: 'the decision was no longer about human life; it was an economic choice between the cost of a recall versus the cost of foregoing a recall. Ultimately, hundreds died or suffered severe burns'.[94] By 1978, Ford had been forced to pay millions in compensation, to recall 1.5 million vehicles to modify the fuel tank and its reputation had been severely tarnished but, most significantly, hundreds of people had lost their lives because of Ford's economic rationalism.

Parrhesiastes – speaking truth to power

Foucault described *parrhesiastes*, which is a Greek term for 'speaking truth to power', as a type of resistance.[95] *Parrhesiastes* is enacted in an asymmetrical power relation, with the person who speaks in a position of lesser authority. The act of speaking has the effect of disrupting or unsettling the status quo. The speaker talks openly about what he/she knows to be true. In speaking so openly, the *parrhsiastes* take risks and may even place themselves in the way of danger. In this regard James O'Toole reflects in *Time* magazine on the naming of three women in 2002 as 'Persons of the Year' for revealing fraud and corruption in their respective organizations:[96]

> In 2002, Enron's Sherron Watkins, WorldCom's Cynthia Cooper, and the FBI's Coleen Rowley were recognized as *Time* magazine's 'Persons of the Year' for courageously bringing news to the men at the top of their respective organizations

that those leaders preferred not to hear. As *Time* reported, the honored trio weren't looking to curry favor, weren't looking for publicity, didn't want to be whistle-blowers, and all three – primary breadwinners in their families – courted great risk in terms of their jobs and careers. Sadly, not only did their warnings about serious ethical violations go unheeded by their bosses, the women then were marginalized, isolated, scorned, and reviled by their organizations for their efforts to save them. So why did they dare to speak truth to power? Their motivations differed, but the actions of all three were rooted in what they saw as a moral imperative to act.

Speaking truth to power involves many risks, not just for the speaker but for others who may be impacted as well. O'Toole suggests that if speaking truth to power is to be a positive virtue (see Box 10.8), it must fulfil specific preconditions:

Before speaking truth to power can be considered virtuous, the act must meet seven criteria:

1. It must be truthful.
2. It must do no harm to innocents.
3. It must not be self-interested (the benefits must go to others, or to the organization).
4. It must be the product of moral reflection.
5. It must come from a messenger who is willing to pay the price.
6. It must have at least a chance of bringing about positive change (there is no virtue in tilting at windmills).
7. It must not be done out of spite or anger.[97]

Box 10.8 Positive in the negative, negative in the positive

Counterintuitively the job of CEO can be a barrier to gaining truthful information about the company. Direct reports filter information to be seen in their best light. As Hal Gregersen, CEO of the MIT Leadership Center explains: 'Power and prestige insulate most CEOs from ideas and information that might alert them to looming opportunities or threats'.[98] Walt Bettinger, CEO of Charles Schwab, describes this as a dilemma that takes two forms: 'people telling you what they think you want to hear, and people being fearful to tell you things they believe you don't want to hear'.[99] Executives therefore need to put effort into breaking down the barriers that surround them, so a broad range of organizational stakeholders have access and can voice their concerns, insights and suggestions. It also requires a change in mindset where the CEO becomes a better listener and better at asking questions, remaining open to the idea that they might have limited or wrong information and, accordingly, may have made wrong decisions.

Gregersen suggests there are specific signs to which the CEO can also attune herself or himself: this is when the people around them become 'unusually uncomfortable, and uncharacteristically quiet'. Detecting these signals can help these people frame questions to uncover unknown information.

Whistleblowing

A way of enacting resistance and *parrhesiastes* or *speaking truth to power* in the organizational context is whistleblowing (also referenced in O'Toole's reflections cited above about *Time* magazine's 2002 'Persons of the Year').[100] The types of alleged wrongdoing exposed by a whistleblower may include the violation of state or company regulations, policies or laws; activities deemed to threaten the public interest or security and various forms of corruption or fraud.[101] Whistleblowers may bring attention to alleged wrongdoing both by reporting to people within the organization such as a supervisor or an ombudsperson, or to external bodies such as the media, government, law enforcement authorities or other stakeholders. Being a whistleblower takes great courage, as they often have to face retaliation from those whom they accuse of wrongdoing (see Box 10.9 for an ancient example).

Box 10.9 Antigone: an ancient case with relevance to organizations today

Separately, management scholars James O'Toole[102] and Alessia Contu[103] make reference to Antigone, the heroine of a play written some 2,400 years ago by Greek playwright Sophocles[104] as an example of *parrhesiastes*, to consider the role played by whistleblowers in raising awareness to expose illegal or unethical practices within an organization.

The play *Antigone* opens in the aftermath of a battle between Antigone's brothers, Eteocles and Polyneices, each fighting to be the sole ruler of the city-state of Thebes, in which each dies in the battle. Their uncle Creon, the Theban king, orders Eteocles' body to be honoured for his loyalty to Creon with a proper burial, while Polyneices' body should be left as food for wild animals as punishment for attacking the city to overthrow Creon. For the Greeks, this is a severe punishment as they held a proper burial as necessary for going on to the afterlife. Antigone, who loves both of her brothers, tries to persuade her sister Ismene to join her in burying their brother Polyneices' body in resistance to Creon's decree that anyone caught doing so will be put to death. Ismene cannot be persuaded to violate Creon's decree, as his word is the law. Antigone responds that the 'divine' law of the gods supersedes the law of any mortal man.

Figure 10.7 Sebastian Norbin's depiction of Antigone violating Creon's decree by burying her brother Polyneices.[105]

Alone, Antigone sets out to bury her brother's body (Figure 10.7). When she is caught, she makes no apology for doing what is just. Antigone is locked up in a cave without food or water. Creon's son, Haemon, pleads for her release, telling his father that he and Antigone have engaged to be married. Antigone eventually commits suicide and when Haemon learns of her death he kills himself. When Creon's wife Euridice receives news of her son's death, she too ends her life. The proud Creon is diminished to nothing for his hubris in violating divine law – he has his kingdom but has lost his family and the favour of the gods.

Modes of retaliation that whistleblowers may face include legal action with criminal charges, social stigma, being demoted and losing privileges such as an office or position, or being fired from their job. In the aftermath of the Global Financial Crisis (GFC) laws protecting whistleblowers were strengthened in the US and other countries. The GFC left a trail of casualties that included institutions that were considered impenetrable such as Lehman Brothers, as well as small businesses and individuals who lost employment, places of residence and entire retirement savings. Most blame for the crisis landed with the Wall Street banking sector.[106] A two-year US Senate inquiry described the causes of the crisis as 'high risk, complex financial products; undisclosed conflicts of interest; the failure of regulators, the credit rating agencies, and the market itself to rein in the excesses of Wall Street'.[107] Seeking to learn from past mistakes and ensure a better future, government reforms have been enacted across the globe to ensure greater accountability and transparency. President Obama signed the Dodd-Frank Wall Street Reform and Consumer Protection Act into law in July – 2010[108] (since repealed by the Trump administration – although, according to the Brookings Institution, the structure of the act remains mainly intact).[109] The Act promotes regulatory and risk management processes as well as ethical standards and accountability. It also empowered the Securities and Exchange Commission to establish a Consumer Protection Fund, worth hundreds of millions of dollars, to provide financial rewards to encourage whistleblowers to report corruption.

Questions concerning the legitimacy and moral responsibility of the whistleblower are the subject of ongoing ethical debate. While one perspective sees whistleblowing as the unethical breach of confidentiality, especially in industries that handle sensitive client or patient information, a competing view sees whistleblowing as an act of civil disobedience aimed at protecting the public from corporate and state wrongdoing. A few of the most high profile whistleblowers that have brought attention to alleged corporate wrongdoing are listed in Table 10.5. Some have lost their jobs and faced prosecution for bringing attention to areas of concern, while others have been awarded significant payments through court processes.

Courage

Monica Worline and Robert Quinn have theorized the courage it takes to resist misconduct in organizations. Courage is required to disrupt the organizational status quo through organizational actions of initiative taking, ethical decision making, perseverance, innovation, speaking up, dissenting and whistleblowing.[113] Worline and Quinn invoke the American transcendentalist philosopher Henry David Thoreau's statement concerning 'action from principle' in doing what is 'right'[114] to theorize organizational

Table 10.5 Famous whistleblowers who exposed alleged organizational wrongdoing

2002	Sherron Watkins	Enron	Watkins was Vice President of Corporate Development at former energy giant Enron when in August 2001 she sent an email alerting then-Enron CEO Kenneth Lay to accounting irregularities in Enron's financial reports. Watkins was jointly named as one of *Time* Magazine's three 'Persons of the Year 2002'.[110]
2003	Courtland Kelly	General Motors	Kelly was head of inspection and quality assurance at General Motors when he found that some of the company's car models had faulty ignition switches, which cut power to the vehicle while in motion.[111] After repeatedly reporting his concerns to his supervisors, with minimal response, in 2003 he opened a case against the company, which he lost. The faults were eventually linked to fatalities and in 2014 the company was fined $35 million by the US government.
2009	Linda Almonte	JP Morgan Chase	Almonte was the Chase Assistant Vice President who brought attention to the bank's corrupt debt collection practices that harmed customers.[112] When filing debt collection cases Chase frequently calculated incorrect fees and interest, leading to judgments for wrong amounts. The company also practiced 'robo-signing', forging signatures on affidavits and other documents without the signer's permission. Almonte filed a lawsuit regarding the corrupt practices under the Dodd Frank Act whistleblower programme and in 2015 the company was required to pay $166 million in penalties and at least $50 million in consumer restitution.

courage as principled action that challenges the values enabled or constrained by various organizational forms (for more on Thoreau and his courageous resistance see Box 10.10). More specifically, they define organizationally courageous principled action as 'individually embodying the highest ideals of the organization even in violation of regular routines and protocols'.[115] Or, in other words: 'when people must draw on their intuitive, emotional, interpersonal, and cognitive resources in order to undertake actions in line with the highest goals of the organization but not part of the accepted routine or status quo'. Worline theorizes that such organizational courage requires the internalization of two important dimensions, which she describes as: 'the simultaneous expression of individuation, an individual's ability to stand apart from the crowd; and involvement, an individual's ability to internalize the values and aims of the collective'.[116]

> ## Box 10.10 Henry David Thoreau, an inspirational and influential example of courageous resistance
>
> One of the great theorists of resistance to the immoral imposition of power is the American poet and philosopher Henry David Thoreau (1817–1862). Author of 20 volumes of works, Thoreau's most famous publications are *Walden, or Life in the Woods* and *Civil Disobedience*, originally titled as *Resistance to Civil Government*. The book *Walden* describes his two years, two months and two days experiment with living apart from society in the natural surroundings of Walden Pond in

Massachusetts.[117] Thoreau believed that by living in nature, independent of the material facilities of civilization, he was taking back his own inner power or soul. He found that in nature he needed little to live, producing his own food and living in a small cabin he built with his own hands. Describing his experiment in his book *Walden*, Thoreau compresses his time at Walden Pond into a single year comprising the four seasons, seasons that he interprets as symbolizing human growth and experienced by those on a spiritual quest. Today *Walden* is regarded as a classic of American literature, exploring natural simplicity, beauty and harmony as exemplars for the development of just cultural and social situations and institutions.

While living in the small cottage that he had built at Walden Pond, Thoreau went one day into the local town of Concord where he by chance met the regional tax collector who demanded that Thoreau pay his taxes for the previous six years. Thoreau refused out of principle, on account of his opposition to the Mexican–American War and American practices of slavery. Thoreau condemned the Mexican–American War, viewing the US as a foreign occupying force that had subjugated Mexico for purposes of expanding slave territory. He was therefore arrested and spent the night in jail. The following day he was released when an anonymous benefactor, possibly his aunty, in violation of his will, paid his taxes. Thoreau's experience of being jailed had a significant influence in cementing his commitment to the cause of resisting government injustice. Two years subsequent to this episode he delivered a public address titled 'The rights and duties of the individual in relation to government', wherein he described his tax resistance and made his case for standing up to morally reprehensible state laws or else be implicated in the perpetrating of injustice: 'Law never made men a wit more just; and, by means of their respect of it, even the well-disposed are daily made the agents of injustice' (p. 38). He advocated that when the state law is unjust, 'then, I say, break the law' (p. 45). A later revision of this address was published as *Resistance to Civil Government*, also known as *Civil Disobedience*.[118]

Thoreau's *Civil Disobedience* had 'left a deep impression' on Mahatma Gandhi (1869–1948). It inspired him to resist British rule in India through non-violent non-cooperation, which helped energize the divided independence movement and win new supporters to the cause.[119] Gandhi took inspiration from Thoreau's argument that,

> If a thousand men were not to pay their tax bills this year, that would not be a violent and bloody measure, as it would be to pay them, and enable the State to commit violence and shed innocent blood. This is, in fact the definition of a peaceable revolution … When the subject has refused allegiance, and the officer has resigned his office, then the revolution is accomplished.

Someone inspired by both Thoreau and Gandhi was Dr Martin Luther King, who applied non-violent resistance in opposing racial segregation, bringing attention to the cause that resulted in changes to legislation that saw the collapse of formal segregation in the USA. King acknowledged the influence of Gandhi's example and teachings of satya, satyagraha and ahimsa in his acceptance of the Nobel Peace Prize in 1964, commending 'the magnificent way Mohandas Gandhi' provided as a 'successful precedent' for using 'only the weapons of truth, soul force, non-injury and courage ... to challenge the might of the British Empire'.[120]

Recognizing that courageous action takes different forms in different organizational contexts, Worline and Quinn provide an analysis of organizational courage based upon the competing values framework that accounts for four different types of organizational design: bureaucracy, clan, market and adhocracy.[121] The competing logics that drive these forms have value implications, which in turn have implications for the enactment of courageous principled action:

- In a bureaucracy (such as that theorized by Weber and discussed earlier) where obedience, conformity and discipline are valued, courage can be called upon in questioning outdated rules or blowing the whistle on unethical behaviour.
- In a clan organization that values loyalty, trust and unity by promoting shared goals and rewards that may lead to groupthink and a false sense of homogeneity, courage may be required to enact individual initiative and express personal ambition.
- In a market organization that promotes competition, rugged individualism and ambition that may be damaging relationships and any sense of community, courage will be required for violating cultural norms by being honest, compassionate and trusting of one's peers.
- In an adhocracy that values innovation, initiative and adaptability, courage is critical for addressing ambiguity, poor coordination and a lack of focus by taking responsibility and holding oneself accountable for organizational outcomes.

What is particularly interesting about Worline and Quinn's analysis of courage using this framework of various organizational forms is that it reveals that courageous action need not be viewed as something that is called for only in the face of non-routine challenges. Rather, depending on the type of organization, different manifestations of courage may be required for challenging the status quo as an ongoing workplace accomplishment. They further theorize that courageous principled action may be important for instigating and maintaining organizational change when the organizational form is no longer a proper fit to its environment.

Final comments

Power and its use is often considered as reprehensible and a source of individual corruption. However, it depends how power is used. Power may be a positive force when used appropriately in the pursuit of right and good ends. In this chapter using a framework of power over, power to, power with and power within, we have explored various power relations. More specifically, we have explored the potential of positive power as social relational processes that are generative, empowering and facilitative of individual and collective flourishing. In contrast, we have distinguished between negative power as relations that are imposed against a person's will, and positive power as relations that an individual voluntarily enters into.

Want more?

Surprisingly there is very little published literature on positive organizational power. However, the following resources will give you a deeper understanding of some of the topics discussed in this chapter. For a critical reflective analysis of positive (but also negative) power within organizations, including analysis using Etzioni and Clegg's models of organizational power, read Simpson, Clegg and Freeder's article 'Power, compassion and organization'.[122] In discussing organizational compassion as a mode of power relations, the authors also provide a concise overview of organizational power theory. For a more informed understanding of polyphony, consider Kornberger, Clegg and Carter's article 'Rethinking the polyphonic organization: managing as discursive practice'.[123] The authors elaborate on the concept of the polyphonic organization by exploring polyphony in Kafka's reading of the story of the Tower of Babel and applying it to the organizational context. To better understand *parrhesiastes* and whistleblowing in the contesting of truth and power in organizations read Weiskopf and Tobias-Miersch's (2016) paper 'Whistleblowing, parrhesia and the contestation of truth in the workplace'.[124] The authors situate their analysis within the context of the case of whistleblower Guido Strack, a former section leader of the Publications Office of the European Union.

Glossary

Authoritative power   Authoritative power involves individuals voluntarily consenting to submit themselves to the will of another because they regard doing so as bowing to a legitimate imperative.

Charismatic authority   Charismatic authority relies on an individual's exceptional qualities of heroism, character or humanity for attracting followers – sometimes with the appeal of a new vision of life, promises of ending different forms of suffering and achieving greater prosperity and wellbeing.

Coercive domination   Coercive power is imposed by force and is therefore generally viewed as illegitimate domination or negative power over others, who are forced to act in a manner that they would not ordinarily do.

Courage   Organizational courage is defined by Worline and Quinn as principled action enacted on individual initiative by drawing on resources to uphold an organization's highest values and ideals, even when doing so violates the status quo of regular organizational routines.

Groupthink   Organizational members ignoring important counterfactual information and making poor decisions in an effort to maintain group harmony is described as groupthink.

Negative power   Negative power is manipulative, coercive, violent, dominating, constraining, antagonistic, destructive and inhibitive.

Panopticon   The panopticon design proposed by Jeremy Bentham involved prison cells arranged in a circular shape around a central watch-tower, with the guard unseen by prisoners who accordingly never knew when they were being watched. The guard's ability to watch prisoners unseen would induce prisoners to objectify themselves in terms of society's gaze, ensuring that they enact self-discipline, self-control and self-regulation in accordance with the expectations of society.

Parrhesiastes A Greek term for 'speaking truth to power', generally in an asymmetrical power relation, with the person who speaks in a position of lesser authority. The act of speaking has the effect of disrupting or unsettling the status quo. The speaker talks openly about what they know to be true.

Personalized charisma Personalized charisma prioritizes personal ambitions over that of followers and a collective organization. Leaders with personalized charisma feel that their followers and organization exist for their own benefit. These leaders willingly act in a manner that is authoritarian, exploitative, narcissistic, self-aggrandizing and non-egalitarian.

Polyphony The recognition and encouragement of conflicting and competing voices within an organizational context, as opposed to insisting on organizational members artificially conforming to a singular language, generating homogenized monotonic communication.

Positive power Positive power relations are voluntarily entered into (as opposed to coercively imposed) and are generative, empowering and facilitative in their effects.

Power Power is a multidimensional construct that is a fundamental property of any system and is necessary for facilitating and enabling structures. Power is essentially social relations that mould the unfolding or inhibition of capabilities, choices and change. It is not a thing with essential qualities but rather relations between people struggling for meaning.

Power over The probability that actor A in a social relation can influence actor B to carry out their will. Coercive power-over is enacted by force whereas authoritative power-over relies on voluntary submission.

Power to Facilitative empowerment supporting an individual's *power to* act and enact their will without interference.

Power with Coactive *power with* facilitates personal development and growth through collaborative and democratic governance practices.

Power within *Power within* relates to an individual's personal sense of their own self-worth and self-understanding. Included herein is the capacity and ability to be accountable for one's emotional responses and choices and thereby live with a sense of inhalable freedom of will.

Rational–legal authority Rational-legal authority is based upon belief in the legality of rules, policies and systems, organized in a rational manner towards the achievement of agreed-upon objectives, as well as in the legitimacy of those holding positions of authority from which they can issue commands.

Resistance The opposing of initiatives imposed from above that violate the will of others affected by the imposed initiative is referred to as resistance. When the imposition infringes on individual freedoms and liberties and minimizes personal power within, such resistance to domination might be seen as a type of positive power within. Management tends to frame any resistance encountered as necessarily illegitimate because it is unauthorized. From this perspective, any resistance to anything management decrees will always be illegitimate, irrespective of the substantive strength of objections.

Socialized charisma Socialized charisma is directed towards addressing the needs of followers and an organization more broadly. Leaders with socialized charisma demonstrate inclusiveness, egalitarianism and empowerment.

Traditional authority Traditional authority relies on the authority of culture, customs and conventions and belief in the sanctity of 'immortal' traditions.

Whistleblower A person who brings attention to and exposes illegal or unethical practices within an organization – literally someone who sees a criminal committing a crime and alerts authorities by blowing a whistle.

Notes

1 Amy Allen (2013).
2 Naím (2014); Nye Jr (2011).
3 Clegg, Courpasson and Phillips (2006, pp. 2–3).
4 Clare Hollingworth, then a young reporter, reported the story in the scoop of the century in the *Daily Telegraph*, on Tuesday, August 29, 1939, when she accidentally saw massed German troops and tanks at the Polish border. World War II was about to be unleashed. Clare lived to be 105 and died in 2017.
5 Barron (2018).
6 Baker (2015).
7 Rottinghaus and Vaughn (2015).
8 McCombs (2013).
9 Koehn (2013, p. BU1).
10 Title of a text included in Abraham Lincoln's Classroom (The Lehman Institute, n.d.). The text is based on Burlingame (2013). The excerpts included in this box are extracted from that text.
11 Pfeffer (2010, p. 177).
12 Haugaard (2012a); VeneKlasen, Miller, Budlender and Clark (2002).
13 Lounsbury and Carberry (2005)
14 Weber (1978, p. 53).
15 Retrieved from: https://commons.wikimedia.org/wiki/File:Max_Weber_1894.jpg. Work is in the public domain.
16 Weber (1922/1978).
17 Bass and Steidlmeier (1999).
18 Potts (2016).
19 Chamorro-Premuzic (2012).
20 Klein and House (1995).
21 Author: Kanu Gandhi. Retrieved from: https://commons.wikimedia.org/wiki/File:Gandhi_writing_1942.jpg. Work is in the public domain.
22 Author: Associated Press. Retrieved from: https://commons.wikimedia.org/wiki/File:Queen_Elizabeth_II_-_1953-Dress.JPG. Work is in the public domain.
23 Author: United States Senate. Retrieved from: https://commons.wikimedia.org/wiki/File:BarackObamaportrait.jpg. Image in the public domain.
24 Source: German Federal Archives. Retrieved from https://commons.wikimedia.org/wiki/File:Bundesarchiv_Bild_183-S33882,_Adolf_Hitler_retouched.jpg. This file is licensed under the Creative Commons Attribution-Share Alike 3.0 Germany license.
25 Author: mylerdude. Retrieved from https://commons.wikimedia.org/wiki/File:Stevejobs_Macworld2005.jpg. This file is licensed under the Creative Commons Attribution 2.0 Generic license.
26 Author: Manfredo Ferrari. Retrieved from: https://commons.wikimedia.org/wiki/File:Mutter_Teresa_von_Kalkutta.jpg. This file is licensed under the Creative Commons Attribution-Share Alike 4.0 International license.
27 Howell (1988); Popper (2002).
28 Clegg, Kornberger and Pitsis (2005).
29 Chaplin (1936).
30 Vance (2003).
31 *Film Daily* (1936).
32 Parsons (1963, 1964).
33 Clegg, Courpasson and Phillips (2006); Giddens (1968).
34 Foucault (1980).
35 Foucault (1977).
36 Christie (1993).
37 Source: Jeremy Bentham (https://commons.wikimedia.org/wiki/File:Panopticon.jpg), 'Panopticon', marked as public domain, more details on Wikimedia Commons: https://commons.wikimedia.org/wiki/Template:PD-old.
38 Carter, McKinlay and Rowlinson (2002).
39 Wray-Bliss (2003).

40 Josserand, Teo and Clegg (2006); McKenna, Garcia-Lorenzo and Bridgman (2010).
41 Courpasson (2000, 2005).
42 Barker (1993).
43 Etzioni (1961).
44 Clegg and Dunkerley (2013 [1980]).
45 Simpson, Clegg and Freeder (2013).
46 Haugaard (2012b).
47 Follett (1924)
48 Source: www.vectorstudy.com/management_gurus/mary_parker_follett.htm. Retrieved from https://commons.wikimedia.org/wiki/File:Mary_Parker_Follett_(1868-1933). This file is licensed under the Creative Commons Attribution-Share Alike 2.5 Generic license.
49 Follett and Metcalf (1941/2003).
50 Groysberg, Lee, Price and Cheng (2018).
51 Mackey and Sisodia (2013).
52 Mackey and Sisodia (2013, p. 97).
53 Foucault (1978, p. 140).
54 Page (2011).
55 Logue, Jarvis, Clegg and Hermens (2015).
56 Ezrati (2018).
57 Derived from information on NationMaster.com.
58 Comittee to Protect Journalists (2017).
59 Trianfi (2017).
60 McGill and Slocum (1993).
61 Dimitroff, Schmidt and Bond (2005).
62 Janis (1982).
63 Clegg (1989).
64 Mowbray, Wilkinson and Tse (2015).
65 Burris (2012).
66 Gregersen (2017).
67 Mowbray, Wilkinson and Tse (2015).
68 Edmondson (1999).
69 Cunha, Simpson, Clegg and Rego (2019).
70 Kornberger, Clegg and Carter (2006).
71 Retrieved from https://commons.wikimedia.org/wiki/File:Confusion_of_Tongues.png. This work is in the public domain.
72 Boje (2002).
73 Marx (1844/2009).
74 Nietzsche (1968).
75 Nietzsche (1998).
76 Nietzsche (2001).
77 Johnsen (2015).
78 Frankl (1959).
79 Pattakos and Dundon (2017, p. 45).
80 Pattakos and Dundon (2017, p. 191).
81 Source: Victor Frankl. Retrieved from: Prof. Dr. Franz Vesely (https://commons.wikimedia.org/wiki/File:Viktor_Frankl2.jpg), 'Viktor Frankl2', https://creativecommons.org/licenses/by-sa/3.0/de/legalcode.
82 Frankl (1959, p. 86).
83 Beck (1976).
84 Weick (1979, p. 133).
85 Manz, Adsit, Campbell and Mathison-Hance (1988); Neck and Manz (1996); Seligman and Schulman (1986).
86 Stewart, Courtright and Manz (2011, p. 203).
87 Ellis (1962).
88 Seligman (2011, p. 105).
89 Seligman (2011, p. 106).
90 Foucault (1978 p. 95).

91 Jermier, Knights and Nord (1994).
92 Locke (2014, p. 4).
93 Gioia (1992).
94 Anand, Ashforth and Joshi (2004, p. 13).
95 Foucault (2001).
96 O'Toole (2006, p. 45).
97 O'Toole (2006, p. 74).
98 Gregersen (2017, p. 78).
99 Cited by Gregersen (2017, p. 78).
100 Contu (2014).
101 Near and Miceli (2013).
102 O'Toole (2006).
103 (Contu, 2014).
104 Sophocles (2005).
105 Author: VladoubidoOo. Retrieved from https://commons.wikimedia.org/wiki/File:Sébastien_Nor blin_Antigone_et_Polynice.JPG. This file is licensed under the Creative Commons Attribution-Share Alike 3.0 Unported license.
106 Schechter (2010); Tasini (2009).
107 United States Senate (2011, p. 1).
108 US Congress (2010).
109 Klein (2018).
110 (Lacayo and Ripley, 2002).
111 (Higgins and Summers, 2014).
112 (Danner, 2015).
113 Worline (2012).
114 Thoreau (2016, p. 15).
115 Worline and Quinn (2003, p. 145).
116 Worline (2012, p. 304).
117 Thoreau (2006).
118 Thoreau (2016).
119 Gandhi and Dalton (1996, p. 136).
120 King Jr (1964, p. 12).
121 Cameron and Quinn (2005).
122 Simpson, Clegg and Freeder (2013).
123 Kornberger, Clegg and Carter (2006).
124 Weiskopf and Tobias-Miersch's (2016).

References

Allen, A. (2013). *The politics of our selves: Power, autonomy and gender in contemporary critical theory.* New York: Columbia University Press.

Anand, V., Ashforth, B. E., & Joshi, M. (2004). Business as usual: The acceptance and perpetuation of corruption in organizations. *Academy of Management Perspectives*, 18(2), 39–53.

Baker, P. (2015). Abraham Lincoln, the one President all of them want to be more like. *The New York Times*, April 15, A11.

Barker, J. R. (1993). Tightening the iron cage: Concertive control in self-managing teams. *Administrative Science Quarterly*, 38, 408–437.

Barron, C. (2018). 10 things you may not know about Abraham Lincoln. *Washington Post*, January 11. (www.washingtonpost.com/lifestyle/kidspost/10-things-you-may-not-know-about-abraham-lincoln/2018/02/09/87511a54-0768-11e8-b48c-b07fea957bd5_story.html?noredirect=on&utm_term=.69468a727049).

Bass, B. M., & Steidlmeier, P. (1999). Ethics, character, and authentic transformational leadership behavior. *The Leadership Quarterly*, 10(2), 181–217.

Beck, A. T. (1976). *Cognitive therapy and the emotional disorders* (2nd ed.). Madison, CT: Published by International Universities Press.

Boje, D. M. (2002). Stories of the storytelling organization: A postmodern analysis of Disney as "Tamara-Land". In S. R. Clegg (Ed.), *Central currents in organization studies* (Vol. 7, pp. 29–66). London: Sage.

Burlingame, M. (2013). *Abraham Lincoln: A life* (Vol. 2). Baltimore, MD: John Hopkins University Press.

Burris, E. R. (2012). The risks and rewards of speaking up: Managerial responses to employee voice. *Academy of Management Journal*, 55(4), 851–875.

Cameron, K. S., & Quinn, R. E. (2005). *Diagnosing and changing organizational culture: Based on the competing values framework*. Chichester: John Wiley & Sons.

Carter, C., McKinlay, A., & Rowlinson, M. (2002). Introduction: Foucault, management and history. *Organization*, 9(4), 515–526.

Chamorro-Premuzic, T. (2012). The dark side of charisma. *Harvard Business Review*, 12. Online.

Chaplin, C. (Writer). (1936). *Modern times*: United Artists.

Christie, I. R. (1993). *The Benthams in Russia: 1780–1791*. Oxford: Berg.

Clegg, S. R. (1989). *Frameworks of power*. London: Sage.

Clegg, S. R., Courpasson, D., & Phillips, N. (2006). *Power and organizations*. London: Sage.

Clegg, S. R., & Dunkerley, D. (2013 [1980]). *Organization, class and control*. Oxon: Routledge.

Clegg, S. R., Kornberger, M., & Pitsis, T. (2005). *Managing and organizations: An introduction to theory and practice*. London: Sage Publications.

Committee to Protect Journalists. (2017). 58 journalists killed in Russia motive confirmed. From Committee to Protect Journalists. (https://cpj.org/killed/europe/russia/).

Contu, A. (2014). Rationality and relationality in the process of whistleblowing: Recasting whistleblowing through readings of Antigone. *Journal of Management Inquiry*, 23(4), 393–406.

Cooper, H. (2010). 'Obama signs legislation overhauling financial rules', *New York Times*, July 21. Available at: https://www.nytimes.com/2010/07/22/business/22regulate.html?hp.

Courpasson, D. (2000). Managerial strategies of domination: Power in soft bureaucracies. *Organization Studies*, 21, 141–162.

Courpasson, D. (2005). *Soft constraint: Liberal organizations and domination*. Copenhagen: Copenhagen Business Press/Liber.

Cunha, M. P. E., Simpson, A. V., Clegg, S. R., & Rego, A. (2019). Speak! Paradoxical effects of a managerial culture of 'speaking up'. *British Journal of Management*, 30(4), 829–846.

Danner, P. (Producer). (2015). Regulators slap JPMorgan Chase. June 17. (www.expressnews.com/business/local/article/Regulators-slap-JPMorgan-Chase-6373817.php).

Dimitroff, R. D., Schmidt, L., & Bond, T. (2005). Organizational behavior and disaster: A study of conflict at NASA. *Project Management Journal*, 36(2), 28–38.

Dodd-Frank Wall Street reform and consumer protection act. (2010).

Edmondson, A. C. (1999). Psychological safety and learning behavior in work teams. *Administrative Science Quarterly*, 44(2), 350–383.

Ellis, A. (1962). *Reason and emotion in psychotherapy*. Secaucus, NJ: L. Stuart.

Etzioni, A. (1961). *Complex organizations: A sociological reader*. New York: Holt, Rinehart and Winston.

Ezrati, M. (2018) The German swindle built into the Euro. *Forbes*, January 23. (www.forbes.com/sites/miltonezrati/2018/01/23/the-german-swindle-built-into-the-euro/#4d7c3e4827d) accessed September 12, 2018.

Film Daily. (1936). Reviews, Wid's Films and Film Folk. *Film Daily*, February 7.

Follett, M. P. (1924). *Creative experience*. New York: Longmans, Green and Co.

Follett, M. P., & Metcalf, H. C. (1941/2003). *Dynamic administration: The collected papers of Mary Parker Follett: Early sociology of management and organizations*. Abingdon: Routledge.

Foucault, M. (1977). *Discipline and punish: The birth of the prison* (A. Sheridan, Trans.). New York: Pantheon.

Foucault, M. (1978). *The history of sexuality: An introduction* (Vol. 1). New York: Vintage.

Foucault, M. (1980). *Power/knowledge: Selected interviews and other writings, 1972–1977*. New York: Harvester Wheatsheaf.

Foucault, M. (2001). *Fearless speech*. Los Angeles, CA: Semiotext(e).

Frankl, V. E. (1959). *Man's search for meaning*. Boston, MA: Beacon Press.

Gandhi, M., & Dalton, D. (1996). *Gandhi: Selected political writings*. Indianapolis, IN: Hackett Publishing.

Giddens, A. (1968). 'Power' in the recent writings of Talcott Parsons. *Sociology*, 2, 257–272.

Gioia, D. A. (1992). Pinto fires and personal ethics: A script analysis of missed opportunities. *Journal of Business Ethics*, 11(5-6), 379–389.

Gregersen, H. (2017). Bursting the CEO bubble. *Harvard Business Review*, 95(2), 76–83.

Groysberg, B., Lee, J., Price, J., & Cheng, J. (2018). The leader's guide to corporate culture. *Harvard Business Review*, 96(1), 44–52.

Haugaard, M. (2012a). Editorial: Reflections upon power over, power to, power with, and the four dimensions of power. *Journal of Political Power*, 5(3), 353–358.

Haugaard, M. (2012b). Rethinking the four dimensions of power: Domination and empowerment. *Journal of Political Power*, 5(1), 33–54.

Higgins, T., & Summers, N. (Producer). (2014). GM recalls: How general motors silenced a whistle-blower. June 17, 2017. (www.bloomberg.com/news/articles/2014-06-18/gm-recalls-whistle-blower-was-ignored-mary-barra-faces-congress).

Howell, J. M. (1988). Two faces of charisma: Socialized and personalized leadership in organizations. In J. A. Conger, & R. N. Kanungo (Eds.), *Charismatic leadership: The elusive factor in organizational effectiveness* (pp. 213–236). San Francisco, CA: Jossey-Bass.

Janis, I. L. (1982). *Groupthink*. Boston, MA: Wadsworth.

Jermier, J., Knights, D., & Nord, W. (1994). *Resistance and power in organizations*. London: Routledge.

Johnsen, C. G. (2015). *Who are the post-bureaucrats*. Copenhagen: Copenhagen Business School.

Josserand, E., Teo, S., & Clegg, S. R. (2006). From bureaucratic to post-bureaucratic: The difficulties of transition. *Journal of Organizational Change Management*, 19(1), 54–64. doi: 10.1108/09534810610643686.

King, M. L., Jr. (1964). *Nobel lecture by Martin Luther King*. New York: The King Center.

Klein, A. (2018). *No, Dodd-Frank was neither repealed nor gutted. Here's what really happened*. Brookings Institution. (www.brookings.edu/research/no-dodd-frank-was-neither-repealed-nor-gutted-heres-what-really-happened/).

Klein, K. J., & House, R. J. (1995). On fire: Charismatic leadership and levels of analysis. *The Leadership Quarterly*, 6(2), 183–198.

Koehn, N. F. (2013, 27 January). Lincoln's School of Management. *New York Times*. (www.nytimes.com/2013/01/27/business/abraham-lincoln-as-management-guru.html).

Kornberger, M., Clegg, S. R., & Carter, C. (2006). Rethinking the polyphonic organization: Managing as discursive practice. *Scandinavian Journal of Management*, 22(1), 3–30.

Lacayo, R., & Ripley, A. (Producer). (2002). Persons of the year 2002: The whisteblowers. *Time Magazine*, June 17, 2017 (http://content.time.com/time/magazine/article/0,9171,1003998,00.html).

The Lehman Institute (Producer). (n.d.). Abraham Lincoln's Classroom. September 6, 2018 (www.abrahamlincolnsclassroom.org/abraham-lincoln-in-depth/abraham-lincoln-and-power/#alp).

Locke, J. (2014). *Second treatise of government: An essay concerning the true original, extent and end of civil government*. Hoboken, NJ: John Wiley & Sons.

Logue, D. M., Jarvis, W. P., Clegg, S., & Hermens, A. (2015). Translating models of organization: Can the mittelstand move from Bavaria to Geelong? *Journal of Management & Organization*, 21(01), 17–36.

Lounsbury, M., & Carberry, E. J. (2005). From king to court jester? Weber's fall from grace in organizational theory. *Organization Studies*, 26(4), 0170–8406.

Mackey, J., & Sisodia, R. S. (2013). *Conscious capitalism: Liberating the heroic spirit of business*. Boston, MA: Harvard Business Press.

Manz, C. C., Adsit, D., Campbell, S., & Mathison-Hance, M. (1988). Managerial thought patterns and performance: A study of perceptual patterns of performance hindrances for higher and lower performing managers. *Human Relations*, 41(6), 447–465.

Marx, K. (1844). The economic and philosophical manuscripts. In K. Marx, & F. Engels. (Eds), (2009). *The economic and philosophic manuscripts of 1844 and the communist manifesto* (pp. 13–141). New York: Prometheus Books.

McCombs, G. M. (2013). Abraham Lincoln, management guru! Lessons for library leadership on resilience, true grit, and bouncing forward. *Portal: Libraries and the Academy*, 13(3), 227–231.

McGill, M. E., & Slocum, J. W. (1993). Unlearning the organization. *Organizational Dynamics*, 22(2), 67–79.

McKenna, S., Garcia-Lorenzo, L., & Bridgman, T. (2010). Managing, managerial control and managerial identity in the post-bureaucratic world. *Journal of Management Development*, 29(2), 128–136.

Mowbray, P. K., Wilkinson, A., & Tse, H. H. (2015). An integrative review of employee voice: Identifying a common conceptualization and research agenda. *International Journal of Management Reviews*, 17(3), 382–400.

Naím, M. (2014). *The end of power: From boardrooms to battlefields and churches to states, why being in charge isn't what it used to be*. New York: Basic Books.

Near, J. P., & Miceli, M. P. (2013). Organizational dissidence: The case of whistle-blowing. *Citation Classics from the Journal of Business Ethics*, 153–172. Springer.

Neck, C. P., & Manz, C. C. (1996). Thought self-leadership: The impact of mental strategies training on employee cognition, behavior, and affect. *Journal of Organizational Behavior*, 17(5), 445–467.

Nietzsche, F. (1968). *The will to power* (W. Kaufmann & R. J. Hollingdale, Trans.). New York: Vintage Books.

Nietzsche, F. (1998). *On the genealogy of morals* (D. Smith, Trans.). New York: Oxford University Press.

Nietzsche, F. (2001). *The gay science* (J. Nauckhoff & A. Del Caro, Trans.). Cambridge: Cambridge University Press.

Nye, J. S. Jr., (2009). Get smart: Combining hard and soft power. *Foreign Affairs*, 160–163.

Nye, J. S. Jr. (2011). *The future of power*. New York: Public Affairs.

O'Toole, J. (2006). Speaking truth to power. In W. Bennis, D. Goleman, & J. O'Toole (Eds.), *Transparency: How leaders create a culture of candor* (pp. 45–92). San Francisco, CA: Jossey-Bass.

Page, R. (2011). *Co-determination in Germany-a beginners' guide* (Vol. 33). Düsseldorf: überarbeitete Auflage, Arbeitspapier, No. 33, Hans-Böckler-Stiftung.

Parsons, T. (1963). On the concept of political power. *Proceedings of the American Philosophical Society*, 107(3), 232–258.

Parsons, T. (1964). Evolutionary universals in society. *American Sociological Review*, 29(3), 339–357.

Pattakos, A., & Dundon, E. (2017). *Prisoners of our thoughts: Viktor Frankl's principles for discovering meaning in life and work*. San Francisco, CA: Berrett-Koehler Publishers.

Pfeffer, J. (2010). *Power: Why some people have it-and others don't*. New York: HarperCollins.

Popper, M. (2002). Narcissism and attachment patterns of personalized and socialized charismatic leaders. *Journal of Social and Personal Relationships*, 19(6), 797–809.

Potts, J. (2016). Charisma is a mysterious and dangerous gift. *Aeon*, August 3 (https://aeon.co/ideas/charisma-is-a-mysterious-and-dangerous-gift).

Rottinghaus, B., & Vaughn, J. (2015). New ranking of U.S. presidents puts Lincoln at No. 1, Obama at 18; Kennedy judged most overrated. *Washington Post*, February 16 (www.washingtonpost.com/news/monkey-cage/wp/2015/02/16/new-ranking-of-u-s-presidents-puts-lincoln-1-obama-18-kennedy-judged-most-over-rated/?utm_term=.3d0c31ee8b17).

Schechter, D. (2010). *The crime of our time: Why Wall Street is not too big to jail*. New York: The Disinformation Company.

Seligman, M. E. P. (2011). Building resilience. *Harvard Business Review*, 89(4), 100–106.

Seligman, M. E. P., & Schulman, P. (1986). Explanatory style as a predictor of productivity and quitting among life insurance sales agents. *Journal of Personality and Social Psychology*, 50(4), 832–838.

Simpson, A. V., Clegg, S., & Freeder, D. (2013). Power, compassion and organization. *Journal of Political Power*, 6(3), 385–404.

Sophocles. (2005). *Antigone* (J. E. Thomas Trans. P. Moliken & E. Osborne Eds.). Delaware: Prestwick House.

Stewart, G. L., Courtright, S. H., & Manz, C. C. (2011). Self-leadership: A multilevel review. *Journal of Management*, 37(1), 185–222.

Tasini, J. (2009). *The audacity of greed: Free markets, corporate thieves, and the looting of America.* New York: Ig Publishing.

Thoreau, H. D. (2006). *Walden.* New Heaven, CT: Yale University Press.

Thoreau, H. D. (2016). *Civil disobedience* (B. P. Taylor Ed.). Ontario: Broadview Press.

Trianfi, B. (Producer). (2017). Little hope for independent media in St. Petersburg (https://ipi.media/little-hope-for-independent-media-in-st-petersburg/).

United States Senate. (2011). *Wall Street and the financial crisis: Anatomy of a financial collapse.* Washington (www.hsgac.senate.gov//imo/media/doc/Financial_Crisis/FinancialCrisisReport.pdf?attempt=2).

Vance, J. (2003). *Chaplin: Genius of the cinema.* New York: Harry N Abrams Inc.

VeneKlasen, L., Miller, V., Budlender, D., & Clark, C. (2002). *A new weave of power, people & politics: The action guide for advocacy and citizen participation.* Oklahoma City, OK: World Neighbors.

Weber, M. (1922/1978). *Economy and society: An outline of interpretive sociology.* Berkeley, CA: University of California Press.

Weick, K. E. (1979). *The social psychology of organizing (Topics in social psychology series).* Columbus, OH: McGraw-Hill Humanities.

Weiskopf, R., & Tobias-Miersch, Y. (2016). Whistleblowing, parrhesia and the contestation of truth in the workplace. *Organization Studies*, 37(11), 1621–1640.

Worline, M. C. (2012). Courage in organizations: An integrative review of the "difficult virtue". In K. M. Cameron, & G. M. Spreitzer (Eds.), *The Oxford handbook of positive organizational scholarship* (pp. 304–315). New York: Oxford University Press.

Worline, M. C., & Quinn, R. E. (2003). Courageous principled action. In K. S. Cameron, J. E. Dutton, & R. E. Quinn (Eds.), *Positive organizational scholarship: Foundations of a new discipline* (pp. 138–157). San Francisco, CA: Berrett-Koehler Publishers.

Wray-Bliss, E. (2003). Quick fixes, management culture and drug culture: Excellence and ecstasy, BPR and brown. *Culture and Organization*, 9(3), 161–176.

11 The positive organization of progress

Summary and objectives

Historically the relationship between business and society has been contested. This chapter explores the nature of that relationship from three perspectives. The *ethical* perspective will provide a review of a range of philosophical ideas related to what the normative relationship between entrepreneurship and society *ought to be*. Considering what have been the dominant impacts of organizations on society, the *empirical* perspective demonstrates both negative and positive effects. From a *prudential* (*or pragmatist*) perspective, the focus is on how leaders exercise judgement in pursuing policies with the practical objective of minimizing the harmful effects of business organizations on society and maximizing the positive benefits. This third domain analysis of positive possibilities forms the primary focus of this chapter as we consider a range of practical business models emphasizing social benefits over a narrow emphasis on profit maximization.

Towards socio-economic wellbeing

Organizations are social by constitution. They are social constructs designed, reproduced and changed by human ingenuity: some people are employed to do business with suppliers or customers, other people own them, and yet others manage them (although at the senior levels managers may also be significant shareholders) and their effects, spatial, environmental, economic and social, can have significant local and global impact. There is obvious potential for both positive and negative outcomes. Yet, so often, an emphasis on efficiency, productivity and profitability leads to management by numbers on a spreadsheet (see the Ford Pinto case in Chapter 10) that is oriented to metrics of the good that stress only narrow conceptions of profit and loss rather than the sum of human wellbeing. The social impact of organizations is under-theorized in management research and under-emphasized in management practice.[1]

This chapter explores the role of capitalist organizations in society. These are organizations whose prime motive, by definition, is to devise forms of organizational ingenuity with which to try and make profits for investors. Critical scholars stress the social and material impacts of business on society while pursuing these profits, while managerial scholars tend to be more interested in enhancing organizational efficiency in so doing. We will seek to steer a course that avoids criticism and managerialism as *a priori* points of departure. The normative assumption that organizations have a fundamental role to play in the development of societies frames our enquiries. The role may be enacted in more or less good ways. For instance, we would argue that normatively only fascists could support the organizational ingenuity that delivered the Holocaust:[2] some societies are premised on evil institutions that routinely deliver death or, at best, human bondage to those who toil within them.[3] Normatively, we prefer the organizational ingenuity that delivers more rather than less organizational democracy, equality and efficiency and does so both peacefully and profitably with regard for those bodies for whom the claim of species being, the ability of members of the species to recognize themselves as such, can be made.

Surplus is important for all forms of investment, including production of a better society to justify this ethical blindness. It is not, however, so important as to justify ethical blindness as to its provenance. If it were, slavery and forced labour would not be stigmatized and exploitative labour relations would be celebrated. Note, however, that, by Kelly's well-grounded estimation,[4] supported by the Global Slavery Index's estimates,[5] the stigma may not be too strong: there are in excess of 46 million slaves in the contemporary world, while some estimates put the number as high as 70 million. Note also that there would not be strong support for the 'flexible arrangements' of the gig economy. As Talentino writes in *The New Yorker*:[6]

> It does require a fairly dystopian strain of doublethink for a company to celebrate how hard and how constantly its employees must work to make a living, given that these companies are themselves setting the terms … the American obsession with self-reliance … makes it more acceptable to applaud an individual for working himself to death than to argue that an individual working himself to death is evidence of a flawed economic system. The contrast between the gig economy's rhetoric (everyone is always connecting, having fun, and killing it!) and the conditions that allow it to exist (a lack of dependable employment that pays a living wage) makes this kink in our thinking especially clear.

Accordingly, the major concern of this chapter discusses how business organizations might contribute towards social wellbeing. As our measure of success, we focus not on the contribution of business towards economic growth. Wealth being a means towards an end, we are more concerned with how business organizations can contribute towards the ends of enhanced human rights protections, health, longevity, security and peace. We organize the material discussed in this chapter using a framework with three areas of analysis: (1) ethical (2) empirical and (3) prudential (Table 11.1).[7]

The *ethical* perspective tries to answer the question of: 'what ought to be'? It is concerned with values and has philosophy as its foundation. This domain is normative in prescribing that organizational activity ought to promote social wellbeing. Organizational activity is good in as much as it achieves the objective of enhanced social

Table 11.1 Three domains of analysis.

Analysis/perspective	Basis	Question	Discipline
Ethical	Values	What ought to be?	Philosophy
Empirical	Facts	What is?	Science
Prudential	Judgement	What can be?	Policy

wellbeing, while it is bad in as much as it fails in this achievement. Our review of the literature will touch on more than two thousand years of Western thought, from the classical Greek philosopher Socrates to the medieval Church and Enlightenment philosophy. The benefit of such a broad review is that it introduces us to some of the most influential thinking that has formed the foundational bedrock of Western civilization through the ages to the current day.

Our *empirical* analysis focusses on providing a descriptive understanding of the relationship between organizational activity and society, with a focus on the question of: 'what is'? Here we are concerned with observing actual phenomena by drawing on scientific observation as our foundation as we consider economic data collected over centuries. The analysis suggests that the organization of business activity has both positive and negative social impacts. The question, then, is how to maximize the benefits while inhibiting the harmful effects, which is the focus of our final major section.

The *prudential* analysis focusses on considering how the pragmatics of judgement influence the contingencies associated with business organizations generating profits while reducing social harm and fostering social benefits. Our primary question here concerns: 'what can be'? We address this question by considering the role of policy in informing organizational practices. We consider practical actions organizations can take and are taking to be a force for good in the world, using models such as corporate social responsibility, creating shared value, stakeholder theory, conscious capitalism, sustainability and B Corps. While considering these different models, we will also reflect on their limitations. In keeping with the positive objectives of this textbook, the third prudential analysis will form the chapter's major focus.

The ethical approach: a philosophical overview

A widely held assumption of our time is that business organizations drive societal progress by creating jobs, producing needed products and services, and investing in innovative technologies that solve human problems. This assumption is a relatively recent view, emerging in the 17 and 18th centuries with the enlightenment and advent of industrial capitalism. It is a view socially constructed in quite specific ways. We can gain insight into these by contrasting them with past constructions.

Through much of history, philosophers, religious leaders and rulers viewed the merchant as socially malignant. Those fortunate enough to have aristocratic and noble forms of life did not truck, trade or barter other than in primary products that their estates produced, the fruits of which they might spend in the noble pursuits of hunting, shooting, fishing and the social life of courtly society. The bias against trade was deep seated in the texts of classical education with which nobility, or at least the male half of it, would have had some familiarity.

Classical philosophers

For the classical philosopher Socrates (469–499 BC; Box 11.1, Figure 11.1), as reported in Plato's *Republic*, the ideal form of government is aristocracy, a just government ruled by the philosopher (lover of wisdom) king who emphasizes virtue.[8] Third best is oligarchy, or rule by the wealthy merchant, emphasizing the accumulation of wealth. In between is timocracy, or rule by the spirited warrior class, emphasizing honour. The least good forms of governance are democracy (or rule by the masses emphasizing

Figure 11.1 The Death of Socrates (centre, with Plato at the base of the bed), by Jacques-Louis David 1787.[9]

freedom) and tyranny (emphasizing the ruler's retention of power by any means). For Socrates, the problem with oligarchy, or rule by the merchant, is its inherent instability, in that it widens the gap between the rich and the poor, culminating in mass revolt by the underclass leading to democracy, which, in his view, would eventually lead to tyranny, as the unruly nature of the demos revealed itself through social disorder. Plato had a negative experience with Athenian democracy, which sentenced his teacher Socrates to death as a legal consequence of his asking politico-philosophic questions that were disconcerting to the city's elites.

Aristotle also distrusted merchants. He emphasized a state governed by a virtuous middle class of free men (women were not included) heading self-sufficient households, where independent craftsmen, or slaves deemed unworthy of citizenship, provided material needs. The possession of sufficient wealth was granted as necessary for civic engagement (voting in the agora and military duty to defend the city) and the exercise of virtuous liberality and magnanimity in sacrificing for the common good. The active pursuit of wealth through trade was regarded as morally hazardous – 'the trafficking in goods' through commerce, where wealth is the means and objective of exchange, was viewed not only as counter to political virtue but also individual moral wellbeing: 'the citizens should not live a vulgar … or a merchant's way of life', Aristotle wrote, 'for this sort of way of life is ignoble and contrary to virtue'.[10] Athenian bankers, merchants and moneylenders were denied citizenship.[11]

Early Christian Church attitudes

The Christian Gospels and early Church Fathers were similarly suspicious and even hostile towards merchants and trade (Figure 11.2). According to the Apostle Mark, Jesus drove out all of those 'that sold and bought in the temple', as he 'overthrew the tables of the moneychangers, and the seats of them that sold doves'.[12] The Apostle Matthew reports that, in his Sermon on the Mount, Jesus preached 'For where your

Figure 11.2 Christ driving money changers from the temple by El Greco, 1568.[15]

treasure is, there will your heart be also', and 'Ye cannot serve God and mammon'.[13] The *Decretum*, a collection of canon law from the middle of the 12th century, referenced these passages declaring: 'The man who buys in order that he may gain by selling it again unchanged as he bought it, that man is of the buyers and sellers who are cast forth from God's temple'.[14]

In the late Middle Ages, a more urban economy arose with the development of cities as the bonds of feudalism were increasingly weakened by peasant revolt, bubonic plague and pestilence, the latter caused by calorific shortfalls because of the exhaustion of available land with the available technology and diminishing yields in the face of an increasing population.[16] New financial institutions began to emerge in the wealthy city states that developed as interstices of capitalism in the feudal economy, notably with the crucial historical development of a banking system in the affluent medieval cities of Florence, Venice and Genoa. As banking flourished in the heart of Roman Catholic Europe the Church began to reconsider its endorsement of biblical injunctions against the practice.

The Scholastic theologians headed by Thomas Aquinas presented a reconsidered Church position on commerce that reconciled the Church with the views of the texts of the newly rediscovered Aristotle.[17] Private property was held to be legitimate as it was the basis for the family and social order, where division of labour 'naturally' led to the hierarchy of the estates (status groups). Economic activity was necessary for a family head to support their dependents at a level appropriate to the standards of their estate. Efforts to improve one's position within the social order beyond that naturally ordained was counter to the virtues of humility and meekness and linked to the cardinal sins of lust and greed. To be godly was to know and remain in one's station in life.

Protestants, including English Puritans and Dutch Calvinists, initially also saw the pursuit of wealth as a threat to salvation. The founder of Methodism, John Wesley, observed an associated contradiction in religion and wealth generation:

> religion must necessarily produce both industry and frugality and these cannot but produce riches. But as riches increase, so will pride, and love for the world in all its branches.[18]

This was the central conundrum that the Protestant Ethic resolved when it conjoined with the spirit of capitalism to produce the motive structure for primitive accumulation and its accounting.[19]

No form of wealth generation was more disdained than usury, the lending of money for interest, which the classical philosophers found blameworthy and the Church fathers and medieval theologians held to be sinful. The 23rd chapter of Deuteronomy (the fifth book of the Torah and the Christian Old Testament) stated, 'You may lend with interest to strangers, but to your brother you may not lend with interest'. Whereas medieval Jewish theologians defined the terms 'brother' as related to Jews and 'stranger' to non-Jews, by the 12th century Christian theologians held that 'brother' applied to all men.[20] They further extended the moral stigma associated with usury to other contracts, with great effort enacted in the distinguishing of licit from illicit profits.

As the European economy grew from 1050 to 1300, with agricultural surpluses making possible greater commercial activity, the borrowing of money became more important, creating a dilemma for good Christians. A resolution was found in the 12th century in allowing Jews, who were not subject to canon law, to engage in the sinful activity. Jews, who previously earned their livelihood from agriculture and crafts, thereby came to be associated with moneylending or 'Jewing', something that further stigmatized Christian attitudes towards commerce.[21] Yet the Jewish role as money-lender made them indispensable to medieval political rulers.

Usury remained stigmatized for Protestant theologians. Luther condemned it in his *Long Sermon on Usury* in 1520 and in his treatise on *On Trade and Usury* in 1524. John Calvin allowed moneylending at a maximum rate of up to 5 per cent. However, he banished those who lent money as a profession from Geneva.[22] The Dutch Reformed Church, up until the mid-17th century, excluded moneylenders from communion.[23]

Enlightenment thought

In the 16th century, the unity of Western Christendom was shattered by an era of religiously motivated war that lasted for over a century. Differing views between Catholics and Protestants about salvation, whether it could be bought or had to be earned by good works, tore at the heart of Europe; ironically it came to form the backdrop for moral thinking about capitalism. Enlightenment philosophers such as John Locke sought to direct attention away from religious differences about heavenly salvation in the afterlife towards the common interest of securing peace and prosperity on Earth in the present life, following the earlier social contract theories of Thomas Hobbes in doing so. In the process, the enlightenment philosophers, through the rhetorical process of paradiastole, redesignated virtues as vices and vice versa.[24] Mandeville's (1670–1733) *The Fable of the Bees, or Private Vices, Public Benefits*, published in 1723 (see Box 11.1; Figure 11.3), makes the case that the individual self-interested character dispositions of pride, vanity and luxury, long stigmatized as vices, were in fact necessary conditions for social prosperity. The fable initially describes the development of a beehive from poverty to prosperity. Instead of accepting and appreciating their new circumstances, the bees take a traditional moralistic position and depreciate pride, vanity and luxury as moral vices corrupting the community. Only when Jove grants the elimination of these vices, leading to a restoration of virtue accompanied by primitive conditions, simplicity and poverty, do the bees recognize that the 'vices' were crucial conditions of their lost prosperity:[25]

> Thus Vice nurs'd Ingenuity,
> Which joined with Time and Industry,
> Had carry'd Life's conveniences,
> It's real Pleasures, Comforts, Ease,
> To such a Height, the very Poor
> Liv'd better than the Rich before.

Mandeville's insistence that economic prosperity would cease without individual ambition for luxury and pride was echoed in the century that followed both by proponents such as Voltaire and Adam Smith, as well as by critics such as Karl Marx. The latter agreed with Mandeville's analysis of the vicious basis for commerce but did not share his admiration for the private accumulation of affluence.[26]

Box 11.1 The positive in the negative and the negative in the positive –
Mandeville's paradoxical analysis of private/public virtues/vices

Private vice as public virtue

Pride, vanity and luxury, all evolve from self-love – promoting public benefits for society by generating greater overall industry, trade, employment and prosperity.

Private virtue as public vice

Honesty, thrift and charity evolve from self-denial – promoting the detriment of society as economic activity stagnates, creating widespread poverty.

Figure 11.3 From *The Fable of the Bees, or Private Vices Public Benefits.*[27]

Voltaire's (1694–1778) advocacy of market capitalism was based on an argument that the pursuit of economic self-interest was not as dangerous to society as religious zealotry.[28] A champion of humanistic values of individual freedom, government toleration of intellectual differences and the rule of law, Voltaire saw England as an exemplar for the rest of Europe. In *An Essay upon the Civil Wars*, he advertises a book, *Letters Concerning the English Nation*, written by a French traveller in England, comparing himself with the heroic:

'Merchant of a nobler Kind, who imports into his Country the Arts and Virtues of other Nations' thereby providing 'a Benefit to our Countrymen'.[29] Voltaire's description of the Royal Exchange (later the London Stock Exchange) was to become one of the most famous arguments articulating the beneficial effects of capitalism for society (Figure 11.4):

> Take a view of the royal exchange in London, a place more venerable than many courts of justice, where the representatives of all nations meet for the benefit of man-kind. There the Jew, the Mohametan, and the Christian transact together, as if they all professed the same religion, and give the name infidel to but bankrupts. There the Presbyterian confides in the Anabaptist, and the churchman depends on the Quaker's word. At the breaking up of this pacific and free assembly, some withdraw to the synagogue, and others to take a glass. This man goes to be baptized in a great tub, in the name of the Father, Son, and Holy Ghost: that man has his son's foreskin cut off, whilst a set of Hebrew words (quite intelligible to him) are mumbled over his child. Others retired to their churches, and wait there for the inspiration of heaven with their hats on, all are satisfied.[30]

Herein the stock exchange is portrayed as a harmonizer that brings together adher-ents of diverse faiths in 'pacific and free assembly' in the common pursuit of pros-perity. Adam Smith (1723–1790), a moral philosopher of the Scottish Enlightenment, whom Voltaire declared 'an excellent man',[32] further developed these arguments supporting individual self-interest as the basis for social order in his book, *The Wealth of Nations* (Figure 11.5). Smith argued that a liberal capitalist market economy, in which people have the freedom to compete in pursuing their own self-interest, is the best vehicle for improving the standard of living of the greatest majority of the population, leading to what Smith termed 'universal opu-lence'. He was critical of monopolies, government tariffs, duties and other state-enforced restrictions of his time, reasoning that the market is the fairest and most efficient arbitrator of resources – and yet he argued for government intervention against oligarchic anticompetitive monopolistic practices. His theory of the *invisible*

Figure 11.4 The Royal Exchange in London, 2009.[31]

Figure 11.5 Adam Smith, engraving, 1790.[35]

hand reasoned paradoxically that self-interest, when channelled through market competition, advanced the common-interest. The merchant:

> [I]ntends only his own gain, and he is in this, as in many other cases, led by an invisible hand to promote an end which was no part of his intention ... By pursuing his own interest he frequently promotes that of the society more effectually than when he really intends to promote it.[33]

Smith was not only concerned with the market's effectiveness in producing better products at lower prices, enhancing society's purchasing power and worldly happiness. As a moral philosopher, he was also concerned with enhancing people's character. In his less well-known but equally important work *The Theory of Moral Sentiments*, published in 1759, Smith discusses market value in terms of its tendency to prompt gentle behaviour and self-restraint in people pursing longer-term objectives through cooperative relations.[34]

Marx's perspective on capitalism

Smith's 'commercial society' was referred to pejoratively by its greatest critic Marx (1818–1883) as 'capitalism', a term now embraced positively by the market's fiercest advocates. Marx articulated two main critiques against capitalism. First, he argued that market competition was inherently a system of exploitation, inequality and political instability. He argued that the *bourgeoisie* (owners of capital and means of production) competing to improve quality while reducing costs could only become wealthier by increasing the exploitation of the increasingly poor *proletariat* (the working class), who, lacking any means of production and capital, could only survive by selling their selves in the form of their labour time and labour power, such that a diminishing share of the value that they produced was returned to them in the form of their exchange value of wages. By contrast, efficient exploitation would deliver an increasing share of surplus value, or profits, to the owners of the means of production. Those owners most efficient at exploitation would grow by swallowing the assets of those less efficient in a tendency towards monopolization. Once conditions reach their highest possible level of human exploitation and concentration of capital, financial liquidity would dry up. The effect, Marx argued, would be economic recession and immiseration with all of the social discontent that accompanies it; large-scale job layoffs, poverty and crime. Capitalism is thereby portrayed as 'vampire like', sucking the lifeblood out of workers and, by extension, from society.[36]

Second, Marx viewed capitalism as morally abhorrent in alienating skilled workers from the products they produce. The effect is to turn artisans into paid labourers, doing routine tasks in assembly lines 'as living appendages' of the machines they now operate. For Marx, the market was a cruel impersonal system that subordinates human dignity (see Box 11.2) to capital, producing four levels of social alienation: (1) people alienated from what they produce, (2) become alienated from their work, (3) from themselves, and (4) eventually from each other. The overall effect of a loss of humanity is the normalization of the conditions that sustain inhumanity.

Marx's book *Capital* (1867) supported his conclusions about the exploitative nature of capitalism with evidence of death and disease from overwork in British factories.[37] His evidence was mostly drawn from reports by government inspectors and newspapers, flagging the abuse of law. His far from balanced presentation doesn't reveal that these examples were the extreme exception rather than the norm. Within the framework of British law ensuring worker protections, capital was not at liberty to exploit workers as much as they might or to the extent Marx argued they did. Marx also does not stress other facts such as the 17 per cent rise in factory workers' average wages between 1830 and 1865[38] and the decline in average factory working hours.[39]

The historical overview of Western thought on the relationship between the organization of wealth generation and social wellbeing is ambivalent but also mostly theoretical. The classicalist and Church assumptions about the incompatibility of wealth generation and social justice and the Enlightenment arguments on the virtues of wealth generation are normative prescriptions based upon specific underlying assumptions. It is only in the case of Voltaire and Marx that we are provided with empirical evidence; however, this is evidence presented selectively to support forgone conclusions.

Box 11.2 Is dignity delicate?

'Dignity is delicate' is the title of an article authored by Remy Debes,[40] associate professor of philosophy at the University of Memphis and the editor of *Dignity: A History* (2017), a volume in the Oxford Philosophical Concepts series. Read the following excerpts and then answer the questions below:

> Dignity has three broad meanings. There is an historically old sense of poise or gravitas that we still associate with refined manners, and expect of those with high social rank. In this sense, dignity is almost synonymous with 'dignified'. Much more common is the family of meanings associated with self-esteem and integrity, which is what we tend to mean when we talk of a person's own 'sense of dignity' or when we say, for example, 'they robbed him of his dignity'. Third, there is the more abstract but no less widespread meaning of human dignity as an inherent or unearned worth or status, which all human beings share

equally. This is its *moralised* connotation ... This moralised connotation is implied in the couplet 'human dignity' ....

... In modern discussions, dignity is usually said to be distinctive in the sense that it is incommensurable: it can't be exchanged for other kinds of worth. The most influential expression of this modern idea comes from Immanuel Kant in *Groundwork for the Metaphysics of Morals* in 1785: 'Whatever has a price can be replaced by something else as its equivalent; on the other hand, whatever is above all price, and therefore admits of no equivalent, has a dignity'. Kant correspondingly argued that we have a categorical duty to treat other human persons 'always at the same time as an end, never merely as a means'. In other words, the distinctive value of dignity demands a special kind of respect, which we express through a self-imposed restriction on our deliberations about what to do or say.

... And yet, the idea of human dignity is beset by hypocrisy. After all, our Western ethos evolved from, and with, the most violent oppression. For 200 years, we've breathed in the heady aspirations of liberty and justice for all, but somehow breathed out genocide, slavery, eugenics, colonisation, segregation, mass incarceration, racism, sexism, classism and, in short, blood, rape, misery and murder. It shocks the imagination.

Questions for reflection

- In your view, which meaning of dignity is more relevant to assess dignity at workplaces?
- Do some managerial and organizational practices aim to 'buy' employees' dignity? Is that possible?
- To what extent do you identify hypocrisy in modern organizations? Why? On what evidence do you base your view?
- In the last part of the article, Debes writes: 'Simply having the idea of human dignity on board hasn't stopped us from leaving a wake of misery and oppression. So, maybe it's time for more humility. Maybe if we assumed there is still much to learn when it comes to the idea of human dignity, we could do better'. In your view, how does this argument matter for improving organizational life?

The empirical approach: evidence of social impacts of organizational activity

What does the empirical evidence tell us about the relationship between organizations, specifically financial organizations, and social wellbeing? Does organizational practice contribute to the objectives of social wellbeing in areas of increased health, longevity, security and peace in society? Here the evidence is a mixed bag because business organizations have both a harmful and beneficial effects on society. We begin with the negative.

Negative social impacts

Voltaire and Adam Smith argued that nations that trade are less inclined to wage war on each other, a rationale that might be extended to organizations. And while Voltaire presented the London Stock Exchange as the embodiment of how trade achieves the objective of international collaboration and peace, there is also evidence of business organizations contributing to violent social conflict through collusion with authoritarian state authorities, through assuming the role of government, through violence and through various forms of human rights abuse.[41]

Violence and collusion with authoritarian states

The part played by the British East India Company (Figure 11.6), described as one of the world's first multinational organizations,[42] in expanding the British Empire provides one such negative example. The 1757 battle of Plassey saw the British East India Company's private army defeat the Nawab of Bengal in armed conflict, making the Company the sovereign ruler of Bengal. In a repeat of this pattern over some years, the Company came to rule most of India. Tax revenue eventually eclipsed profits from trade as the greater source of shareholder dividends. The social injustice of having a private company as sovereign ruler of millions of people led to a popular mutiny by sepoys (Indian solders employed in the East India Company Army) in 1857, in which British civilians were killed. The British Government responded by assuming rule in India and dissolving the company.[43] The British South Africa Company similarly employed a private military that was engaged in capturing African diamond mines, furthering the interests of both the firm and the British state.[44]

Examples of profit-seeking organizations colluding with state authority in undermining the security and rights of sovereign populations is not confined to a past historical era of colonialism, as there are numerous more recent cases (see Box 11.3). For example, doing business with dictatorial regimes, as transpired with IBM maintaining

Figure 11.6 Lord Clive of the British East India Company meets Mir Jafar after the battle of Plassey.[45]

computational machines used in the Nazi concentration camps during WWII, or Coca-Cola, circumventing trade embargos imposed on Nazi Germany that restricted access to the syrup used in the manufacture of Coca-Cola, by creating a new beverage, Fanta, to avoid the embargo.[46]

IKEA's collusion with the oppressive Communist East German Government by contracting prison labourers to manufacture its furniture in the 1970s and 1980s[47] is another case. Many of these prison workers were imprisoned for 'political' crimes that included distributing anti-communist leaflets and they are now seeking compensation. Shell was also criticized in the 1990s for colluding with dictatorial regimes and being complicit in human rights abuses associated with its Nigerian subsidiary and the Government of Nigeria.[48] Despite millions of dollars of royalties being generated, local communities affected by company operations remained impoverished and saw their traditional means of livelihood eroded. It is increasingly typical for multinational mining companies operating in developing countries to employ transnational private armies to protect their interests from violent conflicts that arise between Indigenous communities, governments and multinational organizations.[49] Bobby Banerjee describes such destructive business practices that involve dispossession and even death as necrocapitalism: 'contemporary forms of organizational accumulation that involve dispossession and the subjugation of life to the power of death'.[50]

Box 11.3 Is the wolf no longer in sheep's clothing?

Henry Mintzberg wrote the following in *Rebalancing Society: Radical Renewal Beyond Left, Right, and Center.*[51]

> In December of 2013, *The New York Times* ran an article and editorial about how 'big tobacco' has been using litigation to 'intimidate' and 'bully' poor countries around the world into rescinding regulations intended to control the use of tobacco. The health minister of Namibia referred to having 'bundles and bundles of letters' from the industry about its attempts to curb smoking rates among young women (Tavernise, 2013). But these efforts have not been restricted to poor countries.

The article cited by Mintzberg included the following excerpt:[52]

> Tobacco consumption more than doubled in the developing world from 1970 to 2000, according to the United Nations. Much of the increase was in China, but there has also been substantial growth in Africa, where smoking rates have traditionally been low. More than three-quarters of the world's smokers now live in the developing world. Dr. Margaret Chan, director general of the W.H. O. [World Health Organization], said in a speech last year that legal actions against Uruguay, Norway and Australia were 'deliberately designed to instill fear' in countries trying to reduce smoking. 'The wolf is no longer in sheep's clothing, and its teeth are bared,' she said. Tobacco companies are objecting to laws in both developed and developing nations.

Next, read the following excerpt published in the *Guardian* in January 2018:[53]

> Philip Morris International Inc should not be allowed to claim that its iQOS electronic tobacco device can reduce the risk of tobacco-related diseases compared with cigarettes, an advisory panel to the US Food and Drug Administration [FDA] said on Thursday. The panel concluded that Philip Morris had not proven that iQOS – a sleek, pen-like device that heats tobacco rather than burning it – reduces harm compared with cigarettes. The company's shares were down 2.8 per cent at $107.50 on Thursday afternoon after falling as much as 6.8 per cent.

Questions for reflection

- What is your response to the allegations that tobacco corporations have been bullying and intimidating countries trying to protect their citizens from the harmful effects of tobacco by undertaking legal action? Is it legitimate? If not, how should it be opposed?
- Is the production of iQOS, a tobacco electronic device now produced by Philip Morris International Inc, which heats tobacco instead of burning it and is allegedly less harmful than the traditional cigarettes, more ethical than the cigarette?
- How do you interpret the claims of Philip Morris against those of the FDA?

Human rights violations

Human rights, as norms facilitating the protection of humans from abuse, include the right to a fair trial, to work and to receive fair pay, freedom of religion and political activity, non-discrimination on the basis of gender or ethnicity and the right not to be tortured. These rights exist in morality and in law in some national and international practice, yet they are frequently violated by business, sometimes legally and other times illegally. Nike's outsourcing of manufacturing to companies in developing countries with minimal workplace health and safety regulations and in which minimal wages are paid to child labourers[54] is a case that has received widespread boycotts and condemnation as a form of modern slavery.

As noted in Chapter 1, slavery, often thought obsolete, persists within current organizational practice in a variety of forms and contexts despite international laws guaranteeing human rights (see Box 11.4). Modern slavery, defined as efforts to underpay labour through illegitimate means such as forced threat, ownership/control, abuse, dehumanization, constrained freedom and economic exploitation is facilitated by five specific contexts including:[55]

1   Industry contexts that are highly labour intensive, with elastic demand, low value distribution and low industry legitimacy.
2   Socioeconomic contexts with a disadvantaged population with high poverty and unemployment and low education.

3   Geographic contexts that are highly isolated.
4   Cultural contexts with entrenched inequalities and beliefs.
5   Regulatory contexts that are weak and characterized by a minimal concern for
    protecting human rights.

Another high-profile example of inhumane work conditions involves Apple outsourcing the manufacture of its products to Foxconn in China, where harsh treatment of workers has contributed to unusually high incidences of employee
suicides.[56] Foxconn's initial response to this concern was not to change its workplace practices but to erect nets to catch those committing suicide as they jumped
from the factory dormitory windows.

Multinational companies, particularly IT companies such as Google, Apple and
Facebook, creating elaborate legal structures to avoid paying a fair share of tax[57] have
also sparked widespread public outrage and been described by the International Bar
Association as plunderers of public funds constituting a human rights violation.[58]
Note, however, that it is not the case that public funds are equally distributed, as we
shall see next.

Box 11.4 The Global Slavery Index

The Global Slavery Index conducts an annual study of slavery conditions across
the world, providing three data points for each country: national prevalence of
modern slavery, vulnerability to slavery and the strength of government
responses – ranked from AAA (good) to D (bad). The Index estimated that, in
2016, 45.8 million people were under some form of slavery conditions in 167
countries.[59] The countries with the highest *absolute* numbers of people in modern
slavery are India, China, Pakistan, Bangladesh and Uzbekistan. Several of these
countries provide low-cost labour that produces consumer goods for markets in
Western Europe, Japan, North America and Australia. Other countries, such as
North Korea, Cambodia, Qatar, Democratic Republic of the Congo or Sudan, have
high relative numbers in terms of proportion of population in slavery conditions.
The countries with the lowest estimated prevalence of modern slavery by the proportion of their population are Luxembourg, Ireland, Norway, Denmark, Switzer-
land, Austria, Sweden and Belgium, the US and Canada, as well as Australia and
New Zealand. Here are the 2016 estimates for a couple of countries:

China

*   3,388,400 people living in modern slavery or 0.247 per cent of the
    population.
*   Vulnerability score: 44.66/100.
*   Government response: CCC.
*   Ranked 40 out of 167 nations.

North Korea

- 1,100,000 people living in modern slavery or 4.373 per cent of the population.
- Vulnerability score: 45.84/100.
- Government response: D.
- Ranked 1 out of 167 nations.

Pakistan

- 2,134,900 people living in modern slavery or 1.130 per cent of the population.
- Vulnerability score: 62.47/100.
- Government response: CCC.
- Ranked 6 out of 167 nations.

Australia

- 4,300 people living in modern slavery or 00.018 per cent of the population.
- Vulnerability score: 21.98/100.
- Government response: BBB.
- Ranked 52 out of 167 nations.

Portugal

- 12,800 people living in modern slavery or 0.123 per cent of the population.
- Vulnerability score: 19.27/100.
- Government response: BBB.
- Ranked 49 out of 167 nations.

The co-authors of this textbook were surprised that slavery is so prevalent in their countries. Visit The Global Slavery Index (www.globalslaveryindex.org) to see the statistics for your nation. Hopefully you will not be unpleasantly surprised.

Inequality

A report by Oxfam[60] suggests that in the year 2015 the wealth of the world's richest 1 per cent overtook the wealth of the rest of the world combined. Furthermore, the world's richest 62 people own as much wealth as the poorest 50 per cent of the world's population of 3.6 billion people. Most alarmingly, this skew in income distribution is a worsening trend. The wealth of the richest 62 people rose 45 per cent in the five-year period from 2010, while the wealth of the poorest half of the world fell by 30 per cent. Since the beginning of this century, the poorest half have received just 1 per cent of the increases in global wealth, while more than 50 per cent of that increase has gone to the richest 1 per cent.

Another indicator of widening inequality is the wage differential between the average CEO and the average worker, which has increased at an alarming rate (see Box 11.5). In the USA this wage differential has widened from a ratio of 42:1 in 1980, to 85:1 in 1990 and a staggering 525:1 in 2000.[61] The Global Financial Crisis closed this gap somewhat to 300:1 in 2009 and it has been steadily climbing again each year since, to a ratio of 373:1 in 2014. These ratios are well above that which might be justifiable, considering that higher CEO pay encourages short-term decision-making for fast bottom line results that undermine organizational performance due to diminished investment in the longer term.[62] Moreover, organizations within the same industries tend to perform at a similar level regardless of leadership.[63] Andrew Hill wrote in the *Financial Times*, 'Stratospheric salaries are the biggest obstacle to restoring trust in business':[64]

> Excessive pay is the biggest obstacle to restoration of trust in business. This was true in 2010, when Sir Richard Lambert, then head of the CBI business association, warned it was so out of line that CEOs 'risked being treated as aliens.' It is even truer now, when they have long since left our galaxy and are heading at nanocraft-speed towards the next.

Box 11.5 How much do CEOs make compared with their employees?

To answer the question above regarding the USA, visit the PayScale website: www. payscale.com/data-packages/ceo-pay/full-list. To get a contrasting perspective on 'America's most just companies', visit the website of JUST Capital: https://justcapi tal.com/.

Inequality is a concern not because of the politics of class envy but because it undermines social cohesion, peace and general wellbeing, giving rise to higher crime rates and other social problems such as diminished health and access to education and work opportunities.[65] Inequality also widens the gender gap, disadvantaging females. The resurgence of far right nationalistic extremism across the developed world in recent years, including the election of Donald Trump as US president and the UK's vote to leave the European Union called Brexit (British Exit), is widely viewed as a popular reaction against increasing global inequality on the part of predominantly older, less-skilled and less-educated workers in the developed world that feel they have missed out on the benefits of globalization.[66]

Destructive environmental effects

Organizational operations often have destructive environmental effects that have social impacts. The destructive effects of business organizations on the environment remains a serious issue, particularly considering that the developed world, where most large organizations do business, is responsible for 90 per cent of the world's carbon emissions.[67]

The examples of negative social impact that we have considered demonstrate a concerning record of organizational operations being associated with destructive social outcomes of human rights abuse, exploitation, oppression and violence and widening inequality.

Positive social impacts

Notwithstanding the poor social record of business organizations discussed above, there are also examples of business organizations operating in a manner that promotes social wellbeing: security, peace and prosperity. As Rosling, Rosling and Rönnlund argued, although some things are bad, they are generally becoming better[68] (see Box 11.6).

Prosperity

Economists note that with the arrival of capitalistic business organizations, economic growth, as measured by gross domestic product (GDP), has seen a significant rise. The world's economy was relatively stagnant for 820 years from the year 1000 up until 1820, when it grew just six-fold.[69] With the arrival of capitalism following the Industrial Revolution, however, in the 178-year period between 1820 to 1998 the world economy grew 50-fold, at a rate faster than population growth with, on average, a nine-fold increase in individual incomes. More important for the objective of enhanced social wellbeing discussed in this chapter, world GDP increases translated into an improved standard of living, with increased availability of food, clothing, shelter and health care,[70] and decreases in average weekly working hours and work force participation by children and the elderly.[71]

Box 11.6 'Factfulness' seen through the Gapminder website[72]

Gapminder, an independent Swedish foundation, claims to be 'a fact tank, not a think tank'. It 'promotes a fact-based worldview everyone can understand'. The Foundation promotes 'a new way of thinking about the world and the society which [they] call Factfulness'. If you, the reader, would like to understand how the world has improved over the years, in terms of several social, economic, educational, health and human rights indicators, you might take a look at the Gapminder website (www.gapminder.org/). You will find data per country or aggregated at several levels as trends, maps, ranks, etc. depicted in interesting and even in funny ways. For example, you can see how the interplay between life expectancy and income (GDP/capita) in the world developed since 1800 until today here: www.gapminder.org/tools/#$state$time$ value=1800;;&chart-type=bubbles. In the meantime, have a look at the three screenshots below comparing differences in life-expectancy in the years 1800, 1950 and 2018 (the size of the bubbles represents the country's population) (Figures 11.7a, 11.7b and 11.7c):

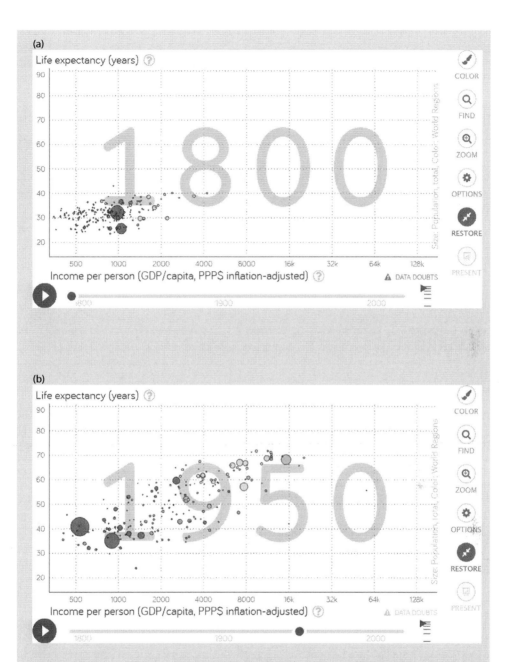

Figures 11.7a, 11.7b and 11.7c Life expectancy 1800, 1950 and 2018 (Gapminder Tools).

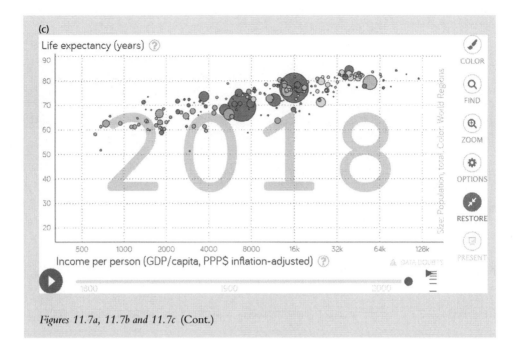

Figures 11.7a, 11.7b and 11.7c (Cont.)

Fighting poverty

University of Michigan Management scholar Prahalad has argued that business leaders, government agencies and donor groups ought to reconsider their perspectives on the poor in developing countries, from seeing them as victims to viewing them as resilient, value-demanding consumers and innovative entrepreneurs.[73] He makes a case that multinational organizations should develop new business models focussed on providing goods and services that address the needs of the 2.7 billion people at the 'base of the [wealth] pyramid' living on less than $2.50 per day (see also Box 11.7). Mass-scale local production and distribution through partnerships with local business owners are real opportunities for bringing down the cost of producing low-value products, as well as providing entrepreneurial opportunities. Prahalad views this approach as one that simultaneously opens up the potential of the world's fastest-growing markets, whilst also helping to alleviate the problem of poverty.

Peace

Can business organizations contribute to peace? This is the question Spreitzer sought to answer empirically in a most novel manner – using cross-country data from existing international databases.[74] As a proxy for peace, Spreitzer used a measure of corruption, Transparency International's corruption perceptions index (CPI), which strongly correlates with the Kosimo peace index and contains responses from people across 102 different countries. Another proxy for peace was unrest, which she assessed using data from The Economist Intelligence Unit (EIU) derived from measures of risk of political instability, armed conflict, social unrest and international disputes and tensions across over 100 different countries. These two proxies of peace (the dependent variables) were correlated with measures of business organizational practices, specifically partici-pative leadership and employee empowerment (the independent variables).

Data on participative leadership was drawn from questionnaire responses from some 17,000 middle managers in 825 business organizations across three industries (food processing, financial services and telecommunications) in 61 countries. Employee empowerment was measured using responses to values surveys from across 55 coun-tries, with an average of 1,400 respondents per country.

Spreitzer found that in countries where the leadership of business organizations is more participative and where employees have greater agency and decision-making authority, there is significantly less corruption and unrest. She additionally found that in countries where employees reported more compliance in unquestioningly following orders from supervisors, there was significantly more unrest.

Acknowledging the limitations of this preliminary research, Spreitzer suggests that busi-ness leaders that offer employees opportunities for voice, empowering them with greater control over their work, provide those employees with critical characteristics of a peaceful society. When employees experience empowerment in the workplace, she suggests, they will seek further possibilities for empowerment, believing they can make a difference in political and civic life, with an overall effect of producing greater peace.

Box 11.7 Cultivating literacy, personal agency and civic engagement through work at Unilever[75]

Unilever's plant in Vinhedo, Brazil, a city where some 50 per cent of the citizens do not complete high school and 20 per cent are illiterate, provides employees with remedial educational opportunities, along with training in technical skills, total qual-ity management and empowerment. Positive organizational effects of these pro-grammes include employees developing confidence and taking more personal responsibility in the workplace, by responding to issues, placing orders and managing budgets. Positive community effects include that employees have a greater sense that their voice counts and that they can make a difference in civic matters as informed and engaged citizens. A positive manifestation of this newfound sense of empower-ment and social responsibility is that employees made efforts to transplant the Unile-ver educational programmes outside of the company, initially to their families and then to the wider community in collaboration with colleges and local government authorities. A hoped-for outcome of enhancing literacy and agency within the com-munity is that citizens may become better equipped for civic engagement, leading to enhanced wellbeing across Brazilian society.

The contribution of organizations towards peace has been advanced by other scholars and practitioners, seeing the promotion of peace and social betterment as a necessary condition for a company's survival. For example, Ryuzaburo Kaku, former president and chairman of Canon, argued:

> Many companies around the world believe that they have a moral duty to respond to global problems such as Third World poverty, the deterioration of the natural environment, and endless trade battles. But few have realized that their survival

actually depends on their response. Global corporations rely on educated workers, consumers with money to spend, a healthy natural environment, and peaceful coexistence between nations and ethnic groups. This reality is to me a great source of hope: at this watershed period in history, it is in the interests of the world's most powerful corporations to work for the advancement of global peace and prosperity. To put it simply, global companies have no future if the Earth has no future.[76]

Thomas Friedman wrote in his book *The World is Flat*:[77]

[W]ith tongue slightly in cheek, I offer the Dell Theory of Conflict Prevention, the essence of which is that the advent and spread of just-in-time global supply chains in the flat world are an even greater restraint on geopolitical adventurism than the more general rising standard of living that McDonald's symbolized. The Dell Theory stipulates: No two countries that are both part of a major global supply chain, like Dell's, will ever fight a war against each other as long as they are both part of the same global supply chain. Because people embedded in major global supply chains don't want to fight old-time wars anymore. They want to make just-in-time deliveries of goods and services – and enjoy the rising standards of living that come with that. One of the people with the best feel for the logic behind this theory is Michael Dell, the founder and chairman of Dell.

... Countries whose workers and industries are woven into a major global supply chain know that they cannot take an hour, a week, or a month off for war without disrupting industries and economies around the world and thereby risking the loss of their place in that supply chain for a long time, which could be extremely costly. For a country with no natural resources, being part of a global supply chain is like striking oil – oil that never runs out. And therefore, getting dropped from such a chain because you start a war is like having your oil wells go dry or having someone pour cement down them.

Other scholars have also pointed out how business organizations may foster peaceful societies. For example, Nancy Adler suggested that global corporations, with more extensive and integrated global experience than most governments and countries, are in a good position to promote social betterment by fostering peace and security.[78] From her perspective, these goals may be accomplished through respecting democracy and human rights, adopting sustainable development actions and policies, promoting health, poverty reduction and more equitable income distribution. By facilitating peace and security, companies also build better conditions for operating and developing their businesses;[79] especially in contexts where environmental problems leading to resource shortage and disease, extreme poverty and excessive income inequalities are a paramount cause of social tension.[80] Prosperity and peace accordingly support each other in a virtuous circle.[81]

In fact, after the destruction of World War II, along with setting up the United Nations to provide a forum for promoting peace among nations, a subsidiary, the World Trade Organization, was also set up to facilitate trade among nations, recognizing that trading partners are less likely to go to war. These arguments draw attention to the possible perverse implications for undermining peace and socio-economic development of political decisions that build new borders and trade barriers. Peter Goodman wrote in *The New York Times*, March 11, 2018:[82]

> In the more than seven decades since the end of the Second World War, leaders of the planet's major economies have operated on a rough consensus that trade offers a potent form of inoculation against the outbreak of military hostilities. The United States and its allies have constructed an economic and security order centered on the notion that communities connected by commerce have a shared interest in maintaining peace. They forged institutions focused on reducing tariffs and other impediments to trade, with the World Trade Organization as the linchpin. But now this collective understanding is under assault by the very power that has championed it most fervently.
>
> … Mr. Trump maintains that Americans have been outwitted by savvier trading partners, with tariffs needed to force jobs to return to the United States. History has proved humbling for those inclined to seek victory through trade conflicts. Commerce has tended to plunge, with the working class suffering lost jobs and diminished livelihoods. Alliances have been frayed, heightening international tensions.

Organizations as 'mediating institutions'

The empirical evidence presented in this section provides some insight into the manner whereby business organizations can act as 'mediating institutions'[83] in promoting greater social wellbeing. Considered in conjunction with negative examples of organizational social impacts presented earlier in the section, it suggests that business organizations are not inherently positive or negative, good or bad. Rather, organizational members, particularly leaders, have a choice in the type of organization they will manage, work for or be associated with in other ways, for example as a supplier or customer. That being the case, it is important to understand the principles that contribute to developing, managing and sustaining positive organizing in a manner that supports greater social wellbeing (see Box 11.8). Here we are concerned with the art of the possible.

Box 11.8 Can, or should, companies learn from Pope Francis?

Jeffrey Pfeffer wrote an article for *Fortune* magazine in September 2015, discussing how companies can learn from Pope Francis. The Pope argues that 'an economy of exclusion and inequality … kills', maintaining that corporations must rather be a source of social betterment. For example, in the *Evangelli Gaudium* Encyclic, Francis argues:[84]

> Just as the commandment 'Thou shalt not kill' sets a clear limit in order to safeguard the value of human life, today we also have to say 'thou shalt not' to an economy of exclusion and inequality. Such an economy kills. How can it be that it is not a news item when an elderly homeless person dies of exposure, but it is news when the stock market loses two points? This is a case of exclusion. Can we continue to stand by when food is thrown away while people are starving? This is a case of inequality. Today everything comes under the laws of competition and the survival of the fittest, where the powerful feed upon the powerless. As

a consequence, masses of people find themselves excluded and marginalized: without work, without possibilities, without any means of escape. Human beings are themselves considered consumer goods to be used and then discarded.

Later in the same document, Francis wrote:

Business is a vocation, and a noble vocation, provided that those engaged in it see themselves challenged by a greater meaning in life; this will enable them truly to serve the common good by striving to increase the goods of this world and to make them more accessible to all.[85]

In the *Laudato Si'* Encyclical Letter, the Pope emphasizes the responsibility of companies in respecting the natural environment, arguing:[86] 'Business is a noble vocation, directed to producing wealth and improving our world. It can be a fruitful source of prosperity for the areas in which it operates, especially if it sees the creation of jobs as an essential part of its service to the common good'.

Inspired by Pope Francis' teachings and messages, Jeffrey Pfeffer wrote:[87]

Although many companies display almost-obligatory boilerplate language thanking their workers in their annual reports, and numerous organizations proclaim a version of 'people are our most important asset,' few businesses consistently put these noble sentiments into practice and manage based on their espoused corporate values. Maybe more should.

… Companies can take care of people during tough economic times and even benefit from doing so. Jim Goodnight – co-founder and CEO of the large, privately owned software company SAS Institute – told me a couple of years ago that during the recent severe recession, people at SAS were concerned for their jobs, even though the company had never laid anyone off. After he put out a notice assuring people there would be no layoffs – but in return asking for their assistance in holding down costs – he was delighted at employees' responses. Staffers cooperated in managing costs and they could work more effectively because they were not distracted by the stress of worrying about their job and their financial security.

The Pope's message reminds us that we are responsible not just for the physical environment, although that is obviously important, but also for the human beings we are contact with and whose livelihoods are entrusted to us. And that includes the people who work inside companies.

Questions for reflection

- Why do employees react positively to companies that 'take care of people during tough economic times'?
- Considering even the material benefits (aside from the ethical imperative) of taking care of employees, why do so many companies act in a less responsible way?

The prudential: policy judgement supporting greater social wellbeing

We now consider the prudential implications of managerial judgement in fostering potential social benefits and minimizing negative effects. Here we consider more pragmatist[88] approaches to organizational theories and actions that can be enacted as a force for positive social transformation.

Corporate social responsibility

Corporate Social Responsibility (CSR) conveys the notion of business organizations self-regulating through the voluntary uptake of socially responsible practices above and beyond what is required by the letter of the law. These practices are taken to be a demonstration of corporate citizenship or corporate conscience.[89] Society expects organizations to act, like any good citizen, in a fair and responsible manner, doing the right thing by others. As fair an expectation as this may sound, there are those who take the ideas of Voltaire and Adam Smith about self-interest providing a social benefit to the extreme and argue that the sole responsibility of business is to maximize profits for shareholders.

Milton Friedman, an American economist who received the 1976 Prize in honour of Alfred Nobel, famously argued that 'greed is good' and that there is no scope for organizations to be socially responsible as they are not people and 'only people have social responsibilities'.[90] Individual managers wanting to contribute to social causes, according to Friedman, could do so with their own private funds, not those of the company they lead. Acting otherwise would amount to stealing from shareholders. Friedman stated that the only social responsibility of business is profit maximization using all facilities available within legal frameworks:

> There is one and only one social responsibility of business – to use its resources and engage in activities designed to increase its profits so long as it stays within the rules of the game.[91]

In contrast to Friedman's views, Martin Wolf, chief economics commentator at the *Financial Times*, wrote:[92]

> Almost nothing in economics is more important than thinking through how companies should be managed and for what ends. Unfortunately, we have made a mess of this. That mess has a name: it is 'shareholder value maximisation'. Operating companies in line with this belief not only leads to misbehaviour but may also militate against their true social aim, which is to generate greater prosperity.

John Kay, a British economist and visiting professor at the London School of Economics, wrote in the *Financial Times*:[93]

> Lehman Brothers and Bear Stearns – the latter the broker-dealer whose mission was to 'make nothing but money' – failed in the long run because the ethos of making 'nothing but money' was not conducive to creating a sustainable organisation. Only profitable companies can survive; but it does not follow, and is not in

fact true, that the ones that survive are those most oriented to making profits. Scrooge is not a happy individual because he does not, until his epiphany, understand that happiness lies not in selfish behaviour but in interaction with others. The happiest people are not necessarily those most determined in their pursuit of personal happiness.

Bower and Paine argue that, although 'most CEOs and boards believe their main duty is to maximize shareholder value, it is not'.[94] Bower and Pain hold that the shareholder centricity is 'flawed in its assumptions, confused as a matter of law, and damaging in practice'.[95] They instead advocate for a 'company-centered model':[96]

> A company's health – not its shareholders' wealth – should be the primary concern of those who manage corporations. That may sound like a small change, but it could make companies less vulnerable to damaging forms of activist investing – and make it easier for managers to focus on the long term.

According to Bower and Pain, corporations perform many functions in society, not just producing goods and services: providing employment, developing technologies, paying taxes, and making several other contributions to the communities in which they operate. They must create value for multiple constituencies and follow ethical standards to guide interactions with all those constituencies, including shareholders and the whole of society. In short, 'they are embedded in a political and socioeconomic system whose health is vital to their sustainability'.[97]

These perspectives contrast with Friedman's view that the only responsibility is to make profit so long as it is within the framework of the law. They indicate an increasing recognition that it is essential for business organizations to operate in a socially responsible manner beyond what is required by the law, as there are many activities that are legal but socially reprehensible. Examples of legal but socially irresponsible practice include some of those cited earlier in this chapter. IKEA's collusion with East German Government authorities in contracting political prisoners to manufacture its furniture,[98] Shell's collusion with the Nigerian government in violating workers' human rights in its African oil refineries,[99] Nike's endorsement of sub-contractors' use of child labourers paid next to nothing to work long hours in unsafe conditions,[100] Apple outsourcing the manufacture of its products to Foxconn in China, where inhumane treatment of workers contributed to unusually high incidences of employee suicides,[101] and Google's elaborate tax evasion strategies[102] are all legal within their jurisdictions but socially irresponsible and therefore reprehensible.

Richard Marens, of California State University, Sacramento, conducted a historical analysis of the history of the notion of CSR, tracing its emergence in the USA in the 1920s and 1930s after the victory of the leaders of business organizations over organized labour fighting for better worker pay and work conditions. In contrast to Europe with its more established democratic institutions and mechanisms of corporate regulation, US Government authorities and the courts mostly sided with business in ruling worker strikes and other forms of resistance illegal:

> State or state-sanctioned use of deadly force was routinely mobilized, or at least threatened, against workers attempting to counter corporate practices.[103]

Ultimately, the labour movement was for the most part crushed, giving the executives of US business organizations unrivalled autonomy in managing their workforces compared with Europe and other parts of the developed world. The triumph also gave business executives greater responsibility for enhancing efficiency, as they could no longer blame union activity for inefficient practices. Having crushed the unions they were posed with the challenge of winning public acceptance from the many who were, had been or might be union members as well as the broader community of relatives, friends and citizens. A response of executives largely adopted by the 1920s was to claim that they managed in accordance with principles of social responsibility. As well as providing employees with a minimum wage adjudged fair by the standards that they had established as well as healthier work environments, a slew of other programmes were rolled out: 'bonuses, profit sharing, piece rates, safety initiatives, recreation, stock plans, educational programs, pensions, mutual funds, clubhouses, suggestion boxes and, especially during World War I, works councils and other employee representation plans for the airing of grievances and the communication of policy changes'.[104]

Through the Great Depression of the 1930s, when there was less need for ideological justification in providing employment in the face of mass recession and unemployment, the reserve army of the unemployed played their disciplining role for those that remained in the workforce. World War II resolved the recession and the ideology: a full employment wartime economy provided the basis for ideological exhortations to work for victory and to support the troops. Not surprisingly, for different reasons, the emphasis placed on CSR saw a period of decline. CSR was to resurface again as a form of softening of the hard edges of various forms of exploitation of nature, society and individuals that accompanied the rise of neoliberalism in the 1980s.

The late 1970s saw the US and UK lose market dominance in manufacturing, particularly with competition from a reemerging Japan and Europe, and especially Germany, which had seen its manufacturing capacity devastated during WWII. Loss of dominance in these areas placed the governments of the developed world under significant financial strain with mounting government debts. The response of the Reagan administration in the US and the Thatcher administration in the UK during the 1980s was a massive programme of economic restructuring, shifting the economies of these countries away from manufacturing towards services.[105] Similar programmes were labelled Economic Rationalism in Australia and Rogernomics in New Zealand.[106] Transition to a services economy was achieved largely by liberalization or breaking up and privatizing what had traditionally been government services (telecommunications, transport, finance, health and education) after deregulating these industries.

The programme that came to be known as neoliberalism was designed to create competition in these areas that, according to *laissez-faire* economic theory, would give citizens (now more commonly labelled as customers) greater choice of better quality products at lower prices. It would also reduce the role of government in society, in theory ensuring greater individual freedoms, the formula being 'small government and lower taxes'. Leading advocates of this approach saw themselves as followers of Adam Smith, to the extent that many, including prize-winning economist Milton Friedman,[107] most famously associated with the Chicago School of Economics, and executives in the Reagan administration, wore Adam Smith ties (see the picture below, Figure 11.8).[108] They glossed over the fact that while Adam Smith opposed government tariffs, he favoured government regulation of business and in fact worked

Figure 11.8 Milton Freedman – note the Adam Smith bust on his tie.[110]

in a government position as Commissioner of Customs in Scotland during his later years. The alternative, a state where the government regulated industry and collected higher taxes to provide a social safety net ensuring greater collective equality, safety and wellbeing for the citizens, was pejoratively referred to as a 'Nanny State'.[109]

Public confidence in self-regulation by business organizations was undermined, however, by corporate crimes, scandals and disasters.[111] While corporate crime was not new, the scale of its impact in a liberalized environment was felt more widely and people began questioning the effectiveness of self-regulation. Eager to regain public support and deflect calls for greater state regulation of industry, the business community sought to provide reassurance to policy makers and the public that it was capable of being responsible for the potential negative effects of business activities. This reassurance materialized as the reemergence of a concern with 'Business Ethics' or, in more corporate parlance, 'Corporate Social Responsibility'. The irony here is that it was the Reagan administration's massive market deregulation and privatization of public services conducted under advice from Milton Friedman that inadvertently contributed to the rebirth of CSR – something Friedman had so vehemently opposed.

Key practices for implementing CSR within business organizations include appointing directors or managers responsible for CSR, developing and publicizing CSR statements and ethical codes of practice, donating to charities and supporting social and environmental causes, enrolling as a member of public forums or environmental groups and publicizing a record of socially responsible practices. Today most large organizations promote themselves as socially responsible, indicating the widespread embrace of CSR.

Claims of CSR practices made by organizations, however, are not necessarily legitimate. Organizations are often accused of adopting CSR merely to engender public and shareholder trust and reduce legal risk, as a cynical public relations exercise of 'window-dressing' designed to pre-empt the government's role as social watch-dog.[112] Business organizations also sometimes use CSR to deflect public attention away from harmful aspects of their business practices. An example advanced by the critics is the McDonald's Corporation's CSR positioning of their relationship with Ronald McDonald House, supporting programmes to improve children's health while simultaneously promoting unhealthy fast-food products that engender harmful eating habits in children and teenagers.[113] Cynicism towards CSR, both by business executives and critics, places business organizations in a Catch 22 situation, where they are damned if they ignore the negative social impacts of organizational operations but also criticized for trying to do something about it.[114]

Creating shared value

Creating shared value (CSV) is a concept that builds upon the notion of CSR, introduced by Michael Porter and Mark Kramer, both of Harvard University (see Figure 11.9). They initially introduced the concept in an article published in 2006 in the *Harvard Business Review* titled 'Strategy & Society: The Link between Competitive Advantage and Corporate Social Responsibility'.[115] These authors challenged the idea that the activities of business organizations and the wellbeing of society necessarily conflict with each other. Rather, they argue that the success of both business and the community are mutually interdependent. Business organizations therefore should identify and enact policy that leverages the natural links between their strategies and CSR, by shifting their focus away from responsibilities and towards a focus on value creation. They consider CSR as often reactionary, being driven by external pressures, reputation management and constrained by budgetary limitations. The interests of society are pitted against the interests of the business organization, highlighting the costs of complying with externally enforced social requirements. CSV, in contrast, is proactive and driven internally by strategic opportunities that provide benefit both for the organization and society. Here the focus is on opportunities for competitive advantage through incorporation of a social value proposition within the organizational strategy.

Porter and Kramer further developed the concept of CSV in a follow-up 2011 article titled 'Creating Shared Value: Redefining Capitalism and the Role of the Corporation in Society'.[116] Acknowledging critiques of capitalism as justified on account of many scandalous socially irresponsible practices focussed on profit maximization without concern for social impacts, the authors argue that capitalism should be redefined through recognition of the opportunities that exist in connecting society and business activity.

Porter and Kramer suggest three strategic areas where business organizations can find opportunities for CSV: (1) reconceiving services, products and markets, (2) redefining value chains, and (3) local and regional cluster development.[118]

First, *reconceiving services, products and markets* can be implemented by innovating to address unmet social needs while improving offers to current customers and markets

Figure 11.9 Creating shared value by linking business strategy to social needs.[117]

and gaining access to new ones. Possibilities for reimagining products and services exist across a range of industries. Hewlett Packard, the US technology company, is creating innovative solutions to address problems in education and health. The costs of delivering education are being disrupted with cloud computing and counterfeit medicine is being combatted with secure labelling. General Electric is addressing health-care affordability and accessibility with its Healthymagination programme,[119] with a goal of developing 100 new products to advance these objectives. In the agricultural sector, Jain Irrigation, the Indian multinational, is addressing water inefficiency with drip-irrigation systems that stand to make a significant impact in both emerging and developed markets from India to the US.

Second, *redefining value chains* can be enacted by improving quality, quantity, price and dependability of inputs and distribution, adopting stewardship of indispensable natural resources while driving both social and economic objectives. Examples include Swiss transnational food company Nestlé creating sustainable supply districts by offering coffee and cocoa growers as well as dairy farmers significant support in rural regions across the world, ensuring the reliable supply of ethically sourced produce. Alcoa, the US lightweight metal company, has invested significant resources in boosting the rate of recycling aluminium cans in the US, potentially reducing billions of tons in greenhouse gas emissions yearly, all the while enhancing cost effective procurement of an important raw material.

Third, *local and regional cluster development* can be supported by contributing towards investment in developing the skills of local suppliers, infrastructure and supporting the rule of law, recognizing that corporations are embedded within their surroundings. Cisco, the US multinational technology conglomerate, provides an example of a company supporting local cluster development. For over a decade, the organization has been investing in IT education through the establishment of some 10,000 academies for training developers and network administrators, thereby enhancing the company's recruitment pool and enabling the emergence of new customers and markets. Anglo American, the South-African-based mining giant, through Anglo Zimele, its investment fund, has invested millions in mining-related small-and-medium-size enterprises in communities around its South African mines. The communities benefit from the creation of thousands of jobs and other forms of economic development, while Anglo American benefits from easier access to quality local suppliers.

Stakeholder theory

Stakeholder theory argues that the numerous groups upon whom organizational practices impact have a legitimate voice that needs to be acknowledged in organizational policy and decision-making. Originally articulated by University of Virginia scholar Edward Freeman in his 2004 book *Strategic Management: A Stakeholder Approach*,[120] stakeholder theory contrasts with shareholder primacy theory, which assumes that the only relevant voice in a corporation is that of shareholders, judging profit maximization and share value increases as the only measure of management success. A stakeholder is defined as 'any group or individual who can affect or is affected by the achievement of the organization's objectives'.[121] Different relevant stakeholder groups include employees, suppliers, customers, financiers, communities, government bodies and the environment as well as trade associations.

Ronald Mitchell, Bradley Agle and Donna Wood have developed a typology of stakeholders based on the attributes of power, legitimacy and urgency.[122] Power concerns the extent to which a stakeholder has the means to impose their will upon a relationship. Legitimacy relates to social expectations of acceptable behaviours or structures. Urgency concerns the criticality or time sensitivity associated with a stakeholder's concerns. Examination of these attributes in combination using a diagram generates eight stakeholder categories with varying managerial implications (see Figure 11.10). Latent stakeholders are characterized by a single attribute:

1   the dormant stakeholder with the single attribute of a claim to power (e.g., such as an employee who has been laid off);
2   the discretionary stakeholder has the single attribute of a claim to legitimacy (e.g., someone who has received corporate philanthropy);

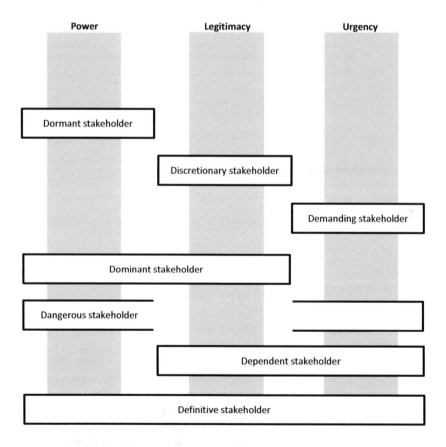

Figure 11.10 Stakeholder typology – according to the combination of their attributes.[123]

3   the demanding stakeholder has the single attribute of a claim to urgency (e.g., a stakeholder with neither legitimacy nor power but prepared to make a lot of noise, believing they have a claim).

While these stakeholders may not demand immediate attention from managers, expectant stakeholders, characterized by more than one attribute, are likely more active in their expectations of a response from the organization. These are:

1   the dominant stakeholder with attributes of power and legitimacy but no urgency (e.g., such as boards of directors, community leaders or significant creditors);
2   the dangerous stakeholder with attributes of power and urgency but no legitimacy (e.g., activists or others comfortable using coercive tactics such as sabotage or terror);
3   the dependent stakeholder with attributes of legitimacy and urgency but no power (e.g., such as community members or the environment);
4   the definitive stakeholder with attributes of power, urgency and legitimacy provides the manager with a definitive mandate to take action on the stakeholder demands.
5   those with no attributes or claims to power, legitimacy or urgency are non-stakeholders.

In project management, where disappointed stakeholder expectations can derail the successful implementation of a project, stakeholder theory is given great attention and applied as a fourfold process.[124] This process involves: (1) identification, recognition and acknowledgement of stakeholders, (2) determining their influence and interest, (3) establishing a plan of communication management, and (4) engaging and influencing the stakeholders. These four steps are conducted through analysis using the following considerations:

•   **High power, interested stakeholders** – manage this group closely, exerting maximum effort to keep satisfied with regular status updates and issue change logs.
•   **High power, less interested stakeholders** – maintain satisfaction with regular updates but not too much communication that becomes information overload. This group could be invited to participate in steering committees and board meetings.
•   **Low power, interested stakeholders** – keep this group sufficiently informed with regular in-person, email and film updates to maintain open communication channels providing certainty that no major concerns are developing.
•   **Low power, less interested stakeholders** – monitor this group, providing regular emails with status reports but not so much information that they become bored.

You might conclude from overviewing these frameworks and directives that stakeholder engagement and management can be a somewhat manipulative way for management to impose their views on those who count or to deflect the concerns of those who might have different perspectives, rather than providing an opportunity for others to express their voices. As with CSR, the adoption of a stakeholder approach to management can also be insincere when used by organizations as a public relations exercise to give a veneer of legitimacy to their socially irresponsible activities. Bobby

Banerjee presents the following striking example from an influential firm claiming to organize around corporate responsibility and stakeholder values:[125]

'The principles that guide our behavior are based on our vision and values and include the following:

- **Respect** – We will work to foster mutual respect with communities and stakeholders who are affected by our operations; we will strive to ensure that our activities, products and services yield a positive impact on the environment, communities and stakeholders where we operate.
- **Integrity** – We will examine the impacts, positive and negative, of our business on the environment and on society, and will integrate human health, social and environmental considerations into our internal management and value system.
- **Communication** – We will strive to foster understanding and support with our stakeholders and communities, as well as measure and communicate our performance.
- **Excellence** – We will continue to improve our performance and will encourage our business partners and suppliers to adhere to the same standards.'

Listed in *Fortune* magazine's 'All-star list of global most admired companies' in 1999 and voted by the magazine as the most 'innovative company in North America' for six years consecutively between 1996 and 2001, reporting revenues of more than 100 billion in 2001,[126] this company was the notorious US energy giant Enron. With the revelation of widespread corruption and accounting fraud practiced all through the 1990s, the company filed for bankruptcy at the end of 2001, its share value dropping from $90.56 in the summer of 2001 to just pennies within less than an month at the end of the year. In the fallout, 20,000 employees lost their jobs and pension funds and it precipitated a worldwide economic crisis.

Conscious capitalism

Conscious capitalism builds on stakeholder theory as an approach by incorporating principles of higher purpose, conscious leadership and conscious culture. Developed by Whole Foods Market's co-Founder and CEO John Mackey (see Box 11.9) and Boston College Professor Raj Sisodia, conscious capitalism has become a worldwide movement.[127] Mackey and Sisodia argue that capitalism correctly practiced has essential qualities of goodness, ethicality, nobility and heroism. Its goodness springs from its ability to create value for stakeholders; its ethicality rests on its foundation of free voluntary exchange; while its noble heroism derives from the power to alleviate human poverty and drive economic prosperity. Four pillars of conscious capitalism differentiating it from alternative business approaches are:

- **Higher purpose** which represents engaging in entrepreneurship for purposes beyond profits to manifest the good, true, beautiful or heroic.
- A **stakeholder orientation** which optimizes value for six groups of stakeholders (customers, employees, suppliers, shareholders, society and the environment) by finding 'win–win–win–win–win–win' or 'win 6' solutions.[128]

- **Conscious leadership** that embodies a commitment to the company's higher purpose, as opposed to profits and power, motivating and inspiring followers to do the same.
- **Conscious culture** that is represented in the 'TACTILE' values: Trust, Authenticity, Care, Transparency, Integrity, Learning and Empowerment.

Box 11.9 Conscious capitalism – the Whole Foods Market way

In the book *Conscious Capitalism: Liberating the Heroic Spirit of Business* John Mackey and Raj Sisodia[129] frequently discuss Whole Foods Market, the US supermarket chain co-founded by Mackey, as an exemplar conscious business. With $13.46 billion reported in 2014 and 91,000 employees, Whole Foods was ranked the 30th largest US retailer.[130] The organization's stated mission is 'to co-create a world where each of us, our communities and our planet can flourish. All the while, celebrating the sheer love and joy of food' (Wholefoodsmarket.com). Its values include selling 'the highest quality natural and organic products available', satisfying, delighting and nourishing customers, supporting employee team member happiness and excellence, serving and supporting local communities, practicing environmental stewardship, and promoting stakeholder health through education in healthy eating.

Figure 11.11 Whole Foods Market in Markham, Ontario.[131]

Value statements are little more than rhetoric if they don't actually inform practice. With obesity on the rise worldwide,[132] Whole Foods Market provides a valuable service as a supermarket that exclusively features foods free from artificial flavours, preservatives, sweeteners, colours and hydrogenated fats. Whole Foods was also the first certified organic grocer in the US to ensure the integrity of its organic products in accordance with the strict standards of the National Organic Program. The organization was also the first US supermarket to commit to eliminating the use of plastic bags in 2008, favouring reusable and recycled paper bags instead, and it purchases a significant portion of its products from local producers. Whole Foods also has policies ensuring the humane treatment of animals such as selling only free-range eggs and not selling meat or milk from cloned animals. In 2005 the company formed the Animal Compassion Foundation, a nonprofit organization with a mission of helping farmers evolve their practices to raise animals in a manner that is natural and humane, ensuring a more knowledgeable and benevolent supply chain.

In 2007, Whole Foods announced its Whole Trade Guarantee that a significant per cent of products imported from developing nations available in its stores would be certified by the Whole Planet Foundation as adhering to a strict criteria stipulating sourcing and payment of fair prices to producers with environmentally and socially responsible practices including providing workers with better wages and labour conditions. The company has also committed to donating 1 per cent of proceeds from Whole Trade certified products to the Whole Planet Foundation to support the provision of micro-loan programmes for producers in developing nations.

In recognition of these policies, Whole Foods Market has received numerous awards such as a first-place social responsibility ranking by *The Wall Street Journal* in 2006, the Environmental Protection Agency's 'Green Power Award' in 2004 and 2005, and 'Partner of the Year' award in 2006 and 2007. Whole Foods has also featured in *Fortune* magazine's annual list of the US's '100 Best Companies to Work For'[133] since the inception of the list in 1998.

Whole Foods Market is not without its critics, but nonetheless it is an example of an incredibly successful organization that embraces positive organizational practices for the benefit all stakeholders. In June 2017 Amazon, the online retail giant, acquired Whole Foods for $13.5 billion.[134] While some price cutting and other changes were immediately implemented with the acquisition, it will be interesting to see if there are changes in values as well.

Mackey and Sisodia argue that not only are conscious businesses better for society and the environment but, in the long run, they are also more profitable. In Sisodia's book *Firms of Endearment*, co-authored with Wolfe and Sheth, the authors create a set of criteria to evaluate conscious businesses that include:[135]

1 Alignment with stakeholder interests.
2 Lower than average compensation of executives.
3 Open-door communication policies.
4 Above industry average employee compensation and training.
5 Recruitment of employees passionate about the company's mission and values.
6 Humanized customer and employee experience.
7 Lower than industry average marketing costs (preferring genuine word-of-mouth customer endorsements over marketing spin).
8 Commitment to the spirit as well as the letter of the law.
9 Focus on company culture as a competitive advantage.

Companies that met these criteria included Costco, Container Store, Honda, IDEO, Johnson & Johnson, New Balance, Patagonia, Southwest Airlines, Starbucks, Timberland, Toyota, UPS and, of course, Whole Foods. Sisodia and colleagues contrast what they term *Firms of Endearment* with another list of 11 companies identified in Jim

Collins' work *Good to Great*.[136] Collins' influential work analyses 11 firms that sustained high stock market performance over a 15-year period from 1982–1998. According to Collins, these organizations, such as tobacco firm Philip Morris and supermarket giant Wal-Mart, built their 'greatness' by developing disciplined cultures emphasizing humble leaders ready to learn from others, engaging the right people for the right job, confronting difficult truths and constant striving for excellence.[137] It turned out the conscious businesses identified in *Firms of Endearment* significantly outperformed both the average performance of the 'great' companies listed in Collins' work and the average performance of the top 500 companies listed on the US S&P stock market over a 15-year period from 1996–2011.

The financial performance of the *Firms of Endearment* is particularly impressive considering that, in contrast to some of the 'great' companies listed in Collins' book that externalize the costs of their doing business on to society, such as the impacts of tobacco on health systems, conscious businesses internalize social costs. Such internalization takes the form of offering above market wages and generous benefits to employees, making significant community investments and being accountable for reducing company environmental impacts.

It is important to point out some of the limitations of the work. Like Collins' *Good to Great*, the work *Firms of Endearment* presents a post-hoc or after the fact analysis. It could be that the selected firms had other attributes contributing to their success and they just so happened to have the culture characteristics that the authors sought to emphasize. As an example, Southwest, one of the world's most successful airlines, attributes its success to its culture supportive both of customers and employees – a key focus of company efforts. The company, however, also has an excellent business model that is superior to other airlines.

Sustainability

Sustainability is defined broadly as 'the capability to advance long-term, multi-faceted quality of life'.[138] The beauty of this definition is that whereas most people think of sustainability as environmental sustainability, this definition incorporates economic, environmental and social concerns. In that sense, this entire chapter could have been framed as being about sustainable business practices, with CSR and stakeholder orientation seen as subsets of sustainability. In the context of this chapter, we are focussed on the social impacts of business organizations. Nonetheless we should give some consideration to the environment because although business sustainability is most frequently discussed in the context of the natural environment, serious sustainability scholars emphasize the interactional relations between the environment and socio-economic activity.

Sustainability can be trifurcated into social, environmental and economic considerations, sometimes referred to as 'the 3 Ps' (people, planet and profit).[139] Note that all three components are relevant and influence each other. For example, a company cannot be socially and environmentally responsible if it does not provide sufficient financial resources to invest in clean energy, and in employees' training, development and wellbeing. A socially and environmentally responsible company is more likely to attract customers that make the company more profitable.

Triple bottom line

Acknowledging the relationships between business, the environment and society, companies are increasingly adding two additional bottom lines to accounting practices by adopting triple bottom line (TBL or 3BR) accounting frameworks.[140] Whereas in traditional accounting the bottom line refers to financial profit and loss recorded at the bottom of a ledger of incomes and expenses, TBL seeks to reflect the full costs of doing business. TBL stresses that business organizations have responsibilities not just to its shareholders but also to a broad range of stakeholders. While the standards for assessing financial performance are well established, assessing social impacts is particularly challenging as compared with environmental impacts. A critique of TBL is that it treats the environmental and social dimensions as external to the organization as opposed to integrating them within the core of the organizational identity.[141]

Environment

The effects of business practices on the physical environment are quite visible and accordingly salient. Melting icebergs, stranded polar bears, felled forests, landscape reshaped by mining activity along with air and water pollution are not easily hidden and make dramatic media images. A company's carbon footprint (see Box 11.10), the amount of greenhouse gases (i.e., CO_2, N_2O, methane, etc.) released into the environment by the company's activities, can be calculated easily enough on the basis of the amount of energy (gas, electricity, water, fuel, paper and waste) used in company operations such as heating and lighting, running machinery and transportation of people and goods. Increasingly organizations are adopting carbon neutral policies. They are also taking account of the carbon emissions of their supply chains.[142] Organizational carbon neutrality is achieved first by reducing emissions and second by offsetting all remaining company carbon emissions with the planting of trees, or purchasing carbon credits from organizations that provide certified offset projects which include planting forests, reducing deforestation, establishing green energy plants such as wind-farms and hydraulic dams and even providing villagers in developing countries with more fuel-efficient cook-stoves. Carbon offsetting projects often provide wider social benefits in developing counties additional to carbon reduction, including jobs, education, food security, biodiversity, as well as enhanced health and wellbeing.

Box 11.10 Calculating your carbon footprint

Calculate your own household carbon footprint using the following free online tool: www.carbonfootprint.com. If you have the information available, you can also calculate the carbon footprint of a business you are familiar with.

Questions for reflection

- What is your carbon footprint as compared with other average households of a similar size?
- What steps could you take to reduce your emissions?
- Would you consider offsetting some of your irreducible emissions to become carbon neutral?

Social sustainability

While environmental impacts can be relatively easy to measure, reduced life expectancy and impeded mental and physical health are less tangible. Even high visibility cases of violence by or towards current or past employees have multiple potential causes. Such behaviour is frequently regarded as uncharacteristic and beyond the employer's control and responsibility. Developing valid and reliable measures of the social impacts of organizational practices, using them to gather data and publicizing the findings is therefore all the more difficult but also all the more important.[143] The resultant public attention provides organizations and government legislators with greater impetus for attending to the human sustainability implications of their practices. Increasingly organizations publicly listed on the stock exchange are required to report not only on their profits and losses but also to disclose exposure to economic, environmental and social sustainability risks. As an example, the Australian Securities Exchange (ASX) introduced such a requirement of all listed companies in 2014.[144] Financial profits, however, remain the main focus, with environment and social issues being treated as factors that pose a potential risk to the objective of high financial performance.

B Corp – benefit corporation

B Corp (see Box 11.11) is one approach to providing external assessment and certification of organizational social and environmental impacts that has been gaining in momentum since its founding in 2006 in the USA.[145] B Corp certification is a third-party certification issued by B Lab, a global non-profit organization with offices across the developed world, to for-profit companies. The emergence of the B Corp model corresponds to the erosion of trust in business organizations and an effort by social entrepreneurs to depend less on public subsidies and donations. To qualify for and maintain certification as a B Corp, organizations follow a three-step process:[146]

1   Meet performance requirements by taking an online assessment of social and environmental performance and meeting the minimum score requirement of 80 out of 200 points. Companies must provide supporting documentation prior to their being certified. Included within the assessment are measures of the company's impacts in areas of governance, employees, the community, the environment, as well as products or services provided by the organization. The assessment and certification are for the entire organization.
2   Meet legal requirements by integrating B Lab stakeholder commitments into organizational governance documents. These legal requirements include: (a) changing company by-laws and articles of incorporation by incorporating a commitment to consider stakeholder interests; (b) a definition of stakeholder as including employees, customers, the community, the environment, suppliers and shareholders; (c) the non-prioritization of one stakeholder group over any other; and (d) a stipulation that the organization's values must endure in the event that the organization comes under new ownership, management or investors.
3   Pay an annual fee ranging from $500 to $50,000 as determined by the annual company revenue.

B Corp certification is reviewed every two years and 10 per cent of B Corps are randomly selected each year for an onsite review. To ensure B Corp's credibility, its certification standard operates under principles of independence, transparency, comprehensiveness, comparability and dynamism. The 30-odd members of the B Lab Standards Advisory Council have the authority to make independent decisions whether or not they have B Lab's support, making recommendations for improvements to the B Corp assessment on a biennial basis. New versions of the B Corp assessment are released only after a 30-day public consultation period.

As of September 2018, there are almost 2,619 certified B Corporations across 60 countries and 150 industries, all driven by the shared purpose of 'using business as a force for good'.[147] Wendy Stubbs conducted interviews with 14 Australian B Corps and found that these organizations tend to view profit not as a goal but as a means towards achieving positive societal ends.[148] They further regard the B Corp model as 'a tool for change', that provides 'a common collective identity for internal and external validation'. Focussing on societal impacts rather than profit maximization, B Corps seek to gain legitimacy for this mode of sustainable entrepreneurship by influencing the business community and government representatives.

Box 11.11 B Corp[149]

The new corporate form known as benefit corporation, or B Corp, aims to hybridize social and for-profit companies: it has been defined as 'legally a for-profit, socially obligated, corporate form of business, with all of the traditional corporate characteristics but with required societal responsibilities' (Figure 11.12). This new form implies certification[150] covering a number of categories attesting the organization's commitment to social good. Legally, a B Corp is not a different type of identity but a member of a voluntary association, subject to assessment according to pre-defined standards. While looking for profit, the B Corp also needs to deliver a general public benefit.

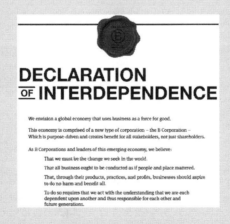

Figure 11.12 B-Corp's Declaration of Interdependence.[151]

Government roles

A fundamental tenet of free market capitalism is that government intervention in the market is undesirable (see Box 11.12). The market is regarded as invariably the best monitor of supply and demand, communicating through price movements what is fair value for a given product or service. Heavy-handed government interventions will create market distortions where certain industries are artificially propped up by bail-outs. Market distortions, however, are not just created by government interventions. They can also arise from business organizations acting in unethical, monopolistic or anti-competitive ways. Even Adam Smith recognized that government regulation had an important role to play in the free market, using both encouragement and coercion to ensure business organizations acted ethically, responsibly and competitively. The roles of government in this regard are threefold:

* The **legislative role** ensures that business organizations comply with ethical responsibilities and that society is not harmed as a result of unethical and illegal business activities.
* The **supervisory role** ensures that large business organizations with market dominance do not abuse their position by engaging in monopolistic anti-competitive practices. Monitoring and supervising business takeovers and mergers, which are subject to antitrust law, is a particularly important area of oversight to ensure the market remains competitive.
* The **incentivizing role** encourages sustainability among business organizations by stimulating desirable practices. For example, governments can encourage desirable behaviour by offering reduced taxes for businesses that demonstrate sustainable practices and imposing surcharges on organizations with high external social costs (such as the burden that alcohol and tobacco impose on the health system) and high carbon emissions that pollute the environment.[152] Companies penalized for wasting energy or improper waste disposal would be less likely to engage in such activities.

Box 11.12 The positive in the negative and the negative in the positive: the role of government in business activity

Too little government oversight

* Anti-competitive monopolization of key industries – undermining the benefits of free market capitalism and creating greater social inequality.
* Worker exploitation – underpay, unsafe conditions, discrimination, child labour.
* Consumer and greater societal harm through the promotion of harmful products or services.

Too much government intervention

* Dampens individual ambition and overall economic activity.
* Infringes individual freedoms.
* Creates a state of fear.

Since the 1980s with the advance of neoliberalism, the trend in much of the world has been towards less government oversight. Interestingly, it is also since this period, particularly over the last decade, that we have seen the trend of growing inequality, where the 1 per cent own more than the 90 per cent, as discussed earlier in the chapter. Oxfam sees government as playing an important role in reversing this trend by ensuring that:

- workers are paid a living wage with a cap on executive rewards and bonuses to narrow the wage differentials gap;
- women are paid as much as their male counterparts and compensated for unpaid care and receive equal inheritance and land rights, thereby narrowing the gender gap;
- government addresses lobbying, reduces the cost of medicine, taxes wealth as opposed to consumption and engages in targeted progressive spending to address inequality.[153]

Despite government having an important guardianship role to play in ensuring that business organizations do not harm society, there is a difference between not harming someone and acting in their best interests. For the most part, government authority has, however successfully, been focussed on ensuring that business organizations do no harm. The point of this chapter has been to consider how business organizations can do better than that and be a force for social wellbeing. It would be impossible and undesirable for government to oversee the operations of all business organizations to the extent of forcing all businesses to embrace the mission of being a force for good. This is a mission that business organizations can choose to embrace or not. If they do so, the rewards, a different type of reward related to a more healthy society, just may include prosperity (and profits) as well.

Final comments

The impacts of business activities may be positive or harmful, depending to a great extent on how organizations are managed. Leaders and members of business organizations have a choice in whether they will conduct their organizational activities in a manner that is harmful or beneficial to society. As Rosabeth Moss Kanter argued, 'instead of being mere money generating machines', great companies 'combine financial and social logic to build enduring success'.[154] Naturally, even the most well-intentioned leaders that aim to benefit the whole of society may produce unintendedly bad consequences. Meeting the needs of some stakeholders may negatively affect satisfying the needs of other stakeholders.

Sustainability is thus a work in progress, an imperfect purpose, a challenge full of difficulties and obstacles. Moreover, as with all good things, there is also potential for misuse and abuse, with the same caveat being applicable to some of the models presented here – enlightened business practices may be used as a façade for deflecting criticism and engaging in business as usual. To reduce those risks, governments can play an important role in providing the legal-regulatory frameworks and supervision to ensure that business organizations at the very least are restricted in causing social harm and at best are facilitated in pursuing a higher mission of being a force for good. As Lynn Forester de Rothschild wrote in the *Financial Times*:[155]

Markets mostly encourage a near maniacal focus on short-term financial results, tolerance of disparities of opportunity, and an apparent disregard for the common good. If these tendencies are left unchecked, the public cannot be expected to show faith in capitalism.

Sustaining such faith:

> is a tough task requiring leadership and co-operation between businesses, philanthropies, individuals and governments. It will mean investments must be measured not just by short-term returns but by the development of human capital, management of innovative potential, compensation aligned with true value creation, supply chains that are sustainable and measurable evidence of the overall contribution of the enterprise to society.[156]

Lynn does not see corporate behaviour changing until there is 'a critical mass of investors and customers who demand long-term thinking and higher ethical standards'.[157] We close this chapter by asserting that all of us must assume a proactive role in fostering sustainable businesses that operate as engines of socio-economic progress.

Want more?

To further explore the ideas of leading philosophers and social scientists on moral and political implications of capitalism over the centuries read *The Mind and the Market: Capitalism in Western Thought* by historian Jerry Z. Muller, published by Anchor.[158] Bobby Banerjee's *Necrocapitalism* traces the history of multinational organizations, focussed specifically on the darker side.[159] Moving from the darkness into a more positive light, Jennifer Oetzel and colleagues in *Business and Peace: Sketching the Terrain*[160] summarize research on the potential role business can play in facilitating peace, focussing specifically on the ways organizations can engage in reducing conflict by promoting economic development, external valuation and the rule of law. Identifying organizations that are actually doing business in a more sustainable and socially responsible manner, Wendy Stubbs in her article "Characterising B Corps as a sustainable business model: an exploratory study of B Corps in Australia"[161] interviews Australian business leaders who run 'B Corps' or benefit organizations.

Glossary

Authoritarian state   A mode of government where power is centralized under the control of an individual or elite group with minimal or no constitutional accountability and where public freedoms are subordinated to the state.

B Corp   A (generally for-profit) organization certified by B Lab, a global non-profit organization with offices across the developed world, as meeting rigorous standards of environmental and social accountability, performance and transparency.

Capitalistic organizations   Organizations functioning within the capitalistic system that are organized through markets, in one of which people lacking capital, the vast majority, sell their labour time, whose engagement will be controlled by managers representing the owners of capital.

Conscious capitalism   An approach to capitalism that builds upon stakeholder theory by incorporating principles of higher purpose, conscious leadership, and conscious culture exemplifying the 'TACTILE' values: Trust, Authenticity, Care, Transparency, Integrity, Learning and Empowerment.

Corporate social responsibility   Conveys the notion of business organizations self-regulating through the voluntary uptake of socially responsible practices above and beyond what is required by the letter of the law as a demonstration of corporate citizenship or corporate conscience.

Creating shared value (CSV)   Challenges the idea that the activities of business organizations and the wellbeing of society necessarily conflict, rather arguing that the success of both is mutually interdependent. CSV is driven by strategic opportunities that provide benefit both for the organization and society with a focus on incorporating a social value proposition within organizational strategy.

Ethical approach   Seeks to establish whether a practice is right or wrong on the basis of philosophical reasoning related to the actions contributing towards or inhibiting virtuous or moral conduct.

Human rights   Norms facilitating the protection of humans from abuse, including the right to a fair trial, to work and receive fair pay, freedom of religion and political activity, and non-discrimination on the basis of gender or ethnicity.

Modern slavery   Efforts to underpay labour through illegitimate means such as forced threat, ownership/control, abuse, dehumanization, constrained freedom and economic exploitation.[162]

Necrocapitalism   'Contemporary forms of organizational accumulation that involve dispossession and the subjugation of life to the power of death.'[163]

Pragmatism   Pragmatism considers thought as an instrument or tool for prediction, problem solving and action. In science, it is argued that the function of thought is not to describe, represent or mirror reality but to change it purposively.

Prudential   Drawing on judgement and wisdom to make thoughtful choices that maximize positive outcomes.

Self-regulation   Business organizations (or industry bodies) self-monitoring compliance with legal, safety and ethical standards rather than being monitored and having standards enforced by government enforcement agencies.

Social impact   Social effects of government policy and organizational activity on wider society, where indicators might include health, longevity, education and other indicators of wellbeing.

Stakeholder theory   Holds that the numerous groups impacted by (and that have impact on) organizational practices have a legitimate voice that needs to be acknowledged in organizational decision making. Relevant stakeholder groups include employees, suppliers, customers, financiers, communities, government bodies, the environment and trade associations.

Sustainability   Cultivating the capability for advancing wellbeing and quality of life by attending to multifaceted social and environmental concerns[164] in the long term.

According to the *Report of the World Commission on Environment and Development: Our Common Future* (United Nations) 'Sustainable development is development that meets the needs of the present without compromising the ability of future generations to meet their own needs'.[165]

Triple bottom line   An accounting framework that acknowledges the relationships between business, the environment and society. It adds two additional bottom lines to the accounting ledger to account for what is sometimes referred to as 'the 3 Ps': people, planet and profits.

Wellbeing   The physical (health), emotional (psychological), material (food, shelter, work, wealth) and spiritual (aesthetic beauty, art, religion) conditions of an individual or a group.

Notes

1 Pfeffer (2010).
2 Clegg (2009).
3 Clegg, Courpasson and Phillips (2006).
4 Kelly (2016).
5 Crane (2013).
6 Talentino (2017).
7 Adapted from Riemer, Simon and Romance (2013).
8 Plato (1992)
9 Artist: Jacques-Louis David (1748–1825). Location: Metropolitan Museum of Art. Retrieved from: https://commons.wikimedia.org/wiki/File:David_-_The_Death_of_Socrates.jpg. This work is marked as being in the public domain.
10 Aristotle (2013, p. 202).
11 Millett (2002).
12 Mark 12:15–16, The Bible: Authorized King James version (1997).
13 Mathew 6:21–24, The Bible: Authorized King James version (1997).
14 Cited in Tawney (1926, p. 35).
15 Artist: El Greco. Location: National Gallery of Art. Retrieved from: https://commons.wikimedia.org/wiki/File: El_Greco_13.jpg. This work is marked as being in the public domain.
16 Anderson (1974).
17 Muller (2003).
18 Cited in Weber (1930, p. 118).
19 Weber (1930).
20 Muller (2010).
21 Muller (2010).
22 Tawney (1926).
23 Schama (1988).
24 Skinner (1996).
25 Mandeville (1806, p. 6).
26 Muller (2003).
27 Author: Bernard Mandeville. Retrieved from: https://commons.wikimedia.org/wiki/File:The_fable_ of_the_bees-_or,_private_vices_publick_benefits_Fleuron_T077573-4.png (see also, Fleuron, a database of 'Eighteenth-Century Printers' Ornaments': https://fleuron.lib.cam.ac.uk/static/ornament_ images/067260030000150_0.png).This work is marked as being in the public domain.
28 Muller (2003).
29 Voltaire (1928, p. ii).
30 Voltaire (1778, pp. 38–39).
31 Author: Rev Stan from London, UK. Retrieved from: https://commons.wikimedia.org/wiki/ File: Royal_Exchange_(3624902569).jpg. This file is licensed under the Creative Commons Attribution 2.0 Generic license.
32 Muller (1995, p. 15).
33 Smith (1817, p. 199).
34 Smith (2010).
35 Author: John Kay. Retrieved from: https://commons.wikimedia.org/wiki/File:Adam Smith1790.jpg. This work is marked as being in the public domain.
36 Marx (2018, p. 163).
37 Marx (2018).
38 Blang (1997).
39 Hoppen (2000).

40 Debes (2018).
41 Banerjee (2008b).
42 Clegg (2016).
43 Robins (2007).
44 Thomas (1996).
45 Author: Francis Hayman. *c*.1762. Location: National Portrait Gallery. Retrieved from: (https://commons.wikimedia.org/wiki/File:Clive.jpg). This work is marked as being in the public domain.
46 Wilson (1993).
47 Connolly (2012).
48 Wheeler, Fabig and Boele (2002).
49 Mbembe (2008).
50 Banerjee (2008b, p. 1541).
51 Mintzberg (2014, p. 19).
52 Tavernise (2013, p. A1).
53 Reuters (2018).
54 Bennett and Lagos (2007).
55 Crane (2013).
56 Chan, Pun, and Selden (2013); Clegg, Cunha and Rego (2016).
57 Fisher (2014).
58 Cohn (2013).
59 Data from www.globalslaveryindex.org/, accessed on July 8, 2018.
60 Oxfam International (2016).
61 Trottman (2015).
62 Cebon and Hermalin (2015).
63 Dalton, Daily, Ellstrand and Johnson (1998).
64 Hill (2016, p. 10).
65 Dalton, Daily, Ellstrand and Johnson (1998).
66 Jacobs and Mazzucato (2016); Mohamand (2016).
67 Gore (2015).
68 Rosling, Rosling and Rönnlund (2018).
69 Wolf (2004).
70 Easterlin and Angelescu (2012).
71 Barro (1997).
72 From the Gapminder website: www.gapminder.org/about-gapminder/.
73 Prahalad (2006); Prahalad and Hart (2002).
74 Spreitzer (2007).
75 Spreitzer (2007).
76 Kaku (1997, p. 55).
77 Friedman (2005, pp. 586–587).
78 Adler (2008).
79 Fort and Schipani (2004).
80 Adler (2008); Fort and Schipani (2004, 2007).
81 Adler (2008).
82 Goodman (2018, p. B3).
83 Fort and Schipani (2004, p. 102).
84 Pope Francis (2013, pp. 45–46).
85 Pope Francis (2013, pp. 160–161).
86 Pope Francis (2015, p. 151).
87 Pfeffer (2015).
88 Pragmatism is associated with the American philosophers Pierce, James and Dewey. James perhaps captured the essential element for our prudential perspective when he affirmed that 'Ideas … become true just in so far as they help us to get into satisfactory relations with other parts of our experience' (James, 1907, p. 34). So, if we want to improve social wellbeing, the important point is to find those ideas that seem to work to improve it: the prudent person is, in pragmatic terms, the wise person.
89 Gatewood and Carroll (1991).

90 Friedman (1970).
91 Friedman (1967, p. 133).
92 Wolf (2014, p. 7).
93 Kay (2014, p. 7).
94 Bower and Paine (2017, p. 50).
95 Bower and Paine (2017, p. 52).
96 Bower and Paine (2017, p. 52).
97 Bower and Paine (2017, p. 58).
98 Connolly (2012).
99 Wheeler, Fabig and Boele (2002).
100 Bennett and Lagos (2007).
101 Chan, Pun and Selden (2013).
102 Fisher (2014).
103 Marens (2012, p. 64).
104 Marens (2012, p. 64).
105 Peck and Tickell (2002).
106 Journalists in New Zealand coined the term Rogernomics to describe the neoliberal eco-
    nomic policies followed by Finance Minister Roger Douglas in the 1980s. It was character-
    ized by market-led restructuring and deregulation and the control of inflation through tight
    monetary policy, a floating rather than fixed exchange rate and reductions in fiscal deficits.
107 The recipient of the Sveriges Bank prize in honour of Alfred P. Nobel, which is not a Nobel
    Prize.
108 *Time* magazine (1981).
109 Daube, Stafford and Bond (2008).
110 UPI. Retrieved from: https://commons.wikimedia.org/wiki/File:Milton_Friedman_1976.jpg.
    This work is marked as being in the public domain.
111 Wray-Bliss (2007).
112 Henderson (2001).
113 McWilliams and Siegel (2001).
114 Morsing, Schultz and Nielsen (2008).
115 Porter and Kramer (2006).
116 Porter and Kramer (2011).
117 Adapted from Bockstette and Stamp (2011).
118 Porter and Kramer (2011).
119 http://healthymagination.gehealthcare.com/en/about.
120 Freeman (1984).
121 Freeman (1984, p. 46).
122 Mitchell, Agle and Wood (1997).
123 Adapted from Mitchell, Agle and Wood (1997, p. 874).
124 Association for Project Management (2016).
125 Banerjee (2008a).
126 *Fortune* magazine (2014).
127 Mackey and Sisodia (2013).
128 Mackey and Sisodia (2013, p. 34).
129 Mackey and Sisodia (2013).
130 National Retail Federation (2015).
131 Author: ChadPerez49. Retrieved from: https://commons.wikimedia.org/wiki/File:Whole_
    Foods_Markham_Canada.jpg. This file is licensed under the Creative Commons Attribution-
    Share Alike 4.0 International license.
132 Caballero (2007).
133 *Fortune* magazine (2014).
134 Taylor (2018).
135 Sisodia, Wolfe and Sheth (2007).
136 Collins (2001).
137 The difficult truth of selling cancer did not seem to trouble Philip Morris unduly, however,
    any more than the maintenance of prohibitions against employees organizing collectively in
    unions troubled Wal-Mart.

138 Starik, Stubbs and Benn (2016, p. 403).
139 Fisk (2010).
140 Hall (2011).
141 Scerri and James (2010).
142 Benjaafar, Li and Daskin (2013).
143 Pfeffer (2010).
144 ASX Corporate Governance Council (2014).
145 Stubbs (2017a, 2019).
146 B-Lab (2014).
147 www.bcorporation.net/.
148 Stubbs (2017b).
149 Source: Hiller (2013).
150 www.bcorporation.net/Certification-Overview.
151 Source: www.bcorporation.net.
152 Stubbs and Cocklin (2008).
153 Oxfam International (2016).
154 Kanter (2011, p. 66).
155 Rothschild (2014, p. 9).
156 Rothschild (2014, p. 9).
157 Rothschild (2014, p. 9).
158 Muller (2003).
159 Banerjee (2008).
160 Oetzel, Westermann-Behaylo, Koerber, Fort and Rivera (2009).
161 Stubbs (2016).
162 Crane (2013).
163 Banerjee (2008b, p. 1541).
164 Starik, Stubbs and Benn (2016).
165 www.un-documents.net/wced-ocf.htm.

References

Adler, N. J. (2008). Corporate global citizenship: Successful partnership with the world. In C. C. Manz, K. S. Cameron, K. P. Manz, & R. D. Marx (Eds.), *The virtuous organization: Insights from some of the world's leading management thinkers* (pp. 181–208). Singapore: World Scientific.

Anderson, R. M. (1974). Population dynamics of the cestode Caryophyllaeus laticeps (Pallas, 1781) in the bream (*Abramis brama* L.). *The Journal of Animal Ecology*, 43(2), 305–321.

Aristotle. (2013). *Aristotle's politics* (C. Lord, Trans., 2nd ed.). Chicago, IL: University of Chicago Press.

Association for Project Management. (2016). *Stakeholder management*. Association for Project Management (www.apm.org.uk/body-of-knowledge/delivery/integrative-management/stakeholder-management/), accessed December 29, 2016.

ASX Corporate Governance Council. (2014). *Corporate governance principles and recommendations*. (www.asx.com.au/documents/asx-compliance/cgc-principles-and-recommendations-3rd-edn.pdf)

Banerjee, S. B. (2008a). Corporate social responsibility: The good, the bad and the ugly. *Critical Sociology*, 34(1), 51–79.

Banerjee, S. B. (2008b). Necrocapitalism. *Organization Studies*, 29(12), 1541–1563.

Barro, R. J. (1997). *Macroeconomics*. Cambridge and London: MIT Press.

Benjaafar, S., Li, Y., & Daskin, M. (2013). Carbon footprint and the management of supply chains: Insights from simple models. *IEEE Transactions on Automation Science and Engineering*, 10(1), 99–116.

Bennett, W. L., & Lagos, T. (2007). Logo logic: The ups and downs of branded political communication. *The Annals of the American Academy of Political and Social Science*, 611(1), 193–206.

B-Lab. (2014). *Performance requirements*. B-Lab (www.bcorporation.net/become-a-b-corp/how-to-become-a-b-corp/performance-requirements), accessed January 8, 2017.

Blang, M. (1997). *Economic theory in retrospect* (5th ed.). Cambridge: Cambridge University Press.

Bockstette, V., & Stamp, M. (2011). *Creating shared value: A how-to guide for the new corporate (r)evolution.* FSG (http://admin.csrwire.com/system/report_pdfs/1225/original/HP_Shared_Value_Guide.pdf), accessed December 29, 2016.

Bower, J. L., & Paine, L. S. (2017). The error at the heart of corporate leadership. *Harvard Business Review*, May–June, 50–60.

Caballero, B. (2007). The global epidemic of obesity: An overview. *Epidemiologic Reviews*, 29(1), 1–5.

Cebon, P., & Hermalin, B. E. (2015). When less is more: The benefits of limits on executive pay. *Review of Financial Studies*, 28(6), 1667–1700.

Chan, J., Pun, N., & Selden, M. (2013). The politics of global production: Apple, Foxconn and China's new working class. *New Technology, Work and Employment*, 28(2), 100–115.

Clegg, S. R. (2009). Bureaucracy, the Holocaust and techniques of power at work. *Management Revue*, 4(20), 326–347.

Clegg, S. R. (2016). The East India Company: The first modern multinational. In C. Dörrenbächer, & M. Geppert (Eds), *Multinational corporations and organization theory: Post millennium perspectives* (pp. 43–67). Bingley: Emerald.

Clegg, S. R., Courpasson, D., & Phillips, N. (2006). *Power and organizations*. Thousand Oaks, CA: Sage.

Clegg, S., Cunha, M. P. E., & Rego, A. (2016). Explaining suicide in organizations: Durkheim revisited. Business and Society Review, 121(3), 391–414.

Cohn, M. (2013). *Tax avoidance seen as a human rights violation.* (www.accountingtoday.com/news/Tax-Avoidance-Human-Rights-Violation-68312-1.html).

Collins, J. C. (2001). *Good to great: Why some companies make the leap … and others don't.* London: Random House.

Connolly, K. (Producer). (2012). Ikea says sorry to East German political prisoners forced to make its furniture. *The Guardian*, November 17 (www.theguardian.com/business/2012/nov/16/ikea-regrets-forced-labour-germany).

Crane, A. (2013). Modern slavery as a management practice: Exploring the conditions and capabilities for human exploitation. *Academy of Management Review*, 38(1), 49–69.

Dalton, D. R., Daily, C. M., Ellstrand, A. E., & Johnson, J. L. (1998). Meta-analytic reviews of board composition, leadership structure, and financial performance. *Strategic Management Journal*, 19(3), 269–290.

Daube, M., Stafford, J., & Bond, L. (2008). No need for nanny. *Tobacco Control*, 17(6), 426–427.

Debes, R. (2018). 'Dignity is delicate', *Aeon*, 17 September. Available at: https://aeon.co/essays/human-dignity-is-an-ideal-with-remarkably-shallow-roots.

Easterlin, R. A., & Angelescu, L. (2012). Modern economic growth and quality of life: Cross-Sectional and time series evidence. In K. C. Land, A. C. Michalos, & M. J. Sirgy (Eds.), *Handbook of social indicators and quality of life research* (pp. 113–136). London and New York: Springer.

Fisher, J. (2014). Fairer shores: Tax havens, tax avoidance, and corporate social responsibility. *Boston University Law Review*, 94(1), 337–366.

Fisk, P. (2010). *People planet profit: How to embrace sustainability for innovation and business growth.* London: Kogan Page.

Fort, T. L., & Schipani, C. A. (2004). *The role of business in fostering peaceful societies.* Cambridge: Cambridge University Press.

Fort, T. L., & Schipani, C. A. (2007). An action plan for the role of business in fostering peace. *American Business Law Journal*, 44(2), 359–377.

Fortune Magazine. (2014). *100 best companies to work for.* Fortune Magazine (http://archive.fortune.com/magazines/fortune/best-companies/2014/list/), accessed January 8, 2017.

Francis, P. (2013). *Evangelii gaudium.* Vatican City: Vatican Press.

Francis, P. (2015). *Laudato Si'.* Vatican City: Vatican Press.

Freeman, R. E. (1984). *Strategic management: A stakeholder approach.* London: Pitman Publishing.

Friedman, M. (1967). *Capitalism and freedom.* Chicago, IL: University of Chicago Press.

Friedman, M. (1970). The social responsibility of business is to increase its profits. *The New York Times*, September 13, SM12.

Friedman, T. L. (2005). *The world is flat*. New York: Picador, Farrar, Straus and Giroux.

Gatewood, R. D., & Carroll, A. B. (1991). Assessment of ethical performance of organization members: A conceptual framework. *Academy of Management Review*, 16(4), 667–690.

Goodman, P. S. (2018). Tariffs, and tough talk by Trump, upset a global consensus on trade. *The New York Times*, March 12, B3.

Gore, T. (2015). *Extreme carbon inequality: Why the Paris climate deal must put the poorest, lowest emitting and most vulnerable people first.* (https://policy-practice.oxfam.org.uk/publications/extreme-carbon-inequality-why-the-paris-climate-deal-must-put-the-poorest-lowes-582545).

Hall, T. J. (2011). The triple bottom line: What is it and how does it work? *Indiana Business Review*, 86(1), 4–8.

Henderson, D. (2001). *Misguided virtue: False notions of corporate social responsibility*. Wellington: New Zealand Business Roundtable.

Hill, A. (2016). Four ways to bring galactic executive pay down to earth. *Financial Times Europe*, 19 (April), 10.

Hiller, J. S. (2013). The benefit corporation and corporate social responsibility. *Journal of Business Ethics*, 118(2), 287–301.

Hoppen, K. T. (2000). *The mid-Victorian generation, 1846–1886*. Oxford: Oxford University Press.

Jacobs, M., & Mazzucato, M. (2016). *The Brexit-Trump Syndrome: It's the economics, stupid.* (http://blogs.lse.ac.uk/politicsandpolicy/the-brexit-trump-syndrome).

James, W. (1975). Pragmatism: a new name for some old ways of thinking (1907). Cambridge: Harvard University Press.

Kaku, R. (1997). The path of Kyosei. *Harvard Business Review*, July–August, 55–63.

Kanter, R. M. (2011). How great companies think differently. *Harvard Business Review*, 89(11), 66–78.

Kay, J. (2014). Rationality is at work in the season of forced goodwill. *Financial Times Europe*, 24 (December), 7.

Kelly, A. (2016). 46 million people living as slaves, latest global index reveals. *The Guardian*, June 1 (www.theguardian.com/global-development/2016/jun/01/46-million-people-living-as-slaves-latest-global-index-reveals-russell-crowe), accessed September 14, 2018.

Mackey, J., & Sisodia, R. S. (2013). *Conscious capitalism: Liberating the heroic spirit of business*. Boston, MA: Harvard Business Press.

Mandeville, B. (1806). *The fable of the bees; or, private vices, public benefits*. London: T. Ostell.

Marens, R. (2012). Generous in victory? American managerial autonomy, labour relations and the invention of Corporate Social Responsibility. *Socio-Economic Review*, 10(1), 59–84.

Marx, K. (2018). *Capital* (Vol. 1). Champain, IL: Modern Barbarian Press.

Mbembe, A. (2008). Necropolitics. In S. Morton, & S. Bygrave (Eds.), *Foucault in an age of terror* (pp. 152–182). London: Palgrave Macmillan.

McWilliams, A., & Siegel, D. (2001). Corporate social responsibility: A theory of the firm perspective. *Academy of Management Review*, 26(1), 117–127.

Millett, P. (2002). *Lending and borrowing in ancient Athens*. Cambridge: Cambridge University Press.

Mintzberg, H. (2014). *Rebalancing society: Radical renewal beyond left, right, and center*. Henry Mintzberg, (www.mintzberg.org/sites/default/files/rebalancing_society_pamphlet.pdf).

Mitchell, R. K., Agle, B. R., & Wood, D. J. (1997). Toward a theory of stakeholder identification and salience: Defining the principle of who and what really counts. *Academy of Management Review*, 22(4), 853–886.

Mohamand, S. (Producer) (2016). *Trump victory reminds us why we must look at politics and inequalities*. Institute of Development Studies, November 10 (www.ids.ac.uk/opinion/trump-victory-reminds-us-why-we-must-look-at-politics-and-inequalities).

Morsing, M., Schultz, M., & Nielsen, K. U. (2008). The 'Catch 22' of communicating CSR: Findings from a Danish study. *Journal of Marketing Communications*, 14(2), 97–111.

Muller, J. Z. (1995). *Adam Smith in his time and ours: Designing the decent society*. Princeton, NJ: Princeton University Press.

Muller, J. Z. (2003). *The mind and the market: Capitalism in Western thought*. New York: Anchor.

Muller, J. Z. (2010). *Capitalism and the Jews*. Princeton, NJ: Princeton University Press.

National Retail Federation. (2015). Top 100 retailers chart 2015. National Retail Federation (https://nrf.com/2015/top100-table), accessed January 1, 2017.

Oetzel, J., Westermann-Behaylo, M., Koerber, C., Fort, T. L., & Rivera, J. (2009). Business and peace: Sketching the terrain. *Journal of Business Ethics*, 89(4), 351–373.

Oxfam International. (2016). *Economy for the 1%: How privilege and power in the economy drive extreme inequality and how this can be stopped*. Oxford (www.oxfam.org.au/wp-content/uploads/2016/01/an-economy-for-the-1-percent.pdf).

Peck, J., & Tickell, A. (2002). Neoliberalizing space. *Antipode*, 34(3), 380–404.

Pfeffer, J. (2010). Building sustainable organizations: The human factor. *The Academy of Management Perspectives*, 24(1), 34–45.

Pfeffer, J. (2015). What Starbucks can learn from Pope Francis. *Fortune*, September 28 (http://fortune.com/2015/09/28/starbucks-pope-francis/).

Plato. (1992). *Republic* (G. M. A. Grube & C. D. C. Reeve, Trans.). Indianapolis, IN: Hackett.

Porter, M. E., & Kramer, M. R. (2006). Strategy & society. The link between competitive advantage and corporate social responsibility. *Harvard Business Review*, 84(12), 78–92.

Porter, M. E., & Kramer, M. R. (2011). Creating shared value. *Harvard Business Review*, 89(1/2), 62–77.

Prahalad, C. K. (2006). *The fortune at the bottom of the pyramid*. New Delhi: Pearson Education India.

Prahalad, C. K., & Hart, S. L. (2002). The fortune at the bottom of the pyramid. *Strategy + Business*, (26), 1–14.

Reuters. (2018). US panel rejects Philip Morris claim iQOS tobacco device cuts disease risk. *The Guardian*, January 25 (www.theguardian.com/us-news/2018/jan/25/us-panel-rejects-philip-morris-claim-iqos-tobacco-device-cuts-disease-risk).

Riemer, N., Simon, D. W., & Romance, J. (2013). *Challenge of politics*. Washington, DC: Sage.

Robins, N. (2007). This imperious company. *Journal of Corporate Citizenship*, 27, 31–42.

Rosling, H., Rosling, O., Rosling-Rönnlund, A. 2018. *Factfulness: Ten Puzzles That Help You Understand the World*. London: Sceptre.

Rothschild, L. F. (2014). Capitalism thrives by looking past the bottom line. *Financial Times*, May 21, 9.

Scerri, A., & James, P. (2010). Accounting for sustainability: Combining qualitative and quantitative research in developing 'indicators' of sustainability. *International Journal of Social Research Methodology*, 13(1), 41–53.

Schama, S. (1988). *The embarrassment of riches: An interpretation of Dutch culture in the Golden Age*. Berkeley, CA: University of California Press.

Sisodia, R., Wolfe, D., & Sheth, J. N. (2007). *Firms of endearment: How world-class companies profit from passion and purpose*. Upper Saddle River, NJ: Wharton School Publishing.

Skinner, Q. (1996). *Reason and rhetoric in the philosophy of Hobbes*. Cambridge: Cambridge University Press.

Smith, A. (1817). *An inquiry into the nature and causes of the wealth of nations* (Vol. 2). Edinburgh: Adam and Charles Black.

Smith, A. (2010). *The theory of moral sentiments*. New York: Penguin.

Spreitzer, G. (2007). Giving peace a chance: Organizational leadership, empowerment, and peace. *Journal of Organizational Behavior*, 28(8), 1077–1095.

Starik, M., Stubbs, W., & Benn, S. (2016). Synthesising environmental and socio-economic sustainability models: A multi-level approach for advancing integrated sustainability research and practice. *Australasian Journal of Environmental Management*, 23(4), 402–425.

Stubbs, W. (2016). Characterising B Corps as a sustainable business model: An exploratory study of B Corps in Australia. *Journal of Cleaner Production*, 144, 299–312.

Stubbs, W. (2017a). Characterising B Corps as a sustainable business model: An exploratory study of B Corps in Australia. *Journal of Cleaner Production*, 144, 299–312.

Stubbs, W. (2017b). Sustainable entrepreneurship and B corps. *Business Strategy and the Environment*, 26(3), 331–344.

Stubbs, W. (2019). Strategies, practices, and tensions in managing business model innovation for sustainability: The case of an Australian BCorp. *Corporate Social Responsibility and Environmental Management*, 26(5), 1063–1072.

Stubbs, W., & Cocklin, C. (2008). Conceptualizing a "sustainability business model". *Organization & Environment*, 21(2), 103–127.

Talentino, J. (2017). The gig economy celebrates working yourself to death. *The New Yorker*, March 22 (www.newyorker.com/culture/jia-tolentino/the-gig-economy-celebrates-working-yourself-to-death), accessed September 14, 2018.

Tavernise, S. (2013) Big tobacco steps up its barrage of litigation. *The New York Times*, December 13, A1.

Tawney, R. H. (1926). *Religion and the rise of capitalism*. New Brunswick: Transaction.

Taylor, K. (2018. March 2). Here are all the changes Amazon is making to whole foods. *Business Insider*, (www.businessinsider.com/amazon-changes-whole-foods-2017-9/?r=AU&IR=T)

Carroll, R., & Prickett, S. (Eds.), *The Bible: Authorized King James version*. (1997). Oxford: Oxford University Press.

Thomas, A. (1996). *Rhodes: The race for Africa*. New York: St. Martin's Press.

Time Magazine. (1981). A cravat for conservatives. *Time Magazine*, 118(1), Online.

Trottman, M. (Producer). (2015). Top CEOs make 373 times the average U.S. worker. *Wall Street Journal*, May 13 (http://blogs.wsj.com/economics/2015/05/13/top-ceos-now-make-373-times-the-average-rank-and-file-worker/).

Voltaire. (1778). *Letters concerning the English nation*. London: J. and R. Tonson, D. Midwinter, M. Cooper and J Hodges.

Voltaire. (1928). *An essay upon the civil wars of France: Extracted from curious manuscripts*. London: Richard W. Ellis, The Georgian Press.

Weber, M. (1930). *The protestant ethic and the spirit of capitalism and other writings* (T. Parsons, Trans.). London: Routledge.

Wheeler, D., Fabig, H., & Boele, R. (2002). Paradoxes and dilemmas for stakeholder responsive firms in the extractive sector: Lessons from the case of Shell and the Ogoni. *Journal of Business Ethics*, 39(3), 297–318.

Wilson, S. (1993). Historicism. *The Year's Work in Critical and Cultural Theory*, 3(1), 164–189.

Wolf, M. (2004). *Why globalization works*. New Haven, CT: Yale University Press.

Wolf, M. (2014). Opportunist shareholders must embrace commitment. *Financial Times Europe*, August 27, 7.

Wray-Bliss, E. (2007). Ethics at work. In D. Knights, & H. Willmott (Eds.), *Introducing organizational behaviour and management* (pp. 506–533). Boston, MA: Thomson Learning.

Epilogue

12 The positive–negative dialectic

Summary and objectives

In this final chapter we consider the ways in which the positive and the negative are inextricably linked. Doing so enables us to consider the nuances and mutual dependencies between opposites in organizational phenomena as the positive produce negative effects and vice versa. To consider these paradoxical relationships, the chapter is structured in the following way. It starts with a common criticism of POS as not accounting for the complexity of real people and organizations. That POS may sometimes be naïve does not mean that it always has to be so: certainly the desire to see only the good can lead to simplistic views of POS but more nuanced views are available. Positivity and negativity coexist, with each, dialectically, defining the limits of the other such that the positive is not merely the absence of the negative. The presence of the negative in the positive and of the positive in the negative is an always-present possibility. The positive may be rare but its glimpses are worth a great deal in a world in which dialectics are overwhelmingly negative.

In dreams

The positivity of new age culture and the many thousands of mostly American self-help gurus who help themselves, in varying degrees, to some of the business it generates, celebrates the power of dreams. A case in point is Rhonda Byrne, a self-help author, who suggests[1] 'Whatever big thing you are asking for, consider having the celebration now as though you have received it'. However, this delusional thinking does not fit reality. Gabriele Oettingen, a professor of psychology at New York University and the University of Hamburg, wrote:[2]

> Indulging in undirected positive flights of fancy isn't always in our interest. Positive thinking can make us feel better in the short term, but over the long term it saps our motivation, preventing us from achieving our wishes and goals, and leaving us feeling frustrated, stymied and stuck. If we really want to move ahead in our lives, engage with the world and feel energised, we need to go beyond positive thinking and connect as well with the obstacles that stand in our way. By bringing our dreams into contact with reality, we can unleash our greatest energies and make the most progress in our lives. Now, you might wonder if positive thinking is really as harmful as I'm suggesting. In fact, it is. In a number of studies

over two decades, my colleagues and I have discovered a powerful link between positive thinking and poor performance.

In an article published in the *Harvard Business Review* in 1994, Chris Argyris, a major organizational theorist, warned against the risks of what he called 'positive thinking at any price'.[3] He observed that the focus on positive values, such as job satisfaction and high morale, could be destructive and 'plainly counterproductive'.[4] In this final chapter we critically discuss the positive approach to organizations in order to extract the best from its conceptual potential, sorting metaphorical wheat from chaff, in a realistic way.

The chapter is informed by intimations of paradox and duality: the positive and the negative intertwine and blend in a process of permanent dialectics. To prevent naïve views of the positive (see Box 12.1 for a 'possibilitist' approach), we conclude with a fine-grained analysis of how the positive can become negative and how the negative may sometimes become positive. We discuss how good and positive effects can be drawn from apparently negative conditions or events, such as in the transformation of 'poison into medicine',[5] the importance of errors as sources of learning, as well as the development of post-traumatic growth after a tragic experience. We thus close the book with a discussion of the complex and nuanced relationship between positive and negative.

Box 12.1 'Bad and better' – a 'possibilitist' approach

Bill Gates considered *Factfulness*, a book authored by Hans Rosling, Ola Rosling and Anna Rosling Rönnlunf, as 'one of the most important books I've ever read – an indispensable guide to thinking clearly about the world'.[6] While it is refreshing that some extremely rich and powerful men actually read books in contemporary times, irrespective of their tastes in doing so, when the power of narrative sustained by anything other than a tweet seems to be in serious decline, the book in question has an ethical purpose that is empirically based: it presents empirical evidence that the world is a much better place than almost of us (including normal citizens, experts from different fields, and even Nobel Prize winners) think – in domains such as education, work, health, life expectancy, levels of poverty, children and women rights. However, several human instincts, most of them resulting from evolutionary reasons (e.g., paying more attention to dangers and negativity than to positivity was crucial to our ancestors' survival), lead us to focus mostly on the negative side of life in the world. The media and their readers are caught by the 'negative instincts' and create a vicious circle. By focussing on 'bad' things, we neglect that things are much better. Naturally, the world is awash with plenty of dramatic problems and events yet the authors argue that there is no conflict between celebrating the progress that has been made and continuing to fight further. To those who consider them as optimistic, the authors reply that they are 'serious possibilists' instead:[7]

> People often call me an optimist, because I show them the enormous progress they didn't know about. That makes me angry. I'm not an optimist. That

makes me sound naive. I'm a very serious 'possibilist'. That's something I made up. It means someone who neither hopes without reason, nor fears without reason, someone who constantly resists the overdramatic worldview. As a possibilist, I see all this progress, and it fills me with conviction and hope that further progress is possible. This is not optimistic. It is having a clear and reasonable idea about how things are. It is having a worldview that is constructive and useful.

The authors use the following analogy to argue that things may be considered as both 'bad and better':[8]

Think of the world as a premature baby in an incubator. The baby's health status is extremely bad and her breathing, heart rate, and other important signs are tracked constantly so that changes for better or worse can quickly be seen. After a week, she is getting a lot better. On all the main measures, she is improving, but she still has to stay in the incubator because her health is still critical. Does it make sense to say that the infant's situation is improving? Yes. Absolutely. Does it make sense to say it is bad? Yes, absolutely. Does saying 'things are improving' imply that everything is fine, and we should all relax and not worry? No, not at all. Is it helpful to have to choose between bad and improving? Definitely not. It's both. It's both bad and better. Better, and bad, at the same time.

In this book, we adopt the same 'possibilist' perspective. Although many things keep going bad in organizations, very significant progress has occurred in many areas. Instead of focussing on the bad with a negative perspective, it is important to adopt a 'possibilist' approach and focus on the organizational betterment.

POS's possibilities

Spreitzer and Cameron point out, 'some may want to dismiss POS as saccharine, naïve or irrelevant in the face of threatening economic conditions'.[9] Certainly, compared with the metaphors of everyday strategic management, centred on pursuits of competition, penetration, destruction, domination and inimitability, the language of POS seems weak by contrast. Seeking human growth rather than destruction is hardly the talk of strategy. The language of business and management has, in fact, appropriated and thus been influenced by the language and thinking of the military. Guerrilla warfare, targeting, strategy, plans and operations, as well as the continued influence of classical military theorists such as Sun Tzu and Von Clausewitz, suggest that business is not for the weak. In this context, POB represents the realism of a resister with a flower before the guns of the state – which is precisely what happened in the Carnation Revolution.[10] Resistance, as happened in Portugal on April 25, 1974, can be positive.

Being 'positive', as it is represented in scholarly disciplines, is not ignorant about the risks of naïve interpretations. Positive approaches have been critiqued for denying the negative in a misplaced criticism. Positive approaches aim to make the organizational world better by leveraging human strengths without denying either the existence of the negative or its inevitability. Moreover, positive approaches consider that the negative may be a premise or standing condition for better things to grow, flourish and build the positive. The definition of positive psychology presented in Chapter 1 is clear in terms of elucidating the importance of the negative in the study of the positive. Positive scholars should be well aware of the role of negativity in human life, knowing that 'the study of health, fulfilment and well-being is as meritorious as the study of illness, dysfunction, and distress'.[11]

There is much that is negative in present-day organizational practices: millions of slaves around the world (see Chapter 11)[12] coexist with other contemporary modes of human exploitation including human trafficking and child labour.[13] Work-related suicides, systematic bullying, toxic leadership, extreme goals and gross disregard for community, ecology and environment all epitomize the intoxicating power that organizations can bestow on those who organize. Suffering, dissatisfaction, interpersonal conflicts, disasters, disagreements, losses, bankruptcies – are all *normal* elements of individuals' and organizations' life. A few carnations can help mark, and sometimes make, a difference. Resistance in everyday politics can be positive and the same is true of resistance in everyday organization.[14] From a managerial perspective, resistance to executive fiat is negative; from a less marginal, interested and particularistic perspective, this negativity is the very source of positivity.

Some habitual criticism of positive approaches

The criticisms with which POS has been confronted are important to consider in order to develop a balanced view. Ignoring them would go against a number of ideas mentioned in this book, namely that the positive process is continuous and fragile. Hence, heeding the critique is of fundamental importance to developing more robust interpretations of positivity. In this section we aim to do so. Respecting the negative is important to manage positively.

Positive managers are dreamy people

Carlos Enrique Cavalier, CEO of Colombia's Alquería, is described as *coordinador de sueños*, coordinator of dreams.[15] In management and organization studies, one of the most respected of academics, James March, explains that reality is not incompatible with dreams.[16] Great leaders are moved by purpose but aware of reality. Those who inspire others are enthused by dreams but connected with reality. Aiming at building a better world through better organization is not incompatible with acknowledging the dark side of life. Much of how organization and organizing is done in too many places is deplorable from any ethical perspective that values the quality of existence: zero-hour contracts, abusive relations, slavery and other forms of subjugation that darken the human spirit, as well as evident disregard for nature and culture, blight all too many societies as too frequent sins of organization, sins that dull, depress and destroy the vitality of the human spirit.

Idealistic assumptions about people

An obvious criticism of stressing the positive is that it assumes a world that does not exist. In this world, people are respectful and power is used 'with' rather than 'over' others. Having such rosy beliefs could indeed be complicated when confronting people whose world views are rooted in respect for domination rather than difference. As Adam Grant has shown, it is important to give but it is equally important not to be a naïve giver.[17] Naïveté is not positivity. The world is not pre-categorized in terms of the good and the bad. What the POS approach defends is that it is better to adopt positive assumptions than limit oneself through negative assumptions. Not everybody has good intentions; nonetheless, assuming the negative as ineluctable will not create a path towards the positive.

False expectations

The pressure for positivity has been associated with false expectations, namely that it will produce good outcomes in a smooth way. Positivity is a difficult journey: more than hedonism, it incorporates a eudemonic component. Living with a purpose can be a source of pain and suffering: consider the case of Nelson Mandela. The positive is not painless and those with unrealistic views of self or their jobs may find themselves disappointed with the challenges and the hurdles it imposes.[18] Those who are obsessed with being happy, who take it as a birth right, are more likely to be more deluded (and possibly more narcotized in their failure to live up to expectations) than those who espouse the view that the pursuit of happiness is a path fraught with perils rather than an assured destination. As Laura King argued, 'The pursuit of happiness is rarely successful when done for its own sake. When happiness is the explicit goal, the pursuit is likely to backfire'.[19]

The positive is recklessly optimistic

Reckless optimism is not virtuous optimism. The world is full of examples of burst optimism. Speculative bubbles are a good example.[20] Expressions of virtue are a matter of balance. An excess of a good thing is bad. Moreover, pessimism may be the most 'positive' (i.e., virtuous) way to deal with some realities. Would you want a very optimistic CEO at the helm of a nuclear plant in your city? Remembering that compassion means 'suffering with', would we want to have uncompassionate coworkers?

Positive approaches promise that everything will turn out well

The positive and the negative are both part of life – as we have repeated almost as a mantra. Being positive does not mean that 'every little thing is gonna be alright'. It means that even in the face of adversity one can strive to be resilient. Pain and suffering are part of the experience of life. Ignoring them would be foolish, not positive. While pain is unavoidable it can sometimes lead to growth and to a greater sense of wellbeing. Perhaps one would not go so far as to agree with Nietzsche that whatever does not kill one makes one stronger: in certain instances this might be the case but as with most generalizations it is best related to specific contexts of application.[21]

In the name of the positive, people are invited not to make waves

Positive people can be represented as those who do not 'make waves' or who are 'nice': the drive for positivity can become an instrument of domination under the banner of the positive. When it happens, the ideology of the positive becomes as negative as any other authoritarian norm. In positive organizations, processes such as speaking up and tempered radicalism are seen as possible and legitimate. When positivity is elevated to the only acceptable ideology, it is positive no more. Organizations with a happiness philosophy may be a source of domination for those employees feeling disempowered (because of the design of their work or hierarchical relations) or who are suffering (e.g., because of personal and family problems) and feel that demonstrations of negativity are inappropriate in context.

In the name of the positive, people are invited not to assume errors and mistakes

To err is all too human but hiding one's mistakes is typical of organizations or teams ruled by fear, not by a positive approach. If an authoritarian rule of always being 'positive' prevails, errors can be hidden to preserve a desired image – fear is present. However, one of the most important facets of being authentically positive in organizations refers to the escape from fear. Positively organized units (dyads, teams, organizations) free individuals from the fear of signalling or assuming problems or mistakes. Positive organizations recognize mistakes as powerful sources of learning, as expressed in the concept of psychological safety (see Chapter 7).

Positive thinking is a superior state

Developing positive assumptions about people does not mean that everybody should be 'up'. Human life is nuanced; there are moments for the whole range of emotions. Forced happiness is the opposite of happiness; it is a sad tyranny of happiness as a regime, irrespective of the context and situation. Organizations exhorting their people to do being happy in an expressive manner are not promoting happiness but imposed role-play. In other words, people are being dominated. Cultivating civilized relationships is compatible with multiple states of mind.

Positive organizations are smooth and frictionless

In a caricature, positive organizations have no conflicts, no hassles, no frictions, no worries. Such places do not exist other than in the lyric of *Heaven*: heaven is a place where nothing ever happens.[22] No friction is a fiction: as Kelly pointed out, 'a world without discomfort is utopia'.[23] No matter how positive they are, positive organizations are human constructions. They are imperfect but there can be aesthetics in their imperfection.[24] Friction is inevitable but conflicts can be productive – they result from diversity, divergence and engagement. Good organizations know how to absorb and use the shock waves resulting from conflicts and turn them into productive sources of collective growth.

The above criticisms, as well as others (see Table 12.1), are important for several reasons. First, they help to define better what positive means. By embracing their

Table 12.1 Some important criticisms of positive organizing

Criticism	Argument	Clarification
Positive managers are dreamy people	Positive managers are unrealistic; they are motivated by idealism.	Yes if they are dilettantes; no, where dreams are complemented by an accurate sense of reality.
Idealistic assumptions about people	The positive movement holds unsustainable views about people and organizations.	People are different and naïveté can be harming. But holding negative assumptions about people will hardly do any organizational good.
Positive managers hold a romantic view of the positive	Given the above, positive projects a romantic view of the world.	It is important to consider that positive can be a path to demanding personal journeys. Leading with purpose and passion can even have a Quixotic side.[27]
The positive is recklessly optimistic	Because of its assumptions, the positive leads to optimistic views of the world that are misleading.	Reckless optimism is negative as exemplified by speculative bubbles. Excessive optimism is not virtuous (the virtue is in the middle).
Everything will be alright	The 'self-help' critique: the positive will materialize if we wish fervently enough.	Positive organizing is realistic: organizations are not exempt from pain and suffering, and assuming otherwise would be foolish.
In the name of the positive, people are invited to not make waves	The positive would invite people to be good team players and therefore to hide their disagreements.	This practice is prevalent in organizations with normal assumptions. Tempered radicals, devil's advocates and principled dissenters should all be welcome in positive organizations.
People will become less accountable	People will be inclined to see mistakes as normal, on the assumption that to err is human. This will breed complacency through niceness.	Covering up mistakes is more likely to happen in organizations where normal assumptions prevail. Positive organizing involves protecting psychological status, which increases accountability.
Positive organizations are smooth and frictionless	Positive organizations are a fiction: they are organizations without friction.	This represents a caricature of the positive: an organization in a pre-celestial stage or an organizational nirvana. It is not a reflection of positive organizations – these are viewed as real and imperfect.

concerns, it is possible to improve the validity of the concept. Second, they alert positively oriented scholars and managers to their possible excesses. Being uncritical about the limits and perversions of one's thinking may have dramatic consequences. Finally, they point out that perverse appropriations of the positive as an ideology rather than as a process orientation can be a source of human suffering, a form of tyranny which can be difficult to resist and to confront. Hence the positive is always dialectically linked to the negative: that's the important message from the critics. Using Hernes' process language, 'instead of assuming that things stay the way they are, they are constantly threatened with disappearance, at least in their present form'.[25] Embedded bad may well be stronger than emergent good[26] such that a positive organization is a fragile construction.

Positive and negative: how do they relate?

The idea that the positive and the negative are two sides of the same coin is an old one with many instances. Light is relative to darkness; beauty exists relative to ugliness; poverty relative to wealth; happiness relative to misery; victory relative to defeat; strength relative to weakness; movement relative to stasis, and so on. As the Greek philosopher Heraclitus (540–480 BC) observed, life is simultaneously tragic and comic. The way up is the same as the way down and we meet the same people going both ways, as is so often remarked.[28] It is by being denied what we want that we give value to what we prize. Sometimes the prize is its exclusivity as a positional good – it is valuable because one has possession of it and others do not.[29] If others did also possess it the value would be diminished.

The same logic of duality applies to positive organizational behaviour: it acknowledges the simultaneity of positive and negative, as in the Yin-Yang. The Yin-Yang represents the duality of things. Duality refers to opposites as mutually constituting. For instance, good and evil, day and night, love and hate, imply one another. In organizations, the same is valid for stability and change, exploration and exploitation, differentiation and integration.

We have presented positive and negative as existing in relation. Before closing, we discuss this relationship in a textured way. What does it mean to exist in relation? In this section, we explore four angles that can be applied to explore the positive–negative relationship: dualistic opposition or Manichaeism, golden mean, positivity ratios and paradoxes (see Table 12.2 for a graphic depiction). We do so with a reference to virtue, defined by Newstead and his colleagues as the human disposition to think, feel and act in ways that contribute to excellence and goodness, an emphasis that is at the very core of recent positive approaches, in contrast with previous humanistic approaches to organizations.[30]

Manichaeism

A first approach to what is virtuous and positive consists in taking positive as the opposite of negative. In this dualistic approach, organizations and their members are confronted with binary categorizations: either one is virtuous or non-virtuous. Such an orientation is expressed when executives are accused of wrongdoing while others are positioned as exemplary ethical role models. The inherent tension underpinning this categorization is powerful because it renders positive and negative as clear-cut categories with well-defined boundaries. Such simplicity, however, comes at the cost of ignoring the grey areas of liminality, where categories get blurred,[31] where wrongdoing is normalized[32] and where even the best leaders have flaws.[33] In a dualistic account, virtuosity is a binary construct. This view is present in media accounts of organizations that construct heroes and villains, as well as in the notion of 'bad apples'[34] or bad barrels. In reality, heroes can become villains and bad apples have nuanced relationships with bad barrels, making it difficult to draw the Manichaean line separating good and bad (Figure 12.1), unlike the rigid dualism between good and evil taught by the prophet Mani.

Golden mean

Some authors represented the positive as a line or a continuum with the positive situated at the (elevated) middle, representing a golden mean approach[36] (see Table 2.2, in Chapter 2). Aristotelian approaches to virtues advance an important framework.[37]

Figure 12.1 Mani, prophet and founder of Manichaeism.[35]

Virtue is the exercise of dynamically being in the middle. It corresponds to the cultivation of a harmonious state of equilibrium in which the extremes are avoided. As Crossan and her colleagues have explained, 'Aristotle conceived of virtues as desirable mean states between vices of deficiency and vices of excess'.[38] In this perspective, strengths are a product of equilibrium. A good thing in excess becomes vicious; strengths can become weaknesses.

The positivity ratio and curvilinearity

A third approach to the positive–negative relationship is curvilinearity, which presents the positive in the light of ratios: after a certain threshold, the positive loses its essence. This idea is well presented in several domains of management and business ethics. For example, an excess of success can lead to architectures of simplicity;[39] an excess of exploitation can limit the capacity for exploration;[40] an excess of positive emotions may make creativity less likely.[41] In business ethics, an excess of self-control can reduce ethical behaviour,[42] and leaders can be seen as *too* ethical, which will degrade the quality of the relationship with followers[43] and the efficacy of their leadership. Ratios make the role of non-linearity explicit.

Paradoxes

A fourth conceptual stream consists of exploring positivity as paradox. Paradox has been defined as 'contradictory yet interrelated elements that exist simultaneously and persist over time'.[44] The theory of organizational paradox is gaining prominence, as illustrated by the recent proliferation of research and the growing recognition that there is benefit in exploring the coexistence of contradictory elements in organizational phenomena.[45] This surge of interest can be explained by the acceptance that paradoxes are constitutive of organization, structurally rooted,[46] normal.[47] The relevance of applying a paradox lens to the discussion of positive phenomena has been captured by March and Weil, who noted that 'virtue only makes complete sense to somebody who has experienced the pleasures of sin'.[48] Knowledge of the positive implies experience of the negative.

Table 12.2 Virtuousness in organizations: a typological approach

	Positional	Processual
Oppositional	*Manichaeism* A *or* not-A Explanation: • there is a division between virtue and the lack of it; • this division defines the boundary between what is ethical and what is not; • Virtue stands in opposition with non-virtue.	*Curvilinear* Explanation: • there can be too much of a good thing (after a threshold is attained); • forces are theorized in terms of rations or thresholds; • a good thing can *itself* become a bad thing; • medicine can become poison.
Dual	*Golden mean* − ←Golden mean→ + Explanation: • strengths as a matter of balance; • balance as a point between extremes; • balance can become stabilized as people gain the habit and the behaviour becomes routinized; • the perspective importantly points out that forces need to be equilibrated; • it presents forces as dualistic; • it is underpinned by a dualistic understanding of the forces in tension.	*Paradox* Explanation: • extremes are interdependent, mutually constitutive; • balance is dynamic and unstable; • effort to equilibrate balance is continuous as the system is dynamic; • this dynamism is underpinned by a tour de force between synergies and trade-offs; • organizations can precipitate states of imbalance when they gain comfort with some force; • therefore, keeping the tension productive is a continuous and effortful process; • virtues can be vices, as they are two sides of the same conceptual coin.

We are not the first to note the presence of tension and paradox in positive organization studies.[49] The paradoxical tension between positive and negative has been explicitly described as defining POB.[50] The recognition of this tension did not lead to significant theoretical development in terms of approaches to becoming positive. This gap is surprising given the rich references to tension and paradox that can be found in management research on topics with which positive approaches deal. Yam, Christian, Wei, Liao and Nai, for example, studied sense of humour, theorizing it as a 'broad bandwidth' trait construct.[51] Humour can be positive by facilitating the establishment of rapport but it can also be demeaning and detrimental to interactions. It is positive when it is respectful and negative when it is aggressive and diminishing of the target.

In the latter case, it reduces engagement. Therefore, humour is positive *and* it is negative. Positive organizational scholarship emphasized the importance of positive emotions, namely positive affect[52] but negative emotions are also relevant for the production of positive outcomes, including creativity and productivity.[53] These are only two of the many possible examples of tensions in positive constructs.

In spite of the presence of paradoxical tensions in positive themes and constructs, the exploration of paradox and its conceptual and practical implications for positive organizing have been under-theorized, especially from a process perspective.[54] A conceptual vacuum results, notably regarding the understanding of how positive becomes negative (or vice-versa), how paradoxes persist, how contradictions can be tackled in such a way that they are used synergistically. In order to use a paradoxical lens to study positivity, we focus on virtues in organizations and how to understand them as rich in synergy and trade-off. By seeing paradox as a combination of synergy and trade-off, two core forces of paradox,[55] the relations between these two forces are endogenous, in the sense that each element contains the seed of its opposite, meaning that the positive and the negative compose a duality (Figure 12.2).

Synergy represents a higher-level articulation of opposites that transforms tension into complementarity. Trade-off, a common characteristic of life in organizations,[57] refers to the oppositional side of paradox. Paradox can be a source of tension, psychological discomfort, as well as the permanent risk of unbalancing.[58] Viewed from a paradox perspective, positivity, given its constitutive tensions and dualities, is a fragile process, one in which established states could be reversed; dualities framed as dualisms, positives becoming negatives. From a paradox perspective, the positive is not the denial or the absence of the negative but rather the dynamic interplay of positive and negative. Strengths and virtues are expressions of the constitutive tensions from phenomena that imply and negate one another. A paradox lens can inform the study of positive phenomena with a dynamism and conceptual granularity that will help to explain how positivity and negativity interact in nuanced ways. We explore the issue in the next section. We discuss how the themes of the chapters composing the book are rich in evidence of how the positive and negative are more intricately linked than is often assumed. Only one or a few illustrations per chapter are discussed, without

My nose grows now!

Figure 12.2 The Pinocchio paradox.[56] (Considering that Pinocchio's nose grows when he lies, what happens when he says that his nose is growing?).

any pretension of completeness, in order to obtain wide focus on the question: how does the positive become negative?

Exploring negative themes in positive approaches

Individual strengths

Some personal characteristics are normally portrayed as positive while their effects may be negative, at least in some circumstances. For example, more grateful individuals tend to experience more wellbeing and to develop better interpersonal relationships.[59] However, expressing gratitude can be problematic in competitive interactions and negotiations: counterparts may infer that gratitude implies forgiveness and will be more likely to exploit the grateful individuals for selfish gain.[60]

Several other positive characteristics may have negative consequences. Extraversion, for example, has been associated with leadership in the sense that extraversion is a facilitator of leadership. As Judge and Cable pointed out, however, it is a positive disposition that can be used in a negative way.[61] Extraversion facilitates power[62] but potentially reduces the inclination to listen, listening being a critical leadership skill. Extraverted leaders may be less effective at leading teams constituted with proactive team members: 'although extraverted leadership enhances group performance when employees are passive, this effect reverses when employees are proactive, because extraverted leaders are less receptive to proactivity'.[63]

Grit is important to persevere towards long-term goals despite obstacles and failures. Unless it is combined with prudence and humility, grit will have a dark side: grittier individuals may persist in unfeasible courses of action and are more susceptible to escalation of commitment or the sunk-cost fallacy. Or consider the case of optimism as energizing. There is abundant evidence that optimism, if not combined with a realistic outlook, can become problematic. An excess of optimism may lead people to discount dangers resulting in disastrous consequences. Confidence, or self-efficacy, constitutes another strength that may turn into weakness. Napoleon Bonaparte was a confident leader. Before attacking Russia, he won 35 military victories and suffered only three defeats, the latter early in his career. In June 1812 he marched towards Russia as the head of an army of 500,000. In December, less than 20,000 reached home safely, after a tragic defeat. The cumulated successes developed a sense of invincibility that partly explains why his self-confidence was transformed into arrogance and hubris as he prepared the Russian campaign against a winter that he had never experienced and guerrilla scorched-earth tactics with which he had not been familiar.[64] A great quality developed into a serious defect – not because self-confidence is per se a defect but because its fruits emerge only when it is combined with other strengths such as humility, prudence and wisdom; especially wisdom.

Authenticity[65] is also typically portrayed as a positive characteristic. It seems difficult to speak against being authentic but authenticity may be less valuable than it seems. People can display authentic irresponsibility,[66] while 'frank' and 'honest' leaders can be authentic bullies. Being authentic is not a free pass to say whatever one wants in the name of authenticity. There are several reasons for this. Leadership is a role and leaders are its actors. Acting necessarily comports a dose of in-authenticity. Roles shift over time as individuals move from one leadership situation to another. In the process, they have to express feelings and competences that may not yet have been achieved, which forces them to fake. As Ibarra has shown, faking can be a signal of growth rather than a symptom of lack of character.[67]

Emotions and the dark side of emotional intelligence

As discussed in Chapter 4, positive emotions are useful, most of the time, in organizational contexts.[68] Organizational contexts are too complex to be qualified as simply positive or negative, however. Human emotions are complex and work frequently involves contradictory emotional demands that elicit a mix of contradicting emotional states. In other words, people do not necessarily feel 'positive' or 'negative'.[69] A demanding goal, for example, can be received with a mix of thrill and fear. It is the interplay between thrill and fear that allows the individual to face the demanding goal with a mixture of both perseverance and caution, grit and prudence, confidence in the possibilities to reach the goal and fear of the inherent risks. Fear or thrill alone is less energizing than both working together.

Emotional intelligence (EI) is another quality that contains a potential dark side. While the initial theorizing and research on EI seemed to suggest that teaching EI in schools, workplaces and hospitals would lead to more caring communities, enthusiasm for EI has been tempered by emerging studies uncovering its dark side. A new body of evidence indicates that people can consciously develop their emotional skills not just as a force for good but also as a tool for manipulation.[70] Some manipulative leaders can be highly emotionally aware and practice emotion regulation to hide their true feelings and fabricate favourable impressions. They sometimes use knowledge of what others feel to play on their heartstrings and influence them in acting against their own personal interests. Sensitivity towards others can also be used to demean and embarrass others for personal gain. Kilduff, Chiaburu and Menges provide a poker analogy: 'a poker player with high EI can detect the emotions of other players around the table and use that information to advantage, while simultaneously controlling and regulating self-emotional display'.[71]

Work as flourishing

Work should provide meaning and personal growth. Purpose has been presented as infusing work with meaning. But purpose can be problematic. People who approach their work with a strong sense of purpose may incur a number of problems and difficulties. They may develop idealized understandings of their jobs. These idealized understandings, in turn, may fail to be validated by reality. As a result, individuals that initially approached work with a strong sense of mission may feel disappointed because reality does not match their noble expectations. Moreover, those people who find meaning in their work may become so deeply involved that they ignore other dimensions of life. They risk what has been called 'extreme working'.[72] Extreme workers are so excessively available to their work that they can become workaholics. Purpose may thus create empty lives, lives with no meaning outside the work sphere.

As relational interactive phenomena (see Chapter 6), organizations may stimulate positive forms of *interaction* that backfire. Researchers have praised the importance of compassion. Compassion has been devised as a quiet force that elevates organizations but even the noblest forms of interaction comport risks and potential negative consequences. Compassion can be fatiguing. Organizations devoid of compassion are impoverished environments but compassion can constitute a burden for those expressing it, especially those in managerial roles. Their efforts to express support may be viewed as in-role behaviours and fail to be appreciated by others as genuine acts of care.[73] This raises the question of who takes care of the caretakers? Additionally, having compassionate feelings toward other people may lead to closing the eyes or underestimating the seriousness of their unethical behaviours.

The same is valid for empathy, the ability to understand and share the emotions of other people. Empathy is viewed as positive because it is critical to understand other people's perspectives and points of view despite research exposing the limits of empathy. Empathy may be an essential quality of leaders but it can produce negative effects. Waytz presented three.[74] First, empathy can be exhausting. Jobs requiring intense levels of empathy (such as nursing or social assistance) can result in compassion fatigue, the inability to empathize due to stress, and burnout. Second, investing empathy in one person can reduce the willingness to invest empathy in another. Therefore, if someone invests empathy in his/her team, he/she may be less inclined to be empathic at home. Finally, empathy can erode ethical behaviour. One leader may be so attuned with someone else's suffering that she/he will engage in ethically questionable actions to help the other. More inclination to cheat exists when it is meant to help another person. Excessive empathy, or the excess of a certain type of empathy, therefore, can be problematic. Empathy can lead to condescendence or complacency with regards to behaviours that deserve toughness. This can provoke unwanted behaviours, for example in terms of ethical complacency.

Teams

Research showing that team dynamics can produce negative impacts is rich and diverse. Teams can be powerful engines of organizational learning and renewal but they can also be stifling. The well-known phenomenon of groupthink (see Chapter 7) shows that processes that are required for teams to function, such as cohesion, can become problematic after a point. The need to be a good team player can reduce the potency of teams by stimulating people to hide their doubts and convictions. A good intention, such as the desire to protect the team, can ultimately be a source of team failure. The excess of cohesiveness destroys teams. Research also indicates that diversity is good but it may be destructive. The phenomenon of diversity is a complex one that can have an impact on team performance positively or negatively.[75] Research on fault lines suggests that some forms of diversity may create divisions inside teams and these divisions originate subgroups that compete. Diversity, when expressed in this way, can originate problematic consequences.

A final illustration of the dark side of teams is group-shift. It is sometimes said that 'two heads are better than one' but this may not always be true. Group-shift represents the phenomenon of the initial positions of individual members of a group becoming exaggerated toward a more extreme collective position. In teams, individuals may collectively take risks that they would not take individually, or they may make more conservative decisions than if they made the decision individually. The shift occurs because of several reasons. For example, the group diffuses responsibility, the individuals feel that mutual support will emerge in case of failure, with individuals lose perspective and discernment when they observe that they share the choice with other members.

Leadership

The literature on leadership displays numerous instances of the negative effects of leaders and leadership. The best example is perhaps that of charismatic leaders. John Potts, a professor of media at Macquarie University in Australia, argued 'Charisma is a mysterious and dangerous gift'.[76] There is a romantic view of charisma that transforms leaders into heroes, special characters with identities that become widely projected.[77] These leaders are sometimes viewed as charismatic saviours.[78] Charisma, however, is a double-edged sword: charismatics often enforce malign forms of power (Figure 12.3). Leaders such as Hitler, Mao and Pol Pot projected power to exclude the 'impure'. The fact that expressions of destructive charisma are often supported by visions of virtuous rhetoric does not render them less evil.[79] Admittedly, for the followers of these leaders, their visions should have indeed been viewed as positive. Hence the question: who defines the meaning of positive? What is positive for some can be negative for others. The negative in the short run may be seen as positive in the long run and vice versa.

Workplaces

Organizations can transform workplace positivity into negativity in several ways. Ciulla emphasized the case of 'bogus empowerment', a form of empowerment that aims to reduce or remove dissent. This is accomplished via the creation of cultures of 'niceness'. Cultures of niceness assume that social harmony is the absence of conflict – the opposite of Follett's thinking (see Chapter 1): 'if no one complains and yells at work, then there is social harmony'.[81] Leaders of niceness lead in a way that is 'unauthentic, insincere, and disrespectful' of others.[82] Instead of genuine empowerment, this form of management amounts to little more than 'sugar-coated manipulation' that deprives people of their voice and dignity.[83]

Also, organizations aim to project images of positivity and sometimes go to great lengths to do so, not only when companies do good (e.g., environmental certification) but also when they do bad (tolerance of sexual abuse).[84] VW, the German carmaker, presented itself as a company at the vanguard of environmental conscience. This

Figure 12.3 Benito Mussolini and Adolf Hitler – epitomes of the dark side of charisma.[80]

image was shattered when the company found itself involved in a massive emissions scandal. The company engaged in a fraudulent system to measure emissions in order to pass the criteria established by the US authorities. A culture of fear instilled by all too powerful leaders contributed significantly to this process.[85] Good intentions may be neutralized by bad management practices.

Power

Supposedly positive practices can be framed negatively when the local political landscape is taken into account. For example, help seeking and giving, demonstrations of compassion and other positive processes can be received negatively. These processes take place inside complex circuits of power and the nature of these circuits informs the way they will be received. Some organizations deliberately create cultures of helping – IDEO being famous for that.[86] In some contexts, however, helping can be framed as a demonstration of weakness: those who need help can be categorized as less competent than those who do not need it, therefore reducing their power and status. Therefore, even those who need it the most can avoid a positive process.

In the same vein, some organizations adopt positive orientations such as the value of speaking up. But speaking up depends not only on the formal adoption of the value itself but also upon how local power dynamics support or counter it.[87] People speak up or avoid doing so, depending on how they see the power relations in their organizations, especially in terms of the receptivity of the boss. When a boss is not receptive to comments or feedback, their organizational value is neutralized. In other words, power permeates the expression of most processes discussed in this book. In the case of speaking up, the realities of power can stimulate people to enjoy the silence rather than express voice, even when the organization formally claims otherwise.

Progress

The role of organizations is central in tackling some of the world's most pressing issues.[88] Organizations embrace their social responsibility, define energizing purpose and engage with communities. However these positive approaches sometimes are pious expressions of nothingness. Messages do not always correspond to reality, creating organizational cynicism. The case of VW, mentioned above, offers a good illustration of rhetoric without substance.[89] But even some genuine forms of positive impact are sometimes negative in the long run. Microcredit is a case in point: it started as a solution for a number of pressing societal problems but was in some cases used in ways that adulterated the original, turning a good idea into an exploitative practice.[90] Corporate social responsibility actions, particularly philanthropic ones, may also be problematic if resources are spent in ways that put the sustainability of the organization at risk.

An overall perspective

The illustrations presented in this section show that even organizations intending to do good may end up producing nefarious results. Several explanations account for this reversal of good into bad. First, organizations are complex systems, in relation with complex environments.[91] As such, they cannot fully anticipate the outcomes of their actions. As Weick explained, 'events in organizations are held together and regulated by dense, circular, lengthy strands of causality'.[92] Positive circles can create unexpected and undesired consequences via long strands of causality.

Second, as humans, including managers too, have limitations in terms of understanding the long-term consequences of their actions (see Box 12.2),[93] what appears to be good in the short run may reveal negative consequences in the long run. For example, improving established solutions is wiser in the short run, instead of trying radical innovations. But the perfecting of current processes in the absence of exploratory efforts may, over time, reduce an organization's competitiveness.[94] Third, organizations are rife with paradox, which means that one positive process contains the seeds of its opposite, negative equivalent. Helping a colleague may lead the colleague to wait for help instead of taking the initiative. Being sincere may hurt others' feelings. Saving the company may require firing employees. Promoting an employee implies not promoting other candidates. Being a competitive company may put other companies in trouble and lead them to adopt downsizing efforts.

Box 12.2 Utopia to dystopia?

Bill Joy, founder of Sun Microsystems, wrote a disturbing text, 'Why the future doesn't need us', published by *Wired* magazine.[95] Joy presents a dystopian view of the evolution of technologies such as artificial intelligence, robots, deep learning, etc. In his account, the human species is creating conditions for its own extinction.

The process can be summarized as follows: as we develop ever more intelligent machines, the machines will be able to evolve their own capacities. Once we start the process it is not possible to predict where it ends. The question then is: how can one tell where it will all end?

Joy's message is powerful: the attempt to create utopian societies often ends up in dystopias. Once opened, Pandora's box cannot be closed again. After reading the article reflect on the dynamics between utopia and dystopia.

Exploring positive themes in negative approaches

Given the paradoxical relation of positive and negative, it is not surprising that negative processes may, on some occasions, hold positive consequences. Moreover, in some circumstances, adopting a negative stance may be necessary to achieve a positive outcome. In this section we do not aim to defend the deliberate adoption of negative practices; we rather show that becoming and being positive is complex. We do so by considering a collection of negative approaches than can produce positive effects. One must however acknowledge that several negative approaches that produce those 'positive effects' are ethically unacceptable. We discuss the issue here to show that reality is more textured than the Manichaean approaches tend to assume (see Table 12.3 for a synthesis). Organizations, individuals and leaders are not purely positive *or* entirely negative entities – they may be both.

Table 12.3 Positive and negative in POB themes

Theme	How positive turns negative	How negative turns positive
Individual strengths	A positive trait or state (e.g. self-confidence, optimism) becomes a liability because of excess. *Illustration*: an excessive agreeableness may be a cause of management failure.[126]	Stubbornness can produce positive organizational outcomes. *Illustration*: the LED bright lighting technology, which originated a multi-billion-dollar industry, was the product of a deviant scientist at Nichia, who continually violated the orders to stop his research.
Emotions	An excess of positive emotions creates a Pollyannaish mindset, putting people in their comfort zone. *Illustration*: optimistic assumptions about the role of markets in the regulation of the banking sector have been advanced as a cause of the banking crisis.[127]	Dissatisfaction can produce positive change and creative solutions. *Illustration*: when properly approached, dissatisfaction can lead to creativity and improvement.[128]
Flourishing	A romantic view of one's work purpose potentially creates disappointment. *Illustration*: idealized representations of work in animal shelters may lead to frustration, as people find obstacles to their inner mission and work with others with distinct representations of work.[129]	Poor work conditions can be circumvented through crafting or bricolage. *Illustration*: entrepreneur Tim Grayson was not stopped by the lack of relevant resources; he transformed lack into abundance.[130]
Interactions	Interactions driven by too much positivity lead to a culture of niceness, in which important but controversial issues are not faced. *Illustration*: a leader avoids difficult conversations in order to protect social harmony.	A harsh boss is not necessarily an impediment of development. Demanding bosses can be powerful agents of follower development. *Illustration*: tough interactions are sometimes productive, when leaders genuinely contribute towards the growth of the followers.[131]
Teams	Cohesion is so high that it traps the team in groupthink dynamics. *Illustration*: NASA's decision to launch the Challenger was partly a result of the groupthink phenomenon.[132]	Conflict and good fights are inherent to good teamwork and better decision-making. *Illustration*: voicing disagreement within a plane's cockpit contributes to reinforcing aviation safety.[133]
Leadership	A charismatic leader orients people toward disaster. *Illustration*: Hitler's charismatic leadership.	Fear and demanding leadership can push people to extraordinary levels of performance. Leader dominance can be good, as dominant leaders tend to provoke extremeness – positive or negative.[134] *Illustration*: in some circumstances, leaders have to be tough to challenge followers and make them more aware of negative realities.
Workplaces	An organization's public defence of reputation, for example, as an environmentally friendly organization, leads the organization to cheat in order to protect its public identity. The positive façade hides a negative core.	Crisis offers opportunities for regeneration. *Illustration*: at Korean Air, a plane crash was used to revise and improve the safety practices of the company. For example, to reduce power distance, English replaced Korean as the work language.

(*Continued*)

Table 12.3 (Cont.)

Theme	How positive turns negative	How negative turns positive
	Illustration: by self-presenting as an environmentally friendly organization, VW may have been more resistant to admitting a problem with emissions.	
Power	Close, intimate relations with powerful groups (supposedly a form of power with) lead to corrupt practices. *Illustration*: Volkswagen's relations with unions were so close that it caused a public scandal when it was discovered that ensuring labour peace involved prostitution services.	Top down power, often presented as negative, can be necessary to facilitate transformation. *Illustration*: the adoption of digital technologies or any other transformational efforts often demand a directive approach to gain momentum.[135]
Progress	Practices of social responsibility can exclude vulnerable stakeholders, therefore reducing social impact where it is more needed. *Illustration*: companies in extractive industries assume sophisticated CSR policies while destroying the livelihoods of indigenous communities.[136]	Embracing opposition can be a source of organizational contribution for the creation of shared value. *Illustration*: in the face of the protests of 65,000 Greenpeace activists, Timberland showed an openness that contributed to the transformation of an escalating crisis into a moment of growth through collaborative dialogue.[137]

Individual strengths

Negative traits tend to be intoxicating. Yet sometimes they can project positive effects. For example, arrogance may have benefits in some circumstances. Arrogance and displays of power project 'leadership' – at least in some contexts. Therefore, in spite of the defence of humility as an important quality of leaders, people can be sensible to the 'impression of power' and react more positively toward leaders who are not humble than to those who behave humbly. Luke Johnson, a British entrepreneur, wrote in the *Financial Times*:[96]

> We should not expect entrepreneurs to be humble, nor even apologetic when their grand designs come crashing down. By necessity they tend towards overweening self-belief. But such pride and arrogance are required if the status quo is to be challenged with radical new ideas; after all, weak characters give up too soon – harried by regulators, safety obsessives and the overcautious.

Other traits such as narcissism can also be positive. Narcissism can be problematic, but productive narcissists have an extra capacity to initiate change. The success of narcissistic leaders such as Jan Carlzon or Steve Jobs (Figure 12.4) to trigger fundamental change in their organizations is an illustration of how something that is typically negative can be rendered productive or even essential for achieving positive results, such as transformation.[97] Naturally, narcissism alone is not enough – research suggests that it is the combination of narcissism and humility that matters if leaders are to gain more positive effects.[98]

Figure 12.4 Steve Jobs: humble narcissist?[99]

Creativity may be considered a virtue (see Table 2.2 in Chapter 2). In knowledge-based economies, it is viewed as critical for organizational renewal. Yet there can be another side to creativity: creative people may be more dishonest. The explanation is the following: a creative mindset makes it easier for people to justify their actions. This ease of justification, in turn, can trigger unethical behaviour. The process was demonstrated in an experimental context.[100] For organizations, this observation suggests that even processes that are represented as positive can and do have a downside. Less than ethical inclinations can lead to positive organizational outcomes – in the short run. Stimulating creativity, therefore, implies ethical leadership but ethical leadership can be a deterrent to creativity, given that it imposes normative pressures that can counter originality.

Emotions

Life in organizations implies positive and negative emotions, both being intimately connected. Positive emotions broaden and build, while negative emotions are important for increasing focus and for stimulating learning: the constructive tension between positive and negative emotion is crucial for learning to unfold.[101] Negative emotions, in some circumstances, may help individuals to be more creative.[102] They may also lead leaders to get some results: while the leader's positive affective displays are likely to inspire creativity, a leader's negative affective displays may promote their analytical performance.[103]

This may explain why some leaders use negative emotions to elicit positive results. For example, Steve Jobs and Jeff Bezos in business and Alex Ferguson and José Mourinho in sports used negative emotions, including anger, to stretch the capabilities of their followers.[104] This style of leadership, to be productive, involves a measure of consent but this consent does not render their leadership 'nicer'. Therefore leaders not only lead with positive emotions but also through a broad emotional bandwidth. Leaders who know when to use negative emotions can improve organizational performance without damaging relationships. As Robert Sutton put it, 'sometimes, being a temporary asshole can improve a subordinate's performance'.[105] Naturally, one should ask if that is ethically legitimate! One may also ask if such performance is sustainable and has no counterproductive effects.

Flourishing

Well-designed jobs support work motivation. But a well-designed job is more than a given. Bad jobs can be crafted and turned into good by individuals themselves, as discussed in Chapter 5. Therefore, the positive can emerge from poorly designed jobs when people find a sense of purpose. Hence, negative can lead to positive through a personal effort to infuse one's job with meaning. This contrasts with romantic views of purpose that do not produce any good. Romanticized representations of purpose can lead to a personal sense of frustration and disappointment. A measure of realism and even an awareness of the negative side of work are important for the pursuit of good jobs. Flourishing may imply finding purpose in adversity. In the same way, flourishing implies growing pains as expressed by the paradox of excellence (see Chapter 1).

Interactions

Transparency and candour have been praised as important organizational qualities. Jack Welch, the famous former CEO of GE, defended the role of candour for business leaders (although he himself had been nicknamed 'Neutron Jack' because of his reputation 'for eliminating people while leaving buildings standing').[106] But Stanford University's Jeffrey Pfeffer departed from the Fleetwood Mac song 'Little Lies' to defend that being untruthful can be more positive than being candid. He defends that people claim that they value honest and candid feedback but mostly they really expect their 'wonderfulness' to be validated.[107] In the same vein, research on prosocial lies indicates that compassion increases the tendency for lying to help others.[108]

Interactions marked by non-transparency can be critical for sustaining positive environments and transparency can cause the degradation of interactions. The case of ingratiation is illustrative. Ingratiation has been presented as a fundamental means for building and maintaining social capital. Those who do the ingratiation validate the target's sense of worth. In the process, however, they may develop feelings of resentment towards the target of their ingratiation.[109] Ingratiation delivers socio-emotional benefits to the receiver at the cost of the sender's positive self-regard. What is good for one party corrodes the relationship. This can lead to a disturbing discrepancy: the target develops a positive understanding of a relationship that the receiver increasingly sees as negative. Research has shown that feelings are not necessarily reciprocated and they can even be misleading. Ingratiates can observe others doing the same and see that such behaviour is supported and rewarded by the leader. This can, in turn, cause envy. Subordinates may convey to their superiors messages that indicate the presence of levels of social capital that do not necessarily exist below the surface. On the basis of this belief, managers may consider that the social capital in their teams is already satisfactory, which prevents them from investing more in its creation, which ends up increasing the dissatisfaction of the subordinates that are an active part in the construction of the environment of their dislike. When they ingratiate persistently they will deepen the very dissatisfaction that they complain about.

Teams

The quality of niceness is often practiced in teams. Good team-workers are presented as people who 'do not make waves' or do not 'rock the boat'. However, teams that exaggerate the value of harmony may instead produce the extreme form of niceness called groupthink. To avoid groupthink, organizations need to instil some dose of an ingredient often perceived as negative: conflict. Good teamwork involves the tolerance of conflict.[110] Conflict around substance is critical to protect a team's appreciation of diversity. If the propensity for harmony reduces the capacity to withstand conflict, groups will be deprived of one of their most important qualities, that of diversity and constructive disagreement. Conflict must be handled with care, though. A meta-analytical study of top management teams showed that dissent produces dysfunctional effects;[111] negative interpersonal relationships may strain the process of integrating diversity productively.

A combination of divergence (diversity, variability) works better when combined with displays of convergence (mutual consideration and respect), as evidenced by Ashforth and Reingen in their study of the Natura food cooperative. This resonates with the important notion that conflict over substance, but not over people, constitutes a productive combination. In other words, it is not conflict per se that is positive, but it is the generative handling of it by people who know how and when to converge and how and when to diverge, that leads to good outcomes.

Leadership

Leaders cannot avoid the negative. Leadership involves choices and choices have consequences. Leadership is about change but change, as a duality, implies resistance. In other words, to lead is to induce change but the induction of change triggers resistance. Leaders thus must accept that their actions have negative consequences and that leadership with no negative consequences is an illusion.

The positive advocates a caring approach but there is ample evidence of the positive effects of fear and even of violence. Leaders such as Steve Jobs, Jeff Bezos and Elon Musk have used the power of fear to achieve change. The power of fear is patent in the movie *Whiplash*.[112] As noted by Lindebaum and Courpasson, the relationship between the main characters, young drummer Andrew Neiman and his sadistic teacher Terence Fletcher, creates a dynamic process: Neiman accepts the humiliation imposed upon him by Fletcher because, to reach the level of achievement he desires, he admits that he needs to be pushed to the limit.

As Morris Holbrook explains, this type of coaching can sometimes be productive even though deeply flawed from a human perspective, given the lack of compassion.[113] Violence can be accepted by the target in pursuit of achievement. By pushing followers beyond their limits, autocratic leaders can sometimes be loved and feared simultaneously, providing a hierarchically ordered reality that projects positive effects in cases where followers accept the style.[114] The admiration and fascination for a leader and the accomplishments she/he makes possible can, for some observers and subjects, justify the acceptance of domination. People rationalize such acceptance by thinking that without a measure of self-sacrifice nothing truly admirable can be achieved. In this sense, abusive leaders may drive exceptional performance in the short term. However, from an ethical approach, such a practice is unacceptable and unlikely to last the course.

The negative long-term consequences must be considered. The case of VW is illustrative of the long-term implications of leadership by fear. CEOs Piech and Winterkorn ruled as autocrats.[115] Some subordinates viewed their dominance as a sign of commitment to quality. Their leadership style created the conditions for the emissions scandal to incubate. People with reservations kept their opinions to themselves and the consequence was that the organization's reputation was severely damaged. Fear cuts like a knife and some cuts can go very deep: even when over-demanding goals are defined, people are not able to voice their doubts in order not to irritate the boss. The result is the creation of an organization that exists in reality only insofar as it represents the imagination of the ruler: all else is buried, hidden, deep, existentially corroding life and being in the organization.

Great workplaces

Organizations tend to be sensitive to institutional pressures for legitimacy reasons. As a result, they often feel pressured to comply with standards not for substantial reasons but because they feel compelled to do so. When that happens, there is a decoupling between the organization's discourse and its actual practice. As a result, they sometimes claim to adopt practices that do not correspond to what they really do. VW's alleged involvement with sustainability offers a case in point. It is thus necessary to accept that it is more positive to assume organizational limits and present the organization realistically than to follow the latest fashion superficially or decide some policy because of public or political pressure. What is sometimes perceived as negative, such as resisting pressures for certain practices, may in the end be more positive than simply complying. For example, consider the case of a Western provider of internet services confronted with the pressure to abandon the Chinese market because of autocratic government that controls its content. Is it better to align with the pressure in the West or to stay and try to do something to change the system?

Power organizing relations

As Follett defended (see Chapters 1 and 10), *power with* tends to be more productive than *power over*. In other words, respecting people and giving them voice tends to be superior to forms of leadership based on the imposition of power over others. However, using power in a top-down way, with limited voice and participation, can be adequate to effect transformational change. For example, experts in the field of digital transformation defend that in order to embrace a digital strategy organizations need strong, top-down leadership.[116] Therefore, leadership involves the use of *power over* as a lever of change in a way to achieve a situation of power (to do something innovative) that is nuanced rather than uniform. *Power with* can be philosophically superior to *power over*, but leaders need to be able to know how to use *power over* and *power to* if desired change is to happen.

The positive is often equated with a soft power approach but it is better perceived as the use of smart power, a combination of hard and soft forms of power. Or as a product of contingencies: in some situations, fear may be a signal that the current situation is untenable and that change is mandatory.[117] Being led by a leader who is disagreeable but generous may be a source of action rather than paralysis – bearing in mind that being a giver (see Chapter 6) is not the same as being nice.[118]

It is also important to note that the negative power[119] (i.e., the resistance aimed at stopping the activity of powerful authorities) may be a form of resistance towards perverse leadership and organizational activities, thus contributing to saving the organization from unethical activities and reputational damages. Whistleblowing is likely the most relevant and complex form of resistance.[120] Erika Kelton discussed in *Forbes* magazine '14.7 billion reasons why Volkswagen should have welcomed whistle-blowers' instead of having punished them.[121] When some forms of 'negative power' are supported and permitted, organizations are more able to avoid external 'delations' that produce huge damages to organizational reputation. As Kelton argues:[122]

> A serious commitment to correcting problems exposed by employees can make a big difference, but it can't be faked. Research has found that nine out of 10 employees first turn to someone inside the company to complain about wrong-doing. More often than not, it's only when employees are retaliated against, ignored or fired that they go to the government and blow the whistle.

Juliet Macur also wrote in *The New York Times* that the 'First Medal of Rio Olympics Deserves to Go to ... a Whistle-Blower' – Grigory Rodchenkov, the former director of Russia's anti-doping lab, who spoke out about Russian doping:[123]

> What makes him a hero in today's Olympic movement – one of the current heroes, I should say – is that he was brave enough to blow the whistle on Russia's state-sponsored doping program ... Because Rodchenkov told his story, there just might be fewer dopers competing in the Rio Games next month. His efforts could also embolden other whistle-blowers to come forward and expose cheating in sports. This could be a watershed moment for Olympic sport in its longstanding battle with dopers.

Organizations as engines of progress

Organizations tackle critical human problems and they often try to use this to their benefit by showing their credentials, but when they proclaim the importance of a given value, they have to be consequential. If an organization puts shareholders above all other stakeholders, it should assume it. When an organization establishes its consideration for the environment, it should act as a motor of environmental progress. When an organization, say VW, proclaims its defence of the environment and falsifies its emissions, it is doing harm to itself. As Ewing described:

> the deployment of defeat devices at the same time that Volkswagen trumpeted its commitment to the environment seems like an extreme case of corporate cognitive dissonance.[124]

Therefore, something potentially perceived as negative, such as a limited inclination towards social responsibility, can be more positive and authentic than expressions of virtue that are window-dressing – and nothing more. Realistically, an organization that assumes that the business of business is business is more transparent than one that projects false images of corporate responsibility. When Patagonia assumed that it would use durable water repellent (DWR) because of its importance to the quality and durability of its products, in spite of its negative environmental implications, it was being more positive than companies that pretend that they care about the environment. Instead of being passive, however, the company embraced the product quality–environmental sustainability tension to explore new possibilities for solving the DWR problem, which reveals genuine commitment rather than mere green rhetoric.[125]

If the positive is so good, why is it so rare?

Considering the benefits of positivity discussed throughout the book, positive organizations should be abundant. Yet they are not. In this section we advance possible explanations of why positive organizing is rare.

Inadequate understanding of the meaning of 'positive'

Organizations sometimes resist positive approaches because they interpret the meaning of positive in an inadequate way. Positive is equated with naïvety: in a dog-eat-dog world of competition, the positive approaches should be handled with care. This understanding is well captured in the idea that nice guys finish last, in the consideration that power is a negative force, in the acceptance that competition means the avoidance of collaboration. In fact, givers can finish first, power can be a positive force for good and competition may involve a measure of collaboration, as reflected in the notion of coopetition.

The meaning of positive is also often misinterpreted as a consequence of biased Darwinian assumptions about humans. Darwinianism is incomplete as an explanation of human behaviour.[138] Human beings contain the worst and the best – not just the worst. Over millions of years, humans' survival depended on both competition *and* cooperation, helping others *and* stealing from them, exhibiting sharing *and* selfish behaviours.

Normality is considered normal – even when it is not

The assumptions christened by Heynoski and Quinn (see Chapter 1) as normal are predominant. They tend to be considered the standard. Most people are socialized in these type of norms and tend to reproduce them. The positive is the extra-ordinary, that which escapes the prevailing paradigm. Therefore, being positive constitutes a deliberate departure from the norm. Considering the prevalence of normal, the positive paradigm is an effortful deviation and may be met with reservations. In short: the fact that a specific negative practice is *normal*, in that it is the most common way in which things are done, does not mean that such a practice is inherent to social/organizational existence. Slavery was *normal* for centuries – nowadays, it is considered as *abnormal* because a positive deviance approach re-categorized *normalcy*.

Personal reservations

The application of positive approaches may be countered by the lack of personal adherence, mainly from powerful figures within academia and the business community. Jim Mallozzi, an adopter of the principles of POS, described the experience at his company:

> about 50 to 60 per cent of the people, if you're lucky, will get it pretty much out of the box. About 20 to 30 per cent of the folks kind of sit on the sideline and

say, 'Is this just Jim's management thing du jour?' About 10 per cent of the people will positively reject everything that I talk about. They will just say, 'It doesn't make any sense. Sorry, it's not working for me.' And that's okay. I don't argue with them. They will be out of alignment with where we're trying to drive the organization, and they should go to a place where they will be in alignment. I quickly encourage them to go there.[139]

Effortful construction of positivity is demanding

Positive approaches are hard to implement, implying relentless effort – including against pseudo-realistic opposition. Being a boss because of one's position in the hierarchy is certainly less demanding than leading on the supposition that one has no inherent formal power if legitimacy and consent are lacking for one's actions, as is the case with positive leadership. Positive organizations are the result of concerted, consistent and coordinated efforts by groups of people. It is difficult to sustain these processes. If organizations tolerate bad examples, if they do not practice the values that they formally espouse, if they suspend positivity in face of adversity, positivity will prove ephemeral.

Moreover, leading positively is an act of courage, involving the willingness to speak up, to express one's vulnerabilities, to counter what is considered normal. Humanity and organizational progress have emerged from the courage of individuals and minorities who believed that positivity, ethics and human dignity are always a work in progress – and therefore must be continuously pursued, in spite of obstacles, failures and setbacks. Remember, for example, that the assumption of *homo economicus*, once considered undebatable, was initially questioned by a minority and is nowadays assumed as representing a biased interpretation of human beings' motivation.

Simplistic understandings of positive management

Managing positively implies breaking with a number of normal practices, such as long working hours, and the adoption of a configuration of layered, mutually reinforcing practices, involving forms of tacit knowledge, built locally over time. In other words, the creation of positive organizations is not the application of a recipe. When organizations embrace good practices as a formula, they often do so incompletely, adopting simplistic versions of the practice, emphasizing the observable and more superficial dimensions. Therefore, positive practices put in place as a formula differ markedly from the configurational elements that are developed over time, which render positive management as a source of competitive advantage.[140]

Positivity as an exercise in humility

Being positive is an exercise in grounded rather than obsequious humility. Power often finds its recognition in forms of obsequiousness on the part of the dominated that are assumed to be a display of consent to the rule of the leader. Such displays are helpful to neither party nor to organizations that tolerate them.

Positive organizational members are aware of how much they depend on others. Maintaining one's groundedness may be difficult when one ascends the organizational ladder: power changes cognition and even the humble may lose humility. Keltner called this dynamic the paradox of power: people ascend to power because they consider others but, once in power, they tend to care less about these others, forgetting the reasons why they have emerged as powerful in the first place.[141] Therefore, conserving humility can constitute a difficult exercise of self-leadership. The power paradox claims many victims in organizations and constitutes an obstacle to positive management as it diminishes empathy and attention to others. Extreme reflexivity is called for: 'why am I doing this in this way?' is a question that should be uppermost.

Positivity is a historical and path-dependent process

Hackman pointed out that organizational positivity is often conceived in an a-historical perspective.[142] This criticism is important, as previous organizational histories may make the construction of positivity a difficult endeavour. When organizations have histories that counter the positive, it will be difficult for them to convince people that the good intentions of positive management are genuine. The proposal of the positive can instead give rise to cynicism – which will render future efforts in a positive direction even harder. One has to acknowledge that this cynicism is sometimes understandable and must be seen as 'legitimate', representing a wise interpretation. In fact, the positive narrative is sometimes used for mere manipulation. However, the problem emerges from how positive approaches are used and implemented. Love is sometimes used in manipulative ways but this does not mean that love is bad; what is bad is how, in using it, it may be used to use others.

Positivity is a secondary result

As Ewing reports in his book on the emissions scandal of VW, the fact that CEO Piech adopted a dictatorial style and stimulated a corrupted culture (for example, sending workers' representatives to bordellos in order to assure labour peace) was ignored by shareholders because he 'delivered'. Organizations thus ignore the negative because economic results are positive. If effectiveness is the dominant factor, the positive is no more than a nice to have – if possible, when possible. Unfortunately, the consequences are often perverse in the long run, as shown by scandals such as Volkswagen[143] and Wells Fargo.[144] Al Dunlap, nicknamed 'chainsaw' because of his rudeness, brutality and aggressive management style, was hired to save Sunbeam: he had got 'results' in other companies.[145] He was fired two years after having held the company's helm. Hired as a saviour, he ended up being the 'gravedigger' of the company, which filed for bankruptcy in 2001.

Negativity is always close

Positivity is a process more than a state. By this we mean that organizations, as Quinn remarked, are always in the process of becoming something different: they can become more positive or more negative. Order and disorder are twin siblings (Figure 12.5).[146] Positivity, moreover, is a fragile process, which critically depends upon the nature of relationships. It depends on leader influence, namely top leadership example. If top managers do not support it, it will be made more fragile. It is wise for leaders to consider positive organizations as works in progress, constantly on the verge of negativity.

Figure 12.5 What do you see in the picture?
('Pavilhão do Conhecimento', Lisbon, Portugal.)[148]

Because bad is stronger than good,[147] in the sense that it attracts people's attention more immediately, bad interactions will render the positive fabric of organizations especially vulnerable.

Making positive more abundant

The discipline of positive organization studies is sometimes portrayed as a field with utopian, unrealistic foundations; a cauldron of good intentions with no practical justification. In the 'real world' there would be no place for such a naïve understanding of organization. The criticism should be heeded rather than ignored. A positively balanced approach is necessary to create better workplaces, not to design perfect organizations but to improve existing designs; not to replace hard work with fun but to create meaningful and engaging workplaces.

We conclude with a few reflections on how anyone can be a positive change agent (see Box 12.3):

- Each person is but one element in humanity but the multitude of humanity is composed of us. In other words: we can all potentially make the difference. The Arab Spring became a series of revolutionary movements in Northern Africa and the Middle East with mixed positive and negative results. One man with no special position of privilege in society ignited the Arab Spring. This man, Mohamed Bouazizi, a successful but accidental revolutionary, inadvertently ignited the Middle East, in various ways, for good or ill. Gandhi, Mandela and other positive deviants decided not to neutralize their power. Instead, they used it to create the better world they imagined.
- Small things count. One of the conclusions of exercises such as the composition of one's reflected best self (see Chapter 2) is that people sometimes remember seemingly minor but highly relevant interactions. In other words, we often have an impact without even knowing it.
- It is important not to be naïve. Being positive will not lead anyone to be loved by everybody else. Leading and managing positively is *managing* nonetheless: it involves the use of power, decision-making, resource distribution and a number

of practices that will necessarily produce friction and tension. Aiming at being positive at any price is going to produce negativity and toxicity.

- Managing positively is about doing right things and doing things right. A high sense of purpose in the absence of good execution amounts to little more than organizational delusion. Organizations need vision, purpose and idealism but they also need good execution, hard work and pragmatism.[149]
- Finally, positivity is a process. It requires constant maintenance. It never sustains itself.

There is no such a thing as a perfect organization but organizations can develop perfective views of themselves, aspiring to become better and more humane. Positive businesses and organizations are not states but processes. The organizations we used to illustrate our arguments may have been positive but it is possible that some of them stopped being so in the very moment the book reaches you. Other organizations may have been criticized here but developed positive practices later. Organization is becoming; positive organizing is about becoming better.

Box 12.3 Teaching humility and curiosity

In *Factfulness*, Hans Rosling and his co-authors wrote that, to foster a possibilist approach (see Box 12.1) toward world betterment, 'we should be teaching our children humility and curiosity'.[150] They also stated:

> Being humble, here, means being aware of how difficult your instincts can make it to get the facts right. It means being realistic about the extent of your knowledge. It means being happy to say 'I don't know.' It also means, when you do have an opinion, being prepared to change it when you discover new facts. It is quite relaxing being humble, because it means you can stop feeling pressured to have a view about everything, and stop feeling you must be ready to defend your views all the time. Being curious means being open to new information and actively seeking it out. It means embracing facts that don't fit your worldview and trying to understand their implications. It means letting your mistakes trigger curiosity instead of embarrassment.

Questions for reflection

- Do you consider that students in business schools should be taught the virtues of humility and curiosity to foster their 'possibilist' perspective about organizational betterment?
- Or do you consider that such teachings are more effective in children?
- Why are several scholars and businesses so sceptical about positive approaches? Are they devoid of humility and curiosity? Or are they filled with cynicism emerging from their own experiences and lessons learned in business school?

Implications for managing positively

Before closing, we stress that positive prescriptions should be handled with care. Attempts to create thriving human communities of work are not a prescription or an organizational design. As Conlin summarized, 'some … attempts at mood elevation and enforced fun sound like the work of the happiness police'.[151] We defend no happiness police. On the contrary, positivity should be allowed to flourish in different and unique ways. As Norem and Chang have pointed out, people are complex and should not be approached as if they are similar.[152] 'One size fits all models' should be carefully avoided. What works for a given person at a given moment is not necessarily what will help another person or the same person in a different moment. Another may perceive what one person regards as optimism as a lack of conscience.

Even though evidence on the positive consequences of optimism and positivity abounds, it does not mean that people should be pressed to be optimistic, happy or positive. Classifying processes as positive should be done with care and respect for individual differences and motivations. After all, life is *more positive* when both *positive and negative* sides are handled with realism.

Final comments

Terence Mitchell's analysis of the evolution of the field of organizational behaviour asks what is the goal of the discipline and its researchers? He answers in the following way:

> organizations can be both better places for people to work as well as more effective … [in] how people are treated; how organizational processes designed to manage, lead, and motivate can be more caring and inclusive; and how behavior can be ethical, with organizations contributing to the growth, health, and humanity of their employees.[153]

The second quote is from Csikszentmihalyi, who wrote: 'Business that does not contribute to human growth and well-being is not worth doing, no matter how much profit it generates in the short run'.[154] We couldn't agree more! Bon Voyage.

Want more?

Having mostly suggested positive-oriented works, in this chapter we focus on good readings that accentuate the negative. We start with three important articles by Collinson[155], Fineman[156] and Hackman.[157] These articles offer a good understanding of the criticism of the positive in organization studies. The critical perspective of Caza and Carroll[158] may also be helpful. Ehrenreich's *Brightsided* is also a powerful book on the dangers of the positive as well as Davies' *The Happiness Industry*.

Glossary

Dualism   Processes that are viewed as opposing and negating one another, such as change and resistance. The same process may be interpreted as a duality.

Duality   Processes that are viewed as interdependent, mutually constituting and contradictory, such as change and resistance. The same process may be interpreted as dualism.

Golden mean   The Aristotelian perspective according to which virtue is the exercise of dynamically being in the middle (e.g., bravery or courage is the middle of two extremes: cowardice and recklessness). (See Chapter 2.)

Manichaeism[159]   A dualistic approach according to which the world (including individuals and organizations) is confronted with binary categorizations: either one is virtuous or non-virtuous, good or bad, God or Evil.

Niceness   The understanding of social harmony as the absence of conflict and divergence.

Paradox   'Contradictory yet interrelated elements that exist simultaneously and persist over time.'[160]

Positivity ratio   The ratio between the positive and the negative (e.g., between positive and negative emotions, or between optimism and pessimism).

Notes

1   Byrne (2008).
2   Oettingen (2016).
3   Argyris (1994, p. 85).
4   Argyris (1994, p. 85).
5   Crane (2013).
6   In the cover of Rosling, Rosling and Rönnlunf (2018).
7   Rosling, Rosling and Rönnlunf (2018, p. 69). Although three authors co-author the book, it is written in the first-person singular, probably as a tribute to the first author, Hans Rosling, who died on February 7, 2017.
8   Rosling, Rosling and Rönnlunf (2018, p. 71).
9   Spreitzer and Cameron (2012, p. 86).
10   Maxwell (2009).
11   Linley et al. (2006, p. 6).
12   Henriques (2014).
13   Crane (2013).
14   Courpasson, Dany and Clegg (2012).
15   Tinjacá (2015).
16   March (2003); Patriotta (2019).
17   Grant (2013).
18   Schabram and Maitlis (2017).
19   King (2008, p. 436).
20   Teeter and Sandberg (2017).
21   Nietzsche (1977).
22   Harrison and Byrne (1979).
23   Kelly (2016, p. 12).
24   Weick (1999).
25   Hernes (2014, p. 45).
26   Baumeister, Bratslavsky, Finkenauer and Vohs (2001).
27   March and Weil (2013).
28   Heraclitus seems to have been the first to remark that the path up and down are one and the same (see Kahn, 1979).
29   Hirsch (1977).
30   Newstead, Macklin, Dawkins and Martin (2018).
31   Cunha, Guimarães-Costa, Rego and Clegg (2010).

32 Palmer (2012).

33 Rego, Cunha and Clegg (2012).

34 Trevino and Youngblood (1990).

35 Retrieved from: https://commons.wikimedia.org/wiki/File:Mani.jpg. This work is in the public domain.

36 Crossan, Mazutis and Seijts (2013).

37 Sison, Hartman and Fontrodona (2012).

38 Crossan, Mazutis and Seijts (2013, p. 570).

39 Miller (1993).

40 March (1991).

41 Rego, Cunha, Reis Júnior, Anastácio and Savagnago (2018), Rego, Sousa, Marques and Cunha (2012).

42 Joosten, Van Dijke, Van Hiel and De Cremer (2014).

43 Stouten, Van Dijke, Mayer, De Cremer and Euwema (2013).

44 Smith and Lewis (2011, p. 382).

45 Van der Byl and Slawinski (2015), Schad, Lewis, Raisch and Smith (2016).

46 Putnam (2013).

47 Putnam, Fairhurst and Banghart (2016, p. 66).

48 March and Weil (2003, p. 57).

49 Cameron (2008).

50 Cameron (2008).

51 Yam, Christian, Wei, Liao and Nai (2018).

52 Frederickson (2001).

53 Ashkanasy, Humphrey and Huy (2017).

54 Langley, Smallman, Tsoukas and Van de Ven (2013).

55 Li (2016).

56 Author: i. Retrieved from: https://commons.wikimedia.org/wiki/File:Pinocchio_paradox_Large_Print.svg. This file is made available under the Creative Commons CC0 1.0 Universal Public Domain Dedication.

57 Weick (1992).

58 Vince and Broussine (1996).

59 Emmons and McCullough (2003), Emmons and Mishra (2011), Polak and McCullough (2006).

60 Yip, Lee, Chan and Brooks (2018).

61 Judge, Piccolo and Kosalka (2009).

62 Guinote (2017).

63 Grant, Gino and Hofman (2011, p. 528).

64 Kroll, Toombs and Wright (2000).

65 Lehman, O'Connor, Kovács and Newman (2018).

66 Wassenaar, Dillon and Manz (2015).

67 Ibarra (2015).

68 Ashkanasy, Humphrey and Huy (2017), Judge and Kammeyer-Muellar (2008).

69 Ashkanasy, Humphrey and Huy (2017).

70 Kilduff, Chiaburu and Menges (2010).

71 Côté et al. (2011, p. 130).

72 Hewlett and Luce (2006).

73 Togel, Kilduff and Anand (2013).

74 Waytz (2016).

75 Mayo, Kakarika, Mainemelis and Deuschel (2017).

76 Potts (2016).

77 Meindl, Ehrlich and Dukerich (1985).

78 Khurana (2004).

79 Clegg, Cunha and Rego (2012).

80 Author: Ladislav Luppa. Retrieved from: https://commons.wikimedia.org/wiki/File:Mussolini_a_Hitler_-_Berl%C3%ADn_1937.jpg. This file is licensed under the Creative Commons Attribution-Share Alike 3.0 Unported license.

81 Ciulla (1998, p. 335).

82 Ciulla (1998, p. 336).

83 Shahinpoor and Matt (2007).
84 Whiteman and Cooper (2016).
85 Ewing (2017).
86 Amabile, Fisher and Pillemer (2014).
87 Cunha, Simpson, Clegg and Rego (2019).
88 Eisenhardt, Graebner and Sonenshein (2016).
89 Rhodes (2016).
90 Sandberg (2012), see also www.theatlantic.com/business/archive/2011/01/lies-hype-and-profit-the-truth-about-microfinance/70405/.
91 Tsoukas (2017).
92 Weick (1979, p. 13).
93 Bansal, Kim and Wood (2018).
94 Miller (1992).
95 www.wired.com/2000/04/joy-2/.
96 Johnson (2014, p. 10).
97 Maccoby (2000).
98 Owens, Wallace and Waldman (2015), Zhang, Ou, Tsui and Wang (2017).
99 Author: Derzsi Elekes Andor. Retrieved from: https://commons.wikimedia.org/wiki/File:Steve_Jobs_(1).JPG. This file is licensed under the Creative Commons Attribution-Share Alike 3.0 Unported license.
100 Gino and Ariely (2012).
101 Vince (2016).
102 George and Zhou (2007).
103 Van Knippenberg and Van Kleef (2016).
104 Mourinho with diminishing results for Manchester United at the time of writing the first draft of this book; by the time of its completion he had moved to lead Tottenham Hotspur.
105 Sutton (2017, p. 25) – please note the importance of the words 'sometimes' and 'temporary'.
106 Holusha (1992).
107 Pfeffer (2016).
108 Lupoli, Jampol and Oveis (2017).
109 Keeves, Westphal and McDonald (2017).
110 Eisenhardt, Kahwajy and Bourgeois (1997).
111 Samba, Van Knippenberg and Miller (2018).
112 Chazelle (2014).
113 Holbrook (2016).
114 De Hoogh, Greer and Den Hartog (2015).
115 Ewing (2017, p. 118).
116 Westerman, Bonnet and McAfee (2014).
117 Lebel (2017).
118 Grant (2013).
119 Rus (1980).
120 Culiberg and Mihelic (2017). Also see Kenny (2019) who charts ways in which it can be positive without necessarily destroying its instigator.
121 Kelton (2016).
122 Kelton (2016).
123 Macur (2016).
124 Ewing (2017, p. 154). A defeat device is a software program that is installed to 'defeat' the test of emissions.
125 O'Rourke and Strand (2017).
126 Hogan, Curphy and Hogan (1994), Judge, Piccolo and Kosalka (2009).
127 De Grauwe (2009).
128 Zhou and George (2001).
129 Schabram and Maitlis (2017).
130 Baker and Nelson (2005).
131 Zhang, Waldman, Han and Li (2015).
132 Esser and Lindoerfer (1989).
133 Hagen (2013).

134 Tang, Crossan and Rowe (2019).
135 Westerman, Bonnet and McAfee (2014).
136 Banerjee (2018).
137 Swartz (2010).
138 O'Hear (1997); also, as Flannery (2002) establishes, it is not universally applicable that competition rather than cooperation furthered species survival.
139 In Cameron and Plews (2012, p. 104).
140 Vermeulen (2017, 2018).
141 Keltner (2016).
142 Hackman (2009).
143 Ewing (2017).
144 Independent Directors of the Board of Wells Fargo & Company (2017).
145 Hall, Khurana and Madigan (1999), Kellerman (2004).
146 Vásquez, Schoeneborn and Sergi (2016).
147 Baumeister, Bratslavsky, Finkenauer and Vohs (2001).
148 Author: Joseolgon. Retrieved from https://commons.wikimedia.org/wiki/File:Pavilh%C3% A3o_do_Conhecimento_(23).jpg. This file is licensed under the Creative Commons Attribution-Share Alike 4.0 International license.
149 March and Weil (2003).
150 Rosling, Rosling and Rönnlunf (2018, p. 249).
151 Conlin (2008, p. 34).
152 Norem and Chang (2002).
153 Mitchell (2018, p. 16).
154 Csikszentmihalyi (2003, p. 35).
155 Collinson (2012).
156 Fineman (2006).
157 Hackman (2009).
158 Caza and Carroll (2012).
159 'Manicheism is a defunct religion, born in Mesopotamia in the 3rd century AD and last attested in the 16th century in China. Its founder [was] Mani (*c*.216–76)' (*Routledge Encyclopaedia of Philosophy*: www.rep.routledge.com/articles/thematic/manicheism/v-1).
160 Smith and Lewis (2011, p. 382).

References

Amabile, T., Fisher, C. M., & Pillemer, J. (2014). IDEO's culture of helping. *Harvard Business Review*, 92(1–2), 54–61.

Argyris, C. (1994). Good communication that blocks learning. *Harvard Business Review*, July–August, 77–85.

Ashforth, B. E., & Reingen, P. H. (2014). Functions of dysfunction: Managing the dynamics of an organizational duality in a natural food cooperative. *Administrative Science Quarterly*, 59(3), 474–516.

Ashkanasy, N. M., Humphrey, R. H., & Huy, Q. (2017). Integrating emotions and affect in theories of management. *Academy of Management Review*, 42(2), 175–189.

Austin, E. J., Farrelly, D., Black, C., & Moore, H. (2007). Emotional intelligence, Machiavellianism and emotional manipulation: Does EI have a dark side?. *Personality and individual differences*, 43(1), 179–189.

Baker, T., & Nelson, R. E. (2005). Creating something from nothing: Resource construction through entrepreneurial bricolage. *Administrative Science Quarterly*, 50(3), 329–366.

Banerjee, S. B. (2018). Transnational power and translocal governance: The politics of corporate responsibility. *Human Relations*, 71(6), 796–821.

Bansal, P., Kim, A., & Wood, M. O. (2018). Hidden in plain sight: The importance of scale in organizations' attention to issues. *Academy of Management Review*, 43(2), 217–241.

Baumeister, R. F., Bratslavsky, E., Finkenauer, C., & Vohs, K. D. (2001). Bad is stronger than good. *Review of General Psychology*, 5(4), 323–370.

Byrne, R. (2008). *The secret daily teachings*. New York: Simon & Schuster.

Cameron, K. S. (2008). Paradox in positive organizational change. *The Journal of Applied Behavioral Science*, 44(1), 7–24.

Cameron, K. (2010). Five keys to flourishing in trying times. *Leader to Leader*, 2010(55), 45–51.

Cameron, K., & Plews, E. (2012). Positive leadership in action:: Applications of POS by Jim Mallozzi, CEO, Prudential Real Estate and Relocation. *Organizational Dynamics*, 41(2), 99–105.

Caza, A., & Carroll, B. (2012). Critical theory and positive organizational scholarship. In G. M. Spreitzer & K. S. Cameron (Eds.), *The Oxford handbook of positive organizational scholarship* (pp. 965–978). Oxford: Oxford University Press.

Chazelle, D. (2014). *Whiplash (motion picture)*. New York: Sony.

Ciulla, J. B. (1998). Leadership and the problem of bogus empowerment. In J. B. Ciulla (Ed.). *Ethics, the heart of leadership* (pp. 63–86). Westport, CT: Praeger.

Clegg, S., Cunha, M. P., & Rego, A. (2012). The theory and practice of utopia in a total institution: The pineapple panopticon. *Organization Studies*, 33(12), 1735–1757.

Collinson, D. (2012). Prozac leadership and the limits of positive thinking. *Leadership*, 8(2), 87–107.

Conlin, M. (2008). Glum chums? Call in the happiness police. *Business Week*, August 25, 34.

Courpasson, D., Dany, F., & Clegg, S. (2012). Resisters at work: Generating productive resistance in the workplace. *Organization Science*, 23(3), 801–819.

Crane, A. (2013). Modern slavery as a management practice: Exploring the conditions and capabilities for human exploitation. *Academy of Management Review*, 38(1), 49–69.

Crossan, M., Mazutis, D., & Seijts, G. (2013). In search of virtue: The role of virtues, values and character strengths in ethical decision making. *Journal of Business Ethics*, 113, 567–581.

Csikszentmihalyi, M. (2003). *Good business: Leadership, flow and the making of meaning*. New York: Viking.

Culiberg, B., & Mihelic, K. K. (2017). The evolution of whistleblowing studies: A critical review and research agenda. *Journal of Business Ethics*, 146, 787–803.

Cunha, M. P., & Clegg, S. (2018). Persistence in paradox. In M. Farjoun, W. Smith, A. Langley, & H. Tsoukas (Eds), *Perspectives in process organization studies* (pp. 14–34). Oxford: Oxford University Press.

Cunha, M. P., Guimarães-Costa, N., Rego, A., & Clegg, S. R. (2010). Leading and following (un)ethically in limen. *Journal of Business Ethics*, 97, 189–206.

Cunha, M. P., Simpson, A. V., Clegg, S., & Rego, A. (2019). Speak! Paradoxical effects of a managerial culture of "speaking up". *British Journal of Management*, 30(4), 829–846

Davies, W. (2015). *How the government and big business sold us well-being*. London: Verso.

De Grauwe, P. (2009). Lessons from the banking crisis: A return to narrow banking. *CESifo DICE Report*, 7(2), 19–23.

De Hoogh, A. H., Greer, L. L., & Den Hartog, D. N. (2015). Diabolical dictators or capable commanders? An investigation of the differential effects of autocratic leadership on team performance. *The Leadership Quarterly*, 26(5), 687–701.

Eisenhardt, K. M., Graebner, M. E., & Sonenshein, S. (2016). Grand challenges and inductive methods: Rigor without rigor mortis. *Academy of Management Journal*, 59(4), 1113–1123.

Eisenhardt, K. M., Kahwajy, J. L., & Bourgeois, L. J. (1997). How management teams can have a good fight. *Harvard Business Review*, 75(77–86), 177.

Emmons, R. A., & McCullough, M. E. (2003). Counting blessings versus burdens: An experimental investigation of gratitude and subjective well-being in daily life. *Journal of Personality and Social Psychology*, 84, 377–389.

Emmons, R. A., & Mishra, A. (2011). Why gratitude enhances well-being: What we know, what we need to know. In K. Sheldon, T. Kashdan, & M. F. Steger (Eds.). *Designing the future of positive psychology: Taking stock and moving forward* (pp. 248–262). New York: Oxford University Press.

Esser, J. K., & Lindoerfer, J. S. (1989). Groupthink and the space shuttle challenger accident: Toward a quantitative case analysis. *Journal of Behavioral Decision Making*, 2(3), 167–177.

Ewing, J. (2017). *Faster, higher, farther: The inside story of the Volkswagen scandal*. New York: Random House.

Fineman, S. (2006). On being positive: Concerns and counterpoints. *Academy of Management Review*, 31(2), 270–291.

Flannery, T. (2002). *The future eaters: An ecological history of the Australasian lands and people*. New York: Grove Press.

Frederickson, B. L. (2001). The role of positive emotions in positive psychology: The broaden-and-build theory of positive emotions. *American Psychologist*, 56, 218–226.

George, J. M., & Zhou, J. (2007). Dual tuning in a supportive context: Joint contributions of positive mood, negative mood, and supervisory behaviors to employee creativity. *Academy of Management Journal*, 50(3), 605–622.

Gino, F., & Ariely, D. (2012). The dark side of creativity: Original thinkers can be more dishonest. *Journal of Personality and Social Psychology*, 102(3), 445–459.

Grant, A. M. (2013). *Give and take: A revolutionary approach to success*. Harmondsworth: Penguin.

Grant, A. M., Gino, F., & Hofman, D. A. (2011). Reversing the extraverted leadership advantage: The role of employee proactivity. *Academy of Management Journal*, 54(3), 528–550.

Guinote, A. (2017). How power affects people: Activating, wanting, and goal seeking. *Annual Review of Psychology*, 68, 353–381.

Hackman, J. R. (2009). The perils of positivity. *Journal of Organizational Behavior*, 30, 309–319.

Hagen, J. U. (2013). *Confronting mistakes: Lessons from the aviation industry when dealing with error*. New York: Palgrave Macmillan.

Hall, B. J., Khurana, R., & Madigan, C. (1999). *Al Dunlap at Sunbeam*. Harvard Business School Case. 899–218 (revised December 2003). Boston, MA: Havard Business School.

Harrison, J., & Byrne, D. (1979). *Heaven, fear of music*. New York: Sire Records.

Hernes, T. (2014). *A process theory of organization*. Oxford: Oxford University Press.

Hewlett, S. A., & Luce, C. B. (2006). Extreme jobs: The dangerous allure of the 70-hour workweek. *Harvard Business Review*, 84(12), 49–59.

Hirsch, F. (1977). *The social limits to growth*. London: Routledge & Kegan Paul.

Hogan, R., Curphy, G. J., & Hogan, J. (1994). What we know about leadership: Effectiveness and personality. *American Psychologist*, 49(6), 493.

Holbrook, M. (2016). Reflections on jazz training and marketing education: What makes a great teacher? *Marketing Theory*, 16(4), 429–444.

Holusha, J. (1992). A softer 'Neutron Jack' at G.E. *The New York Times*, March 4, D0001.

Ibarra, H. (2015). The authenticity paradox. *Harvard Business Review*, 93(1–2), 53–59.

Independent Directors of the Board of Wells Fargo & Company. (2017). *Sales practices investigation report*. April 10.

Johnson, L. (2014). The Virgin Galactic crash and the need for risk-takers. *Financial Times Europe*, November 5, 10.

Joosten, A., Van Dijke, M., Van Hiel, A., & De Cremer, D. (2014). Being 'in control' may make you lose control: The role of self-regulation in unethical leadership behavior. *Journal of Business Ethics*, 121(1), 1–14.

Judge, T. A., & Kammeyer-Muellar, J. D. (2008). Affect, satisfaction, and performance. In N. M. Ashkanasy & C. L. Cooper (Eds.), *Research companion to emotion in organizations* (pp. 136–151). Cheltenham: Edward Elgar.

Judge, T. A., Piccolo, R. F., & Kosalka, T. (2009). The bright and dark sides of leader traits: A review and theoretical extension of the leader trait paradigm. *The Leadership Quarterly*, 20(6), 855–875.

Kahn, C. (1979). *The art and thought of Heraclitus: Fragments with translation and commentary*. Cambridge: Cambridge University Press.

Keeves, G. D., Westphal, J. D., & McDonald, M. L. (2017). Those closest wield the sharpest knife: How ingratiation leads to resentment and social undermining of the CEO. *Administrative Science Quarterly*, 62(3), 484–523.

Kellerman, B. (2004). *Bad leadership*. Boston, MA: Harvard Business School Press.

Kelly, K. (2016). *The inevitable: Understanding the 12 technological forces that will shape our future*. New York: Viking.

Keltner, D. (2016). *The power paradox*. New York: Allen Lane.

Kelton, E. (2016). 14.7 billion reasons why Volkswagen should have welcomed whistleblowers. *Forbes*, June 29 (http://forbes.com/sites/erikakelton/2016/06/29/14-7-billion-reasons-why-volkswagen-should-have-welcomed-whistleblowers/#6277d9f662bc).

Kenny, K. (2019). Whistleblowing: Toward a new theory. Cambridge, MA: Harvard University Press.

Khurana, R. (2004). *Searching for a corporate savior: The irrational quest for charismatic CEOs*. Princeton, NJ: Princeton University Press.

Kilduff, M., Chiaburu, D. S., & Menges, J. I. (2010). Strategic use of emotional intelligence in organizational settings: Exploring the dark side. Research in organizational behavior, 30, 129–152.

King, L. A. (2008). Interventions for enhancing subjective well-being: Can we make people happier and should we? In M. Eid & R. J. Larsen (Eds.), *The science of subjective well-being* (pp. 431–448). New York: Guilford Press.

Kish-Gephart, J. J., Harrison, D. A., & Treviño, L. K. (2010). Bad apples, bad cases, and bad barrels: meta-analytic evidence about sources of unethical decisions at work. *Journal of Applied Psychology*, 95(1), 1–31.

Kroll, M. J., Toombs, L. A., & Wright, P. (2000). Napoleon's tragic march home from Moscow: Lessons in hubris. *Academy of Management Executive*, 14(1), 117–128.

Langer, E. J. (1989). *Mindfulness*. Reading, MA: Addison-Wesley/Addison Wesley Longman.

Langley, A., Smallman, C., Tsoukas, H., & Van de Ven, A. H. (2013). Process studies of change in organizations and management: Unveiling temporality, activity and flow. *Academy of Management Journal*, 56(1), 1–13.

Lebel, L. D. (2017). Moving beyond fight and flight: A contingent model of anger and fear spark proactivity. *Academy of Management Review*, 42(2), 190–206.

Lehman, D. W., O'Connor, K., Kovács, B., & Newman, G. E. (2018). Authenticity. *Academy of Management Annals*, 13(1), 1–42.

Li, P. P. (2016). Global implications of the indigenous epistemological system from the East: How to apply yin-yang balancing to paradox management. *Cross Cultural & Strategic Management*, 23(1), 42–77.

Linley, A. P., Joseph, S., Harrington, S., & Wood, A. M. (2006). Positive psychology: Past, present, and (possible) future. *The Journal of Positive Psychology*, 1(1), 3–16.

Lupoli, M. J., Jampol, L., & Oveis, C. (2017). Lying because we care: Compassion increases prosocial lying. *Journal of Experimental Psychology: General*, 146(7), 1026–1042.

Maccoby, M. (2000). Narcissistic leaders: The incredible pros, the inevitable cons. *Harvard Business Review*, 78(1), 68–78.

Macur, J. (2016). First medal of Rio Olympics deserves to go to … a whistleblower. *The New York Times*, July 20, B8.

March, J. G. (1991). Exploration and exploitation in organizational learning. *Organization Science*, 2(1), 71–87.

March, J. G., & Weil, T. (2003). *On leadership*. Malden, MA: Blackwell.

Maxwell, H. (2009). Portugal: "The revolution of the carnations", 1974–75. In A. Roberts & T. M. Ash (Eds.), *Civil resistance and power politics: The experience of non-violent action from gandhi to the present* (pp. 144–161). Oxford: Oxford University Press.

Mayo, M., Kakarika, M., Mainemelis, C., & Deuschel, N. T. (2017). A metatheoretical framework of diversity in teams. *Human Relations*, 70(8), 911–993.

Meindl, J. R., Ehrlich, S. B., & Dukerich, J. M. (1985). The romance of leadership. *Administrative Science Quarterly*, 6(3), 78–102.

Miller, D. (1992). The Icarus paradox: How exceptional companies bring about their own downfall. *Business Horizons*, 35(1), 24–35.

Miller, D. (1993). The architecture of simplicity. *Academy of Management Review*, 18(1), 116–138.

Mitchell, T. R. (2018). A dynamic, inclusive, and affective evolutionary view of organizational behavior. *Annual Review of Organizational Psychology and Organizational Behavior*, 5, 1–19.

Newstead, T., Macklin, R., Dawkins, S., & Martin, A. (2018). What is virtue? Advancing the conceptualization of virtue to inform positive organizational inquiry. *Academy of Management Perspectives*. doi: 10.5465/amp.2016.0162.

Nietzsche, F. (1977). *Twilight of the idols and the anti-christ*. Trans. R. J. Hollingdale. Harmondsworth: Penguin.

Norem, J. K., & Chang, E. C. (2002). The positive psychology of negative thinking. *Journal of Clinical Psychology*, 58, 993–1001.

O'Hear, A. (1997). *Beyond evolution: Human nature and the limits of evolutionary explanation.* Oxford: Clarendon Press.

O'Rourke, D., & Strand, R. (2017). Patagonia: Driving sustainable innovation by embracing tensions. *California Management Review*, 60(1), 102–125.

Oettingen, G. (2016). Don't think too positive. *Aeon*, July 25 (https://aeon.co/essays/thinking-positive-is-a-surprisingly-risky-manoeuvre).

Owens, B. P., Wallace, A. S., & Waldman, D. A. (2015). Leader narcissism and follower outcomes: The counterbalancing effect of leader humility. *Journal of Applied Psychology*, 100(4), 1203–1213.

Palmer, D. (2012). *Normal organizational wrongdoing: A critical analysis of theories of misconduct in and by organizations.* Oxford: Oxford University Press.

Patriotta, G. (2019). Imagination, Self-Knowledge, and Poise: Jim March's Lessons for Leadership. *Journal of Management Studies*, 56(8). 1517–1768.

Pfeffer, J. (2016). Tell me lies, tell me sweet little lies: The many positive functions of being untruthful. *People + Strategy*, 39(4), 32–35.

Polak, E., & McCullough, M. E. (2006). Is gratitude an alternative to materialism? *Journal of Happiness Studies*, 7, 343–360.

Potts, J. (2016). Charisma is a mysterious and dangerous gift. *Aeon*, August 3 (https://aeon.co/ideas/charisma-is-a-mysterious-and-dangerous-gift).

Putnam, L. L. (2013). Primary and secondary contradictions: A literature review and future directions. *Management Communication Quarterly*, 27(4), 623–630.

Putnam, L. L., Fairhurst, G. T., & Banghart, S. (2016). Contradictions, dialectics, and paradoxes in organizations: A constitutive approach. *Academy of Management Annals*, 10(1), 65–171.

Rego, A., Cunha, M. P., & Clegg, S. (2012). *The virtues of leadership: Contemporary challenge for global managers.* Oxford: Oxford University Press.

Rego, A., Cunha, M. P., Reis Júnior, D., Anastácio, C., & Savagnago, M. (2018). The optimism-pessimism ratio as predictor of employee creativity: The promise of duality. *European Journal of Innovation Management*, 21(3), 423–442.

Rego, A., Sousa, F., Marques, C., & Cunha, M. P. (2012). Optimism predicting employees' creativity: The mediating role of positive affect and the positivity ratio. *European Journal of Work and Organizational Psychology*, 21(2), 244–270.

Rhodes, C. (2016). Democratic business ethics: Volkswagen's emissions scandal and the disruption of corporate sovereignty. *Organization Studies*, 37(10), 1501–1518.

Rosling, H., Rosling, O., & Rönnlunf, A. R. (2018). *Factfulness: Ten reasons we're wrong about the world – And why things are better than you think.* London: Sceptre.

Rus, V. (1980). Positive and negative power: Thoughts on the dialectics of power. *Organization Studies*, 1(1), 3–19.

Samba, C., Van Knippenberg, D., & Miller, C. C. (2018). The impact of strategic dissent on organizational outcomes: A meta-analytic integration. *Strategic Management Journal*, 39(2), 379–402.

Sandberg, J. (2012). Mega-interest on microcredit: Are lenders exploiting the poor? *Journal of Applied Philosophy*, 29(3), 169–185.

Schabram, K., & Maitlis, S. (2017). Negotiating the challenges of a calling: Emotion and enacted sensemaking in animal shelter work. *Academy of Management Journal*, 60(2), 584–609.

Schad, J., Lewis, M. W., Raisch, S., & Smith, W. K. (2016). Paradox research in management science: Looking back to move forward. *Academy of Management Annals*, 10(1), 5–64.

Shahinpoor, N., & Matt, B. F. (2007). The power of one: Dissent and organizational life. *Journal of Business Ethics*, 74, 37–48.

Sison, A., Hartman, E. M., & Fontrodona, J. (2012). Reviving tradition: Virtue and the common good in business and management. *Business Ethics Quarterly*, 22(2), 207–210.

Smith, W. K., & Lewis, M. W. (2011). Toward a theory of paradox: A dynamic equilibrium model of organizing. *Academy of Management Review*, 36, 381–403.

Stouten, J., van Dijke, M., Mayer, D.M., De Cremer, D. & Euwema, M.C. (2013). Can a leader be seen as too ethical? The curvilinear effects of ethical leadership. *The Leadership Quarterly*, 24(5), 680–695.

Sutton, R. I. (2017). *The asshole survival guide*. Harmondsworth: Portfolio Penguin.

Swartz, J. (2010). Timberland's CEO on standing up to 65,000 angry activists. *Harvard Business Review*, September, 39–43.

Tang, J., Crossan, M., & Rowe, W. G. (2019). Dominant leaders: Heroes or villains? *Organizational Dynamics*, 48(1), 1–7.

Teeter, P., & Sandberg, J. (2017). Cracking the enigma of asset bubbles with narratives. *Strategic Organization*, 15(1), 91–99.

Tinjacá, A. M. (2015). Construí un sueño común para lograrlo con mi equipo. El Espectador, September 27 (http://elespectador.com/noticias/economia/construi-un-sueno-comun-lograrlo-mi-equipo-articulo-589075), accessed July 14, 2017.

Togel, G., Kilduff, M., & Anand, N. (2013). Emotion helping by managers: An emergent understanding of discrepant role expectations and outcomes. *Academy of Management Journal*, 86(2), 334–357.

Tsoukas, H. (2017). Don't simplify, complexify: From disjunctive to conjunctive theorizing in organization and management studies. *Journal of Management Studies*, 54(2), 132–153.

Van der Byl, C. A., & Slawinski, N. (2015). Embracing tensions in corporate sustainability: A review of research from win-wins and trade-offs to paradoxes and beyond. *Organization & Environment*, 28(1), 54–79.

Van Knippenberg, D., & Van Kleef, G. A. (2016). Leadership and affect: Moving the hearts and minds of followers. *The Academy of Management Annals*, 10(1), 1–42.

Vásquez, C., Schoeneborn, D., & Sergi, V. (2016). Summoning the spirits: Organizational texts and the (dis)organizing properties of communication. *Human Relations*, 69(3), 629–659.

Vermeulen, F. (2017). *Breaking bad habits*. Boston, MA: Harvard Business Review Press.

Vermeulen, F. (2018). A basic theory of inheritance: How bad practice persists. *Strategic Management Journal*, 39(6), 1603–1629.

Vince, R. (2016). Emotion and learning. *Journal of Management Education*, 40(5), 538–544.

Vince, R., & Broussine, M. (1996). Paradox, defense and attachment: Accessing and working with emotions and relations underlying organizational change. *Organization Studies*, 17(1), 1–21.

Wassenaar, C. L., Dillon, P. J., & Manz, C. C. (2015). Authentic irresponsibility: Quo vadis? *Organizational Dynamics*, 44(2), 130–137.

Waytz, J. (2016). The limits of empathy. *Harvard Business Review*, 94(1), 70–73.

Weick, K. E. (1979). The social psychology of organizing (2nd ed.). New York: McGraw-Hill.

Weick, K. E. (1992). Agenda setting in organizational behavior. *Journal of Management Inquiry*, 1(3), 171–182.

Weick, K. E. (1999). The aesthetic of imperfection in orchestras and organizations. In M. P. Cunha & C. A. Marques (Eds.), *Readings in organization science* (pp. 541–563). Lisboa: ISPA.

Westerman, G., Bonnet, D., & McAfee, A. (2014). *Leading digital: Turning technology into business transformation*. Boston, MA: Harvard Business Press.

Whiteman, G., & Cooper, W. H. (2016). Decoupling rape. *Academy of Management Discoveries*, 2(2), 115–154.

Yam, K. C., Christian, M. S., Wei, W., Liao, Z., & Nai, J. (2018). The mixed blessing of leader sense of humor: Examining costs and benefits. *Academy of Management Journal*, 61(1), 348–369.

Yip, J. A., Lee, K. K., Chan, C., & Brooks, A. W. (2018). *Thanks for nothing: Expressing gratitude invites exploitation by competitors*. Harvard Business School, Working Paper 18-081.

Zhang, H., Ou, A. Y., Tsui, A. S., & Wang, H. (2017). CEO humility, narcissism and firm innovation: A paradox perspective on CEO traits. *The Leadership Quarterly*, 28(5), 585–604.

Zhang, Y., Waldman, D. A., Han, Y.-L., & Li, X.-B. (2015). Paradoxical leader behaviors in people management: Antecedents and consequences. *Academy of Management Journal*, 58(2), 535–565.

Zhou, J., & George, J. M. (2001). When job dissatisfaction leads to creativity: Encouraging the expression of voice. *Academy of Management Journal*, 44(4), 682–696.

Index

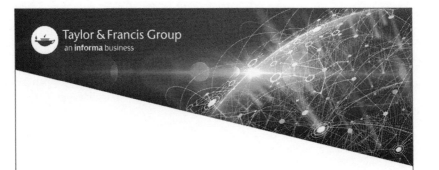